Studies in Diversity Linguistics

Editor: Martin Haspelmath

In this series:

1. Handschuh, Corinna. A typology of marked-S languages.
2. Rießler, Michael. Adjective attribution.
3. Klamer, Marian (ed.). The Alor-Pantar languages: History and typology.
4. Berghäll, Liisa. A grammar of Mauwake (Papua New Guinea).
5. Wilbur, Joshua. A grammar of Pite Saami.
6. Dahl, Östen. Grammaticalization in the North: Noun phrase morphosyntax in Scandinavian vernaculars.
7. Schackow, Diana. A grammar of Yakkha.
8. Liljegren, Henrik. A grammar of Palula.
9. Shimelman, Aviva. A grammar of Yauyos Quechua.
10. Rudin, Catherine & Bryan James Gordon (eds.). Advances in the study of Siouan languages and linguistics.
11. Kluge, Angela. A grammar of Papuan Malay.
12. Kieviet, Paulus. A grammar of Rapa Nui.
13. Michaud, Alexis. Tone in Yongning Na: Lexical tones and morphotonology.
14. Enfield, N. J. (ed.). Dependencies in language: On the causal ontology of linguistic systems.
15. Gutman, Ariel. Attributive constructions in North-Eastern Neo-Aramaic.
16. Bisang, Walter & Andrej Malchukov (eds.). Unity and diversity in grammaticalization scenarios.
17. Stenzel, Kristine & Bruna Franchetto (eds.). On this and other worlds: Voices from Amazonia.
18. Paggio, Patrizia and Albert Gatt (eds.). The languages of Malta.
19. Seržant, Ilja A. & Alena Witzlack-Makarevich (eds.). Diachrony of differential argument marking.
20. Hölzl, Andreas. A typology of questions in Northeast Asia and beyond: An ecological perspective.
21. Riesberg, Sonja, Asako Shiohara & Atsuko Utsumi (eds.). Perspectives on information structure in Austronesian languages.

ISSN: 2363-5568

Perspectives on information structure in Austronesian languages

Edited by

Sonja Riesberg

Asako Shiohara

Atsuko Utsumi

Sonja Riesberg, Asako Shiohara & Atsuko Utsumi (eds.). 2018. *Perspectives on information structure in Austronesian languages* (Studies in Diversity Linguistics 21). Berlin: Language Science Press.

This title can be downloaded at:
http://langsci-press.org/catalog/book/201
© 2018, the authors
Published under the Creative Commons Attribution 4.0 Licence (CC BY 4.0): http://creativecommons.org/licenses/by/4.0/
ISBN: 978-3-96110-108-5 (Digital)
    978-3-96110-109-2 (Hardcover)

ISSN: 2363-5568
DOI:10.5281/zenodo.1402571
Source code available from www.github.com/langsci/201
Collaborative reading: paperhive.org/documents/remote?type=langsci&id=201

Cover and concept of design: Ulrike Harbort
Typesetting: Wataru Okubo
Proofreading: Amir Ghorbanpour, Bev Erasmus, Bonny Sands, Elizabeth Zeitoun, Ikmi Nur Oktavianti, Jeffrey Pheiff, Jeroen van de Weijer, Joseph Lovestrand, Mykel Brinkerhoff, Natsuko Nakagawa, Prisca Jerono, and Vadim Kimmelman
Fonts: Linux Libertine, Libertinus Math, Arimo, DejaVu Sans Mono
Typesetting software: XƎLATEX

Language Science Press
Unter den Linden 6
10099 Berlin, Germany
langsci-press.org

Storage and cataloguing done by FU Berlin

Contents

Preface and Acknowledgements iii

I Information status and NP marking

1 Referential cohesion in Bunun: A comparison of two genres
   Rik De Busser 3

2 Stance, categorisation, and information structure in Malay
   František Kratochvíl, Nur Izdihar Binte Ismail & Diyana Hamzah 41

3 Attention focus and information packaging in Vera'a demonstratives
   Stefan Schnell 81

4 Two definite markers in Manado Malay
   Asako Shiohara & Anthony Jukes 115

II Information structure and syntactic constructions

5 Information structure in Sembiran Balinese
   I Wayan Arka & I Nyoman Sedeng 139

6 Constituent order and information structure in Indonesian discourse
   Dwi Noverini Djenar 177

7 Austronesian predication and the emergence of biclausal clefts in Indonesian languages
   Daniel Kaufman 207

8 The role of information structure for morphosyntactic choices in Tagalog
   Anja Latrouite & Arndt Riester 247

9 Information structure in Sumbawa: A QUD analysis
   Arndt Riester & Asako Shiohara 285

Contents

10 Preposed NPs in Seediq
   Naomi Tsukida   313

III Information structure and prosody

11 Some preliminary observations on prosody and information structure in
   Austronesian languages of Indonesia and East Timor
   Nikolaus P. Himmelmann   347

12 Focus and prosody in Tagalog
   Naonori Nagaya & Hyun Kyung Hwang   375

13 On the perception of prosodic prominences and boundaries in Papuan Malay
   Sonja Riesberg, Janina Kalbertodt, Stefan Baumann & Nikolaus P. Himmelmann 389

Index   415

Preface and Acknowledgements

Information structure is a relatively new field to linguistics and has only recently been studied for smaller and less described languages. This book brings together contributions on information structure in Austronesian languages, covering all subgroups of the large Austronesian family (including Formosan, Central Malayo-Polynesian, South Halmahera-West New Guinea, and Oceanic). Its major focus, though, lies on Western Malayo-Polynesian languages. A number of chapters investigate two of the largest languages of the region, i.e. Tagalog and (different varieties of) Malay, others study information structural phenomena in smaller, underdescribed languages. The book emerged from a series of workshops on information structure in Austronesian languages between 2013 and 2016 that were organized by Atsuko Utsumi (Meisei University) and Asako Shiohara (Tokyo University of Foreign Studies) and which took place at the Research Institute for Languages and Cultures of Asia and Africa (ILCAA), Tokyo University of Foreign Studies. The book is divided into three major parts, which roughly reflect the different topics of these workshops. Part one subsumes chapters on the topic of NP marking and reference tracking devices. In part two, contributions investigate how syntactic constructions, such as, for example, cleft constructions or passives, may reflect different information structural categories. Finally, the third part studies the interaction of information structure and prosody.

We gratefully acknowledge the generous funding of the Linguistic Dynamics Science Project 2 (Research Institute for Languages and Cultures of Asia and Africa, Tokyo University of Foreign Studies (2013-2015AY), principal investigator: Toshihide Nakayama) which made it possible to hold the workshops in the first place and to invite its participants to come to Tokyo. During the process of editing this book, SR has been supported through the Volkswagen Foundation, the German Research Foundation (DFG) within the SFB 1252 "Prominence in Language" at the University of Cologne, and by the Australian Research Council (ARC) within the "Centre of Excellence for the Dynamics of Language" at the Australian National University. AS received funding through the Linguistic Dynamics Science 3 program (LingDy3) and the JSPS project "A collaborative network for usage-based research on less-studied languages."

We want to thank all of the contributors for the good collaboration. Special thanks to those who helped us with the internal reviewing process. For external reviewing we would like to express our gratitude to Sander Adelaar, Laura Arnold, Abigail Cohn, Carmen Dawuda, Michael Ewing, Katja Jasinskaja, Kurt Malcher, Gabriele Schwiertz, Aung Si, Volker Unterladstetter, and Akira Utsugi. Maria Bardají Farré, Lena Rennert,

Preface and Acknowledgements

and Katherine Walker have helped with some of the editorial work and proof reading, and Wataru Okubo has done a wonderful job in converting the manuscripts into LaTeX and preparing them for publication. A big thank you also to Sachiko Yoshida for doing all the admin work for the workshops and other volume-related issues.

Sonja Riesberg, Köln
Asako Shiohara, Tokyo
Atsuko Utsumi, Tokyo

Part I

Information status and NP marking

Chapter 1

Referential cohesion in Bunun: A comparison of two genres

Rik De Busser
National Chengchi University

> This chapter investigates how referential expressions are involved in establishing and maintaining textual cohesion in Bunun, an Austronesian language of Taiwan, and how this behaviour varies across genres. Relying on a model of referential cohesion inspired by systemic-functional grammar, it explores differences and similarities for encoding referential continuity across sentence boundaries in oral and narrative text. It concludes that, contrary to initial expectation, and despite considerable formal differences in how referential expressions are realized, at a more fundamental level the properties of referential cohesion are unexpectedly stable across genres.

1 Introduction

1.1 Cohesion

Now more than four decades ago, Halliday & Hasan (1976) published their seminal work on the linguistic subsystem that helps creating coherent text by establishing connections between related semantic elements in that text. More specifically, it is "a set of lexicogrammatical systems that have evolved specifically as a resource for making it possible to transcend the boundaries of the clause — that is, the domain of the highest-ranking grammatical unit" (Halliday & Matthiessen 2004: 532). They referred to this subsystem as cohesion and to the connections as cohesive ties, and described it as the set of "relations of meaning that exist within the text, and that define it as text" (Halliday & Hasan 1976: 4). This means that its realization is not confined by clause or other grammatical boundaries, but typically operates on the scale of text or discourse.

It also implies that there is no isomorphic relationship between grammatical devices and cohesive effects; cohesion pertains to semantic relationships within texts that "may take any one of various forms" (Halliday & Hasan 1976: 13). The original proposal, which has been integrated in Halliday's systemic-functional grammar (Halliday 1994; Halliday & Matthiessen 2004; Halliday & Matthiessen 2014), distinguishes four types of relationships:

Rik De Busser. 2018. Referential cohesion in Bunun: A comparison of two genres. In Sonja Riesberg, Asako Shiohara & Atsuko Utsumi (eds.), *Perspectives on information structure in Austronesian languages*, 3–40. Berlin: Language Science Press. DOI:10.5281/zenodo.1402535

1. REFERENCE establishes cohesive ties between linguistic elements through various forms of spatio-temporal and personal deixis, and through comparison.

2. ELLIPSIS covers all phenomena that establish cohesive links by omitting a grammatical unit, or by swapping it for a placeholder element.[1]

3. CONJUNCTION creates logical or spatio-temporal ties between propositions, typically through various grammatical mechanisms for clause linking.

4. LEXICAL COHESION is established between lexical elements through repetition and various semantic relationships.

The markers for each of the four types of cohesive relationship are indicated in the following examples.

(1) English
  a. Reference
     *That man's dog is **much larger than** my cat.*
  b. Ellipsis
     *How many cookies are left? I took twelve Ø. **So did** you.*
  c. Conjunction
     ***When** it shut down, something went wrong. **In short**, it caught fire.*
  d. Lexical organization
     ***Emperor penguins protect** their **chicks** from the **cold** by **putting** the **little fluff balls** on their **feet**.*

In (1a), *that* points to a referent that exists outside the text (exophoric reference), the phrase *much larger than* connects *that man's dog* and *my cat*, and the possessive form *my* creates an exophoric link to the speaker. In (1b), ellipsis in the second clause indicates that the head of *twelve Ø* refers to the same set of referents as *cookies* in the first clause. The substitutive construction *so did* in the third clause indicates that its subject performed the same action, *take [cookies]*, as the first person in the second clause. In (1c), *when* creates a relationship of simultaneity between the first and second clause, and *in short* indicates that the third clause summarizes the previous discourse. Finally, the penguin-related lexical items in (1d) arrange themselves in a complex of lexical cohesive relationships (see Figure 1).

---

[1]Halliday & Hasan (1976: 88–141) called the latter substitution and originally considered it to be a separate cohesive category, meant to account for forms like *one* in English expressions such as *You can choose the blue candy or the red one*. They acknowledged that both substitution and ellipsis established cohesive ties by replacement, either by zero or by a placeholder (Halliday & Hasan 1976: 88) and both are subsumed under ellipsis in Halliday (1994) and later publications.

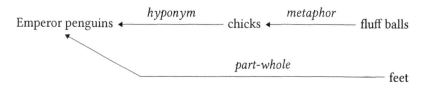

Figure 1: Schema of a cohesive chain

As the examples illustrate, markers of cohesion are highly heterogeneous in their grammatical and relational properties. What they have in common is that they establish cohesive ties, that is, semantic connections between linguistic elements (words, phrases, clauses, etc.) that are typically asymmetrical and express that the discourse segments in which they occur are to be interpreted as part of a coherent whole. These ties, either in isolation or by combining into longer chains, weave through a text. Together with thematic structure (theme/rheme contrasts) and focus structure (given/new), cohesion thus creates 'texture' (Halliday 1994: 334; Halliday & Matthiessen 2004: 579), the perception of a text or discourse as a connected whole. Texture in turn is "one aspect of the study of coherence, which can be thought of as the process whereby a reading position is naturalized by texts for listener/readers" (Martin 2001: 35).

Importantly, this implies that Hallidayan systemic-functional grammar "does *not* equate cohesion with coherence" (Martin 1992: 27; see also Martin 2001). Cohesion is merely one of the linguistic systems responsible for textual coherence. Later work on coherence often merged the two concepts, and typically reduced the phenomenon to a semantic-pragmatic component responsible for combining clause-level propositions into larger rhetorical structures (see e.g. Mann & Thompson 1987; Kehler 2002; Kehler 2004).

In sum, cohesion is an information-structuring device that, by establishing semantic connections between a heterogeneous set of linguistic units within a text, assists language users in interpreting that text as a cohesive, connected whole. In doing so, it is one of the subsystems responsible for structuring the distribution of information elements on a textual (supra-sentential) level.

Cohesion has been explored extensively in theoretical and applied linguistics, but overwhelmingly in the context of English (Halliday & Hasan 1976; Connor 1984; Martin 1992; Abadiano 1995; Tanskanen 2006; Crossley & McNamara 2012) and occasionally other major languages (Aziz 1988 on Arabic; Hickmann & Hendriks 1999 on English, French, German and Mandarin; Kruger 2000 on Afrikaans; Hassel 2005 on English, German and Norwegian). Work on minority languages is much less common. In the Austronesian world, the only studies I am aware of are Ezard (1978) on Tawala, Flaming (1983) on Wandamen, and Benn (1991) on Central Bontoc. The first two are literal applications of Halliday & Hasan's framework to their languages; Benn employs a number of frameworks, including Halliday & Hasan's, for his analysis of the discursive structure of Central Bontoc ritual texts.

This chapter adapts Halliday & Hasan's original model to fit the needs of analysing the role of referential expressions in establishing the cohesive texture of Bunun texts. It investigates the role cohesion plays in establishing genre distinctions through a small-scale pilot study.

1.2 Genre and cohesion

Genres or registers can be defined as specific types of texts or discourse with sets of "relatively stable" properties associated with the "thematic content, style, and compositional structure" that reflects the specific needs of well-defined contexts in which they were realized (Bakhtin 1986: 60).

Distinctions between genres are marked through various linguistic means. Biber (1995: 28) makes a basic distinction between register markers and register features. The former are linguistic cues that are specific to a certain register or genre and therefore directly indicate that a text belongs to it. An anecdotal example is the phrase *a long time ago in a land far, far away* introducing a fairy tale. Register features are linguistic elements that are not genre-specific, but whose frequency or distribution is in certain situations indicative of a specific register or genre. For instance, imperatives are relatively common in recipes, but they occur in many other genres as well. Cohesion falls into the latter category.

Research on the relationship between genres and their indicators has mainly focussed on the "relative distributions of surface linguistic features, such as adjectives, nominalizations, passives, and various clause types" (Biber 1995: 12). Even Biber, who went well beyond previous studies by focussing on complex feature bundles, mainly concentrates on morphosyntactic features that can be straightforwardly extracted from the surface realization of the text (see Biber 1995: 94–104; also Biber & Conrad 2009: 217–226). Given that genre is associated with the global discursive and semantic features of texts, one should probably assume that these grammatical features serve as proxy indicators of certain structural elements of meaning, discourse organisation and information structure.

Cohesion is an important determinant of the distribution of information in text, so it is reasonable to assume that it is interconnected with the global properties of text structure, and therefore contributes to (Halliday & Hasan 1976) or closely interacts with genre (Martin 1992; Martin 2001). There are a number of reasons why one would expect consistent correlations between cohesion and genre, many linked to the accessibility of linguistic information (Lambrecht 1994: 74–116; Ariel 1991).

First, expectation patterns related to the nature and quantity of assumed background knowledge and explicitly expressed information are often genre-specific. Specialized genres assume a greater volume of background knowledge than more generalized genres. For example, the presupposed background knowledge in an informal conversation is different from that in an academic textbook (Biber & Conrad 2009: 14–15). This affects the need for explicitly expressing cohesive relationships between elements in a text.

Second, differences in genre commonly correlate with differences in modes of realization, which in term influences the options for realizing cohesion. For instance, oral and written genres diverge in which cohesive strategies they employ (see e.g. Fox 1987; Givón 1993). Textual coherence in writing is partly realized through meta-linguistic means, such as writing conventions and punctuation, not available in oral discourse. Because of the visual nature of the written medium, information is also more readily, and longer, accessible. All things being equal, one would therefore expect that oral genres tend to have a more dense cohesive structure (or a larger presence of other coherence-creating mechanisms) than their written equivalents, in order to reach an equal level of coherence.

For certain types of cohesive relationships, the link between cohesion and genre is well understood. For instance, it is uncontroversial that "genre-specific conventions [...] play a significant role in anaphoric patterning in conversation and writing" (Fox 1987: 2). Research explicitly comparing cohesive patterning across genres is scarce, but the influence of cohesion on the realization of individual genres is the subject of a number of studies. The above-mentioned Benn (1991) investigates cohesion in single genre (written essays) in Central Bontoc. Another example are Malah & Rashid (2016) who, based on Hoey (1991), explore the role of content words in establishing the cohesive properties of English language Nigerian newspaper texts.

One important question is in which manner exactly cohesion indicates genre in text or – from a comparative perspective – how its realizations are indicative of differences between genres. Halliday & Hasan suggest that "the possible differences among different genres and different authors [are] in the numbers and kinds of tie they typically employ" (Halliday & Hasan 1976: 4). In other words, one would expect that (1) cohesive density, and (2) the nature of the connections between elements in cohesive relationships varies between genres.

This chapter investigates whether, and to what extent, these two hypotheses are true for two text genres, oral narrative and biblical translations, in a Bunun speech community. It compares the cohesive density and the morphosyntactic and semantic-pragmatic properties of cohesive ties in these two types of texts.

Similar to Malah & Rashid (2016), this chapter not discuss all aspects of cohesion as they were introduced in Halliday & Hasan (1976). Rather, the discussion focuses on referential cohesion, the conceptually coherent subset of cohesive ties that is involved in establishing relationships between referential items. Its exact delineation is discussed in §1.4. Before this is possible, I first introduce the Bunun language, its dialects and the genres involved in the present analysis.

1.3 Bunun dialects

Bunun is one of around sixteen Austronesian languages spoken on Taiwan (Li 2008). It has five extant dialects that are classified into a Southern (Isbukun), Central (Takbanuaz and Takivatan) and Northern branch (Takibakha and Takituduh). Within the Isbukun dialect, at least three distinct varieties are spoken in Kaohsiung, Taitung, and Nantou. Between dialects, especially between Isbukun varieties and dialects of the other branches, there is a fair amount of phonological, lexical, and grammatical differentiation (see Li 1988 for an overview of phonological and lexical variation). Only the Takivatan and Isbukun dialects are relevant to the present discussion.

(2) Bunun

    a. Takivatan (fieldwork, observed)
       mun-ʔisaq=ʔas
       ALL-where-2S.SUBJ
       'Where are you going?'

    b. Isbukun (Lilian Li, pers. comm.)
       ku-ʔisaʔ   kasuʔ   ma-tuktuk lukis
       ALL-where   2S.SUBJ   DYN-chop wood
       'Where do/did you go to chop wood?'

Example (2a–2b) illustrates the degree of discrepancy between the two dialects.[2] The coda of the question word (/q/ in Takivatan, /ʔ/ in Isbukun) is illustrative of a systematic phonological contrast. In near-identical contexts, both dialects use different allative prefixes. Finally, whereas Takivatan prefers a pronominal clitic in subject positions like this, Isbukun uses a free pronoun that does not exist in Takivatan (see Table 1 and Table 2).

Bunun dialects have a verb-initial constituent order and what has been called a Western Austronesian or Philippine-type voice system (see French 1987; Foley 2007; Riesberg 2014 for general overviews), which in Bunun distinguishes at minimum between actor (AV), undergoer (UV), and locative voice (LV), marked by suffixes on the verb. In (3a), *siða* is actor voice and as a result unmarked; the UV in (3b) is indicated by a suffix *-un*, and the LV in (3c) by *-an*.

(3) Takivatan Bunun

    a. Actor voice ((fieldwork, elicited))
       na-siða qaimaŋsuð.
       IRR-take thing
       'I will pick up things.'

    b. Undergoer voice ((fieldwork, text corpus))
       maŋmaŋ ni   siða-un.
       many   NEG take-UV
       '… a lot were not caught.'

    c. Locative voice ((fieldwork, text corpus))
       maqtu pa-siða-an-in   ŋabul vanis.
       can   CAUS.DYN-take-LV-PRV deer   wild.boar
       '… and we could catch deer and wild boar.'

---

[2]The following changes were made to graphemic conventions: z > ð, ' > ʔ, ch > ʤ, ng > ŋ

Certain analyses additionally include instrumental, beneficiary, and resultative object voices, but these forms are relatively uncommon and can be further ignored here.

The remainder of this section gives a short overview of various deictic paradigms, since these are relevant to the discussion at hand. All five Bunun dialects have sets of free and bound personal pronouns. Paradigmatic distinctions are largely equivalent, but the pronominal sets have formally diverged and have been analysed as expressing different grammatical distinctions in Takivatan and Isbukun. Tables 1 and 2 give the pronominal paradigms for both dialects.[3]

Table 1: Personal pronouns in Takivatan Bunun

(a)	Subject		Non-subj.		Poss.	Loc.
	Free	Bound	Free	Bound		
1S	sak, saikin	-(ʔ)ak	ðaku, nak	-(ʔ)uk	inak, ainak, nak	ðakuʔan
2S	—	-(ʔ)as	suʔu, su	—	isu, su	suʔuʔan
3S	(see b)	-(ʔ)is	(see b)	—		
1I	ʔata, inʔata	—	mita	—	imita	mitaʔan
1E	ðamu, sam	-(ʔ)am	ðami, nam	—	inam, nam	ðamiʔan
2P	amu	-(ʔ)am	muʔu, mu	—	imu, mu	muʔuʔan
3P	(see b)	—	(see b)	—		

(b)	Subject & Non-subject		
	Prox	Med	Dist
3S	isti	istun	ista
3P	inti	intun	inta

Some of the more systematic differences are worth mentioning. Third person pronouns in Takivatan differentiate between proximal, medial and distal forms and do not have distinct subject and non-subject forms. They can therefore be interpreted as a subset of demonstratives (Table 3). In contrast, Isbukun third person pronouns do not encode a deictic contrast. Singular forms all appear derived from the stem *sia*, which in Takivatan is an anaphoric form that appears in a number of grammatical positions (De Busser 2009: 467–474). Plural forms all derive from the stem *nai*. Zeitoun (2000: 72) suggests

---

[3] The Takivatan data on personal pronouns is from De Busser (2009: 441); the Isbukun data from the Kaohsiung variety in Huang & Shih (2016: 85). The latter mark vowel length by grapheme doubling. This distinction is non-phonemic in Bunun: generally, monosyllabic roots tend to have lengthened vowels, irrespective of the environment in which they occur. To make comparison easier, long vowels in the Isbukun examples are represented by single vowel graphemes. Subject and non-subject forms are analysed and glossed differently in De Busser (2009) and Huang & Shih (2016), in this might reflect subtle differences in the grammatical distribution of these forms. Again, to make comparison easier, this terminology has here been homogenized.

Table 2: Personal pronouns in Isbukun Bunun

	Subject		Non-subj.		Poss.	Loc.
	Free	Bound	Free	Bound		
1S	saikin	-ik	ðaku	-ku	inak	ðakuan
2S	kasu(n)	-as	su	-su	isu	suan
3S	saia, sai(n)	—	saidʒia	—	isaidʒia, isia	siʔaan dʒia
1I	kata	-ta	ita, mita	-ta	imita	mitaan
1E	kaimin	-im	ðami	—	inam	ðamian
2P	kamu(n)	-am	mu	-mu	imu	muan
3P	nai, nian (VIS), naia (NVIS)	—	nai (VIS), naidʒia (NVIS)	—	inai (VIS), inaidʒia (NVIS)	naian dʒia (NVIS)

that variant forms within each category code a visibility distinction. The element *dʒia* on third person forms is in all likelihood a distal determiner enclitic, making their status of as personal pronouns contentious.

Demonstrative pronouns vary substantially between dialects. De Busser (2017: 95–97) describes an elaborate paradigm for Takivatan; see Table 3.

Table 3: Free demonstratives in Takivatan Bunun

		PROX	MED	DIST	USPEC
S	VIS	aipi	aipun	aipa	aip
	NVIS	naipi	naipun	naipa	naip
P	VIS	aiŋki	aiŋkun	aiŋka	—
	NVIS	naiŋki	naiŋkun	naiŋka	—
GNR	VIS	aiti	aitun	aita	—
	NVIS	naiti	naitun	naita	—
PAUC	VIS	—	—	(ainta)	—
	NVIS	—	naintun	(nainta)	—

None of these forms has so far been attested in Isbukun. The demonstrative forms described in Huang & Shih (2016: 95) distinguish case and distance, but not visibility. However, their paradigm consists of fully transparent combinations of the form *sia* or the spatial adverbs *di* and *adi* 'there' with various bound determiners (see Table 4), which encode both distinctions mentioned above.

Finally, all Bunun dialects have two sets of bound determiners, which encode a distance contrast and can occur on a variety of word classes including verbs (see De Busser 2009: 427–440 for an explanation).

Table 4: Determiners in Isbukun and Takivatan Bunun

		Takivatan	Isbukun (Taitung & Kaohsiung)	Isbukun (Nantou)
D1	PROX	-ki	-in	-in
	MED	-kun	-an	-an
	DIST	-ka	-a	-a
D2	PROX	-ti	-dʑin	-tin
	MED	-tun	-tan	-tan
	DIST	-ta	-dʑia	-tia

Again, there are formal differences, this time even between different varieties of the Isbukun dialect. The distinction between D1 and D2 appears to be fundamentally different in the two dialects. De Busser (2009: 426–440); De Busser (2017) argues that in Takivatan the difference between the two sets is semantic in nature; in Isbukun, the difference is associated with case (D1 = NOM, D2 = OBL; see Huang & Shih 2016: 95; Zeitoun 2000: 76). Bound determiners are optional, and are considerably more common in Takivatan than in other dialects.

The paradigms above serve as illustrations of the degree of differentiation between Takivatan and Isbukun, and give an overview of some of the paradigms that are relevant to the present analysis, as they directly influence the difference between different text genres in Bunun.

1.4 Narrative genres in Bunun

This chapter compares two narrative genres, traditional oral narrative text and biblical narrative, as they occur in a single Takivatan Bunun language community in the village of Bahuan at the East Coast of Taiwan.

Traditional narrative texts, despite being transmitted orally, are by nature not improvised. In traditional Bunun communities, both expository and narrative texts in formal settings follow relatively strict conventions that govern amongst other things: (1) who has the right to speak and when; (2) how certain traditional knowledge should be presented; and (3) which formal aspects, such as formulae related to politeness and the veracity of the narration, should be included in specific oral genres. Many of these conventionalized aspects of stories appear to be the result of an ongoing consultation process between the elders, or a larger group of members, of the community. Transgressions of these rules are usually pointed out by authoritative members of the community, usually male elders.

A second genre with which many Bunun people are confronted on a nearly daily basis are biblical narratives. Presbyterian and Catholic missionaries introduced Christianity after the end of the Second World War, and it is an important part of contemporary Bunun culture. From the 1940s onwards, especially the Presbyterian Church, through the Bible Society of Taiwan, has been active in translating biblical texts into the Bunun language.

Bible translations are intricate undertakings that typically involve a translation team consisting of translators, native language consultants, and theologians. Especially in cultures that have little historical affinity with the Judaeo-Christian tradition, this process is more than simply translating texts: it requires the meticulous transposition of an alien conceptual universe with its associated lexical and grammatical framework (see De Busser 2013). This makes it nearly impossible to produce translations for every dialect of Bunun.

The present Bunun Bible translation (Bible Society in Taiwan 2000) will be referred to as the Bunun Bible. It is the authoritative translation containing the full New Testament and an abbreviated Old Testament, and is heavily based on the Isbukun dialect. Despite this, it is used in almost all Bunun churches, irrespective of their denomination or the dialect area to which they belong. From a language planning perspective, this made a lot of sense: Isbukun is the largest dialect, has the widest geographical spread, and has been studied most extensively. This is not to say that the Bunun Bible is a written mirror of any specific Isbukun variety: the translation process rather resulted in a supra-dialectal written standard for Christian texts in Bunun, which is also used for other religious text genres such as hymns.

An interesting consequence is that, although many Bunun are reading or listening to excerpts of the Bible on a regular basis, especially "to members of Takbanuaz, Takivatan, Takibakha and Takituduh communities, the language of their Bible is not closely related to the common vernacular" (De Busser 2013: 67). Since the discrepancy between Isbukun and the Takivatan dialect is considerable, the result is a situation in which two dominant narrative genres in the Takivatan language community have relatively divergent dialectal characteristics.

This leads to a question: how and to what extent do language users in non-Isbukun communities interpret the content of these texts that belong to related genres but have quite distinct lexical and grammatical characteristics? To an extent, this is a matter of lexical and grammatical overlap between dialects. However, an additional question concerns the cohesive fabric of these two types of texts. Given the differences between grammatical paradigms that are central to establishing cohesion, such as personal pronouns, demonstratives, and determiners, how do language users keep tab of issues such as thematic integrity, topic continuity, and the general distribution of information in a narrative progression?

The present study will investigate this issue by looking at how these two different narrative genres realize cohesion, and in a particular subset of cohesive relations that is here referred to as referential cohesion.

1.5 Referential cohesion

The basic framework for my analysis of referential cohesion is set out in De Busser (2017). Halliday & Hasan (1976) consider cohesion to be the aggregate set of cohesive ties, semantic relationships that exist between meaningful elements in a text. Cohesive ties are directional: they point from a textual source, which will be called the Reference (Rc), to a second element, which can exist inside (4a) or outside the text (4b).

(4) a. Rc points to text-external Rt
    maq **aipa**   Rc [→ Rt: object in external reality]
    what DEM.S.DIST.VIS
    'What is that?'

   b. Rc points to text-internal Ta
    maq-a   ainak-a   **tama-ka**   tu-tuða   tu   miqðiq daiŋʔað
    DEFIN-LNK 1S.POSS-LNK father-K.DIST INTENS-real COMPL difficult large
    aipa.   Ta ← Rc
    DEM.S.DIST.VIS
    'As for my father, he really had a lot of difficulties.'

When this element is linguistic in nature, I call it a Target (Ta). Targets are themselves References that point back to previous targets. In doing so, they create cohesive chains, referential strands of different length that 'weave' through a text. Eventually, the final Reference of each chain points to a concept that exists outside the textual universe; this is called the Referent (Rt) of the cohesive chain and is in effect its ultimate Target (Halliday & Hasan 1976: 329; De Busser 2017: 107–108). This is schematised in Figure 2.

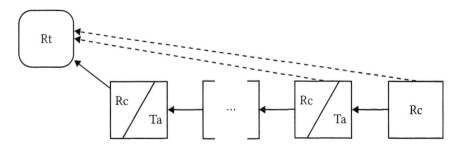

Figure 2: Schema of a cohesive chain

Together with other linguistic mechanisms, such as prosody, event expression, and contextual information, cohesion allows language users to interpret a text as a coherent whole operating in a context. It does this by expressing "the continuity that exists between one part of the text and another" (Halliday & Hasan 1976: 299). In doing so, cohesion forms an interface between the local and global distribution of information elements in a text. This interaction is given to be complex, but one specific example in which referential cohesion interacts with clause-internal information structural devices is by the "Theme tell[ing] the hearer where to start from in the interpretation of a message, and the cohesive ties signal how the message latches on to other parts of the discourse" (Hasselgård 2004: 68).

A crucial aspect of Halliday & Hasan's (1976) model is that cohesive ties are inherently semantically motivated, and therefore do not correspond to a single grammatical mechanism or exist between fixed classes of words or other linguistic elements. Somewhat contradictorily, Halliday & Hasan partly rely on grammatical criteria to distinguish different types of cohesion: they make a basic distinction between grammatical cohesion, which is expressed by grammatical means such as function words and grammatical constructions, and lexical cohesion, which is expressed through content words. These two categories further break down in an assortment of subtypes, based on a combination of semantic and grammatical criteria (see Halliday & Hasan 1976: 324).

This chapter takes a different approach; it focuses exclusively on referential cohesion, "the set of cohesive relations that create referring relationships between linguistic forms and referents" (De Busser 2017: 107). These are all linguistic expressions that can be targeted by deixis (or simply, that can be pointed at). In essence, this combines Halliday & Hasan's category of reference, with the exclusion of comparative reference, and their category of lexical cohesion, with the exclusion of collocation.

The criterion for establishing referential cohesion is semantic: all words and sub-lexical elements that are involved in establishing referential meaning are included in the cohesion analysis irrespective of their word class or grammatical status. Their involvement in reference is determined by their ability to be indicated by deictic expressions. The only formal restriction is that (with the exception of lexical compounds) phrases and other multi-word units are excluded, to prevent the data selection process from becoming too arbitrary. Word classes that have so far been implicated in referential cohesion in Bunun are: (1) nouns; (2) personal pronouns (see Table 1 and Table 2); (3) demonstrative pronouns (see Table 3); (4) bound demonstrative articles (see Table 4); (5) the anaphoric marker *sia* and its derivations; (6) numerals; (7) words expressing time, manner and location; (8) question words; and (9) certain verbal roots.

It is appealing to equate referential cohesion to anaphora resolution, but this is only so in a very broad sense. Phoric reference is typically seen as a grammatical property of language that is involved in referent tracking and uses fixed morphosyntactic strategies to establish relationships of identity between expressions and their antecedents (see for instance Huang 2000). On the other hand, referential cohesion, though obviously involved in reference tracking, is a semantic property of language that creates meaning relations between two referential expressions. These are not always relations of identity (although they can be), and neither do they necessarily have straightforward morphosyntactic correlates. For instance, the cohesive tie between *bantas* 'legs' and the preceding word *bunun* 'man' is meronymic in nature, and the fact that both are nouns is not grammatically determined.

(5) T3.8a
itu ***bunun-ʤia*** ***bantas*** *mas buhtuŋ hai ʤinsu*
this.here people-DIST.OBL leg OBL joint TPC immediately
is-tamasað-an
TRANSFER-strength-LV
'This man here, his legs and joints immediately became powerful, ...'

1 Referential cohesion in Bunun: A comparison of two genres

The fact that cohesion is involved in shaping the general structure of a text suggests that it varies between and is therefore indicative of genre (Martin 2001). One of the goals of this research is to try to establish the nature of this variation. One possibility suggested by Halliday & Hasan (1976: 4) is that "among different genres and different authors in the numbers and kinds of tie they typically employ." Another option is that genres vary in cohesive density, the number of cohesive elements or cohesive chains relative to text length. I will investigate both possibilities in the next section by analysing three short text segments.

2 Cohesion analysis

2.1 Data

The present study is a small-scale comparison of oral and biblical narrative as it occurs in the Takivatan Bunun speech community in the village of Bahuan (Chinese name: Mayuan) at the East Coast of Taiwan. It consists of the analysis of three text excerpts (T1, T2, and T3), which are given in their entirety with cohesive elements underlined in the Appendices. All three are part of larger narratives; segment boundaries were chosen to extract internally coherent sub-narratives.

The first two texts, T1 and T2, are traditional oral narrative sequences. They feature two elderly men, both fluent speakers of Takivatan Bunun and both around 75 years old at the time of recording. Text T1 is an account of a hunt and is part of a long story in which the speaker, Vau Taisnunan, recounts his life story. In text T2, Tulbus Manququ recounts how the traditional Bunun hunters used prophetic dreams to determine the appropriate time for the hunt.

Text T3 is an excerpt from the Acts of the Apostles in the Bunun Bible (Bible Society in Taiwan 2000), in which the apostles Peter and Paul heal a cripple. As mentioned in §1.2, it is a written text that is the product of a complex translation process. The spelling of the original text in the Bunun Bible was adapted to make it consistent with the Takivatan Bunun texts and make it adhere to a one-grapheme-per-phoneme principle (see Footnote 1).

2.2 Methodology

All elements in these texts that could be unambiguously identified as having a referential function were marked for analysis. Importantly, this means that non-expressed (ellipted) elements are not included, despite having a referential value. In contrast with the coding scheme in Halliday & Hasan (1976: 329–355), no prior assumption is made about the word class (or morphological class) of the elements involved; so far only the nine linguistic classes mentioned in §1.5 have been attested in referential cohesive relationships.

In the data set the following information about each Reference, and the nature of its cohesive tie to its Target and Referent are encoded:

1. The location of a Reference in the text;

2. Its word class (see §1.5 and Table 5);

3. Its Target and the location of the Target in the text (this is not relevant for exophoric links);

4. The Referent of its cohesive chain, i.e. the text-external entity (or event) to which the Reference eventually refers;

5. The ontological type of the Target, i.e. whether the immediate Target of a Reference refers an event, a location or time, or a textual element (see Table 6);

6. The phoric status of the cohesive tie, i.e. whether it is a anaphoric, cataphoric, or exophoric link (see Table 7);

7. The relationship between the concept indicated by a Reference and the concept indicated by its Target (see Table 8).

The first four data points provide information about the structural properties of cohesive chains; the information in 5–7 relates to conceptual and informational properties of individual cohesive ties. The Referent (data point 4) of referential expressions is indicated by unique names that allow us to track cohesive chains. Targets of cohesive ties can belong to a number of distinct ontological types (data point 5). Most commonly they are concrete or abstract entities in the real world, but they can also be reified events, physical or temporal locations, or textual elements; this is discussed in §3.2. The phoric status (data point 6) indicates whether a Reference points to a Target that precedes it (anaphoric reference), follows it (cataphoric reference) or exists outside the textual universe (exophoric reference).

Finally, data point 7 encodes the conceptual relationships between References and their Targets. Possible values are adapted from the set of relations subsumed under Halliday & Hasan (1976: 277–282) category of reiteration, complemented by Peirce's fundamental semiotic relationships that exist between signifiers and semiotic objects (metaphor, metonym, symbol; see Merrell 2001). The following relationships are distinguished:

Identity: Relations in which the Reference refers to the same concept as its Target. This can be because it is a literal repetition, a personal or demonstrative deictic, a synonym, or a near-synonym.

Hyponym/hyperonym/co-hyponym: Relations dictated in terms of category membership. Hyponyms refer to other concepts of which they are a subclass; hyperonyms refer to concepts of which they are a superclass; co-hyponyms are terms that have the same immediate superclass.

Part/whole/co-part: Relations that defined in terms of meronymy (see example 4 above).

Antonym: Relations based on conceptual opposition.

Metaphor: Relations based on similarity, other than identity.

Metonym: Relations based on proximity or, more generally, contiguity.

Symbol: Relations based on conventional semantic connections that cannot be reduced to any of the previous six relations.

Originally envisaged to be applicable to lexical cohesion alone, these relations here extend to all referential cohesive ties. In the present sample, no metaphoric and symbolic relations have been attested. The referential cohesion analysis of the sample texts is included in the Appendix.

The next section compares the distribution of these data in the three text samples in order to investigate the following questions:

1. How similar or different are oral (T1 & T2) and biblical narrative (T3) in terms of referential cohesion?

2. How do systematic differences manifest themselves?

3. Given that biblical texts are strongly influenced by the Isbukun dialect, to what extent are differences the result of dialect differentiation and to what extent of genre differentiation?

On a more fundamental level, these questions provide an insight in how Takivatan speakers deal with the genre innovation that biblical narrative has brought to their literary repertoire.

§3.1 discusses the distribution of word classes in the three texts (data point 2), and §3.2 that of various functional properties (data points 5–7). In §3.3, I look at the global properties of cohesion in oral and biblical narrative text. Note again that this exploratory study uses a relatively small text sample.

3 Discussion

3.1 Word class

Let's first have a look at how different word classes are involved in the expression of referential cohesion. Table 5 shows the distribution of word classes of References in the three text excerpts used in the present analysis (please take into account that these results are indicative only).

In line with expectation, nouns are the dominant word class by a considerable margin in all texts and both text types: referential cohesion prototypically involves reference to concrete or abstract entities, and cross-linguistically these are typically expressed by nouns. However, the relative proportion of nouns is significantly higher in biblical text than it is in oral narratives (44.59% in T3 vs. 25.45% in T1+T2). In oral narratives, this relative scarcity of nouns is offset by a relative abundance of place and time words. In

Table 5: Word class of References (Rc) of cohesive ties

	Oral narrative						Biblical narr.	
	T1		T2		T1+T2		T3	
	%	#	%	#	%	#	%	#
anaph. marker	10.71	3	3.70	1	7.27	4	5.41	4
article	14.29	4	14.81	4	14.55	8	4.05	3
dem. pronoun	10.71	3	0	0	5.45	3	0	0
place word	10.71	3	14.81	4	12.73	7	2.70	2
manner word	0	0	0	0	0	0	0	0
noun	21.43	6	29.63	8	25.45	14	44.59	33
numeral	3.57	1	0	0	1.82	1	2.70	2
pers. pronoun	3.57	1	3.70	1	3.64	2	29.73	22
time word	14.29	4	7.41	2	10.91	6	1.35	1
question word	0	0	0	0	0	0	1.35	1
verb	10.71	3	25.93	7	18.18	10	8.11	6
TOTAL	100	28	100	27	100	55	100	74

the absence of any indication that these word classes behave differently in the Takivatan and the Isbukun dialect, the most likely explanation for these discrepancies is that it is a genre distinction. In oral narratives, especially when they concern historical accounts of a personally experienced past, the temporal and geographical anchoring of events is probably more important than in stories of a distant past that are mainly intended as moral lessons. Conversely, Biblical narrative often puts great emphasis on the symbolic significance of names and places; more than half of the nouns in T3 are proper names. This is evident when the distributions of ontological types of Targets are compared in both genres (Table 6 below).

A second categorial inversion between the two genres can be observed in the distribution of demonstrative (anaphoric markers, determiners, and demonstratives) and personal deixis (personal pronouns). In oral narratives, demonstrative reference accounts for 27.27% of all referential expressions, and person pronouns for a mere 3.64%. In the biblical excerpt, personal pronouns make up 29.73% of all References, and the three demonstrative classes combined only 9.46%. It is not clear how this discrepancy can be explained as a genre distinction: oral narratives represent a highly speaker-centric form of storytelling and one would assume a relatively high proportion of personal pronominal reference. In this case, the difference is more likely due to dialect variation. For instance, as suggested in §1.3, bound determiners are much (the data suggests three times) more common in Takivatan than in other dialects including Isbukun. We also saw that, whereas Takivatan has a highly developed free demonstrative paradigm, putative demonstratives in Isbukun are all complex forms involving deictic determiners. Conversely, the Isbukun pronominal paradigm is more complex than that in Takivatan. In the sample, the most highly developed deictic paradigm also has the highest relative frequency in each language variety.

Interestingly, verbs sometimes express referential cohesion. This happens most commonly with verbs derived from nouns or locative words.

(6) T2.1b
taŋus-aŋ mati-**bahi**.
first   PROG-have.prophetic.dream
'... they interpreted a prophetic dream beforehand.'

(7) T1.2b
mina-**baʔav**   tupa naip   tu:
ABL-high.location say DEM.S.NVIS COMPL
'... Tiang had returned, he had come back from the mountain and told us: ...'

3.2 Conceptual dimensions

This section investigates the distribution of referential cohesive elements in terms of their conceptual-semantic properties (data points 5–7 in §2.2). It first looks at the ontological type of the Target. As mentioned above, referential expressions indicate concepts that can be targeted by deixis. One would assume that the prototypical Target of a referential cohesive expression is a material entity of some sort. Table 6 shows that this is not always the case.

Table 6: Ontological type of the Target of the cohesive tie

	Oral narrative						Biblical narr.	
	T1		T2		T1+T2		T3	
	%	#	%	#	%	#	%	#
Entity	39.29	11	29.63	8	34.55	19	78.38	58
Event	–	–	18.52	5	9.09	5	1.35	1
Location / Time	60.71	17	48.15	13	54.55	30	16.22	12
Text	–	–	3.70	1	1.82	1	4.05	3
TOTAL	100	28	100	27	100	55	100	74

In biblical narrative (T3) entities indeed make up more than two-thirds of the Targets of cohesive reference, the majority unsurprisingly people or concrete objects in the narrative world, e.g. *Pitilu* 'Peter' (T3.1c), *naidʒia* 'they < Peter and John' (T3.3c) or *kim* 'gold' (T3.6b). However, in the oral narrative sample this is only one-third. More than half of Targets in T1 and T2 refer to a spatial or temporal location, such as *laqaiban* 'route' (T1.3b), *ʔita* 'there (distal)' (T2.2a) or *[tupa]-ka* '[say] at that time' (T2.4g). In the previous section, I already explained that this discrepancy is genre-related. Traditional oral narratives in Bunun culture are typically anchored in the immediate spatio-temporal context; in Biblical stories, on the other hand, identifying time and place is only of secondary importance relative to the need to keep track of people and objects that populate an unfamiliar narrative universe and commonly have a symbolic significance.

Counterintuitively, 9.09% of referential expressions in T1 and T2 and 1.35% in T3 refer to events. These generally are instances of event reification: events are reinterpreted as quantifiable objects, with a certain materiality and well-defined boundaries (Quine 1985; Zacks & Tversky 2001). Finally, a number of referential cohesive ties have a metatextual function: rather than referring to anyone or anything in the narrative universe, they point towards part of the text itself. This type of cohesive tie corresponds to what Himmelmann (1996) and others refer to as discourse deixis. In Bunun dialects, these discourse deictic links are always expressed by *sia*, which in Takivatan, and possibly also in other dialects, is a specialized anaphoric marker and typically refers back to a phrase, clause or larger text segment in the immediate context (for shorter segments, typically the preceding sentence). For instance, in T3.3b the form *sia* in *sia masaniŋsiŋ pisvaŋduan* 'the aforementioned Holy Temple' refers back to an identical phrase in the previous sentence T3.2d, which in turn refers back to *masaniŋsiŋ pisvaŋduan* 'the Holy Temple' (T3.1c), the first mention of this particular Referent in the story.

Table 7: Phoric function of the cohesive tie

	Oral narrative						Biblical narr.	
	T1		T2		T1+T2		T3	
	%	#	%	#	%	#	%	#
Exophoric	10.71	3	25.93	7	18.18	10	16.22	12
Anaphoric	89.29	25	74.07	20	81.82	45	79.73	59
Cataphoric	–	–	–	–	–	–	4.05	3
TOTAL	100	28	100	27	100	55	100	74

Table 7 gives an overview of the distribution of phoric functions of the cohesive ties in the sample. Anaphoric reference is dominant in all genres: most referents central to the text are introduced near the beginning and tend to persist throughout the story. This also explains why exophora are less common: they often occur towards the front of the text. Cataphoric reference is rare and in the present sample is only attested in biblical narrative.

Finally, Table 8 gives a breakdown of the types of conceptual relationships between References and their Targets.[4] It is important to realize that these relationships are conceptual rather than lexical semantic distinctions: they hold between the concepts indi-

---

[4] Totals in Table 8 do not add up to 100% because exophoric cohesive ties have no associated conceptual relationship.

cated by referential expressions, and not only lexemes, as is the case in Halliday & Hasan (1976). This makes it possible, for instance, to establish a part-whole relationship between the noun ʔima 'hand' (T3.7a) and the pronoun isaidʒia '3S.POSS' (T3.7a).

Table 8: Cohesive relationship between Rc and Ta

	Oral narrative						Biblical narr.	
	T1		T2		T1+T2		T3	
	%	#	%	#	%	#	%	#
Identity	67.86	19	40.74	11	54.55	30	55.46	41
Hyponym	7.14	2	11.11	3	9.09	5	–	–
Hyperonym	–	–	7.41	2	3.64	2	–	–
Cohyponym	–	–	–	–	–	–	2.70	2
Part	–	–	3.70	1	1.82	1	8.11	6
Whole	3.57	1	–	–	1.82	1	2.70	2
Copart	–	–	–	–	–	–	1.35	1
Antonym	7.14	2	–	–	3.64	2	–	–
Metaphor	–	–	–	–	–	–	–	–
Metonym	7.14	2	7.40	2	7.27	4	9.46	7
Symbol	–	–	–	–	–	–	–	–
TOTAL	92.86	26	70.37	19	81.82	45	83.78	59

The introduction mentioned that referential cohesion is not necessarily identificational and is therefore not exclusively "concerned with resources for tracking participants in discourse" (Martin 2001: 38). However, from the data it is clear that this is an important aspect of cohesion: in both text genres, around 55% of all cohesive ties establish relationships of identity, and their function relates to reference tracking. Among the general semiotic relationships (metaphor, metonym, symbol), only metonymy is attested in the sample.

One possible minor difference between genres is that oral narrative appears to prefer hyponymic relationships, and biblical texts meronymy. However, this is in all likelihood an incidental difference resulting from the biblical story having as its main theme the miraculous healing of a physical handicap. Superficially, differences between oral and Biblical narratives appear almost non-existent, contrary to Halliday & Hasan's (1976: 4) expectation that genres differ in the types of cohesive ties they employ.

In conclusion, despite differences between the frequency distribution of word classes in the two genres (see §3.1), and despite the fact that they have their origins in different dialects of Bunun, oral and biblical narratives are largely similar in terms of the relative distribution of phoric properties and types of cohesive ties. The most conspicuous difference between the two genres is in the ontological type of the Target: cohesive ties in oral narratives have a higher tendency to refer to location or time, biblical narrative tends to refer more to material entities.

3.3 Global properties

The final section of this discussion examines the global properties of referential cohesion in the three Bunun text samples. As mentioned, it has been asserted that one of the ways in which cohesion might exhibit genre-dependent variation is through consistent differences in its density. In other words, the "number and density of such networks is one of the factors which gives to any text its particular flavour or texture" (Halliday & Hasan 1976: 52). Biber (1995: 187–193) suggests that this is indeed the case for Korean: the degree to which cohesive relations, including referential cohesion, are explicitly expressed varies widely between text genres. In this study, I measure density in Bunun text in three different ways:

Referential density: The total number of words relative to the total number of References (or cohesive ties) in a text.[5] Referential density gives a general impression of how much real estate cohesive referential expressions take up in a text. Note that it does not really measure which percentage of words are referential expressions, since References can be morphemes and a single word can therefore contain more than a single Reference (see e.g. *daiða-ki* 'there-K.PROX' in T1.2b).

Cohesive density: The number of cohesive chains in a text relative to the total number of words. This is a proxy indicator of what in the quote by Halliday & Hasan above is referred to as the density of the cohesive network, that is, how many cohesive chains weave themselves through a text of a normalized length.

Cohesive referential density: The number of cohesive chains in a text relative to the number of References. This measure indicates the average length of cohesive chains in a text, in terms of its average number of referential expressions.

Table 9 calculates these three density metrics for the three texts and the two genres in the present sample.

Table 9: Global properties of the text segments

	Oral			Biblical
	T1	T2	T1+T2	T3
# of words	62	80	142	179
# of referential expressions (Rc)	28	27	55	74
# of cohesive chains	7	9	16	19
Referential density (words / Rc)	2.214	2.963	2.582	2.419
Cohesive density (chains / words)	0.113	0.113	0.113	0.106
Referential cohesive density (Rc / chains)	4	3	3.438	3.895

---

[5]This measure is equivalent to Abadiano's (1995: 308) cohesive density.

While referential density and referential cohesive density both seem to be vacillating around a central value, the most surprising result is that the value for cohesive density is almost completely equal (0.11) across texts and genres. Especially in a small sample, where a certain degree of instability is expected, it is not very likely that this is a spurious result. This is very much against initial expectation, as cohesive density is one of the factors that one would most expect to vary across text types. For instance, in planned written text, such as our biblical narrative, tracking entities and spatio-temporal locations is cognitively less demanding than in oral narration, where visual cues that allow the listener to reaffirm the status of activated concepts are not available. The basic assumption would therefore be that written narration does not need to be as cohesively dense as oral narration.

Not only is this not the case, the present sample suggests that cohesive density is a constant, at least in Bunun. This is the opposite of "the possibility of cross-linguistic universals governing the patterns of discourse variation across registers and text types" that Biber (1995: 359) is looking for: what we have here is a property of the supra-clausal information structure of language that appears to be impervious to personal or genre-based variation. The reasons for the stability of this value are at present unclear. One possibility is that languages have a tendency to evolve towards a cohesive equilibrium, in which texts are as cohesive as necessary to make them coherent but not more so, an equivalent on a textual level of Haiman's (1983) competition between iconicity and expressiveness.

4 Conclusion

This leads us to an unexpected conclusion. Despite the evident grammatical differences between oral and biblical narratives in the sample, caused by dialect and genre differentiation, the conceptual properties of their underlying referential cohesive structures are surprisingly similar: against initial expectation, no major systematic differences can be observed in the phoricity or functional type of cohesive relationships. Even more so, the data suggests that, in defiance of lexical and grammatical variation in the two genres and dialects, the cohesive density of the two genres under investigation is invariant. This may point towards a cohesive constant underlying the structure of Bunun texts, though further research will need to verify this.

There are a small number of systematic differences between the two text genres. In terms of the referential type of the concepts they encode, referential cohesive ties in oral narrative tend to refer more to spatial or temporal location and those in Biblical narrative more to entities. This corresponds to a predilection for place and time words in the former genre, and for nouns in the latter. I argued above that this distinction is in all likelihood due to genre-based informational demands. On the other hand, a contrast in the frequency of demonstrative and personal deixis is probably rooted in dialect-related grammatical differences.

The present study is intended as a pilot, a fact-finding mission. Despite its modest data set, it has come up with interesting and unexpected results, but future research is necessary to test whether the present results will stand when tested against larger, statistically valid and more diversified data sets, and to find out whether regularities can be found in any of the lower-level categories. A number of questions regarding the invariance in cohesive density need to be answered. Will the cohesive density constant hold up in a larger sample with more genre distinctions and dialects? If so, how can it be explained? And does a similar phenomenon exist in other languages?

Acknowledgments

The research in this chapter was made possible by grant 104-2410-H-004-139- from the Ministry of Science of Technology, Taiwan. Many thanks to the anonymous reviewers for their insightful comments and suggestions.

Abbreviations

?	function unknown	GNR	generic
1E	first person exclusive	HESIT	hesitation marker
1S	first person singular	HUM	human
2S	second person singular	INCH	inchoative
3P	third person plural	INTENS	intensifier
3S	third person singular	INTER	interjection
ABL	ablative prefix expressing movement from	IRR	irrealis
		LNK	linker
ALL	allative prefix expression movement toward	LOC	locational prefix expressing position in or at
ANAPH	anaphoric marker	LV	locative voice
ART	article	MED	medial
ASSOC	associative	N	noun
ATTR	attributive marker	NEG	negator
AV	actor voice	NSUBJ	non-subject form
CAUS	causative	NUM	numeral
COMPL	complementizer	NVIS	non-visible
COORD	coordinator	OBL	oblique case marker
CV	CV reduplication	P	plural
D1	determiner paradigm 1	PAUC	paucal
D2	determiner paradigm 2	PLACE	place word
DEFIN	definitional marker	POSS	possessive
DEM	demonstrative	PROG	progressive
DIST	distal	PRON	pronoun
DYN	dynamic	PROX	proximal
EMO	emotive	PRT	particle
ENUM	enumerator	PRV	perfective

Q	question word	TIME	time word
RECIP	reciprocal	TPC	topicalizer
RESOBJ	resultative object	USPEC	underspecified
S	singular	UV	undergoer voice
STAT	stative	V	verb
SUBJ	subject form	VIS	visual
SUBORD	subordinator		

Appendix

T1: Segment oral narrative

Source: Takivatan Bunun Corpus
Corpus location: TVN-008-002:130-134
Speaker: Vau Taisnunan, M, 75 y
Location and time: Bahuan (Mayuan), 2006
The excerpt below was previously published as example 22 in De Busser (2017).

Text

(8) *Aupa tuða niaŋ tu nanu sanavan minsumina Tiaŋ, minabaʔav tupa naip tu:*

   a. *aupa tuða ni-aŋ   tu   nanu **sanavan** min-suma-in-a   **Tiaŋ***
      thus real NEG-PROG COMPL really evening INCH-return-PRV-LNK T.

   b. *mina-**baʔav**   tupa **naip**   tu*
      ABL-high.location say DEM.S.NVIS COMPL

   'But, when it wasn't really evening yet, Tiang had returned, he had come back from the mountain and told us: ...'

(9) *Na, maqtu laqbiŋina, naʔasa dusa ta matiskun, maluʔumi han baʔav daiðaki, pinkaunun isian baʔavta, ŋabul.*

   a. *na maqtu   **laqbiŋin**-a   na-asa   **dusa-ta**   ma-tiskun*
      well be.possible tomorrow-LNK IRR-have.to two-T.DIST DYN-in.a.group

   b. *maluʔum-i   han **baʔav**   daiða-ki*
      disperse-PRT be.at high.location there-K.PROX

   c. *pinkaun-un i-sia-an   **baʔav**-ta   **ŋabul***
      go.up-UV LOC-ANAPH-LV high.location-T.DIST deer

   'Well, tomorrow is possible, two of us will have to go together, and disperse when we get to this place, and we will climb upwards to the deer that is in that place above.'

(10) *A, namaqaisaq dauka, saqnutai du sia ʔukai laqaiban.*

   a. *a   na-ma-qaisaq   **dau-ka***
      INTER IRR-DYN-in.that.direction EMO-K.DIST

b. *saqnut-ai-du   sia   ʔuka-i   **laqaiban***
      get.stuck-PRT-EMO ANAPH NEG.have-PRT route

      'A, if he will go in that direction, he will get stuck there, without a way out.'

(11) *Mei, mei kahaul duna ʔuka duduma laqaiban, aupa tuða, maupa tupina.*
   a. *mei   mei   ka-**haul**   dun-a*
      already already come.from.below line-LNK
   b. *ʔuka   du-duma   **laqaiban***
      NEG.exist RED-other route
   c. *aupa tuða maupa tupa-in-a*
      thus real thus   say-PRV-LNK

      'The track is coming from below, and there is no other way out, it really is like that, thus he told us.'

(12) *Ansaisaŋa Atul Daiŋ tu "nis, matiŋmutin tamudana madav."*
   a. *ansais-aŋ-a   **Atul daiŋ** tu*
      forbid-PROG-ENUM A.   large COMPL
   b. *ni-is   ma-**tiŋmut**-in   ta-mu-dan-a   maðʔav*
      NEG-3S.F STAT-morning-PRV ?-ALL-road-LNK embarrassed

      'But Big Atul forbade us: "no, when it has become morning, we will leave, it is embarrassing.'

(13) *Na, ʔukin aipa ʔita namudanin, musbai naipa maqmut.*
   a. *na   ʔuka-in   **aipa**   **ʔita**   na-mu-dan-in*
      well NEG.have-PRV DEM.S.DIST.VIS there.DIST IRR-ALL-go-PRV
   b. *mu-isbai   **naipa**   **maqmut***
      ALL-cause.to.move DEM.S.DIST.NVIS night.time

      'Well, it will not be there anymore, it will be gone, it will have run away during the night.'

Cohesion analysis

Table 10 contains an analysis of referential cohesive elements in text T1 above. Numbers in the headers refer to the data points referred to in §2.2.

Table 10: Referential cohesion analysis T1

(1) Reference (Rc)	Rc word class (2)	(3)	Target (Ta)	Referent (4)	Functional role Ta (5)	Phoric function (6)	Rel. Rc-Ta (7)
1a *sanavan* 'evening'	TIME		(prev. text)	time of day	Loc/Time	Exophoric	Identity
1a *Tiaŋ* 'T.'	N		(prev. text)	Tiaŋ	Entity	Anaphoric	Identity
1b *[mina-]baʔav* 'come from the mountain'	V	1a	*Tiaŋ* 'T.'	location deer	Loc/Time	Anaphoric	Identity
1b *naip* 'DEM.S.NVIS'	DEM	1a	*sanavan* 'evening'	Tiaŋ	Entity	Anaphoric	Identity
2a *laqbiŋin[-a]* 'tomorrow'	TIME		(prev. text)	time of day	Loc/Time	Anaphoric	Metonym
2a *dusa-ta* 'two'	NUM			we	Entity	Exophoric	Hyponym
2a *[dusa]-ta* 'ART.ENT.DIS'	ART	1b	*[mina-]baʔav* 'come from the mountain'	location deer	Loc/Time	Anaphoric	Identity
2b *baʔav* 'high location'	V	2a	*[dusa]-ta* 'ART.ENT.DIS'	location deer	Loc/Time	Anaphoric	Identity
2b *daiðal-ki* 'that place'	PLACE	2a	*laqbiŋin* 'tomorrow'	location deer	Event	Anaphoric	Identity
2b *[daiða]-ki* 'ART.EVT.PROX'	ART	2b	*daiða-ki* 'that place'	time of day	Loc/Time	Anaphoric	Identity
2c *i-sia-an* 'the place of that one'	ANAPH	2b	*daiða-ki* 'that place'	location deer	Loc/Time	Anaphoric	Identity
2c *[i-]sia[-an]* 'ANAPH'	ANAPH		(*dapana* 'foot prints') [008-002:125]	deer	Entity	Anaphoric	Whole
2c *baʔav[-ta]* 'high location'	PLACE	2c	*i-sia-an* 'the place of that one'	location deer	Loc/Time	Anaphoric	Identity
2c *[baʔav]-ta* 'ART.ENT.DIST'	ART	2c	*sia* 'ANAPH'	location deer	Entity	Anaphoric	Identity
2c *ŋabul* 'deer'	N	2c	*-ta* 'ART'	deer	Entity	Anaphoric	Identity
2c *[na-ma-qaisaq-dau]-ka* 'ART.EVT.DIST'	ART	2c	*baʔav-ta* 'high location'	location deer	Loc/Time	Anaphoric	Identity
3a *sia* 'ANAPH'	ANAPH	2c	*ŋabul* 'deer'	deer	Entity	Anaphoric	Identity
3b *laqaiban* 'route'	N			route deer	Loc/Time	Exophoric	Identity
3a *[ka-]haul* 'below'	V	3a	*[na-ma-qaisaq-dau]-ka* 'ART.EVT.DIST'	location deer	Loc/Time	Anaphoric	Antonym
3b *laqaiban* 'route'	N	3b	*laqaiban* 'route'	route deer	Loc/Time	Anaphoric	Identity
4a *dun* 'line'	N	4a	*dun* 'line'	route deer	Loc/Time	Anaphoric	Identity
4b *laqaiban* 'route'	N			route deer	Loc/Time	Anaphoric	Identity
5a *Atul daiŋ* 'Big Atul'	N		(*nas-Atul daiŋ* 'the erstwhile Big Atul') [008-002:126]	Atul	Entity	Anaphoric	Identity
5b *[niʔ]-is* '3S.F'	PRON	3b	*sia* 'anaph'	deer	Entity	Anaphoric	Identity
5b *[ma-]tiŋmut[-in]* 'morning'	TIME	2b	*[daiða]-ki* 'ART.SIT.PROX'	time of day	Loc/Time	Anaphoric	Hyponym
6a *aipa* 'DEM.S.DIST.VIS'	DEM	3b	*[niʔ]-is* '3S.F'	deer	Entity	Anaphoric	Identity
6a *ʔita* 'there.DIST'	PLACE	4a	*[ka-]haul* 'below'	location deer	Loc/Time	Anaphoric	Antonym
6b *naipa* 'DEM.S.DIST.NVIS'	DEM	5a	*aipa* 'DEM.S.DIST.VIS'	deer	Entity	Anaphoric	Identity
6b *maqmut* 'night time'	TIME	4b	*[ma-]tiŋmut[-in]* 'morning'	time of day	Loc/Time	Anaphoric	Metonym

T2: Segment oral narrative

Source: Takivatan Bunun Corpus
Corpus location: TVN-012-001:38-41
Speaker: Tulbus Manququ, M, 75 y
Location and time: Bahuan (Mayuan), 2006

Text

(14) *Maqai maqabasi tupa tu madaiŋʔaði namuqumaka taŋusaŋ matibahi.*

    a. *maqai ma-**qabas**-i   tupa tu   ma-**daiŋʔað**-i*
       if   DYN-in.former.times-PRT say   COMPL STAT-old-PRT
       *na-mu-**quma**-ka*
       IRR-ALL-field-K.DIST

    b. *taŋus-aŋ mati-**bahi***
       first   PROG-have.prophetic.dream

    'If in the old days the elders said they wanted to work on the land, they interpreted a prophetic dream beforehand.'

(15) *Namaqun ʔita maqai masihala bahia, tudip, na, sintupadu tu maqai ʔitun asa namasihal kakaunun.*

    a. *na-maqun ʔita*
       IRR-cut.off there.DIST

    b. *maqai ma-sihal-a   **bahi**-a   tudip*
       if   STAT-good-SUBORD prophetic.dream-SUBORD that.time

    c. *na   sin-tupa-du   tu   maqai ʔitun*
       well RES.OBJ-say-EMO COMPL if   there.MED

    d. *asa   na-ma-sihal   ka-kaun-un*
       be.able IRR-STAT-good CV-eat-UV

    'And when they wanted to go there to harvest (lit: when they wanted to cut off things in that place), if the dream was good, that meant in those days that if you were there, you could eat very well.'

(16) *A maqai dipi madiqla bahia tupa tu asa ni ʔituni nalauq, nitu na ... masihala kakauna sanasia maqai, amin tu maqai ʔitun namuqða kuðaki madiqla bahi, na haiða matað.*

    a. *a   maqai **dip**-i   ma-diqla **bahi**-a*
       INTER if   then-PRT STAT-bad prophetic.dream-LNK

    b. *tupa tu   asa   ni   ʔitun-i*
       say COMPL have.to NEG there.MED-PRT

    c. *nalauq   ni   tu   na ma-sihal-a   ka-kaun-a*
       otherwise NEG COMPL well STAT-good-LNK CV-eat-LNK

d. sana-*sia*   maqai
    ACCORDING.TO-ANAPH if

e. amin tu   maqai ʔitun   na-muqða kuða-*ki*
    all   COMPL if   there.MED IRR-again work-K.PROX

f. ma-diqla **bahi**
    STAT-bad prophetic.dream

g. na   haiða matað
    well have die

'And if the dream was bad, then they said that you must not go there, because otherwise you would not eat well, if you followed the rule, but if anyone at all went back to that place to work, and there was a bad dream, people would die.'

(17) A, maqai mataisaq ... matataisaq a madadaiŋʔað tu, ... maqai munʔitaʔa mavia mataisaq tu saduʔuki siatu, sinsusuað bunuað masmamua mavisqai, mavilasa tu-paka madadaiŋʔað tu na maqtu munquma istaʔai nakasihalain kakaunun namasihala bunun.

a. a   maqai ma-taisaq
    INTER if   DYN-dream

b. ma-ta-taisaq   a   **madadaiŋʔað** tu
    DYN-CV-dream INTER elder   COMPL

c. maqai mun-ʔita   a   ma-via   ma-taisaq   tu
    if   ALL-there.DIST HESIT DYN-why DYN-dream COMPL

d. saduʔu-*ki* sia   tu
    see-K.PROX ANAPH COMPL

e. sin-su-suað   **bunuað** mas-ma-muav ma-visqa-i
    RES.OBJ-CV-sow plum   BE-CV-excessive STAT-abundant.with.fruit-PRT

f. mavi-*las*-a
    CONTAIN-fruits-LNK

g. tupa-*ka*   madadaiŋʔað tu
    tell-K.DIST elder   COMPL

h. na   maqtu   mun-**quma** ista-ai
    well be.possible.to ALL-field   3S.DIST-PRT

i. na-ka-sihal-in   ka-kaun-un
    IRR-ASSOC.DYN-good-PRV CV-eat-UN

j. na-ma-sihal-a   **bunun**
    IRR-STAT-good-LNK people

'And if they dreamt... if the elders dreamt that, if they went over there, they suddenly dreamt that they saw that the plum tree had grown so that it was full of fruits and had large fruits, then the elders would say that it was permitted for them to the land to work, and they would produce good fruits, and the people would also be fine.'

Table 11: Referential cohesion analysis T2

(1)	Reference (Rc)	Rc word class (2)	(3)	Target (Ta)	Referent (4)	Functional role Ta (5)	Phoric function (6)	Rel. Rc-Ta (7)
1a	ma-qabaʃ[-i] 'in the old days'	V			in former times	Loc/Time	Exophoric	
1a	ma-daiŋ-ʔað[-i] 'elders'	N			elders	Entity	Exophoric	
1a	[na-mun-lquma[-ka] go work on the land'	V			land	Loc/Time	Exophoric	
1a	[na-mun-quma]-ka 'over there'	ART			location land	Loc/Time	Exophoric	
1b	[mati-]bahi 'have a prophetic dream'	V			dream	Event	Exophoric	
2a	ʔita 'there.DIST'	PLACE	1a	[na-mun-lquma[-ka] go work on the land'	land	Loc/Time	Anaphoric	Identity
2b	bahiʃ[-a] 'prophetic dream'	N	1b	[mati-]bahi 'have a prophetic dream'	dream	Event	Anaphoric	Hyponym
2b	tudip 'that time'	TIME	1a	[ma-qabaʃ]-i 'in the old days'	in former times	Loc/Time	Anaphoric	Hyponym
2c	ʔitun 'there.MED'	PLACE			village	Loc/Time	Exophoric	
3a	dipʃ[-i] 'then'	TIME	2b	tudip 'that time'	in former times	Loc/Time	Anaphoric	Metonym
3a	bahiʃ[-a] 'prophetic dream'	N	2b	bahiʃ[-a] 'prophetic dream'	dream	Event	Anaphoric	Hyponym
3b	ʔitun[-i] 'there.MED'	PLACE	2a	ʔita 'there.DIST'	land	Loc/Time	Anaphoric	Identity
3d	[sana-]sia 'according to the aforementioned'	V			text	Text	Anaphoric	
3e	ʔitun 'there.MED'	PLACE	3b	ʔitun[-i] 'there.MED'	land	Loc/Time	Anaphoric	Identity
3e	[kuðaʃ]-ki '(the work) in this place'	ART	3e	ʔitun 'there.MED'	land	Loc/Time	Anaphoric	Identity
3f	bahi 'prophetic dream'	N	3a	bahiʃ[-a] 'prophetic dream'	dream	Event	Anaphoric	Identity
4b	madadaiŋʔað 'elders'	N	1a	ma-daiŋ-ʔað[-i] 'elders'	elders	Entity	Anaphoric	Identity
4c	[mun-]ʔita '(go) over there'	V	3e	ʔitun 'there.MED'	land	Loc/Time	Anaphoric	Identity
4d	[sadu?a]-ki '(see) here'	ART	3f	bahi 'prophetic dream'	dream	Event	Anaphoric	Metonym
4d	sia 'ANAPH'	ANAPH	4b	madadaiŋʔað 'elders'	elders	Entity	Anaphoric	Identity
4e	bunuað 'plum'	N			plum tree	Entity	Exophoric	
4f	[mavi-]lasf[-a] '(be full of) fruits'	V	4e	bunuað 'plum'	plum tree	Entity	Anaphoric	Hyperonym
4g	[tupa]-ka '(say) at that time'	ART	3a	dipʃ-iʃ 'then'	in former times	Loc/Time	Anaphoric	Part
4g	madadaiŋʔað 'elders'	N	4d	sia 'ANAPH'	elders	Entity	Anaphoric	Identity
4h	[mun-]quma 'go to the field'	V	4c	[mun-]ʔita '(go) over there'	land	Loc/Time	Anaphoric	Identity
4h	istaʃ[-ai] '3S.DIST'	PRON	4g	madadaiŋʔað 'elders'	elders	Entity	Anaphoric	Identity
4j	bunun 'people'	N	4h	istaʃ[-ai] '3S.DIST'	elders	Entity	Anaphoric	Hyperonym

T3: Segment Biblical narrative

Source: *Tama Dihanin tu Halinga. The Bunun Bible in Today's Taiwan Bunun Version* (Bible Society in Taiwan 2000)
Corpus location: Acts 3:1-10

Text

(18) *Aiða tu hanian, masa tauŋhuvalin tu ʥintau, Pitilu mas Iuhani hai kusia Masaniŋsiŋ Pisvaŋduan.*

　　a. *ʔaiða tu　　　hanian*
　　　　exist COMPL day

　　b. *masa　tauŋhuvali-in tu　　ʥin-ta*
　　　　WHEN noon-PRV　　ATTR HOUR-three

　　c. *Pitilu mas Iuhani hai kusia masaniŋsiŋ pisvaŋduan*
　　　　Peter OBL John　TPC use　holy　　　　temple

　　'There was a day, when it was three at noon, that Peter and John were using the Holy Temple.'

(19) *Isia tupaun tu Manauað Ilav ʥia hai, aiða tu taʥini maisna tausʔuvaðun mapiha, kaupa hanian ansahanun mas bunun mapunsia ilav ʥia, makikisaiv mas nakuŋadah sia Masaniŋsiŋ Pisvaŋduan tu bunun.*

　　a. *i-sia　　　tupa-un tu　　manauʔað ʔilav-ʥia　　　hai*
　　　　POSS-ANAPH say-UV COMPL beautiful　door-DIST.OBL TPC

　　b. *ʔaiða tu　　　taʥini　maisna tausʔuvað-un ma-piha*
　　　　exist COMPL one.HUM from　give.birth-UV STAT-cripple

　　c. *kaupa hanian ansahan-un mas bunun ma-pun-sia　　　　ʔilav-ʥia*
　　　　each　day　　carry.to-UV OBL person DYN-CAUS.ALL-ANAPH door-DIST.OBL

　　d. *ma-ki-kisaiv　mas na-ku-ŋadah　　　sia　　masaniŋsiŋ pisvaŋduan*
　　　　DYN-RED-give OBL IRR-ASSOC.ALL-lower ANAPH holy　　　　temple
　　　tu　bunun
　　　ATTR person

　　'At what was called the Beautiful Gate, there was one man who was cripple from birth, and people carried him every day and put them at that door, and he begged to people that went down into the Holy Temple.'

(20) *Sadu saia tu Pitilu mas Iuhani hai nakuŋadah sia Masaniŋsiŋ Pisvaŋduan, at makisaiv naiʥia.*

　　a. *sadu saia　　tu*
　　　　see　3S.NOM COMPL

b. *Pitilu mas **Iuhani** hai na-ku-ŋadah sia masaniŋsiŋ*
Peter OBL John TPC IRR-ASSOC.ALL-lower ANAPH holy
pisvaŋduan
temple

c. *at makisaiv **naiʥia***
and make.give 3P.OBJ

'He saw that Peter and John were about to enter the Holy Temple and made them give (money) [tried to ask them for money].'

(21) *Naia hai samantuk saiʥia tupa Pitilu tu: "Sadua kasu maðami!"*

a. *naia hai samantuk saiʥia*
3P.NOM TPC keep.close.watch.on 3S.OBL

b. *tupa **Pitilu** tu*
say Peter COMPL

c. *sadu-a **kasu** ma-ðami*
see-LNK 2S.NOM DYN-1E.OBL

'They looked straight at him, and Peter said as follows: "You look at us!"'

(22) *Saia hai samantuk naiʥia, asa usiðan maðmað.*

a. *saia hai samantuk naiʥia*
3S.NOM TPC keep.close.watch.on 3P.OBL

b. *asa u-siða-an maðmað*
want ABLE.TO-take-LV which.things

'He looked straight at them, he wanted to be able to get something from them.'

(23) *Pitilu hai tupa saiʥia tu: "Ukan saikin kim mas sui, haitu nasaivan ku kasu mas inak tu iskakaupa: Mapakasia saikin mas itu takisia Naðale tu Iesu Kilistu tu ŋan tupa masu tu, mindaŋkaða mudan!"*

a. ***Pitilu** hai tupa **saiʥia** tu*
Peter TPC say 3S.OBL COMPL

b. *ʔuka-an **saikin** **kim** mas sui*
NEG.have-LV 1S.TOP.AG gold COORD money

c. *haitu na-saiv-an-ku kasu mas i-nak tu iskakaupa*
although IRR-give-LV-1S.NSUBJ 2S.NOM OBL POSS-1S.N ATTR everything

d. *ma-paka-sia **saikin** mas itu taki-sia **Naðale** tu*
DYN-RECIP-ANAPH 1S.TOP.AG OBL this.here ORIGIN-ANAPH Nazareth ATTR
***Iesu Kilistu** tu ŋan*
Jezus Christ ATTR name

e. *tupa **masu** tu*
say 2S.OBL COMPL

f. *mindaŋkað-a mu-dan*
   stand.up-LNK ALL-go

   'Peter told him: "I do not have gold or money here, but I will give you everything I have here. I use the name of Jesus Christ who comes from Nazareth to tell you: stand up and walk."'

(24) *Pitilu hai maʔalak mas isaidʒia tu tanaskaun ima, sidaŋkað saidʒia.*

   a. **Pitilu** hai ma-ʔalak mas **isaidʒia** tu   tanaskaun ʔima
      Peter TPC DYN-lead OBL 3S.POSS ATTR right   hand

   b. *si-daŋkað* **saidʒia**
      ?-stand   3S.OBL

   'Peter led him by the right hand, and helped him to stand.'

(25) *Itu bunun dʒia bantas mas buhtuŋ hai dʒinsu istamasaðan, at mataidaða, matuduldul, kitŋab mudadan.*

   a. itu   **bunun-dʒia**   **bantas**   mas **buhtuŋ** hai **dʒinsu**
      this.here people-DIST.OBL leg.and.foot OBL joint   TPC immediately
      is-tamasað-an
      TRANSFER-strength-LV

   b. at   mataidaða matuduldul kitŋab mu-da-dan
      and jump   stand   begin ALL-RED-road

   'This man here, his legs and joints immediately became powerful, and he jumped up and stood, and he began to walk.'

(26) *Saia hai taskun naidʒia kuŋadah sia Masaniŋsiŋ Pisvaŋduan, madʒishahainað mudadan, matumashiŋ mas Sasbinað Dihanin.*

   a. **saia**   hai   taskun **naidʒia**   ku-**ŋadah** sia
      3S.NOM TPC do.together 3P.NSUBJ ASSOC.ALL-lower ANAPH   holy
      masaniŋsiŋ pisvaŋduan
      temple

   b. *madʒishahainað mu-da-dan*   matumashiŋ mas **Sasbinað Dihanin**
      gleeful   ALL-RED-road thank   OBL God

   'Together with them he entered the Holy Temple, and gleefully walk over and he thanked God.'

(27) *Bunun hai sadu saidʒiaa tu mudadan, at matumashiŋ mas Sasbinað Dihanin, at dʒiŋhuða, au pa sahal naia tu saia hai takisia Masaniŋsiŋ Pisvaŋduan tu Manauað Ilav malʔanuhu makisasaiv tu bunun.*

   a. **bunun** hai sadu **saidʒia**-a tu   mu-da-dan
      people TPC see 3S.OBL-LNK COMPL ALL-RED-road

   b. at   matumashiŋ mas **Sasbinað Dihanin**
      and thank   OBL God

c. *at ʤiŋhuða*
   and be.startled

d. *aupa sahal **naia** tu*
   because clearly 3P.NOM COMPL

e. ***saia** hai taki-sia masaniŋsiŋ pisvaŋduan tu*
   3S.NOM TPC have.origins.in-ANAPH holy temple ATTR
   manauʔað ʔilav** malʔanuhu sa-makisaiv tu **bunun
   beautiful door sit.down SEE-beg ATTR person

   'People saw him walk, and thank God, and they were startled, because they recognized him as the man that used to beg sitting down at the Beautiful Door that was the entrance to the Holy Temple.'

Table 12: Referential cohesion analysis T3

(1)	Reference (Rc)	Rc word class (2)	(3)	Target (Ta)	Referent (4)	Functional role Ta (5)	Phoric function (6)	Rel. Rc-Ta (7)
1a	hanian 'day'	N	1b	ʤin-ta 'three o'clock'	time of story	Loc/Time	Exophoric	
1b	tauɲhuvaliʃ-in] 'having become noon'	V			time of day	Loc/Time	Cataphoric	Metonym
1b	ʤin-ta 'three o'clock'	NUM	1a	hanian 'day'	time of day	Loc/Time	Anaphoric	Part
1c	Pitilu 'Peter'	N			Peter	Entity	Exophoric	
1c	Iuhani 'John'	N			John	Entity	Exophoric	
1c	masaniŋsiŋ pisvaŋduan 'the Holy Temple'	N			temple	Entity	Exophoric	
2a	i-sia 'POSS-ANAPH'	ANAPH	1c	masaniŋsiŋ pisvaŋduan 'the Holy Temple'	temple	Entity	Anaphoric	Identity
2a	manauʔað ʔilavʃ-ʤia] 'beautiful door-DIST.OBL'	N	2a	i-sia 'POSS-ANAPH'	door	Entity	Anaphoric	Part
2a	[manauʔað ʔilavʃ-ʤia 'beautiful door-DIST.OBL	ART	2a	i-sia 'POSS-ANAPH'	location temple	Loc/Time	Anaphoric	Metonym
2b	taʤini 'one.HUM'	NUM			cripple	Entity	Exophoric	
2b	mapiħa 'STAT-cripple'	N	2b	taʤini 'one.HUM'	cripple	Entity	Anaphoric	Identity
2c	hanian 'day'	TIME			every day	Loc/Time	Exophoric	
2c	bunun 'person'	N			people	Entity	Exophoric	
2c	[ma-pun-]sia 'DYN-CAUS.ALL-ANAPH'	V	2a	manauʔað ʔilavʃ-ʤia] 'beautiful door-DIST.OBL'	door	Entity	Anaphoric	Metonym
2c	ʔilavʃ-ʤia] 'door-DIST.OBL'	N	2c	[ma-pun-]sia 'DYN-CAUS.ALL-ANAPH'	door	Entity	Anaphoric	Metonym
2c	[ʔilavʃ-ʤia 'door-DIST.OBL'	ART	2a	[manauʔað ʔilavʃ-ʤia	location temple	Loc/Time	Anaphoric	Identity
2d	na-ku-ŋaðah 'IRR-ASSOC.ALL-lower'	PLACE	2c	ʔilavʃ-ʤia] 'door-DIST.OBL'	location temple	Loc/Time	Anaphoric	Metonym
2d	sia 'ANAPH'	ANAPH	1c	masaniŋsiŋ pisvaŋduan 'the Holy Temple'	temple	Text	Anaphoric	Identity
2d	masaniŋsiŋ pisvaŋduan 'the Holy Temple'	N	2a	i-sia 'POSS-ANAPH'	temple	Entity	Anaphoric	Identity
2d	bunun 'person'	N	2c	bunun 'person'	people	Entity	Anaphoric	Cohyponym
3a	saia '3S.NOM'	PRON	2b	mapiħa 'STAT-cripple'	cripple	Entity	Anaphoric	Identity
3b	Pitilu 'Peter'	N	1c	Pitilu 'Peter'	Peter	Entity	Anaphoric	Identity
3b	Iuhani 'John'	N	1c	Iuhani 'John'	John	Entity	Anaphoric	Identity

(1) Reference (Rc)	Rc word class (2)	(3)	Target (Ta)	Referent (4)	Functional role Ta (5)	Phoric function (6)	Rel. Rc-Ta (7)
na-ku-ŋadah 'IRR-ASSOC.ALL-lower'	V	3b	*na-ku-ŋadah* 'IRR-ASSOC.ALL-lower'	location temple	Loc/Time	Anaphoric	Identity
sia 'ANAPH'	ANAPH	3b		temple	Text	Anaphoric	Identity
masaniŋsiŋ pisvaŋduan 'the Holy Temple'	N	3b	*masaniŋsiŋ pisvaŋduan* 'the Holy Temple'	temple	Entity	Anaphoric	Whole
naidʒia '3P.OBJ'	PRON	3c	*Pitilu* 'Peter' + *Iuhani* 'John'	Peter and John	Entity	Anaphoric	Identity
naia '3P.NOM'	PRON	4a	*naidʒia* '3P.OBJ'	Peter and John	Entity	Anaphoric	Identity
saidʒia '3S.OBL'	PRON	3a	*saia* '3S.NOM'	cripple	Entity	Anaphoric	Identity
Pitilu 'Peter'	N	3b	*Pitilu* 'Peter'	Peter	Entity	Anaphoric	Identity
kasu '2S.NOM'	PRON	4a	*saidʒia* '3S.OBL'	cripple	Entity	Anaphoric	Identity
[ma-]ðami 'DYN-1E.OBL'	PRON	4c	*naia* '3P.NOM'	Peter and John	Entity	Anaphoric	Identity
saia '3S.NOM'	PRON	4c	*kasu* '2S.NOM'	cripple	Entity	Anaphoric	Identity
naidʒia '3P.OBJ'	PRON	5a	*[ma-]ðami* 'DYN-1E.OBL'	Peter and John	Entity	Anaphoric	Identity
maðmað 'which.things'	Q	5b		possessions	Entity	Exophoric	Identity
Pitilu 'Peter'	N	6a	*Pitilu* 'Peter'	Peter	Entity	Anaphoric	Identity
saidʒia '3S.OBL'	PRON	6a	*saia* '3S.NOM'	cripple	Entity	Anaphoric	Identity
saikin '1S.NOM'	PRON	6a	*Pitilu* 'Peter'	Peter	Entity	Anaphoric	Identity
sui 'money'	N	6b	*maðmað* 'which.things'	possessions	Entity	Anaphoric	Part
kim 'gold'	N	6b	*maðmað* 'which.things'	possessions	Entity	Anaphoric	Part
[na-saiv-an]-ku '-1S.N'	PRON	6b	*saikin* '1S.NOM'	Peter	Entity	Anaphoric	Identity
kasu '2S.NOM'	PRON	6a	*saidʒia* '3S.OBL'	cripple	Entity	Anaphoric	Identity
i-nak 'POSS-1S.N'	PRON	6c	*[na-saiv-an]-ku* '-1S.N'	Peter	Entity	Anaphoric	Identity
iskakaupa 'everything'	N	6b	*sui* 'money'	possessions	Entity	Anaphoric	Whole
[ma-paka-]sia 'DYN-RECIP-ANAPH'	V	6b-6c		do	Event	Anaphoric	Identity
saikin '1S.NOM'	PRON	6c	*i-nak* 'POSS-1S.N'	Peter	Entity	Anaphoric	Identity
[taki-]sia 'ORIGIN-ANAPH'	V	6d		Nazareth	Loc/Time	Cataphoric	Identity
Naðale 'Nazareth'	N	6d	*Naðale* 'Nazareth'	Nazareth	Loc/Time	Exophoric	Identity
Iesu Kilistu 'Jesus Christ'	N	6d		Jesus	Entity	Exophoric	Identity
ŋan 'name'	N	6d		name	Entity	Exophoric	Identity
masu '2S.OBL'	PRON	6e	*kasu* '2S.NOM'	cripple	Entity	Anaphoric	Identity
Pitilu 'Peter'	N	6d	*saikin* '1S.NOM'	Peter	Entity	Anaphoric	Identity
isaidʒia '3S.POSS'	PRON	6e	*masu* '2S.OBL'	cripple	Entity	Anaphoric	Identity
ʔima 'hand'	N	7a	*isaidʒia* '3S.POSS'	hand of cripple	Entity	Anaphoric	Part
saidʒia '3S.OBL'	PRON	7a	*isaidʒia* '3S.POSS'	cripple	Entity	Anaphoric	Identity

1 Referential cohesion in Bunun: A comparison of two genres

(1)	Reference (Rc)	Rc word class (2)	(3)	Target (Ta)	Referent (4)	Functional role Ta (5)	Phoric function (6)	Rel. Rc-Ta (7)
8a	bunun[-dʒia] 'people-DIST.OBL'	N	7b	saidʒia '3S.OBL'	cripple	Entity	Anaphoric	Identity
8a	[bunun]-dʒia 'people-DIST.OBL'	ART	3b	na-ku-ŋadah 'IRR-ASSOC.ALL-lower'	location temple	Loc/Time	Anaphoric	Metonym
8a	bantas 'leg'	N	8a	bunun[-dʒia] 'people-DIST.OBL'	limb	Entity	Anaphoric	Part
8a	buhtuŋ 'joint'	N	8a	bantas 'leg'	limb	Entity	Anaphoric	Copart
9a	saia '3S.NOM'	PRON	8a	bunun[-dʒia] 'people-DIST.OBL'	cripple	Entity	Anaphoric	Identity
9a	naidʒia '3P.OBJ'	PRON	5a	naidʒia '3P.OBJ'	Peter and John	Entity	Anaphoric	Identity
9a	[ku-]ŋadah 'ASSOC.ALL-lower'	PLACE	8a	bunun[-dʒia] 'people-DIST.OBL'	location temple	Loc/Time	Anaphoric	Metonym
9a	sia 'ANAPH'	ANAPH	3b	masaniŋsiŋ pisvaŋduan 'the Holy Temple'	temple	Text	Anaphoric	Identity
9a	masaniŋsiŋ pisvaŋduan 'the Holy Temple'	N	3b	masaniŋsiŋ pisvaŋduan 'the Holy Temple'	temple	Entity	Anaphoric	Identity
9b	Sasbinað Dihanin 'God'	N			God	Entity	Exophoric	
10a	bunun 'person'	N	2d	bunun 'person'	people	Entity	Anaphoric	Cohyponym
10a	saidʒia[-a] '3S.OBL-LNK'	PRON	9a	saia '3S.NOM'	cripple	Entity	Anaphoric	Identity
10b	Sasbinað Dihanin 'God'	N	9b	Sasbinað Dihanin 'God'	God	Entity	Anaphoric	Identity
10d	naia '3P.NOM'	PRON	10a	bunun 'person'	people	Entity	Anaphoric	Identity
10e	saia '3S.NOM'	PRON	10a	saidʒia[-a] '3S.OBL-LNK'	cripple	Entity	Cataphoric	Identity
10e	[taki-]sia 'ORIGIN-ANAPH'	V	10e	masaniŋsiŋ pisvaŋduan 'the Holy Temple'	temple	Entity	Anaphoric	Identity
10e	masaniŋsiŋ pisvaŋduan 'the Holy Temple'	N	9a	masaniŋsiŋ pisvaŋduan 'the Holy Temple'	temple	Entity	Anaphoric	Identity
10e	manauʔað ʔilav 'beautiful door'	N	2d	na-ku-ŋadah 'IRR-ASSOC.ALL-lower'	door	Entity	Anaphoric	Identity
10e	bunun 'person'	N	10e	saia '3S.NOM'	cripple	Entity	Anaphoric	Identity

References

Abadiano, Helen R. 1995. Cohesion strategies and genre in expository prose: An analysis of the writing of children of ethnolinguistic cultural groups. *Pragmatics* 5(3). 299–324.
Ariel, Mira. 1991. The function of accessibility in a theory of grammar. *Journal of Pragmatics* 16(5). 443–463.
Aziz, Yellow Y. 1988. Cohesion in spoken Arabic texts. In Erich H. Steiner & Robert Veltman (eds.), *Pragmatics, discourse and text: Some systemically inspired approaches*, 148–157. London: Pinter.
Bakhtin, Mikhail M. 1986. The problem of speech genres. In Caryl Emerson & Michael Holquist (eds.). Trans. by Vern W. McGee, *Speech genres and other late essays*, 60–102. Austin, TX: University of Texas Press.
Benn, Keith Laurence. 1991. *Discourse approaches to cohesion: A study of the structure and unity of a Central Bontoc expository text*. Manila: De La Salle University. (MA thesis).
Biber, Douglas. 1995. *Dimensions of register variation: A cross-linguistic comparison*. Cambridge: Cambridge University Press.
Biber, Douglas & Susan Conrad. 2009. *Register, genre, and style*. Cambridge: Cambridge University Press.
Bible Society in Taiwan (ed.). 2000. *Tama dihanin tu halinga [the Bunun Bible in today's Taiwan Bunun Version]*. Taipei: The Bible Society in the R.O.C.
Connor, Ulla. 1984. A study of cohesion and coherence in English as a second language students' writing. *Paper in Linguistics* 17(3). 301–316.
Crossley, Scott A. & Danielle S. McNamara. 2012. Predicting second language writing proficiency: The roles of cohesion and linguistic sophistication. *Journal of Research in Reading* 32(2). 115–135.
De Busser, Rik. 2009. *Towards a grammar of Takivatan Bunun: Selected topics*. Melbourne: La Trobe University. (Doctoral dissertation).
De Busser, Rik. 2013. The influence of Christianity on the Bunun language: A preliminary overview. In *Proceedings of the International Workshop on "Special Genres" in and around Indonesia*, 59–76. Tokyo: Research Institute for Languages, Cultures of Asia & Africa, Tokyo University of Foreign Studies.
De Busser, Rik. 2017. Spatial deixis, textual cohesion, and functional differentiation in Takivatan Bunun. *Oceanic Linguistics* 56(1). 89–121.
Ezard, Bryan. 1978. Insights on cohesion from Tawala. *Oceanic Linguistics* 17(2). 107–132.
Flaming, Rachel. 1983. Cohesion in Wandamen narrative. *NUSA: Linguistic Studies of Indonesian and Other Languages in Indonesia* 15. 41–49.
Foley, William A. 2007. The place of Philippine languages in a typology of voice systems. In Peter Austin & Simon Musgrave (eds.), *Voice and grammatical relations in Austronesian languages*, 22–44. Stanford, CA: CSLI Publications.
Fox, Barbara A. 1987. *Discourse Structure and Anaphora: Written and Conversational English*. Cambridge: Cambridge University Press.
French, Koleen Matsuda. 1987. The focus system in Philippine languages: An historical overview. *Philippine Journal of Linguistics* 18(2)/19(1). 1–27.

Givón, Talmy. 1993. Coherence in text, coherence in mind. *Pragmatics and Cognition* 1(3). 171–227.

Haiman, John. 1983. Iconic and Economic Motivation. *Language* 59. 781–819.

Halliday, M. A. K. 1994. *An introduction to Functional Grammar*. 2nd edn. London: Arnold.

Halliday, M. A. K. & Ruqaiya Hasan. 1976. *Cohesion in English*. London: Longman.

Halliday, M. A. K. & Christian M. I. M. Matthiessen. 2004. *An introduction to Functional Grammar*. 3rd edn. London: Hodder Arnold.

Halliday, M. A. K. & Christian M. I. M. Matthiessen. 2014. *Halliday's introduction to Functional Grammar*. 4th edn. London: Routledge.

Hassel, R. Chris. 2005. *Shakespeare's religious language: A dictionary*. New York: Continuum.

Hasselgård, Hilde. 2004. The role of multiple themes in cohesion. In Karin Aijmer & Anna-Brita Stenström (eds.), *Discourse Patterns in spoken and written corpora*, 65–87. Amsterdam: John Benjamins Publishing Company.

Hickmann, Maya & Henriëtte Hendriks. 1999. Cohesion and anaphora in children's narratives: A comparison of English, French, German, and Mandarin Chinese. *Journal of Child Language* 26(2). 419–452.

Himmelmann, Nikolaus P. 1996. Demonstratives in narrative discourse: A taxonomy of universal uses. In Barbara Fox (ed.), *Studies in anaphora*, 205–254. Amsterdam: John Benjamins Publishing Company.

Hoey, Michael. 1991. *Patterns of lexis in text*. Oxford: Oxford University Press.

Huang, Hui-chuan J. (黃慧娟) & Chao-kai (施朝凱) Shih. 2016. *An Introduction to Bunun Grammar*. Taipei: Council of Indigenous Peoples.

Huang, Yan. 2000. *Anaphora: A cross-linguistic study*. Oxford: Oxford University Press.

Kehler, Andrew. 2002. *Coherence, reference, and the theory of grammar*. Stanford, CA: CSLI Publications.

Kehler, Andrew. 2004. Discourse coherence. In Laurence R. Horn & Gregory L. Ward (eds.), *The handbook of pragmatics*, 241–265. Malden, MA: Blackwell.

Kruger, Alet. 2000. *Lexical cohesion and register variation in transition: "The merchants of Venice" in Afrikaans*. Pretoria: University of South Africa. (Doctoral dissertation).

Lambrecht, Knud. 1994. *Information structure and sentence form: Topic, focus and the mental representations of discourse referents*. Cambridge, UK: Cambridge University Press.

Li, Paul Jen-Kuei. 1988. A comparative study of Bunun dialects. *Bulletin of the Institute of History and Philology, Academia Sinica* 59(2). 479–508.

Li, Paul Jen-Kuei. 2008. The great diversity of Formosan languages. *Language and Linguistics* 9(3). 523–546.

Malah, Helen Tan, Zubairu & Sabariah Md Rashid. 2016. Evaluating lexical cohesion in Nigerian newspaper genres: Focus on the editorials. *International Journal of Applied Linguistics and English Literature* 6(1). 240–256.

Mann, William C. & Sandra A. Thompson. 1987. *Rhetorical structure theory: A theory of text organization*. Marina del Rey, CA: Information Sciences Institute.

Martin, James R. 1992. *English text: system and structure.* Philadelphia: John Benjamins Publishing.
Martin, James R. 2001. Cohesion and texture. In Deborah Schiffrin, Deborah Tannen & Heidi E. Hamilton (eds.), *The Handbook of discourse analysis*, 35–53. Malden, MA: Blackwell.
Merrell, Floyd. 2001. Charles Sanders Peirce's concept of the sign. In Paul Cobley (ed.), *The Routledge companion to semiotics and linguistics*, 28–39. London: Routledge.
Quine, Willard V. 1985. Events and Reification. In E. Lepore & B. McLaughlin (eds.), *Actions and events: Perspectives on the philosophy of Davidson*, 162–171. Malden, MA: Blackwell.
Riesberg, Sonja. 2014. *Symmetrical voice and linking in Western Austronesian languages.* Berlin: Mouton de Gruyter.
Tanskanen, Sanna-Kaisa. 2006. *Collaborating towards coherence: lexical cohesion in English discourse.* Amsterdam: John Benjamins Publishing.
Zacks, Jeffrey M. & Barbara Tversky. 2001. Event structure in perception and conception. *Psychological Bulletin* 127(1). 3–21.
Zeitoun, Elizabeth. 2000. *A reference grammar of Bunun (*布農語參考語法*).* Taipei: 遠流.

Chapter 2

Stance, categorisation, and information structure in Malay

František Kratochvíl
Palacký University, Olomouc, Czech Republic

Nur Izdihar Binte Ismail
Nanyang Technological University, Singapore

Diyana Hamzah
Temasek Laboratories, Singapore

This chapter describes the expression of referents in Singaporean Malay using a parallel corpus of elicited narratives. We demonstrate that the speaker's epistemic stance affects how discourse is constructed. The speaker's epistemic stance is apparent in referent categorisation: referents can be categorised either as "familiar", when taking a strong epistemic stance, or as "unfamiliar", when taking a neutral stance. We show that referent categorisation is more fundamental than the information structure notions of *new*, *old*, or *given*. Familiar human or animate referents are expressed with proper names and are pivotal for organising the narrative plot: by constructing other discourse-persistent referents in relation to the familiar referent, their description and tracking simplifies. Human and animate referents categorised as unfamiliar are expressed with nominals. Their descriptions and tracking are more elaborate, involving demonstratives and discourse particles, whose function lies in the coordination of joint attention. Inanimate referents are rarely subject of strong epistemic stance and are therefore expressed with nominals. Their discourse-persistence is the best predictor of how elaborate their description and tracking are.

1 Introduction

One of the fundamental functions of human language is balancing the information disparity between the speaker and the hearer. It has been argued that the speaker and hearer both operate under the assumption that the world presents itself in the same way to their interlocutor. Under such an assumption, the speaker can "trade places" with the hearer, and can predict and mitigate obvious disparities (Rommetveit 1976; Zlatev 2008; Duranti 2009; 2010).

František Kratochvíl, Nur Izdihar Binte Ismail & Diyana Hamzah. 2018. Stance, categorisation, and information structure in Malay. In Sonja Riesberg, Asako Shiohara & Atsuko Utsumi (eds.), *Perspectives on information structure in Austronesian languages*, 41–80. Berlin: Language Science Press. DOI:10.5281/zenodo.1402537

The above information-disparity problem is examined through the study of information structure, i.e. the structural arrangement of various types of information, such as *new, old, given, topic, focus*, etc. (cf. Prince 1981; Gundel et al. 1993; Lambrecht 1994; Gundel & Fretheim 2004).

In a broader perspective, however, the complexity of expression of the *new, old* and *given* reflects the speaker's stance towards the utterance, reality, and the hearer. This *stance*, or *alignment* is manifested in the amount of information disclosed in order to mitigate disparity (cf. Du Bois 2007).[1]

Du Bois' framework conceptualises stance as the process of evaluation and positioning towards the object of stance and the mutual alignment between subjects emerging from the interaction (Du Bois 2007: 171). Stance is achieved through overt communicative means towards any salient dimension of the sociocultural field (Du Bois 2007: 163). This process is visualised in Du Bois' original *stance triangle*, reproduced here in Figure 1.

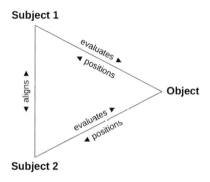

Figure 1: Du Bois' *stance triangle* (Du Bois 2007: 161)

We demonstrate that the compositional vectors of *stance*, namely *evaluation, positioning*, and *alignment* can be applied to the study of information structure and referent expression. We expand the understanding of Du Bois' *evaluation* to include the choice in identifying a referent and *referent categorisation*, a term borrowed from Stivers et al. (2007). The categorisation *positions* the speakers towards the object differently in terms of their epistemic stance. The choice has consequences for the construction of subsequent discourse, as will be documented in §3.

2 Methodology, participants, and language situation

The data for this paper consists of a set of elicited narratives in Singapore Malay. These narratives were collected using four stimuli sets: (i) Getting the Story Straight (San Roque et al. 2012), (ii) Pear Story (Chafe 1980), (iii) Frog Story (Mayer 1969), and (iv) Jackal

---

[1] In Malay/Indonesian, an important work on this aspect of language is Englebretson (2007), which primarily deals with the choice of pronouns and its consequences.

and Crow (Carroll et al. 2011). The stories allow us to make a systematic comparison of how our subjects categorise a variety of referents (human, animate, inanimate, singular, plural, etc.). By comparing how referents are introduced and tracked, we reveal the consequences of the categorisation for discourse construction. We rely on the annotation guidelines of the *RefLex Scheme* to distinguish various types of referents and their expressions (Riester & Baumann 2017).

In this section, we describe the Malay spoken in Singapore (2.1), our participants (2.2), and the stimuli used here (2.3–2.6). The instances where we consulted our Singapore Malay Corpus are distinguished with corpus text identifiers.[2]

2.1 Malay in Singapore

The Malay language connects diverse varieties that form the Malayic subgroup of Austronesian. In all probability from Southern Sumatra, Malay varieties are now spoken throughout Indonesia, Brunei, Malaysia, Singapore and southern Thailand (Adelaar 2004). In Singapore, Malay has always had a special status, given its former role as the administrative language and lingua franca and for its political value in the region (Alsagoff 2008).

Apart from the symbolic status of the national language of Singapore, Malay is one of the four official languages of Singapore, alongside English, Mandarin Chinese and Tamil. Malay is the assigned *mother tongue* of the ethnic 'Malays' in Singapore, a label comprising people of Malay, Javanese, Boyanese, and Sundanese descent as well as other smaller groups from the peninsula and archipelago, which make up 13.3% of the resident population (Kuo & Jernudd 1993; Singapore Department of Statistics 2015).[3]

Standard Singapore Malay is the formal written and spoken variety taught in schools and used in formal contexts (government and media). It is similar to the standard variety used in Malaysia, with the addition of certain lexical items relevant to the local context. Colloquial Singapore Malay is the informal spoken variety. In the past, a number of contact varieties emerged, with distinct syntactic, grammatical and phonological features (Sasi Rekha d/o Muthiah 2007). The best studied among them include: (i) Singapore Baba Malay, a Malay creole influenced by Hokkien, which is typically spoken by the Peranakan population in Singapore (Lee 2014), (ii) Singapore Bazaar Malay, a Malay-lexified pidgin influenced by Hokkien which was the traditional lingua franca for interethnic communication (prior to the rise of English) and is typically spoken by Singaporean Chinese, and (iii) Singapore Indian Malay, a Malay-lexified pidgin influenced by Bazaar Malay and Indian languages which is typically spoken by Singaporean Indians (Adelaar & Prentice 1996; Daw 2005; Sasi Rekha d/o Muthiah 2007). Rising levels of bilingualism with English introduce contact features such as code-switching, borrowing of lexicon and structural convergence with Singlish.

---

[2]Our Singapore Malay Corpus consists of about 100 conversations and narratives (spontaneous, planned and elicited), counting about 62,000 words.

[3]The 2015 census reveals that English-Malay bilinguals make up 86.2% and 14.0% of the Malay and Indian resident population, respectively, and that Malay remains the dominant home language of the Malay resident population aged 5 years and over (78.4%) (Singapore Department of Statistics 2015).

2.2 Participants

Our participants are all Singapore Malays from diverse linguistic backgrounds. JUR, ISM, and ISH grew up in monolingual Malay families, only beginning their English studies when they entered primary school at the age of seven. AM, YAN, and SI grew up in Malay-dominant bilingual families. While their exposure to English was earlier, all three attended Malay-speaking kindergartens, and YAN and SI went on to private religious schools, where the medium of instruction was Malay and English. MIZ grew up in an English-dominant bilingual family, while LQ, HZ and NZ came from families where bilingualism was more balanced. Their formal education in English and Malay also began in kindergarten. After kindergarten, AM, MIZ, LQ, HZ, and NZ went through the mainstream Singapore education system, where the medium of instruction was English.

2.3 Getting the Story Straight (San Roque et al. 2012)

The first stimuli collection is a graphic mini-novel depicting in 16 pictures the transformation of a man, through a descent into jail caused a change of heart, from someone who drinks and beats his wife into a loving father and husband, as shown in Figure 2.

Figure 2: Getting the Story Straight storyline (San Roque et al. 2012)

In the original set-up (see text 1 in Table 1), the pictures were presented in a stipulated sequence to two participants who negotiated and constructed the narrative. When finished, they presented it to a newly arrived third participant. The entire experiment lasted about 20 minutes. The word counts offer a measure of the verbal effort with the second set-up, when the correct picture sequence is presented to a speaker who narrates it. No negotiation took place, since the second participant was instructed to take on the role of the listener. The task lasted only about five minutes on average, and required much less verbal effort (see texts 2–11).

2.4 Pear Story (Chafe 1980)

The second stimuli set is the *Pear Story*, a six-minute film. Set in the countryside, it depicts a loose sequence of events happening around an orchard, where a farmer is picking pears. A man walks by with a goat, and a boy on the bicycle comes to collect the fruit. When he later falls and the load of pears spills on the road, three other boys come to his help, who each receive a pear in return. We recorded two versions.

2.5 Frog Story (Mayer 1969)

Frog Story is a picture book for children (see Figure 3) widely used for language comparison. It is the story of a boy whose pet frog escaped from its jar, so he sets out with his dog to find it. We recorded two versions of this story, listed in Table 3.

Figure 3: Frog Story storyline (Mayer 1969)

2.6 Jackal and Crow (Carroll et al. 2011)

Jackal and Crow consists of nine pictures presenting a version of the famous Aesop fable of The Fox and the Crow. The fox is drawn to be identifiable as a jackal, wolf, or dog, and the crow holds a fish, instead of cheese.

Figure 4: Jackal and Crow storyline (Carroll et al. 2011)

We again used two set-ups. The 2013 version is a narration of the picture sequence by a single speaker, while the 2014 version follows the original guidelines of Carroll et al. (2011) and is a negotiation of two speakers, who construct the narrative for a third participant.

Table 1: Collected versions of *Getting the Story Straight* (San Roque et al. 2012)

	text name	words
1.	2014.MLZ.GettingTheStoryStraight	2235
2.	2017.NI.GettingTheStoryStraight.JUR	247
3.	2017.NI.GettingTheStoryStraight.ISM	249
4.	2017.NI.GettingTheStoryStraight.MIZ	572
5.	2017.NI.GettingTheStoryStraight.AM	355
6.	2017.NI.GettingTheStoryStraight.YAN	437
7.	2017.NI.GettingTheStoryStraight.SI	512
8.	2017.NI.GettingTheStoryStraight.ISH	239
9.	2017.NI.GettingTheStoryStraight.LQ	214
10.	2017.NI.GettingTheStoryStraight.HZ	380
11.	2017.NI.GettingTheStoryStraight.NZ	227

Table 2: Collected versions of *Pear Story* (Chafe 1980)

	text name	words
1.	2013.CA.PearStory	169
2.	2013.LN.PearStory	442

Table 3: Collected versions of *Frog Story* (Mayer 1969)

	text name	words
3.	2013.OG.FrogStory	963
4.	2013.SS.FrogStory	387

Table 4: Collected versions of *Jackal and Crow* (Carroll et al. 2011)

	text name	words
1.	2013.OG.JackalAndCrow	212
2.	2014.MLZ.JackalAndCrow	660

3 Stance and referent categorisation

In §1, we linked stance to the notion of *referent categorisation*. Referent categorisation refers to the choice a speaker makes by identifying the referents for the hearer. A fundamental dichotomy exists between *proper names* and *descriptions* (nominal expressions).

Categorisation with proper names positions the speaker as familiar with the object of stance. According to Sacks & Schegloff (2007), proper names satisfy two discourse-organisational preferences: (i) recognitional preference and (ii) minimised reference. For the first, it is easier to work out the reference to something familiar, even if familiarity is only constructed. The second is a preference for a stable, and perhaps a single, reference form, so that the expression-referent pair is stable. Proper names meet both requirements, but nominal expressions require more recognitional effort on the part of the hearer. In addition to speaker's stance, the choice of a proper name reveals aspects of speaker's identity, such as their relation to the topic and their self-positioning within the community (cf. Barešová 2016: 13). In a constructed narrative, the identity is symbolic.

Categorisation with *descriptions* reveals the speaker's neutral epistemic stance.[4] The hearer's effort is greater in both recognition and maintaining reference, as will be apparent in §4.

The effect of referent categorisation on discourse structure is most obvious among the eleven versions of *Getting the Story Straight* (see §3.1), and is also detected in the *Frog Story* (see §3.2). In contrast, the referent categorisation in the *Pear Story* is uniform. For categorisation of inanimate referents, their discourse role is the most important factor. Discourse-persistent referents require more elaborate descriptions than "props" (see §3.3).

3.1 Human referent categorisation in *Getting the Story Straight*

The main participants in *Getting the Story Straight* are: a farmer, his wife, child, and friends. The farmer is present in all frames, while the other characters play a less central role, sometimes restricted to a single frame.

More than half of our subjects categorise the farmer with a proper name (usually a common Malay name such as *Adam, Halim, Samad,* or *Zamri*), making it a referential pivot for other human referents (farmer's family and friends). This strategy is in line with the *preferences for person reference* formulated in Sacks & Schegloff (2007: 24). Proper names are prototypical and ideal recognitional devices (Sacks & Schegloff 2007: 25) and their use is therefore referentially effective. The RefLex scheme classifies the first use of proper names as *r-unused-unknown* (Riester & Baumann 2017: 10). Example (1) illustrates that to track the given referent (RefLex *r-given*) proper names can be repeated.

(1) Singapore Malay (2017.SI.12–14)
 [*Abu*] *kedengaran me-racau-racau ber-tanda dia sudah mabuk.* [*Abu*]
 PN   audible   AV-talk.incoherently AV-sign 3SG already drunk   PN

---

[4]The term *descriptions* is synonymous with *nominal expressions*.

mula ber-cerita yang bukan-bukan. Ini lazim   ber-laku   apabila [Abu]
start AV-tell   REL nonsense   PROX common AV-happen when   PN
mabuk kerana minum   minuman keras itu.
drunk because consume alcohol   DIST

'Abu was heard to rave, which was a sign that he was drunk. Abu started to tell untrue stories. This habitually happened when Abu was drunk from drinking alcohol.'

The neutral epistemic stance leads to the categorisation of the farmer with a nominal expression as a *petani* 'farmer' (RefLex *r-new*).[5] Because the referent will persist in discourse, it is typically introduced with a classifier phrase (cf. Hopper 1986: 317). We will return to this point in the discussion of example (6) and again in §3.3.

The farmer's family and friends are always introduced through expressions of their relationship to the farmer, such as *isteri=nya* 'his wife' in (2). The RefLex scheme characterises such expressions as *r-bridging-contained* (Riester & Baumann 2017: 9). The bridging containment is realised by possessive constructions available in Malay. It is interesting that when the farmer is given a name, his wife is usually given one too (e.g. *Alia, Hawa, Huda, Laila*), as in (2).[6]

(2)   Singapore Malay (2017.MIZ.01)
      kedua-dua Zamri dan [isteri-nya   Alina] ber-kerja seperti pekebun.
      both   PN   and wife-3POSS   PN   AV-work as   farmer
      'Both Zamri and his wife Alina work as farmers.'

The categorisation of the child seems independent of the speaker's stance towards the farmer and his wife. In our data, the child is rarely categorised with a proper name. In several versions, although depicted in Frame 2 as held by her mother, the child is introduced only in the domestic violence scene, as in (3).

(3)   Singapore Malay (2017.YAN.12)
      sambil men-dukung [anak-nya], Huda mem-beritahu Halim bahawa dia tidak
      while AV-hold   child-3POSS PN AV-tell   PN   COMP   3SG not
      mem-punyai apa-apa hubungan   sama sekali dengan Khalid ... dengan Leyman.
      AV-have   any   relationship at.all   with PN   with   PN
      'While carrying her child, Huda told Halim that she did not have any relationship with Khalid [sic], ...with Leyman.'

---

[5] A wealth of literature is dedicated to various aspects of the Malay noun phrase. The relevant devices are (i) classifiers (Hopper 1986; Chung 2000; 2008; Cleary-Kemp 2007; Chung 2010; Salehuddin & Winskel 2012); (ii) demonstratives (Himmelmann 1996; Williams 2009), (iii) relative clauses (Cole & Hermon 2005), (iv) the linker *yang* (van Minde 2008), and (v) the definite *-nya* (Rubin 2010).

[6] The bridging anaphor between the possessive *-nya* and its target *Zamri* is highlighted using the RefLex scheme convention, i.e. the target of the anaphora is underlined and the referential expression is in square brackets.

2 Stance, categorisation, and information structure in Malay

Plurality is an important feature of human referents: the farmer's friends are always introduced in a reduplicated form as *kawan-kawan* 'friends'. The possessive =*nya* may associate them with the topical farmer. In some versions, the gossiping friend is named (e.g. *Rashid, Wahid*). Both strategies are combined in AM's version, where the friends are first introduced as a group in an earlier sentence, and then the gossiper is named as *Rashid*, as shown in (4).

(4) Singapore Malay (2017.AM.08)
[*Rashid*] *menceritakan bahawa dia pernah ter-nampak isteri Pak Samad telah*
PN AV.tell COMP 3SG once INVOL-see wife Mr PN already
meng-gatal dengan Encik Romi semasa dia sedang mem-beli barang rumah di
AV-chat.up with sir PN when 3SG PROG AV-buy item home in
pasar.
market
'Rashid told everyone that he had seen Pak Samad's wife flirting with Mr. Romi while she was buying household items at the market.'

The old man, who sees the fight between the farmer and his wife (Figure 2, frame 5), is usually categorised as a relative (usually as the father of the spouse) using a possessed noun, as in (5). This is a type of *r-bridging-contained*, where the possessor is already known from the context. The introduction is abrupt, because the old man calls the police right away, so there is no time or need to provide any other details.

(5) Singapore Malay (2017.AM.14)
[*Papa Laila*] *ter-nampak perkara ini lalu me-lapor-nya, lalu*
father PN INVOL-see event PROX then AV-report-3 then
me-lapor-kan-nya ke polis.
AV-report-APPL-3 to police
'Laila's father saw the incident and reported it, reported it to the police.'

The neutral stance leads to a nominal categorisation of the old man as a neighbour, using an enumerated classifier phrase, as in (6).[7] In the RefLex Scheme, such a referent is classified as *r-new* (Riester & Baumann 2017: 11). It should be noted that the neutral stance to the old man does not exclude a strong stance to the farmer and his wife, whom SI categorises with proper names.

(6) Singapore Malay (2017.SI.23)
kebetulan kejadian tersebut di-lihat oleh [*se-orang jiran*].
coincidentally event mentioned PV-see by one-CL.HUMAN neighbor
'Coincidentally, the incident was seen by a neighbour.'

---

[7]Hopper (1986) described the role and use of classifiers and provided parameters conducive to the use of classifiers based on written nineteenth-century Malay (pp. 313–314). According to Hopper, the primary function of classifiers is to grant discourse-new nouns prominence and the ability to become topics, whose referents are "individuated" and "persistent in discourse" (p. 319).

Categorisation of the policemen and court officials is fairly uniform, using various types of nominals. Bare nouns such as *polis* 'police', or a group compound *pihak polis* 'police force' are the most common.[8] Within the RefLex scheme, the referent is classified as *r-unused-known*, because we assume that it is generally known and that appeal can be made to the local security force to stop violence. The only case where an indefinite description (quantified classifier phrase) is used is shown in (7). This may be a consequence of enumeration, which in Malay requires a classifier phrase.

(7) Singapore Malay (2017.SI.24)
tidak lama selepas itu, [dua orang polis] datang dan mem-berkas Adam.
not long thereafter two CL.HUMAN police come and AV-arrest PN
'Not long afterwards, two policemen came and arrested Adam.'

Proper names open up a referent-internal perspective: for example, the abuse by the farmer can be presented from the perspective of his wife or the court, and their stance can be constructed. This is shown in (8), where the farmer, introduced as *Adam*, is referred to as *suami-nya* 'her husband', embedding him in a kinship relation with expected norms of behavior. HZ's version uses the same strategy to mark the wife's perspective in the same point of the narrative (see Table 6). The speaker can establish and/or maintain differential perspective to the same referent in this way (cf. Enfield 2007: 107).

(8) Singapore Malay (2017.SI.25)
Semasa Hawa di-panggil untuk mem-buat kenyataan di balai polis, Hawa
when PN PV-call to AV-make statement in station police PN
kelihatan teruk di-cederakan oleh [suami-nya] sehingga mata, kepala
appearance dreadful PV-injure.CAUS by husband-3POSS so.that eye head
dan leher-nya perlu di-balut.
and neck-3POSS need PV-dress.wound
'While Hawa was called in to make a statement at the police station, she seemed badly hurt by her husband, to the point where her eyes, head, and neck had to be bandaged.'

3.2 Categorisation of human referents in *Frog Story* and *Pear Story*

The two versions of *Frog Story* show a similar pattern as *Getting the Story Straight*. A stronger epistemic stance leads to categorisation of the boy with a proper name. The stronger stance allows the speaker to fabulate the boy's character, emotions, and habits, as in (9), where the dog is described as the boy's *anjing kesayangan* 'beloved dog', and the frog is expressed with a possessive phrase (*r-bridging-contained*).

---

[8]The root *pihak* is used in other group compounds such as *pihak berkuasa* 'authority, agency', *pihak lawan* 'opposition', *pihak musuh* 'enemy, enemies', and *pihak pengurusan* 'management'.

(9) Singapore Malay (2013.SS.FrogStory.01)
Pada suatu malam sebelum tidur [Abu] dan [anjing kesayangan dia] sedang
on one night before sleep PN and dog beloved 3SG PROG
me-renung [katak-nya].
AV-study frog-3POSS
'One night before sleeping Abu and his beloved dog were watching his frog.'

In an inverted manner, the speaker's neutral epistemic stance is reflected in a categorisation with descriptions. In (10), both the boy and his dog are categorised with indefinite nominals (RefLex Scheme: *r-new*). The friendship between the dog and the boy is constructed later, and is not included in the first description of the dog.

(10) Singapore Malay (2013.OG.FrogStory.01)
Pada suatu hari, ada [se-orang anak kecil], budak lelaki, yang mem-punyai
on one day exist one-CL.HUMAN child small boy REL AV-own
[se-ekor anjing] sebagai teman-nya.
one-CL.ANIMAL dog as friend-3POSS
'Once, there was a little boy, who had a dog as his friend.'

Both available versions of the *Pear Story* contain no proper names. New human referents (*r-new*) are categorised with enumerated classifier phrases and inanimates with bare nouns.[9]

3.3 Categorisation of non-human referents

Let us now turn to the *Jackal and Crow* texts, which describe a simple plot without human referents.[10] Neither of the texts uses proper names; instead, participants are introduced into the discourse with enumerated classifier phrases (RefLex *r-new*), as in (11). The fragment also contains two presentational clauses, headed by the verb *terdapat* 'exist, be attested in the world, be found'. Vague quantification with *beberapa* 'several, few', or with reduplicated plural forms such as *ikan-ikan* '(a variety of) fish' does not require a classifier.

(11) Singapore Malay (2013.MLZ.JackalCrow.140–141)
Pada zaman dahulu, terdapat [se-ekor burung gagak]. Dah beliau
in past exist one-CL.ANIMAL crow already 3SG.HON
ternampak beberapa bakul yang terdapat ikan-ikan.
INVOL-see few basket REL exist RED-fish
'Once upon a time, there was a crow. And it saw several baskets filled with fish.'

---

[9] Our findings agree with those reported by Sukamto (2013), who studied written narratives of the *Pear Story* in Indonesian.
[10] As mentioned in §2.6, two set-ups were used to collect the two texts. For the analysis of the MLZ version, we are only concerned with the final summary of the story given to the third participant.

The second text shows the same pattern. Animate non-human referents are categorised as descriptions, expressed with a classifier phrase, if the referent will become a topic. In (12), the referent *burung gagak* 'crow' is introduced as the subject of an inverted existential clause headed by *ada* 'exist'. The inversion puts the focus on the predicate (Sneddon et al. 2012: 270). The subject is quantified (the numeral *se-* + the classifier *ekor* (animate)), as well as the object of the relative clause (*beberapa* 'several'). A similar use of classifiers and quantification in introducing new referents is reported in Hopper (1986: 319) for the nineteenth-century written autobiography known as *Hikayat Abdullah*.

(12) Singapore Malay (2013.OG.JackalCrow.02)
 Pada satu hari ada [se-ekor   burung gagak] yang men-jumpai beberapa
 on   one day exist one-CL.ANIMAL crow   REL AV-discover several
 bakul ikan.
 basket fish
 'Once, there was a crow that found several baskets of fish.'

Although the fish is already mentioned as the content of the basket, as introduced in (12), this does not grant the fish the status of given information. It requires an upgrade from being a 'prop' to become a discourse-persistent referent (cf. Hopper 1986: 319). Analogous to other discourse-persistent referents, the single fish, which is to be picked up by the crow, is introduced with a classifier phrase, as in (13).

(13) Singapore Malay (2013.OG.JackalCrow.03)
 Jadi burung gagak itu meng-ambil [se-ekor   ikan] untuk jadi   bahan
 so   crow   DST AV-pick   one-CL.ANIMAL fish to   become   matter
 makan-nya untuk hari itu.
 food-3POSS for   day DIST
 'So the crow took a fish (OR one fish) as its meal for the day.'

It is interesting to note that the tree, on which the crow lands, is not mentioned at all in the second version. In the first version, its expression is unusual, requiring a placeholder, suggesting retrieval problems, as in (14). After the correct label is retrieved, it is realised as an N-DEM structure, with the reduced proximate *ni*, requiring resolution in the physical context. The RefLex scheme classifies such referents as *r-environment*. This is, however, a non-standard solution in the context of the narrative.

(14) Singapore Malay (2013.MLZ.JackalCrow.147)
 Dia LAND   kat ker..., apa   ni..., pokok ni.
 3SG CS.land at PART   what PROX   tree PROX
 'It landed on what..., what's this..., on this tree.'

The above examples illustrate what Hopper (1986: 313) refers to as *props*. Event settings are described with bare nouns, which are occasionally enumerated, or reduplicated (*beberapa bakul ikan, ikan-ikan*). Props are easily omitted where the context and world knowledge enable the hearer to construct them regardless.

To summarise, the speaker epistemic stance is most apparent in the categorisation of humans. A stronger epistemic stance leads to the use of proper names for the key characters. We will show in §4 that the tracking of such characters is simpler than of those humans categorised as nominals. For non-human participants, the speaker's epistemic stance is less relevant than what Hopper (1986: 319) termed as *persistence in the discourse*. Future topics are introduced in a more elaborate way (typically with a classifier phrase) than *props*. Incidental props have only short persistence and require no tracking (cf. Hopper 1986: 320). Table 5 summarises the effects of stance and discourse role on the categorisation and expression of referents in our Malay corpus. We should keep in mind that elaborate descriptions can combine a nominal and a proper name, as in (2). For the sake of our hierarchy postulated here, we consider the proper name to be an indication of the speaker's stronger epistemic stance.

Table 5: Effect of stance and discourse role on referent categorisation

REFERENT CATEGORY	EPISTEMIC STANCE	
	STRONG	NEUTRAL
+human	proper name	classifier phrase
+animate	?	classifier phrase
−animate, +discourse-persistent	classifier phrase	
−animate, −discourse-persistent	bare noun	

4 Categorisation and referent tracking

Many referents persist in discourse for some time (Hopper 1986: 317) and dedicated constructions indicate their status as given (RefLex r-given). In this section, we show that the initial stance and categorisation have global consequences for referent tracking.

Human referents categorised with proper names, discussed in §3, are tracked with proper names and pronouns, usually *dia* and *ia*. Particles, demonstratives and other markers are used rarely. In contrast, human referents categorised with nominals are tracked in a more elaborate way, requiring a greater effort from the hearer. A range of devices are used, including repetition, and synecdoche; marking with demonstratives, particles, or relative clauses are all common ways of tracking.

Figure 5 and Figure 6 visualise the categorisation and tracking of referents in two quite distinct versions of *Getting the Story Straight*. The expressions are time-aligned as they appear in the story.[11] Continuous lines mean that the referent is not only discourse-persistent but also topical. Whenever the line is interrupted, another topical referent appears. Two lines coincide when a reference is made to more than one referent, either

---

[11]The following abbreviations are used in Figure 5 and 6 and the tables in the remainder of this chapter: CL classifier, N noun, NUM numeral, PN proper name, POSS possessor, PRO pronoun, and RED reduplication.

with plural pronouns (*mereka* 'they'), or with possessive constructions (indexing both the possessed and the possessor).

Figure 5 illustrates the minimisation of reference: proper names are systematically followed by pronouns (cf. Heritage 2007: 260), but other devices are not used. As the narrative shifts, a proper name is used to activate the referent and the pronoun tracking it within the local macro-event, usually corresponding to a single picture. In two places, the speaker used synecdoche (N[N]), which corresponds to the blue line dropping to the bottom of the chart.

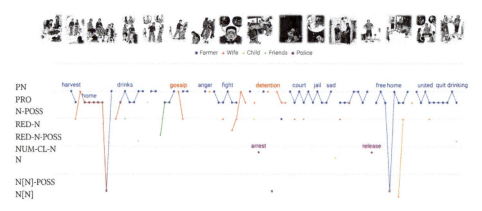

Figure 5: Storyline visualisation of the referential devices in SI version of *Getting the Story Straight*

Figure 6 shows that the referents are introduced with a classifier phrase (NUM-CL-N) or with a possessor phrase (N-POSS), and are tracked almost without exception with pronouns. Particles *pun*, *pula* and the demonstrative *tersebut* are used to reactivate a given referent as a topic.

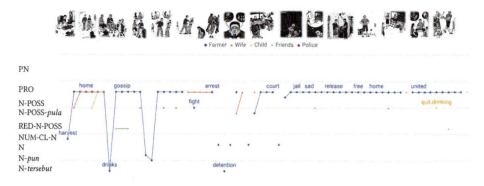

Figure 6: Storyline visualisation of the referential devices in HZ version of *Getting the Story Straight*

Detailed discussion of the patterns visualised in Figure 5 and Figure 6 and those attested in other texts follow. Demonstratives and the particles *pun*, *pula*, and *lagi* will be treated in §5. We are only concerned with the nominal expression of referents; zero anaphora, word order alternations, and verbal morphology will be discussed elsewhere.

4.1 Tracking of human referents

The most common way to track human referents is with pronouns, followed by repetition and synecdoche. The main characters of *Getting the Story Straight* (the farmer and his wife), regardless of their categorisation as familiar or unfamiliar, can be tracked by pronouns. Repetition of the proper name or the nominal expression is also common. In a complex sentence, proper names are restricted to the first mention and tracked with personal pronouns in subsequent positions, such as *dia* and *-nya* in (15).

(15) Singapore Malay (2017.AM.09)
er... [Zamri] sangat marah dengan pengetahuan ini, dan [dia], dan [dia]
HESIT PN very angry by knowledge PROX and 3SG and 3SG
telus... terus balik rumah untuk marah isteri [-nya].
 immediately return home to scold wife-3POSS

'Zamri was very angry upon receiving this information, and he immediately went back home to scold his wife.'

Multiple named referents are tracked with the plural *mereka*, as in (16).

(16) Singapore Malay (2017.YAN.01)
Seperti hari-hari biasa, *Halim bersama isteri-nya Huda akan ke kebun*
as everyday accustomed PN together wife-3POSS PN will to garden
mereka untuk memetik buah-buah labu yang telah pun masak.
3PL to AV.pick RED-fruit pumpkin REL already ADD ripe

'As on a normal day, Halim and his wife Huda would go to their garden to pick pumpkins that had ripened.'

Referents categorised with proper names are tracked with pronouns, even where another topic is present. This is the case in (17), where the speaker comments on the loss of appetite experienced by the farmer in jail. The farmer, called *Halim* in this version (see (16)), is tracked with the possessive *-nya* to background his experiencer role and to highlight his experience.

(17) Singapore Malay (2017.YAN.22)
Selera [*-nya*] *juga ter-ganggu dan* [*dia*] *tidak dapat*
appetite-3POSS also AFF-upset and 3SG not manage AV-finish
meng-habiskan makanan yang di-berikan.
food REL PV-give

'His appetite was affected and he couldn't finish the food he was given.'

Topical kinship terms, such as *isteri-nya* 'his wife' in (18), are tracked with pronouns. Interestingly, the proper name *Jack* in the complement clause cannot become the antecedent of *dia*. This suggests that Malay anaphoric pronouns target the local topic, or that embedded proper names are not felicitous as antecedents for pronouns.

(18) Singapore Malay (2017.LQ.07)
Isteri-nya   ber-kata yang Jack salah faham   dan [dia] setakat beli
wife-3POSS AV-say COMP PN misunderstand and 3SG so.far buy
barang-barang pasaran sahaja.
things   market only

'His wife said that Jack misunderstood and that she only bought goods from the market.'

As mentioned in the discussion of Figure 5, proper names are tracked with pronouns where one description is a paraphrase of an earlier one, or follows from it in a logical way, as in (19).

(19) Singapore Malay (2017.YAN.30–31)
[Halim] mem-beritahu berapa   seksa-nya   hidup di dalam penjara.
PN   AV-tell   how.much torturous-INTENS life   inside prison
[Dia] me-luahkan rasa   kesal   [-nya] di atas perbuatan   ganas
3SG   AV-express feeling repent-3POSS at   action violence-3POSS past.time
[-nya] tempoh hari akibat   mabuk me-minum minuman keras.
          in.result drunk   AV-drink alcohol

'Halim told them what a torment life in prison was. He expressed his feelings of regret over his brutal actions a few days ago, the result of being drunk from drinking liquor.'

In (20), a single macro-event in three sentences characterises the farmer's ordeal in jail. The proper name *Adam* is used only in the first sentence, and tracked with *dia* '3SG' subsequently.

(20) Singapore Malay (2017.SI.29–31)
Sewaktu di dalam penjara, [Adam] tidak henti-henti menangis. [Dia] tidak
while   inside jail   PN   not   RED-stop   AV.cry   3SG   not
lalu   untuk makan. [Dia] hanya duduk menangis di dalam penjara yang gelap
happen to   eat   3SG   only sit   AV.cry   inside jail   REL dark
lagi berbau itu.
ADD smell DIST

'While in jail, Adam did not stop crying. He could not eat. He only sat crying in the jail that was dark and smelly.'

We have shown that proper names are tracked with pronouns, and that their repetition creates a rhythm of sub-events. This strategy applies to the main character, the farmer.

2 Stance, categorisation, and information structure in Malay

A somewhat different strategy is used to track the farmer's wife and child. Apart from repetition, particularly common is synecdoche (RefLex *r-given*); the farmer's wife and child are referred to as *keluarga* 'family', as in (21). In another version, the farmer's status is characterised as *berumah-tangga* 'married, having a family', or the couple is referred to with *suami-isteri*.

(21) Singapore Malay (2017.AM.26)
Pak Samad cuba mengeratkan hubungan-nya dengan [keluarga-nya].
Mr PN try AV.strengthen relationship-3POSS with family-3POSS
'Pak Samad tried to improve his relationship with his family.'

In one version of *Frog Story*, the boy is categorised with a proper name and tracked by repetition and pronouns (see Table 8). His dog and frog are categorised and tracked with possessives, highlighting their relationship to the boy.

(22) Singapore Malay (2013.SS.FrogStory.11)
Kemudian Abu dan [anjing-nya] memanggil-manggil [katak-nya] lalu
subsequently PN and dog-3POSS RED-call frog-3POSS through
tingkap [bilik-nya].
window room-3POSS
'Then Abu and his dog called repeatedly for his frog through the window of his room.'

Categorisation with descriptions reflects the speaker's neutral epistemic stance (see also §3). Tracking of such referents is more elaborate and besides repetition, pronouns and zero anaphora also include demonstratives and particles (see also §5).

Another tracking strategy involves relativisation. Unlike demonstratives or particles, however, relativisation can embed another perspective. In the final scenes of *Pear Story*, the farmer is puzzled by seeing three boys walking by with his pears. The farmer is not aware that the boy who took one of his baskets shared the fruit with these boys when they helped him to pick up the scattered fruit. LN resolved this by constructing the three boys as new, taking up the farmer's perspective, as in (23). Notice that the noun *pear* combines with *tadi*, conforming to the all-knowing perspective of the speaker-storyteller.

(23) Singapore Malay (2013.LN.PearStory.31)
Kemudian dia ter-nampak tiga, [tiga orang budak yang sudah
subsequently 3SG INVOL-notice three three CL.HUMAN child REL already
me-makan pear tadi].
AV-eat pear previous
'Then he saw three…, three boys who were eating the pears from earlier on.'

In CA's version in (24), the passing boys are presented as the subject of an inverted intransitive clause and modified by a relative clause referring to the pears received for their help.

(24) Singapore Malay (2013.CA.PearStory.13)
 <unclear> datang [tiga budak] yang mem-bantu budak yang <unclear> makan
          arrive three boy   REL AV-help   boy   REL   eat
 buah yang di-petik.
 fruit REL PV-pick

 '[While he was thinking], coming there were three boys who helped the [fallen] boy, eating the harvested fruit.'

Relative clauses are utilised in *Pear Story* to distinguish between the children (boy, girl, and the three boys). In the case of the boy, reference is made to his fall, as in (25). The false start with code-switching may reveal the decision-making of the speaker as to how to most effectively categorise the boy, i.e. with reference to boys who helped, or with reference to the fall. In general, the more elaborate descriptions distinguishing the children confirm our point about the simplifying effect of strong epistemic stance on referent categorisation and tracking.

(25) Singapore Malay (2013.LN.PearStory.25)
 Budak yang CHILDRE... [budak yang ter-jatuh tadi   itu pun] terus
 boy   REL CS.children boy REL INVOL-fall RECENT DIST EVENT direct
 menunggang basikal-nya   kembali.
 AV.ride   bicycle-3POSS back

 'The boy that children..., the boy who fell just now continued riding his bicycle.'

Table 6 summarises the expressions of the participants in *Getting the Story Straight*, in the order in which they appear in the narrative (the first mention is underlined). The horizontal line divides the texts into two groups according to the epistemic stance, taking the categorisation of the farmer as a criterion. Above the line are seven texts where the farmer (and usually also his wife) is categorised with a proper name. In the remaining four texts, the speaker's neutral epistemic stance is apparent in the categorisation of the farmer with a description. In contrast, categorisation of the police and friends is more uniform.

The most significant patterns, discernible in the table, are the following: (i) the speaker's strong epistemic stance is reflected in the categorisation of prominent referents with proper names; (ii) repetition and pronouns are used to track them; (iii) neutral stance leads to categorisation with descriptions, typically an enumerated classifier phrase; (iv) various types of NPs (including demonstratives and particles) and pronouns are used for tracking; and (v) the farmer's wife, child and friends are referred to with possessive phrases.

4.2 Tracking animate and inanimate referents

Tracking of non-human referents (animate and inanimate) shows a split pattern, a more diverse one to track animates, especially when fabulated as capable of inner speech (thoughts, plans, or emotions). Inanimate referents, on the other hand, are rarely tracked

2 Stance, categorisation, and information structure in Malay

Table 6: Categorisation and tracking of prominent human referents in *Getting the Story Straight*

version	farmer	wife	child	friends	police
MLZ	PN [a], PRO [b], N(+*itu*+*pun*)	PN, PRO, N-POSS(+*itu*), N[N]	N-POSS [c]	RED-N-POSS [d]	N[N] [e]
MIZ	PN, PRO	N-POSS + PN, PRO [f], N-POSS, N[N]	N-POSS, PRO, N[N]	RED-N-POSS, PRO	N[N], PRO
AM	PN (+*pun*), PRO	N-POSS + PN, PRO, N[N]	N-POSS [g], N[N]	RED-N-POSS, PRO	N, N+*pun*
YAN	PN, PRO	N-POSS + PN, PRO, N[N]	N-POSS, N[N]	PN, PRO, N[N]	NUM-CL-N, N[N]
SI	PN, PRO, N-POSS [h]	N-POSS + PN, PRO, N-POSS, N[N]	N -POSS, N[N]	PN + N-POSS, PRO, RED-N-POSS	
ISH	PN, PRO, [N] [i]	PN, PRO, N-POSS, N[N] [j]	(RED-)N-POSS	RED-N -POSS	N[N]
LQ	NUM-CL-N + PN, PRO, N[N]	NUM-CL-N, PRO, N[N]-POSS [k]	NUM-CL-N + PN, PRO, [N] -POSS [l]	RED-N-POSS, PRO	N[N]
JUR	N, PRO, N+*itu*, N+*pun*	N-POSS, N, PRO	N-POSS, PRO+NUM [m], N[N]	RED-N-POSS, PRO	N [n]
ISM	N, PRO, N+*pun*	N-POSS, PRO	N-POSS	RED-N -POSS	N
HZ	NUM-CL-N, PRO(+*pun*), N-POSS [o], N+*tu*+*pun*, N+*pula*, N+*tersebut*	N[N]-POSS, PRO, N+*pula*	N[N]-POSS	RED-N-POSS	N
NZ	NUM-CL-N, PRO(+*pun*), N-POSS+*pun*, N[N]+(*i*)*tu*+*pun*, N+*tersebut*	N[N]-POSS (+*pun*),	[N]-POSS	N-POSS, RED-N+*tersebut*, N-POSS	N +*tersebut*, [N]+*pula*

[a] PN: proper name
[b] PRO: pronominal element, including *dia*, *mereka* and *-nya*
[c] N-POSS: possessed noun with an optional possessive *-nya*, e.g. *anak-nya* 'their child', *isterinya* 'his wife', *bapak Halim* 'Halim's father', etc.
[d] RED-N: reduplicated noun with N repetition and synecdoche, e.g. *kawan-kawan*(-*nya*) or *teman-teman*(-*nya*) 'this friends'
[e] N[N]: both N repetition and synecdoche, e.g. *pihak berkuasa* 'authorities' or *keluarga* 'family, i.e. wife and child'
[f] includes also *kedua-dua mereka* 'both of them' (i.e. wife and child)
[g] not referred to in the first picture frame where it occurs, but later
[h] the farmer, named here *Adam* is referred to as *suami-nya* 'her husband', when his wife is reporting to the police
[i] [N]: synecdoche *suami-isteri* 'couple, husband and wife'
[j] N[N]: both N repetition and synecdoche *suami-isteri* 'couple, husband and wife'
[k] N[N]-POSS: repetition and synecdoche, including possessive marking
[l] [N]-POSS: synecdoche *keluarga-nya* 'his family'
[m] PRO-NUM: pronoun combined with a numeral, to refer to both the child and her mother, e.g. *mereka dua-dua* 'both of them'
[n] N: simple repetition only
[o] N-POSS: possessed noun *suami-nya* 'her husband' used when wife's perspective is given

beyond their first introduction. Discourse-persistent inanimate referents are tracked with various types of NPs, but never with pronouns. Table 7 and Table 8 summarise the tracking devices in *Frog Story* and *Jackal and Crow*.

Table 7: Categorisation and tracking of referents in *Jackal and Crow*

version	crow	basket	fish	jackal	tree
MLZ	NUM-CL-N PRO[b], N(+*pun*), *the*+N[d]	QUANT-N-RC	RED-N N, N+*itu*	N [a] PRO(+*pun*)[c]	N-DEM
OG	NUM-CL-N PRO, N[N][e] N[N]+*itu*	QUANT-N	N N N+*itu*	NUM-CL-N PRO N N+*itu*(+*pun*)	n.a.

[a] bare noun is followed by the additive focus particle *pula* in (43), but we analyse it as scoping over the entire clause
[b] both the honorific *beliau* and default *dia* are used
[c] a range of 1st, 2nd and 3rd person pronouns are used
[d] codeswitching is used: *the gagak* 'the crow'
[e] N[N]: the crow is referred to as *burung gagak* 'crow', or as *burung* 'bird'

Table 7 shows that referent categorisation and tracking in *Jackal and Crow* is quite uniform. A single referent, the tree in which the crow perches, is completely omitted by OG. In contrast, the two versions of *Frog Story* display the same epistemic stance variation as the *Getting the Story Straight* texts, as shown in Table 8.

We now turn to the tracking of non-human referents. For animate referents, repetition and pronouns are common. In (26), the frog (*katak Abu* 'Abu's frog') is tracked with the possessive -*nya*, partly because the frog is fabulated as an experiencer (capable of emotion), and thus the description of the boy and dog is consistent with the frog's perspective.

(26) Singapore Malay (2013.SS.FrogStory.54)
 Nampaknya [katak Abu] sangat merindui kawan-kawan-nya .
 apparently frog PN very miss RED-friend-3POSS
 'Apparently Abu's frog missed his friends.'

In (27), personal pronouns *dia* and *beliau* (honorific) refer to the crow, where the honorific is a clue of speaker's sarcasm.

(27) Singapore Malay (2013.MLZ.JackalAndCrow.141–2)
 Dah [beliau] ter-nampak beberapa bakul yang terdapat ikan-ikan. SO [dia]
 already 3SG.HON INVOL-see few basket REL exist RED-fish CS.SO 3SG

2 Stance, categorisation, and information structure in Malay

Table 8: Categorisation and tracking of referents in *Frog Story*

version	boy	dog	frog	jar	forest	bees	rodent	hole[a]
OG	NUM-CL-N PRO, N-POSS N[N](+*itu*)	NUM-CL-N PRO, N-POSS, N+*itu*(+*pun*)	NUM-CL-N PRO, N-POSS N+*itu*	NUM-CL-N PRO, N[N]+(*itu*)	NUM-CL-N N(+*itu*)	N-RC N(+*itu*)	NUM-CL-N N[N](+*itu*)	NUM-CL-N N-POSS PP[b]
SS	PN PN, PRO(+*pun*), (RED-)N-POSS	N-POSS PRO(+*pun*) (RED-)N-POSS	N-POSS N-POSS N+*itu*	N-POSS N-POSS N+*itu*	N	N-RC RED-N	n.a.	NUM-N-PP N+*itu*

	owl	rock	branch	antlers	deer	water	log	frogs
OG	NUM-CL-N PRO, N(+*itu*)	NUM-N N+*itu*	NUM-N-RC N+*itu*	N-POSS	NUM-CL-N PRO, N+*itu*	N-RC N	NUM-N [c] N+*itu*	N-POSS [d] PRO, N[N], NUM-CL-N+*itu*
SS	NUM-CL-N N+*itu*	NUM-N N+*itu*	NUM-N-RC [e] N+*itu*	N-POSS N+*itu*	N N+*itu*	N [f] N+*itu*	N-RC N	N-POSS NUM-CL-N N[N](+*itu*)

[a] the cavity occupied by the owl
[b] PP: prepositional phrase: the hole referred to as *di dalam* 'inside'
[c] the constituent could be interpreted as a compound *satu akar pokok* 'a tree root' or a possessive construction *satu akar pokok* 'a root of the tree'
[d] realised as a possessor in *bunyi-bunyi katak* 'frog sounds' and treated as given thereafter
[e] realised as *satu ranting pokok yang...* 'a tree branch that ...'
[f] realised together with *antlears* as *tanduk rusa* 'deer antlers'

    pergi ah, terbang, terbang, terbang, [dia] pergi dekat ikan tu, zoop!
    go PART fly fly fly 3SG go near fish DIST INTER
'And he (the crow) saw several baskets filled with fish. So he went, flew, he came to the fish and went *zoop*.'

The same version contains a mini-dialogue, shown in (28), where the first and second person pronouns refer to the jackal and crow, respectively. The follow-up comment where the speaker praises his own story-telling performance is another clue of the speaker's sarcasm.

(28)   Singapore Malay (2013.MLZ.JackalAndCrow.164)
    [*Saya*] nak dengar suara [*awak*] yang merdu lah. Chey, macam betul aja.
    1SG want hear voice 2SG REL sweet PART INTER, kind genuine PART
    'I want to hear your sweet voice, hey that kind of sounds just right.'

A summary of the categorisation and tracking of non-human given referents in *Jackal and Crow* and *Frog Story* is given in Table 7 and Table 8. The common pattern is the limited variation in the description of inanimates, and the lack of tracking thereof. When tracked, the default is to include the demonstrative *itu*, which will be discussed in §5.1.

Finally, Table 9 shows that the categorisation and tracking of referents in *Pear Story* is fairly uniform. Neither speaker takes a strong epistemic stance, with the result that the

61

tracking of the children is quite elaborate to distinguish the boy with the basket, from the girl on the bike and the boys who help him pick up spilled fruit.

Table 9: Categorisation and tracking of referents in *Pear Story*

version	farmer	fruit	baskets	shepherd	boy	bicycle	girl	3 boys
CA	NUM-CL-N, PRO, N+*tadi* *si*+N+*itu*	N	NUM-N[a]	n.a.	NUM-CL-N, PRO, N+*itu*	N	n.a.	NUM-N [b] PRO, N(+NUM)
LN	NUM-CL-N, PRO, N+*itu*, N+*tadi*	N	N-PP[c]	N-POSS, PRO	NUM-CL-N, PRO, N+*lagi*+*tadi*+*itu*	N	NUM-CL-N	NUM-CL-N [d], PRO+*pun* PRO+*tadi*, NUM-CL-N RED-N-POSS

[a]NUM-N: quantified noun, e.g. *tiga bakul* 'three baskets'
[b]NUM-N: enumerated noun phrase *tiga lagi budak kanak-kanak* 'three small boys'
[c]N-PP: noun with a locative prepositional phrase locating the baskets in relation to the tree
[d]realised as *tiga orang dak laki* 'three boys'

The effect of stance and discourse role on the tracking of referents is summarised in Table 10, whose structure parallels that of Table 5 above.

Table 10: Effect of stance and discourse role on referent tracking

	EPISTEMIC STANCE	
REFERENT CATEGORY	STRONG	NEUTRAL
+human	PN, PRO	PRO, N(+*itu*/PART)
+animate	PRO(+PART), N-POSS/+*itu*	PRO, N(+*itu*/PART)
−animate, +discourse-persistent	PRO, N-POSS/+*itu*	N(+*itu*)
−animate, −discourse-persistent	n.a.	

5 Maintaining joint attention

In the previous two sections we discussed the role of stance for referent categorisation and tracking. This section focuses on another aspect of interaction and balancing of information disparity. This interactive aspect is part of Du Bois' stance model, conceptualised as the alignment between the interlocutors (cf. Du Bois 2007: 171). As Du Bois puts it: *I evaluate something, and thereby position myself, and thereby align with you* (2007: 163). Du Bois' *alignment* falls within a larger notion of *joint attention*, which is a type of social cognition (cf. Tomasello 1995). Diessel (2006) applies the notion of joint attention to demonstratives, whose primary roles he identifies in (i) locating referents relative to the deictic centre, and (ii) coordinating the interlocutors' joint attention (Diessel 2006: 469).

While demonstratives are certainly the most prominent joint-attention coordinating devices in Malay (cf. Himmelmann 1996; Williams 2009), Malay possesses a number of adnominal markers with a similar function, most importantly *pun* and *pula*. In this section, we analyse the use of Malay demonstratives and other adnominal markers in relation to coordination of interlocutors' joint attention and show how the use of these devices is related to epistemic stance and referent categorisation. The data suggests that neutral stance and nominal expression of referents correlate with the use of demonstratives. By taking a neutral stance, the speaker expects greater recognitional effort on the side of the hearer and compensates by providing more clues so that joint attention can be maintained. We will demonstrate that these clues are demonstratives and particles. While key characters of the story do not require the use of these clues frequently, they are used whenever a more peripheral participant becomes a topic.

5.1 Malay demonstratives

Malay demonstratives (both long and short forms) may introduce new information and track "persistent" referents throughout discourse (Himmelmann 1996: 241). The use of demonstratives has implications for how the perspective of the hearer is constructed in interaction, as either having or lacking access to the intended referent (Williams 2009), and indicates the speaker's stance. Our discussion of the data again follows the referential hierarchy, starting with human referents.

In the following fragment, the farmer is tracked with a demonstrative phrase. Such use is common in texts where the referent was categorised with a description.[12] The speaker prevents a possible misalignment with the hearer by using the demonstrative and putting focus on the farmer, as affected by *polis* 'police', the local topical agent, which moves the plot.

(29) Singapore Malay (2017.JUR.18)
      Polis tiba   dan menangkap [petani itu].
      police arrive and AV.seize   farmer DIST
      'The police arrived and caught the farmer.'

Another example is given in (30), which immediately follows (50). The distal *itu* puts the gardener in focus, and constructs the child's perspective as not recognising her father. The distal form does not have any spatial meaning here, because the man has just arrived in the scene. Instead, it creates an emotional distance, and marks the stance of the child. It locates the responsibility for the non-recognition within the child, and ultimately in the abusive behaviour of her father.[13]

(30) Singapore Malay (2017.ISM.21)
      Anak-nya   tidak kenal kepada [pekebun itu].
      child-3POSS not   know to   gardener DIST
      'His child did not recognise the gardener.'

---
[12] An overview of all the expressions of key referents in *Getting the Story Straight* can be found in Table 6.
[13] Williams (2009) describes a similar use of demonstratives in Indonesian conversation. Djenar (2014) shows that *nih* and *tuh* have presentative, directive and expressive functions, and explains why *tuh* is used for recognitional and discourse deixis.

The most common way to track discourse persistent non-human referents is with N+*itu*. The demonstrative has a similar function as the English definite article, marking the given referential status of the referent. The distal form does not imply any contrast or any spatial relation, and its function is purely referential in marking the given referent and perhaps aids the hearer in identifying the referent. We do maintain the gloss DIST in (31), but a gloss GIV for *given* would be equally plausible.

(31) Singapore Malay (2013.OG.FrogStory.03)
Umm. Dan mereka ber-main bersama-sama tiap-tiap malam, di mana [anjing
HESIT and 3PL   AV-play RED-together RED-each night where dog
itu] akan tidur di bawah [katil [budak lelaki itu]], sementara [katak itu] akan
DIST will sleep below   bed   boy   DIST while   frog DIST will
tidur di dalam peti gelas-nya.
sleep inside   glass.jar-3POSS

'Mmm. They played together every night and the dog would sleep under the boy's bed while the frog slept in its jar.'

The above characterisation of *itu* as a definite marker is further supported by the code-switching patterns. Speakers of Colloquial Singaporean Malay frequently code-switch in English across genres. Consider now (32), where the NP contains the English definite article *the*, where one would expect *itu*. The English *then* corresponds to the eventive *pun*, which will be discussed in §5.4.

(32) Singapore Malay (2013.MLZ.JackalAndCrow.167)
THEN THE gagak, THEN THE   gagak nyanyi
CS.then CS.DEF crow CS.THEN CS.DEF crow sing

'Then the raven sang.'

The following two examples from *Frog Story* are a pair, where (33) shows the categorisation of a pair of adult frogs in the final episode of the story. A description consisting of a possessive construction presents the frogs indirectly as "emitters" of the sound.

(33) Singapore Malay (2013.OG.FrogStory.30)
Selepas itu, mereka um, jalan ke satu ah, lagi satu uh, akar uh, pokok ya,
thereafter 3PL   PART move to one HESIT other one PART root PART tree yes
dan budak lelaki itu suruh anjing-nya diam, kerana dia men-dengar ah,
and boy   DIST ask   dog-3POSS silent because 3SG AV-hear   HESIT
[bunyi-bunyi katak] di belakang mm, dahan pokok itu ya.
RED-noise   frog   behind   PART branch trunk DIST yes

'After that, they walked to another tree root, and the boy instructed his dog to be quiet because he heard frog noises behind the tree trunk.'

Subsequently, the frogs are tracked with N+*itu* (RefLex *r-given*).

(34) Singapore Malay (2013.OG.FrogStory.31)
Jadi dengan senyap, mereka dekat berhampiran dengan um, [katak itu], dan,
so   with   silence 3PL   near adjacent   with   PART frog   DIST and
akhirnya mereka jumpa dua ekor   katak di belakang um, pokok itu, ya.
finally   3PL   find   two CL.ANIMAL frog   behind   PART tree   DIST yes

'So with silence, they approached close to the frog and finally they met two frogs behind the tree.'

The proximal *ini* is used less frequently and does entail that the referent is spatially proximate. The viewpoint from which the proximity is constructed can shift and be located within the participants. In (35), the boy's perspective is taken to refer to the frogs, as well as to the relative temporal *ini* 'now', located within the story.

(35) Singapore Malay (2013.OG.FrogStory.33)
Jadi mm, selepas   budak lelaki itu, ber-cerita-kan kepada kedua, uh,
so   PART subsequently boy   DIST AV-tell-APPL   to   couple PART
[ibu   dan bapa   katak ini], bahawa ia   mahu mem-bawa balik, uh   katak
mother and father frog   PROX COMP   3SG wish AV-carry   return PART frog
yang sebelum   ini   berada di rumah-nya.
REL previously PROX be   in house-3POSS

'So after the boy explained to both the father and mother frog that he wanted to bring back that frog that before this was in his house.'

Apart from the spatial *ini* and *itu*, there are three more deictic forms which do not have spatial uses, but are common in discourse: *tadi* 'recently mentioned', *tersebut* 'aforementioned', and *si* 'familiar', which will be described below. Their use correlates with a neutral epistemic stance and categorisation with descriptions, except for *si*, which expresses familiarity and therefore marks a stronger epistemic stance.

The demonstrative *tadi* 'recently mentioned' is a dedicated anaphoric form derived from an adverbial meaning 'earlier' (Sneddon et al. 2012: 133). It is likely grammaticalised to the adnominal position through a *yang* modifier construction: *N yang tadi* > *N tadi*. In one version of the *Pear Story*, it tracks the farmer picking fruit. The example given in (36) is beautiful, because it verbalises the intention behind using *tadi* in the preceding phrase *kita patah balik...* 'let us return back'.

(36) Singapore Malay (2013.CA.PearStory.11)
Jadi bila,   kita   patah balik kepada [perkebun tadi],   masa dia turun
so   when 1PL.INCL turn.back to   farmer   RECENT time 3SG descend
daripada pokok dia nampak tadi,   dia nampak agak   aneh kerana sebab
from   tree   3SG see   recently 3SG see   slightly weird because reason
masa dia naik   ada tiga   bakul.
time 3SG climb be   three basket

'So back to the farmer from earlier, the time he came down from the tree he found it weird as he last saw three baskets.'

The anaphoric demonstrative *tersebut* 'aforementioned, that' is used with expressions referring to the farmer in *Getting the Story Straight*. Singapore Malay speakers base some of their stylistic preferences on their formal education; the use of particles and of the demonstrative *tersebut* strikes native speakers as formal and rote-like. In NZ version, where *tersebut* is used more than in all the other texts combined, the particle is used to track the farmer, his friends and the police (see Table 6). Apart from tracking, *tersebut* puts the focus on the given referent. We gloss it as GIVEN.FOC and translate it with the English *that*, which can also have a focusing role. Its use correlates with the neutral epistemic stance and categorisation of referents with descriptions. Its extensive use by NZ is illustrated in (37). We believe that the frequent use is a personal characteristic of NZ, rather than a general pattern.[14]

(37) Singapore Malay (2017.NZ.05–08)
Dalam kemarahannya itu   dia pun   menumbuk isterinya.   Se-orang
in   anger-3POSS   DIST 3SG EVENT AV.punch   wife-3POSS one-CL.HUMAN
orang tua yang ter-lihat   [kejadian tersebut] pun,   uh,   mmm, memanggil
old.man   REL   INVOL-see event   GIVEN.FOC TOP2 HESIT HESIT   AV.call
polis   dan [polis tersebut   pun]   uhhh, menangkap [lelaki tersebut]. Di
police and police GIVEN.FOC EVENT HESIT AV.catch   man   GIVEN.FOC in
balai   polis pula, uh,   isteri-nya   pun   mem-beritahu keterangan tentang
station police then   HESIT wife-3POSS TOP2 AV-report   testimony about
[kejadian tersebut] kenapa ia   terjadi. Suami-nya   pun takut dengan,
event   GIVEN.FOC why   3SG happen husband-3POSS TOP2 afraid with
aah, apa   yang akan menjadi terhadapnya.
HESIT what REL   will   happen about-3
'In his anger he then punched his wife. An old man who saw that incident then called the police and those police then caught that man. Then at the police station, his wife explained that incident and why it had happened. Her husband then got frightened over what would happen to him.'

In our corpus, the demonstrative *si* is used sparsely. Traditional grammars attribute *si* a diminutive function (Sneddon et al. 2012: 146) and report that it is never used in address terms, but only in reference to somebody who is not the hearer (Sneddon et al. 2012: 374). The *Wiktionary* entry for *si* contains an accurate characterisation; in addition to 'friendly connotation', 'diminutive', and 'friendly categorisation', it also lists 'generic categorisation', exemplified in (38).

(38) Indonesian (Wiktionary.si#Indonesian)
[*Si ayah*] *harus belajar mengenal* [*si anak*].
   father must learn   AV.know   child
'The father has to learn to know the child.'

---

[14]Note that the NP *seorang tua yang...pun* combines with *pun*, while newly introduced into discourse, but immediately cast as topic. The particle *pun* seems to work in tandem with *tersebut*, where one marks the new topic and the other links explicitly the relevant given referent.

We propose that *si* is a marker of familiarity, restricted to human referents. It is an expression of a strong epistemic stance.[15] *Si* draws interlocutors' attention to a referent by presenting it as familiar, i.e. identifiable within one's knowledge, or recent discourse. Tracking proper names with a *si* phrase follows the *triangular* pattern of person reference identified in (Haviland 2007: 229–230), where a new referent is anchored in relation to both the speaker and the hearer. The *si* phrase is an explicit anchoring effort in relation to the familiar knowledge of the hearer. Within the stance framework proposed by Du Bois (2007), it is also an alignment device which explicitly interacts with the interlocutors' perspective.

It is not relevant that the familiarity is only constructed as such, because existing familiar referents are identified in exactly the same way, as we will show in (41). In (39), a discourse-recent referent marked with *si* is presented. Sukamto (2013) observes a similar pattern in written Indonesian accounts of *Pear Story*. Expressions re-activating the given participants tend to be highly specified, and combine with both *si* and *sang* in the Indonesian texts.

(39) Singapore Malay (2013.CA.PearStory.05)
Semasa dia memetik buah dia atas, ada se-orang   budak me-naiki
when   3SG AV.pick fruit 3SG above exist one-CL.HUMAN boy   AV-travel.by
basikal dan dia ter-nampak buah di dalam bakul itu lalu dia memikir
bicycle and 3SG INVOL-notice fruit inside   basket DIST then 3SG AV.think.about
harus-kah   dia meng-ambil tetapi memandangkan [si   perkebun itu]
need-Q.PART 3SG AV-take   but   considering   FAMILIAR farmer   DIST
begitu perihatin dengan memetik buah di atas pokok lalu dia meng-ambil satu
so   concerned with   AV.pick fruit on.top tree   then 3SG AV-take   one
bakul tampa izin.
basket without approval

'When he picked the fruits above, a boy riding a bicycle saw fruits in the basket. Then he thought whether he should take some, but considering that our farmer was so concerned with picking fruits, he actually took one whole basket without permission.'

In our Singapore Malay corpus, *si* is used invariably to refer to relatives, partners or friends who do not take part in the interaction. The fragment in (40) is taken from an interview with an elderly speaker of Singapore Malay, who describes here how she got engaged. Her future father-in-law used to ask her, whether she had yet found a *mata-air* 'beloved' and whether she liked his son (absent during the exchange).

---

[15]The notion of familiarity is defined by Gundel et al. (1993: 278) as a special cognitive status where the hearer already has a representation in memory, either in long-term memory, absence of recent mention, or in short-term memory, if he has.

(40) Singapore Malay (2016.BandarGirls.202)
Kau suka tak, dengan si... Arsyad?
2SG like not with FAMILIAR PN
'Do you like [our] Arsyad, don't you?'

In (41), a mother asks whether her son, who is preparing for a math exam, is finished with his tutor (absent during the exchange). This is the first mention of the tutor in the conversation, and later in that same conversation, the tutor is tracked with *dia*.

(41) Singapore Malay (2013.SNS.Exam.17)
Abeh tak belajar eh? Dah habis [si dia tu] ajar dah habis?
then not study Q.PART already finish FAMILIAR 3SG DIST teach already finish
'Why don't you prepare anymore? It is done what he [the tutor] taught you?'

In our narrative corpus, human referents categorised with proper names may be accompanied by an appositive *si* phrase. In (42), the vegetable seller is constructed as familiar to the farmer, amplifying the effect of the accusation and explaining the rage that follows.[16]

(42) Singapore Malay (2017.SI.15)
sewaktu sedang mabuk Abu mem-beritahu Adam bahawa dia ter-nampak Hawa,
while PROG drunk PN AV-tell PN COMP 3SG INVOL-see PN
isteri Adam, sedang ber-mesra-mesra bersama [Sani, si penjual sayur] di
wife PN PROG AV-RED-cozy together PN ART seller vegetable in
pasar.
market
'While he was drunk, Abu told Adam that he saw Hawa, Adam's wife, behaving in a friendly way with Sani, [you know] the vegetable seller at the market.'

In summary, Malay *si* interacts with a specific layer of the hearer's memory: either with the recent memory, or with personal knowledge and stereotypes. Marking unknown and unfamiliar referents with *si* is a request for cooperation to either fill out the speaker's intention, and accept the referent in a common ground (in statements), or to supply the relevant knowledge in the next turn (in questions). It is the ultimate device forcing joint attention.[17]

We will now proceed to discuss the Malay particles *pula*, *lagi*, and *pun*, whose function in manipulation of joint attention is even more complex than that of the demonstratives discussed here.

---

[16] The man introduced in the drunk gossip (see Figure 2, frame 4), is sometimes given a name, such as *Encik Romi* in (4), or is referred to with a proper name followed by a nominal marked with *si*, such as *Leyman, si penjual surat khabar* 'Leyman, the news agent'.

[17] There are some interesting parallels with other markers of familiarity, such as the New Zealand *y'know* (Stubbe & Holmes 1995: 69), the Abui hearer-oriented forms (Kratochvíl & Delpada 2015), or the more grammaticalised systems of engagement (Evans et al. 2017a,b).

5.2 Particle *pula*

The Malay particle *pula* (colloquial *pulak*) is traditionally characterised as an additive focus particle (Sneddon et al. 2012: 236). Nomoto (2017: pula(k)) distinguishes between two functions of the Malay *pula*: (i) when placed after the predicate, the particle indexes the speaker's epistemic stance — the situation is marked as not conforming to the speaker's expectation, as surprising, or as evoking doubts; (ii) when combined with nominals, *pula* encodes contrast, but also interacts with expectation.

Both (43) and (44) employ the additive *pula* when the jackal is categorised with a description.[18] In (43), the additive *pulak* marks the existence of the newly introduced jackal as a somewhat unexpected addition to the discourse. The speaker perhaps contradicts the reasonable anticipation of the bird eating the fish, so the appearance of a hungry jackal presents an unexpected twist in the story.[19] After all, the fable is well-known, and it is reasonable to expect that the hearer is familiar with the plot.

(43) Singapore Malay (2013.MLZ.JackalCrow.149)
*Dah   LAND, dia alih-alih ni   ada [musang] **pulak** dia nampak.*
already cs.land 3SG suddenly PROX exist jackal   ADD   3SG see

'And as it landed, the crow suddenly saw that there was also a fox (there).'

In the second text, the jackal is introduced as the subject of an inverted existential clause with an enumerated classifier structure in (44). The jackal is linked to the already known crow with the relative clause, where the crow is the object of the involuntary action verb *terlihat* 'happen to see'. The additive *pula* marks the newly introduced location, effectively extending the space in which the narrative is constructed. In terms of joint attention, the particle forces an update. It constructs the extension of the space in which the story takes place as unexpected or surprising.

(44) Singapore Malay (2013.OG.JackalCrow.04)
*Di satu ladang **pula** ada [se-ekor   serigala] yang terlihat burung gagak*
in one field   ADD exist one-CL.ANIMAL jackal   REL   spot   crow
itu terbang bersama ikan dalam mulut burung itu.
DST fly   together fish inside beak bird   DST

'In a field, there was a jackal that saw the crow flying with the fish in its mouth.'

Example (45) shows the contrastive function of *pula*, where the benefit of the police action for the farmer's wife has to be considered in parallel with the punishment of her husband.

---

[18] Note that there are several additive markers in Malay. Forker (2016: 91) discusses only *pun* as additive, while Goddard (2001: 27) calls both *pun* and *pula* emphatic. Sneddon et al. (2012: 236) considers both *juga* and *pula* additive markers, which indicate that "the focused part is an addition".

[19] Malay speakers in Singapore are taught in Malay language composition classes that the particles *pula* and *pun* make their style "more interesting" or "engaging", and mark the "climax". We believe that at least in some cases, Malay speakers may be using these particles for such "aesthetic" reasons. The aesthetic function of *pun*, as a marker of a particular style is also discussed by Cumming (1991: 107).

(45) Singapore Malay (2017.HZ.09–10)
Dengan itu, dia harus pergi ke, uh, pihak polis dan beritahu tentang apa yang
therefore 3SG must go to HESIT police and inform about what REL
terjadi. Um, [suami-nya pula] berasa amat menyesal akan apa
happen HESIT husband-3POSS CON.FOC feel very AV.regretful about what
terjadi, dan beliau amat risau tentang, um, apa yang akan terjadi
happen and 3SG.HON very uneasy about HESIT what REL will happen
kepada-nya iaitu, um, beliau harus di- di- di-letakkan di dalam lockup dan
to-3 namely HESIT 3SG.HON must PV-place inside jail and
di-belasah oleh pihak polis.
PV-beat.up by police

'So now she had to go to the police and tell them what happened. Her husband (on the other hand) felt very regretful about what had happened, and he was very worried about what would happen to him, that is, he had to be detained in a jail cell and beaten by the police.'

The particle *pula* also occurs with left-dislocated locative elements. Its function appears to be to move the narrative along to another location. We have seen one example of this use in (44) and give another in (46) below.

(46) Singapore Malay (2017.NZ.07)
[Di balai polis pula], uh, isteri-nya pun mem-beritahu keterangan
in station police ADD HESIT wife-3POSS TOP2 AV-report testimony
tentang kejadian tersebut kenapa ia terjadi.
about event GIVEN.FOC why 3SG happen

'Then at the police station, his wife explained that incident and why it had happened.'

By using *pula*, the speaker proposes a broadening or update of joint attention. In this function *pula* is similar to the demonstratives discussed in §5.1, because the "field" of joint attention remains essentially the same. In the next section we will discuss the use of *lagi*, another additive particle, whose use seems to be more restricted, but allows for scope manipulation.

5.3 Particle *lagi*

The particle *lagi* indicates repetition with predicates, but with adnominal quantifiers, it has an additive function. The additive function is illustrated in (47), where the particle highlights that the reference is made to all members of the group (Forker 2016: 84–85).

(47) Singapore Malay (2013.CA.PearStory.08)
Dalam perjalanan pulang budak itu dengan tidak sengaja ter-langgar batu
while drive home child DIST with accident INVOL-hit rock
lalu dibantu oleh [tiga lagi budak kanak-kanak] untuk mengumpulkan,
then PV-help by three more boy child to AV.collect

mem-bangunkan basikal-nya dan buah-buahan yang ter-jatuh.
AV-put.upright   bicycle-3POSS and fruit   REL   INVOL-fall

'On the way home, the boy accidentally bumped into stones and is assisted by three other young children to collect the bicycle and fallen fruits.'

The additive *lagi* also creates a relationship with the boy, who is the topic of the sentence. Within the RefLex scheme, this referent is classified as *r-new*, but the presence of the additive marker suggests that this may be a referential type, not distinguished by the RefLex Scheme. In terms of joint attention manipulation, *lagi* emphasises the existence of another referent which should be included in the focus. Additives are known to be scope sensitive (Forker 2016: 72). In (47), the additive marker follows the quantifier, highlighting the precise quantity of the added referents. In the next section we will discuss the use of *pun*, which essentially marks a proposal for a joint attention shift.

5.4 Particle *pun*

The particle *pun* is more frequent than other particles and demonstratives in our *Getting the Story Straight* corpus. This particle has received much attention in the literature, and is treated in the greatest detail in Goddard (2001), who provides an exhaustive overview of earlier studies (p. 29–30). In our discussion, we adhere to Goddard's analysis. The most common use in our data, is the "second-position *pun*" which highlights the sentence topic (Goddard 2001: 31). Cumming (1991: 107) suggests that *pun* is a resumptive topic marker attached to left-dislocated noun phrases. Its distribution is further affected by *individuation* of the referent, its *semantic role*, its *introduction* into the discourse, and the *eventiveness* of the description. The first function is well attested in our narratives; *pun* frequently marks a switch in topic as participants take over the agency in moving the plot forward. One such sequence is given in (48).

(48) Singapore Malay (2017.ISM.11–13)
Bila polis tiba, [pekebun pun] di-tangkap. Di mahkamah, isteri-nya
when police arrive gardener TOP2 PV-catch   in court   wife-3POSS
memberi, ah, tahu hakim apa yang telah   terjadi. [Pekebun pun]
give   HESIT know judge what REL   already happen gardener TOP2
di-jatuhkan   hukuman penjara.
PV-hand.down jail.sentence

'When the police came, the farmer was arrested. In court, his wife told the judge what had happened. The farmer was then sentenced to a jail term.'

In (49), which follows directly from (21), *pun* amplifies the eventiveness of the sequence (i.e. the progress of the plot). Note that the translation attempts to capture this with the English adverb *then* in both sentences.[20]

---

[20]Note also the use of the active voice in both clauses, highlighting their eventiveness (cf. Djenar 2018: this volume).

(49) Singapore Malay (2017.AM.27–28)
[*Pak Samad pun*] *men-ceritakan pengalaman-nya di dalam penjara dan*
Mr PN EVENT AV-tell experience-3POSS inside prison and
men-jelaskan bahawa dia menyesal dengan tindak-laku-nya. [*Pak Samad pun*]
AV-explain COMP 3SG AV.regret with actions-3POSS Mr PN EVENT
ber-janji dengan anak-nya bahawa dia akan mem-bawa anak-nya ke
AV-promise with child-3POSS COMP 3SG will AV-take child-3POSS to
jalan-jalan keesokan hari.
walk.around the.following.day

'Pak Samad then told the story of his experiences in jail and made it clear that he regretted his actions. Pak Samad then promised his child that he would take him for a walk the next day.'

A similar instance of *pun* amplifying the progress of the plot (i.e. eventiveness) is shown in (50). In colloquial Singapore English, the particle *pun* is often translated with *then*, which has the same function in marking the previous event as completed and a new one as commencing.[21]

(50) Singapore Malay (2017.ISM.19–20)
Dia sangat gembira dapat me-nikmati cahaya matahari. [*Pekebun pun*] *pulang*
3SG very elated get AV-enjoy sunlight gardener EVENT return
ke rumah-nya.
to house-3POSS

'He was very happy that he got to enjoy the sunshine. The farmer then returned to his house.'

Goddard (2001: 54) reports that the *topic focus* function is the most common in his written Malay corpus. In our narrative data, the *event sequence* function is more common. An instance of topic focus is given in (51), where the jackal, upon spotting the crow with the fish, is constructed as talking to itself.

(51) Singapore Malay (2013.MLZ.JackalAndCrow.151)
[*Aku pun*] *lapar ah.*
1SG TOP2 hungry PART

'I am also hungry.'

The presence of *resumptive topic* resets the reference of the third person pronoun *dia* and *ia*. In (52), the jackal is referred to as *ia*, while the fish and crow require nominal expressions. The minimisation of the expression of the topic after it has been focused with *pun* resembles the general tendency for minimisation of reference (Heritage 2007; Sacks & Schegloff 2007). We take this as a signal that *pun* indicates a shift of joint attention to a new "field", which is accompanied by a reset in the scope of anaphoric devices.

---

[21]Hiroki Nomoto has suggested to us that perhaps the core function of the particle is to indicate a clause relationship between two clauses which are told in their order of occurrence, but the particle has to be placed after the subject of the second clause (Nomoto 2017: pun).

(52) Singapore Malay (2013.OG.JackalAndCrow.05–6)
Jadi [serigala itu pun] ingin me-makan ikan itu kerana [ia] sangat lapar.
so   jackal   DIST TOP2 wish AV-consume fish DST because 3SG very hungry
Jadi [ia] fikir [ia] mahu ikan yang di dalam mulut burung gagak itu.
so   3SG think 3SG want fish REL inside mouth crow   DST

'The jackal wanted to eat the fish because it was so hungry. And it thought, it wanted the fish in the crow's mouth.'

Example (53) summarises the outcome for the crow and clearly illustrates the *event sequence* focus function of *pun* (cf. Goddard 2001: 38).

(53) Singapore Malay (2013.MLZ.JackalAndCrow.173)
[Gagak pun] sedih sebab   dia kena tipu, bosan.
crow EVENT sad because 3SG PASS cheat disgusting

'The crow was sad because it got cheated, disgusting.'

The particle *pun* does not occur in our texts with inanimates, but this is just a consequence of the construction of the plot in the narratives which we focus on here. There are instances of its use in our Singapore Malay corpus, such as (54), which describes the shortage of rice during WWII. *Pun* here highlights the food shortage as a local topic and brings the focus on *porridge*, lexically tracking the topic *beras* (RefLex r-given, l-accessible-sub).

(54) Singapore Malay (2016.BIZ.45)
Memang takde jumpa beras, lah, nanti masak, ah, bikin bubur ke, bikin,
indeed not find rice PART later cook TOP make porridge or make
kalau dapat bubur pun dah   bagus lah, sekali-sekali, pun nak taruk
if get porridge TOP2 already good PART occasionally EVENT MOD put
keledek, taruk ubi.
sweet potato put tapioca

'We couldn't of course find rice, when we cooked porridge for instance, if we got porridge it was already very good, once in a while, still we had to add sweet potato and tapioca.'

5.5 Demonstratives and particles

Demonstratives may be followed by the particle *pun*. An eventive *pun* can be seen in (55). The speaker confuses the plot, and refers to the wife where the husband is meant.

(55) Singapore Malay (2017.NZ.04)
Dalam kemarahan, uh, [lelaki itu pun] pergi, uh, pergi ke suami-nya,
in   anger HESIT male DIST TOP2 go HESIT go to husband-3POSS
eh, ke isteri-nya dan marah, dan marah suami-nya   kenapa dia berbual
HESIT to wife-3POSS and angry and angry husband-3POSS why 3SG converse

> dengan lelaki lain.
> with   male other
>
> 'In anger, that man then went to his wife and scolded his husband [sic] for talking to other men.'

In (56), the farmer is described as *suami tu pun*. The particle *pun* prompts the hearer to attend to the temporal sequence, while the demonstrative *tu* places the focus on the same referent. The distal may encode the wife's apprehensive stance towards her husband.

(56) Singapore Malay (2017.NZ.14)
> *Dia mem-beritahu tentang, aah, keadaan-nya   di situ dan bagaimana dia*
> 3SG AV-tell   about   HESIT situation-3POSS there and how   3SG
> *insaf   dan rasa kesan   terhadap kejadian-nya tersebut. Dari hari*
> penitent and feel consequence about   incident-3POSS GIVEN.FOC from day
> *itu, [suami tu pun] tidak me-minum arak   lagi dan tidak ber-campur*
> DIST spouse DIST EVENT not AV-drink alcohol again and not   AV-mix
> *dengan kawan-kawan tersebut.*
> with   RED-friend   GIVEN.FOC
>
> 'He told them about the conditions there and how he regretted and felt the effects of that incident. From that day on, the husband did not drink alcohol any more and did not mix with those friends.'

Multiple demonstratives can combine within a single description, as in (57), where the noun *budak laki* 'boy' is followed by the recent mention *tadi* and *itu*.

(57) Singapore Malay (2013.LN.PearStory.18)
> [*Budak lelaki tadi   yang menunggang basikal itu*] *te-nampak se-orang*
> boy   RECENT REL AV.ride   bicycle DIST INVOL-spot one-CL.HUMAN
> (1s) *budak perempuan yang juga menaiki   basikal yang bertentangan, yang* (1s)
>   child female   REL also AV.travel.by bicycle REL opposite   REL
> *berjalan bertentangan dengan-nya.*
> travel   opposite   with-3
>
> 'The boy who was riding the bicycle saw a girl who was also riding a bicycle in the opposite direction.'

Table 11 sketches the functions of Malay demonstratives and particles in manipulating and directing the interlocutors' joint attention. The effect is captured with simple verb phrases — a conventionalised terminology remains lacking.[22] This representation also draws on the idea of cognitive states developed in Gundel et al. (1993) but takes the attention asymmetry between the interlocutors as a starting point. The effects fall into two groups, depending on whether the "field" of joint attention remains the same or shifts.

---

[22] Tomasello (1995) offers a lucid account of the development of social cognition and the ability to manipulate joint attention in children.

2 Stance, categorisation, and information structure in Malay

Within the same field, the proximal *ini* requires a symmetrical manipulation of joint attention, while the remaining deictic forms indicate a reorientation of attention on the side of the speaker and require a manipulation of the focus on the side of the hearer so that joint attention can be renewed. The most forceful reorientation within the same field is encoded with the epistemic particle *pula(k)*, which indicates a surprise or novelty on the side of the speaker (captured here as "update"). Finally, the particle *pun* encodes a shift of joint attention and entails a reset of anaphora, exemplified in (52).

Table 11: Joint attention manipulating functions of Malay demonstratives and particles

DEMONSTRATIVE	JOINT ATTENTION MANIPULATION	
	SPEAKER	HEARER
si	bring in focus	activate familiar
ini	keep in focus	keep in focus
itu	bring in focus	access
tadi	bring in focus	recall recent
tersebut	bring in focus	recall known
pula(k)	update/broaden	update/broaden
lagi	add in focus	add in focus
pun	shift	shift

6 Conclusions

A systematic comparison of elicited narrative texts organised in a parallel corpus enables us to make several points about Malay discourse and information structure:

- The speaker's stance is reflected in referent categorisation and has consequences for referent tracking.

- The stronger epistemic stance simplifies expression of referents and their tracking, confirming the claim by Sacks & Schegloff (2007) that categorisation of humans with proper names require less recognitional effort, as shown in §4.

- The neutral epistemic stance generally motivates referent categorisation with descriptions, which need to be more elaborate to track referents effectively.

- Taking a stronger epistemic stance, the speaker can construct and maintain differential perspectives on the referents through their categorisation, such as *Adam* vs. *her husband*, or *her father* (Stivers et al. 2007).

- The variation of expression correlates with the referential status of the referent as well. The high referential status allows for tracking with pronouns, but the low status disfavours enumeration and classifiers.

- The topic focus particle *pun* is preferred with more complete expressions of a third person referent, after which the reference can be minimised (zero, *dia*, *ia*, etc.), as argued by Heritage (2007); Sacks & Schegloff (2007).

- Both topical and focused participants are eligible for minimisation, but the remaining referents require a fuller expression, for non-humans typically a N+*itu* phrase.

Future work will focus on the role of word order and verbal morphology as well as on the effect of downgrading the role of the hearer to a silent listener, unable to interact where joint attention is not achieved (DeLancey 1997). Our parallel corpus contains such information in the negotiations preceding the presentation of the agreed narrative.

Acknowledgements

We would like to thank the editors of this volume and three anonymous reviewers for their encouragement and comments on earlier versions of this paper. We would also like to thank the members of the Malay Research Group at the Nanyang Technological University in Singapore for their valuable comments and suggestions: David Moeljadi, Kadek Ratih Dwi Oktarini, Nur Atiqah binte Othman, Hannah Choi Jun Yung, Nur Amirah Binte Khairul Anuar, and Hiroki Nomoto. All the authors gratefully acknowledge the generous support of the Singaporean Malay community. The authors also acknowledge the generous support of the ILCAA Joint Research Project 'Cross-linguistic Perspective on the Information Structure of the Austronesian Languages' (PI Dr Atsuko Utsumi), funded by The Research Institute for Languages and Cultures of Asia and Africa (ICLAA) of Tokyo University of Foreign Studies, as well as the research funding through a Tier 1 project 'Development of Intonational Models for Malay and Singapore English' awarded by the Singapore Ministry of Education Tier 1 Grant MOE2013-T1-002-169 (PI Dr Tan Ying Ying).

Abbreviations

1, 2, 3	person markers	INVOL	involuntary agent *ter-*
AFF	affected	HESIT	hesitation marker
APPL	applicative	MOD	modal auxiliary
AV	active voice	PASS	passive auxiliary *kena*
COMP	complementizer *bahawa, yang*	POSS	possessive
		PROX	proximate
CS	code-switching	PV	passive voice
DEM	demonstrative	TOP	topic
DIST	distal	TOP2	switched topic (Goddard's *topic focus*)
FOC	focus		
INTENS	intensifier		

References

Adelaar, K. Alexander. 2004. Where does Malay come from? Twenty years of discussions about homeland, migrations and classifications. *Bijdragen tot de Taal-, Land-en Volkenkunde* 160(1). 1–30.

Adelaar, K. Alexander & David J. Prentice. 1996. Malay: Its history, role and spread. In Stephen A. Wurm, Peter Mühlhäusler & Darrell T. Tryon (eds.), *Atlas of languages of intercultural communication in the Pacific, Asia, and the Americas*, vol. II (Trends in Linguistics, Documentation 13 1), 673–693. Berlin/New York: Mouton de Gruyter.

Alsagoff, Lubna. 2008. The commodification of Malay: Trading in futures. In Rani Rubdy & Peter Tan (eds.), *Language as commodity: Global structures, local marketplaces*, 44–56. London & New York: Bloomsbury Publishing.

Barešová, Ivona. 2016. *Japanese given names: A window into contemporary Japanese society*. Olomouc: Palacký University Olomouc.

Carroll, Alice, Barbara Kelly & Lauren Gawne. 2011. The jackal and crow picture task. Designed for use by the Social Cognition and Language Project. A collaboration of The Australian National University, Griffith University, University of Melbourne and the Max Planck Institute for Psycholinguistics.

Chafe, Wallace L. 1980. *The Pear Stories: Cognitive, cultural, and linguistic aspects of narrative production*. Norwood, New Jersey: Ablex.

Chung, Sandra. 2000. On reference to kinds in Indonesian. *Natural Language Semantics* 8(2). 157–171.

Chung, Sandra. 2008. Indonesian clause structure from an Austronesian perspective. *Lingua* 118(10). 1554–1582.

Chung, Siaw-Fong. 2010. Numeral classifier buah in Malay: A corpus-based study. *Language and Linguistics* 11(3). 553–577.

Cleary-Kemp, Jessica. 2007. Universal uses of demonstratives: evidence from four Malayo-Polynesian languages. *Oceanic Linguistics* 46(2). 325–347.

Cole, Peter & Gabriella Hermon. 2005. Subject and non-subject relativization in Indonesian. *Journal of East Asian Linguistics* 14(1). 59–88.

Cumming, Susanna. 1991. *Functional change: The case of Malay constituent order*. Vol. 2. Berlin & New York: Walter de Gruyter.

Daw, Khin Khin Aye. 2005. *Bazaar Malay: History, grammar and contact*. Singapore: National University of Singapore dissertation.

DeLancey, Scott. 1997. Mirativity: The grammatical marking of unexpected information. *Linguistic Typology* 1. 33–52.

Diessel, Holger. 2006. Demonstratives, joint attention, and the emergence of grammar. *Cognitive linguistics* 17(4). 463–489.

Djenar, Dwi Noverini. 2014. Nih and tuh as spatial deixis in imagined interaction. *Nusa* 56. 27–46. http://hdl.handle.net/10108/77644.

Djenar, Dwi Noverini. 2018. Constituent order and information structure in Indonesian discourse. In Sonja Riesberg, Asako Shiohara & Atsuko Utsumi (eds.), *A cross-linguistic perspective on information structure in Austronesian languages*. Berlin: Language Science Press.

Du Bois, John W. 2007. The stance triangle. In Robert Englebretson (ed.), *Stancetaking in discourse: Subjectivity, evaluation, interaction*, 139–182. Amsterdam: John Benjamins Publishing Company.

Duranti, Alessandro. 2009. The relevance of Husserl's theory to language socialization. *Journal of Linguistic Anthropology* 19(2). 205–226.

Duranti, Alessandro. 2010. Husserl, intersubjectivity and anthropology. *Anthropological Theory* 10(1). 1–20.

Enfield, N. J. 2007. Meanings of the unmarked: How 'default' person reference does more than just refer. In N. J. Enfield & Tanya Stivers (eds.), *Person Reference in Interaction: Linguistic, Cultural and Social Perspectives* (Language Culture and Cognition), 97–120. Cambridge University Press. DOI:10.1017/CBO9780511486746.006

Englebretson, Robert. 2007. Grammatical resources for social purposes: Some aspects of stancetaking in colloquial Indonesian conversation. In Robert Englebretson (ed.), *Stancetaking in discourse: Subjectivity, evaluation, interaction*, 69–110. Amsterdam: John Benjamins Publishing Company.

Evans, Nicholas, Henrik Bergqvist & Lila San Roque. 2017a. The grammar of engagement I: Framework and initial exemplification. *Language and Cognition* 21. 1–31.

Evans, Nicholas, Henrik Bergqvist & Lila San Roque. 2017b. The grammar of engagement II: Typology and diachrony. *Language and Cognition* 22. 1–30.

Forker, Diana. 2016. Toward a typology for additive markers. *Lingua* 180. 69–100.

Goddard, Cliff. 2001. The polyfunctional Malay focus particle pun. *Multilingua–Journal of Cross-Cultural and Interlanguage Communication* 20(1). 27–59.

Gundel, Jeanette K. & Thornstein Fretheim. 2004. Topic and focus. In Larry R. Horn & Gregory Ward (eds.), *Handbook of pragmatics*, 175–196. Oxford: Blackwell.

Gundel, Jeanette K., Nancy Hedberg & Ron Zacharski. 1993. Cognitive status and the form of referring expressions in discourse. *Language* 69(2). 274–307.

Haviland, John B. 2007. Person reference in Tzotzil gossip: Referring dupliciter. In N. J. Enfield & Tanya Stivers (eds.), *Person Reference in Interaction: Linguistic, Cultural and Social Perspectives* (Language Culture and Cognition), 226–252. Cambridge: Cambridge University Press. DOI:10.1017/CBO9780511486746.011

Heritage, John. 2007. Intersubjectivity and progressivity in person (and place) reference. In N. J. Enfield & Tanya Stivers (eds.), *Person Reference in Interaction: Linguistic, Cultural and Social Perspectives* (Language Culture and Cognition), 255–280. Cambridge University Press. DOI:10.1017/CBO9780511486746.012

Himmelmann, Nikolaus P. 1996. Demonstratives in narrative discourse: A taxonomy of universal uses. In Barbara Fox (ed.), *Studies in anaphora*, 205–254. Amsterdam: John Benjamins Publishing Company.

Hopper, Paul J. 1986. Some discourse functions of classifiers in Malay. In Colette Grinevald Craig (ed.), *Noun classes and categorization*, 309–325. Amsterdam: John Benjamins Publishing Company.

Kratochvíl, František & Benidiktus Delpada. 2015. Definiteness and specificity in Abui. In *Proceedings of the second international workshop on information structure of Austronesian languages*, 179–208. Tokyo: Research Institute for Languages, Cultures of Asia & Africa, Tokyo University of Foreign Studies.

Kuo, Eddie C. Y. & Björn H. Jernudd. 1993. Balancing macro-and micro-sociolinguistic perspectives in language management: The case of Singapore. *Language problems and language planning* 17(1). 1–21.

Lambrecht, Knud. 1994. *Information structure and sentence form: Topic, focus and the mental representations of discourse referents*. Cambridge, UK: Cambridge University Press.

Lee, Nala Huiying. 2014. *Lee, n. H. (2014). A grammar of baba Malay with sociophonetic considerations*. Manoa: University of Hawai'i (Doctoral dissertation).

Mayer, Mercer. 1969. *Frog, where are you?* New York: Dial Press.

Nomoto, Hiroki. 2017. *Bahasa Melayu TUFS Grammar – in Japanese*. http://www.tufs.ac.jp/common/fs/ase/mal/tatabahasa_web/index.html. http://www.tufs.ac.jp/common/fs/ase/mal/tatabahasa_web/index.html.

Prince, Ellen F. 1981. Toward a taxonomy of given-new information. In Peter Cole (ed.), *Radical pragmatics*, 223–255. New York: Academic Press.

Riester, Arndt & Stefan Baumann. 2017. The RefLex scheme: Annotation guidelines. In Jonas Kuhn (ed.), *SinSpec. Working papers of the SFb 732*, vol. 14, 1–31. University of Stuttgart.

Rommetveit, Ragnar. 1976. On the architecture of intersubjectivity. In Lloyd H. Strickland, Kenneth J. Gergen & F. J. Aboud (eds.), *Social psychology in transition*, 201–214. New York: Plenum Press.

Rubin, Aaron D. 2010. The development of the Amharic definite article and an Indonesian parallel. *Journal of Semitic Studies* 55(1). 103–114.

Sacks, Harvey & Emanuel A. Schegloff. 2007. Two preferences in the organization of reference to persons in conversation and their interaction. In N. J. Enfield & Tanya Stivers (eds.), *Person Reference in Interaction: Linguistic, Cultural and Social Perspectives*

(Language Culture and Cognition), 23–28. Cambridge University Press. DOI:10.1017/CBO9780511486746.003

Salehuddin, Khazriyati & Heather Winskel. 2012. Malay numeral classifier usage in caretaker-child talk. *GEMA Online Journal of Language Studies* 12(1). 89–104.

San Roque, Lila, Lauren Gawne, Darja Hoenigman, Julia Colleen Miller, Alan Rumsey, Stef Spronck, Alice Carroll & Nicholas Evans. 2012. Getting the story straight: Language fieldwork using a narrative problem-solving task. *Language Documentation and Conservation* 6. 135–174. http://hdl.handle.net/10125/4504.

Sasi Rekha d/o Muthiah. 2007. *A description of Singapore Indian Malay, a pidgin's pidgin*. Singapore: National University of Singapore MA thesis.

Singapore Department of Statistics. 2015. General Household Survey 2015. In. http://www.singstat.gov.sg/publications.

Sneddon, James N., K. Alexander Adelaar, Dwi N Djenar & Michael Ewing. 2012. *Indonesian: A comprehensive grammar*. 2nd edn. London & New York: Routledge.

Stivers, Tanya, N. J. Enfield & Stephen C. Levinson. 2007. Person reference in interaction. In N. J. Enfield & Tanya Stivers (eds.), *Person Reference in Interaction: Linguistic, Cultural and Social Perspectives* (Language Culture and Cognition), 1–20. Cambridge University Press. DOI:10.1017/CBO9780511486746.002

Stubbe, Maria & Janet Holmes. 1995. You know, eh and other 'exasperating expressions': An analysis of social and stylistic variation in the use of pragmatic devices in a sample of New Zealand English. *Language and Communication* 15(1). 63–88.

Sukamto, Katharina Endriati. 2013. Anaphoric expressions in Indonesian narrative discourse. Paper presented at the 23rd Annual Meeting of the Southeast Asia Linguistics Society (SEALS 23) Bangkok, 29–31 May 2013.

Tomasello, Michael. 1995. Joint attention as social cognition. In Chris Moore & Phil Dunham (eds.), *Joint attention: Its origin and role in development*, 103–130. Hillsdale: Lawrence Erlbaum.

van Minde, Don. 2008. The pragmatic function of Malay yang. *Journal of Pragmatics* 40(11). 1982–2001.

Williams, Nicholas. 2009. Toward a linguistic anthropological account of deixis in interaction: *Ini* and *itu* in Indonesian conversation. In *Colorado research in linguistics*, vol. 22 (June 2009), 1–23. Boulder: University of Colorado.

Zlatev, Jordan. 2008. The co-evolution of intersubjectivity and bodily mimesis. In Jordan Zlatev, Timothy P. Racine, Chris Sinha & Esa Itkonen (eds.), *The shared mind: Perspectives on intersubjectivity*, 215–244. Amsterdam: John Benjamins Publishing Company.

Chapter 3

Attention focus and information packaging in Vera'a demonstratives

Stefan Schnell
Centre of Excellence for the Dynamics of Language & University of Melbourne

> I investigate endophoric uses of demonstratives in the Oceanic language Vera'a (North Vanuatu) in relation to their exophoric use, drawing on different types of linguistic data, in particular conversations during the building of a house and narrative texts. I find that Vera'a demonstratives mark a three-way distinction of speaker-oriented (excluding the addressee) versus addressee-oriented (including the speaker) versus distal (excluding both speaker and addressee). Seeking to determine the core meaning of the three demonstratives that would square with both their exophoric and their endophoric use, I develop the hypothesis that considerations of joint attention focus rather than localisation are its central aspect: speaker-oriented forms are used to *draw* the addressee's attention to an entity, addressee-oriented forms to *maintain* attention to an entity, and distal forms to *delay* attention to an entity. The joint attention meaning of demonstratives in endophoric use yields effects in the domain of information packaging: speaker-oriented forms are used to introduce new information; addressee-oriented forms in specific syntactic contexts yield effects akin to topic and focus; distal forms are used to keep track of background information. Hence, attention focus is the invariable core meaning of Vera'a demonstratives that accounts for all senses in different contexts of use.

1 Introduction

The role of demonstratives in discourse has been the focus of a growing body of corpus-based research, starting with Himmelmann (1996). Recent work has been undertaken for the Australian language Dalabon by Cutfield (2012) and the Oceanic language Logea by Dawuda (2009). The central question concerning the endophoric (inner-textual) usage of demonstratives is its relationship to their exophoric (deictic) usage. One line of thought sees discourse essentially as a metaphorical extension of space (Diessel (1999) and Bühler (1999[1934]: 121)), with spatial distance being equivalent to anaphoric (antecedent) distance, and referent activation. An example of this is Terrill (2001), who examines the function of two demonstratives, *foia* and *oia*, in discourse from Lavukaleve: she finds

Stefan Schnell. 2018. Attention focus and information packaging in Vera'a demonstratives. In Sonja Riesberg, Asako Shiohara & Atsuko Utsumi (eds.), *Perspectives on information structure in Austronesian languages*, 81–113. Berlin: Language Science Press. DOI:10.5281/zenodo.1402539

that the use of these two forms in endophoric use mirrors their function to mark distance distinctions (proximal versus distal) in situational use, so that spatial distance in the physical environment corresponds to antecedent distance within discourse, for instance how many clauses lie between an anaphor and its antecedent within a given text. Other authors stress the speaker/addressee orientation of demonstratives, but still see them merely as anchor points for marking spatial relations between speaker, referent, and addressee. This view is reflected in Margetts (2004). Yet other authors also focus on the speaker/addressee orientation of demonstratives, but see the use of demonstratives as a reflection of communicative interaction that can override 'objectively' determined spatial circumstances (see Enfield 2003 on Lao). In this line of thought, Mosel (2004) shows that Samoan speaker-oriented demonstratives are often used to introduce new information into discourse, whereas speaker-plus-addressee-oriented demonstratives are used for given referents, reflecting the knowledge state of speaker and addressee during discourse production/comprehension rather than their location in space relative to each other or to the entity referred to. This paper lends further support to this latter view, and it links the significance of knowledge states of interlocutors to that of joint attention. On this view, demonstratives can be characterised as linguistic devices that serve to "coordinate the interlocutors' joint focus of attention" (Diessel 2006: 481).

In this paper I present findings from a study of the use of demonstratives in the Oceanic language Vera'a. I argue that Vera'a demonstratives do not have spatial-localising but attention-focussing meaning. Typical for an Oceanic language from Melanesia, Vera'a has a rich inventory of interrelated demonstrative forms that can be divided into three functionally defined sets of forms: 1. speaker-oriented (DEM.SPKR), 2. addressee-oriented (DEM.ADDR), and 3. neither speaker- nor addressee-oriented (distal) (DEM.DIST). In instances of exophoric reference, these forms do not merely serve the localisation of an entity in terms of their distance relative to either speaker, addressee, or both. Rather, it is the awareness state of participants in the communicative situation that is crucial for their exophoric use, serving to coordinate the attention focus of speaker and addressee (Diessel 2006). Thus, addressee-oriented forms are used where speaker and hearer share awareness of a referent and attend to it, even when the referent is located in the speaker's *here-space*. Conversely, speaker-oriented forms can be used where a referent is at a large distance from both speaker and addressee if the speaker believes the addressee to not be aware of or not attending to a referent they want them to attend to. Distal forms are used to refer to something that speaker is not focussing their attention on.

Crucially, the same considerations of attention focus account for the endophoric use of demonstratives in narrative texts (Diessel 2006: 476): here, speaker-oriented forms are restricted to two cases of *Deixis am Phantasma* (Bühler 1999[1934]: 121–140), a subtype of situational use in Himmelmann (1996: 222) (see §3.3 for a more detailed characterisation): 1. announcements of a narrative that is about to be produced by the speaker, and 2. cases of direct speech, where the narrated situation is rendered in analogy to the physical context of the actual speech situation. These uses are classified as exophoric here. In endophoric use, the choice between addressee-oriented and distal forms is sensitive to referential distance; however, the use of addressee-oriented forms can yield

3 Attention focus and information packaging in Vera'a demonstratives

information-packaging effects in specific discourse contexts, often corroborated with other structural properties, for instance left-dislocation and emphatic particles. I argue here that these information-packaging effects do not constitute an extended meaning of demonstratives, but follow straightforwardly from their attention-focussing meaning: speaker-oriented forms are used cataphorically to draw the addressee's attention to the narrative that is about to ensue, whereas addressee-oriented forms are used anaphorically, but serve to reinforce joint attention to already shared and activated information. This latter function then contributes to information-packaging effects, which are essentially a matter of pragmatic inference and the semantics of given syntactic and discourse contexts. Addressee-oriented forms are thus not simply used to mark the activation of a referent, and other forms of reference – typically pronouns – are used for activated referents. Distal forms, on the other hand, are used to re-activate a referent.

The paper unfolds as follows: §2 provides a brief overview of the Vera'a language and its speakers, and the corpus data underlying this study. In §3, I first define the class of demonstratives in Vera'a, and related demonstrative adverbs derived from them, and describe their syntactic distribution. I then turn to the description of exophoric uses, followed by endophoric uses. In §4, I discuss the findings with regard to spatial and attention-focus accounts of demonstratives. In §5, I conclude the paper, and provide an outlook on future research.

2 Language data and methodological notes

Vera'a (ISO 639-3: vra) is an Austronesian language of the Oceanic subgroup spoken by 500 people on the island of Vanua Lava, the largest of the Banks group of islands in North Vanuatu. It belongs to what Kalyan & François (to appear) call the 'Vanuatu linkage'. Vera'a is spoken in close vicinity to Vurës (Malau 2016) and Mwotlap (François 2001), and adult speakers are usually fluent in the former, and often at least understand the latter. All speakers of Vera'a above the age of approx. 3 years speak Bislama, the English-lexified contact language that has the status of Vanuatu's 'national language'. Nonetheless, Vera'a is not severely endangered and it is very vital: most children grow up (until the age of about 3) monolingually with Vera'a, which is used virtually in all domains of everyday communication, except for some church services. Immigrants into the Vera'a community usually acquire Vera'a, but may continue to use their first language with their children in their homes (this concerns mainly women from neighbouring communities who marry into the Vera'a community) (cf. François 2012). The language is endangered only due to the small size of the community, so that a language shift, for instance to Vurës, could potentially occur within a short time frame if the positive attitude towards the language should falter in the future.

This study draws on different types of text data in the Vera'a language documentation that I have been compiling since December 2006 in close collaboration with speakers of the language (http://dobes.mpi.nl/projects/vures_veraa/). The documentation encompasses recordings of a wide range of communicative events, ranging from narratives – produced mainly for the sake of being documented – to public speeches and (very few) casual conversations, which represent the most naturally occurring communicative events. Particularly relevant for this study are a set of video recordings documenting the construction of a larger house (approx. 4 hours), audio recordings of plant (150 descriptions, 30sec average recording length) and fish (254 descriptions, 1.5min average length) descriptions, and a collection of narrative texts (65 narratives of different lengths), most of which were only audio-recorded. Video recordings exist for a handful of narratives, and I will point to specific visual clues where relevant in the discussion to follow. Note, however, that for the purposes of this study, neither gestures nor prosodic structures were taken into account systematically, and a systematic and sound analysis of these two aspects of language use will have to be left for future work on the language. The time-aligned annotation of the audio signal in all recordings was segmented into pause units.

A smaller set of 10 narratives from different male and female speakers of different ages – some traditional legends and myths, some more similar to (moral) fables in the European tradition – contain rich morphosyntactic annotations that serve as the basis for some quantitative examination into the use of demonstratives in Vera'a. The texts show some variation in length, ranging from 178 to 929 clause units. Table 1 gives an overview.

Table 1: GRAID-annotated corpus of Vera'a narrative texts

Text ID	Speaker initials	age group	text type	no. of clause units
ANV	AN	18–25	narrative	208
AS.1	AS	35–50	narrative	224
GABG	GA	35–50	narrative	178
GAQG	GA	35–50	narrative	232
HHAK	HH	18–25	narrative	446
ISAM	IS	50+	narrative	248
ISWM	IS	50+	narrative	608
JJQ	JJ	50+	narrative	929
MVBW	MV	25–35	narrative	314
PALA	PH	35–50	narrative	402
Totals				3789

All of these ten narratives are part of the Vera'a corpus Schnell (2016) within the Multi-CAST collection (Haig & Schnell 2016; https://lac.uni-koeln.de/de/multicast/). Like all other text corpora in Multi-CAST, the Vera'a texts have been annotated according to the GRAID conventions (Haig & Schnell 2014), reading 'Grammatical Relations and Animacy in Discourse'. This annotation scheme has been designed specifically for purposes of research into referentiality, argument structure and discourse structure, as pioneered by Wallace Chafe and Talmy Givón, and associates. Essentially, GRAID annotations couple glosses for form (zero, pronoun, full NP) with those for syntactic functions (s, a, p, etc.), as well as information on person and animacy. The Vera'a corpus also contains annotation of phrasal sub-constituents, merely indicated by symbols for "word to the right of NP head" (⟨rn⟩) and "word to the left of NP head" (⟨ln⟩), and likewise for constituent words in complex verbal predicates. Also, adjuncts and other clause-level constituents, like adverbs and particles, have been annotated as ⟨other⟩.

In the study of demonstratives reported here, GRAID annotations were used systematically together with morphemic glossing: since both layers of annotation are *symbolically associated* (and the respective type has been used for the GRAID tier relative to the morphemic glossing tier in ELAN), all demonstrative forms can be searched with respect to their syntactic function, either as an argument, a clause-level adjunct/particle, or an NP-level satellite constituent. Thus, using ELAN's layered search function, one can easily determine figures for and all instances of say DEM.ADDR forms occurring on NP level by searching for ⟨dem.addr⟩ on the morphemic glossing tier and ⟨rn⟩ on the GRAID tier. It was thus possible to determine a total of 759 instances of demonstrative forms in use in this corpus, comprising 528 basic demonstratives and 231 demonstrative adverbs. Since GRAID triggers basic features of referring expressions, we can also compare quantitatively the use of demonstratives in relation to NPs without demonstratives and other forms, in particular zero and pronoun. This latter investigation is, however, beyond the scope of this paper, and is planned to be undertaken in the future.

In this paper, I generally draw on the wider Vera'a documentation, discussing different types of data in turn. It will thus be clear during the discussion from which type of data a specific example has been drawn. The Vera'a Multi-CAST corpus serves merely to establish a quantitative picture of syntactic distributions of different demonstrative forms in narrative texts.

3 Demonstratives in Vera'a

In this section, I first define demonstratives in Vera'a following Himmelmann (1996) and describe the inventory of basic demonstratives and derived demonstrative adverbs in §3.1, and their syntactic distribution in §3.2. I then turn to their exophoric and endophoric uses in §3.3 and §3.4 respectively. My use of these two terms is adopted from Halliday & Hasan (1976: 33) in the following way: exophora is a direct relationship between a linguistic expression and an extra-linguistic entity; this is essentially the same as deixis. Endophoric relations can be defined in analogy to the definition of anaphora, as stated by Huang (2000: 1):

> [An anaphora; added by Stefan Schnell] is a relation between two linguistic elements, wherein the interpretation of one (called an anaphor) is in some way determined by the interpretation of the other (called an antecedent) [...].

I use endophoric here as a hyperonym to both anaphora and cataphora, where the latter defines a relationship of "carrying forward" rather than backward. Like Huang (2000) for anaphora, I understand endophoric relations as essentially quite vague and general, relying to a large degree on pragmatic inference. Thus, in determining whether a referring expression is exophoric or endophoric (for instance a definite full noun phrase), interlocutors will seek different clues as to whether they require to consider the discourse context of the same text, or whether they should resort directly to the physical surroundings of the speech situation in order to establish its reference. Although some form types are more common than others in one of the two types of relation, referential form classes are generally not specified for their type of reference. For instance, a personal pronoun in Vera'a can be endophoric or exophoric, regardless of the fact that the former use is possibly more common than the latter. Likewise, demonstratives are not *per se* exophoric.

Exophoric uses of demonstratives are attested in two different communicative contexts and related recordings, namely in non-narrative contexts (house building videos, observations) and in or immediately connected to narratives. In the latter context, they come in two different types: 1. the introduction of a narrative, and 2. instances of *Deixis am Phantasma*, in the sense of Bühler 1999[1934]: 131:

> *[...] wenn ein Erzähler den Hörer [...] ins Reich der konstruktiven Phantasie führt und ihn dort mit denselben Zeigwörtern traktiert, damit er sehe und höre, was es dort zu sehen und zu hören [...] gibt. Nicht mit dem äusseren Auge, Ohr usw., sondern mit dem, was man [...] das '"innere"' oder '"geistige"' Auge und Ohr zu nennen pflegt.* [[...] when the narrator leads the hearer [...] into the realm of constructive imagination and treats him to the same deictic words as before so that he may see and hear what can be seen and heard there [...]. Not with the external eye, ear, and so on, but with what is [...] called the "mind's" eye or ear [...] (English translation by Donald Goodwin and Achim Fraser Eschbach)]

Although we may expect this special kind of deictic reference within direct speech to work somewhat differently from deixis within the actual speech act frame, I take the similarities eluded to by Bühler sufficient to treat them basically alike here (but I will point out to the reader what type is represented by any given example). Before turning to the exophoric and endophoric uses of demonstratives, I shall provide a definition of these forms together with their inventory in Vera'a, and outline their syntactic distribution.

3.1 Definition and inventory of demonstrative forms

Vera'a distinguishes three basic forms of demonstrative, marking a three-way opposition between speaker-oriented (DEM.SPKR), addressee-oriented (DEM.ADDR), and distal (DEM.DIST). What is labelled here 'addressee-oriented' is understood as essentially encompassing the sphere of both speaker and addressee, as will become clear below. The three forms fall under the definition put forward by Himmelmann (1996: 210), albeit with one qualification. According to Himmelmann, demonstratives have the following necessary criteria:

3 Attention focus and information packaging in Vera'a demonstratives

(1) Demonstratives are linguistic expressions that
   1. are in a paradigmatic relationship to elements that serve to locate a referent on a distance scale, i.e. proximal, distal, etc.
   2. cannot be used with reference to entities that are uniquely identifiable in a culture (or the world), or in so-called associative anaphora, e.g. where an anaphor is a part of the whole expressed by the antecedent

As for criterion 1, in situational use DEM.SPKR forms can be used to identify a referent that is located close to the speaker, whereas DEM.ADDR forms can be used where it is further away from the speaker, possibly between addressee and speaker. The form DEM.DIST can be used for referents even further away from the speaker, possibly at a large distance from both speaker and addressee. Examples in §3.3 will illustrate these points. While these uses concern the extension of demonstratives, their intentional definition in Vera'a does not draw precisely on the distance parameter, as will become clear in the sections to follow. Moreover, it seems that the Vera'a facts provide some illustrative evidence that the exophoric-situational use is not necessarily basic to the meaning of demonstratives, as assumed in earlier work by Diessel 1999: 93. Instead, my findings support the view that the meaning of demonstratives is general with respect to exophoric and endophoric uses (cf. Himmelmann 1996: 242), and is indeed grounded in considerations of interlocutor interaction and 'attention focus', as found by Enfield (2003) for Lao (cf. also Diessel 2006). Table 2 summarises the inventory of basic and adverbial demonstrative forms. Forms of DEM.SPKR and DEM.ADDR alter between a 'plain' form and a form prefixed with *a-*. The latter is quite likely to represent a crystallised combination of the specific locative article *a* and a demonstrative. The formal distinction is relevant insofar as they correlate with constraints on syntactic distribution: for instance only the prefixed but not the plain forms of basic demonstratives can occur adnominally. Where a form is prefixed, this is indicated by .A in the gloss, for instance DEM.SPKR.A for the prefixed speaker-oriented base form.

Table 2: Inventory of Vera'a demonstrative forms

| | DEM.ADDR | | DEM.SPKR | | DEM.DIST |
	PLAIN	A-FORM	PLAIN	A-FORM	
BASIC	nē	anē	gēn(ē)	agēn(ē)	ē
MANNER	senē	asenē	segēn(ē)	asegēn(ē)	
TEMPORAL	va'anē		va'agēn		
LOCATIVE	('e)kēnē		('e)kēgēn		

Table 2 also lists demonstrative adverbs in addition to basic demonstratives. These are derived from the base forms as follows: manner adverbs are derived by adding a prefix *se-* whose exact meaning and origin are unclear at this stage. Temporal adverbs essentially consist of an adverb *va'a* 'already' plus the base form. Locational adverbs are combinations of the noun *'ekē* 'place' and a basic demonstrative. All three types of adverb can be used adnominally and occupy the same phrase-final slot as base forms (compare example (3)):

(2) n= gie si =n gengen si =n sava senē di =m wōlwōl
 ART= kava or =ART food or =ART what MAN.DEM.ADDR 3SG =TAM1 RED:buy
 ma mē no. (0.6)
 hither DAT 1SG

 '[He gave me money for the work.] Also kava, food, or such things, he bought for me.' MVRP.080

I will be dealing mainly with the use of base form demonstratives in this chapter. However, I will occasionally outline particular usage properties of DEM.SPKR and DEM.ADDR by reference to adverbs where particularly illustrative examples show that the findings presented here apply to the wider demonstrative system.

As for Himmelmann's second criterion, the forms in Table 2 are indeed incompatible with the first usage context, but a single example is attested that is similar to the binding (associative) anaphora example mentioned by Himmelmann (1996: 210):

(3) qōn vōwal e ruwa mē =n gunu-ruō duru =m 'ōgo 'ōgo vaa-van
 night one PERS HUM:DL DAT =ART spouse-3DL 3DL =TAM1 stay stay RED-go
 =n reñe anē ne wotoqtoqo.
 =ART woman DEM.ADDR.A AOR:3SG pregnant

 'One day, (there was) a couple. They stayed and stayed (and after some time) that woman got pregnant.' ANV.001–003

In this example, the speaker first introduces the couple, and two clauses later refers to one in the couple, the woman, using an adnominal DEM.ADDR. This usage would disqualify the forms in question as demonstratives according to Himmelmann's second criterion. Thus, if we take this particular use of a DEM.ADDR form as evidence against its status as a demonstrative we will probably have to conclude that the language does not possess demonstratives at all, given the clear paradigmatic relation of the form with DEM.SPKR and DEM.DIST forms. This would in my view not be a plausible analysis, given the universality of demonstratives (and hence their expectedness in Vera'a) and the otherwise clear indications that the forms in question function like demonstratives in other languages.

There are two possibilities to account for this 'abnormal' use of a demonstrative: firstly, we might be dealing simply with a production mistake, given that it is the only example in the entire corpus. Though this is somewhat speculative, it is not impossible that speakers occasionally 'miscalculate' the identifiability of referents, believing that there is an eligible antecedent expression in the discourse context, although there isn't (Ariel 1990: 72). The second possibility is that Himmelmann's criterion is too narrow, and that Vera'a treats associative anaphora differently from other languages. Which of these two possibilities is more appropriate remains an open question at this point, and is left for future investigations of more, and possibly more varied, discourse data to determine whether such uses are more common with some speakers or in some contexts than our current data suggests.

3.2 Syntactic distribution of demonstrative forms

For base form demonstratives, three syntactic positions and respective functions are attested: NP-internal modifier (adnominal use), argument on clause level (pronominal use), and clause-level adverbs and particles. Table 3 provides figures for the frequencies of uses of DEM.ADDR, DEM.SPKR, and DEM.DIST in all three syntactic contexts, with the restriction that DEM.DIST cannot be used pronominally.

Table 3: Frequencies of basic demonstratives in 10 Vera'a narratives

DEM.ADDR			DEM.SPKR			DEM.DIST		Totals		
ADN	PRO	other	ADN	PRO	other	ADN	other	ADN	PRO	other
255	20	127	21	4	10	74	17	350	24	154

All three forms can be used adnominally, as modifiers in the noun phrase, as shown by the following examples (4) and (5):

(4) ne   'ēn e   ruwa   m̄alm̄ala ē   =s   sag 'i   e   ruwa
    AOR:3SG see PERS HUM:DL girl   DEM.DIST =SIM sit DEL PERS HUM:DL
    m̄alm̄ala anē   so
    girl   DEM.SPKR.A QUOT
    '[...] and then (he) spotted those two girls (who were) sitting (there), and the two girls said: ...'   1.PALA.059–060

(5) no =k   kaka =n   nelño vu' agēnē
    1SG AOR:1SG story =ART voice spirit DEM.SPKR.A
    'I am going to tell this (the following) story: ...'   ISWM.001

The functions of these different forms in adnominal use will be discussed in §3.3 and §3.4. Pronominal use is restricted to DEM.ADDR and DEM.SPKR forms. While DEM.ADDR demonstratives occur as subjects (ex 6) and predicates (ex 7) in non-verbal clauses, all pronominal uses of DEM.SPKR are instances of subjects in non-verbal clauses (ex 8):

(6) nē   =n   tēktēk   mu-n   e   Qo'.
    DEM.ADDR =ART RED:speech POSS.GEN-CS PERS Q.
    'This was Qo''s speech [what Qo' said].'   JJQ.306

(7) bul   wova'al   ē   di   sa   nē
    bunch pawpaw   DEM.DIST 3SG EMPH DEM.ADDR
    'That bunch of pawpaw (over there), it is exactly that [which we had in mind]'
    GABG.075

(8) kamaduō gēn.
    1DL.EX   DEM.SPKR
    'This (is) us.'   2.PALA.125

Pronominal uses of demonstratives are very rare, in particular where DEM.SPKR forms are involved. These cases are in fact restricted to contexts of *Deixis am Phantasma* in narrative texts, to be discussed in §3.3. This corroborates the findings from the sample presented in Himmelmann (1996: 215) for texts from different languages.

Similar to other Oceanic languages (Mosel (2004) on Samoan; Margetts (2004) on Saliba; François (2001) on Mwotlap), basic demonstratives in Vera'a can occur on clause level in clause-final position, for example:

(9) e   raga   anē   =k   tek   so   =n   tōo   me   ma' nē
    PERS HUM:PL DEM.SPKR.A =AOR:NSG say QUOT =ART fowl FUT dead DEM.ADDR
    'And they said: "These chickens will die!"'   ANV.037

(10) dir'ōl =k   ōnōn   'i   unē
     3TL   =AOR   RED:lie   DEL   DEM.SPKR.A
     'They lay down [and shortly after that ...]'   MVBW.109

(11) e   Qo' ne   sag rēn   sag kēkē   ē
     PERS   Q. AOR:3SG sit stuck up   above   DEM.DIST
     'But Qo' is trapped up (in the tree), have you forgotten?'   JJQ.151

(12) kamam   mi'ir sa   gēnē   lē   =n   wio.
     1PL.EX.TAM1 sleep EMPH   DEM.SPKR   LOC =ART   bamboo
     'Let's sleep right here, in the bamboo.'   JJQ.354

In examples (9) and (10), DEM.ADDR forms occur in clause-final position. In (9), it functions as an assertive particle that serves to underscore the speaker's conviction about the truth of a proposition. In (10), it fulfils a clause-combining function, details of which will be discussed in §3.4. The same function is carried out by DEM.DIST in this position (ex 11). Basic DEM.SPKR forms always function as locative adverbs when occurring on clause level (ex 12).

Demonstrative adverbs are used mainly adverbially on clause level (category 'other' in Table 4). However, they do occur – in rare instances – as modifiers in the noun phrase. Table 4 lists the relevant figures for frequencies of use.

I confine myself here to presentation of a single example of a locative adverb in adnominal function (see also example (2) above):

Table 4: Distribution and frequency of demonstrative adverbs in 10 narratives

	DEM.ADDR		DEM.SPKR		TOTALS	
	ADN	other	ADN	other	ADN	other
MANNER	2	57	3	24	5	81
TEMPORAL	1	61	0	5	1	66
LOCATIVE	4	57	1	16	5	73
TOTALS	7	175	4	45	11	220

(13)   'erē 'ama' 'ekēnē   dir =ēm   van se-serge   ma.
       PL   devil   LOC.DEM.ADDR   3PL =TAM1 go RED-together hither
       'The spirits (of) here, they came together here.'   ISWM.281–282

In the following subsections, I will focus on the use of basic demonstratives, and only occasionally turn to the use of demonstrative adverbs.

Before we turn our attention to the different uses of demonstratives, it should be noted that adnominal demonstratives are the only NP-level element that directly influences the referential interpretations of NPs. Pre-head articles are merely phrase markers whose only function is the marking of the type of phrase, and the subtype of NP (common versus personal). NPs with adnominal demonstratives are definite, and have an identifiable referent. We will see below that this is merely an entailment of demonstratives, and not their core meaning. NPs without demonstratives are likewise regularly used in contexts where their referent is identifiable, but they are also compatible with discourse-new reference. As for pronominal uses of demonstratives, these may be relatively rare in the corpus because third person pronouns are regularly used for anaphoric and – to a lesser degree – deictic reference to identifiable entities. As indicated above, this paper will be confined to the development of a first hypothesis concerning the use and meaning of Vera'a demonstratives. A systematic corpus study of the use of demonstratives in competition with other types of referring expressions will be left for future work on the language.

3.3 Exophoric use of Vera'a demonstratives

The exophoric functions of demonstratives are often seen as basic, for instance in Diessel (1999). While it is the exophoric use of demonstratives that defines the class as a whole in Himmelmann's (1996) definition, it is questionable whether spatial considerations are part of the core meaning of demonstratives. Himmelmann himself doubts this, as do do studies like Enfield (2003), as well as later work by Diessel (2006). My findings concerning the use of demonstratives in Vera'a lend further support to the view that the basic function of demonstratives is in interlocutor interaction and attention focussing.

The purpose of this section is to provide an outline of exophoric uses of the three demonstratives in Vera'a. I will here draw on two types of data, namely the house building video and observation where speakers point to entities and locations in the physical environment of the recording. Secondly, I will illustrate the same patterns of demonstrative use in instances of *Deixis am Phantasma* in the direct speech of characters pointing to entities within the narrated reality. The last type of exophoric use to be discussed here is in a narrative's frame, in particular where a narrative is announced just prior to its narration, and where it is wrapped up after the last events have been reported.

It should be noted here that at this stage, no more systematic investigation of situational uses of demonstratives – like the studies by Enfield (2003) on Lao and Margetts (2004) on Saliba – has been carried out for Vera'a as yet. This is, however, not strictly necessary for understanding their use in narrative discourse, as will become clear below. The basic distinctions of speaker orientation, addressee orientation, and distal interpretation is relatively clear from the few examples in the video recordings (the house-building recording and a subset of narratives), and is the only one relevant for their use in narrative discourse. We will see in some examples here that even in exophoric use, information-related categories are more relevant than spatial considerations.

Vera'a demonstratives are participant-oriented, which does not so much draw on distance relative to the speaker, but on considerations as to whether the addressee (or the speaker) can be regarded as sharing some *here-space* with the referent. In this system, DEM.SPKR forms are strictly associated with the speaker, as can be seen from the following two examples where the DEM.SPKR form contributes the location of an object near the speaker, but outside of the immediate perception of the addressee:

(14) **woqe'enge agēnē**   *'erē mom kal 'i*   [...]
     wood   DEM.SPKR.A PL   put   up   DEL

  'This wood here [in speaker's hand], put (it) up, I have just cut (it).'
                                                                HouseBuilding10_FQ.005

(15) n   *gasel luwo mu-m*   **gēn**
      ART knife big   POSS.GEN-2SG   DEM.SPKR

  'Your bush knife is here [where I am]!'   observed

Example (14) is taken from a house building recording. In this situation the speaker is holding a piece of wood in his hand and is about to pass it up to someone standing on the scaffold, so that it becomes a strut in the house's rafter. In uttering (14), he brings this new piece of roof structure to the other person's attention. Examples like (15) can be observed daily in the Vera'a community. Here, the speaker is sitting in a sleeping house and shouts out to the addressee, who is searching for his knife outside and inside the kitchen house. One crucial aspect concerning the use of DEM.SPKR is that it seems to entail the speaker's assumption that the addressee is not attending to the entity in question (and is possibly not familiar with it). This is illustrated by the following examples of direct speech involving situational use within narratives. Here, the speaker is drawing the addressee's attention to something that is not only clearly not in their *here-space*, but is also presented in such a way that the addressee is not aware of it:

3 Attention focus and information packaging in Vera'a demonstratives

(16) *ruwa =n nō-k ēn bē agēnē n= bē nō-k*
HUM:DL =ART POSS.DOM-1SG ART water DEM.SPKR.A ART= water POSS.DOM-1SG
anē ga mana nē.
DEM.SPKR.A STAT power DEM.ADDR
'Hey you two, I have some water here. This water of mine has magic powers.' AS.
1.100–101

(17) *n qō gēnē wo =n mañra gēnē no me gis gidē =k van.*
ART pig DEM.SPKR and =ART money DEM.SPKR 1SG FUT hold 1PL.IN =AOR go
'I have a pig here, and some money here. I'll take it and then let's go.'
ISWM.219

In both examples, the referent is presented as new to the addressee. Once attention has been established in (16), the speaker uses the DEM.ADDR form in the following clause which further elaborates on the referent. The data examined thus far lend themselves to the following hypothesis: DEM.SPKR forms are used where an entity is only in the *here-space* of the speaker, excluding that of the addressee, and where the addressee is not yet attending to that entity.

By contrast, DEM.ADDR forms are used where the referent is not exclusively in the speaker's *here-space*, for instance where addressee also has perceptual access to it or where it is in the addressee's *here-space*. The following two examples illustrate this:

(18) *o kēnē nē ga tēlēglēg.*
INTERJ LOC.DEM.ADDR DEM.ADDR STAT askew
'No, there, that one is (still) uneven [not horizontal].'
HouseBuilding04_PB.008

(19) [...] *le rieg ēn ñara gasel anē* [...]
take out ART mouth knife DEM.SPKR.A
'Remove that (blade of that) knife!.'
HouseBuilding09_JJ.009

Again, both examples stem from the house building video recordings. In (18), the speaker is first looking at the measuring string between two posts on the other side of the house's plane. The string is used to check whether both posts have the same height, and here the speaker states that it is not horizontal yet. The adjustment of the string is the main thing that is happening at this stage, and the speaker can assume everybody to be attending to it. In (19), the speaker – standing outside the scaffold – is referring to the knife lying in the middle of the house's plane, surrounded by other builders. One of these in fact then approaches the knife, apparently following the request. Everybody in this scene can be regarded as being aware of the knife lying there. We can assume that the use of a DEM.SPKR form would have triggered the addressees' turning their heads towards the speaker, the *here-space* exclusive to the speaker.

Equivalent examples can be found in direct speech within narrative texts where both characters, the speaker and the addressee, are rendered as being aware of an entity and attending to it:

(20) **nē**   =n   ēn   men nē
      DEM.ADDR =ART ART   bird DEM.ADDR

   '[discussion among characters after hearing some noise out in the bush] "That [what we are hearing here] is a bird, believe me!" (There is a bird singing.)'
   MVBW.061

(21) o   bul   wēwē wova'al ne   vōwal sarēnē ga   mine **ne'ē**   sa
      INTERJ friend fruit pawpaw NUM one up.there STAT ripe DEM.ADDR EMPH
      gidu   me   gen nē
      1DL.IN FUT eat DEM.ADDR

   'Oh friend, that one ripe pawpaw fruit up there, that's the one we will eat, I tell you.'   GABG.051–052

The second example also illustrates the omnipresent potential ambiguity between exophoric-situational and endophoric-tracking use: as will become clear below, DEM.ADDR forms are also the ones used for given-activated referents – i.e. those referents already attended to by both speaker and addressee – and DEM.ADDR forms could here be understood as referring to the entity both characters attend to in the depicted physical environment, or the referent in the depicted discourse of direct speech. Example (16) illustrates a similar ambiguity in the second clause, where the magic water just presented to the two is taken up again in the second clause.

The following examples of direct speech illustrate the same functional aspect of DEM.ADDR forms, this time used adnominally:

(22) dir =m   gal no ma   no =m   rem   a   =n   woqe'enge **anē**.
      3PL =TAM1 lie 1SG hither 1SG =TAM1 climb LOC.SP =ART tree   DEM.SPKR.A

   'They tricked me into coming here, and I climbed up this tree.'   JJQ.182–183

(23) 'ei   bulsal nik   ē   dada   sēvēe lē =n   bē   nanara **anē**
      INTERJ friend 2SG AOR:2SG RED:do how LOC =ART trunk tree.sp DEM.SPKR.A

   'Hey, friend, what are you doing on this Nanara trunk here?'   GAQG.034

Summarising the observations concerning the use of DEM.ADDR, the following can be stated: 1. the entity in question is not clearly located in the speaker's *here-space* and is not clearly excluded from that of the addressee, and 2. both speaker and addressee attend to it, or are at least aware of it.

Comparing the use of DEM.SPKR and DEM.ADDR forms, we can conclude that the former are used where the entity is excluded from the addressee's *here-space* and is being brought to the addressee's attention just at the time of utterance, and the latter is used where the converse situation holds, i.e. where an entity is not excluded from the addressee's *here-space* and both speaker and addressee are already attending to it at the beginning of the utterance. This hypothesis would be falsified, for instance, by examples where a DEM.ADDR form is used for an entity clearly in the *here-space* of the speaker but not the addressee – for instance where both are separated by a wall or so, as in example (15) above – or where a DEM.SPKR form is used when clearly both speaker and addressee were already attending to the entity at the beginning of the utterance. Such examples have not been identified in the data.

The decisive factor in the use of these two forms is the inclusion versus exclusion of the addressee, rather than the speaker's *here-space*. This is illustrated by the following example where the referent of the NP 'head post' is in the speaker's *here-space*, but not excluded from that of the addressee. The speaker here appeals to the fact that the addressee – in this case myself behind/next to the camera – is attending to the post, pointing the camera at it and him:

(24) di ne 'i-'iris e raga a sag kēkē a =n wōlwōlo
 3SG AOR:3SG RED-even PERS HUM:PL LOC.SP up above LOC.SP =ART cross
 ē nē =n wōqa'ag qi'i nē no =s 'ar'ar
 DEM.DIST DEM.ADDR =ART post head DEM.ADDR 1SG =SIM RED:carve
 anē.
 DEM.ADDR.A

 'So that it is becoming even with the others up there on that cross (beam). This is the head post, you know, that one I am cutting.' HouseBuilding08_JJ.002–003

This shows that DEM.ADDR forms are used where the addressee is assumed to be aware of or attending to the entity in question, for instance looking straight at it as in this example. The DEM.SPKR forms are, on the other hand, restricted to uses where only the speaker has perceptual access to or is aware of the entity in question, as was illustrated by example (15) above. The relevant functional aspect of DEM.SPKR forms, distinguishing them from DEM.ADDR forms, is that they are exclusive to the speaker's access.

The hypothesis that DEM.SPKR forms are associated with a strictly speaker-delimited *here-space* receives further support from the observation that DEM.SPKR forms cannot be used as expansions of the speaker's *here-space* to include that of the addressee, or a wider spatial dimension. For such contexts – where English would use *here* – DEM.ADDR forms are used. In the following example, taken from an account of local history recounting the resettlement of Vera'a speakers at the location of the contemporary village, the speaker refers to the village of Vera'a, where the recording is taking place:

(25) lē =n masōgi dir =ēm mul kal ma kēnē
 LOC =ART time 3PL =TAM1 move up hither LOC.DEM.ADDR

 'When they came up here [to today's Vera'a village, where the recording takes place]...' BSVH.066

The same is illustrated by the following examples from direct speech within narratives: in (26) and (27), the speaker refers to the house where he, his associates and the addressee are.

(26) kamam ē mi-mi'ir ros a vie kamam mi'ir wal
 1PL.EX NEG.GEN1 RED-sleep NEG.GEN2 LOC.SP where 1PL.EX:TAM1 sleep INTENS
 sa kēnē
 EMPH LOC.DEM.ADDR

 'We didn't sleep anywhere (else), we slept right here!' JJQ.396

(27) kamam ne gitag   ēn   m̄o-mam   [...] kamam ga   mi'ir wal   sa
      1PL.EX ?? not.exist ART POSS.HOUSE-1PL.EX   1PL.EX STAT sleep INTENS EMPH
      lē =n   nim̄ē anē
      LOC =ART house DEM.SPKR.A

'We don't have another house that we could move to. We slept in this house right here!' JJQ.425

The respective DEM.SPKR forms of locative adverbs are used only where the addressee is clearly not included in the speaker's *here-space*, as in the following example of direct speech where a character is inviting a group of people from far down the coast to stay at his place:

(28) van ma   gēdē   me 'og kēgen.
      go hither 1PL.IN FUT stay LOC.DEM.SPKR

'(You guys) come here, and we will stay here together.' JJQ.273

That attention focus is the driving force behind the choice between DEM.ADDR and DEM.SPKR forms is further supported by examples where DEM.SPKR forms are used with referents that are clearly situated at an enormous distance from the position of the speaker. The crucial point is that it is *not in the addressee's here-space*. Moreover, it seems that the speaker in this example intends to draw the addressee's attention to something new, or something the speaker would assume the addressee not to be aware of at a given point. The most blatant example illustrating this point comes from another instance of direct speech in a narrative: in (29), a boy asks his father about a light that is far away in the bush (and the video shows the narrator pointing into the distance when depicting the boy's gesture, while looking to the other side to address his father), using the DEM.SPKR form:

(29) lē =n   qōñ ne   vōwal Wowōt   ne   vesir e   'ama-gi   so   mam
      LOC =ART night NUM one   pers.name AOR:3SG ask PERS father-3SG QUOT dad
      ba =n   bur agēnē   =n   sava
      but =ART light DEM.SPKR.A =ART what

'Then one day, Wowot would ask his father: "Dad, but this light here [pointing gesture], what is that?"' ISWM.075–076

The explanation for the use of a DEM.SPKR form in line with our hypothesis is that here the speaker has the light in mind and now wants to direct his father's attention to it so he can ask him about it. Similarly in the following example, the group of people – already featured in examples (26) – (28) – is looking for a place to sleep to hide from the evil spirit who had invited them to stay with him. The group has been sleeping in different parts of the house, hiding from the spirit who wants to kill them. In example (30), one member of the group gives them away to the spirit by telling him the actual place they spent the night in:

(30) kamam mi'ir sa **gēnē** lē =n wio
    1PL.EX sleep EMPH DEM.SPKR LOC =ART bamboo

'["Where did you sleep?" And then Tagarqonqon said:] "We slept right here, in the bamboos [We slept in the (bamboo) struts.]"' JJQ.354

This example contrasts with examples (26) and (27) – taken from the same context. Here the speaker draws the addressee's attention to something new, rather than the house, that the addressee is familiar with, aware of and shares his *here-space* with. Specifically, the speaker here points to a more specific place within the house that – given the context – the addressee was not aware of. Finally, an example from the house building video illustrates the same idea. In (31), the speaker – standing next to the camera and commenting on what is happening in the frame – points to different spots where the side posts of the house are going to be located, thereby drawing the attention of the addressee – me in this case, behind the camera – to these different locations:

(31) rōv'ē 'i so =n 'aval-gi a kēl sar **gēnē** dir =ēk mom
    close DEL CPL =ART side-3SG LOC.SP back bushwards DEM.SPKR 3PL =AOR put
    qē =n 'erē qa'aga (0.4) wo dir =ēk qē'ēg kēl ēn 'aval-gi
    finish =ART PL post and 3PL =AOR begin back ART side-3SG
    agēnē. (0.3)
    DEM.SPKR.A

'It's almost like that side further bushwards, they have put all the posts, and then they will start on this side over here.' HouseBuilding05_IS.008–009

Here, the speaker first points away from the two of us towards the bushwards side of the plane of the house, using a DEM.SPKR form, and then turn to the other side, again using a DEM.SPKR form. This consecutive pointing to new locations and referents seems similar to the listing use of proximal demonstratives in Samoan (Mosel 2004), and is compatible with the idea that such forms are used to draw the addressee's attention to the next, new point in the series.

Finally, DEM.DIST forms are used where an entity is not associated with the speaker or addressee, and is not to become the focus of attention. Example (25) above illustrates this: the speaker uses a DEM.ADDR form when referring to the post he is cutting, assuming that the addressee is also attending to it. But in the immediately preceding clause, he refers to the cross beam of the house's scaffold that is outside of what speaker and addressee will then be attending to, and relevant only as background. The DEM.DIST form is used here. DEM.DIST forms are also used where the speaker cannot fully attend to the referent in question because it is outside their perception. This is the case in (32), where Cat is asking Rat about the pawpaw that only Rat has access to:

(32) o bul rōv-rōv'ē nik e kur kirm̄ō =n **gako wova'al ē**
    INTERJ friend RED-close 2SG 2SG:AOR gnaw break =ART stalk pawpaw DEM.DIST

'Hey friend, will you almost have gnawed through that pawpaw stalk?'
    GABG.083

I conclude that the DEM.ADDR and the DEM.SPKR forms are both used where the speaker seeks joint attention focus with the addressee; DEM.DIST forms, on the other hand, are used where the referent is outside of the interlocutor's attention sphere, and relevant only generally but not right here, or simply impossible to attend to conjointly. Obviously, this can be the case where the referent is at a greater distance from both speaker and hearer, hence its characterisation as distal.

Lastly, DEM.SPKR forms are often used in two further contexts that belong to narrative texts, but are to be classified as exophoric-situational since they involve consideration of the communicative situation of the narration itself. The first of these are cases of *Deixis am Phantasma* (Bühler 1999[1934]) where a narrator uses the physical environment and/or their own body to illustrate aspects of the depicted reality of the narrative (see also Himmelmann 1996: 224). Thus, in (33) the speaker shows where a character is holding the different kinds of leaves (to signal his peaceful mindset). In (34), the narrator demonstrates how a piece of breadfruit is broken off. For this latter example, two interpretations seem possible: one in terms of the manner of breaking it off, and one in terms of the dimensions (size, shape) of the piece. In (35), the speaker illustrates the dimensions of a rock wall.

(33) di ga gis ēn du m̄ēl **val-gi** **agēnē** wo =n seg
3SG STAT hold ART leaf tree.sp opposite-3SG DEM.SPKR.A and =ART tree.sp
val-gi **agēnē**.
opposite-3SG DEM.SPKR.A
'He was holding a *m̄ēl* leaf in this hand here, and a *seg* leaf on the other side here.'
ISWM.258

(34) 'ubu-gi =m 'uq rak den ēn menre-gi ne vōwal
grandparent/child-3SG =TAM1 break.off out ABL ART piece-3SG NUM one
segēnē [...]
MAN.DEM.SPKR
'His grandma broke off a piece (of breadfruit) like this.' MVB.149

(35) kel qa-qañ luwo **segēn**.
big RED-walling big MAN.DEM.SPKR
'a wall big like this.' ISWM.175

These uses of DEM.SPKR forms are compatible with the hypothesis outlined above that these forms function to establish joint attention. The respective narrator is pointing out aspects of his body and corresponding aspects of the narrated reality that he believes the audience is not aware of. Similarly, and occasionally hard to distinguish from *Deixis am Phantasma*, narrative frames and meta-comments are essentially exophoric in nature. Narrative frames are those passages where a narrative is introduced or ended, or where the narrator makes meta-narrative comments, for example stating that the narrative will soon come to an end. As for the former case, speakers often start a narrative by referring to the act of narrating or the narrative (as a textual whole) that is going to follow. In these cases, DEM.SPKR forms are used, as can be seen from the following two examples:

(36) no =k   kaka =n   nelño vu'   agēnē
     1SG =AOR:1SG story =ART voice- spirit DEM.SPKR.A
     'I am going to tell the following story:'   ISWM.001

(37) no ga   moros no =k   dedicatem ēn kaka agēnē   mē =n   e
     1SG STAT want 1SG =AOR:1SG dedicate ART story DEM.SPKR.A DAT =ART PERS
     raga   m̃ērm̃ēre
     HUM:PL kid
     'I want to dedicate this story to the children [...]'   MVBW.004

A similar context featuring DEM.SPKR use is the following, where the narrator announces a song to follow, sung in this case by another person, and meant to be sung by a character in the story:

(38) lē =n   nes 'a   bēne   di =m   van esegēn
     LOC =ART song ASS.SP OBL.PRO 3SG =TAM1 go DEM.SPKR.A
     'The song belonging to it [i.e. the story] goes like this:' HHAK.091

Hence, we are dealing here with cataphoric uses of the speaker-oriented forms, which are notionally similar to *this-new* (Wald 1983: 93) uses in English, and which square with the attendance-establishing hypothesis: the function of DEM.SPKR forms here is to get the audience to attend to the story to come, which of course they are not familiar with, and which metaphorically rests with the speaker up to that point where they start the narration. As observed by Himmelmann (1996) for a range of languages, these instances of cataphoric reference with speaker-based forms to introduce new information are often restricted to discourse-deictic use, and this is true for Vera'a as well. Hence, DEM.SPKR forms are used cataphorically in this way only where an event or content noun is involved, as in examples (36–38).

Conversely, at the end of a story, narrators conclude the narration with reference back to the story, stating that it has come to an end. Interestingly, in these instances no demonstrative is ever used to modify the noun 'story'. However, a locative adverb of the DEM.ADDR series is used to refer to that end point in the story, for example:

(39) kaka wunva   di =m   diñ   wuva ekēnē.
     story probably 3SG =TAM1 reach only LOC.DEM.ADDR
     'The story, it is probably over at this point.'   ISWM.361

(40) ba =n kaka =m   qē'   sa   kēnē.
     but =ART story =TAM1 finish EMPH LOC.DEM.ADDR
     '[...and what happened to them I don't know], but the story is over right here.'
                                                                  MVBW.137

This context is not clearly exophoric, but can be seen as an instance of endophoric and discourse-deictic use. Two observations seem relevant here. For one thing, these examples highlight that DEM.ADDR forms are not markers of definiteness in endophoric use, since the NPs 'story' are clearly to be understood as definite in both examples. For another thing, the use of DEM.ADDR locative adverbs suggests a spatial metaphor for discourse, where narrators frequently make meta-comments by referring to the point of the narration where 'we are' at a specific point (cf. Diessel 2006: 475). That DEM.ADDR is used is motivated by the speaker's assumption that the addressee is conjointly attending to the narration, and to that moment in it.

Finally, there are examples where a story is referred back to by a plain DEM.ADDR form, which seems to be most similar to endophoric discourse-deictic use:

(41) so nē'ē =n ni'i kaka wo =n nes [...]
?? DEM.ADDR =ART small story and =ART song

'So this is a little story and song [about how the incubator bird builds its nest].'

GATG.065

The DEM.ADDR form is used in these instances because the speaker assumes that the addressee is familiar with the referent and attending to it.

In sum then, Vera'a has a three-way system of demonstratives. The choice of forms is driven primarily by considerations of attention focus and information management: DEM.DIST forms are used where an entity is outside the *here-space* of both speaker and addressee, and joint attention to it is not relevant or cannot be obtained. DEM.SPKR forms are used where an entity is in the *here-space* of the speaker, excluding the addressee. It is used where the speaker seeks to draw attention to an entity that only they are currently familiar with or aware of. DEM.ADDR forms are used where speaker and addressee share a *here-space* with regard to the entity in question, and the speaker assumes the addressee to already be attending to the entity in question. The crucial aspect of this system is that it has a marked speaker-oriented *here-space* and attention focus, and that wherever the addressee is seen as sharing *here-space* and attention, the DEM.ADDR form is used. The functions of DEM.SPKR and DEM.ADDR forms are essentially different in that only the former alters the focus of attention. The function of DEM.ADDR is to maintain joint attention focus on an entity for what follows. This can then yield different pragmatic effects, as can be seen from the following examples (42) and (43):

(42) ei **nike anē** sa =s dada kel ēn nak mu-k
INTERJ 2SG DEM.ADDR.A EMPH =SIM RED:do back ART canoe POSS.GEN-1SG

'Hey, so is it you who has been putting my canoe back up all the time?' JJQ.064

(43) 'ei **kamadu anē** =m van ma sir nik anē.
INTERJ 1DL.EX DEM.ADDR.A =TAM1 go hither for 2SG DEM.ADDR.A

'Hey, we came here because of you, [because we want to be together with you].'

1.PALA.059–061

In (42), the DEM.ADDR-marked pronoun occurs in left-dislocated position, which is in other cases also associated with topicalisation. Here, however, it is clear that the referent has a role more akin to what has been called focus (Krifka 2008, Lambrecht 1994), picking out a referent from a putative open set (someone who can do things). Likewise, the use of a DEM.ADDR form with the pronouns in (43) would be hard to motivate by considerations of identification, or topic marking. If anything, it seems, the subject pronoun would have to be construed as a 'topic', whereas the PP complement would be in 'focus' – 'we are not here just for the dancing or other people, but for *you*'. These examples thus underscore the point that demonstratives do not serve as markers of definiteness, since the personal pronouns already entail definiteness. Instead of definiteness, demonstratives seem to bear functions in the domain of information structure. However, it is also clear from these examples that they do not mark specific information-structural roles like 'topic' or 'focus'. Rather, in my view, the use of DEM.ADDR forms is motivated here by the same considerations of maintained attention focus as in other uses discussed thus far, and this has the effect of an inference that what follows is in some way relevant for the entities thus expressed. Given other structural properties, like left-dislocation and emphatic marking, this may produce a 'focus effect' (Matić & Wedgwood 2013). Moreover, it does seem to have the effect of singling out entities as 'information packages' (Ozerov 2015), the interpretation of which depends on the discourse context. I will take up this point in §4 and §5.

3.4 Endophoric use of Vera'a demonstratives

I now turn to endophoric uses of demonstratives within narrative texts, excluding its frame, meta-comments, and direct speech. I call this instance of discourse 'narration text'. The functions of demonstratives in this context are typically associated with anaphora and referent tracking (called 'tracking use' in Himmelmann 1996), but also with considerations of information packaging (Diessel 1999). In what follows I will go through the uses of demonstratives in different syntactic contexts. It should be noted at this point that I will be dealing almost exclusively with the use of DEM.ADDR and DEM.DIST forms since DEM.SPKR forms are very restricted in this context, occurring practically only in one interesting case which will be discussed first. It will be made clear in §4 below that the virtual absence of DEM.SPKR forms in narration text follows straightforwardly from their attention-establishing cataphoric function discussed in §3.3.

3.4.1 Speaker-oriented forms in narrative discourse

The only example of a DEM.SPKR form in narration text is the following, where the narrator seems to slip into the report of a character's thought:

(44) *di ne van ma ne rērē e ruwa agēn ō di rōs.*
3SG AOR:3SG go hither AOR:3SG head PERS HUM:DL DEM.SPKR.A INTERJ 3SG NEG2

'Then she would come over and take a closer look at "these two here, no, not him".' ISWM.326

This appears to be one of many examples from Vera'a narratives where a narrator seems to slide seamlessly from the narration text into direct speech or thought. As in this example, such cases often feature interjections. Thus, in this example direct thought and narration text are not clearly marked off. The use of a DEM.SPKR form here in fact already represents an instance of *Deixis am Phantasma*, and it is motivated by the same attention-directing principles discussed above. Hence, for the remainder of this section, I will be dealing only with DEM.ADDR and DEM.DIST forms.

3.4.2 Plain addressee-oriented forms on clause level in narration text

Plain, i.e. unprefixed, DEM.ADDR forms are very rare in narration text. One recurrent occurrence is their pronominal use in subject function. Their function here is discourse-deictic, as in the following example (45):

(45) **nē**   =n   tēktēk   mu-n   e   Qo'.
     DEM.ADDR =ART speech POSS.GEN-CS PERS PERS.NAME
     'That was Qo' talking there.'   JJQ.308

The DEM.ADDR form here refers back to the last few intonation units in which the narrator clarifies that it was the hero of the story, Qo', who said these things. As in exophoric use, a DEM.ADDR form can occur in clause-final position in narration text. Here, however, they seem to have a somewhat different function in maintaining the addressee's attention to a specific point in a narrative:

(46) di   =m   'ōg kelkel   'ōg kelkel   n-   me' ne   onon   rōw
     3SG =TAM1 stay RED:back stay RED:back ART= reef AOR:3SG RED:lie at.sea
     nē'   di   =m   'ōg kelkel   [...] vavavavan.
     DEM.ADDR 3SG =TAM1 stay RED:back   RED-go
     'He was staying up (on the island), and the reef was lying down at the sea. So now he [the man] was spending his time (there) [and one night he was dreaming, the reef came to him in his dream].'   ISAM.048

Such instances of DEM.ADDR forms are relatively rare in the corpus, and more data needs to be analysed before more substantial conclusions can be drawn. Nonetheless, I would like to argue that the use of the DEM.ADDR form here has the same function of maintaining joint attention to a specific point in a narration. This then has two related effects in this context, I believe. For one thing, it yields a simultaneity effect: while the reef is sitting down at the shore the man is up at the top of the shore. It also seems to have the effect of keeping the reef relevant for the following propositions, leading over to its appearance in the man's dream. Although these interpretations would have to be further substantiated, they do seem to square with the information-packaging effects to be discussed in §4.

3.4.3 Adnominal use of addressee-oriented versus distal demonstratives in narration text

DEM.ADDR forms occur adnominally in cases where the referent in question has been mentioned in the immediate context. A typical usage context is where the referent was introduced in the previous clause and is then taken up immediately again, for example:

(47) duru =k 'ēn ma =n lumgav ne vōwal **lumgav ne vōwal**
3DL =AOR see hither =ART young.man NUM one young.man NUM one
anē di ne laa-laka senē wo ne virig ma [...]
DEM.ADDR.A 3SG AOR:3SG RED-dance MAN.DEM.ADDR and AOR:3SG rush hither

'Then the two spotted a young man. And the young man, he danced, and then (he) came over, [and sat down under the wild kava plant].' 1.PALA.044–045

(48) van ma diñ ēn bē **bē ne vōwal anē** =n so-gi =n
go hither reach ART water water NUM one DEM.ADDR.A =ART name-3SG =ART
Bē'elmamgin.
PLACE.NAME

'Went here and reached a river. This (some) river, its name (is) Bē'elmamgin [lit. 'Cold to dive water'].' AS.1.071–073

(49) ote mu-n e ni'i- reñe anē ne ma' e duru =k
mum POSS.GEN-CS PERS small- female DEM.ADDR.A AOR:3SG dead DISC 3DL =AOR
'ēn ...eh =n 'ama-gi ne 'ēn gōr ēn ni'i- reñe anē
see COR =ART father-3SG AOR:3SG see secure ART small- female DEM.ADDR.A
vaavan 'e =n **'ama-gi anē** ne ma'.
RED-go DISC =ART father-3SG DEM.ADDR.A AOR:3SG dead

'Then the mother of the little girl died. So her father looked after the little girl, on and on, and then her father died.' ANV.005–007

These examples show again that DEM.ADDR forms do not merely mark an NP as definite, and this is also clear from its compatibility with personal pronouns, see §3.3 above. Moreover, the total of 361 adnominal uses of demonstrative forms (including all adverbs) accounts for only a small fraction of full (lexical) NPs with given referents in our corpus, hence givenness/identifiability is likewise not *marked* by demonstratives. This was also made clear with respect to reference back to the story in narrative frames. The point is further supported by examples where DEM.ADDR is used with personal names or, as in the following example (50). Typically, these are nouns meaning 'older same-sex sibling, firstborn' or 'younger same-sex sibling, lastborn', with couples of siblings typically featuring as heroes in Vera'a literature.

(50) wo **'isimēre anē** ne 'añ vē'ē =n dudu vada ne
and firstborn DEM.ADDR.A AOR:3SG hand release =ART leaf pandanus NUM
vōwal.
one

'(The devil was then sucking in the sea again, and the sea current [that arose from that] brought the canoe [the two siblings are sitting in] ever closer to him.) So then the older sister let go of a pandanus leaf.' 2.PALA.091

This example also underscores that DEM.ADDR forms are not merely used to differentiate between referents, since this function can be clearly ascribed to the use of the noun itself.

In contrast to DEM.ADDR forms, DEM.DIST forms are used adnominally where the referent of the NP has been mentioned a while ago in the previous discourse, for example:

(51) duru =k   wos   ēn ñar   wos   ēn ñar   anē
     3DL =AOR hammer ART canarium.nut hammer ART canarium.nut DEM.ADDR.A
     dir'ōl da =n wig me big 'ō   sa   =n rōrō'   ē   alē   duru
     3TL do =ART wig FUT eat carry EMPH =ART k.o.cabbage DEM.DIST INTERJ 3DL
     =k   wos   ēn ñar.
     =AOR hammer ART canarium.nut

   'So they would smash up the canarium nuts. Smash up the canarium nuts to make wig (a kind of nalot (Bislama), i.e. K.o. pudding), which was to be had with that cabbage (that they had gotten earlier on). All right, so they smashed the canarium nuts (and then started making nalot).' AS.1.028–030

(52) wede di =m   luwo di ne   le =n nak   susu   ē.
     rain 3SG =TAM1 big 3SG AOR:3SG take =ART canoe RED-paddle DEM.DIST
     'Then the rain became big, and it took out that canoe.' JJQ.104–105

A DEM.DIST form can also be used where the referent is merely evoked by or inferable from earlier happenings, as is the case in the following example:

(53) ba di =m   gis ēn menre- kōlōv- 'ar-'ara ē   ne   mul 'ō'
     but 3SG =TAM1 hold ART piece chipping RED-chop DEM.DIST AOR:3SG go carry
     lē =n   lōlō-   imē.
     LOC =ART iniside- house
     'But he took a piece of that chipping, and took it home with himself.' JJQ.052

Here, the actual chopping of the tree was mentioned seven intonation units away, and the DEM.DIST form is used because it requires the addressee to re-activate this event to relate the 'piece of chipping' to it. But apparently its inferability via frame semantics is sufficient to warrant the use of a DEM.DIST form that is otherwise used for individually given referents. Though there is good reason to assume that the DEM.DIST form in the previous examples is an NP-internal constituent, its position is nonetheless ambiguous between NP- and clause-final, the latter being another possible slot for both DEM.ADDR and DEM.DIST forms (see below). For the sake of completeness, the following example shows a DEM.DIST form in a subject NP. This is likewise an instance of inference, since the dancing was mentioned ten intonation units before inside a character's direct speech who states that they want to dance:

(54) **laklaka ē**   =m   van.
     dance   DEM.DIST =TAM1 go
     'And then that dance happened.' ISWM.319

In this example, the narrator is referring back to the idea of holding a dance for the hero of the story, who is temporarily dead. After this was mentioned first by some of the characters ten intonation units earlier, it was reported how people were walking to the place where the dead would have to be found and the dances would take place.

3.4.4 Addressee-oriented and distal demonstratives in clause combining constructions

The prefixed basic DEM.ADDR form can occur in clause-final position where it is used in clause combining constructions. In the following examples, it occurs in clause-final position and the event described therein comes to an end once the second one sets in:

(55) dir =m suō kal wal diñ sar ma **anē** e Qo'
3PL =TAM1 paddle up once reach inland hither DEM.ADDR.A PERS PERS.NAME
ne lañ wōr wal ēn nak.
AOR:3SG slap split once ART canoe

'And as they had just come up on the shore, Qo' smashed the canoe to pieces.'
JJQ.257

(56) alē duru =m inin va-van **anē** e Dōl so o
INTERJ 3DL =TAM1 RED:drink RED-go DEM.ADDR.A PERS PERS.NAME QUOT INTERJ
no man qē'.
1SG PFV finish

'All right, so the two of them drank and drank until [up to this point, and then...] Dōl said: "I am done. (The kava has kicked in.)"'   1.AS.039–040

In other instances, the two events are depicted as taking place simultaneously:

(57) lē =n masōgi di =m sagsag **anē** ba di ne susur lik
LOC =ART time 3SG =TAM1 RED:sit DEM.ADDR.A but 3SG AOR:3SG RED:tie more
ēn aklē dudu woqe 'enge.
ART some- leaf tree

'And as he was sitting (up at the top of the shore), he also assembled some leaves (to make some decoration for himself).'   ISAM.076

(58) ba dir'ōl =s vanvan **anē** =n 'isimēre mal lama'i so =n 'ama'.
but 3TL =SIM RED:go DEM.ADDR.A =ART lastborn REM.PFV know CPL =ART devil

'But as the three were walking along, the younger sister had already realised that is was a devil.'   2.PALA.018–019

These examples of DEM.ADDR uses are similar to the use of the plain form in (46). In yet other cases, the first clause marked by a clause-final DEM.ADDR form expresses a state of affairs that is a presupposition for the proposition of the following clause, expressing for example the reason for that proposition holding, as in the following example:

(59) so Qo' di ne sag 'i **anē** [...] di e lama'i ros so di
?? PERS.NAME 3SG AOR:3SG sit DEL DEM.ADDR.A 3SG NEG1 know NEG2 CPL 3SG
me 'isiw siviē.
FUT climb.down how

'(And then they turned towards Gaua). But Qo', he was sitting up there, [that darag towla it is so big so] he didn't know how to climb down.'   JJQ.171–172

Generally speaking, clause-final DEM.ADDR forms seem to have the effect of interpreting the preceding clause as immediately relevant for the interpretation of the subsequent clause. By contrast, clause-final DEM.DIST forms have the effect of steering away from the proposition expressed in its clause, while keeping it on hold for future reference. The following example (60) is taken from the same story as (59), and occurs long before that latter. The DEM.DIST-marked clause expresses the same state as the DEM.ADDR-marked one in (59); but here, the subsequent clause is not immediately related to that proposition, but instead shows a shift in topic and theme, now dealing with Qo''s brothers and their moving away from him. The story then goes on to recall how they steal his wife and canoe and travel to Gaua. Qo''s situation is then taken up again in the clause preceding the one in (59).

(60) e   Qo'   ne   sag rēn   sag kēkē ē   sag wo e   **raga**
     PERS PERS.NAME AOR:3SG sit stuck up above DEM.DIST sit and PERS HUM:PL
     'i-'isi-gi   *anē*   van rōw   lē   =n   vunuō.
     RED-younger.same.sex.sibling-3SG DEM.ADDR.A go   down LOC =ART village

'So Qo' was now stuck up there (in the tree). Sat (there) while his brothers went down to the village. (They stole his wife and his canoe, and paddled off with it.)'
JJQ.151–152

Noteworthy in this example is also the switch of topic in the second clause and the concomitant use of an adnominal DEM.ADDR form. Another illustrative example involving a clause-final DEM.DIST form shows its theme-switching effect: in (61), the context is that two men find a turtle at the beach and tie it up to pick it up later. After these recountings, the two men walk away from the beach and up the shore to their home village. The following discourse is about the men's reporting back to their chief and the villager's planning to go down, cook the turtle, and hold a feast. The clause-final DEM.DIST forms in this instance have the effect of signalling this momentary switch in scene before the narration turns back to this referent later:

(61) *ge'ew'i ne*   wil   'alañ   **ēn nuō ē**   qē'   duru =k
     other AOR:3SG turn.over upside.down ART turtle DEM.DIST finish 3DL =AOR
     vrig kal kēl   lē   =n   lōlō   vunu
     rush up back LOC =ART inside village

'And then the other one turned the turtle over onto its back, and after that the two ran back up into the village.'   GAQG.057–058

Regarding this particular example, it should be noted again that the position and function of the DEM.DIST form is ambiguous here. The discussion of other examples of adnominal DEM.DIST forms above would suggest that its use in (61) is not to be classified as adnominal, since the turtle had just been the theme of the preceding discourse, and it seems more plausible to interpret it as clause-final, bringing about the effect outlined here. This conclusion should, however, be taken as preliminary, and further examples are required to substantiate – or falsify – it.

4 Discussion: Attention and information

I first summarise the findings from the discussion of exophoric and endophoric uses, and then present a preliminary analysis of these. In exophoric use, DEM.SPKR forms are used where only the speaker is familiar with or aware of an entity, and attends to it. The form is used in order to draw the addressee's attention to the same entity, thereby establishing a joint attention focus. Relevant contexts exemplified above are those where only the speaker can see (or otherwise perceive) the entity; where the speaker assumes that the addressee is not familiar with an entity, for instance the story in introductions to narratives; where the speaker assumes the addressee to be unaware of the entity to be talked about, for instance the piece of wood brought to a house builder, the enacting of bodily aspects in *Deixis am Phantasma*, or the light seen at night in the bush. The last example makes it clear that spatial considerations are not the relevant ones: what counts instead is the awareness-state of the speaker, and their assumptions concerning that of the addressee. Obviously, in communication the speaker will always be aware of the entities they verbalise and elaborate upon, thus speaker-oriented forms are naturally used when the addressee is assumed to lack that awareness or knowledge (see Mosel 2004 for the same point on Samoan proximal demonstratives). The DEM.SPKR forms are, however, never used cataphorically for new referents in a narrative, and it seems possible that this kind of use is typologically very restricted (English *new-this*), as already remarked by Himmelmann (1996), a tendency corroborated by the case of Vera'a. As for locative adverbs, DEM.SPKR forms are used where the speaker perceives their location as not overlapping with that of the addressee.

The addressee-oriented forms, DEM.ADDR, are used where the speaker assumes the addressee to already be aware of and attending to an entity. With the plain forms in pronominal function within exophoric use, this concerns mostly immediately perceived sensations, like sounds. In endophoric use, these pronominal instances of DEM.ADDR forms have discourse-deictic functions, referring back to the immediately preceding discourse. In adnominal use, the forms are used where the entity in question is already being attended to by the addressee. One effect of its use is that the referent has to be understood as individuated, whereas an unmarked NP can always have class reference; and given that Vera'a does not distinguish generic from specific contexts in other parts of the grammar, for instance tense, aspect, mood-marking, this is an omnipresent potential ambiguity. In narrative texts, a DEM.ADDR form is used adnominally in NPs whose referents are identifiable from the immediately preceding discourse context. This can be seen as equivalent to established attention to an entity in exophoric contexts. Their use does not *mark* the NP as having an identifiable referent, since most other NPs with such identifiable referents are unmarked, and DEM.ADDR forms also occur with pronouns and proper names. My hypothesis is that their use is connected to considerations of information packaging (see below). Finally, DEM.ADDR forms are used in clause-combining constructions where the clause they mark is immediately relevant for the interpretation of the subsequent clause.

Distal forms are used in exophoric contexts where an entity is outside of the speaker's and the addressee's interaction space, and also not within speaker's *here-space*. This was illustrated with an example from the house building video where the speaker refers to the cross beam of the scaffold, but obviously then wants the addressee to focus their attention on the wood in his hands. In endophoric use, a DEM.DIST form is used adnominally where a referent is being re-activated, and is used clause-finally at thematic or episodic shifts.

Comparison of DEM.ADDR and DEM.DIST forms reveals that the latter are used merely to activate information, but not to focus on it, whereas the former have the effect of demanding focus of attention. This was demonstrated in example (4), repeated here as (62):

(62) ne   'ēn e   ruwa   m̄alm̄ala ē   =s   sag 'i   e   ruwa   m̄alm̄ala
     AOR:3SG see PERS HUM:DL girl   DEM.DIST =SIM sit   DEL PERS HUM:DL girl
     anē   so
     DEM.ADDR.A QUOT

'[…] and then (he) spotted those two girls (who were) sitting (there), and the two girls said: …'   1.PALA.059–060

The use of a DEM.DIST form in the first mention of 'the girls' functions to re-activate the referent who had been mentioned before, but the few intonation units immediately before this dealt exclusively with the young man's dancing. In the second clause, a DEM.ADDR form is used, and here seems to have a topicalising effect, signalling that the clause is about them. This suggests furthermore that information packaging and referent activation are two different aspects of discourse structure, as illustrated in Vallduví (1993: Chapter 2), although this is often blurred in a Givón'ian sense of 'topic' that seems to conflate notions dealt with under the headings 'discourse referent', 'discourse topic', and '(sentence) topic' in other work.

But does a DEM.ADDR form as such have a topicalising function, or even 'topic-marking' function, as is sometimes claimed for Oceanic languages? At least in Vera'a, the answer should be no. We have seen in examples above that DEM.ADDR forms are in fact found to mark pronouns that are clearly in a relation one would traditionally call 'focus', namely where the pronoun is left-dislocated and marked with the emphatic marker *sa*. As outlined above, I suggest here that DEM.ADDR forms are not 'polyfunctional' in any way, sometimes 'marking or expressing topics', and in other contexts 'marking or expressing focus'. Instead, I analyse these uses in the spirit of Matić & Wedgwood (2013), Ozerov (2014) and Ozerov (2015) as *bringing about an effect* that is compatible with both 'topic' and 'focus', as discussed in the literature (Lambrecht 1994, Krifka 2008). In this way, a topicalising effect is merely brought about by the DEM.ADDR form meaning 'addressee keep attention focused on this', which can trigger the inference that something relevant will be said about the entity in question. Likewise, keeping attention focus can have the effect of stressing someone's involvement in a state-of-affairs, as in the examples where someone is asked whether he was the one who put a tree back up.

The clause-combining uses of DEM.ADDR forms can be accounted for in a similar manner: namely, they have the effect of holding a proposition in attention focus. Given the maintained attention to the proposition, it is interpreted as immediately relevant for the proposition to follow, so that the latter is interpreted as being *about* the former. The use of DEM.DIST forms, on the other hand, has the general function of activating a referent, but not making it the attention focus. In clause-combining constructions, this bears the effect of topic and/or theme/episodic shift, together with the expectation that the previous episode may be relevant in some way at a later point in the discourse.

Therefore, the use of demonstratives in exophoric and endophoric contexts follows straightforwardly from their meaning related to attention focus, as shown in Table 5. This meaning of demonstratives can be stated as relatively slim, much in the spirit of Enfield (2003). All readings summarised above are the result of these stable meanings interpreted by interlocutors in relevant contexts.

Table 5: Meaning of demonstratives in Vera'a

speaker-oriented	you do not attend to this
addressee-oriented	I and you attend to this
distal	I do not attend to this

5 Conclusions

In conclusion, demonstratives in Vera'a bear attention-focusing meaning in the sense of Diessel (2006), and their interpretative effects result from interaction of speaker and addressee in relevant communicative contexts, much in the spirit of Enfield (2003). Spatial considerations are not primary, that is to say that orientation with regard to speech-act participants is not spatial, but communicative-interactional, relating to dimensions of knowledge and attention coordination. The interactional interpretations triggered by the different meanings of demonstratives produce different effects in different contexts, which means that we do not need to assume polysemy for demonstratives. I conclude that their meaning is absolutely stable across exophoric and endophoric uses, and sub-uses therein.

Finally, it should be noted again that more extensive examination of more video data – which has been collected in large amounts over the past ten years – is necessary to substantiate the extensional aspects of demonstratives in exophoric use, and this should be done in future research. Thus, for instance it would be interesting to see whether Vera'a speakers can use a speaker-oriented form to point to something unnoticed by the addressee on the latter's body or clothing, and the like. Possibly also the use of certain stimuli (like the MPI space games) may help clarify some usages. I do believe, however, that even these initial observations from the currently available data are sufficient to draw up the basic outline of the system as done here. Moreover, it should be noted that spatial considerations as observable in video data are not an objective heuristic to explain the use of demonstratives, as illustrated convincingly by Enfield's (2003) examination of such data in Lao. It seems that Vera'a presents another illustrative example of the salience of interactional pragmatics considerations in accounting of multi-contextual uses of demonstratives.

Acknowledgements

The research reported in this contribution was made possible through the following research grants: Australian Research Council DECRA, awarded to the author (grant no. DE120102017), and two VolkswagenStiftung's DoBeS grants (grant no. II/81 898 and II/84 316) awarded to Catriona Hyslop-Malau (PI) for the documentation of the Vurës and the Vera'a language. I also wish to acknowledge the ongoing support for my research within the ARC Centre of Excellence for the Dynamics of Language and the School of Languages and Linguistics at the University of Melbourne. I warmly thank everyone in the Vera'a community who have been so kind and generous to host me for more than ten years of our joint effort to document the Vera'a language.

I would like to thank Birgit Hellwig for her insightful comments on a very early version of this paper. Furthermore, I thank two anonymous reviewers for their comments on the submitted manuscripts, and suggestions for improvement. All remaining errors are of course my own responsibility.

Abbreviations

1	1st person	IN	inclusive
2	2nd person	INTENS	intensifier
3	3rd person	INTERJ	interjection
A	*a* prefix	LOC	locative
ABL	ablative	MAN	manner
ADDR	addressee-oriented	NEG.GEN	general negation
ADN	adnominal	NSG	non-singular
AOR	aorist	NUM	numeral article
ART	common article	OBL	oblique
ASS	associative	PERS	personal article
COR	correction	PFV	perfective
CPL	complementizer	PL	plural
CS	construct suffix	POSS.DOM	domestic possession
DAT	dative	POSS.GEN	general possession
DEL	delimitative aktionsart	POSS.HOUSE	house possession
DEM	demonstrative	PRO	pronoun
DISC	discourse marker	QUOT	quotative
DIST	distal	RED	reduplication
DL	dual	REM.PFV	remote perfective
EMPH	emphatic	SG	singular
EX	exclusive	SIM	simultaneous
FUT	future	SP	specific
GRAID	Grammatical Relations and Animacy in Discourse	SPKR	speaker-oriented
		STAT	stative
		TAM	tense-aspect-mood
HUM	human	TL	trial

References

Ariel, Mira. 1990. *Accessing noun-phrase antecedents*. London: Routledge.

Bühler, Karl. 1999[1934]. *Sprachtheorie: Die Darstellungsfunktion der Sprache*. Frankfurt: UTB.

Cutfield, Sarah. 2012. *Demonstratives in Dalabon: A language of south-western Arnhem Land*. Melbourne: Monash University (Doctoral dissertation).

Dawuda, Carmen. 2009. *Discourse functions of demonstratives and place adverbs with exophoric reference in Logea, an Oceanic language of Papua New Guinea*. Melbourne: Monash University dissertation.

Diessel, Holger. 1999. *Demonstratives: Form, function and grammaticalization*. Amsterdam & Philadelphia: John Benjamins Publishing Company.

Diessel, Holger. 2006. Demonstratives, joint attention, and the emergence of grammar. *Cognitive Linguistics* 17(4). 463–489.

Enfield, N. J. 2003. Demonstratives in space and interaction: Data from Lao speakers and implications for semantic analysis. *Language* 79(1). 82–117.

François, Alexandre. 2001. *Contraintes de structures et liberté dans l'organisation du discours*. Paris: Université Paris-IV Sorbonne (Doctoral dissertation).

François, Alexandre. 2012. The dynamics of linguistic diversity: Egalitarian multilingualism and power imbalance among northern Vanuatu languages. *Language use in Melanesia. Special issue of International Journal of the Sociology of Language* 214. 85–110.

Haig, Geoffrey & Stefan Schnell. 2014. *Annotations using GRAID: Grammatical relations and animacy in discourse: Manual version 7.0*. Köln: Universität zu Köln. https://lac.uni-koeln.de/en/multicast/.

Haig, Geoffrey & Stefan Schnell. 2016. *Multi-CAST: Multilingual Corpus of Annotated Spoken Texts*. Cologne: Language Archive Cologne. https://lac.uni-koeln.de/de/multicast/.

Halliday, M. A. K. & Ruqaiya Hasan. 1976. *Coherence in English*. London & New York: Routledge.

Himmelmann, Nikolaus P. 1996. Demonstratives in narrative discourse: A taxonomy of universal uses. In Barbara Fox (ed.), *Studies in anaphora*, 205–254. Amsterdam: John Benjamins Publishing Company.

Huang, Yan. 2000. *Anaphora: A cross-linguistic study*. Oxford: Oxford University Press.

Kalyan, Siva & Alexandre François. to appear. Freeing the comparative method from the tree model. In Ritsuko Kikusawa & Laurence Reid (eds.), *Let's talk about trees: Tackling problems in representing relationships among languages*. Osaka: National Museum of Ethnology.

Krifka, Manfred. 2008. Basic notions of information structure. *Acta Linguistica Hungarica* 55(3–4). 243–276.

Lambrecht, Knud. 1994. *Information structure and sentence form: Topic, focus and the mental representations of discourse referents*. Cambridge, UK: Cambridge University Press.

Malau, Catriona. 2016. *A grammar of Vurës*. Berlin & Boston: de Gruyter Mouton.

Margetts, Anna. 2004. Spatial deixis in Saliba. In Gunter Senft (ed.), *Deixis and demonstratives in Oceanic languages*, 37–57. Canberra ACT Australia: Pacific Linguistics.

Matić, Dejan & Daniel Wedgwood. 2013. The meaning of focus: The signifcance of an interpretation-based analysis. *Journal of Linguistics* 49(1). 127–163.

Mosel, Ulrike. 2004. Demonstratives in Samoan. In Gunter Senft (ed.), *Deixis and demonstratives in Oceanic languages*, 141–174. Canberra ACT Australia: Pacific Linguistics.

Ozerov, Pavel. 2014. *Information packaging in colloquial Burmese*. Melbourne: La Trobe University (Doctoral dissertation).

Ozerov, Pavel. 2015. Information structure without topic and focus. Differential Object Marking in Burmese. *Studies in Language* 39(2). 386–423.

Schnell, Stefan. 2016. Vera'a. In Geoffrey Haig & Stefan Schnell (eds.), *Multi–CAST: Multilingual Corpus of Annotated Spoken Texts*. Cologne: Language Archive Cologne.

Terrill, Angela. 2001. Activation levels in Lavukaleve demonstratives: Oia versus foia. *Linguistic Typology* 5. 67–90.

Vallduví, Enric. 1993. *The information component.* Philadelphia: University of Pennsylvania (Doctoral dissertation).

Wald, Benji. 1983. Referents and topic within and across discourse units: Observations from current vernacular English. In Flora Klein-Andreu (ed.), *Discourse perspectives on syntax,* 91–116. New York: Academic Press.

Chapter 4

Two definite markers in Manado Malay

Asako Shiohara
Tokyo University of Foreign Studies

Anthony Jukes
La Trobe University

> This chapter discusses referential strategies in Manado Malay (MM), a variety of trade Malay spoken in North Sulawesi, with special focus on how a lexical NP is marked according to the information status of the referent. Like some other Malay varieties, MM uses two strategies to indicate definiteness: articles and the third person singular possessive. The articles are derived from demonstratives and used for direct situational and anaphoric reference, while the possessive is used for reference in which some kind of association is required for identification. An article and a possessive may co-occur in one NP. The semantic domain each form covers is not exclusive to the other but rather belongs to intrinsically different semantic dimensions. Thus, the MM system enables speakers to mark that the referent is textual-situationally accessible and, at the same time, associable to the larger shared situation.

1 Introduction

This paper discusses referential strategies employed in lexical NPs in Manado Malay (hereafter MM). There, forms functionally similar to what is called the "definite marker" in other languages are grammaticalizing from two distinct sources: one is from the third person singular possessive marker *depe* and the other is from the demonstratives.

MM is a variety of trade Malay spoken in Indonesia by upwards of 2 million people in North Sulawesi, the Sangir and Talaud archipelagos to the north, and Gorontalo to the west. It seems to have developed from North Moluccan Malay, but it has developed independently since the 17th century (Paauw 2008: 43–44). Until relatively recently, first language speakers were mainly found in the city of Manado, while elsewhere MM was used as a second language by speakers of the indigenous Minahasan and Sangiric languages. In recent decades MM has become the first language of virtually the entire population of the region. Although most of the Minahasan and Sangiric languages are still

Asako Shiohara & Anthony Jukes. 2018. Two definite markers in Manado Malay. In Sonja Riesberg, Asako Shiohara & Atsuko Utsumi (eds.), *Perspectives on information structure in Austronesian languages*, 115–135. Berlin: Language Science Press. DOI:10.5281/zenodo.1402541

spoken, even elderly people grew up with MM and it could be considered a "joint" first language, while for many people of all ages, it is their first or even their only language.

The notion of monolingual MM speakers requires some clarification. The education system, media, and government administration largely use standard Bahasa Indonesia (BI), and so everyone is exposed to this variety and code switching and mixing are pervasive. Some speakers are clear about the significant grammatical and lexical differences between BI and MM, and they call MM "Melayu Manado" or "Bahasa Manado", recognizing that it is not the same as BI. Others do not have this meta-awareness and believe that the language that they speak is BI. As noted by Paauw, "Manado Malay and Indonesian (and, in particular, colloquial Indonesian) have been converging to the point that speakers of Manado Malay, to varying extents and often subconsciously, employ Indonesian vocabulary and constructions when using Manado Malay, and it is often difficult to draw a line between the two languages" (Paauw 2008: 44).

The data sources of this study are (i) translation/elicitation from standard Indonesian sentences, (ii) semi-spontaneous monologue that was obtained using a procedural video as stimulus, and (iii) an unpublished MM-BI dictionary compiled by the Pusat Penerjemahan Bahasa (PPB, Translation Centre) in Tomohon. The last item was particularly useful and the authors would like to thank Albert Polii for making it available to us.

The structure of this chapter is as follows: §2 provides a brief overview of the NP structure of MM. In §3, we will examine the semantic function of the two definite marking devices, that is, articles and the third person possessive *depe* based on elicited and published data, and provide a brief comparison to the other Malay varieties. In §4, we will see larger texts elicited using a procedural video and confirm the usage of the two devices discussed in §3. In §5, we look at the MM definite marking strategy from a cross-linguistic perspective.

2 NP structure in MM

Before discussing the referential strategy of MM, we will show the NP structure in MM, largely based on Prentice (1994: 424–429). (1) is the structure that Prentice suggests. Note that Prentice calls the demonstrative "deictic".

(1) (article) (POSSESSOR+*pe*) N$_{head}$ (attributive N/V)[1]

Two articles *tu* and *ni*, "both translatable by *the*" (Prentice 1994: 424), are derived from the distal demonstrative *itu* and proximal demonstrative *ini*, respectively. "The articles both mark the referent of the following noun as being known to both speaker and addressee, while *ni* has the added function of indicating geographical temporal and/or psychological proximity to the speaker" (Prentice 1994: 424). Examples (2a–b) are examples from Prentice (1994: 424).

---

[1]Quantifiers may precede or follow the head noun according to its pragmatic status, which we will not go into further in this research.

(2)   a. *tu   anging*
          ART wind
          'the wind (e.g. which blew down my coconut palms.)'
      b. *ni   anging*
          ART wind
          'the wind (e.g. which is blowing now.)'

Prentice suggests that the demonstratives may either precede the head-noun alone or follow the combination of article + noun, as shown in Example (3a–d).

(3)   'that island' or 'those islands'/ 'this island' or 'these islands'
      a. *itu pulo*
          that island
      b. *ini pulo*
          this island
      c. *tu   pulo itu*
          ART island that
      d. *ni   pulo ini*
          ART island this

We assume that Prentice's data was collected in the 1980s and 1990s. More recent MM data shows that the pre-predicate slot is more frequently, though not exclusively, filled by the article. Thus, phrases like (2a–b) or (3c–d) are more common than ones like (3a–b).

In more recent MM data, the form *tu* may co-occur with either the demonstrative *itu* or *ini*, as seen in *tu ruma itu* in example (4) and *tu parkara ini* 'this problem' in example (5).

(4)   *Tu   ruma itu ancor   lantaran da kena   bom waktu prang.*
      ART.D house that broken because PST affected bomb time war
      'That house is broken because it was bombed in the war.'   (PPB:2)

(5)   *Tu   parkara ini so   lama nyanda klar-klar.*
      ART.D issue   DEM.P PFV long NEG   solved
      'This issue has not been solved (lit. finished) for a long time.' (PPB:62)

Example (4) and (5) suggest that the form *tu* has undergone semantic bleaching, as it is neutral regarding the distance to the reference point.

The occurrence of the determiners *tu* and *ni* exhibits a syntactic restriction in that they only occur with S, A, and P but not with an oblique. Consider examples (6) and (7) below, which Prentice (1994: 430) provides to show word order variation in the MM transitive clause. Examples (6) and (7) both denote almost the same proposition in which "I" is the actor, the basket is the location, and the rice is the theme; and the non-agent NP occurs with the determiner *tu* only when it is P.

(6) *Kita so isi tu   loto   deng padi.*
    1SG PFV fill ART.D basket with rice
    'I have already filled the basket with rice.'

(7) *Kita so isi tu   padi di loto.*
    1SG PFV fill ART.D rice at basket
    'I have already filled the rice with a basket.'

In possessive structures, the possessor noun or pronoun precedes the head (the possessed item) being followed by the possessive marker *pe*, the short form of *punya* 'have' in standard Malay. Table 1 contains the paradigm of possessives with personal pronouns and a lexical noun.

Table 1: Possessives

1SG	*kita / ta pe*	*kita pe anak* 'my child'
1PL	*torang / tong pe*	*torang pe anak* 'our child'
2SG	*ngana pe*	*ngana pe anak* 'your (SG.) child'
2PL	*ngoni pe*	*ngoni pe anak* 'your (PL.) child'
3SG[2]	*dia pe / depe*	*depe anak* 'his/ her/ its child'
3PL	*dorang / dong pe*	*dorang pe anak* 'their child'
lexical noun	NOUN *pe kamar*	*anak pe kamar* 'a child's room'

Among the forms presented in Table 1, the long form of the first-person possessive (*kita pe*) and the short form of the third person (*depe*) are not shown in Prentice (1994: 424). However these forms, especially *depe*, are much more frequently observed in current MM than their alternatives.

In MM, the possessor is obligatorily marked when the referent of the matrix NP is possessed by, or has a part-whole relation to, a referent whose identity is clear from the previous utterance – thus, in sentences (8) and (9), the possessive obligatorily occurs.

(8) *Tu   anak pe gaga.   depe   mata basar deng depe   mulu kacili.*
    ART.D child POSS beautiful 3SG.POSS eyes big   and 3SG.POSS mouth small
    'How beautiful the child is. Her eyes are big, and her eyes are big, and her mouth is small.' (elicited)

(9) *Sayang ini   pohon, depe   ujung so   potong.*
    pity   DEM.P tree   3SG.POSS tip PFV cut
    '(This) poor tree, the (its) top has been chopped off.' (elicited)

---

[2] The third person pronouns *dia* (SG) and *dorang* (PL) may refer to both animate and inanimate referents, and so may the possessives, as seen in sentence (8) and (9) among others.

4 Two definite markers in Manado Malay

The article and possessive may co-occur in pre-head noun position, as seen in examples (10) and (11), suggesting they are assigned to separate syntactic positions.[3]

(10) Serta tu   depe   ubi milu deng sambiki so   mandidi.
     after ART.D 3SG.POSS potato corn and pumpkin PFV   boil
     'after the potato, corn and pumpkin are boiled.' (elicited narrative, speaker D: 45)

(11) Dia no tu   / ni   kita pe   papa.
     3SG PTC ART.D / ART.P 1SG POSS father
     He is my father. (lit. the my father)   (PPB dictionary:89)

This co-occurrence also suggests that they each have semantic functions independent of each other. We will return to this point in §4.

As will be seen in the section that follows, the use of *depe* partially overlaps with that of English definite article *the*, but not all *depe*-marked NPs refer to a so-called definite referent.

In example (12), neither the possessor *ayang* 'chicken' or *de* '3SG' in the possessive is referential, but used attributively.[4]

(12) Kita suka **ayang** pe   kaki, mar nyanda suka **depe**   dada.
     1SG like chicken POSS leg   but NEG   like 3SG.POSS breast
     'I like chicken leg meat, but not chicken breast meat.'   (elicited)

The development of the articles and possessives that we have seen in this section have been observed in other varieties of Malay, to a lesser or greater extent. We will give a brief comparison in §3. The variation of the position of the demonstratives and the long and short forms of the third person possessives mentioned above illustrate the transitional status of the two strategies.

3 Semantic functions of the articles and the possessive construction

As mentioned in the introduction, MM has developed two types of definite markers, the sources of which are the demonstratives and possessives. Their compatibility in one NP (e.g. *tu depe ruma* 'the house of him/her/it) implies that each device has a function

---

[3]As for the status of possessives, Lyons (1999: 130–134) proposed a typological distinction of DG language and AG language; in the former, the possessive is assigned to the determiner position and, in the latter, to the adjectival or some other position. The compatibility of the article and possessive, seen in sentences (10) and (11), suggests that MM belongs to the latter (AG) type.

[4]Note that the antecedent of *depe* in example (12) is the expression *ayang* 'chicken', not the referent of the expression *ayang* 'chicken'. (See Krifka & Musan 2012: 23 on the distinction of expression givenness and denotation givenness.) This type of anaphorical usage is not observed in the third person possessive pronoun in many other languages, such as English *its* or *nya* in standard Indonesian. Thus, the sentence '*I like chicken leg meat, but not its breast meat' cannot be accepted as the English counterpart of example (12).

119

independent of each other. In this section, we will examine the semantic function of each strategy, mainly based on MM sentences obtained as translations of target sentences from standard Indonesian and utterances observed in every day conversation.

Hawkins (2015: Chapter 3) makes a distinction between four major usage types of the definite article *the*: anaphoric, immediate situational, larger situational, and associative anaphoric uses.

The MM articles *ni* and *tu* are used in cases similar to the first two types, that is, anaphoric use and immediate situational use. In sentence (13), the two forms are used for making reference to the entity in the speech situation, in sentence (14), one of the two forms *tu* is used for making reference to the entity or situation mentioned in the previous discourse.[5]

(13) *Bole pinjam tu / ni pulpen?*
 may borrow ART.D / ART.P ballpoint.pen
 'May I borrow that ballpoint pen?' (elicited)

(14) *Ada parampuang gaga deng dua anak da masuk ke satu ruangan. kita*
 exist woman beautiful and two child PST enter to one room 1SG
 langsung tahu sapa tu parampuan itu.
 directly know who ART.D woman DEM.D
 'An elegant lady and two children came in the room. I immediately knew who the woman was.'

These two uses correspond with what Lyons (1999: 166, 198) calls "textual-situational ostension". According to Lyons, "what these have in common is that the referent is immediately accessible." Lyons suggested that a primary distinction of definiteness should be made between textual-situational ostension and other usages. The former functionally overlaps with demonstrativeness, and the others do not. A similar view is presented in many previous studies, such as Hawkins (2015: Chapter 3), Himmelmann (1996), and De Mulder & Carlier (2011: 528).

Demonstratives are a well-known source of definite markers in many languages, as suggested by Heine & Kuteva (2002) and Lyons (1999) among others. De Mulder & Carlier (2011: 528) suggest that the crucial semantic shift from demonstratives to the definite article is seen from *direct reference* that corresponds to the direct situational use and anaphoric use of Hawkins, to *indirect reference*, which corresponds to anaphoric associative use and larger situational use.

Notwithstanding the distinct syntactic position in NP from the demonstratives, the uses of the articles in MM have not undergone a semantic shift and have not extended

---

[5] (14) is a sentence obtained as a rough translation of sentence (i) below; an example of anaphoric use of the English definite article is given in Lyons (1999: 3).

(i) An elegant, dark-haired woman, a well-dressed man with dark glasses, and two children entered the compartment. I immediately recognized the woman....

beyond direct reference. Instead, indirect uses are covered by the third person possessive *depe* '3SG.POSS' in MM. In the anaphoric associative use of *the*, the NP refers to something associable to the referent of a previously mentioned NP, while in the larger situational use, the NP refers to something associable to the situation of the utterance itself. In both uses, the hearer is supposed to use shared general knowledge for identification; the hearer and the speaker need to know the referent is associable to the antecedent or the utterance situation in question.

Sentences (15–16) are examples of anaphoric associative uses.[6]

(15) *Kita lebe suka Australia daripada Jepang karna depe sayur-sayur lebe*
1SG more like Australia from Japan because 3SG.POSS vegetable.RED more
sadap deng murah.
tasty and cheap

'I like Australia more than Japan, because vegetables there are tastier and cheaper.' (elicited)

(16) *Kita baru pulang dari pesta kaweng. Depe broid ta pe tamang.*
1SG just come.back from party wedding. 3SG.POSS bride 1SG POSS friend

'I have just come back from a wedding party. The bride was a friend of mine.' (elicited)

Employment of the third person possessive *depe* for this use can be easily explained by its original meaning; the possessive *depe* includes *de*, the shortened form of the third person pronoun *dia* '3SG'. The pronoun *dia* may be used as an anaphor, and in the possessive, it indicates the presence of a whole to part relation between the referent of the pronoun and the matrix NP.

From sentences (15) and (16) above, we can see that the semantic relation between the possessor and the head noun is not limited to the simple whole to part relation that is exemplified in sentence (8) and (9) shown in §2. There may be various relations, such as location, as seen in example (15), and occasion, as in example (16).

However, the semantic range the possessive covers does not seem to perfectly overlap with that of anaphoric associative *the*. Consider example (17), which Lyons (1999: 3) gives as one of the examples of associative use of the English definite article.

(17) I had to get a taxi from the station. On the way, **the driver** told me there was a bus strike.

In sentence (18), a rough MM equivalent of sentence (17), the counterpart of the English definite NP does not receive any explicit marking, as seen in sentence (18).

---

[6]Example (16) is obtained as a rough MM equivalent of sentence (ii) below; an example of associative anaphoric use of English *the* given in Lyons (1999: 3).(ii) 'I have just come back from a wedding party. The bride wore blue.'

(18) Ni   hari kita da   nae taksi dari stasion. Di tenga jalang (*depe   / *tu)
     ART.P day 1SG PFT ride taxi from station at middle way   3SG.POSS ART.D
     sopir se   *tau*   *tadi*   *ada cilaka   brat.*
     driver CAUS know before exist accident heavy

   'I had to get a taxi from the station. On the way **the driver** told me there was a
   serious accident.'   (elicited)

In this situation, we can reasonably associate the referent of *sopir* 'the driver' to *taksi* 'a taxi', and that is the reason the NP undergoes the definite marking in English sentence (17), but that is not the case in MM. The reason may be that the semantic relation between *sopir* 'the driver' and the associated *taksi* 'a taxi' cannot be taken as a possessor-possessed, or whole to part relation, to the MM speakers; one of the MM speakers suggested that he could not use the possessive *depe* here because the driver possessed the taxi, not the reverse. This example may show the difference between the English definite article in associative use and MM possessives; the former may indicate any type of association, while the latter exhibits some limitations which presumably are attributed to the original possessive meaning. At the present stage of our research, however, we do not have enough data to provide the precise condition where the possessive may or may not occur.[7]

The use of *depe* in example (19) and (20) overlaps with the "larger situational use" of *the* in Hawkins's classification, where the referent of the *depe* NP is associable to the utterance situation. Note that there is no clear antecedent of the possessive in these examples.

In sentence (19), the NP *depe cuaca* refers to the weather of the place the speaker and hearer are located in.

(19) *Depe   cuaca   bae.*
     3SG.POSS weather good
     'The weather is nice (today).' (spontaneous utterance obtained from daily
     conversation)

The sentences in (20) are from a Facebook post. Example (20a) is the original Facebook post made with a picture of yams, and (20b) and (20c) are comments posted by two friends of the poster. In both comments, *ubi* 'yam' mentioned in the original post is marked by *tu* and *depe*, and the antecedent of *depe* is not explicitly mentioned.

(20) a. *Slamat pagi,   panen ubi jalar   serta menanam ulang.*
        good.morning harvest yam spread after plant   again
        'Good morning, harvesting yams and then planting them again.'

---

[7] We might be able to infer that if the 'possessed' NP is animate and the 'possessor' NP is inanimate, the marking with *depe* may not be permitted, as it contradicts the concept of possession we intuitively would have.

b. *Mantaap Beng pe besar-besar kang tu **depe ubi**?*[8]
   great Beng very big.RED ITR ART.D 3SG.POSS yam

   'Great Beng the (lit. the its) potatoes are very big, aren't they?'

c. *Banyak tu **depe batata** ada panen.*
   many ART.D 3SG.POSS sweet.potato PST harvest

   'Lots of the (lit. the its) sweet potatoes were harvested.'

The lack of a clear antecedent[9] in sentences (19) and (20) shows that the form *depe* does not function as the possessive marker. Instead, we can claim that the form *depe* plays a similar semantic role to the larger situational use of *the*, whichever label we give to it in MM grammar. In this use, the referent is identified by two processes: one is identifying the nature of the "shared" larger situation intended by the speaker, and the other is identifying the referent using the "shared" knowledge that presupposes the existence of the referent in the situation (Hawkins 2015).

A similar type of development from the possessive to the definite marker is observed in other languages that are not genetically related, such as Amharic (Rubin 2010) and Yucatec Maya (Lehmann 1998: 86–88), as well as colloquial Indonesian, as mentioned in §3. This development can be explained by an affinity between the association and indication of the part-whole relation. Hawkins (2015: 123–124), in discussing the similarity of associative anaphoric and larger situational use, claims that "(T)he notion 'part-of' seems to play an important role in defining the number of possible associates. The trigger (of the association) must conjure up a set of objects which are generally known to be part of some larger object or situation." (For a more recent and precise discussion of the development from possessive to definite marker, see Fraund 2001; Gerland 2014; 2015).

---

[8]The commentator uses the spelling of *bsr2* and *dp* for *besar-besar* and *depe*, respectively, in her original post.

[9]We asked the commenter to identify the antecedent of *depe* in sentence (20)c several times, but her answers were not consistent. Her response may show that the referent of the antecedent is not a concrete entity that can be clearly mentioned. We might be able to insist that the third person pronoun *de* refers to the implied "shared situation", but the claim may not be accepted, because the third person pronoun *dia*, from the long form of *de* in *depe*, may not refer to the situation or proposition. Consider the three pairs of sentence (i). A situation or proposition can be referred to only by the demonstrative *begitu*, not by the third person pronoun *dia*.

(i) a. *Albert so nya mo pusing deng orang laeng pe emosi. So bagitu Albert pe kalakuan.*
      Albert PFV NEG want bothered with person other POSS emotion PFV like.that Albert POSS behavior

      'Albert doesn't want to be bothered with other people's feelings. The character of Albert is like that.' (elicited)

   b. *Albert so nya mo pusing deng orang laeng pe emosi. *Dia Albert pe kalakuan.*
      Albert PFV NEG want bothered with person other POSS emotion 3SG Alert POSS behavior

      '(Intended meaning) Albert doesn't want to be bothered with other people's feelings. That's the character of Albert.'

Other varieties of Malay exhibit similar developments to a greater or lesser extent. Adelaar & Prentice (1996: 675) suggest that the use of the short form of the demonstratives *ni* and *tu* as well as forms such as *pu* or *pun* (derived from *punya* 'have' as possessive marker) are among several morphosyntactic features shared among trade Malay varieties, which Adelaar & Prentice (1996: 675) call Pidgin-Derived Malay (PDM) varieties. Regarding the development of demonstratives into the definite markers, Adelaar (2005: 212–217) points out the anaphoric use of the short forms of demonstratives *tu* and *ni* in Ambon Malay and Cocos Malay; they also underwent semantic bleaching similar to that of MM. Similar types of development are reported in both Papuan Malay (Kluge 2017: 384–388) and Ternate Malay (Litamahuputty 2012: 263, 277).

The development of the possessive into a definite marker is also observed in colloquial Indonesian, in which the third person possessive enclitic =*nya* is used to indicate identifiability, exhibiting functions similar to MM *depe* in associative anaphoric use and larger situational use (Englebretson 2003: 161–168). A rather different distribution was observed in Baba Malay, spoken in Malaka and Singapore by "Strait-born" Chinese. In Baba Malay, the articles *ini* and *itu* cover larger semantic domains, including associative anaphoric use and larger situational use (Thurgood 2001: 477–480), although the third person possessive suffix -*nya* also has similar functions to the articles (Thurgood 1998: 132–135).

4 Determiners and possessives in elicited procedural text

4.1 Method

In this section, we will see larger texts elicited by a short cooking video as stimulus to confirm the syntactic and semantic functions of the two strategies outlined in the previous sections. The advantage of employing this method for elicitation is that (i) this type of non-linguistic stimulus enables us to collect more naturalistic data without the influence of a medium language, and (ii) the reference tends to be clear in the text obtained through this method when compared to purely spontaneous utterance in which the referent of each NP may not always be easily identified (see Majid 2012 for details of elicitation methods using stimulus materials.)

The video employed as stimulus here is titled *Tinutuan* 'Manadonese porridge'. The video was shot by one of the authors and is available from https://youtu.be/cyJanYZjXoo. We asked four speakers of MM (H, I, D and A) to watch the video and give a commentary in MM. In the video, the main dish *tinutuan* 'Manadonese porridge' and the side dishes *tahu goreng* 'fried tofu' and *dabu-dabu* 'chili sauce' are cooked. The outline of the cooking process is shown in Table 3.

4 Two definite markers in Manado Malay

Figure 1: *Tinutuan* 'Manadonese porridge', *tahu goreng* 'fried tofu' and *dabu-dabu* 'chili sauce'.

Table 2: MM speakers who provided the narrative

Name	Age	From	Mother tongue
H	65	Beo, Talaud	Talaud
I	36	Beo, Talaud	Manado Malay
D	34	Sonder, Minahasa	Manado Malay
A	55	Tomohon, Minahasa	Tombulu

Table 3: Outline of the cooking process

Scene 1:	showing ingredients
Scene 2:	cut and peel hard vegetables such as yam and pumpkin
Scene 3:	put the vegetables and rice into a pan and heat them
Scene 4:	cut and wash the leafy vegetables
Scene 5:	mash the pumpkin in the pan, put the leafy vegetables in the pan and mix all the ingredients
Scene 6:	prepare the side dish *tahu goreng* (fried tofu)
Scene 7:	prepare *dabu-dabu* (chili sauce)
Scene 8:	serve the dish

125

4.2 Results
4.2.1 Referent and general referential strategies observed

There are 45 entities mentioned in the narrations of the four speakers; the range of entities that each speaker mentioned varies depending on the speaker, and the term for the same entity may vary among speakers, too. The referents can be grouped into the semantic categories below.

- The speaker (1 type): *Isye*

- The name of dishes (3 types): *tinutuan* 'porridge', *tahu goreng* 'fried tahu', and *dabu-dabu* or *laburan* 'chili sauce'

- Ingredients (1 type): *bahan-bahan* 'ingredients'

- Base ingredients, i.e. root vegetables and rice (6 types): *ubi* 'potato', *batata* or *ubi manis* 'sweet potato', *ubi kayu* 'cassava', *sambiki* 'pumpkin', *milu* 'corn', *beras merah*, *beras* 'rice', *aer* 'water'

- Leafy vegetables (6 types): *sayor* 'leafy vegetables', *bayam* 'amaranth vegetable', *kangkung* 'water spinach', *gedi* 'aibika leaf', *kukuru, balakama* 'basil', *sarimbata, baramakusu, goramakusu* 'lemongrass'

- Ingredients for side dishes (8 types): *tahu* 'soybean curd, tofu', *bawang merah* 'shallot', *bawang putih* 'garlic', *garam* 'salt', *tomat* 'tomato', *rica* 'chili', *ikan roa* 'dried fish', *minyak kelapa* 'coconut oil'

- An attribute or a part of ingredients (4 types): *kuli* 'skin', *daong* 'leaf', *isi* 'contents, edible part of vegetable', *warna (kuning)* '(yellow) color'

- Cooking tools and so on (6 types): *blanga/panci* 'pan', *kompor* 'stove', *mangko* 'bowl', *pantumbu* 'pestle', *cobe-cobekan* 'mortar', *piso* 'knife'

- Body parts of the cook (2 types): *tangan* 'hand', *jare* 'finger'

- Others (8 types): *cacing* 'worm', *vitamin* 'vitamin', *kelihatan* 'appearance', *nama* 'name', *priksaan* 'test', *hasil* 'result, *pedis* 'spicy (n)', *orang* 'person'

The text length and number and varieties of the referents mentioned vary among the speakers. Table 4 shows the number of words and referents included in each narrative. Each referent can be expressed by either a personal pronoun, a demonstrative pronoun, or a lexical NP. Table 5 counts the occurrences of each strategy.

It should be noted that the argument of the predicate is not expressed when it is salient in discourse; category zero counts such arguments.

The actor (the cook) is not mentioned at all in three of the four narratives and is mentioned only once (by the third person singular pronoun *dia*) in the remaining narrative. Other non-agent arguments are also often not expressed; a series of cooking processes

4 Two definite markers in Manado Malay

Table 4: The number of words and referents included in each narrative

Speaker	Words included	Types of referent mentioned
I	444	41
H	525	38
D	336	27
A	478	32

Table 5: Occurrence of each strategy

Speaker	Zero	Personal pronoun	Demonstrative pronoun	Lexical NP
I	131	8	18	105
H	111	5	12	95
D	112	1	4	78
A	117	6	8	89

is expressed by a co-ordinate clause, and the entity mentioned in the first clause is not expressed in the clauses that follow it. Consider sentence (21), which consists of coordinate clauses expressing a series of actions processing garlic. Here, the actor does not occur throughout the sentence, and the patient, *bawang putih* 'garlic' occurs only once in the first clause, but not in the three clauses that follow.

(21) Aa kase ancor bawang <me->[10] bawang putih so kase ancor ϕ lagi iris-iris ϕ
      ITJ CAUS crush onion   <re->   onion white PFV CAUS crush again slice
      lagi hh campur ϕ di tahu.
      again ITJ mix   at tofu

  'Aa...(she) crushes the onion...the garlic, after crushing, (she) will slice (it) and mix (it) with tofu.' (speaker H 37–38)

In what follows, we focus on how lexical NPs are marked with the articles and/or the possessive. A lexical NP may occur (i) in unmarked form, that is, a bare NP, (ii) with the article *tu* or *ni*, (iii) with possessives *depe* or *dia pe*, (iv) with both the article *tu* and the possessive, (v) with a postposed demonstrative, or (vi) with =*nya*, the third person singular possessive enclitic used in standard Indonesian.

Most of the possessives are that of the third person singular *depe* in the text; the text includes only one example of the lexical noun possessor, *sambiki le pe kuli* [pumpkin also POSS skin] 'pumpkin's skin'.

Table 6 shows the occurrence of the article and the possessive construction.

---

[10]In this utterance, the speaker started to say *bawang merah* 'shallot', and then corrected herself saying *bawang putih* 'garlic'.

Table 6: Occurrence of the determiner and the possessive construction

	Sum of the lexical NPs	Unmarked	ART (tu/ni)	POSS + POSS	tu Pre-posed	DEM Post-posed	=nya	Others
I	105	62	32 (31/1)	8	2	0	0	0	0
H	95	45	3 (1/2)	41	0	0	2[a]	3	1
D	79	47	19 (14/2)	9	2	3	1	0	1
A	88	77	6 (6/0)	3	0	0	1	0	1

[a](ni+ini)

As observed in §2, in current MM the pre-head noun position is much more frequently filled by the article than by a demonstrative. This data confirm the observation; we can see only 3 instances of pre-head noun demonstratives compared to 65 instances of articles. We also mentioned the variation in form of the third person singular possessive. The short form *depe* occurs much more frequently (66 examples) than the long form *dia pe* (3 examples).

The individual narratives exhibit considerable variation in the frequency with which each speaker uses the two strategies – the determiner and the possessive. For example, speaker I prefers to use the article, while speaker H prefers the possessive *depe*. Speaker D uses both in similar frequencies, while speaker A rarely uses either of the markers.

Notwithstanding the difference in preference in using each device, the use in the text maintains the basic semantic function of the determiners and the possessive, which we have shown in §3; the articles mark a textual-situationally given referent, while the possessive *depe* or *dia pe* marks a referent associable to a given referent or utterance situation.

Table 7 shows the distribution of NPs with an article and the possessive *depe* in a textually accessible environment.

Table 7: The distribution of the articles and possessive *depe*

	Articles	Possessive *depe*
Total	59	61
Not textually accessible	3	30
Textually accessible	56	31

Because of the nature of the text, most of the referents are visible to both the speaker and addressee.[11] That makes it difficult to verify how direct situational accessibility affects both devices. The fact that a considerable number of NPs were not marked by either of the devices, however, suggests that situational accessibility is not a crucial factor for either of the markings.

---

[11]The addressee in any given narrative is whichever of the authors was present at the time of recording.

Regarding textual-accessibility, we can see a clear difference of frequency between the articles and possessives. In the 59 occurrences of the NP marked with articles in total, 56 refer to a textually accessible – in other words, previously mentioned, entity.

In contrast to the articles, as expected by the observation of §3, textual-accessibility does not influence the use of the possessive *depe*.

In the following sections, we will see the details of how each strategy works in the text.

4.2.2 Textually accessible use of the article

As mentioned above, in almost all the occurrences the NPs marked with an article refer to a textually accessible referent. The frequency of *tu* is far higher than that of *ni*, as seen in Table 6, which supports Prentice's view that *ni* is semantically marked (see §3). From the text obtained by the experiment, though, we could not clearly see the functional difference between the two articles.

As mentioned in §2, the determiner *tu* occurs with core arguments (S, A, and P). However, not all textually given S and P referents are marked by the determiner. Table 8 shows the frequency of use of the determiner for textually given S and P referents.[12]

Table 8: The frequency of the form *tu* and *depe* marking for a given S and P referent

Speaker	Textually accessible ASP	Marked by ART
I	55	38 (69%)
H	30	3 (10%)
D	35	21 (60%)
A	35	6 (20%)

The preference varies among the speakers. Speaker I and D more frequently used *tu* than the other two speakers. They are younger than the other speakers, and so this may represent a change in progress.

4.2.3 The use of the possessive pronoun

As shown in §2 and §3, the possessive covers anaphoric associative use as a part of its possessive meaning and also covers the larger situational use of Hawkins (2015) as a result of semantic change.

The obligatory marking of the possessor mentioned in §2 is attested by the narratives. Sentence (22) is a typical example.

---

[12] No given A occurs in the four texts.

(22) Serta so ta-kaluar depe   kuli, mo kupas lei   tu   sambiki.
      after PFV PASS-peel 3SG.POSS skin FUT peel again ART.D pumpkin
      'After all the peel has been removed, (then she) will peel the pumpkin, too.' (H 13)

The form *depe* in (22) retains its possessive meaning and indicates that the referent of the whole NP is associable to the referent of previously mentioned NP. In actual sentences, the associative use and larger situation use cannot always be separated clearly.

Consider sentence (23). This is the first sentence in scene 6 (preparation of a tofu dish), and the antecedent of *depe* in the NP *depe tahu* 'the tofu', is not clear, or is at least unavailable in clauses that directly precede sentence (23).

(23) Skarang mo bekeng **depe**   tahu. tahu taro di panci.
      now   FUT do   3SG.POSS tofu tofu put at pan
      'Now (we) want to make the tofu. Put the tofu in the pan.'   (I 052)

Sentence (24) provides a similar example. This is the first sentence in scene 7 (preparation of chili sauce), and the antecedent of *depe* in the NP *depe laburan* 'the sauce', is not clear, or at least is unavailable in the clauses that directly precede it.

(24) Itu mo bekeng depe   laburan.
      that FUT make 3SG.POSS sauce
      'There (she) is going to cook the (its) sauce'.   (D 80)

According to the speaker, in both cases, the possessor is the main topic of the whole text: *tinutuan* 'Manado porridge', fried tofu and chili sauce always come together with the porridge as a side dish and can be considered a part of the dish.

The dish *tinutuan* does have prior mention and we could therefore say that sentences (23) and (24) are examples of anaphoric associative use. But the prior mention of *tinutuan* is made in the very beginning of the whole narrative — far from sentences (23) and (24) (51 and 78 clauses away from each *depe* NP, respectively). It is therefore difficult to consider the NP *tinutuan* to be antecedent of the possessive *depe*. It may be more plausible to think that the referent of *depe* NP is associable with the larger situation in which the utterance was made, that is, watching, and talking about, the cooking process of *tinutuan*.

Table 9 shows the frequency with which each speaker uses *depe*; each use is classified into those that have an antecedent available in directly preceding clauses – in other words, associative anaphoric use and larger situational use.
Differences among speakers are observed in their use of larger situational *depe*.

As seen in Table 9, one of the four speakers (Speaker H) showed a marked preference for wider topic *depe*, while Speaker I did that to a lesser extent. Speaker H's distinct use of *depe* is clearly seen in the beginning of his narrative, where he introduces ingredients immediately after the title *tinutuan* 'Manado Porridge' is shown. Sentence (25) shows that part; here, speaker H marked the NP expressing ingredients with *depe* '3SG.POSS'.

4 Two definite markers in Manado Malay

Table 9: Frequency of the form *depe*

	Lexical NP	Possessive		
		Sum	Associative anaphoric use	Larger situational use
I	105	10	6	4
H	96	43	13	30
D	78	12	3	9
A	89	5	4	1

(25) a. *Mo bekeng masakan nama-nya tinutuan.*
   want make food name-3SG.POSS(BI) tinutuan
   '(She) wants to cook food named tinutuan.' (Speaker H: 01)

   b. *Ado e pe sadap skali ini, aah ini batata, depe batata,*
   ITJ ITJ ITJ delicious very this ITJ this sweet.potato, 3SG.POSS sweet.potato,
   depe ubi.
   3SG.POSS yam
   'Oh, it is very delicious, this is sweet potato, the sweet potato, the yam.'

Unlike H, the other three speakers introduce the ingredients without any marking. In sentence (26), speaker I describes the same scene.

(26) *Bahan-bahan, bete, ubi kayu sambiki milu...*
   ingredients taro sweet.potato pumpkin corn
   'Ingredients...taro, sweet potato, pumpkin, and corn...' (Speaker I: 02)

Differences among speakers are also seen in the description that follows (25) and (26), respectively, which explains the cooking procedure. Sentence (27) is a description that follows sentence (25). Speaker H keeps employing *depe* for referring to the ingredients given in the previous part of his utterance; here, one of the ingredients *batata* 'sweet potato' is marked with *depe*.

(27) *Aah sekarang **depe** batata mo di-kupas kase kaluar depe kuli.*
   ITJ now 3SG.POSS sweet.potato FUT PASS-peel give go.out 3SG.POSS skin
   'Ah, now (she) is going to peel the potato, peel off the skin.' (Speaker H: 11)

In contrast to that, speaker I employs *tu* to mark all the ingredients that were given in the preceding part of the utterance. Sentence (28) is a part of the description that follows sentence (26).

(28) *Pertama kase bersi tu bete, kupas depe kuli.*
   first CAUS clean ART.D taro peel 3SG.POSS skin
   'First, clean the taro, and peel its skin.' (Speaker I: 18)

It should be noted that all the speakers use both strategies to a greater or lesser extent. Speaker H, who very frequently uses *depe*, also uses *tu* twice to mark a textually accessible referent, as in sentence (22), while speaker I, who uses *tu* for most of the textually given referents, also employs larger situational *depe*, as seen in sentence (23) above.

The variation observed in the frequency of each device among speakers, therefore, is not caused by differences in the referential system each of them employs, but by which strategy they prefer to code an anaphoric relation of a referent in the discourse and discourse situation. Speaker I prefers to code a relation of a referent in the previous discourse and therefore uses anaphoric articles more frequently, while speaker H prefers to relate a referent to a shared situation told by the whole discourse and therefore uses the possessive more frequently.

As mentioned in §2, the article and possessive may co-occur in one NP. The elicited text includes three examples of such a co-occurrence. Example (29) below and example (10) above from the elicited text and (20)b and (20)c above, which are spontaneous utterances, show this compatibility. In sentence (29), the article *tu* indicates a textual-situational accessibility and the possessive *depe* indicates that the referent can be associated with the shared larger situation.

(29) Kase ancor **tu**   **depe**   sambiki supaya dapa lia   warna kuning.
      cause smash ART.D   3SG.POSS   pumpkin so.that get   see   color yellow
      '(We) smashed the pumpkin, so that we could see the yellow color.'   (I 42)

This suggests that the semantic domain each device covers is not exclusive to the other and belongs to intrinsically different semantic dimensions; one may mark the referent as textual-situationally accessible and, at the same time, as identifiable through association with the larger situation shared between the interlocutors.

5 Summary and discussion

We have shown referential strategies of MM, with special focus on how a lexical NP is marked according to the information status of the referent. MM has two strategies to mark so-called "definiteness": articles and the third person singular possessive *depe*. The articles are derived from demonstratives and are used for direct situational reference and anaphoric reference, while the possessive is used for references in which some kind of association is required for identification, which corresponds to anaphoric associative use and larger situation use of English in the classification of Hawkins (2015).

Both devices still retain their original semantic functions. The semantic domain of the articles does not extend beyond textual-situational accessibility, a direct semantic extension of the demonstratives; while the possessive does not cover all the "associative" relations that would be expressed by the definite NP in English, as seen in §3.

Demonstratives are a well-known source of definite markers in many languages. MM articles have established a syntactic position in NPs separated from the postposed demonstratives, and especially *tu* (derived from the distal demonstrative) has undergone semantic bleaching. We could expect that the use of the articles might be extended further to indirect reference, such as anaphoric associative or larger situational use (Hawkins 2015). This cross-linguistically plausible scenario, however, seems to be blocked by the semantic extension of the possessive *depe*, at least in the present stage.

The article *tu* and possessive *depe* may co-occur in one NP. This fact suggests that the semantic domain which each form covers is not exclusive to the other and belongs to intrinsically different semantic dimensions; one may mark the referent as textual-situationally accessible and, at the same time, as identifiable through association.

A very similar type of referential system with demonstratives and possessives is observed in Cirebon Javanese, a genetically related language (Ewing 1995; Ewing 2005). In Cirebon Javanese, as in MM, the determiners derived from the demonstratives mark directly shared identifiability, and textual-situational accessibility, while the possessive suffix *-é*, marks identifiability through indirect association. The two devices can frequently co-occur in one NP, because they "are not in some sort of complementary distribution" (Ewing 1995: 80).

Similar, but apparently more grammaticalized patterns of marking are observed in Fehring, a dialect of North Frisian. In Fehring, according to Lyons (1999: 161ff), which is based on the description of Ebert (1971a,b), and De Mulder & Carlier (2011), the strong, less grammaticalized, article is used for textual-situational accessibility, while the weak, more grammaticalized, article is used to indicate anaphoric association, unique entity, and generic entity (De Mulder & Carlier 2011: 529). The two articles exhibit complementary distribution in the pre-head noun determiner slot. The result of definite marking development in MM may be the pattern observed in Fehring.

Another possible development may be that one of the two strategies becomes more dominant than the other. As shown in §4, among the four speakers who have provided narrative data, one elder speaker prefers to use the possessive, while the two younger speakers prefer to use the articles. From this generational difference, we might predict that the article will become dominant and extend its semantic domain to indirect reference in the future.

MM is rapidly obtaining native speakers. As it goes in this direction, processes of standardization or homogenization could be expected to affect the marking of definiteness. The process should be monitored through ongoing research.

Abbreviations

1, 2, 3	the 1st, 2nd, 3rd person	NEG	negation
ART.D	distal article	PASS	passive
ART.P	proximal article	PFT	perfect
CAUS	causative	PFV	perfective
DEM.D	distal demonstrative	PL	plural
DEM.P	proximal demonstrative	POSS	possessive
EXCL	exclusive	PST	past
FUT	future	PTC	discourse particle
ITJ	interjection	RED	reduplication
ITR	interrogative	SG	singular

References

Adelaar, K. Alexander. 2005. Structural diversity in the Malayic subgroup. In K. Alexander Adelaar & Nikolaus P. Himmelmann (eds.), *Austronesian languages of Asia and Madagascar*, 202–226. London: Routledge.

Adelaar, K. Alexander & David J. Prentice. 1996. Malay: Its history, role and spread. In Stephen A. Wurm, Peter Mühlhäusler & Darrell T. Tryon (eds.), *Atlas of languages of intercultural communication in the Pacific, Asia, and the Americas*, 673–693. Berlin: Mouton de Gruyter.

De Mulder, Walter & Anne Carlier. 2011. The grammaticalization of definite articles. In Bernd Heine & Heiko Narrog (eds.), *The Oxford handbook of grammaticalization*, 522–534. Oxford: Oxford University Press.

Ebert, Karen H. 1971a. *Referenz, Sprechsituation und die bestimmten Artikel in einem nordfriesischen Dialect (Fering)*. Vol. 4 (Studien und Materialen). Bredstedt: Nordfriisk Instituut.

Ebert, Karen H. 1971b. Zwei Formen des bestimmten Artikels. In Dieter Wunderlich (ed.), *Probleme und Fortschritte der Transformationsgrammatik*, 159–74. Munich: Hueber.

Englebretson, Robert. 2003. *Searching for structure: The problem of complementation in colloquial Indonesian conversation*. Amsterdam: John Benjamins Publishing Company.

Ewing, Michael. 1995. Two pathways of identifiability in Cirebon Javanese. In *Berkeley Linguistics Society 21: Special Session on Discourse in Southeast Asian Languages*, 72–82.

Ewing, Michael. 2005. *Grammar and inference in conversation: Identifying clause structure in spoken Javanese*. Amsterdam: John Benjamins Publishing Company.

Fraund, Kari. 2001. Possessives with extensive use: A source of definite articles? In Michael Herslund Irène Baron & Finn Sørensen (eds.), *Dimensions of possession*, 243–268. Amsterdam: John Benjamins Publishing Company.

Gerland, Doris. 2014. Definitely not possessed? Possessive suffixes with definiteness marking function. In Thomas Gamerschlag, Doris Gerland, Rainer Osswald & Wiebke Petersen (eds.), *Frames and concept types*, 269–292. Cham: Springer.

Gerland, Doris. 2015. *Possessive suffixes as definite determiners in Indonesian languages*. Paper presented at 5th International Symposium on the Languages of Java (ISLOJ5). Universitas Pendidikan IndonesiaBandung, West Java, Indonesia. 6–7.

Hawkins, John A. 2015. *Definiteness and indefiniteness: A study in reference and grammaticality prediction* (Routledge Library Editions: The English Language). London & New York: Routledge.

Heine, Bernd & Tania Kuteva. 2002. *World lexicon of grammaticalization*. Cambridge: Cambridge University Press.

Himmelmann, Nikolaus P. 1996. Demonstratives in narrative discourse: A taxonomy of universal uses. In Barbara Fox (ed.), *Studies in anaphora*, 205–254. Amsterdam: John Benjamins Publishing Company.

Kluge, Angela. 2017. *A grammar of Papuan Malay*. Utrecht: LOT.

Krifka, Manfred & Renate Musan. 2012. Information structure: Overview and linguistic issues. In Manfred Krifka & Renate Musan (eds.), *The expression of information structure*, 1–44. Berlin: Mouton De Gruyter.

Lehmann, Christian. 1998. *Possession in Yucatec Maya*. Unterschleissheim: LINCOM Europa.

Litamahuputty, Betty. 2012. *Ternate Malay: Grammar and texts*. Utrecht: LOT.

Lyons, Christopher. 1999. *Definiteness*. Cambridge: Cambridge University Press.

Majid, Asifa. 2012. A guide to stimuli-based elicitation for semantic categories. In Nicholas Thieberger (ed.), *The Oxford handbook of linguistic fieldwork*, 54–71. Oxford: Oxford University Press.

Paauw, Scott H. 2008. *The Malay contact varieties of Eastern Indonesia: A typological comparison*. New York: The State University of New York at Buffalo (Doctoral dissertation).

Prentice, David J. 1994. Manado Malay: Product and agent of language change. In T. Dutton & D. T. Tryon (eds.), *Language contact and change in the Austronesian world*, 411–441. Berlin: Mouton.

Rubin, Aaron D. 2010. The development of the Amharic definite article and an Indonesian parallel. *Journal of Semitic Studies* 55(1). 103–114.

Thurgood, Elzbieta A. 1998. *A description of nineteenth century Baba Malay: A Malay variety influenced by language shift*. Manoa: University Hawai'i dissertation.

Thurgood, Elzbieta A. 2001. The development of articles in Baba Malay. *Anthropological Linguistics* 43(4). 471–490.

Part II

Information structure and syntactic constructions

Chapter 5

Information structure in Sembiran Balinese

I Wayan Arka
Australian National University / Universitas Udayana

I Nyoman Sedeng
Universitas Udayana

> This paper discusses the information structure in Sembiran Balinese, an endangered, conservative mountain dialect of Balinese. It presents the first detailed description of the ways topic, focus and frame setter in this language interact with each other and with other elements in grammar. It is demonstrated that Sembiran Balinese employs combined strategies that exploit structural positions, morpho-lexical and syntactic resources in grammar. The description is based on a well-defined set of categories of information structure using three semantic-discourse/pragmatic features of [+/−salient], [+/−given] and [+/−contrast]. This novel approach allows for the in-depth exploration of the information structure space in Sembiran Balinese. The paper also highlights the empirical-theoretical contributions of the findings in terms of the significance of local socio-cultural context, and the conception of information structural prominence in grammatical theory.

1 Introduction

Sembiran Balinese is one of the endangered conservative dialects of Balinese (i.e. *Bali Aga*, or Mountain Balinese). It is spoken by around 4,500 speakers in the mountainous village of Sembiran in northern Bali.[1] Sembiran Balinese has a similar morphosyntax to Plains, or Dataran Balinese, but it is different in that it lacks the speech level system characteristics of Plains Balinese.[2] The noticeable difference is therefore related to the lexical stock, including the pronominal system, which is discussed in §2.

---

[1] SBD should be distinguished from the Plains Balinese dialect, which lexically has been influenced by many other languages, namely, Javanese, Sanskrit, English, Arabic and Indonesian. Morphologically, both dialects have slight differences in prefix and suffix systems, but syntactically, both dialects have the same syntactic marking typology.

[2] Sembiran Balinese lacks the elaborate speech level system of Plains Balinese; however, the data suggests that there has been considerable contact with Plains Balinese, with the speakers being bilingual and fully aware of the politeness and speech level system. For example, the use of code-switching with the polite pronoun *tiyang* in addition to code-switching with Indonesian words was found.

I Wayan Arka & I Nyoman Sedeng. 2018. Information structure in Sembiran Balinese. In Sonja Riesberg, Asako Shiohara & Atsuko Utsumi (eds.), *Perspectives on information structure in Austronesian languages*, 139–175. Berlin: Language Science Press. DOI:10.5281/zenodo.1402543

Sembiran Balinese is relatively underdocumented compared to Plains Balinese. Previous studies on Sembiran Balinese include studies by Astini (1996) on consonant gemination and by Sedeng (2007) on morphosyntax. A more comprehensive documentation of Sembiran Balinese and other *Bali Aga* varieties is needed.

The present paper on information structure in Sembiran Balinese primarily builds on Sedeng's (2007) work. Our paper is the first thorough description of the information structure in Sembiran Balinese, based on a well-defined set of categories of information structure using three features ([+/−salient], [+/−given] and [+/−contrast]). The adopted novel approach makes it possible to map out the information structure in Sembiran Balinese in considerable detail and depth, revealing the intricacies of the semantics, syntax and pragmatics involved. The data provides fresh empirical evidence not only for the distinction of the known major categories of FOCUS vs. TOPIC, but also for the subtle distinction of FRAME SETTER vs. (CONTRASTIVE) TOPIC. Typologically, certain aspects of the information structure patterns observed in Sembiran Balinese are consistent with the patterns found in Plains Balinese (Pastika 2006) and other Austronesian languages with voice morphology, such as Pendau, a language in central Sulawesi (Quick 2005; 2007).

The paper is structured as follows. Grammatical relations and related salient features of Sembiran Balinese are discussed in §2. This is followed by an overview of information structure and the proposal of decomposing topic and focus into three features ([salient], [given] and [contrast]) in §3. The main discussions with the presentation of the data and analysis are presented in §4 for topic, §5 for focus and §6 for frame setting and left-periphery positions. The conclusion and further remarks are provided in the final section.

2 Grammatical relations in Sembiran Balinese in brief

Sembiran Balinese is a conservative dialect of Balinese. The conservative nature is first evident by the retention of an archaic Austronesian feature already lost in Plains Balinese, namely the pronouns *(a)ku/-ku* and *engko/-mu*, as shown in Table 1.

Table 1: Pronominal systems in Sembiran Balinese

PERSON	FREE PRONOUN	BOUND GENITIVE PRONOUN
1	aku, oké, kaka, **icang**	-ku
2	engko, cahi, **nyahi**	-mu
3	**iya**	-a

The pronouns in bold in Table 1 are those that are also shared with Plains Balinese. The bound pronouns in their genitive function in the nominal typically appear with the nasal ligature *-n* and the definite suffix *-e*, leading to the morphologically complex bound forms of *-kune*, *-mune* and *-ane* for the first, second and third persons, respectively. An example is given in (1):

(1) *Engko sa   mutang sa   engko kén panak-mu-n-e.*
     2   PART MID.debt PART 2   to child-2-LIG-DEF
     'You still owe your son/daughter (a ritual).' (Sedeng 2007)

There is also an intriguing difference in which certain intransitive verbs in Sembiran Balinese use the Actor Voice (AV) prefix *N-* with a prenasalised segment retention rather than the middle (MID) voice *ma-* used in Plains Balinese, as shown in (2). This further indicates the conservative nature of Sembiran Balinese given the fact that a prenasalised segment is an ancient and widespread feature of Austronesian languages (Blust 2013: 224); however, it should be noted that this prenasal segment retention only applies for intransitive verbs. In transitive verbs, the nasal property of the AV prefix *N-* assimilates with the initial consonant, resulting in no prenasal segment, e.g. *teguh* 'bite' → *neguh* (<N-teguh) 'AV-bite'.

(2)
Root	Sembiran Balinese	Plains Balinese	Gloss
a. *besen*	*mbesen*	*mabesen*	'send message'
b. *pupur*	*mpupur*	*mapupur*	'make up with powder'
b. *salin*	*nsalin*	*masalin*	'change dress'
c. *kisid*	*ngkisid*	*makasid*	'move'

The morphosyntax of Sembiran Balinese is exactly like Plains Balinese. Following the conventions of language typology (Comrie 1978; Dixon 1979; Croft 2003; Haspelmath 2007; Comrie 2005; Bickel 2011), grammatical relations are represented using the abbreviated labels, as described in (3). These labels, particularly A vs. P and G vs. T, are distinguishable by certain semantic entailment properties (Dowty 1991; Bickel 2011; Witzlack-Makarevich 2011; among others). The same labels are used in this paper when the arguments alternate, e.g. the same label A is used for the most actor-like argument in the active structure (i.e. core A argument) and in its passive counterpart, which is grammatically an oblique A. When necessary, a specific semantic role is specified for clarity, e.g. P: goal, meaning a goal of a three-place predicate that is treated as P as it enters a transitive structure.

(3) Grammatical functions: default generalised semantic relations
    S = sole core argument of an intransitive predicate
    A = most actor-like argument of a bivalent transitive predicate
    P = most patient-like argument of a bivalent transitive predicate
    G = most goal/recipient-like argument of a trivalent predicate[3]
    T = theme of a trivalent predicate

Sembiran Balinese also exhibits a grammatical SUBJECT or PIVOT, which plays a role in complex clause formations, such as control and relativisation. The voice system regulates the selection of a particular role as a pivot, which may also bear a particular discourse

---

[3]Based on applicativisation in Balinese, G is also the generalised role for a source/locative-like argument.

function of topic or focus. In the following examples, which show syntactic control, the verb *mati-ang* 'dead-CAUSE=kill' is in the UV form in (4a). P is selected as the pivot and is therefore controlled by (i.e. understood as the same as) the matrix subject *engko*. In contrast, in (4b), because the verb is in the AV form, the A argument is selected as the pivot and understood as the same as the matrix subject.

(4) a. *Saking engko dot* [__ *mati-ang oké*]?
really 2SG want UV.dead-CAUS 1SG
'You really want me to kill you?'

b. *Glema-néné nagih* [__ *ngmati-ang i rangsasa*].
person-DEF want AV.dead-CAUS ART giant
'This person wants to kill the giant.' (Sedeng 2007: 135)

In terms of word order, Sembiran Balinese is an A/S-V-P (or SVO) language, with an alternative order reflecting different information structure. Sembiran Balinese is like Plains Balinese in its phrase structure, which are schematised informally in (5).

(5)

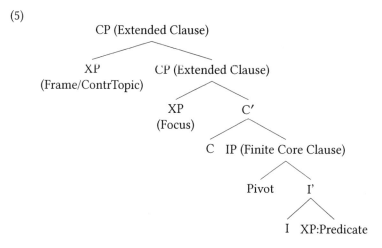

The predicate is not necessarily verbal; hence, XP (with X being any lexical category). The grammatical subject/pivot is part of the finite core clause structure, precisely in Spec, with the IP not shown in (5).

A sentence can have units placed sentence-initially. This type of sentence is analysed as having an extended clause structure. Formally, in terms of X-bar syntax, this extended structure has a unit that is left-adjoined to the clause structure. The adjoined element bears the pragmatically salient discourse functions (DFs), frame/contrastive topic and contrastive focus, typically in that order. The left-most sentence's initial DF position is often called a left dislocated or detached position. The focus position is closer to the core clause (IP) structure. It is called the Pre-Core Slot in Role and Reference Grammar (RRG) (Van Valin 2005; Van Valin & LaPolla 1997). It is a position in [Spec, CP] in terms of the X-bar syntax adopted here.

5 Information structure in Sembiran Balinese

Evidence for the structure shown in (5) is based on the following facts. First, there is evidence associated with interrogatives with question words (QW) in free clauses. The QW focus can appear in situ or can be fronted. When fronted, it must come in [Spec, CP] linearly before the core clause structure (IP). This is exemplified in (6a). In this sentence, the subject *cening* appears in its position within IP; however, the subject can be fronted marked with a topicaliser *en (buat)* 'as for' as in (6b), where it appears before the QW focus expression *buwin pidan*. Note that the fronted constituent *(en) cening* is precisely a contrastive topic. Crucially, this contrastive topic with the explicit marking with *en* cannot come after the QW focus, as can be observed from the unacceptability of (6c).

(6) a. [[*Buwin pidan*]_{Foc} [*cening lakar mlali*]_{IP}]_{CP}?
    again when   [kid   FUT   MID.go.sightseeing
    'When again will you go (there)?'

  b. [[(*En*) *cening*]_{Top}, [*buwin pidan*]_{Foc} [_ *lakar mlali*]_{IP}]_{CP}?
     as.for kid   again when   FUT MID.sightseeing
     'As for you, kid, when again will you go (there)?'

  c. *[[*buwin pidan*]_{Foc} [*en cening*]_{Top}, [_ *lakar mlali*]_{IP}]_{CP}?

Additional evidence is based on finite complement clauses. Complement clauses are structurally CP with QWs like *pidan* 'when', *apa* 'what/if', *ken* 'which' and *nyen* 'who' that can function like complementisers, appearing as part of the CP taking the finite clause, as in example (7a). An important point to note from (7a) is that the adverbial phrase *buwin mani* 'tomorrow' is part of the complement clause CP, as in the partial phrase structure tree shown in (7b). While appearing before *apa*, it is an adjunct of the embedded clause, not of the matrix clause. The matrix clause has its own temporal adjunct, namely *ibi* 'yesterday'. Also note that the adverbial *buwin mani* is fronted, resulting in a focus interpretation that is indicated by capital letters in the free translation.

(7) a. *Meme ibi   ntakon* [*buwin mani   apa* [*ia teka mai*]_{IP}]_{CP}.
       mother yesterday AV.ask   again tomorrow if   3SG come here
       'Mother yesterday asked whether TOMORROW he would come here.'

  b.
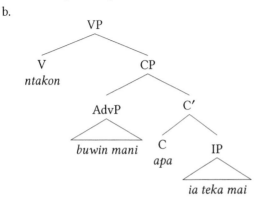

The evidence that there is a focus position associated with CP positions before IP is based on the exclusive focus marker *ane*, which is also a relativiser. The syntactic constraint is that it must also be associated with the pivot. Structurally, this means that the presence of *(a)ne* requires that the position [Spec, IP] and the positions before it (i.e. [Spec, CP] and/or C) must be associated with the pivot. Hence, sentence (8b) is correct when *ane* is used to augment the focus expression *icang ba* in (8b). In both, the A argument *icang* is the focus and the pivot, as evidenced by the form of the verb, which is in the AV form.

(8) a. [*Iya*]_{ContrTop}, [[*icang ba*]_{ContrFoc_i} [__*i* *mehang nasi*]_{IP}]_{CP}.
    3SG   1SG PART   PIV AV.give rice
    'As for him, I am the one who provided meals.'

b. [*Iya*]_{ContrTop}, [*icang ba*]_{ContrFoc_i} [*ane*_i [_*i* *mehang nasi*]_{IP}]_{CP}.
   3SG   1SG PART   REL   PIV AV.give rice
   'As for him, I am the one who provided meals.'

c. *[*Iya*]_{ContrTop} *ane*_i [*icang ba*]_{ContrFoc_i} [_*i* *mehang nasi*]_{IP}]_{CP}.
   3SG   REL   1SG   PART   PIV AV.give rice
   'As for him, I am the one who provided meals.'

An attempt to mark the left-most NP (*iya*) with *ane*, as in (8c), is ungrammatical. This is because such marking results in a structure with an intervening argument *icang*, which is referentially distinct from the *ane*-marked NP (*iya*). Given the requirement of *ane*, it causes two referentially different NPs to compete for the pivot argument.

Finally, it should be noted that there may be units in the left periphery positions that are not necessarily arguments of the main verb. They are represented by XP in (5). For example, the verb *ngamah* 'AV.having meals' in (9) appear in the left periphery position. Syntactically, it is not a dependent unit of the predicate *mehang* 'AV.give'. It functions as a frame or presentational topic (cf. Lambrecht 1994: 177–181); that is, it introduces an event of 'eating', evoking and delimiting certain referents in the discourse, including *nasi* 'rice', which is the new focus.

(9) [*En buat ngamah*]_{Frame}, [*icang ba*]_{ContrFoc} *mehang iya nasi*.
    if about AV.eat   1SG PART   AV.give 3SG rice
    'As for eating needs, I am the person who gave him meals.'

Additional details for marked discourse functions in left periphery positions will be provided in §6. There can also be a right-dislocated position in Sembiran Balinese. This is the case for a re-introduced or after-thought topic, which is discussed in §5.3.

3 Information structure: an overview

An information structure (i-str) is a structure by which meanings are packaged to accommodate speaker-hearer needs for effective communication in a given discourse context (cf. Lambrecht 1994: 5; Vallduví & Engdahl 1996: 460; among others). Examples of the units of i-str that are widely discussed in the literature are different types of topic and focus. Topic and focus are expressed by different formal mechanisms in the grammar of a given language, depending on the available morphosyntactic, prosodic and/or lexical resources. In Sembiran Balinese, voice system, structural positions, nominal expressions and prosody are important resources for i-str.[4]

The precise mechanism that underpins the various ways in which information is packaged within and across languages has been subject to intense study (Vallduví & Engdahl 1996; Erteschick-Shir 2007; Dalrymple & Nikolaeva 2011; among others). For the analysis of i-str in Sembiran Balinese in this paper, a parallel model with a LFG-like framework was used, which separates different layers of structures to distinguish predicate argument structure from linear order constituent structure (c-str), surface grammatical relations and information structure. The grammatical relations are represented using labels commonly used by typologists, such as A and P, as in (3). It was also recognised that the pivot is part of the surface grammatical relations.

In the adopted framework, there is no one-to-one relation between these layers of structures. Thus, different sentences in (10) are driven by different forces in information structure. They all have the same (underlying) predicate argument structure, but their argument roles are mapped onto different surface grammatical relations and different discourse functions. For example, the Actor *John* in (10) is the grammatical subject-topic in (10a), but it is a contrastive focus (while still being a pivot) in (10b) and a completive focus and grammatically oblique in (10c). Explicit information about i-str is given as necessary, and this is represented by means of annotations, e.g. as in (11) for sentence (10b).

(10) a. *John killed the robber.*
b. *It's John who killed the robber.*
c. *The robber was killed by John.*

(11) *It is* [*John*]$_{\text{A:Contr.Foc}}$ [*who killed the robber*]$_{\text{VP:Comment|Given}}$.

The information structure itself could be considered to consist of different layers with different possible associations of clausal constituents. For example, the i-str system at the broadest level may operate with two layers showing topic–comment and given (presupposed)–new focus distinctions as seen in Russian, where the topic precedes the comment and the given precedes the focus (Foley 2007; Comrie 1987: 405). Thus, the focus expression always comes later, and not all of the units of the comment belong to the focus. Consider the mini dialogue in (12) from Russian (13).

(12) S: *Maksím ubivájet Aleksé´j-a. (Russian)*
Maxim.NOM kills Alex-ACC
'Maxim kills Alexei.'

---

[4]Prosody is not discussed in this paper. While we are aware of the role of prosody in information structure in (Sembiran) Balinese, we have not conducted specific research on this topic. This is one of the areas that needs further research not only in Sembiran Balinese but also in Plains Balinese.

Q: A   Víktor-a?
    and Victor-ACC
    'And Victor?'

A: Víktor-a   Máksim   zaščiščajet.
    Victor-ACC Maxim.NOM defends
    'Maxim defends Victor.' (Comrie 1987: 96)

(13)   Víktor-a   Máksim   zaščiščajet
        [- topic -]   [- - - - comment - - - -]
        [- - - - - given - - - - -]   [- focus -]

The answer in (12.A) has the same information structure represented in (13), where Viktor is the topic and part of the comment (i.e. Maxim) is given. Additional complications in Balinese Sembiran will be discussed in §5, where part of the comment is fronted and gains a contrastive focus.

Building on earlier studies on information structure (Vallduví & Engdahl 1996; Erteschick-Shir 2007 2007; Dalrymple & Nikolaeva 2011; Krifka & Musan 2012; among others), todefined as a prototypical unmarkedpic and focus were conceptualised as two broad categories forming the information structure space where pragmatic and semantic notions of contrast, salience and givenness are essential. Following Choi (1999: 133), topic and focus were analysed as non-primitive notions. It is proposed that they are decomposable into features that capture the three independent but intertwined cognitive-discourse properties just mentioned: contrast, salience and givenness.

The features [salience] and [givenness] are typically topic-related. They encompass important semantic-pragmatic properties in communicative events, such as the particular frame/entity within/about which new information should be understood (i.e. the "aboutness" of the topic), and the degree of importance/salience/prominence of one piece of information relative to other bits of information in a given context. The latter is related to the "emphatic" element of communication. It reflects the speaker's subjective choice of highlighting one element and making it stand out for communicative purposes.

While often closely linked, salience and givenness are distinct. The two do not always go together. New information (i.e. [–given]), for example, can be [+salient]. This is a situation in which indefinite/generic referents are assigned emphatic focus, which is further discussed in §4.2.

The feature [contrast] captures the explicit choice of one alternative with the strong exclusion of the others in a given contrast set. It can be associated with both topic and focus, which is further discussed in §5.5 and §4.2.

The three features with their values result in eight possible combinations in the i-str space, as shown in (14). The features can be used to characterise fine-grained (sub)categories of topic and focus and to explore how they interact.

(14)   Grammatical functions: default generalised semantic relations
        a. [+salient, +given, +contrast] = contrastive frame/TOP

b. [+salient, −given, +contrast] = contrastive (often fronted) FOC
c. [+salient, −given, −contrast] = new (i.e. first mentioned indefinite) TOP
d. [+salient, +given, −contrast] = default/continuing/reintroduced TOP
e. [−salient, +given, −contrast] = secondary TOP
f. [−salient, −given, −contrast] = new (completive/gap) FOC
g. [−salient, −given, +contrast] = contrastive new FOC
h. [−salient, +given, +contrast] = contrastive secondary TOP

To clarify the complexity of information structure involved in Sembiran Balinese, the conception of common ground (CG) was adopted (Krifka & Musan 2012, and the references therein). Two related aspects of CG should be distinguished: the CG contents and CG management. The CG contents refer to the set of information mutually shared by speech participants in a given context. This information can be a set of presupposed propositions in the immediate/current CG and a set of entities introduced earlier in the discourse or general shared information.

CG is dynamic. It is continuously modified and adapted for communicative purposes throughout a speech event, e.g. by the addition of new information to the CG contents. The speaker generally has control over how to proceed in a speech event depending on his/her communicative interests/goals, possibly also considering the addressee's interests/goals. The way the communicative moves are handled to update and develop the CG is part of CG management.

CG management reflects the speaker's perspective and attention characterised by the properties shown in (14), e.g. what is assumed/presupposed, singled out and contrasted, emphasised or new in a given communicative episode. Thus, in example (10), where the A and P referents 'John' and 'the robber' are both [+given] (i.e. already shared in the CG), the speaker has more than one option to restructure the information depending on his/her interest or attention for effective communication. The use of the passive structure (10c), for instance, reflects the choice that P *robber* is of interest and is considered salient about which the new information, the event of killing, should be understood.

In the following sections, the interactions among the properties shown in (14) in Sembiran Balinese are illustrated in more detail.

4 Focus

Focus has been characterised in the literature in terms of two properties: informational newness and the presence of alternatives. In terms of the features outlined in (14), the first property is captured by the feature [−given]. That is, the focus is the informative, new and non-presupposed part of the proposition (Lambrecht 1994; Valldduví & Engdahl 1996; Dalrymple & Nikolaeva 2014; among others). It is the information added to the CG by (part of) comment expressions in statements, question-answers in dialogues or actions required in commands.

Focus can also be characterised in terms of the presence of alternatives (Krifka 2008; Krifka & Musan 2012). This is particularly clear in the case of the contrastive focus and the contrastive topic, which embeds the focus, as discussed in the previous section. The concept of "alternative" is part of the conception of the set, and according to Krifka, the presence of alternatives is in fact central to the definition of focus. There is a presence of strong alternatives with an overt focus marking in Sembiran Balinese that carry the [+contrast] feature. This is to distinguish it from an unmarked new focus discussed in this section, which is [−contrast], i.e. carrying no overt contrast in the expressions and no (clear) contrastive sets in the current CG other than alternatives due to a general knowledge of things in the world. In §4.1, this general local knowledge in Sembiran Balinese is exemplified to illustrate the point that focus indeed shows the presence of potential alternatives in a given shared local socio-cultural setting. The understanding of the choice of one alternative instead of another in a set is implicit and therefore requires a good understanding of broader information in the CG. It is argued that a focus related to this type of alternative has a weak or implicit 'contrast-like' meaning and is therefore categorised as having a [−contrast]. New focus in Sembiran Balinese is discussed in §4.1, followed by the contrastive and emphatic focusses in §4.2.

4.1 New focus

New/completive focus is defined as a prototypical unmarked focus ([−salient, −given, −contrast]): it has negative values for the relevant features and contains no strong or embedded contrastive element. It is [−given], meaning that the information is not part of the CG (e.g. being asked) or is newly added to the current CG either by the speaker or the addressee as the speech event progresses.

New focus is unmarked in the sense that its expression is assigned no specific tagging to signal a contrast or any other salience, such as structural fronting and/or the use of emphatic markers. New focus is therefore [−contrast, −salient]. An expression with a new focus is a constituent unit that appears in its canonical position. While implying the presence of alternatives (due to general world knowledge), new focus was analysed as [−contrast], as there is no entity present in the current CG with which it is being contrasted.

The clearest instance of a new focus that shows non-presupposed information with the presence of alternatives is related to question-answer pairs. This is exemplified by polarity interrogatives, as in example (15). Polarity interrogatives, as the name suggests, are associated with either 'yes' or 'no' answers. This type of question clearly illustrates the presence of alternatives in a new focus. In (15), *ngara* 'no', instead of the other alternative *ae* 'yes', is the information being asked; hence, it is new.

(15) Context: Men Dora told a story about how she gave her money to somebody but did not get her land certificate, and consequently, she lost her land.

> Question: *Bakat tanah-e?*
> UV.obtain land-DEF
>
> 'Did you get the land?'
>
> Men Dora: [*Ngara*]_Foc, [*ngara*]_Foc *bakat.*
>   NEG   NEG   UV.obtain
>
> 'No, (I) didn't get (it).'

A new focus in relation to content questions such as *nyén* 'who' and *apa* 'what' also implies the presence of alternatives. Thus, the interrogative in (16a) can be analysed as having an information structure with a pragmatic presupposition, as shown in (16b) in the CG. The shared presupposition is that every traditional garden definitely contains certain plants such as oranges, coconuts, and mangoes. The alternatives within this presupposed set of plants are part of the general local semantic field or knowledge in CG. The entity questioned and the answer given (i.e. X = focus) are among the alternatives in the set classified as PLANTS commonly cultivated in the garden, which is *poh* 'mango' in this case.

(16) a. Miasa: *Tanah-anne Patra m-isi apa dowang?*
    land-3SG.POSS Patra AV-contain what PART

'What is Patra's land planted with?'

Dora: [*Poh cenik-cenik*]_Foc. *Mara jani m-isi poh.*
    mango small-RED   new now AV-content mango

'Young mango trees. It has just been planted with mangos.'

b. Presupposition: *Patra's land is planted with X*, where X ∈ PLANTS COMMONLY CULTIVATED IN THE GARDEN
Question: *What is X?*
Answer: X = 'mango' (one of the plants commonly cultivated in the garden)

A new focus in monologue types of genres, such as narratives and descriptions, may also imply alternatives. The speaker in this type of genre, being the sole participant responsible for additional new information to update the CG, often provides new information piece by piece for easy and comprehensible communication with his/her addressee. Crucially, new focus expressions often come with modifiers of some type, flagging one piece of information in the current CG signalling one alternative, possibly in anticipation of more (alternative) information later in the discourse. For example, the speaker (*Men Dora*) tells her story about herself and discusses her children. In the first sentence in her autobiography (17a), the modifier *mara besik*, 'still one' signifies that *panak* 'child' (focus) is just one of the set of children that she will discuss. Later in her story, she discusses other children, including sentence (17b) about her second child. Here, the adverb *buwin* is used to signify similar new information ('giving birth', 'baby[-boy]'). Note that focus expressions include one of the alternatives that is true, e.g. *buwin ninnya* 'male again' is used in (17b) instead of the other alternative 'baby-girl' in accordance with the truth condition of the (updated) CG contents.

(17) a. [Ngelah [panak]$_P$]$_{Emph.Foc}$ [meme]$_{A.Top}$ [mara besik]$_{P.NewFoc}$ madan
AV.have child   mother   still one   MID.name
Butuh Dora.
Butuh Dora
'I (mother) gave birth to the first (lit. still one) child, named Butuh Dora.'

b. Ba   kento   [∅]$_{A.Top}$ buwin sa   ngelah [panak]$_{Foc}$, [∅]$_{S.Top}$ buwin
after like.that   again PART AV.have child   again
[ninnya]$_{Foc}$.
male
'After that, I again gave birth to a child, (and) (he's) again a baby boy.'

In terms of its structural expression, a new focus is typically part of the comment constituent and distinct from the topic; however, the comment constituent may be split, as in (17a) where the comment VP is fronted, leaving the numeral phrase modifier in the object position. The whole predicate in sentence (17a) (i.e. 'giving birth to one child') is actually new in the discourse. The split with fronting the VP can be considered the speaker's way of assigning some type of emphatic prominence to her phases of motherhood with a series of childbirths. At this point of the story, it is about the first baby. Based on the characterisation of the new focus adopted in this paper, *mara besik* 'first child' is a proper new focus in (17a). The fronted VP, which gains emphatic meaning by fronting, can be precisely labelled as the emphatic new focus. It is a marked focus, which is discussed in next section.

4.2 Marked focus: Contrastive and emphatic

A "marked focus" refers to a focus whose information structure contents in the CG are complex, typically characterised by [+contrast, +salient, –given]. The contrastive meaning ranges from a strong one to a subtle (emphatic) one, with complex encoding at the formal expression level. The complexity can be structural, involving the use of an extended clause structure with unit fronting to the left-periphery. It may also be accompanied by specific focus markers. At the content level, the complexity is indicated by the presence of an embedded element of a contrast set.

The presence of a contrast set constrains the contextual interpretation of the focussed element. In Sembiran Balinese, it may range from a focus with a strong contrastive meaning (i.e. the choice of one with a clear exclusion of the other alternative(s) in the understood set) to a focus with an emphatic meaning. Emphatic focus, as the term suggests, encodes a class of salient pragmatic nuances, such as emphasis, affirmation and counter-expectation, which the speaker wants the addressee to pay attention to during communication.

There is no clearly defined difference between contrastive and emphatic meanings, as both are associated with the contextual presence of contrasting alternatives. For simplicity, they are discussed under the broad category of contrastive focus. In Sembiran

Balinese, they both make use of the same linguistic resources. The difference, if any, appears to be a matter of degree, involving how explicit the contrasting entities are present in the contrast set and how strong other pragmatic nuances, such as emphasis and affirmation, are expressed in a given context. The degree of the strengths of these nuances in Sembiran Balinese can often be seen from the extent of marking present, e.g. whether fronting is also accompanied by an overt focus marker. Cases with strong contrast sets are discussed first, followed by cases with subtler emphatic nuances.

Cases for clear contrastive focus can be informally represented, as in (18). The representation shows that X is the contrastive focus if it is the selected member of a contrast set in the current CG, with the other contrasting entity, Y, excluded from the set. The presence of a contrast set is often strong and expressed by some type of structural and/or particle marking. This is exemplified by the question-answer pair from English shown in (19). The question (Q) sets the contrast between two alternatives, which are overtly marked by the disjunction *or* in the question. The answer (A) in (19) selects one ('the white') and excludes the other. The contrastive focus of the answer (19A) can be represented as in (20). Note that what is new in the answer is not the two entities in the set (as they are both present in the CG), rather, it is the selection of one of them.

(18)   Contrastive focus X: $\{[X]_{ContrFoc}, [Y] ...\}_{Foc}$
       [where the contrasting entity, Y, is clearly
       established in the immediate/current CG.]

(19)   Q: Which laundry did John wash, the white or the coloured?
       A: He *washed* the WHITE laundry.   (Erteschick-Shir 2007: 48)

(20) $\{['the white']_{ContrFoc}, ['the coloured']\}_{Foc}$

In Sembiran Balinese, strategies used to express contrast include the following: fronting to the left-periphery position, structural parallelism, lexical items (e.g. antonymous words), polarity particles, focus markers and prosodic prominence (i.e. stress). Fronting is the most common strategy, which is often combined with one or more of the other strategies.

Consider the context of contrastive focus in the second clause in (21). The presence of polarity *ngara* in the first sentence sets one (negative) option in the bipolar contrast set (X in the representation in (22)). The second clause adds new specific information to this negative option by stating that the money was actually corrupted (lit. 'taken and eaten'). Crucially, the speaker provides extra emphasis on this by preposing the VP clause-initially. It therefore bears a contrastive focus, as it indicates that the speaker strongly highlights the negative option, excluding the positive option (Y).

(21)   Context: The secretary officer in the village was trusted to collect the money needed to cover the costs for the issuance of the land certificates for a group of people in the village, including the speaker; however, the money was corrupted by the secretary and the village head.

Tau-tau [*pipis-e*]_{P.Top} [*ngara setor=a   ke kantor*]_{Foc}, [[*juwang=a amah=a di*
know-RED money-DEF NEG   transfer=3 to office   UV.take=3 UV.eat=3 on
jalan]_{ContrFoc}]_{NewFoc} [*ento*]_{P.Piv.Top} [*ajak=a   wakil prebekel-e*]_{NewFoc}.
road   that   accompany=3 deputy head.villate-DEF

'Surprisingly, the money was [not transferred to the (Land) office]_{Foc}, that (money) was [taken and eaten along the way]_{ContrFoc} by him and the village head.'

(22) {[X: 'not transferred','taken and eaten']_{ContrFoc}, [Y: 'transferred']}_{NewFoc}

The example in (23) further illustrates contrastive focus, achieved by using passivisation, whereby the new information is made the subject. Linking an argument with new information (i.e. new focus) to the pivot is rather unusual as far as information structure are concerned; however this is done for a good communicative purpose, namely to achieve an element of surprise associated with the new information. That is, the focus item needs to be fronted to gain the contrast meaning. Note that sentence (23) is a reported speech where the first clause is the reported question asking for water. The second clause is the reported answer. The entity 'blood' is the new focus, as it is the answer to the question. It is also contrastive because it is being contrasted with the expected answer ('water'). This is a folktale, a work of fiction with a giant as the main character. It is full of surprises, e.g. the giant eats human beings and drinks human blood.

(23) a. Context: a story about a girl called *bawang*, who is asked to cook by a giant who eats humans.
  Mara   iya nakon-ang   [yéh]_{P.Foc}, [*getih kanya*]_{P.Top} *tuduh-ang=a.*
  just.time 3SG AV.ask-APPL water,   blood PART   UV.point-APPL=3
  'When she asked for water, it was blood that he pointed at.'
  b. {['blood']_{ContrFoc}, ['water(asked)']}_{NewFocus}

In this example, the contrast set is clearly established through (reported) question and answer pairing. However, in other cases, the elements in the contrast set might be fully understood only in relation to a complex locally/culturally specific CG, not simply the truth condition involved. For example, the element of [+contrast] associated with a counter expectation in the following sentence can be fully understood only in the local cultural setting as described in (24):

(24) Socio-cultural context: the speaker is a poor woman involved in the so-called *ngadas* practice: she was given a female piglet to look after as capital by somebody else. The agreement was that when the pig grew and became a mother-pig with its own piglets, the speaker should pay the owner back using the offspring.
  [*Ba   ada [ukuran lima bulan*]_{NewFoc} [*ubuwin*]]_{Comment} [*kucit-e*]_{P.Top}, [*mara*
  already exist about five month   UV.look.after   piglet-DEF   just

> ukuran setengah]_ContrFoc [gede-n   kucit-e]_S.Top, [mati]_ContrFoc [kucit-e]_S.Top.
> about   half   size-NML piglet-DEF   die   piglet-DEF
>
> 'Presumably, for about five months, I looked after the pig. The size of the pig's body was about half the size of a mature one's, (but) it died unexpectedly.'

Note that the contrastive focus of the last sentence in (24) arises from the fronting of the predicate *mati* 'died'. It is also marked by a prominent prosodic stress, resulting in the speaker's subtle complex meaning of 'surprise, unexpectedness, unwantedness'. This is understood in the socio-cultural context described in (24), where the piglet is not hers but a type of loan capital. The contrastive focus also expresses the speaker's strong feelings of disappointment in contrast to her expectation that it would grow and eventually give birth to offspring. The piglet's death was premature (at around five months of age). It was still relatively small, at half the size of a full-grown pig.

The contrast element in the focus can often be augmented by the use of focus markers in addition to constituent fronting. Here, the use of focus particles *ba* and *jeg* are exemplified in Sembiran Balinese. Sentence (25) illustrates the use of *ba*. This particle appears to have originated from *suba*, the adverb/auxiliary meaning 'already/perfective', which is also often abbreviated as *ba*.[5] Both appear in example (25). The free translation is given here to show the emphatic focus involved, namely the long-awaited and good news about the completion of the making of the shirt material. The focus particle *ba* carries a sense of relief, or of no more thinking/concern on the part of the speaker. Note that it would take days, or even weeks, to complete the weaving. This again points to the fact that the emphatic focus has a subtle meaning that would only be understood in a given local cultural setting.

(25) Context, barter-based economy: the speaker promised to give the person (addressed below as *Nang*[6]) a hand-woven material to create a shirt in return for six-hundred ears of corn that the person had previously given her.
Nang, [ba   tepud ba]_ContrFoc [lakar   baju-ne]_S.Top.
father PERF done PART   material shirt-DEF

'Father, it's done, the material for the shirt.'

The focus particle *jeg* carries a selection of one option instead of the other(s) with negative nuances, such as something unwanted or no other alternative. This is often associated with an event/action carried out against the speaker's/addressee's wishes. This is exemplified in (26) and (27). In (26), the focus marker *jeg* appears with the negative sentence, highlighting the absence of any possession whatsoever on the part of the speaker. In (27), it is an imperative sentence, and the instruction to the addressee is that he must find a doctor, nobody else (e.g. not a shaman), for the mother. Note that in this second sentence, the focus is doubly marked by *jeg* and *ba*.

---

[5]It also has a prepositional-like meaning 'after' as in (*su*)*ba kento* 'after (like-)that'. The grammaticalisation of forms with these meanings has been reported in other languages (cf. Heine & Kuteva 2002: 17, 134).

[6]Nang is the vocative use of *nanang* 'father'. This kin term is used to address the brother of one's father or any male of the same age as one's father.

(26) Context: The speaker had a hard life with many children to raise. This sentence is part of the most difficult time in her life when one of her children was seriously ill:
Kene ojog=a masan parah=sen jeg apa ngara ngelah.
like.this visit=3 time hard=very PART what NEG AV.have
'The worst time hit hard at this time, I had NOTHING whatsoever.'

(27) *Tut Sik, meme* **jeg** **dokter** *ba alih-ang di Jakula nto.*
Tut Sik mother PART doctor PART UV.find-APPL PREP place that
'Tut Gasik, as for me (Mother), you just find a DOCTOR (nobody else) for me in Tejakula.'

The example in (28) illustrates an emphatic focus. It is also achieved by predicate fronting. The speaker describes her husband by placing emphasis on his negative characteristic of being lazy in contrast to an otherwise more positive alternative commonly expected for a good husband. This characterisation of laziness is the first mention of this in the text; hence, it is an emphatic new focus. The contrastive element has no overt expression in the preceding context. It should be understood based on the good values assumed in the community as part of the general CG.

(28) [*Gelema kalud ng-luyur ngara nyak pati me-gaé*]$_{Pred.ContrFoc}$ [*sommah*
  person PART AV-wander NEG want ever AV-work   husband
  meme-né ento]$_{S.Top}$.
  mother-POSS DEM
'A person who's wandering around, not wanting to work, my husband is.'

5 Topic

Topic is defined prototypically in terms of the file-card metaphor (Reinhart 1981; Erteschick-Shir 2007; Krifka & Musan 2012) in relation to the comment part of a sentence and the i-str features given in (14). The following is the definition of topic, adapted from Krifka & Musan (2012: 28):

(29) Definition of topic:
  The prototypical topic constituent of a clause is the one referring to a [+salient] entity in the CG, under which the information of the comment constituent is stored or added.

As mentioned, the [+salient] feature is meant to capture the most important cognitive property of an entity (or a set of entities) in a given context about which attention and additional information is given to increase the addressee's knowledge (in statement), is requested from the addressee (in question), or when an action is requested (in command). This definition is consistent with the traditional concept of "aboutness" topic (Reinhart

1981; Gundel 1988; Lambrecht 1994: 210, among others) and 'attention' (Erteschick-Shir 2007: 44).

The concept of prototype (Rosch 1978; Taylor 1991) was used in the definition in (29) to capture different types of topics, particularly because there may be a less canonical topic, called a secondary topic. While its referent is present in the CG, this topic is not as salient as the default topic, which now becomes the PRIMARY TOPIC.[7] The secondary topic gains its salience in relation to the primary topic; see further discussions in §5.4.

Next, the most common type of topic is discussed first, namely the default topic of a clause, which is also grammatically a pivot.

5.1 Default topic

The term DEFAULT TOPIC is used to refer to the only topic in the basic (i.e. non-extended) clause structure characterised by [+salient, +given, −contrast] properties. Its referent has been established and shared in the CG (i.e. cognitively/pragmatically salient and given). Crucially, it is not contrasted. That is, as far as CG management is concerned, it is a unit without an embedded element of contrast. Grammatically, it is the pivot of the clause, occupying a unique pivot position in the clause structure. As mentioned in §2, the pivot selection and therefore default topic selection is signalled by verbal voice morphology.

The material realisation of the default topic varies for discourse-pragmatic reasons. It can be an overt noun (NP), a free overt pronoun or a zero pronoun. The data suggests that this is determined by the activation and relative adjacency of the relevant entity in the current CG. An overt common noun topic is typically a definite topic, possibly a re-introduced default topic; a pronoun or a zero pronoun is typically a continuing default topic. Each is discussed and exemplified in the next sections.

5.1.1 Common nouns and proper names

Common noun and proper name topics constitute only 18% of the total default topics in Sembiran Balinese. The majority of default topics are pronominals, unexpressed/zero subjects (67%) and overt pronominal subjects (15%).[8] Default topics are typically definite, i.e. having a [+given] property. Nouns gain definiteness in different ways. The most common way in text is a second (or later) mention after it is introduced as the new focus in a previous sentence. For example, in the following excerpt, the noun *jagung* 'corn' is introduced in the first sentence and becomes a definite topic later, flagged by a definite marking (-*e*, *ento*). Likewise, the NP *lakar baju* 'shirt material' becomes the topic after the second mention, referred to by the definite determiner *ento*.

---

[7]The term PRIMARY TOPIC is the default topic in the presence of the secondary topic. They refer to the same kind of topic and are used interchangeably in this paper.
[8]These statistics are based on a limited text corpus of 66,677 words, consisting of traditional folktales and a recording of the personal story of Men Dora. The recording was first transcribed in ELAN, and then the appropriate tagging reflecting grammatical relations and information structure status was done in ELAN, before a simple statistical calculation was undertaken.

(30) Ba   kento, behang=a meme **jagung** tigang atak,   nunun   ntas meme
      after that UV.give=3 mother corn   three two.hundred AV.waive then mother
      lakar   baju, ba   **tepud ento** ... ba   kento, **jagung-e ento** ada a=bulan
      material shirt PERF finish that   PERF that   corn-DEF that exist one=month
      tengah dahar...
      half UV.eat

   'After that, I (mother) was given 600 ears of corns...I then waived shirt material; it was then done...after that, the 600 ears of corn were consumed in about one month and a half...'

A common noun can gain its topicality (i.e. [+given]) even when first mentioned in the discourse through a vocative use. It exophorically refers to the speaker or the addressee in a given context. The noun types that possibly function in this way are typically kin-term nouns. For example, the default topic in (31) is *meme* 'mother', used vocatively to refer to the speaker. This is the first sentence in the autobiography text. It is a topic NP because it is the entity/referent (i.e. the speaker, *Men Dora*) about whom 'giving birth to the first child' is being told.

(31) Context: the speaker Men Dora told her son (i.e. the addressee) about her life.
      Ngelah   panak [meme]$_{\text{A.Top}}$ mara besik, madan   Butuh Dora.
      AV.have child.P mother   still one MID.name B.   Dora

      'I (mother) gave birth to my first child, named Butuh Dora.'

A common noun can also gain its [+given] property through a possessive relation with the addressee. In example (32), the NP *nanang caine*, 'your father' is the default topic of the second sentence. It has not been mentioned in previous sentences. Its referent is part of the shared CG information, as it is the father of the addressee who is also the husband of the speaker.

(32) Context: the speaker told her son (i.e. the addressee) about his father.
      Buina   ngelah   panak mara patpat kento   teh, [nanang]$_{\text{A.PIV.TOP}}$ cahi-ne
      moreover AV.have child.P still   four   like.that PART father   2SG-DEF
      ngalih   somah buwin.
      AV.take wife.P again

      'In addition, when I had given birth to four children, your father took another wife.'

5.1.2 Pronominal topic: Reintroduced and continuing

When a referent is highly active in the CG and established as the default topic, there is often no need to express it overtly; however, if expressed overtly, it is often realised as a pronoun, as in (33a). In this example, the default topic *tiyang*[9] (the speaker *Men Dora*)

---

[9] Note that *tiyang* is a Plains Balinese pronoun (h.r.). Speakers of Sembiran Balinese are also typically fluent in Plains Balinese as well, and code switching is common.

is already salient in the general CG. In the two sentences immediately preceding it, the pronoun is not the topic. It is a topic in an earlier sentence. In this case, it can be classified as a reintroduced topic (see §5.3); however, in the sentences immediately following (33a), *tiyang* (or the speaker, index *i*) is maintained as the default topic. It is realised as a zero pronoun, represented as Ø. The default topic is a continuing topic in these instances. In short, a continuing topic is, like a reintroduced topic, a discourse-level topic, but the referent of a continuing topic is already present in the immediately preceding sentence.

(33) Context: the TOP in the two immediately previous sentences is about the speaker's two last children out of nine children:

a. *Ba   keto mara* [*tiyang*]_{A.Piv.Top_i} *ngelah   panak siya.*
    after that just   1SG   AV.have child nine.

    'Then, after, I gave birth to a total of nine children.'

b. [Ø]_{A.Piv.Top
i} *Ba   nau   ne ba.*
            PERF happy this PERF

    'I was already happy.'

c. [Ø]_{A.Piv.Top
i} *Ba   lupa* [Ø]_{A.Piv.Top} *ba   ngucapang* ...
            PERF forget *i*   PERF AV.mention

    'I forgot to mention (something).'

These data from Sembiran Balinese represent a common pattern where an entity that is highly salient in a series of immediate states of CG is selected as the continuing topic. It is typically formally reduced in its expressions, either as a zero pronoun (67%) or a (clitic) pronoun (15%). This fits well with Givón's (1990: 917) observation that referents that are already active in the CG require minimal coding. This is also consistent with the findings in Plains Balinese (Pastika 2006) and in other Austronesian languages of Indonesia with verbal voice morphology, such as Pendau (Quick 2005); however, in other Austronesian languages with diminishing verbal voice morphology, e.g. in certain dialects of Sasak, the use of pronominal clitics is widespread, and the discourse distribution of nominal and voice types is expected to be different (cf. Wouk 1999).

5.2 New topic

While topic is typically [+given], it can be [−given]. This is the topic whose referent is firstly mentioned in the discourse (i.e. newly introduced in the CG). It is typically introduced by the verb *ada* in Sembiran Balinese. Consider (34), which is the first line of a story. The subject of the first clause is an indefinite NP *tuturan satua*. This is a new topic. Then, the second clause provides more specific information about the new topic.

(34) *Ada* [*tutur-an satua*]_{NewTop}, *madan I   Bapa Sedok.*
      exist tell-NML story   MID.call ART Father Sedok

      'There is a story often talked about called *I Bapa Sedok*.'

The sentence in (35) is in the middle of a story, but it is the first time the referent *nak* 'person' is introduced in the context described in (35). While indefinite and new, *nak* is the topic here, as the information that follows is about this NP, *nak*.

(35) Context: The sentences are about the speaker's bad experience. She was deceived by the village official and lost her money in the process of the issuance of land certificates. Somebody else, called Sumarwi, stepped in to replace her money:
Ada nak   nimbalin, Sumarwi adan-anne neh nimbalin.
exist person AV.replace Sumarwi name-POSS REL AV.replace

'There's a person reimbursing (the money); Sumarwi is the name of the person who reimbursed the money.'

5.3 Reintroduced topic

The term REINTRODUCED TOPIC is used to refer to a topic expression associated with a salient entity already selected as a topic earlier but that is picked up again as a topic in a clause (cf. Givón 1990: 760); hence [+salient, + given]. It is not associated with a contrastive set in the CG, however. The reintroduced topic has been exemplified in (33). In this example, the pronoun exophorically refers to the speaker, so there is no ambiguity issue in its identification.

When there is more than one entity in the CG that the third-person pronoun can refer to, as the default topic, a pronoun may need further specific information provided by a full NP expression. In Sembiran Balinese, this full topic NP may come later in the clause in the right dislocated position. This is exemplified in (36). The pronoun *iya* in the last sentence is potentially ambiguous, as there are other participants in the CG indicated by the indices *i* and *j*. To avoid ambiguity, the speaker provides additional information: 'that (first) co-wife' (underlined) in the right detached position, index *k*. Thus, there are two topic expressions referring to the same entity in this sentence; *iya* is the default topic expression, and the full NP *madu-né ento* is the reintroduced topic.

(36) Context: the speaker is the second of three co-wives reporting what the first co-wife (index k) has said about Sapin, the third co-wife (index i).
'Tawah [I   Sapin-e   ento]_i. [[panak[-a]_i]_j ngara gaen-ang[=a]_A_i banten
strange ART Sapin-DEF that   child-3   NEG make-APPL=3   ritual
behan   Ø_S_i ngara ngelah, orahhang[=a]_A_i aget=se   ...' kento   [iya]_S.Top_k
because   NEG AV.have say=3   lucky=PART   like.that 3SG
m-peta,   [madu-n-né   ento]_Top_k.
AV-mention co-wife-LIG-3POSS DET

'Sapin_i was strange. [Her_i child]_j. She_i didn't make any ritual due to her_j lack of money (when the child unexpectedly died prematurely), and she_i said she was lucky', she_k said, the (first) co-wife_k.'

5.4 Secondary topic

The SECONDARY TOPIC is defined in relation to the default or primary topic. It is defined as 'an entity such that the utterance is construed to be ABOUT the relationship between it and the primary topic (Dalrymple & Nikolaeva 2014: 55). The secondary topic is like the primary topic in that it is pragmatically [+given]: It is present in the (immediate) CG; however, it is less salient than the primary topic. Saliency reflects some type of prominence, which can be assessed based on certain properties related to how it is marked in a given language, e.g. linear order (with the earlier sentence-initial position being more salient than later), linking (with the subject/pivot topic being more prominent than the object topic) and explicit marking (with the focus marked by the contrastive focus marker, which is more prominent than the [unmarked] new focus).

In the English example from Lambrecht (1994: 148), sentence (37) contains two topic expressions, both expressed by the pronouns *he* and *her*. Their referents are already present and salient in the CG due to the preceding (37) and (37) sentences. Sentence (37) is about *John*, referred to by the subject *he*; hence, this is the primary topic. The secondary topic, the object *her*, is part of the comment constituent. The communicative intent of (37) – its new information, the focus constituent of the Comment – is the assertion of the "love-relation" in which Rosa was not loved by John.

(37) a. *Whatever became of John?*
 b. *He married Rosa,*
 c. *but [he]$_{PrimaryTop}$ [[didn't really love]$_{Foc}$ [her]$_{SecondaryTop}$]$_{Comment}$*

The secondary topic, like the primary topic, can also be a continuing topic when its referent is already salient and present in the general CG. It is often the case that two salient entities in the CG alternate between the primary and secondary topic, depending on the focussed predicate involved. Consider the following excerpt from the text in (38), which comes after example (32). The speaker repeats the same message with some new information about her status as one of three co-wives of her husband. Both the speaker and her husband are highly salient in the immediate CG. The speaker (index *i*) is the continuing topic in the three sentences, becoming the primary topic in (38b) and (38c). Her husband, realised as the clitic =a (index *j*), is also the continuing but secondary topic in (38b) and (38c). Note that in (38b), the husband becomes the primary topic of the adverbial clause, realised as a zero pronoun.

(38) a. *Ba kento mara [meme]$_{A.Top\_i}$ ngelah panak patpat,*
 after that just.after mother AV.have child four
 'Then, after, I (mother) gave birth to four children,'
 b. *Ø$_{P.Top1\_i}$ Kalahin[=a]$_{A.TOP2\_j}$ [Ø $_{P.Top1\_j}$ ngallih somah buwin].*
 UV.left=3 AV.take wife again
 'I was left by him to take a new wife again.'

    c. *Madu-telu-ang[=a]*_{A.Top2_j} [*meme*]_{P.Top1}.
       co-wife-CAUS=3   mother
    'I was made one of his three wives.'

In Sembiran Balinese, instances of the secondary topic are typically the A of the UV verbs expressed as (clitic) pronouns. In this case, P is the primary topic, also highly topical and selected as the pivot. Sembiran Balinese is like Plain Balinese, in that in both UV and AV clauses, the A argument is highly topical and even more topical than the U argument. Pastika (2006) presented statistical evidence from a referential distance measure (cf. Givón 1994), which showed that the significant factor for the selection of voice type, AV vs. UV, in Balinese is the topicality of U rather than that of A.

5.5 Contrastive topic

The contrastive topic expression is defined as being associated with [+salient, +given, +contrast] features. That is, like the types of topic discussed thus far, it refers to a referent already present in the CG and is highly salient (e.g. about which comment information is added); however, it differs in that it carries an element of contrast (i.e. [+contrast]). On the expression side, the [+contrast] feature has an explicit marking of some type. On the CG side, it is associated with an established contrast set of referents.

    A contrast is marked in different ways. In the English question-answer example in (39), the contrast set is restricted and established by the nominal *siblings* in question (A) and also by structural parallelism through the coordination accompanied by a parallel prosody in the answer. In this pair of questions and answers, the subject NPs in B are instances of a contrastive topic, analysed as having a focus embedded in the topic (Erteschick-Shir 2007; Krifka & Musan 2012: 30). Focus carries the presence of alternatives (Krifka & Musan 2012), an element also shared with [+contrast]; however, the focus may be simply [−contrast]. That is, new information is added to the common ground without an overt contrastive reference to other entities in the CG, which has been discussed in detail in §4.1. The contrastive topic is represented as a topic with an embedded contrastive focus (ContrFoc). For example, (40): (40i) and (40ii) are the representations of the contrastive topics of clauses B.i and B.ii, respectively. The topics consist of a set of two salient referents in the CG that are commented on by means of their different occupations, which are not shown by the representation in (40).

(39) A: *What do your siblings do?*
       B: i. [[*My SISter*]_{Foc}]_{Top} [*studies MEDicine*]_{Foc}, *and*
           ii. [[*my BROther*]_{Foc}]_{Top} *is* [*working on FREIGHT ship*]_{Foc}. (Krifka & Musan 2012: 30)

(40) i. {['my sister']_{ContrFoc}, ['my brother']}_{Top}
       ii. {['my sister'], ['my brother']_{ContrFoc} }_{Top}

Parallelism by means of coordination, as shown in the English example above, is common cross-linguistically. Parallelism that encodes a contrastive set membership is often achieved by using the same or synonymous lexical items in structurally marked constructions, such as a left-dislocated position.[10] A contrastive topic expressed in this way is found in Sembiran Balinese. This is exemplified by the topic expression *iya ba* in the second clause in example (41a). The partial information structure representation is given in (41b).

(41) a. [*Meme*]$_{P.Top\_i}$ *ngara ajak=a ng-(g)ellah-ang tanah warisan di Pramboan*
 mother NEG invite=3 AV-own-APPL land inheritance in Pramboan
 mapan [*iya ba*]$_{Top\_j}$, [*somah-anne senikan ento*]$_{P\_j}$ *ajak=a.*
 since 3SG EMPH wife-3SG.POSS younger that UV.invite=3
 '[I (mother)] was not invited to share the inherited land in Pramboan because it's [she]$_j$ [his younger wife]$_j$ whom he invited.'

 b. CG: {[['younger wife']$_j$ $_{ContrFoc}$, ['mother']$_i$} $_{Top}$

As seen in (41b), the 'co-younger wife' is the topic, i.e. the salient participant about/to whom a land-sharing invitation was discussed/offered. It is a contrastive topic, with the contrast achieved by means of the contrasting element of negation associated with the same verb *ajak*. The younger co-wife is referred to by *iya*, which appears in the left-dislocated topic position and whose pragmatic effect is augmented by the use of the emphatic particle *ba*. The full NP *somah-anne senikan ento*, which appears in the pivot position, provides additional specific information about *iya*.

Example (42) also illustrates a contrastive topic. The P object *ne*, 'this' refers to the land being discussed. It is topicalised through fronting to the left-most sentence-initial position. This way, it gains its contrastive effect; hence, it is a contrastive topic. Note that the verb is in the AV form with the subject/pivot being the A argument *cahi*. The A argument is also pragmatically prominent, appearing with the focus marker *ba*. Both of the referents of the A and P arguments are present in the preceding sentences, as described in the context description in (42a). The information structure is informally represented in (42b).

(42) a. Context: Bapak, the officer from the Agrarian Office, measured a piece of state-owned land to be granted to Butuh Dora. Two salient entities are involved in the first clause: the addressee *cahi* and the land.
 [*Ne*]$_{Top}$ [*cahi*]$_{A.Piv.Foc}$ *ba ngelahang. Ne ngara ukur Bapak ne.*
 this 2SG PART AV.have.APPL this NEG UV.measure father this
 'As for this piece of land, YOU are the one who owns (it). This one, I didn't measure it.'

 b. CG: {['this land']$_{ContrFoc}$, ['the other land'],}$_{Top}$ {['you']$_{ContrFoc}$, ['the others'], ...}$_{Foc}$

---

[10]Parallelism is a prominent feature of the languages of central and eastern Indonesia, particularly in the domain of ritual language (Fox 1988; Grimes et al. 1997; Kuipers 1998; Arka 2010; Sumitri & Arka 2016). The information structure in a ritual language require further research.

The type of structure given in (42) is of particular interest, as both A and P are equally contrastive, highly salient and already present in the CG. This reflects the interaction between the topic and focus and creates complications regarding the distinction between the primary and secondary topics; however, it appears that in a given structure, only one is selected as the most prominent topic. This is the left-most unit, *ne* 'this (land)', because the rest of the predication is about this referent. This topic functions as the frame setter, which delimits the interpretation of the other parts of the sentence. In terms of CG management, and in line with the definition of topic presented in (29), based on the free translation, it is this topicalised P/object that is closer to the 'about topichood' than the subject *cahi*. The object is more prominent than the subject as far as the information structure is concerned; however, grammatically, there is good cross-linguistic evidence (Keenan & Comrie 1977; Bresnan 2001; among others) as well as language specific evidence, e.g. from reflexive binding in (Sembiran) Balinese (Arka 2003; Sedeng 2007) that the object is less prominent than the subject/pivot.

6 Frame setting and left-periphery positions

6.1 Frame setting and topicalisation

Frame setting, which is exemplified in English in (43), is part of the so-called *delimitation* in information structure (Krifka & Musan 2012). The frame setter *healthwise/as for his health* in this example restricts the predication: the new/gap focus FINE must be understood within the frame of '(his) health'. Note that the topic here is *John*, as the predication of being 'fine' is about him.

(43) Q: How is John?
    A: {Healthwise/As for his health}, he is FINE. (Krifka & Musan 2012: 31)

The frame setter carries the presence of alternatives within a particular specific CG domain set out, or assumed, by the speaker. This specificity property of the CG overlaps with definiteness characterising the topic, captured by the [+given] property in (14). The frame setter therefore resembles a contrastive topic, e.g. the frame setters *healthwise/as for his health* means 'in terms of/talking about his health instead of his other situations'; 'his health' is the specific CG domain within which 'fine' must be understood. However, a frame setter is not exactly the same as a contrastive topic as it might carry only some degree of domain specificity, not the really strong properties of definiteness and saliency captured by [+given] and [+salient] features exhibited in (14). We argue that the frame setter should be characterised as [+salient, ±given, +contrast], where ±given captures the idea of specificity and a low degree of givenness; this is further discussed in §6.3.

In Sembiran Balinese, like in English, the frame setter occupies a clause-external left periphery position. This is a position left-adjoined to the maximal sentence structure of CP in terms of a version of the X-bar syntax in LFG adopted here; see §2, also (Arka 2003). Sentence (44a) is an example of frame setting from Sembiran Balinese. The phrase structure of this sentence is given in (44b).

(44) a. [*En buat ngamah*]~Frame~, [*icang ba*]~ContrFoc~ *mehang iya nasi.*
     if about AV.eat   1SG PART   AV.give 3SG rice
     'As for eating needs, I am the person who gave him meals.'

b.
```
                    CP
                   /  \
                  PP   CP
              (FrSetter) /  \
                       NP   IP
         en buat ngamah, icang ba  mehang iya nasi
```

The predication of 'giving him rice' in (44) must be interpreted in the context of the frame setter of 'eating needs' instead of other needs. There is no co-referential or argument-dependency relation between the frame setter *en buat ngamah* and any element in the predication. The element *nasi* 'rice' is related to the frame setter in a sense through its semantic field, e.g. 'food-related' in this case.

However, there are cases where the frame setter expression can be understood as the syntactic dependent of the predicate. These are cases that are traditionally known as left-dislocation and topicalisation, exemplified in English in (45) and (46), respectively (Foley 2007).

(45) a. Turtles, they make the greatest pets. (Left dislocation)
     b. Mary, I went to university with her.

(46) a. That dish, I haven't tried. (Topicalisation)
     b. For Egbert, I would do anything.

Left-dislocation and topicalisation are similar but different types of constructions. In left-dislocation, the frame setter and a syntactic dependent in the predication are related by means of a pronominal copy. In topicalisation, they are related through a filler-gap relation. In languages such as English, left-dislocation is only available for a pivot/subject. A topicalisation of a subject is ungrammatical, as it would leave the subject position unoccupied, e.g. * *Turtles, – make the greatest pets* (Foley 2007).

In terms of information structure, these topicalised/ left-dislocated units are contrastive topics, as they carry the presence of contrasting alternatives, e.g. 'turtles in contrast to other animals as pets' in (45a).

Example (47) illustrates left-dislocation in Sembiran Balinese. The left-dislocated topic (index i) is anaphorically referenced by the pronoun *iya* in the object position.

(47) [*Beli Dora*]$_i$, *nang tua jua ng-adep-in iya$_i$ nyuh pluk kutus puhun.*
     Beli Dora father old PART AV-sell-APPL 3SG coconut eighteen trees
     'As for Brother Dora, it was uncle who sold eighteen coconut trees to him.'

There is no clear difference between left-dislocation and topicalisation in (Sembiran) Balinese. The pronominal copy involved in left-dislocation can be dropped. Sentence (47) is still acceptable when *iya* is elided, making left-dislocation and topicalisation indistinguishable in Balinese. In addition, the overt third-person pronoun *iya* in (Sembiran) Balinese only refers to animate beings, typically human referents. A definite non-human inanimate referent is expressed by a zero pronoun in Balinese. Thus, when the fronted topic NP is associated with an inanimate entity, the structure never appears with an overt pronominal copy *iya*. This is exemplified in (48), where the fronted topic *nyuh nanange nto* 'father's coconut tree' is in the left periphery position. It is the P argument of the verb *nebus* 'AV.redeem'. In its object argument position, the P argument has no overt realisation, indicated by a Ø. Note that it cannot be overtly realised by *iya*, indicated by (*iya*).

(48) [*Nyuh nanang-é ento*]_{Top} *nagih beli Mudiasir buwin nebus* Ø /
 coconut father-DEF that AV.intend brother Mudiasir again AV.redeem
 (**iya*), *nagih bayah=a ny-(c)icil* Ø, *ngara behang-a kén Man Jantuk.*
 3SG intend pay=3 AV-pay NEG give-PASS by Man Jantuk

'As for Father's coconut tree, (brother) Mudiasi wanted to redeem (it); (he) wanted to pay it in instalments, but it was not accepted by Man Jantuk.'

The fact associated with the definite inanimate referent, such as in (48) and other cases with optional *iya* for a human referent, shows that it is unclear whether the unexpressed argument is a gap (i.e. topicalisation) or a zero pronoun (i.e. left-dislocation). For these reasons, the term topicalisation was used for fronted topic NPs in the left peripheral position for both cases with or without an overt pronominal copy; however, if necessary, the empty position was represented by Ø to make the original position of the fronted NP explicit.

6.2 Ordering of marked topic and focus

When both the topic and focus are fronted to left periphery positions, there are immediate questions. First, what is the constraint, if any, in terms of their order? Second, what does the constraint mean in terms of information structure and the broader grammatical system? The empirical issue in relation to the first question is addressed in this section. The second issue is briefly discussed in the conclusion in §7.

When two marked discourse functions are in the left periphery positions, the order is the frame setter/contrastive topic first, followed by contrastive focus, as informally formulated in (49). This is illustrated in (44). Another example is given in (50); however, when the focus is a question word (QW), the fronted focus can precede the frame setter/contrastive topic (see (54)).

(49) [XP]_{Frame/ConstrTopic} [XP]_{ConstFoc} [IP]core clause

(50) [(*En buat*) *behas*]$_{\text{P.ContrTop}}$, [*iya*]$_{\text{A.Piv.ContrFoc}}$ *lakar meli-ang* Ø; (*en buat*)
 (If about) rice 3SG FUT AV.buy-APPL if about
 céléng]$_{\text{P.ContrTop}}$, [*cahi*]$_{\text{A.Piv.ContrFoc}}$ *ngurus-ang* Ø.
 pig 2SG AV.arrange-APPL

'As for rice, he'll buy it; as for pigs, you have to arrange them.'

In example (50), there are parallel clausal structures with their P arguments *behas*, 'rice' and *celeng*, 'pig' functioning as frame setters, which are also contrastive topics. Note that the structure is in the AV voice with the A being a pivot. The unmarked position of the object P is postverbal, indicated by Ø.

The evidence that these sentence-initial expressions in (50) are topics is that they can be marked by the topic phrasal marker *en buat* 'as for'. They are also frame setters, as they delimit the interpretation of the predication. That is, the action of buying is about/in relation to rice, whereas the other arrangement is in relation to pigs.

Another important point to note from example (50) is that the topic expressions are not definite. They are indefinite/generic, referring to a class of entities called *behas* 'rice' versus another class called *celeng* 'pig'. No particular rice or pig is referred to: any rice or pig would do. In short, this provides evidence from Sembiran Balinese that the topic is not necessarily definite.

There is evidence that the actor pivot arguments, *iya* and *cahi*, in (50) are a contrastive focus because these are units that can be marked by the contrastive focus relativiser (*a*)*ne* – an exclusive property of a pivot. The fact that only a pivot can be relativised is a well-known characteristic of Austronesian languages. Thus, the pivot *iya* can receive *ane*, marking the contrast (51a). In contrast, marking the topicalised P results in an ungrammatical structure, as shown in (51b).

(51) a. [*Behas*]$_{\text{P.ContrTop}}$, [*iya*]$_{\text{A.Piv.ContrFoc}}$ *ane lakar meli-ang.*
 rice 3SG REL FUT AV.buy-APPL

 'As for rice, he is the one who will buy it.'

 b. * [*Behas*]$_{\text{P.ContrTop}}$ *ane*, [*iya*]$_{\text{A.Piv.ContrFoc}}$ *lakar meli-ang.* NOT FOR 'As for
 rice REL 3SG FUT AV.buy-APPL
 rice, he will buy it' or 'It is rice that he will buy.'

Reversing the order with the contrastive focus first and the frame setter/contrastive topic after compromises the acceptability. In contrast to (50), for example, the following is unacceptable:

(52) ?* [*iya*]$_{\text{A.Piv.ContrFoc}}$ [(*en buat*) *behas*]$_{\text{P.ContrTop}}$, *lakar meli-ang* Ø; FOR 'As
 3SG (if about) rice FUT AV.buy-APPL
 for rice, he is the one who will buy it.'

Unlike the previous example in (50), the frame setter/topic in example (53a) is definite:

(53) a. [Ne]_Top [cahi]_A.Piv.Foc ba   ane ngelahang.
       this   2SG   PART REL AV.have.APPL
   'This (land), YOU are the one who owns (it).'

   b. [Ne]_Top ba   [cahi]_A.Piv (ba) ane ngelahang.
      this   PART   2SG   PART REL AV.have.APPL
   'THIS (LAND), YOU are the one who owns (it).'

   c. * [Ne]_Top ba   ane [cahi]_A.Piv (ba) ngelahang.
        this   PART REL 2SG   PART AV.have.APPL
   'NOT FOR 'THIS (land), YOU are the one who owns (it)' or
   'It is THIS (LAND) that YOU are the one who owns it.'

Note that the focus appears with a particle *ba* marking [+contrast]. This particle can be associated with either a topic or a focus; hence, (53b) with both a topic and a focus marked by *ba* is possible. The topic in (53b) has a stronger contrast (indicated by placing its translation of THIS in capital letters) than its counterpart without *ba* in (53a), e.g. with additional affirmation in response to the addressee's question/hesitation.

The unacceptability of (53c) provides further evidence that a contrastive focus cannot precede a contrastive topic in left periphery positions. In this example, an attempt is made to make the first NP a contrastive focus by a *ba* and *ane* marking.

Still, it is possible to have a fronted focus before a topicalised NP in (Sembiran) Balinese. This is the case when the focus is a question word (QW). This possibility stems from the constraint that a fronted QW must be associated with a pivot, an exclusive property of the pivot argument in Balinese (Arka 2003). Consider a transitive predicate such as *alih* 'AV.search' in a declarative sentence, as in (54a). When the A pivot is questioned, the QW can appear in situ, as in (54b). The P object can be topicalised, as in (54c). The QW can be fronted as well, as in (54d). Note that the fronted QW must be associated with the PIV, which is in this case the A argument (index *j*) because the verb is in the AV. While the NP *Men Tiwas* is closer to the verb than the fronted QW, the fronted QW must be associated with the pivot (index j; reading [i]), not the object (reading ii).

(54) a. *Men Sugih ngalih   Men Tiwas.*
       Men Sugih AV.look.for Men Tiwas
   'Men Sugih looked for Men Tiwas.'

   b. *Nyen ngalih   Men Tiwas?*
      who AV.look.for Men Tiwas
   'Who looked for Men Tiwas?'

   c. [*Men Tiwas*]_Top–i [[*nyen*]_Foc [*ngalih*   _i]]_IP?
      Men Tiwas   who   AV.look.for
   '(As for) Men Tiwas, who looked for her?'

   d. [*Nyen*]_Foc_j/*i [*Men Tiwas*]_Top [_j ngalih   _i]?
      who   Men Tiwas   A.PIV AV.look.for P.OBJECT
   i) 'Who was looking for Men Tiwas?'
   ii) * 'Whom Men Tiwas was looking for?'

An adjunct can appear as a frame setter. It may also carry an emphatic or contrastive meaning. Consider the following example in (55), where the adverb *ditu* 'there' in the left periphery position is referentially the same as the sentence-final adjunct PP 'at Butuh Catra's place'. The contrastive-emphatic meaning resulting from the appearance of *ditu* 'there' in the left periphery position is captured by the rather long free translation given the locative adjunct in (55).

(55) Ba kento [ditu sa]$_{\text{Frame\_i}}$ [meme]$_{\text{S.Top}}$ bareng megae [di Butuh
 after like.that there PART mother together MID.work at Butuh

 Catra-ne ento]$_{\text{\_i}}$.
 Catra-DEF that

 'After that, THERE at Butuh Catra's place (i.e. not at other places), I (mother) work together.'

6.3 Scope, contrast, and negation

In this final subsection, we address the issue of the scope of focus/contrast and related complexity due to the interaction of information with negation, topicalisation and pragmatic-contextual implication where local socio-cultural information might also be important. We begin with the different sizes focus can apply.

Units of different sizes can be put into contrast, bearing a new focus, from a broad new focus covering the whole sentence (even a string of sentences) to a narrow(er) new focus involving smaller/lower clausal constituents, such as VPs with their object NPs, just the object NP or oblique PP of a VP or possibly even just the modifier part of the object NP. A (wide) sentence new focus (cf. Lambrecht 1994) is exemplified by the answer sentence in example (56) from English (Foley 1994).[11] The same sentence in different discourse contexts would have a different information structure involving different units of new focus. If the context of the dialogue in (56) already included Los Angeles (LA) as part of the CG information, then LA would not be part of the new focus unit.

(56) Q: What happened?
 A: An earthquake just hit Los Angeles.

Of particular interest are the intricacies of the different sizes of unit being focussed and contrasted through negation. Negation is of particular interest because it illustrates the complexity of a semantic-pragmatic-syntax interface wherein there can be a mismatch between scope in semantics and pragmatic information structure. Consider the yes/no question-answer pair in (57) and its context.

---

[11]Foley distinguishes between focus and new information. He argues that not all the new information is a focus, e.g. a high falling pitch in the answer sentence in (56) would indicate that the last NP Los Angeles is the focus (i.e. the earthquake happened just in Los Angeles not in other cities), while the whole sentence carries new information. Focus in Foley's sense here is equivalent to the emphatic/contrastive focus type captured by the [+contrast] feature.

(57) Context: Men Dora told a story about how she gave her money to somebody but did not get her land certificate, and consequently, she lost her land.

Question: *Bakat   tanah-e?* (=(15))
         UV.obtain land-DEF
'Did you get the land?'

Men Dora: [*ngara*]_{Foc}, [*ngara*]_{Foc} *bakat.*
          NEG   NEG   UV.obtain
'No, (I) didn't get (it).'

Semantically, the negation is wide in scope, as it negates the whole sentence/proposition; however, in terms of information structure, the new information (i.e. new focus) does not cover the whole sentence/proposition. The new focus here is the negative choice itself. A yes/no question offers closed alternatives, and in this instance, the 'no' option is chosen/true. The information conveyed by the other parts of the sentence is not new. The subject topic 'the land' and the A argument ('you') are already understood (i.e. part of the CG) and are therefore elided. The predication encoded by the UV verb 'obtain' is also presupposed information.

A negator can often result in different scopes, possibly with ambiguity, typically when the negation is of the type of normal sentential negation, as exemplified in (58a). Note that, even though the negator *ngara* appears in its preverbal position in this sentence, reading (ii) is possible: it does not negate the predicate *mati*, but only the adjunct *ulihan nyai* following the verb. This reflects the narrow scope of the negation.

(58) a. *Kucit-e   ngara mati ulihan   nyai.*
        piglet-DEF NEG   die because.of 2SG.F
   i. 'The piglet was not dead because of you.'
   ii. 'The piglet was dead not because of you.'

   b. *Kucit-e   mati ngara ulihan   nyai.*
      piglet-DEF die NEG   because.of 2SG.F
   * i. 'The piglet was not dead because of you.'
   ii. 'The piglet was dead not because of you.'

Sentence (58b) exemplifies a constituent negation where the negator immediately precedes the PP. The predicate *mati* is not in the negation scope; hence there is no ambiguity.

Then, the negated unit together with its negator can appear in the left-periphery position to express a contrastive focus, as illustrated by the excerpt from the corpus in (59). In this example, the context provides the contrasting reason for the piglet's death. However, it should be noted that, even without an explicit contrasting element as in (58b), the constituent negation presupposes that something else has caused the death of the piglet; hence the negated adjunct is contrastive focus.

(59) *Ento kucit mati kinnya behan sakiten;* [*ngara* [*ulihan nyai*]]_{Foc} *kada mati.*
    that piglet dead because by sickness NEG   because.of 2SG.F   make dead

'The piglet died because of its sickness; not because of you, (the thing that) caused its death.'

Fronting may give rise to topicalisation, selecting a narrow scope for negation, and the fronted unit appears to behave like a topic. Its status as contrastive topic (or focus) is, however, not immediately clear.

Consider (60), where the negator *ngara* appears in its position preverbally, but its semantic scope is narrow, due to the fronting for the object. That is, the predicate *ngelah*, 'have' is not within its scope of negation. Based on the context, it is understood that the speaker might have other types of produce, but she had no coconuts—the relevant produce needed for the barter.

(60) *Budi luwas ke gunung ngalih sela,   [nyuh]*_{ContrFoc} *ngara ngelah.*
    want go to mountain AV.get sweet.potato coconuts   NEG   AV.have

'I was going to go to the mountain to trade for sweet potatoes, but, as for COCONUTS, I didn't have any.'

The fronted object P *nyuh* to the left-dislocated position is assigned [+contrast]. The question is whether the fronted unit is a contrastive focus, as seen in the fronted adjunct in the preceding example in (59), or a contrastive topic.

We contend that it is neither; it is a frame setter. It is not really the focus, as the focus is in fact the narrow negation with respect to possession of 'coconuts'. It is not really the topic, as it is not definite, and it is actually new as far as the immediate CG context is concerned; hence [-given].

The referent of 'coconut', however, could be thought of as [+salient], as evidenced by the fronting (a common strategy for expressing some kind of salience). It is also salient as far as the local socio-cultural context is concerned. That is, the fronting should also be understood as the speaker's intention to express not only the bipolar sense of contrast in relation to the negation of coconuts, but also in relation to the socio-cultural salience of coconuts vs. other items of farm produce for bartering. The two senses of contrast are represented in (61), with (b) showing the sociocultural-economic contrast set.

(61) a. Truth value contrast:
        {['have no coconuts']_{NegFocus}, ['having coconuts']}_{Frame}
    b. Local cultural-economic contrast:
        {['no coconuts for barter']_{NegFoc} ['other items for barter]}_{Frame}

The data of the types shown above raise an important issue in the analysis of (contrastive) topic and frame setter in terms of the feature space outlined in (14). The challenge is how to capture the different degrees of specificity and salience characterising the CG. The CG may simply be specific in the larger context of a particular domain due to our understanding of the world or due to certain local socio-cultural knowledge. Such referential specificity may not render the referent of an entity definite (i.e. [+given]) but the referent is not totally [-given] either. We propose that such a referent bears a weak given property, represented by [±given] in our proposed feature space; meaning it is 'specific', neither indefinite nor definite; see the discussion of the relationship between (in)definiteness and specificity (Enç 1991). This issue highlights the gradient nature of the information structure categories. Thus, the other features [contrast] and [salient] can also be thought of as gradient in nature, represented in the same way, [±contrast] and [±salient] respectively. Exploring the precise implication of adding this weak dimension as another value to the analysis of information structure is beyond the scope of the present paper.

7 Conclusion and final remarks

New data on information structure from Sembiran Balinese, an endangered conservative mountain dialect of Balinese, has been presented. This is the first detailed study on information structure in this language that outlines the ways the pragmatic functions of the topic and focus interact with each other and with the grammatical functions in the grammar of this language. In a descriptive-empirical context, it has been shown that Sembiran Balinese employs combined strategies, exploiting the available structural positions (e.g. left/right periphery, parallel clausal structures) and morpho-lexical and syntactic resources in grammar (e.g. voice systems and particles) and general local knowledge. Prosody has been identified to play a role in Sembiran Balinese, but its precise role in information structure in this language requires further research.

In an analytical context, the novel approach of the analysis presented is the conceptions of the topic and focus as complex notions, decomposed into three semantic-discourse/pragmatic features of [+/−salient], [+/−given] and [+/−contrast]. Based on these features, the information structure space in Sembiran Balinese was explored. The investigation revealed that the three features of topic and focus interact in complex ways, allowing for different possibilities to characterise different subtypes of the topic and focus in Sembiran Balinese, such as default/primary topic, secondary topic, contrastive topic/focus and new topic/new focus. Throughout the paper, language-specific characterisations and supporting data for these sub-types of topic and focus in Sembiran Balinese have been provided. Thus, this study has contributed to the typology of information structure and the framework by which such a typological study can be conducted.

On a theoretical level, the analysis assumes a modular parallel model of grammar, as in LFG (Bresnan et al. 2015, among others, Dalrymple 2001) and RRG (Van Valin 2005, Van Valin & LaPolla 1997). There have been proposals regarding how i-str units can be formally and precisely mapped onto other layers of structures in grammar (King 1997, Mycock 2013, Butt 2014). The comprehensive classification of the discourse functions of the topic and focus provided in this paper can be formally utilised in existing frameworks.

One theoretical point worth highlighting is the concept of prominence in linguistic theories, and to certain extent, in language typology. Prominence in LFG, for example, has played a key role in the linking/mapping theory to account for cross-linguistic predictability and variations in semantics-syntax interfaces. The basic principle of any theory of linking is harmonious prominence matching: most prominent items across layers tend to require being mapped onto each other. Thus, given the widely agreed cross-linguistic generalisation of the prominence of A>P in semantic-argument structure and the pivot/subject>object in syntactic argument structure, there is a cross-linguistic tendency of A and the Subject to be mapped to each other. In this context, the prominence of the i-str space is included based on the proposed conception, as discussed in §3. The decomposition of the topic and focus into features with values allows for representing the gradient nature of the types of topic and focus thus far identified. Based on the analysis, the presence of the properties (i.e. with + value) contributes to the prominence, which results in the gradience shown in (62).

Some discussion is needed for the gradience of information structure prominence captured by (62). First, the gradience comes with two opposing ends in which the contrastive topic/frame setter is the most prominent category (with all features having plusses) and new/completive focus is the least prominent (with all features having minuses). The plus value should be understood as the presence of the relevant information structure property, possibly with its overt marking. Thus, from the speaker's perspective, a contrastive topic/frame setter encodes an information unit singled out as having some kind of importance, which has been amply demonstrated in the previous discussion as having salient or marked structural and prosodic properties; e.g. fronted, stressed and/or marked by particles; see §5.5 and §6.1. Structurally, it is high in the phrase structure tree; see (5). In contrast, the new/completive focus is the least prominent, as evidenced from its structural and prosodic properties in Sembiran Balinese; e.g. expressed later in the clause (formally low in the phrase structure tree) and linked to a less prominent grammatical function (e.g. P as object, rather than the pivot).

Second, the information structure prominence captured in (62) should be understood as reflecting the general pattern, with typical structural and prosodic correlates as just mentioned. However, there is no one-to-one correlation, and there may be a case where focus structurally comes first and the frame setter/contrastive topic comes second. This is when the focus is linked to the pivot, which is the most prominent grammatical function, as seen in the case with a fronted QW, exemplified in (54). This indicates that grammatical prominence outweighs information structure prominence, at least in (Sembiran) Balinese.

(62)

	1	2	3	4	5	6	7	8
salience	+	+	+	−	+	−	−	−
given	$+^a/\pm^b$	−	+	+	−	+	−	−
contrast	+	+	−	+	−	−	+	−

1=a.ContrTopic; b.FrameSetter
2=ContrFocus (fronted)
3=Default Topic
4=ContrSecondTopic
5=NewTopic
6=SecondTopic
7=ContrNewFoc
8=New/Completive Focus

Third, the prominence is gradient in the sense that there are no discrete or clear boundaries in the ranking of the categories in between the two ends, even though a pattern indicating the ranking of two subclasses is observable in (62): subgroups 2–4 vs. 5–7. Subgroup 2–4 appears to be more prominent than subgroup 5–7. Evidence for this in Sembiran Balinese, for example, comes from the positive values of the information structure features correlating with the structural marking properties. Thus, the default topic comes structurally higher, before the verb, whereas the secondary topic comes later, after the verb.

However, the prominence of member categories within each group is not always clear. For this reason, no boundaries are represented separating them within their own group (62). The labelling and ordering of the members of the second group, 5–7, are for convenience only. More research is needed to determine how new topic (5), secondary topic (6) and non-fronted (contrastive) new focus should be ranked with one another.

Finally, another question regarding prominence is whether the three features are also ranked against each other. While a definite answer to this question requires further verification and investigation (as the element of contrast can be achieved by means of more than one strategy), it appears that [+contrast] outweighs [+givenness]. Evidence for this can be found in the contrastive new focus in (Sembiran) Balinese, which triggers the linking to the pivot, as seen in example (23). That is, when the A is [+given] and P is [+contrast], even though it is new, it triggers the linking to pivot and can claim a position earlier or higher (i.e. more prominent) (phrase-) structurally.

Prominence is a broad and important concept in typological and theoretical linguistics, and this paper has contributed to the empirical basis of this area of research. The notion of contextual CG is central in the information structure analysis, and this paper has also contributed to the empirical basis in this discourse pragmatic research by highlighting the significance of the local socio-cultural information in understanding information structure in Sembiran Balinese. Languages vary in terms of coding resources, and this paper has contributed to descriptive linguistics, showing how linear order and constituency, voice system, and other grammatical-lexical resources interact to convey complex and subtle communicative meanings. More research is required to uncover whether similar patterns and complexities are encountered in the neighbouring languages, and beyond.

Acknowledgements

We thank our Sembiran Balinese consultants for their help with the data. We also thank two anonymous reviewers for their detailed comments and criticism of the earlier version of this paper. We found their feedback very useful for the revision, and the quality of the published paper has been significantly improved by their feedback. All remaining errors are ours.

Abbreviations

1, 2, 3	first, second and third person pronouns	NEG	negator
		NML	nominaliser
A	actor	NOM	nominative
ACC	accusative	P	most patient-like argument of transitive verbs
APPL	applicative		
ART	article	PART	particle
AV	actor voice	PERF	perfect
CAUS	causative	Piv	Pivot
CG	Common Ground	POSS	possessive
DEF	definite	RED	reduplication
Foc	Focus	REL	relativiser
FUT	future	S	subject of intransitive verb
h.r.	high register	SG	singular
LIG	ligature	Top	Topic
MID	middle voice	UV	undergoer voice

References

Arka, I Wayan. 2003. *Balinese morphosyntax: A lexical-functional approach*. Canberra: Pacific Linguistics.

Arka, I Wayan. 2010. Ritual dance and song in language documentation: Vera in Rongga and the struggle over culture and tradition in modern Manggarai-Indonesia. In M. Florey (ed.), *Language endangerment in the Austronesian world: Challenges and responses*, 90–109. Oxford: Oxford University Press.

Astini, Ida Ayu Putu. 1996. *Struktur geminasi bahasa Bali dialek Sembiran*. Denpasar: Linguistics Graduate Program, Universitas Udayana. (MA thesis).

Bickel, Balthasar. 2011. Grammatical relations typology. In Jae Jung Song (ed.), *The Oxford handbook of language typology*, 399–444. Oxford: Oxford University Press.

Blust, Robert. 2013. *The Austronesian languages*. Canberra. http://hdl.handle.net/1885/10191. Revised edition.

Bresnan, Joan. 2001. *Lexical-Functional Syntax*. London: Blackwell.

Bresnan, Joan, Ash Asudeh, Ida Toivonen & Stephen Wechler. 2015. *Lexical-Functional Syntax*. 2nd edn. Oxford: Wiley-Blackwell.

Butt, Miriam. 2014. Question and information structure in Urdu/Hindi. In Miriam Butt & Tracy H. King (eds.), *Proceedings of LFG14*, 158–178. Stanford: CSLI Publications. http://web.stanford.edu/group/cslipublications/cslipublications/LFG/19/lfg14.html.

Choi, Hye-Won. 1999. *Optimizing structure in context: Scrambling and information structure*. Stanford: CSLI Publications.

Comrie, Bernard. 1978. Ergativity. In W. P. Lehman (ed.), *Syntactic typology: Studies in the phenomenology of language*, 329–394. Austin: University of Austin Press.

Comrie, Bernard. 1987. Russian. In Timothy Shopen (ed.), *Languages and their Status*, 91–151. Philadelphia: University of Pennsylvania Press.

Comrie, Bernard. 2005. Towards a typology of ditransitive constructions. In *The Sixth Congress of the Association for Linguistic Typology*. Padang, Indonesia.

Croft, William. 2003. *Typology and universals*. Cambridge: Cambridge University Press. second edition.

Dalrymple, Mary. 2001. *Lexical Functional Grammar*. San Diego: Academic Press.

Dalrymple, Mary & Irina Nikolaeva. 2011. *Objects and information structure*. Cambridge: Cambridge University Press.

Dalrymple, Mary & Irina Nikolaeva. 2014. *Object and information structure*. Cambridge: Cambridge University Press.

Dixon, R. M.W. 1979. Ergativity. *Language* 55. 59–138.

Dowty, D. 1991. Thematic Proto-roles and Argument selection. *Language* 67. 547–617.

Enç, M. 1991. The semantics of specificity. *Linguistic Inquiry* 22(1). 1–25.

Erteschick-Shir, Naomi. 2007. *Information structure*. Oxford: Oxford University Press.

Foley, William A. 1994. Information Structure. In R. E. Asher & J. M.Y. Simpson (eds.), *The encyclopedia of language and linguistics*, 1678–85. Oxford: Pergamon Press.

Foley, William A. 2007. A typology of information packaging in the clause. In Timothy Shopen (ed.), *Language typology and syntactic description*, 2nd edn., 362–446. Cambridge: Cambridge University Press.

Fox, James J. 1988. *To speak in pairs: Essays on the ritual languages of eastern Indonesia*. Cambridge: Cambridge University Press.

Givón, Talmy. 1990. *Syntax: A Functional-Typological introduction*. Amsterdam: John Benjamins Publishing Company.

Givón, Talmy. 1994. *Voice and inversion*. Amsterdam: John Benjamins Publishing Company.

Grimes, Charles E, Tom Therik, Barbara D Grimes & Max Jacob. 1997. *A guide to the people and languages of Nusa Tenggara*. Kupang: Artha Wacana Press.

Gundel, Jeanette K. 1988. Universals of topic-comment structure. In Michael Hammond, Edith Moravczik & Jessica Wirth (eds.), *Studies in syntactic typology*, 209–239. Amsterdam: John Benjamins Publishing Company.

Haspelmath, Martin. 2007. Ditransitive alignment splits and inverse alignment. *Functions of Language* 14(1). 79–102.

Heine, Bernd & Tania Kuteva. 2002. *World lexicon of grammaticalization*. Cambridge: Cambridge University Press.

Keenan, Edward L. & Bernard Comrie. 1977. Noun phrase accessibility and universal grammar. *Linguistic Inquiry* 8. 63–99.

King, Tracy Holloway. 1997. Focus domains and information structure. In Miriam Butt & Tracy Holloway King (eds.), *On-Line Proceedings of the LFG97 Conference*. CSLI On-line Publications.

Krifka, Manfred. 2008. Basic notions of information structure. *Acta Linguistica Hungarica* 55(3–4). 243–276.

Krifka, Manfred & Renate Musan. 2012. Information structure: Overview and linguistic issues. In Manfred Krifka & Renate Musan (eds.), *The expression of information structure*, 1–44. Berlin: Mouton De Gruyter.

Kuipers, J. C. 1998. *Language, identity, and marginality in Indonesia: The changing nature of ritual speech on the island of Sumba*. Cambridge: Cambridge University Press.

Lambrecht, Knud. 1994. *Information structure and sentence form: Topic, focus and the mental representations of discourse referents*. Cambridge, UK: Cambridge University Press.

Mycock, Louise. 2013. Discourse functions of question words. In M. Butt & T. H. King (eds.), *Proceedings of the LFG13 Conference*. Stanford: CSLI Publications.

Pastika, I Wayan. 2006. *Voice selection in Balinese narrative discourse*. Bali-Indonesia: Pustaka Lasaran.

Quick, Phil. 2005. Topic continuity, voice and word order in Pendau. In I Wayan Arka & Malcolm Ross (eds.), *The many faces of Austronesian voice systems: Some new empirical studies*, 221–242. Canberra: Pacific Linguistics.

Quick, Phil. 2007. *A grammar of the Pendau language of central Sulawesi, Indonesia*. Canberra: Australian National University dissertation.

Reinhart, Tanya. 1981. Pragmatics and Linguistics: An analysis of sentence topics. *Philosophica* 27. 53–94.

Rosch, Eleanor. 1978. Principles of categorization. In E Rosch & B. Llcyd (eds.), *Cognition and categorization*, 27–47. Hillsdale: Lawrence Erlbaum.

Sedeng, I Nyoman. 2007. *Morfosintaksis bahasa Bali dialek Sembiran: Analisis tatabahasa peran dan acuan [The morphosyntax of Sembiran Balinese: A Role and Reference Grammar Analysis]*. Denpasar: Universitas Udayana dissertation.

Sumitri, Ni Wayan & I Wayan Arka. 2016. Bahasa ritual dan kekuasaan tradisional etnik Rongga [Ritual language and traditional power in Rongga]. In *Proceedings of the KIMLI 2016 (the International Conference of the Indonesian Linguistics Society)*, 669–674. Denpasar-Bali: Universitas Udayana.

Taylor, John R. 1991. *Linguistic categorization: Protoypes in linguistic theory*. Oxford: Clarendon Press.

Vallduví, Enric & Elisabet Engdahl. 1996. The linguistic realisation of information packaging. *Linguistics* 34. 459–510.

Van Valin, Robert D. 2005. *Exploring the syntax-semantics interface*. Cambridge: Cambridge University Press.

Van Valin, Robert D. & Randy J. LaPolla. 1997. *Syntax: Structure, meaning and function*. Cambridge: Cambridge University Press.

Witzlack-Makarevich, Alena. 2011. *Typological variations in grammatical relations*. University of Leipzig dissertation.

Wouk, Fay. 1999. Sasak is different: A discourse perspective on voice. *Oceanic Linguistics* 38. 91–114.

Chapter 6

Constituent order and information structure in Indonesian discourse

Dwi Noverini Djenar
The University of Sydney

> This study draws on theories of information structure to examine the findings from Cumming's (1991) study showing changing preferences in constituent order in Indonesian. Cumming found that predicate-initial clauses, an important grammatical resource for encoding events in Classical Malay, are diminishing in Indonesian, and agentive clauses are now preferred. Based on data from fictional discourse and television reports, three clause structures are examined: [*meN*-V], [*di*-V-*nya*] and [*ia* V]. I show that the use of [*meN*-V] to denote successive events and to mark the climactic portion of a story episode illustrate most dramatically the preference for agentive clauses in Indonesian. I also argue that [*di*-V-*nya*] remains an important resource for encoding events but its pragmatic function seems to have weakened. This clause type is now mainly used to mark a new focus, drawing the addressee's attention to a particular event or series of events. Meanwhile, objective voice [*ia* V] is also used to encode events; however, unlike [*di*-V-*nya*] which is structurally different from [*meN*-V], the use of [*ia* V] alongside agentive clause structure [*ia meN*-V] creates an impression of structural symmetry and can serve two goals simultaneously: marking event and signalling a new focus. It could be that, as the pragmatic force of [*di*-V-*nya*] is weakening, [*ia* V] is increasingly preferred for marking focal events.

1 Introduction

In her work on constituent order in Malay, Cumming (1991) makes an important observation regarding syntactic change in this language, arguing that the predominant VSO order in Classical Malay has gradually given way to SVO order in Indonesian and Malaysian.[1] She points out that predicate-initial clauses, an important grammatical resource for encoding "eventiveness" in Classical Malay, are diminishing in Indonesian, and agentive clauses are now preferred (Cumming 1991: 199). Eventiveness, in her term, refers to "a related class of phenomena having to do more with characteristics of an event

---

[1] Cumming uses the term "Modern Indonesian" to refer to contemporary Standard Indonesian, and 'Malay' to the language of which Indonesian and Malaysian national languages are varieties (1991: 2).

Dwi Noverini Djenar. 2018. Constituent order and information structure in Indonesian discourse. In Sonja Riesberg, Asako Shiohara & Atsuko Utsumi (eds.), *Perspectives on information structure in Austronesian languages*, 177–205. Berlin: Language Science Press. DOI:10.5281/zenodo.1402545

than with characteristics of its participants"; while some phenomena "are primarily related to the inherent semantics of the event", others "have more to do with the way the event is presented" (Cumming 1991: 123). Eventiveness is also associated with high discourse transitivity and event sequentiality (Cumming 1991: 161–162). Cumming (1991: 176) notes that in Indonesian, predicate initial clauses with passive morphology such as [di-V-nya] are still used to encode eventiveness but eventiveness is not the only motivation for this passive morphology. Such clauses tend to be "especially eventive" (Cumming 1991: 176). Clauses with pre-predicate patient indicate that the patient is treated as "topical", that is, it has either been mentioned in the immediately preceding clause or a few clauses back and needs recalling (Cumming 1991: 176).[2]

In this study, I examine Cumming's findings in light of more recent data from standard Indonesian.[3] My goal is to demonstrate that, although the data support Cumming's observation, the preference in Indonesian is for events to be encoded with [meN-V] clauses, and that predicate initial clauses such as those encoded with [di-V-nya] are marked, there seems to be a further development since her study. I focus my discussion on the interaction between three types of clause structure – agentive clauses with [meN-V], [di-V-nya] 'passive' clauses, and objective clauses with [ia V] – to show the following. First, [meN-V] clauses are indeed preferred for encoding various events, including successive events, irrespective of whether they are performed by the same agent or different agents. Cumming (1991: 175) states that in Indonesian, [di-V-nya] passive morphology is reserved for "especially eventive" clauses that mark the "climactic portion" of a story episode. The data in this study show that [meN-V] clauses are also used for this purpose. These provide strong support for Cumming's finding that the preference in Indonesian is for agentive clauses.

Second, the function of [di-V-nya] appears to be weaker now than Cumming found in her data. Events encoded by [di-V-nya] in the present data do not need to be "especially eventive" or to occur in the climactic portion of a story episode; rather, [di-V-nya] is mainly used to signal a new focus. A switch from [meN-V] to [di-V-nya] invites the addressee/reader to turn their attention to a different event or series of events. The switch may indicate a shift from a series of descriptive clauses to an eventive one, or from a series of eventive clauses to a different event or series of events.

Third, in addition to [di-V-nya], another type of clause is also employed to mark a new focus, namely objective clause with free third person pronoun ia '3SG'. The objective clause structure [ia V] is often preceded and followed by [ia meN-V] agentive clauses. A switch from [ia meN-V] to [ia V] signals a new focus, similar to a switch from [meN-V] to [di-V-nya], but whereas [di-V-nya] marks a structural difference from [meN-V], the

---

[2] "Topical" in Cumming's (1991) sense is slightly different from "topic" in theories of information structure adopted here. Cumming's use of the term considers the tracking of a referent across clauses and narrative episodes, and the position of the participant relative to other participants in narrative, whereas topic in the information structure theories is defined at clause or sentence level. Nevertheless, in both cases, a topic referent is understood as one that has been previously mentioned and hence can be presupposed.

[3] Cole et al. (2008) distinguish between standard Indonesian that is the formal variety of the language and the "prescriptive standard" variety, i.e., the highly institutionally prescribed variety. No such distinction is made in this study.

use of [ia V] objective clause alongside [ia meN-V] agentive clause creates an impression of structural sameness. In both cases, the third person pronoun ia '3SG' is preverbal, thus highlighting the continuity of the third person as agent (or actor in intransitive clause) through explicit mention of the agent. In events encoded by [meN-V] clauses, agent continuity tends to be indicated with zero.

I draw on theories of information structure advanced by Lambrecht (1994), Gundel (1999), Gundel et al. (1993) and Gundel & Fretheim (2004) to demonstrate how a switch from [meN-V] clauses to [di-V-nya] or [ia V] can be explained as a shift to a new focus. As will be shown, a switch to a different grammatical construction functions to draw the addressee's attention to a particular action or series of actions the agent is performing which cannot presupposed from the previous clauses. Drawing on the notion of "topic" in these theories is also useful for explaining why one participant, and not another, is referred to with zero in a series of [meN-V] clauses as well as what the relation is between the topic participant and the focal elements in the clause. More generally, examining the functions of the different clause structures in terms of information structure is helpful for explaining why clauses occur in the structures that they do.

Most of the data for this study are taken from six Indonesian novels. One of the novels was published in 1977, and the others between 2002 and 2012. I chose fiction rather than other types of text based on the following considerations. First, fictional texts contain numerous instances of clause chains and different clause structures, including [di-V-nya] clauses which may be rare in other text types, thus enabling us to examine the interaction between the different clause structures. Second, Cumming's findings on Indonesian were based on fictional texts, hence using data from the same text type but a different period is helpful for showing in what respects her findings are current and how they can be extended. I include examples from television news broadcast to show that the arguments I offer are also relevant for non-fictional texts.

This chapter is structured as follows. §2 provides a description of the different clause structures to be analysed and introduces Cumming's (1991) "trigger" system. §3 provides an overview of "topic" and "focus", key concepts in information structure, to facilitate the analysis of the three Indonesian clause types in §4, §5, and §6 respectively. The study concludes in §7 with a summary of findings and suggestions for further research.

2 Agent trigger and patient trigger clauses

In her study, Cumming (1991: 29) discusses different clause structures in terms of "trigger". She distinguishes three types of clause: the intransitive clause, the "agent trigger" (AT) clause and "patient trigger" (PT) clause, the latter two being types of transitive clauses. "Trigger" is a syntactic role label for "the participant which is a) obligatory, and b) functions as the shared argument or 'pivot' in clause combining" (1991: 31), and whose semantic role "triggers" the verb morphology. In the AT clause, the trigger has the semantic role of agent, while in the PT clause, it has the semantic role of patient. I adopt her terminology here.

In Indonesian AT clauses, the agent typically precedes the verb and the verb is generally prefixed with *meN-*, as shown in (1).

(1) *Mel **meng-ambil** kimono.*
    Mel MEN-fetch   kimono
    'Mel **fetched** (her) kimono.' (Nuranindya 2009: 14)

PT clauses are of two types. The first has [*di-*V] verbal morphology. In this clause type, the agent, when expressed, occurs in an adjunct phrase typically marked by *oleh* 'by', as shown in (2). This type of PT clause is also referred to in the literature as "passive" or "passive type 1" (Sneddon et al. 2010).

(2) *Sepasang   suami   istri yang sedang   pergi ke tahlilan keluarga di   Cirebon*
    one.couple husband wife REL in.process go   to *tahlilah* family   LOC Cirebon
    ***di-serang** oleh geng motor.*
    DI-attack   by   gang motor
    'A husband and wife, who went to a family *tahlilan* event in Cirebon, were attacked by a motorcycle gang.'[4] (*Fokus Pagi, Indosiar*, 9/11/2015)

A related clause type is one where [*di-*V] is followed by the cliticised third person agent *–nya* '3SG'. The enclitic *–nya* is attached to the verb rather than to the preposition *oleh* 'by' in an adjunct phrase (*olehnya* 'by her/him/it'). In example (3), [*di-*V-*nya*] occurs with pre-predicate patient.

(3) *Dan setelah pamili ini   agak   berada   sedikit, kamar itu **di-pakai-nya** sebagai*
    and after   family this rather wealthy a.little room that DI-use-3SG   as
    kandang anjing yang baru   di-beli-nya. Lit. 'And after the family became a
    kennel dog   REL recently DI-buy-3SG
    little wealthy, the room **was used by him/her** as a kennel for the dog they had bought.'
    'After the family became a little wealthy, they used the room as a kennel for the dog s/he had just bought.'   (Idrus, cited in Kaswanti Purwo 1988: 204; my translation)

[*di-*V-*nya*] clauses also occur with post-predicate patient, as in (4).

(4) *Babu itu me-lihat air   yang berkilauan. [...]. Kemudian **di-ambil-nya** abu,*
    maid that MEN-see water REL BER-shine   then   DI-get-3SG   ash
    di-siram-kan pada air   kencing dan [...].
    DI-pour-APPL LOC water urine   and
    'The maid looked at the shining liquid. [...]. Then **she took** some ashes and **sprinkled** (them) on the urine and [...].' (Pramoedya Ananta Toer 1963: 25–26; cited in Kaswanti Purwo 1988: 219; translation from Kaswanti Purwo 1988: 219)[5]

---

[4] *Tahlilan* is a Muslim social gathering to commemorate the dead.
[5] For consistency, I use my own glossing in this example rather than the original.

6 Constituent order and information structure in Indonesian discourse

As Cumming's (1991) and Hopper's (1979) studies show, [*di*-V-*nya*] is a common device for marking foregrounding in Classical Malay. Foregrounding clauses, in Hopper's definition, are clauses denoting "events belonging to the skeletal structure of the discourse" (Hopper 1979: 213). These are clauses that move a story along temporally, in contrast to backgrounding material that do not. Cumming (1991: 123) uses the term "eventiveness" rather than "foregrounding" to place less emphasis on the participants and more on the characteristics of the event. The frequent use of this structure in Malay texts has led to its conventionalisation as a structure denoting an action performed by some third person agent. Kaswanti Purwo (1988: 205) suggests that [*di*-V-*nya*] is "the type of *di*- used to describe a series of chronologically ordered punctiliar actions by a single actor". This is certainly true of example (5) below.

(5) **Di-cuci-nya** muka-nya, kemudian **di-lap-nya** kering-kering, lalu kembali ke
 DI-wash-3SG face-3SG then DI-wipe-3SG dryly then return to
 kamar-nya.
 room-3SG

 'She$_i$ **washed** her face$_j$, she$_i$ **wiped** [ ]$_j$ dry, then [ ]$_i$ returned to her room.'
 (Krisna 1977: 119)

However, [*di*-V-*nya*] is not the only construction that can be used to encode successive actions by a single actor, as will be shown later in this chapter. In Indonesian, [*di*-V-*nya*] is found mainly in written discourse, particularly in older fictional narrative (the example in (5) is taken from a novel published in 1977). As we saw in (4), [*di*-V] is also used to encode such actions. This example is from a collection of short stories published in 1963 by acclaimed writer Pramoedya Ananta Toer. In more contemporary texts, this is more likely to be rendered in either in [*meN*-] AT clauses or a combination of AT and PT clauses, as will be discussed in §4, §5 and §6.

The second type of PT clause contains an unprefixed verb with the agent in pre-predicate position, either in the form of a clitic, such as in *ku*- '1SG' in (6), or a free pronoun, such as *ia* '3SG' in (7).[6] This type of PT clause is better known in the literature as "objective voice" – henceforth OV (Arka & Manning 1998; Cole et al. 2008; Kroeger 2014). This study is mainly concerned with OV clauses containing the third person pronoun *ia*.[7]

(6) **Ku-guyur** seluruh tubuh-ku dengan air dari keran wudu.
 1SG-pour.water entire body-1SG with water from tap wudu

 'I **poured water on** my body with water from the *wudu* tap.'[8] (Kumalasari 2006: 12)

---

[6]The agent may also be proper name or kin term.
[7]Beside *ia*, the third person pronoun *dia* is also used in Indonesian. The latter is not discussed in this study.
[8]*Kran wudu* is the tap Muslims use to get water from to wash their face, hands, and feet in preparation for prayer.

(7) *Buku-buku yang semula   berserakan di atas tempat tidur, meja dan lantai*
    book-RDP REL   previously scattered   LOC top place sleep table and floor
    ia masuk-kan[9] *ke dalam kotak kardus.*   Lit. 'The books which were
    3SG put.in-APPL DIR inside box cardboard
    previously scattered on the bed, table and floor, **he put** in cardboard boxes.'
    '**He put the books** which were previously scattered on the bed, table and floor in
    cardboard boxes.'   (Kurniawan 2002: 195–196)

Cumming (1991: 34) uses the following shorthand to refer to the different types of constituent order: V>T for clauses in which the predicate occurs before the patient, and T>V for those the patient precedes the predicate (in her terms, "predicate before trigger" and "trigger before predicate" respectively). She categories OV clauses with pre-predicate agent such as in (6) as PT clauses and not AT clauses even though the agent is in pre-predicate position (and the order of the constituents is therefore A V P). Her argument for doing so is that in this type of construction, the preverbal agent occupies the same slot as the prefix *di-* in passive. Nevertheless, as I argue later in this study, the choice of the free pronoun *ia* instead of the enclitic *–nya* is pragmatically and stylistically meaningful.

The foregoing examples show that events can be encoded in different ways, such with [*meN*-V] AT clause, [*di*-V] or [*di*-V-*nya*] PT clauses with either pre-predicate or post-predicate patient and OV clause with proclitic or a free pronoun as agent. Given these different possibilities, what motivates the use of PT clauses and what is the functional difference between PT clauses with T>V order and that with V>T order? As Cumming argues, PT clauses with post-predicate patient (V>T order) are an important grammatical resource for encoding eventiveness in Classical Malay while pre-predicate patient (T>V order) in PT clauses indicates the topical status of the patient. I argue that in contexts where both AT and PT clauses are used, a switch from AT clauses to a PT clause marks a shift in focus. By switching to a PT clause, the writer signals that there is new information and the reader is invited to direct their attention to it. In the next section, the notions of "topic" and "focus" are explained.

3 Topic and focus

"Topic" and "focus" in the sense of Lambrecht (1994), Gundel (1977), Gundel (1999), Gundel & Fretheim (2004), and Gundel et al. (1993) are relational pragmatic categories. Topic is defined in terms of aboutness: "the thing which the proposition expressed by the sentence is ABOUT" (Lambrecht 1994: 118; emphasis in original). The term "topic" designates the "entity" or "the discourse referent" about which the proposition is construed (Lambrecht 1994: 127). A topic must be referential, individuated (Gundel & Fretheim 2004: 187), and cognitively active, i.e., it is mentioned in the sentence or clause, and not merely inferred. In the example below (from Lambrecht 1994: 127; capitalisation in original), the

---

[9]Indonesian has two applicative suffixes, -*kan* and *-i*. In this study I treat [*di*-V-*kan*] and [*di*-V-*i*] as a subset of [*di*-V].

6 Constituent order and information structure in Indonesian discourse

expressions 'Pat', 'she', and 'her' all refer to the same entity, and that entity is construed as being what the propositions are about. The referent of these topic expressions is identifiable through the mention of the proper name 'Pat' and the third person pronominal forms 'she' and 'her'.

(8)   a. Pat said they called her TWICE.
       b. Pat said she was called TWICE.
       c. Pat said SHE was called.
       d. Pat said they called HER.

Van Valin & LaPolla (1997: 204) explain that topics "either name a topic referent in the discourse, or they are simply involved in the expression of a semantic relation between a topic referent and a predication." Topics that have the former function are generally coded as lexical NPs, while those in the latter function, are "most often" coded as zero or unstressed pronouns. In terms of syntactic coding for topic and focus, Van Valin & LaPolla (1997: 205) provide a useful scale of acceptability, shown below in Figure 1.

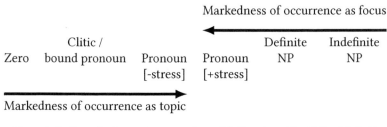

Figure 1: Coding of referents in terms of possible functions (Van Valin & LaPolla 1997: 205)

This figure shows that zero coding is the least marked coding for a topic, while indefinite NP is the least marked coding for a focus. According to Van Valin & LaPolla (1997: 205), "while indefinite NPs can be topics under special contextual circumstances, it is impossible for a focal element to be zero". Zero correlates with the referent's cognitive status as active (Givón 1975: 379).

Focus, like topic, is defined relationally; focus is a relational notion that "determines the main predication in the sentence, that predication being assessed relative to topic" (Gundel & Fretheim 2004: 190). Lambrecht (1994: 213) defines it as "the semantic component of a pragmatically structured proposition whereby the assertion differs from the presupposition". The difference between a pragmatic presupposition and a pragmatic assertion has to do with the difference between what the hearer is assumed to know at the time of hearing the sentence, and what s/he is expected to know as a result of hearing it, as spelt out below (Lambrecht 1994: 52; capitalisation in original).

PRAGMATIC PRESUPPOSITION: the set of propositions lexicogrammatically evoked in a sentence which the speaker assumes the hearer already knows or is ready to take for granted at the time the sentence is uttered.

183

PRAGMATIC ASSERTION: the proposition expressed by a sentence which the hearer is expected to know or take for granted as a result of hearing the sentence uttered.

The relation between topic and focus is one between "pragmatically non-recoverable to the recoverable component of a proposition". Focus creates a new state of information in the mind of the addressee (Lambrecht 1994: 218), thus is often conflated with Chafe's (1994) notion of "new information" in his discussion on referent accessibility; however, as Lambrecht (1994: see chapter3) stresses, the two are not the same.

(9) Q: When did you move to Switzerland?
    A: When I was SEVENTEEN.
    (Lambrecht 1994: 48, 217)

The stressed element in the answer is identified as the focus. What makes the proposition informative is *not* the fact that the person was seventeen years of age at some point in her life (which is the pragmatic presupposition in this example), but that s/he moved to Switzerland at the time she was seventeen (the pragmatic assertion). The assertion (focus) thus stands in relation to the topic (the person moving) and the action of the topic referent (i.e., moving to Switzerland). Similarly, in (10), the referent of 'Bill' is cognitively active (it is mentioned in the question Q). However, Bill is the focus here because in the presupposition 'speaker saw x' where 'x = Bill', it is "new" information. This is an example of what Gundel & Fretheim (2004: 182) call "contrastive focus".

(10) Q: Did you see John or Bill?
     A: Bill.
     (Van Valin & LaPolla 1997: 205)

Lambrecht (1994: 221–235) distinguishes between argument-focus, predicate-focus, and sentence-focus structures. Argument-focus structure is a sentence in which the focus is the missing argument in an open proposition (similar to "narrow focus" in Givón 1975). This is illustrated in (11). Here the focal element 'car' is the argument of the proposition.

(11) Q: I heard your motorcycle broke down?
     A: My CAR broke down.
     (Lambrecht 1994: 48, 223)

In predicate-focus structure, the predicate is the focus, and the subject with all its elements are in the presupposition.

(12) Q: What happened to your car?
     A: My car/it broke DOWN.
     (Lambrecht 1994: 48, 223)

In sentence-focus structure, it is both the subject and predicate in the sentence (minus any topical, non-subject elements) that constitute the focus (e.g., in presentative constructions).

(13) Q: What happened?
　　A: My CAR broke down.
　　　(Lambrecht 1994: 48, 223)

All languages have some grammatical means for marking topic and focus, including morphosyntax, prosody, word order, or any combination of these (Van Valin & LaPolla 1997: 201). With regard to Indonesian PT clauses, Cumming (1991: 175) notes that the position of patient relative to the predicate provides an indication of its topical status (or "thematic" in Kaswanti Purwo's 1988: 226 term). Pre-predicate position suggests topicality, while post-predicate position indicates the patient is "not made prominent" and "not highlighted". As will be shown in §5, PT clauses are marked and they are not always used to indicate a climactic point in a story. Agentive [*meN*-V] clauses can also be used to mark a climactic portion, as will be shown in §4. Drawing on the notions of focus and topic helps us explain the significance of pre-predicate patient by taking into account its relation to the predicate, as well as the significance of the referent of the patient argument in the discourse.

4 *MeN*- clauses

One of the most important findings in Cumming's (1991) study is that modern Indonesian strongly shows a preference for AT clauses. A recent study by Shiohara (2015) supports this finding. Using short videos showing a young person performing a series of actions (e.g., breaking an egg into a bowl, whisking the egg, adding some milk, then whisking it again) for data elicitation, Shiohara's study shows that of all the transitive clauses found, 88.5% were AT, while the remaining clauses were rendered in PT (8.6% in *di*- passive and 2.9% in objective voice). Shiohara's study tells us that the preference for [*meN*-V] clauses is most dramatic when successive actions by the same agent are involved. It also shows that [*meN*-V] primarily occurs in eventive clauses, contrary to Kaswanti Purwo's (1988: 226) claim that they tend to be used for backgrounding. In what follows I show that the preference for [*meN*-V] persists even when there are multiple referents that are accorded the status of agent and a switch in the semantic function of the participant is involved (cf. Foley & Van Valin 1984). Moreover, [*meN*-] AT clauses are also used to mark the climactic portion of a story episode, unlike in older texts where PT is preferred for this purpose.

Two examples from the novel *Lelaki Harimau* 'Man Tiger' (Kurniawan 2004) show how a series of AT clauses can be used to encode a series of actions performed by two different participants, with a switch in the semantic function of one participant – from patient to agent – but without the accompanying change in the verbal morphology. The excerpt in (14) is included here to provide a context for the AT examples in (15) and to show the switch from PT to AT. The protagonist, Margio, has just killed the man who had courted his mother and made her pregnant but refused to marry her. Margio is subsequently captured for his deed and detained at the local military office. The information about his arrest is rendered in PT with T>V order, signalling to the reader to pay attention to the event that describes the capture. The referent 'Margio' is shown as the "topical" patient, as indicated by its pre-predicate position (Cumming 1991: 175). As will be further discussed in the next section, PT clauses are commonly used to attract the reader's attention to a new focus.

(14) *Kini, ketika malam telah runtuh ke bumi mengapungkan bintang-bintang dan bulan sepotong tergantung enggan, lampu-lampu dinyalakan di pelataran rumah dan pinggir jalan, dan codot tak lagi tampak beterbangan disebabkan hitam yang menghapus hitam tubuhnya,* **Margio diseret Joni Simbolon ke rayon militer**. *Selalu begitu sebelum seseorang dibawa ke kantor polisi, sebab tanpa itu para prajurit tak punya lagi keriangan di dunia republik yang tak ada perang.*

'Now, when night has fallen on the earth making the stars appear floating and a piece of moon is hanging reluctantly, the lights lit on the front yards and along the streets, and the bats no longer flying around as the darkness hides the blackness of their bodies, **Margio is being dragged by Joni Simbolon to the local military office**. That always happens before someone is taken to the police station, because otherwise, the soldiers would no longer be able to have fun in a republic where there is no war happening.' (Kurniawan 2004: 37; my translation)[10]

In the immediately following discourse, shown in (15), the author switches to AT to describe two successive events depicting what Margio's captors did to him. In the first clause, the agent (Joni Simbolon and his friends) is referred to with the third person plural pronoun *mereka* 'they', while the patient (Margio), with the enclitic *–nya* '3SG'. These pronominal forms indicate the presupposed status of the two participants. In the second [*meN-V*] clause, the referent of 'Joni Simbolon (and his friends)' is coded as zero (reflecting its topic status), while 'Margio' is mentioned with the enclitic *-nya* '3SG' again. These two [*meN-V*] clauses are followed by a switch in the semantic function of the patient participant. Margio, coded as zero, is now actor of the intransitive clause *meringkuk di satu dipan* 'curled up on a wooden bed' and agent of the subsequent AT transitive clauses.

(15) *Mereka* **me-ngurung-nya** *di   dalam sel,* **meng-ganti pakaian-nya** *dengan*
     3PL   MEN-cage-3SG   LOC inside cell   MEN-change clothes-3SG   with
     seragam hitam bau   kapur barus   dan lemari   kayu, **me-ringkuk** *di   satu*
     uniform black smell chalk barus.tree and wardrobe wood MEN-curl.up LOC one
     dipan   **meng-hadap-i** *susu hangat yang tak di-cecap-nya,* **meng-hadap-i**
     wooden.bed MEN-face-APPL milk warm   REL   NEG DI-taste-3SG   MEN-face-APPL
     sepiring   nasi ikan tongkol yang tak di-lumat-nya.
     one.plate rice fish tuna   REL   NEG DI-devour-3SG

   'They_i **put him_j in a cell**, [ ]_i **changed his_j clothes** into a black uniform smelling of mothballs and wooden wardrobe, [ ]_j **curled up** on a wooden bed [ ]_j **facing** (a

---

[10] In this translation I provide as close a translation as possible to the original to facilitate the discussion. This is slightly different from the published English translation (see Kurniawan 2015; translated by Labodalih Sembiring).

glass of) warm milk he_j didn't drink, [ ]_j **facing** a plate of tuna rice he_j didn't devour.'
(Kurniawan 2004: 37; my translation)

In this excerpt, the referent of 'Margio' is treated as highly continuous; he is mentioned with the enclitic *-nya* '3SG' in the first two clauses, followed by zero in the subsequent three (main) clauses. In the final two clauses, the reader is told that Margio is not touching the food given to him. The author uses the same predicate in these clauses and also relative clauses, creating parallel structures of the kind [V NP *yang tak di*-V-*nya*]. As discussed later in this chapter, parallelism is an important stylistic resource fiction authors often draw on to produce a rhythmic effect.

(16) a. *meng-hadap-i susu hangat yang tak di-cecap-**nya***
MEN-face-APPL milk warm REL NEG DI-taste-3SG

'face (a glass of) warm milk **he** didn't drink'

b. *meng-hadap-i sepiring nasi ikan tongkol yang tak di-lumat-**nya***
MEN-face-APPL one.plate rice fish tuna REL NEG DI-devour-3SG

'face a plate of tuna rice that **he** didn't devour'

Below is a summary of the different clauses and arguments (expressed arguments are italicised, while the zero is rendered in square brackets).

1. *Margio*_i is captured by *Joni Simbolon and his friends*_j.
2. *They*_j put *him*_i in a prison cell.
3. [ ]_j changed *his clothes* to a prison uniform.
4. [ ]_i curls up on the wooden bed.
5. [ ]_i faces *a glass of warm milk* he didn't drink.
6. [ ]_i faces *a plate of tuna rice* he didn't devour.

We can see in this example that [*meN*-V] AT clauses are the preferred construction for encoding agency even when there are multiple agents and the agency is switched between different human referents. In addition, stylistic considerations are also important in the presentation of events. The string of [*meN*-V] clauses and the repeated [NP *yang tak di*-V-*nya*] relative clauses create a rhythmic effect and an impression of quick, successive actions. Though the last three AT clauses are not foregrounding clauses, the rhythmic effect remains and this is due to the repetition of *meN-* verbs (*meringkuk* 'curl up' and *menghadapi* 'face something', the latter being used twice in succession) and the relative clauses in (16).

Another example showing [*meN*-V] used in succession is given in (17). This example describes a physical clash between Margio's sister, Maesa Dewi, and a luminous shadow. These two participants are overtly mentioned in the initial AT clause.

(17) *Maesa Dewi*ᵢ *me-lihat bayangan cemerlang*ⱼ *yang tak di-kenal-i-nya*ᵢ,
Maesa Dewi MEN-see shadow brilliant REL NEG DI-recognise-APPL-3SG
me-mancar mem-beri silau kepada mata-nya, **men-desak-nya**ᵢ *ke belakang*
MEN-shine MEN-give blinding toward eye-3SG MEN-force-3SG to back
dan suatu benturan **meng-hantam** *kepala-nya*ᵢ *saat itu* []ᵢ **me-nentang**
and INDEF knock MEN-whack head-3SG moment that MEN-hit
dinding pintu di belakang, []ⱼ **meng-henti-kan-nya**ᵢ *sejenak sebelum* []ᵢ
wall door LOC back MEN-stop-APPL-3SG for.a.moment before
me-rosot *dan tumbang ke lantai.*
MEN-slide.down and collapse to floor

'Maesa Dewiᵢ saw a luminous shadowⱼ, which sheᵢ did not recognise, [ ]ⱼ shone brightly, giving her eyes a blinding light, [ ]ⱼ **pushed her**ᵢ backwards and a knock hit her head at that moment (until) [ ]ᵢ **knocked** the back door, [ ]ⱼ **stopped her** momentarily before [ ]ᵢ **slid down** and [ ]ᵢ **fell to the floor.**' (Kurniawan 2004: 34)

The chain of events with the different participants and their semantic roles is summarised below (as previously, expressed participants are shown in italics, and the zero is indicated as square brackets).

1. *Maesa Dewi*ᵢ (Agent) saw *a luminous shadow*ⱼ (Patient).

2. [ ]ⱼ (Agent) shone brightly, giving *her*ᵢ *eyes* (Patient) a blinding light.

3. [ ]ⱼ (Agent) pushed *her*ᵢ (Patient) backwards.

4. [ ]ᵢ (Agent) knocked the back door (Patient).

5. [ ]ⱼ (Agent) stopped *her*ᵢ (Patient) momentarily.

6. [ ]ᵢ (Undergoer) slid down.

7. [ ]ᵢ (Undergoer) fell to the floor. (note: this event is encoded with a bare verb.)

With the exception of the first two clauses, the clauses in this example are eventive, as indicated by the punctual verbs. The referent of 'Maesa Dewi' is presented as agent in the initial clause, then patient and undergoer in the following clauses. The use of zero in subject position throughout this long example potentially creates referential confusion and slows down processing: is it the shadow or Maesa Dewi that slid down and collapsed? However, this potential confusion is resolved by the discourse context. In the subsequent clauses, Maesa Dewi is described as lying down as if frozen, unable to speak and her memory hazy. All the clauses in this story episode are rendered in [*meN*-V] AT clauses and most of them denote quick, successive actions by different agents/actors. In this example, as with example (15), the repetition of [*meN*-V] produces vividness and a sense of immediacy as well as a rhythmic effect. It seems that for the author, creating this kind of effect is more important in this long sentence than avoiding potential referential

6 Constituent order and information structure in Indonesian discourse

confusion. These examples provide evidence that in contemporary Indonesian, [*meN*-V] serves the kind of pragmatic function previously encoded with [*di*-V-*nya*].

The next two examples are from television news reports aired in 2015 and 2017, showing [*meN*-V] AT clauses marking the climactic portion of a story episode. In these examples, a PT clause with [*di*-V] is used to mark an event that leads to the climax and one subsequent to it. The first example of [*meN*-V] occurs in (19). This example follows directly from the sentence in example (2), repeated below as (18) for convenience. When this news item was broadcast, the sentence was read like a headline about a husband and wife couple being attacked by people in a motorbike. This headline is rendered in PT.

(18) *Sepasang suami istri yang sedang pergi ke tahlilan keluarga di Cirebon*
SE-couple husband wife REL in.process go to *tahlilan* family LOC Cirebon
di-serang oleh geng motor.
DI-attack by gang motor
'A husband and wife, who went to a family *tahlilan* event in Cirebon, **were attacked by a motorcycle gang**.'[11] (*Fokus Pagi, Indosiar*, 9/11/2015)

Following the headline, a series of chronological events were reported, as shown in (19). The first clause contains a [*di*-V] PT clause with pre-predicate patient, the second has a [*meN*-V] clause with zero agent, and the third, another [*di*-V] clause also with pre-predicate patient. The agentive [*meN*-V] clause marks the climax of the story, while the first and third PT clauses inform the addressee of the event that leads to and follows this climax respectively. The pre-predicate patient (*pasangan suami istri itu* 'the husband and wife couple') in the PT clauses indicates its "topical" status.

(19) *Naas pasangan suami istri itu **di-pepet** oleh kendaraan*
bad.luck couple husband wife that DI-press.against by vehicle
*bermotor lalu **me-nyerang** dengan senjata tajam, kemudian sang istri*
have.engine then MEN-attack with arm sharp then DEF wife
di-tusuk. (Lit. 'Bad luck, the husband and wife couple was pressed against by a
DI-stab
motorbike then attack with a sharp object, after which the wife was stabbed.')
'Bad luck for the husband and wife couple$_i$, a motorbike$_j$ approached them$_i$ and [ ]$_j$ attacked [ ]$_i$ with a sharp object, then stabbed the wife.'
(*Fokus Pagi, Indosiar*, 9/11/2015).

A similar example is shown in (20) but with the post-climactic event rendered in an intransitive clause marked by the prefix *ber-*. This example is taken from a news item about a crime committed against Novel Baswedan, a senior investigator for Indonesia's *Komisi Pemberantasan Korupsi* 'Commission for the Eradication of Corruption'. Novel was reported as walking home from the nearby mosque at five am when two people in a motorbike rode towards him and threw acid on his face. The initial [*di*-V] PT clause

---
[11] *Tahlilan* is a Muslim social gathering to commemorate the dead. *Pak* is a short form of *bapak*, a kin term used to address or refer to one's father and adult males in general.

alerts the addressee to new information, while the [*meN*-V] marks the eventive clause and the climax of the story.[12] The pre-predicate patient in the PT clause indicates the patient's "topical" status. The following [*ber*-V] clause describes what happens after the climax.

(20) *Tiba-tiba   Novel **di-datang-i** dua orang bersepeda motor dan langsung*
suddenly-RDP Novel DI-come-APPL two person on.bicyle motor and immediately
***me-nyiram-nya** dengan air   keras. Novel lalu **berteriak** dengan*
MEN-pour-3SG   with   water hard Novel then scream   with
sekencang-kencangnya.
as.loud.as.possible-RDP

'Suddenly Novel$_i$ **was approached** by two people$_j$ on a motorbike and [ ]$_j$ **threw** acid **on him**$_i$. Novel **screamed** as loudly as he could.' (*Eksklusif: Wawancara Novel Baswedan, Aiman, Kompas TV*, 3 July 2017)

To summarise, this section has discussed, first, the use of [*meN*-V] clauses to encode a series of events involving different agents. In the examples shown, vividness and a sense of immediacy are created through successive use of [*meN*-V] in both transitive and intransitive clauses involving different referents in subject position (in the role of either agent, actor or undergoer). I discussed two examples from the same novel, so one might argue that the preference for [*meN*-V] clauses is particularised to the author of that novel (i.e., Eka Kurniawan). However, as Cumming (1991) and Kaswanti Purwo (1988) have amply shown through their examples, the use of [*meN*-V] or [*di*-V-(*nya*)] clauses to denote successive actions is common in Indonesian fiction. What seems to be a new development is the strong preference for AT even when agency is switched among participants. This section has also shown that [*meN*-V] clauses can mark the climactic portion of a story episode, with non-eventive clauses marked by [*di*-V] and [*ber*-V] preceding and following them. This is the opposite of the kind of pattern in older texts studied by Cumming and Kaswanti Purwo, where PT is the preferred clause type for marking climax and AT for backgrounding.

5 *Di*-V-*nya* and topic-focus distinction

Some have argued that [*di*-V-*nya*] clauses with post-predicate patient are ergative (see Hopper 1979: 232–233; Arka & Manning 1998: 14). However, others disagree (e.g., Cumming & Wouk 1987; Cumming 1991: 33–34; Kroeger 2014). The debate will not be entered into here; in this study I follow Cumming (1991) in considering [*di*-V-*nya*] as a type of PT clause. One of the common environments in which [*di*-V-*nya*] appears in Indonesian is where it is preceded and followed by AT clauses. A switch from AT clauses to a [*di*-V-*nya*] clause signals a shift to a new focus and serves as an invitation to the addressee/reader to take notice. This is exemplified in (21).

---

[12]In this example, the verb contains the applicative suffix –*i*. As mentioned, this is treated as [*di*-V].

6 Constituent order and information structure in Indonesian discourse

(21) Almashira₍ᵢ₎ **mem-buka** gorden biru muda bermotif vineyard, **me-natap-i**
 Almashira MEN-open curtain blue light have.pattern vineyard MEN-gaze-APPL
 tetes hujan deras yang mem-basah-i jendela kamar-nya yang ter-letak
 drop rain hard REL MEN-wet-APPL window bedroom-3SG REL TER-position
 di tempat yang paling private di rumah-nya, alias di loteng.
 LOC place REL most private LOC house-3SG none.other.than LOC upstairs
 Di-ambil-nya*₍ᵢ₎ *sweter-nya*₍ⱼ₎ *yang gombrong dan nyaman, lalu
 DI-get-3SG sweater-3SG REL loose and comfortable then
 me-makai-kan-nya*₍ⱼ₎ *di tubuh-nya yang langsing.
 MEN-put.on-APPL-3SG LOC body-3SG REL slim

 'Almashira₍ᵢ₎ **opened** the light blue curtain with a vineyard motif, **stared at** the raindrops falling on the window of her bedroom which is located in the most private section of her house, namely upstairs. <u>She₍ᵢ₎ **grabbed**</u> her loose and comfortable sweater₍ⱼ₎, and **put it**₍ⱼ₎ **on** her slim body.' (Karina 2008: 7)

Here, the initial clause describes the protagonist *Almashira* opening the curtain in her bedroom and subsequently staring at the raindrops falling on her window. *Almashira* is the agent in the AT clauses in this sentence. The first clause (referring to Almashira opening the curtain) is eventive, while the second (Almashira staring at the raindrops) is a process (descriptive). In the second sentence, a switch to PT with *di-V-nya* occurs. This switch marks a shift from a non-eventive clause in the previous sentence (Almashira staring at the raindrops) to an eventive one (Almashira fetching her sweater). The switch to [*di-V-nya*] also coincides with a new sentence. The [*di-V-nya*] clause is then followed by a return to AT. In this AT clause, the agent, which is mentioned in the PT clause with the clitic –*nya* '3SG', is now rendered with zero, indicating the referent's status as topic. Meanwhile, the patient argument (the referent of *sweternya* 'her sweater') is now rendered also with the clitic –*nya* '3SG'.

Cumming (1991: 175) suggests that a switch to PT is usually associated with the "climactic portion" of a story episode and creates a feeling of vividness or immediacy. However, this argument does not apply to (21). The excerpt is taken from the opening paragraph of the novel *Circa* (Karina 2008) and this is the first time that the reader is introduced to the protagonist and her actions. The switch from a descriptive clause (Almashira staring at the rain drops) to the [*di-V-nya*] clause (Almashira fetching her sweater) draws our attention to new information but does not indicate a climactic point in the episode. Moreover, the patient cannot be considered topical either as it has not been mentioned previously. The PT clause merely introduces a new event that contrasts from the descriptive clause in the previous sentence. Once this event has been introduced, a switch back to AT with zero agent follows.

Compare (21) with the example below from the novel *Senja di Jakarta* by Mochtar Lubis published in 1970 (quoted without gloss in Cumming 1991: 174) where [*di-V-nya*] marks the climactic portion of the story episode. Here Dahlia's actions of arranging Hasnah's hair, taking a lipstick from her bag and applying it on Hasnah's lips form successive actions and all are rendered in PT. The beginning and end of the episode are rendered in AT.

(22) *Dahlia memegang rambut Hasnah, mengambil sisir, dan asyik mengerjakan rambut Hasnah. Mula-mula Hasnah membantah, akan tetapi tidak diperdulikan Dahlia. Setelah **rambut Hasnah disusunnya, diambilnya cat bibir** dari tasnya, dan **digincunya bibir Hasnah**. Dia mengambil kaca dari dinding, memegang kaca di depan Hasnah, dan berkata, "Nah, lihat, kan cantik?"*

'Dahlia grasped Hasnah's hair, took a comb, and zealously did Hasnah's hair. At first Hasnah rebelled, but (she) was ignored by Dahlia. After **she had arranged Hasnah's hair, she took a lipstick** from her bag and **painted Hasnah's lips**. She took a mirror from the wall, held the mirror before Hasnah, and said, "Now, look, aren't you pretty?"'

Although the beginning and end of example (21) are also marked by AT, the sense of immediacy generated by the series of quick, successive actions in (22) is largely absent. In (21), the use of [*di*-V-*nya*] merely signals to the reader that the protagonist is now performing an action that contrasts with the one before. I would argue that [*di*-V-*nya*] with post-predicate patient in both examples marks a new focus. By using this clause structure, the author is making a pragmatic assertion (about what action the agent is performing and in relation to what kind of patient referent), expecting the reader to know what the proposition is only after reading the clause. This assertion cannot be presupposed; so, for example, in (21) Almashira fetching her sweater cannot be presupposed after reading about her opening the window and staring at the raindrops. Using [*di*-V-*nya*] with V>T order is a grammatically effective way of alerting the reader to the new information.

In a similar example, shown earlier in (5) and repeated below as (23) with a fuller context, a switch from AT to PT with V>T order is found. Here a series of AT clauses is followed by a series of PT clauses. As with the previous examples, the switch from the AT to PT (the PT clauses are underlined in the English translation) does not mark the climactic part of a story episode but rather, a shift in focus.

(23) Rosna **me-langkah** ke dalam, **mem-buka** pintu tengah, lalu **pergi** menuju
 Rosna MEN-step to inside MEN-open door middle then go toward
 kamar mandi setelah ia **meng-ambil** *handuk yang ter-gantung di sampiran.*
 room bath after 3SG MEN-fetch towel REL TER-hang LOC clothes.line
 ***Di-cuci-nya muka-nya**, kemudian **di-lap-nya** kering-kering, lalu kembali ke*
 DI-wash-3SG face-3SG then DI-wipe-3SG dryly then return to
 kamar-nya.
 room-3SG

'Rosna **stepped inside, opened** the door in the middle (of the room), and then **headed** towards the bathroom after she **fetched** a towel that was hanging on the rail. <u>She washed</u> her face$_i$, then <u>she wiped</u> [ ]$_j$ dry, after which [ ]$_i$ returned to her room.' (Krisna 1977: 119)

Here, Rosna is described as performing a series of actions (stepping inside, opening the middle door, fetching a towel and going towards the bathroom), and these actions are rendered in AT clauses with *meN-* verbs and an intransitive clause with a bare verb (***pergi** menuju kamar mandi* 'headed towards the bathroom'). The switch to the [*di-V-nya*] PT clause marks the beginning of a different series of actions (i.e., washing and drying the face). These are actions for the purpose of which the preceding series of actions are taken (i.e., Rosna walking to the bathroom and fetching a towel on the way are performed for the purpose of washing and drying her face). It is in this way that we can understand the PT clauses as being narratively significant. In the first PT clause, the patient *mukanya* 'her face' cannot be presupposed (Rosna could have washed her hands rather than her face, for instance). Furthermore, the actions denoted by the PT clauses, although significant, cannot be considered climactic. The excerpt describes the protagonist Rosna performing the series of actions in preparation to speak to Benda, the man she has been wishing to date. Although the actions of washing and drying the face are significant within the context of the episode where Rosna is concerned to making herself presentable to Benda, they are only part of the series of events that lead to the climax. Later in the episode, the reader is told that Benda, who is waiting for her in the living room while Rosna freshens herself, decides to leave suddenly and not engage romantically with her, leaving Rosna deeply disappointed. It is that part of the episode in my view that marks the climactic portion.

It is possible to render the focal action(s) rendered in PT in (21) and (23) as AT clauses, as shown in the reconstructed examples in (24) and (25), but these clauses merely denote a series of chronological events rather than signal a shift to a different event (or a new series of events) the author wants the reader to pay particular attention to.

(24) *Ia **mengambil** sweter-nya$_j$ yang gombrong dan nyaman,   lalu*
      3SG MEN-take   sweater-3SG REL loose   and comfortable then
      ***me-makai-kan-nya**$_j$ di tubuh-nya yang langsing.*
      MEN-put.on-APPL-3SG LOC body-3SG REL slim

      'She **grabbed** her loose and comfortable sweater, and **put it on** her slim body.'
      (adapted from Karina 2008: 7)

(25) *Ia **men-cuci** muka-nya, kemudian **me-lap**   kering-kering, lalu kembali*
      3SG MEN-wash face-3SG   then   MEN-wipe-3SG dryly-RDP   then return
      ke kamar-nya.
      to room-3SG

      'She$_i$ **washed** her face$_j$, then **wiped** [ ]$_j$ dry, after which [ ]$_i$ returned to her room.'
      (adapted from Krisna 1977: 119)

In the original examples we saw earlier in (23), it is the entire PT clauses, and not individual elements within them, that are treated as focus. This exemplifies what Lambrecht (1994: 233) calls "sentence focus", the type of focus where the scope extends to the entire clause, and not only the predicate or an argument. To explain how the focus is determined, let us turn to example (2) again, repeated below without the gloss.

(26) *Almashira*ᵢ **membuka** *gorden biru muda bermotif vineyard,* [ ]ᵢ **menatapi** *tetes hujan deras yang membasahi jendela kamarnya yang terletak di tempat yang paling private di rumahnya, alias di loteng.* **Diambilnya**ᵢ *sweternya yang gombrong dan nyaman, lalu* [ ]ᵢ **memakaikannya**ⱼ *di tubuhnya*ᵢ *yang langsing.*

'Almashiraᵢ **opened** the light blue curtain which a vineyard motif, [ ]ᵢ **gazed at** the drops of water coming from the pouring rain that is wetting her bedroom window which is located in the most secluded part of her house, namely upstairs. **She grabbed** her loose and comfortable sweater, then [ ]ᵢ **put it**ⱼ **on** herᵢ slim body' (Karina 2008: 7)

Here we have the protagonist, *Almashira*, mentioned in the initial clause as opening the curtain in her bedroom. This clause is rendered in a [*meN*-V] AT clause. The referent of the name *Almashira* is rendered as zero in the following [*meN*-V] clause, indicating that it is now treated as topic. In the [*di*-V-*nya*] PT clause that follows, the referent is referred to with enclitic –*nya*, while in the subsequent "resumptive" [*meN*-V] AT clause, it is rendered as zero, once again indicating her status as topic. In this example, the entire PT clause is the focus because the event denoted by it adds new information. The patient *sweternya yang gombrong dan nyaman* 'her loose and comfortable sweater' cannot be the only focal element although it adds new information to the presupposition 'the person fetched x', where 'x = *sweternya yang gombrong dan nyaman*', because saying so does not explain why [*di*-V-*nya*] occurs, and why the patient is in post-predicate position (V>T order). It is grammatically and semantically acceptable to have the patient placed in pre-predicate position: *Sweternya yang gombrong dan nyaman dipakainya* 'She put on her loose and comfortable sweater' (T>V order). However, the switch to the PT clause puts the highlight not only on the sweater but also on the fact that Almashira is grabbing it and putting it on, thus it is the event that is focal, not only the patient argument. The PT clause is a grammatical device that informs the reader to direct their attention to a new focus. In this sense, it is similar in function to presentatives marked by particle *lah* in Classical Malay (see Cumming 1991: 90 for examples). Cumming points out that the use of *lah* to mark presentativeness is greatly diminished in Indonesian. It could be that switching from AT clauses to a PT clause is one mechanism that Indonesian writers use for this purpose.

The focal status of the PT clause can be shown by using an adapted version of the tests in Lambrecht (1994: 223). A focus element can occur on its own as an open proposition. Thus below, the entire PT clause can occur as the open proposition in (27a), but the predicate alone cannot do so, as shown in (27b).

(27) a. Sentence-focus
    Q: *Apa yang terjadi?*   'What happened?'
    A: *Diambilnya sweternya.*   'She grabbed her sweater.'
  b. Predicate-focus
    Q: *Apa yang terjadi pada sweternya?* 'What happened to her sweater?'
    A: *DIAMBILNYA sweternya.*   'She grabbed.'

6 *Constituent order and information structure in Indonesian discourse*

Applying the same tests to the first PT clause in example (5) and (23), repeated below without the gloss, the open proposition in (29a) makes sense, while (29b) and (29c) which put the stress on *dicucinya* 'she washed' and *mukanya* 'her face' respectively, are awkward. The proposition in (29b) would be more appropriately responded to with an AT clause (*Dia* MENCUCI *mukanya* 'She WASHED her face'); similarly, a more suitable response to (29c) would be to front the patient (MUKANYA *yang dicucinya* 'It is HER FACE that she washed'). This suggests that the focus of the first PT clause extends to the entire clause rather than being limited to the predicate or the patient argument.

(28)   ***Dicucinya***$_i$ *mukanya*$_j$, *kemudian* ***dilapnya***$_i$ *kering-kering, lalu kembali ke kamarnya.*

'She$_i$ washed her face, she$_i$ wiped [ ]$_j$ dry, then [ ]$_i$ returned to her room.' (Krisna 1977: 119)

(29)   a. Sentence-focus
              Q: *Apa yang terjadi?*   'What happened?'
              A: *Dicucinya mukanya.*   'She washed her face.'
         b. Predicate-focus
              Q: *Apa yang dilakukannya?*   'What did she do?'
              A: *DICUCINYA mukanya.*   'SHE WASHED her face.'
         c. Argument-focus
              Q: *Apa yang dilakukannya?*   'What did she do?'
              A: *Dicucinya* MUKANYA.   'She washed HER FACE.'

The question that remains now is: what is the status of the second *di-V-nya* clause (*dilapnya kering-kering* 'she wiped it dry')? I propose that in this case too, the focus extends to the entire clause. Here, the patient in the preceding clause (*mukanya* 'her face') is now presupposed and occurs as zero, indicating its topic status. If it were expressed, the clause would appear as *dilapnya mukanya kering-kering* or *dilapnya kering-kering mukanya*, both meaning 'she wiped her face dry'.

The topic status of the patient *mukanya* 'her face' can also be shown, for example, by applying a combination of left- and right-dislocation test (cf. Gundel & Fretheim 2004: 186). Gundel & Fretheim (2004: 186) state that "the structure most widely and consistently associated with topic marking is one in which the constituent referring to the topic of the sentence is adjoined to the left or right of a full sentence comment/focus". I apply a combination of left- and right-dislocation to test the topic status of the referent of *mukanya* 'her face'. The resulting sentence is well-formed though, I submit, it would be more likely to occur in spoken language rather than written language (as Gundel & Fretheim (2004: 188) also note with regard to right dislocation construction in Norwegian).

(30)   a. *Dilapnya kering-kering.*
              'She wiped [it] dry.'
         b. *Kalau mukanya, dilapnya kering-kering, mukanya itu.*
              'As for her face, she wiped it dry, that face of hers.'

One might argue that the topic in the clause *dilapnya kering-kering* is the referent of the enclitic *-nya* '3SG' (i.e., the referent of 'Rosna'), and not the referent of *mukanya* 'her face'. However, as mentioned, *di-V-nya* is conventional in the sense that this structure presupposes an action performed by some third person agent, therefore *-nya* '3SG' is presupposed as its structural element, not as the topic of the PT clause. The same left-/right-dislocation topic test therefore does not apply. The resulting sentence below is nonsensical (note: in the test below, the enclitic must be rendered as a free pronoun in the 'as for' phrase for well-formedness).

(31) a. *Dilapnya kering-kering.*
      'She wiped [it] dry.'
   b. *Kalau **dia**, dilapnya kering-kering, **dia** itu.*
      'As for her, she wiped [ ] dry, she is.'

Treating [*di-V-nya*] clauses with V>T order (i.e., PT clauses with post-predicate patient) in terms of sentence focus sits well with Hopper's (1979) argument that this structure marks foregrounding in Classical Malay. The series of [*di-V-nya*] clauses with V>T order in (28) and also those in (22) denote focal events that move the stories along the temporal axis. By using a series of [*di-V-nya*] clauses the authors invite the reader to pay particular attention not to a single new event in the narrative, as is the case with a switch from AT clauses to a single PT clause, but rather to sustain their attention throughout a series of events. To strengthen this argument we can compare with a switch from AT clauses to a single PT clause in (32). This example describes a young man feeling shocked at seeing a torn picture of an ex-girlfriend who had left him. The initial main clause contains the serial verbs *tertegun melihat* 'stunned in seeing'. The [*di-V-nya*] PT clause marks a shift from these process verbs to an event (picking up the picture). The return to an AT clause after the PT clause marks a return to a process (the agent staring at the picture). (Note: as indicated in the subscript, the referent of *-nya* in *dipungutnya* 'he picked up' is not coreferential with that in *menatapinya* 'he stared at it' in the following clause.) The PT clause marks an event, while the AT clauses occur as descriptive clauses.

(32) *Cowok berparas   kutu buku ini **tertegun me-lihat** salah.satu potongan*
      guy   have.the.look lice book this stunned MEN-see one.of   cut
      *gambar yang terasa begitu familiar di   ingatan-nya. Perlahan **di-pungut-nya**$_i$*
      picture REL feel   so   familiar LOC memory.3SG slowly   DI-pick.up-3SG
      *ujung kertas itu, **me-natap-i-nya**$_j$ lama dengan berbagai luapan*
      corner paper that MEN-stare.at-APPL-3SG long with   various explosion
      emosi   bermain di   refleksi   mata-nya yang nanar.
      emotion play   LOC reflection eye-3SG REL wild

   'This guy with the bookish face was stunned (at) seeing a piece of a picture which felt so familiar in his memory. Slowly **he picked up** the corner of the paper, [ ] stared at it for a long time with all sorts of emotions reflecting in his wild eyes.'   (Karina 2008: 9)

Here, as in (28), the PT clause *dipungutnya ujung kertas itu* 'he picked up the corner of the paper' is focal and its domain spans the entire clause. In the "resumptive" AT clause, the agent occurs as zero while the patient is expressed as *–nya* '3SG'. However, this AT clause with zero agent sounds rather awkward, but this is possibly due to the fact that the situation is narrated in the third person but incorporates the point of view of the character. The relative clause *yang terasa begitu familiar di ingatannya* 'which feels so familiar in his mind' is told from the point of the view of the narrator but the situation is viewed from the perspective of the character (as indicated by the scalar/intensifier adjective *begitu familiar* 'so familiar'). This technique of presenting point of view, known as 'free indirect discourse' (see e.g., Cohn 1978; Fludernik 1993; Maier 2014), is widely used in fictional texts.

To summarise, I have argued in this section that the switch from an AT clause to a [*di*-V-*nya*] PT clause marks a shift in focus, signalling a new event (or a series of new events) that contrasts with what occurs before. The next section shows that [*di*-V-*nya*] is not the only PT form used for this purpose. The OV structure [*ia* V] serves a similar function but with an added pragmatic function of creating an impression of structural symmetry.

6 PT clauses with *ia*, repetition, and parallelism

In this section, I consider the interaction between OV clauses with the free third person pronoun *ia* '3SG', [*ia* V], and AT clauses containing the same pronoun [*ia meN*-V] to show that, similar to the switch from [*meN*-V] AT clauses to a [*di*-V-*nya*] clause (or a series of clauses), the switch from [*ia meN*-V] to [*ia* V] marks a shift of focus. The use of [*ia* V] also serves an additional function, namely producing a "synchronising" effect between the OV and AT clauses through an appearance of structural similarity. In both of these clause types, the agent *ia* '3SG' is in pre-predicate position. When *ia* '3SG', either in [*ia* V] or [*ia meN*-V], is repeated across clauses, the repetition creates an impression of parallel structures.

Consider example (33). Here Alma, the sister of the guy with the bookish face mentioned in (32), is described as sympathetic to her brother's situation and doing her best to console him. An AT clause with [*ia meN*-V] occurs in the first sentence, followed by [*ia* V] OV clause in the first clause of the second sentence. Subsequent clauses in this sentence are rendered in [*meN*-V] once again but with zero agent. In the previous examples we saw a PT clause being preceded and followed by AT clauses; here we see a similar pattern of AT clauses preceding and following an OV clause, marking the OV clause as focal.

(33) *Sesaat **ia** juga **merasakan** emosi yang sama. Dengan perasaan tak menentu, **ia** palingkan wajahnya, merenung, lalu kembali **menepuk** punggung abangnya dengan ceria.*

'For a moment **she**$_i$ also **felt** the same emotion. Feeling uncertain, **she**$_i$ **turned away**, [ ]$_i$ **thought for a while**, and then [ ]$_i$ **tapped** her brother on the back cheerfully.' (Karina 2008: 9)

The referent of *ia* in the OV clause *ia palingkan wajahnya* 'lit. she turned her face away' is coreferential with *ia* in the preceding sentence *ia juga merasakan emosi yang sama* 'she also felt the same emotion'; in both cases the referent is presupposed and treated as topic. In this clause, it is the entire clause *ia palingkan wajahnya* that constitutes the focus. The NP patient *wajahnya* 'her face' cannot, on its own, be treated as the focus because *palingkan* 'turn away' and *wajahnya* 'her face' are in relations of entailment (*memalingkan* 'turn away' entails *memalingkan wajah* 'turning (one's) face away'). Thus in the test for focus shown in (34), interpretation (34a) makes sense, while (34b) is odd.

(34) Ia paling-kan wajah-nya.
    3SG turn.away-APPL face-3SG
    'She turned away.'
    a. PRAGMATIC PRESUPPOSITION: 'the person did x'
       PRAGMATIC ASSERTION: 'x = turn away'
    b. PRAGMATIC PRESUPPOSITION: 'the person turned away x'
       PRAGMATIC ASSERTION: 'x = her face'

The occurrence of the free pronoun *ia* '3SG' in the AT and OV clauses is significant not only because the pronoun is the controller for the zero in the following [*meN*-V] clauses, but importantly, because the repetition of this pronoun in the different clause structures creates "stylistic alignment" through structural parallelism. Repetition, as Tannen argues, is a common device for promoting a heightened sense of involvement in spoken and written discourse, and "rhythmic synchrony" is an important and widespread feature in both conversational and written fictional discourse (Tannen 2007: 32). Repetition and parallel structures in texts also aid processing (Carlson 2002). By using the [*ia* V] OV clause rather than [*di*-V-*nya*] PT clause, the author thus achieves several goals simultaneously: signalling a new focus, creating a rhythmic effect and thus promoting heightened involvement by stylistically aligning the OV clause with the preceding and following AT clauses, and highlighting the continuity of the third person agent. The series of clauses in this example are reproduced below.

(35) *ia$_i$ merasakan emosi yang sama*   'she$_i$ felt the same emotion'
     ia$_i$ palingkan wajahnya   'she$_i$ turned her face away'
     [ ]$_i$ *merenung*   '[ ]$_i$ thought for a while'
     [ ]$_i$ *menepuk punggung abangnya*   '[ ]$_i$ tapped her brother's back'

It is important to mention here that repetition and parallel structures can be achieved not only by aligning [*ia meN*-V] with [*ia* V]. In the earlier examples, we saw that the repetition of [*meN*-V] AT clauses and [*di*-V-*nya*] PT clauses to denote a series of events by the same agent can also produce a similar effect. What is interesting about [*ia* V] clause in (33) is that, the effect is achieved through an "impression of sameness" between this OV clause and the [*ia meN*-V] AT clause. This sameness is created by the repetition of the free pronoun *ia* '3SG' in pre-predicate position. While multiple occurrences of the same clause structure denote a series of actions performed in quick succession by the same agent (Cumming 1991: 174; also see Kaswanti Purwo 1988: 225), the pragmatic and stylistic effects that result from the use of different clause structures, to my knowledge, have not been discussed. Taking these effects into account helps us understand why different grammatical structures are chosen, not only what types of events they encode.

Both Cumming (1991: 175–178) and Kaswanti Purwo (1988: 222–228) have noted that the position of the patient in PT clauses tells us something about its information status. The patient in [*ia* V] OV clauses can occur in post-predicate position, as seen earlier in (33), or in pre-predicate position, as in (7). According to Kaswanti Purwo (1988: 222), one of the environments in which pre-predicate patient can occur is where there is a gap between the last mention of the NP and the current mention.[13] Cumming (1991: 177) also notes that the patient in this position is treated as "topical", i.e., the referent has been mentioned "in the immediately previous clause or several clauses back, and is of some importance" (1991: 179). Both of these observations are borne out in an example from the acclaimed novel *Cantik itu Luka* 'Beauty is a Wound' by Eka Kurniawan, given below. I include the excerpt in (36) to give a context for the OV clause V>T order in (37).

The excerpt begins with the description of Dewi Ayu, the protagonist, waking early to go to the toilet. A wealthy woman who made her money from working as a prostitute, Dewi Ayu was taken to a prison camp along with others from her village when the Japanese came to Indonesia. Not wanting to lose her precious jewellery, she decided that the best way to safeguard it was to swallow some of the pieces (six gold rings) and she buried the rest in the broken toilet at the back of her house. She did this before leaving for the camp. At the camp, she safeguards the rings by retrieving them from her faeces when she defecates and swallowing them again afterwards. The [*ia meN*-V] AT transitive clauses occur twice.

(36) **Dewi Ayu** *yang terbiasa bangun pagi sekali untuk buang air segera bergegas ke toilet, namun antrian panjang telah menunggu. [....] Cara terbaik adalah mengambil air dengan kaleng margarin Blue Band-nya, dan pergi ke halaman belakang sel. Di sana, di antara pohon ketela yang entah ditanam siapa,* **ia menggali** *tanah seperti seekor kucing, dan berak di lubangnya. Setelah cebok dengan menyisakan sedikit air,* **ia mengorek** *tainya untuk menemukan keenam cincinnya. Beberapa perempuan lain melihat cara beraknya yang buruk, dan menirunya dalam jarak yang cukup berjauhan; mereka tak tahu ia punya harta karun.*

'Dewi Ayu, who is used to getting up very early to pass stool, quickly rushed to the toilet, but a long queue was already waiting [....] The best alternative is (for her to) get water using the Blue Band margarine tin, and go to the yard behind the cell. Over there, between cassava trees planted by some unknown person, **she dug** the ground like a cat, and defecated in the hole. After rinsing herself and leaving some water aside, **she poked through** her faeces to find her six rings. Some women saw

---

[13] According to Kaswanti Purwo (1988: 222), the other two environments in which the patient occurs pre-verbally are a) when two NPs are contrasted and b) when an NP is promoted from oblique position to argument position.

how bad her manner of passing stool was, and [ ] imitated her from a distance; they didn't know she had some treasure.' (Kurniawan 2002: 67; my translation)

Immediately following (36) is the sentence with an OV clause and pre-predicate agent, shown in (37). This clause is followed by another a [*meN*-V] AT clause but with zero agent.

(37) *Cincin-cincin tersebut   ia_i cuci dengan sisa   air, dan*
ring-RDP   aforementioned 3SG wash with   leftover water and
me-nelan-nya_j   kembali.
MEN-swallow-3SG again

'She washed the rings with the remaining water, and [ ]_i swallowed them_j again.'   (Kurniawan 2002: 67)

In the OV clause, the pre-predicate patient *cincin-cincin tersebut* 'the rings' is the topic. It occurs as a definite NP and the referent is presupposed, having been mentioned in the previous discourse. Its topic status can be shown for example, by applying the same left- and right-dislocation test from Gundel & Fretheim (2004) that we applied to the previous examples.

(38) *Kalau cincin-cincin tersebut, ia cuci dengan sisa air, cincin-cincin itu.*

'As for the rings, she rinsed (them) with the remaining water, those rings.'

The OV predicate *ia cuci dengan sisa air* is focal in relation to the topic expression *cincin-cincin tersebut* 'the rings'. The test below shows that the predicate can stand alone as an open proposition in answer A, whereas the [*ia* V] phrase in answer B is slightly odd when it occurs on its own as a response to the question Q.

(39) Q: *Apa yang terjadi pada cincin-cincin tersebut?*
'What happened to the rings?'
A: *Ia cuci dengan sisa air.*
'She washed (them) with the remaining water.'
B: *Ia cuci.*
'She washed (them).'

This analysis supports the idea that the relation between topic and focus is in some respects like that between "topic" and "comment" (Gundel & Fretheim 2004: 175) in topic-comment constructions. The [*ia* V] OV clause is similar to topic-comment in that the pre-predicate patient (*cincin-cincin tersebut* 'the rings') is the topic, and the elements to its right (*ia cuci dengan sisa air* 'she washed with the remaining water') are a comment about the topic. Also the pre-predicate patient is "topical" in Cumming's sense in that the referent is accorded some importance in the episode, and this is reflected in its syntactic position. As indicated in (36), the six rings are significant in relation to the protagonist; they are valuable belongings the protagonist wants to protect. They are also important in

6 Constituent order and information structure in Indonesian discourse

the subsequent episode where the reader is told that the rings saved Dewi Ayu financially. After being released from the camp, she was able to survive by pawning them and the rest of the jewellery she could retrieve.

The "topical" status of the patient referent (in Cumming's sense) can also be inferred from the previous discourse and does not need to have been explicitly mentioned in prior discourse. The excerpt in (40) describes the character Kliwon tidying up his room in preparation for leaving home. The example is taken from an episode where Kliwon is depicted as a young, budding left-wing activist about to leave his hometown to take up university study in Jakarta. Among his belongings are books that are scattered around his room. The pre-predicate patient *buku-buku* 'books' is the topic of the second sentence. The referent of this NP is presupposed by virtue of its association with the patient NP in the preceding sentence (*semua barang-barangnya* 'all his belongings') and inferable from a mention in prior discourse where the reader learns that Kliwon has been given a book by his socialist mentor.

(40) **Ia** telah **me-ngemas** semua barang-barang-nya, dengan harapan jika ia pergi
3SG PERF MEN-pack all belonging-RDP-3SG with hope if 3SG go
me-ninggalkan-nya, semua dalam keadaan rapi. **Buku-buku** yang semula
MEN-leave-3SG/PL all LOC condition neat book-RDP REL previously
berserakan di atas tempat tidur, meja dan lantai **ia masukkan** ke dalam kotak
scattered LOC top place sleep table and floor 3SG put.in to inside box
kardus dan **me-numpuk-nya** rapi di sudut kamar.
cardboard and MEN-stack.up-3SG/PL neat LOC corner room

'**He** has **packed up** all his belongings, with the hope that if he has to go away leaving them behind, all would be in a neat condition. **He put the books** which were lying on the bed, table and floor in cardboard boxes and [ ] **stacked them up** neatly in the corner of the room.' (Kurniawan 2002: 195–196)

The example begins with an eventive AT clause containing completive marker *telah*. Two successive events follow, encoded by eventive OV clause with pre-predicate patient and eventive AT clause respectively. The pre-predicate position of the patient *buku-buku* 'books' suggests that the switch to OV is made mainly to direct the reader's attention to a new focus. After this, the author resumes his use of AT. As with (37), the multiple occurrences of *ia* create an impression of parallel structures, and together with the zero in the final clause, highlight the continuity of the human agent.

To summarise this section, the foregoing discussion has shown [*ia* V] OV clauses can be used to introduce a new focus, similar to [*di*-V-*nya*] PT clauses discussed in the previous section. In both cases, the clause highlights the agentivity of the human topic referent.[14] The difference is that, the repetition of the free pronoun *ia* '3SG' across OV and AT clauses gives a "synchronising" effect; that is, it makes both [*ia* V] OV clauses and [*ia meN*-V] AT clauses appear structurally similar. In contrast, the occurrence of

---

[14] Agentivity is understood here in the sense of Cruse (1973: 21) as referring to "an action performed by an object which is regarded as using its own energy in carrying out the action", where "object" includes "living things, certain types of machine, and natural agents".

a [*di*-V-*nya*] PT clause among [*meN*-V] AT clauses marks the event encoded by it as structurally different. One could argue, then, that [*di*-V-*nya*] is more marked than [*ia* V]. Further research could support this argument with quantitative evidence.

7 Conclusion

In this paper I have discussed different clause structures – [*meN*-V] AT clauses, PT clauses with [*di*-V-*nya*] and [*di*-V], and [*ia* V] OV clauses (considered here as a type of PT) – to show that in Indonesian, eventiveness can be encoded by means of any of these structures. Thus the preference for AT clauses in Indonesian cannot be understood narrowly as a preference for eventive clauses, or that eventiveness is coded only by AT clauses. The foregoing analysis shows that each clause type has similar as well as different functions, summarised as follows. First, [*meN*-V] clauses used to denote successive events, either involving the same agent or different agents in transitive clauses and actor or undergoer in intransitive clauses, and to mark the climactic portion of a story episode, illustrate most dramatically the preference in Indonesian for agentive clauses in SVO order. Kaswanti Purwo (1988: 226) points out that *meN*- verbs tend to occur in subordinate, backgrounding clauses. Meanwhile, Cumming (1991: 203) found that the "basic" clause type in Indonesian novels is AT with T>V order; PT clauses with V>T order, though still used to encode eventiveness, are marked. As we saw, [*meN*-V] occurs in both eventive/foregrounding and backgrounding clauses. Precisely whether and how [*meN*-V] AT clauses are used to encode eventiveness in Indonesian is a question that needs to be explored further. For now, it will have to be sufficient to say that these clauses can be used to encode both.

Second, PT clauses with [*di*-V-*nya*] remain an important resource for encoding eventiveness in Indonesian but their function is now mainly to signal a new focus, drawing the addressee/reader's attention to a particular event (or series of events) that contrasts with the event or state that comes before. In §4 I showed that [*di*-V] clauses occur with pre-predicate patient, indicating the patient's "topical" status. It may be that these clauses are mainly used to highlight patient continuity, while [*di*-V-*nya*] is primarily used to emphasise a particular event the agent is performing. Further research would be able to confirm this early observation.

Third, OV clauses with [*ia* V] structure are also used to encode eventiveness. Its co-occurrence with [*ia meN*-V] AT clauses emphasises the continuity of the third person agent and creates an impression of structural symmetry. The repetition of *ia* '3SG' across two different clause types produces a rhythmic effect much desired in fictional texts. To what extent rhythm and structural symmetry are also important considerations in other types of texts (e.g., news reporting) is an interesting topic that can be explored in a larger study. Such a study would also be able to inform us whether, with the weakening in pragmatic force of [*di*-V-*nya*], [*ia* V] is now preferred for marking focal events.

The majority of the data on which this study is based are taken from fictional narrative. Whereas Shiohara (2015) tested Cumming's findings using experimental data, I have drawn on fictional narrative to approximate the kind of data that Cumming used in drawing her generalisations. The results presented here might invite questions regarding genre; that is, the arguments I have raised might be objected to as valid only for narrative discourse. However, I hope to have demonstrated that they are also relevant for television news discourse. Finally, stylistic preferences can vary greatly between language users, as Cumming (1991: 174–175) herself has also noted. By including news discourse and fictional texts by different authors I hope to have shown that the choice of constituent order is not just a matter of individual style.

Acknowledgements

I am grateful to Sander Adelaar, Michael Ewing, Nerida Jarkey, Umar Muslim, and two anonymous reviewers for taking the time to patiently read the earlier versions of this paper and offering insightful comments. I have tried my best to incorporate their suggestions but no doubt inconsistencies remain, and for these I alone claim responsibility.

Abbreviations

1	first person	LOC	locative
2	first person	NEG	negation
3	third person	PERF	perfective
APPL	applicative	RDP	reduplication
DEF	definite article	REL	relative clause
DIR	directional	SG	singular
INDEF	indefinite		

References

(Producer unknown). 2017. *Eksklusif: Wawancara Novel Baswedan*. Jakarta. Aiman [Television program].
Anonymous. 2015. *Fokus pagi*. Jakarta. Television broadcast.
Arka, I Wayan & Christopher Manning. 1998. Voice and grammatical relations in Indonesian: A new perspective. In Miriam Butt & Tracy Holloway King (eds.), *Proceedings of the LFG98 conference*. CSLI Publications: Stanford.
Carlson, Katy. 2002. *Parallelism and prosody in the processing of ellipsis sentences*. New York: Routledge.
Chafe, Wallace L. 1994. *Discourse, consciousness, and time: The flow and displacement of conscious experience in speaking and writing*. Chicago: University of Chicago Press.
Cohn, Dorrit. 1978. *Transparent minds: Narrative modes for presenting consciousness in fiction*. Princeton, New Jersey: Princeton University Press.
Cole, Peter, Gabriella Hermon & Yanti. 2008. Voice in Malay/Indonesian. *Lingua* 118. 1500–1553.
Cruse, D. A. 1973. Some thoughts on agentivity. *Journal of Linguistics* 9(1). 11–23.

Cumming, Susanna. 1991. *Functional change: The case of Malay constituent order.* Vol. 2. Berlin & New York: Walter de Gruyter.

Cumming, Susanna & Fay Wouk. 1987. Is there 'discourse ergativity' in Austronesian languages? *Studies in Ergativity.* Lingua 71. 271–297.

Fludernik, Monika. 1993. *The fictions of language and the language of fiction.* London: Routledge.

Foley, William A. & Robert D. Van Valin. 1984. *Functional syntax and universal grammar.* Cambridge, UK: Cambridge University Press.

Givón, Talmy. 1975. Focus and the scope of assertion: Some Bantu evidence. *Studies in African Linguistics* 6. 185–205.

Gundel, Jeanette K. 1977. Where do cleft sentences come from? *Language* 53. 543–559.

Gundel, Jeanette K. 1999. On different kinds of focus. In Peter Bosch & Rob van der Sandt (eds.), *Focus: Linguistic, cognitive, and computational Perspectives,* 293–305. Cambridge: Cambridge University Press.

Gundel, Jeanette K. & Thornstein Fretheim. 2004. Topic and focus. In Larry R. Horn & Gregory Ward (eds.), *Handbook of pragmatics,* 175–196. Oxford: Blackwell.

Gundel, Jeanette K., Nancy Hedberg & Ron Zacharski. 1993. Cognitive status and the form of referring expressions in discourse. *Language* 69(2). 274–307.

Hopper, Paul J. 1979. Aspect and foregrounding in discourse. *Syntax and Semantics* 12. 213–241.

Karina, Sitta. 2008. *Circa.* Jakarta: Gramedia Pustaka Utama.

Kaswanti Purwo. 1988. Voice in Indonesian: A discourse study. In Masayoshi Shibatani (ed.), *Passive and Voice,* 195–242. Amsterdam: John Benjamins Publishing Company.

Krisna, Asbari-Nurpatria. 1977. *Kondektur ibu kota.* Jakarta: UP Kresno.

Kroeger, Paul. 2014. Passive agents in Malay: The binding properties and discourse functions of agentive =nya. In Siaw-Fong Chung Chung & Hiroki Nomoto (eds.), *Current trends in Malay linguistics,* 57. 5–29: NUSA.

Kumalasari, Ade. 2006. *Dengerin dong, Troy.* Jakarta: Gramedia Pustaka Utama.

Kurniawan, Eka. 2002. *Cantik itu luka.* Yogyakarta: AKY Press and Penerbit Jendela.

Kurniawan, Eka. 2004. *Lelaki harimau.* Jakarta: Gramedia Pustaka Utama.

Kurniawan, Eka. 2015. *Man tiger: A novel.* London: Verso. (transl. by Labodalih Sembiring).

Lambrecht, Knud. 1994. *Information structure and sentence form: Topic, focus and the mental representations of discourse referents.* Cambridge, UK: Cambridge University Press.

Maier, Emar. 2014. Language shifts in free indirect discourse. *Journal of Literary Semantics* 43(2). 143–167.

Nuranindya, Dyan. 2009. *Canting cantiq.* Jakarta: Gramedia Pustaka Utama.

Shiohara, Asako. 2015. Voice in eventive coordinate clauses in Standard Indonesian. *Clause Combining in the Languages of Indonesia* 59. 47–67.

Sneddon, James N., K. Alexander Adelaar, Dwi Noverini Djenar & Michael C. Ewing. 2010. *Indonesian reference grammar.* 2nd edn. St Leonards: Allen & Unwin.

Tannen, Deborah. 2007. *Talking voices: Repetition, dialogue, and imagery in conversational discourse.* 2nd edn. New York: Cambridge University Press.

Toer, Pramoedya Ananta. 1963. *Cerita dari Blora.* Jakarta: Balai Pustaka.
Van Valin, Robert D. & Randy J. LaPolla. 1997. *Syntax: Structure, meaning and function.* Cambridge: Cambridge University Press.

Chapter 7

Austronesian predication and the emergence of biclausal clefts in Indonesian languages

Daniel Kaufman
Queens College & ELA

> Information structure is tied up closely with predication in predicate-initial Philippine-type languages. In these languages, subjects are presupposed and the predicate position operates as a default focus position. The present paper argues that there is no need for biclausal focus constructions in these languages due to the nominal properties of their event-denoting predicates. Non-Philippine-type Austronesian languages develop a stronger noun/verb distinction that I argue ultimately gives rise to biclausal focus constructions. The building blocks of biclausal clefts in Indonesian languages are analyzed as well as the nature of predication in Philippine-type languages. Finally, I discuss a paradox in the syntax of definite predicates in Philippine-type languages. In a canonical predication, the less referential portion (the predicate) precedes the more referential portion (the subject). However, when both portions are definite the relation is reversed such that the more referential portion must be initial. I tie this to animacy effects found in other Austronesian languages in which a referent higher on the animacy scale must linearly precede one that is lower.

1 Introduction

Languages vary widely in their strategies for indicating pragmatic relations such as FOCUS and TOPIC. In the simplest case, a language may employ dedicated morphological markers which combine directly with focused or topical constituents. More common perhaps is the use of dedicated syntactic positions, typically on the left periphery of the clause, which host focused or topicalized constituents. Finally, all languages are thought to express basic information structure via prosodic means, although the actual implementation differs significantly from language to language. Parallel to pragmatic relations such as TOPIC and FOCUS, all languages possess a basic SUBJECT-PREDICATE relation which is partly independent of pragmatics but which also intersects with the phenomena of topic, focus and presupposition. While there has been notable success in the definition and analysis of pragmatic relations over the last several decades, the true nature

Daniel Kaufman. 2018. Austronesian predication and the emergence of biclausal clefts in Indonesian languages. In Sonja Riesberg, Asako Shiohara & Atsuko Utsumi (eds.), *Perspectives on information structure in Austronesian languages*, 207–245. Berlin: Language Science Press. DOI:10.5281/zenodo.1402547

of the subject-predicate relation remains one of the most fraught topics in the history of linguistics, with its beginnings in the work of Aristotle and Plato. Indeed, as Davidson (2005: 83) states with regard to predication, "It is a mark of Plato's extraordinary philosophical power that he introduced a problem that remained unresolved for more than two millennia." As could be surmised solely from the disagreement among syntactic analyses of English, a robust *cross-linguistic* definition of predicate and subject remains even more elusive. Copular clauses and cleft structures are of special interest here as notional predicates can occupy the canonical syntactic position of the subject (and vice versa) in these sentence types. In the present work, I am concerned with the interplay between the subject-predicate relation and information structure in Austronesian languages. Specifically, I would like to answer the following three questions:

(i) What is the evidence for biclausal cleft structures in Philippine-type[1] versus Indonesian languages? (§3)

(ii) How and why do biclausal cleft structures come into being outside of Philippine-type languages? (§4)

(iii) What does it mean to be a predicate in Philippine-type languages? (§5)

We can briefly preview the answers put forth below. With regard to (i), I argue that a genuine cleft structure in Indonesian languages emerges from a more symmetric Philippine-type system where true biclausal clefts do not exist. In regard to (ii), I show how a distinction between plain modification and modification by relative clause develops in Indonesian languages and how old functional morphology is recruited to mark relative clauses. Finally, regarding (iii), I argue that the predicate-subject relation in Philippine-type languages is determined by the *relative referentiality* of the two basic parts of a proposition similar to copular clauses in more familiar languages. The more referential half of the predication (i.e. the subject) follows the less referential half (i.e. the predicate). An interesting complication is that when both the predicate and the subject are referential, the part of the predication higher on the referentiality/animateness scale precedes the one lower on the scale. That is, the principle which derives the normal predicate-initial order in Philippine-type languages appears to be reversed in these cases.

Languages that sit on the border of the Philippine-type and non-Philippine-type are especially interesting in regard to information structure. In §4, I examine Balantak as a language that appears to be transitioning from monoclausal to biclausal focus constructions. This in turn sheds light on the development of biclausal constructions in languages that have diverged even further from the Philippine-type, such as Malay/Indonesian.

In §2, I attempt to define all the relevant categories in terms that are as theory-neutral as possible. The relevant notions for our purposes are subject and predicate (§2.1), prag-

---

[1] "Philippine-type languages" refer to a typological grouping rather than a geographic or phylogenetic one. It is used here to refer to Austronesian languages with a historically conservative set of (3 or 4) voices (following Blust 2002). Crucially, in Philippine-type languages, these voices are symmetrical in that a predicate can only bear one voice at a time and the agent argument is not demoted in the non-actor voices, as it would be in a canonical passive.

matic relations such as topic, focus and presupposition (§2.2), and the various types of clefts together with their component parts (§2.3).

2 Defining the terms

2.1 Subject and predicate

Several streams in philosophy of language, semantics and even formal syntax have taken a purely taxonomic approach to the notion of predicate with the goal of seeking a unifying trait in these types. The philosophical literature, in particular, is replete with claims such as "predicates ascribe" and "predicates designate". One of Frege's most important contributions to our current understanding of predicate involved viewing it as an element with *unsaturated* arguments; in his words, "not all parts of a thought can be complete; at least one must be unsaturated or predicative; otherwise they would not hold together" (Frege 1892/1997: 193).[2] For Frege, linguistic elements such as names and definite descriptions could not be classified as predicates as they cannot be naturally thought of as having unsaturated arguments in the way that "runs" has a single unsaturated argument and "punches" has two unsaturated arguments. But the fact that languages routinely place definite descriptions, names and even pronouns in the predicate position of clauses that bear all the morphosyntactic hallmarks of canonical predication poses an immediate empirical challenge to Frege's view of predicates as a natural class of *linguistic* elements.[3] Under the direct or indirect influence of Frege, a large body of work in syntax has treated such sentences as something other than pure predications. This has led, for instance, to a taxonomic tradition in the study of copular sentences (Mikkelsen 2011), in which copular clauses can come in specificational, equational and identificational flavors which largely correlate to the referentiality of the "predicate".

For present purposes, the notions SUBJECT and PREDICATE can be defined following type-theoretic predicate logic. Namely, the subject and predicate are the two constituents that combine to yield a TRUTH VALUE. It is not always a trivial matter to determine what types of strings have a truth value and which do not. In the simple case, we can compare the modification relation in (1) with the predication in (2).

(1) Tagalog
 ang matangkad na dalaga
 NOM tall   LNK girl
 'the tall girl'

---

[2] As a reviewer notes, an important aspect of Frege's contribution was to assimilate all types of predication to verbal predication. In Fregean semantics, predicates can be defined simply as categories with unsaturated terms.

[3] As noted by Modrak (1985), among others, philosophers have chiefly attempted to explain metaphysical predication, which only bears an incidental relation to linguistic predication. Patterns of linguistic predication across human language have thus not played a major role in philosophical investigations.

(2) Tagalog
    Matangkad ang dalaga.
    tall   NOM girl
    'The girl is tall.'

Tagalog speakers understand (1) as having a potential reference in the world but not a truth value, whereas the opposite intuition holds for (2) (which nonetheless contains the referring expression *ang dalaga* 'the girl'). In (1), the entire string consists of a single Determiner Phrase (DP) marked with the nominative case determiner *ang*. In (2), the string contains two major phrases, a predicate, followed by the nominative marked DP.

Himmelmann (1986) takes the key feature of predications to be "challengeability": "A predicative structure always allows for – or even demands – a yes-no reaction" (Himmelmann 1986: 26). This view, correctly, I believe, draws a strong line between predication on the one hand and modification, secondary predication and even subordinate predication on the other hand, a distinction which not all theories abide by. I also agree here with Himmelmann in understanding predicates to be crucially a relational concept rather than an inherent property of certain types of linguistic elements.[4]

A particularly vexed question in Philippine linguistics regards which of the two arguments of a basic transitive clause should be considered the "subject", with all possible answers having been posited by different analysts (including "none of the above", see Schachter 1976). In (3), we see three variations on a patient voice clause and in (4) we see the same kind of variations in an actor voice clause.[5] Following a type-theoretic approach, we can see that there is an important difference between the (b) and (c) sentences. In an out-of-the-blue setting, (3b) and (4c) are judged to have truth values but (3c) and (4b) are not. The latter two sentences are not ungrammatical, but they must depend on the preceding discourse to obtain a truth value. That is, as long as anyone ate the tofu, (3b) will be judged true but (3c) cannot be judged as true or false even if we know that Juan ate something. Similarly, for just anyone to have eaten tofu does not make the actor voice sentence in (4b) true. In order for it to be evaluated as true or false, the preceding discourse has to provide the reference for the elided nominative argument.

---

[4] I prefer though to rely on *the potential for a truth value* rather than the notion of challengeability as the latter cannot cleanly apply to imperatives and interrogatives. While some views on questions and imperatives take them to lack truth values, questions and imperatives seem to me best understood as other (non-assertive) things we do with truth values. Declaratives assert that a proposition is true or false; yes-no questions request the hearer to posit a true or false judgement on the proposition; content questions request a value to make a proposition with a variable true; imperatives demand that the addressee make the proposition true. None of these acts could be executed if the proposition itself had no truth value. Thus, just as *Dog* is not a predication, neither is *Dog?* a possible yes-no question, nor *Dog!* a command. I believe these facts can be unified in any approach that sees speech acts as *operations on truth values* rather than restricting truth values to assertions.

[5] In the non-actor voices, the agent is expressed in the genitive case, treated by some as ergative case, while the argument selected by the voice morphology is expressed in the nominative/absolutive case.

7 Austronesian predication and biclausal clefts in Indonesian languages

(3) TAGALOG

    a. *K<in>áin-Ø ni Juan ang tokwa.*
        <BEG>eat-PV GEN Juan NOM tofu
        'Juan ate the tofu.'

    b. *K<in>áin-Ø ang tokwa.*
        <BEG>eat-PV NOM tofu
        'The tofu was eaten.'

    c. *%K<in>áin-Ø ni Juan.*
        <BEG>eat-PV GEN Juan
        'Juan ate (it).'

(4) TAGALOG

    a. *K<um>áin ng tokwa si Juan.*
        <AV.BEG>eat GEN tofu NOM Juan
        'Juan ate tofu.'

    b. *%K<um>áin ng tokwa.*
        <AV.BEG>eat GEN tofu
        '(S/he) ate tofu.'

    c. *K<um>áin si Juan.*
        <AV.BEG>eat NOM Juan
        'Juan ate.'

The key generalization then is that a predicate must combine with a nominative/absolutive (in Tagalog, *ang* marked) argument to obtain a truth value. On this basis, we can refer to the *ang* phrase as the subject and the clause-initial phrases in the above examples as the predicate. Precisely parallel facts have been observed for several Polynesian languages, such as East Futunan and Tongan (Dukes 1998; Tchekhoff 1981; Biggs 1974). Dukes (1998) sums up the Tongan situation in a way that describes Philippine-type languages equally well:

> An omitted ergative argument need not presuppose any particular referent in the discourse and may in fact be interpreted existentially in much the same way an omitted agent in an English passive is interpreted. When an absolutive is omitted however, it must be interpreted referentially as a null pronoun picking out some previously mentioned individual. As Biggs puts it, native speakers of these languages consider sentences which are missing an absolutive to be 'incomplete', whereas sentences missing ergatives are not.

Note that this definition of subject is completely independent from the "subject" as identified by classic syntactic diagnostics like those posited by Keenan (1976), e.g. binding relations, raising and control, many of which converge on the more agentive argument of a transitive clause, as in English, and only some of which seem to pick out the *ang* phrase.[6] The concept of the subject-predicate relation as posited above is inherently symmetrical; the subject and predicate are simply the two (topmost) constituents which are combined to yield a truth value. However, few if any human languages treat these constituents symmetrically. There are clearly distinct positions for subject and predicate in the vast majority of described languages in the world.[7] Certain types of copular clauses, however, are apparently reversible in many languages but with subtly different entailments. Jespersen (1937/1984; 1965) notes the distinct meanings of 'my brother' in the following passage:

> Now, take the two sentences:
> > *My brother* was captain of the vessel, and
> > *The captain* of the vessel was my brother.
>
> In the former the words *my brother* are more definite (my only brother, or the brother whom we were just talking about) than in the second (one of my brothers, or leaving the question open whether I have more than one). (Jespersen 1965: :153)

Based on a family of similar observations, Jespersen develops the idea that choice of subject and predicate is based on relative familiarity. We can therefore conceptualize predication as an inherently *symmetrical* relation but one whose syntactic expression is highly sensitive to referentiality. That is, the more referential of the two elements in a predication relation will be mapped to a position which we can, following tradition, refer to as "subject" and the less referential of the two will be mapped to a position we call the "predicate".[8] In English, a subject initial language, there is only one way to make a predication between *Mary* and *a linguist*, that is, by treating *Mary* as the subject and mapping *a linguist* to the predicate, as in (5). We say that Philippine-type languages are "predicate-initial" because the less referential component of the predication relation is clause-initial while the more referential component follows it, as shown in (6). Just as in

---

[6] The *ang* phrase relation of Tagalog which I refer to here as subject has, in fact, been given so many names over the years to distinguish it from the subject of a hierarchical argument structure that it is hard to keep track. Among others, we find, "predicate base", "pivot", "topic", and the neutral *ang* phrase. (See Blust 2002, Ross 2006, Kroeger 2007 and Blust 2015 for good summaries of the terminological and conceptual challenges presented by Austronesian voice and case.) I maintain the term subject here because of the familiarity of the subject-predicate relation, which is specifically relevant here. Moreover, the hierarchical relations between co-arguments of a predicate (e.g. the relation between subjects and objects) is not relevant for our purposes and so we can avoid the usual confusion. These are, however, very different relations that should be kept separate terminologically and theoretically, as for instance in Foley & Van Valin (1984).

[7] Diverging from most generative syntacticians, den Dikken (2006) does argue for a symmetrical view of predication but applies the term very broadly to include phenomena that are generally analyzed as modification. Heycock's (2013) overview of predication in generative syntax shows how far this line of work has diverged from the traditional Aristotelian concept of a predicate as part of a bipartite proposition that yields a truth value.

[8] This is also very much in line with the view of predication developed by Williams (1997: 331), who treats referential NPs as potential predicates: "It is sometimes thought that a predicate cannot be 'referential'. It seems to me though that the best we can say is that the predicate is less "referential" than its subject, and that what we really mean is something having to do with directness of acquaintance." Concomitantly, for Williams (1997: 323), "A phrase is not predicational in any absolute sense, but only in relation to its subject."

7 Austronesian predication and biclausal clefts in Indonesian languages

English, the relative referentiality of the two parts of the predication determines their position in the clause. Reversing the order, as in (6b), results in ungrammaticality.

(5) English
   a. Mary is a linguist.
   b. *A linguist is Mary.

(6) Tagalog
   a. *Abogado si   Jojo.*
      lawyer NOM Jojo
      'Jojo is a lawyer.'
   b. **Si   Jojo abogado.*
      NOM Jojo lawyer

I would thus like to take a Jespersonian approach here, which does not rely on purported universal properties of subjects (e.g. "referring") or predicates (e.g. "unsaturated"). Having established this still informal, but hopefully workable, concept of predication, we turn to the impressive flexibility of Philippine languages in mapping lexical categories to the predicate and subject positions, as exemplified in (7). This was noted by Bloomfield (1917) for Tagalog and discussed extensively in the subsequent literature (Gil 1993; Himmelmann 1987; 1991; Foley 2008; Schachter & Otanes 1982; Kaufman 2009a).

(7) Tagalog
   a. *K<um>a~káin   ang laláki.*
      <AV>IMPRF~eat NOM man
      'The man is eating.'
   b. *Laláki ang k<um>a~káin.*
      man   NOM <AV>IMPRF~eat
      'The eating one is a man.'

In a very simplistic schema, we can conceive of English and Tagalog differing as in (8) and (9). Whereas the English clausal spine makes crucial reference to lexical categories such as NP and VP, Philippine-type phrase structure seems to refer primarily to the functional categories PredP and SubjP which can in turn host phrases of any lexical category (XP and YP below).[9]

---

[9]Proponents of this view, in one form or another, include Scheerer (1924); Lopez (1937/1977); Capell (1964); Starosta et al. (1982); Egerod (1988); DeWolf (1988); Himmelmann (1991); Lemaréchal (1991); Naylor (1975; 1980; 1995); Kaufman (2009a). Byma (1986), on the other hand, and most subsequent syntacticians (Richards 2000; Rackowski 2002; Aldridge 2004), have defended (or assumed) an analysis in which Tagalog is also structured like (8). Richards (2009a,b) explicitly argues that all predications in Tagalog are mediated by a verbal element but that this element is null in most copular clauses. For reasons of space, I refer the reader to Kaufman (forthcoming) for a rebuttal of this view.

(8) ENGLISH-TYPE PHRASE STRUCTURE

NP   VP
(Subj) (Pred)

(9) PHILIPPINE-TYPE PHRASE STRUCTURE

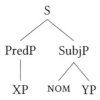

In order to understand how phrases are mapped to the predicate and subject position in Philippine-type languages we must first define the crucial pragmatic concepts that come into play. We turn to this in the following subsection.

2.2 Pragmatic relations

Presupposition and focus are often described in shorthand as old information and new information, respectively. While this evokes the right idea, Lambrecht (1994) argues against such oversimplified definitions. I follow Lambrecht's definitions for the relevant categories, as given below.[10]

(10) **Presupposition, assertion, focus and topic** (Lambrecht 1994: 52, 213, 131)

   a. PRAGMATIC PRESUPPOSITION: The set of propositions lexico-grammatically evoked in a sentence which the speaker assumes the hearer already knows or is ready to take for granted *at the time the sentence is uttered*.

   b. PRAGMATIC ASSERTION: The proposition expressed by a sentence which the hearer is expected to know or take for granted *as a result of hearing the sentence uttered*.

   c. FOCUS: The semantic component of a pragmatically structured proposition whereby the assertion differs from the presupposition.

   d. TOPIC: A referent is interpreted as the topic of a proposition if in a given situation the proposition is construed as being about this referent, i.e. as expressing information which is relevant to and which increases the addressee's knowledge of this referent.

---

[10] Abbott (2000) offers an alternative view of presuppositions as *non-assertions* rather than information known to the hearer. This may well fit the Austronesian data better but I leave this question to further work. A good overview of the issues and literature surrounding presuppositions is found in Kadmon (2000).

7 Austronesian predication and biclausal clefts in Indonesian languages

While the Tagalog *ang* phrase is often referred to as "topic" in different analytic traditions, it has been shown clearly by Naylor (1975), Kroeger (1993) and Kaufman (2005) to have no inherent pragmatic status beyond its definiteness or referentiality. Tagalog and, it would seem, all other Philippine languages have a bona fide topic position on the left periphery. In Tagalog, the fronted pragmatic topic, is followed either by the topic marker *ay* or a pause. In Tagalog, but not all Philippine languages, there is also a dedicated focus position on the left periphery of the clause which hosts oblique phrases, exemplified in (11).

(11) Tagalog
 [*Sa Manila*]$_{FOC}$=ka=ba *p<um>unta*?
 OBL Manila=2S.NOM=QM <AV.PRF>go
 'Did you go to MANILA?' ('Was it to Manila that you went?') (Kaufman 2005: 182)

The presence of an oblique phrase in the focus position in the left periphery bifurcates the sentence into a focus and a presupposition. In the above, 'to Manila' is the focus and it is presupposed that the addressee had gone somewhere. The question would be inappropriate if this information was not already part of the discourse in the same way that 'Was it to Manila that you went?' would be inappropriate in an out-of-the-blue context. On the other hand, a phrase in the left peripheral topic position followed either by the topic marker or a pause, needs to either be in the discourse already or contrasted with a similar argument that belongs to the same set. In (12), the fronted oblique phrase can serve as a contrastive topic, pragmatically akin to English, 'What about Naga, have you gone there?'. Note that the topic is further outside the clause and thus does not host second position clitics. Furthermore, it does not trigger a presupposition. The question in (12) is still felicitous without it being in the discourse that the addressee went somewhere.

(12) Tagalog
 [*Sa Naga*], *p<um>unta=ka=ba*?
 OBL Naga <AV.PRF>go=2S.NOM=QM
 'To Naga, did you go (there) already?'

With this brief introduction we are now prepared to turn to the mapping of these pragmatic categories on to phrase structure across several Austronesian languages.

2.3 Clefts

Cleft structures make use of the subject-predicate relation to satisfy requirements of information structure. Subjects are canonically (but not necessarily) topic-like and predicates canonically (but not necessarily) align with the focused constituent of a clause. Thus, focused subjects and presupposed predicates constitute non-canonical alignments which languages may either tolerate or avoid by means of various syntactic mechanisms. Languages with a high tolerance for focused subjects, such as English, will allow such a subject to be merely marked by intonation, as in (13a). However, an option also exists to shift such a focused subject into the predicate position, as in the *it*-cleft sentence in (13b) (Lambrecht 1994).

(13) a. Only [John]$_{FOC}$ knows Jane.
      b. It's only [John]$_{FOC}$ who knows Jane.

At the same time, the presupposition of an English *it*-cleft is demarcated syntactically by means of a relative clause. Thus, while both (13a) and (13b) contain a presupposition 'X knows Jane', its pragmatic status is only reflected syntactically in (13b), by means of the relative clause *who knows Jane*. The English *it*-cleft can thus be said to create a more transparent mapping between the syntactic and pragmatic structure of the clause.

Other languages do not tolerate non-canonical mappings such as that in (13a). For instance, the Malay/Indonesian adverb *saja* 'only', which must combine with a focused constituent preceding it, cannot associate with a subject in a simple declarative clause, as shown in (14a). Instead, a cleft structure is required in which the presupposed predicate is packaged as a relative clause, as shown in (14b).

(14) Indonesian
      a. *Presiden (*saja) bisa menilai   kinerja menteri.*
         president   only can AV:evaluate output minister
         'A president can evaluate a minister's output.'
      b. *Presiden saja yang bisa menilai   kinerja menteri.*
         president only RELT can AV:evaluate output minister
         'Only a president can evaluate a minister's output.'

As seen in (15), no special manipulation is required in order to narrowly focus the predicate or a part thereof, as this respects the canonical mapping between predicate and focus.

(15) Indonesian
      Presiden bisa menilai   kinerja menteri saja.
      president can AV:evaluate output minister only
      'A president can only evaluate a minister's output.'

Most interestingly, we find that the Austronesian tendency to express presuppositions syntactically manifests itself in Philippine English, as well. Whereas English can employ prosodic focus alone in a sentence like (16), Philippine English will invariably employ a TH-cleft (to be introduced below) in the same function, as seen in (16) and (17). The Tagalog equivalent is given in (18).

(16) US ENGLISH
      JOHN will carry your bag.

(17) PHILIPPINE ENGLISH
      John will be the one to carry your bag.

7 Austronesian predication and biclausal clefts in Indonesian languages

(18) Tagalog
    *Si   Juan **ang** mag-da~dala   ng   bag mo.*
    NOM Juan NOM AV-IMPRF~carry GEN bag 2SG.GEN
    'JUAN will carry your bag.' (Lit. 'Juan will be the one to carry your bag.')

Clefts thus function to transparently bifurcate the sentence into a focus and a presupposition. As seen in the difference between English and Indonesian above, languages differ as to the extent to which they require such transparency. In terms of the syntactic hallmarks of cleft sentences, Lambrecht (2001) offers the following definition:

(19) CLEFT CONSTRUCTION (Lambrecht 2001: 467)
A cleft construction is a complex sentence structure consisting of a matrix clause headed by a copula and a relative or relative-like clause whose relativized argument is coindexed with the predicative argument of the copula. Taken together, the matrix and the relative express a logically simple proposition, which can also be expressed in the form of a single clause without a change in truth conditions.

There are two components in (19). The structural component defines clefts as a biclausal structure containing a relative clause in a larger copular sentence. The semantic component of the definition relates clefts to simpler monoclausal sentences by virtue of their similar meaning. The cleft and the monoclausal structure differ in information structure and implicature but not in their basic truth conditions.

Lambrecht advocates for a taxonomy of English clefts as in (20), where caps indicates focus:

(20) CLEFT TYPES (Lambrecht 2001: 467)
    a.   I like CHAMPAGNE.   Canonical sentence
    b.   It is CHAMPAGNE (that) I like.   IT cleft
    c.   What I like is CHAMPAGNE.   WH cleft (pseudo-cleft)
    d.   CHAMPAGNE is what I like.   Reverse WH cleft
                                                                        (reverse/inverted pseudo-cleft)

In (20a) we find the canonical monoclausal sentence which is roughly equivalent in its truth conditions to the following clefts. The *it*-cleft places the focused phrase in the predicate position of a copular clause in which a dummy pronoun is the subject. The presupposition is packaged as a relative clause.[11] The types in (20c) and (20d) are termed alternatively *wh*-clefts or pseudo-clefts (although I will use only the latter term in the following). Here, there is no dummy subject. A relative clause headed by an interrogative pronoun like 'what' is in a copular construction with a focused phrase. In English, this type is reversible so that the presupposition can be the subject of the matrix clause, as in the standard pseudo-cleft exemplified in (20c), or the predicate of the matrix clause, as

---

[11]The precise relation between the two clauses in the English *it*-cleft has been subject to rather intense scrutiny, summed up recently by Reeve (2010).

in the inverse pseudo-cleft exemplified in (20d). To Lambrecht's taxonomy, we can add the "TH-cleft", in (21), first identified as a separate type by Ball (1977). Here, the relative clause modifies a definitely determined semantically bleached noun phrase, e.g. 'the one', 'the thing', etc.

(21)   a.   The one/thing I like is CHAMPAGNE.   TH-cleft
          b.   CHAMPAGNE is the one/thing I like.   Reverse/inverse TH-cleft

The syntax of clefts accommodates information structure in several ways. In structures like the English *it*-cleft (*It's JOHN who bit me*), part of the focus semantics derives from mapping a phrase to the object position of a copular structure, a more hospitable position for focused material than the subject position. In all types of cleft sentences, the presupposition is clearly demarcated by packaging it as a relative clause of some type.

It is clearly not the case that relative clauses always contain a presupposition outside of cleft sentences. For instance, the relative clause subject in (22) does not presuppose that someone will come after closing time. The sentence in (23), however, does entail such a presupposition, and this shows that it is the determiner or demonstrative that gives rise to the presupposition rather than anything inherent to the relative clause itself.[12]

(22)   Any customer who arrives after closing time will not be served.

(23)   I will take care of those customers who arrive after closing time.

In addition to determiners of a relativized noun, a phrase headed by an interrogative pronoun can be at least partly responsible for projecting a presupposition. A certain chess hustler in Greenwich Village used to rile his opponents with the following rhetorical question during the heat of a match:

(24)   Do you know what I like about your game? Absolutely nothing!

The jarring quality of the answer is the effect of canceling the presupposition in the question. The infelicity of the following cleft sentences in (25) makes this clear. That the presupposition does not come directly from the relative structure can again be seen in the felicitous (26), which contains a relative clause headed by the quantifier 'nothing', and which carries no presupposition.

(25)   a.   %Nothing is what I like about your game.
          b.   %What I like about your game is nothing.

(26)   There is nothing that I like about your game.

---

[12] See Kroeger (2009) for a similar point with regard to mistaken assumptions about headless relative clauses. As Kroeger shows for Tagalog, the presuppositions in such constructions are triggered by the determiners rather than the relative structure itself. Note that Kroeger (1993) claims that the subject actually precedes the predicate in Tagalog translational equivalents to English cleft sentences. On this view, *sino* 'who' would be the subject in a sentence like (27). Kroeger (2009: fn.3), however, recants this position and views (apparent) headless relatives like *ang dumating* 'the one who arrived' in (27) as being in subject position. This change in perspective was prompted by Tagalog's similar behavior to Malagasy as analyzed by Paul (2008) and Potsdam (2009), who offer several pieces of evidence for the predicatehood of (non-adjunct) interrogative phrases.

We can say then that relative clauses pave the road for presuppositions without necessarily triggering them directly. As we will see in the following section, what triggers the presuppositional reading in putative Philippine-type clefts is the definite semantics of the nominative case marking determiner (e.g. Tagalog *ang*). Unlike English, interrogative pronouns are never employed for this purpose in Philippine-type languages.

3 The syntactic structure of Austronesian clefts

A key point of variation between Philippine-type and non-Philippine-type Austronesian languages can be exemplified with the following example form Tagalog (27) and formal Indonesian/Malay (28).

(27) Tagalog

    a. *Sino **ang** d<um>ating?*
       who NOM <AV.BEG>arrive
       'Who arrived?'

    b. *D<um>ating **ang** guro.*
       <AV.BEG>arrive NOM teacher
       'The teacher arrived.'

(28) Formal Indonesian/Malay

    a. *Siapa **yang** datang?*
       who RELT arrive
       'Who arrived?'

    b. *Datang abang-nya...*
       arrive elder.brother-3S.GEN
       'His brother arrived...' (Hikayat Pahang 128:9)

Nearly all Philippine-type languages require some form of case marking on clausal arguments. In (27), this can be seen for Tagalog in the case marking determiner *ang*, which can be glossed nominative or absolutive (see Kaufman 2017 for discussion), but whose function is also tightly bound up with a definite/specific reading of the following NP (Himmelmann 1997).[13] There are two crucial things to note in this comparison. First, while Philippine-type languages require such case markers, only few Austronesian languages of Indonesia employ case marking on arguments (see Himmelmann 2005). The relativizer *yang* is strongly preferred in the subject question in (28a) but would not be acceptable in (28b) and can thus be easily distinguished from *ang* in Tagalog and the equivalents in other Philippine languages. Second, the case markers of Philippine languages do not discriminate between apparent verbal and nominal complements. Constantino (1965) was

---

[13]The precise semantics of *ang* has been debated in the literature. A non-definite reading can be obtained in Tagalog with *ang isang*... NOM one:LNK. However, without the presence of the numeral *isa* 'one', felicitous use of *ang* requires familiarity on the part of the hearer. For this reason, I maintain that definiteness, rather than specificity, best captures the pragmatic function of *ang*.

Table 1: Philippine sentence patterns following Constantino (1965)

Tagalog	kina:ʔin	naŋ	ba:taʔ	aŋ	maŋga
Bikolano	kinakan	kan	a:kiʔ	aŋ	maŋga
Cebuano	ginka:ʔun	han	bataʔ	aŋ	maŋga
Hiligaynon	kinaʔun	saŋ	ba:ta	aŋ	pahuʔ
Tausug	kyaʔun	sin	bataʔ	in	mampallam
Ilokano	kinnan	dyay	ubiŋ	ti	maŋga
Ibanag	kinan	na	abbiŋ	ik	maŋga
Pangasinan	kina	=y	ugaw	su	maŋga
Kapampangan	pe:ŋa=na	niŋ	anak	iŋ	maŋga
	eat:PV.PRF	GEN	child	NOM	mango

'The child ate the mango.'

Table 2: Philippine sentence patterns following Constantino (1965)

Tagalog	maŋga	aŋ	kina:ʔin	naŋ	ba:taʔ
Bikolano	maŋga	aŋ	kinakan	kan	a:kiʔ
Cebuano	maŋga	aŋ	ginka:ʔun	han	bataʔ
Hiligaynon	pahuʔ	aŋ	kinaʔun	saŋ	ba:ta
Tausug	mampallam	in	kyaʔun	sin	bataʔ
Ilokano	maŋga	ti	kinnan	dyay	ubiŋ
Ibanag	maŋga	ik	kinan	na	abbiŋ
Pangasinan	maŋga	su	kina	=y	ugaw
Kapampangan	maŋga	iŋ	pe:ŋa=na	niŋ	anak
	mango	NOM	eat:PV.PRF	GEN	child

'It was the mango that the child ate.'

the first to show that this is a far reaching characteristic of Philippine languages with the comparisons in Table 1 and Table 2. In no Philippine language do putative pseudo-clefts contain an overt relative marker, a *wh*-element, a dummy head noun, or any extra sign of nominalization. The voice marked words that serve as predicates in Table 1 are simply bare complements to the determiner in Table 2.

It turns out there is good reason for this symmetry. Starosta et al. (1982) first noted that the well-known Austronesian "voice" paradigm appeared to involve a reanalysis of nominalizations as voice markers, as shown in (29). [14]

---

[14] Unlike the rest of the forms in (29), the actor voice morpheme *<*um*> is not thought to have developed from a nominalizer, as it can be reconstructed to the proto-Austronesian verbal paradigm (Ross 2002; 2009; 2015).

(29) Austronesian voice morphology
*-en PATIENT NOMINALIZER > PATIENT VOICE
*-an LOCATIVE NOMINALIZER > LOCATIVE VOICE
*Si- INSTRUMENTAL NOMINALIZER > INSTRUMENTAL VOICE
*<um> AGENT VOICE/NOMINALIZER

I argue in Kaufman (2009a) that the large number of morphological and syntactic similarities between nouns and verbs can be attributed to the reanalysis in (29). This receives further support from Ross (2009), who shows that Puyuma, a Formosan language, maintains a division of labor where the verbs of Philippine-type main clauses are restricted to relative clauses. Another set of verbal morphology, now only used in a subset of Philippine-type languages for imperatives and subjunctives, is used to mark main clause verbal predicates in Puyuma.[15] It seems then that the reanalysis of relative clauses as main clause predicates in an earlier Austronesian proto-language had the effect of erasing any significant differences between relative clauses and main clauses in the daughter languages. If words formed with the morphology in (29) are nominalizations, it is no surprise that they can serve as direct complements of determiners such as seen above in Table 2. There is no need to relativize the verb phrase in sentences such as those in Table 2 if the verb is already akin to a thematic nominalization. To make this concrete, we could compare the patient voice morpheme in (29) to English -ee in *employee*. English allows for the two semantically similar sentence in (30).

(30) a. George is the one Jane employs.
      b. George is Jane's employee.

Clearly, direct relativization from a finite clause is far more common and productive in English than thematic nominalization. But in Austronesian, thematic nominalization, as in (30b), was developed to an unusual degree for the purpose of forming relativizations and these then spread to main clauses.[16] A consequence of this, particularly important for focus constructions, is that apparent clefts in Philippine-type languages are monoclausal, just as English (30b) is monoclausal. The key facts are reviewed below.

3.1 Apparent Philippine-type clefts: monoclausal or biclausal?

A reasonable analysis of the English pseudo-cleft is shown in (32), which can be compared to the canonical monoclausal declarative sentence in (31).

---

[15]Forms which take this set of morphology, referred to as the dependent paradigm by Wolff (1973) and the non-indicative paradigm by Ross (2002), cannot serve as the complement of a determiner or case marker in Philippine languages (Kaufman 2009a: 25).

[16]While this is unusual, it is not unique. Shibatani (2009) notes typological similarities between the use of thematic nominalizations in Austronesian and similar phenomena in Qiang, Yaqui, Turkish and Quechua. With regard to terminology, I refer below to these historically nominalized predicates, i.e. "Philippine-type verbs", as participles rather than verbs or nouns. The term participle is preferable because these forms have an intermediate status between plain nouns and the historical verbs of Austronesian, the latter which have been relegated to non-indicative contexts in Philippine languages.

(31)
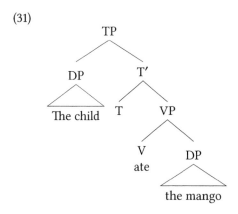

(32)
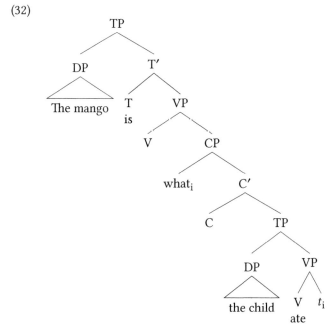

The English pseudo-cleft is considered biclausal because it contains two separate extended projections of a verb phrase, headed by *is* in the matrix clause and *ate* in the relative clause in (32). Each domain can mark categories like tense, negation and agreement independently. In contrast, the monoclausal (31) only contains a single domain for tense, negation and agreement. There is little reason to believe such a distinction exists in Philippine-type languages. The translational equivalents of (31) and (32) in Tagalog both appear monoclausal, as suggested by the analysis in (33) and (34). The only difference is that the participle (descended historically from a nominalization) is in the predicate position in (33) and in the subject position in (34). We can treat both cases, however, as copular clauses, indicated by the (null) Cop in both structures.

7 Austronesian predication and biclausal clefts in Indonesian languages

(33)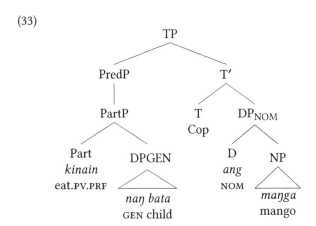

(34)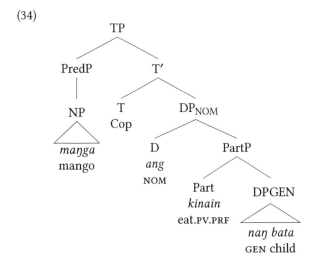

One of the few arguments that has been adduced in favor of a biclausal structure for sentences such as (34) is a putatively asymmetric pattern of clitic placement.[17] As discussed

---

[17]The notion that apparent clefts in Philippine languages are biclausal is widespread although often not explicitly argued for. Nagaya (2007: 348), for instance, analyzing Tagalog information structure in an RRG framework, states "A cleft construction in Tagalog is an intransitive clause where its single core argument is a headless relative clause, and its nucleus is a noun phrase coreferential with the gap in the headless relative clause." as illustrated in his (i), where S represents a gap in the relative clause.

(i) Si Boyet₍ᵢ₎ ang [p<um>atay [S₍ᵢ₎] kay Juan].
    NOM Boyet NOM <AV>kill   OBL Juan
    'The who killed Juan is Boyet.' (Nagaya 2007: 348)

Even in non-derivational frameworks such as RRG, the gap strategy employed commonly for relative clauses in Indo-European languages is typically applied to the analysis of Tagalog without consideration of alternative analyses.

223

in detail in Kaufman (2010b), Tagalog pronominal clitics are positioned after the first prosodic word in their syntactic domain. Aldridge (2004: 320), assuming that such clitics strictly take the clause as their domain, presents the data in (35) as an argument for the biclausal structure of apparent clefts. If such sentences were monoclausal, it would stand to reason that clitics could follow the interrogative directly as in (35b), but such a pattern is ungrammatical.

(35) Tagalog (Aldridge 2004: 319)
    a. *Ano ang g<in>a~gawa=mo?*
       what NOM <BEG>IMPRF~do.PV=2S.GEN
       'What are you doing?'
    b. **Ano=mo ang g<in>a~gawa?*
       what=2S.GEN NOM <BEG>IMPRF~do.PV

Second position clitics, however, are not only clause-bound; they are also bound within the DP, as can be seen in the following comparison with the possessive clitic *=ko* 1SG.GEN. With a bare predicate like *kaibigan* 'friend', as in (36a), the possessive clitic attaches to the first element in the clause, in this case, negation. When the predicate is a case marked DP, as in (36b), the associated genitive clitic cannot take second position in the clause and must attach after the first prosodic word within the DP.

(36) Tagalog
    a. *Hindi[=ko]=siya kaibigan[?=ko].*
       NEG=1S.GEN=3S.NOM friend=1S.GEN
       'He is not a friend of mine.'
    b. *Hindi[*=ko] siya ang kaibigan[=ko].*
       NEG=1S.GEN 3S.NOM NOM friend=1S.GEN
       'He is not the friend of mine.'

Similarly, in an event-denoting predication such as (37), second position clitics cannot follow the predicate when they originate within a case-marked DP.

(37) Tagalog
    Na-dapa[*=ko] ang kapatid[=ko].
    BEG-fall=1S.GEN NOM sibling=1S.GEN
    'My sibling fell.'

Aldridge (2004), citing data similar to (36), essentially comes to the same conclusion.[18] But if this generalization is correct, then the earlier clitic argument from (35) for a biclausal cleft structure is neutralized. Clitics are unable to escape from a DP and thus the genitive clitic in (35), representing an agent embedded in a nominative phrase, cannot follow the interrogative.

---

[18] Aldridge (2004: 262): "I assume that DP is a strong phase, not permitting movement from it. However, a predicate nominal is not, so the clitic would be able to move."

3.2 True biclausal clefts in Austronesian languages

The nominal properties of "Philippine-type verbs" is largely lost south of the Philippines (Kaufman 2009b). Consequently, Malay, even in its earliest attested stages, does distinguish relative clauses syntactically through the use of *yang*. As shown earlier in (28), Indonesian-type relativizers like *yang* are functionally distinct from Philippine-type case marking determiners. We can further see in (38) and (39) how Indonesian-type relativizers are distinguished syntactically from the "linker" or "ligature" found in most Philippine-type languages. First, *yang* is not required to mediate adjectval modification, as seen in (38a). Second, it can head a phrase without a preceding noun, as seen in (38b). The Philippine linker/ligature differs on both of these counts. It must mediate all instances of modification, as shown in (39a) and cannot surface without a preceding phrase.[19]

(38) Indonesian
 a. *rumah (yang) besar*
  house RELT big
  'big house'
 b. *(yang) ini*
  RELT this
  'this one'

(39) Tagalog
 a. *bahay*(na) malaki*
  house LNK big
  'big house'
 b. *(*na) ito*
  LNK this
  'this'

A relative clause referring to the agent is built on an actor voice VP with the addition of the relativizer *yang*, as in (40a). As can be seen in (40b), the plain VP cannot stand in subject position with the same function.[20]

The presence of a dedicated relativizer is one crucial piece of evidence for the biclausal nature of the construction. An additional piece of evidence is the optional presence of the copular element *adalah*.

---

[19] See Yap (2011) for a further discussion of *yang* and its expanding functions in the history of Malay.

[20] Verb phrases can also stand in subject position, typically with the help of a demonstrative, when functioning as event nominalizations, as in (i).

 (i) TP[DP[VP[Menilai kinerja mentri] itu] susah].
  AV:evaluate output minister that difficult
  'Evaluating the output of ministers is difficult.'

(40) Indonesian
   a. *Yang menilai   kinerja menteri adalah Presiden.*
      RELT AV:evaluate output minister COP   president
      '(The one) who evaluates the output of a minister is the president.'[21]
   b. **Menilai   kinerja menteri adalah Presiden.*
       AV:evaluate output minister COP   president

The innovation of a copula in Indonesian languages has yet to be studied systematically. The copula *adalah* was innovated in the attested history of Malay from a presentative use of the existential *ada* in combination with the emphatic *lah*. Although English-like cleft constructions employing both the copula and a relative clause can be found in modern Indonesian, there remain restrictions on the use of the copula that are not well understood. Specifically, we find that the copula is rejected in questions like (41b), a constructed minimal pair with the attested (41a).

(41) Indonesian
   a. *Dia adalah yang di-tua-kan di   antara sesamanya.*
       3S COP   RELT PV-old-APPL PREP among colleague
      'It's him who is treated as an elder among colleagues.'[22]
   b. *Siapa (*adalah) yang di-tua-kan?*
       who   COP   RELT PV-old-APPL
      'Who is treated as an elder?'

In line with the historical development of *adalah*, it is likely that it selects for a focused complement or at least avoids a presupposed one. This is supported by the fact that the copula is again possible when the interrogative is in-situ, as in (42).[23]

(42) Indonesian
   Yang di-tua-kan (adalah) siapa?
   RELT PV-old-APPL COP   who
   'The one treated as an elder is who?'

The use of a dedicated relativizer and copula in Indonesian (non-adjunct) content questions and focus constructions shows that this language has developed bona fide biclausal cleft sentences where Philippine-type languages still employ an equational monoclausal structure. Unfortunately, the difference between Philippine-type and non-Philippine-type Austronesian languages in this regard has not been given much attention by syntacticians. The default hypothesis has treated languages like Indonesian as simply having

---

[21] http://nasional.republika.co.id/berita/nasional/politik/16/01/06/o0iwuo354-jokowi-yang-menilai-kinerja-menteri-adalah-presiden
[22] http://nasional.kompas.com/read/2014/09/19/06431611/Artidjo.Korupsi.Kanker.yang.Gerogoti.Negara
[23] The ungrammaticality of post-interrogative copulas and copula stranding is not addressed by Cole & Hermon (2000).

overt markers for what are null functional elements in Philippine-type languages.[24] In the next section, we explore how the morphological glue of biclausal constructions is recruited from existing lexical and functional elements as part of a larger argument that such constructions are relatively recent innovations in the history of Austronesian.

4 How to jerry-rig an Austronesian biclausal cleft

We can posit a structure such as the one in (43) for an English TH-cleft (introduced earlier in §2.3). The focus here lies in the subject position while the presupposition is packaged as a DP containing a relative clause. Note that there are multiple elements within the presupposition that are special to this construction.

(43)

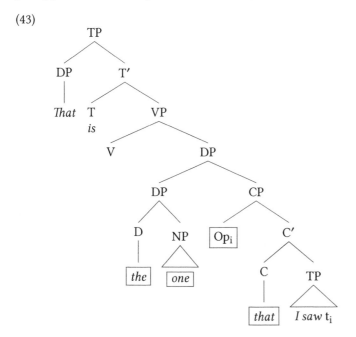

The DP proper contains a determiner and a semantically bleached noun, in this case *one*. The modifying CP contains a complementizer *that* and, ostensibly, a null operator in the position otherwise reserved for interrogative elements. That these layers are distinct

---

[24]Potsdam (2009) enumerates the pseudo-cleft analyses proposed for wh-questions across a diverse set of Austronesian (including both Philippine-type and non-Philippine-type) languages: Palauan (Georgopoulos 1991), Malay (Cole et al. to appear), Indonesian (Cole et al. 2005), Tsou (Chang 2000), Tagalog (Kroeger 1993; Richards 1998; Aldridge 2004; 2002), Seediq (Aldridge 2004; 2002), Malagasy (Paul 2001; 2000; Potsdam 2006a,b), Maori (Bauer 1991; 1993), Niuean (Seiter 1980), Tuvaluan (Besnier 2000), Tongan (Otsuka 2000; Custis 2004). Chung (2010) specifically traces the analysis of content questions in Philippine-type languages as pseudo-clefts to Seiter (1975). While such analyses appear well supported for many non-Philippine-type languages, it does not seem justified to assume the same structure for Philippine-type languages.

is seen both in historical stages of English, as exemplified in (44), and in non-standard modern English, (45).

(44)   Middle English (Chaucer's *Prolog* 836, cited in Curme 1912)
        He which   that   hath the shortest shall beginne.
        he RELT.PRON COMP has   the shortest shall begin
        'He who has the shortest shall begin.'

(45)   Here I am, in this room, because of an organization whose work that I deeply, deeply admire.[25]

In (46), the DP 'an organization', is modified by a CP which contains both an interrogative phase, 'whose work', moved to its left periphery and the complementizer 'that'.

(46)

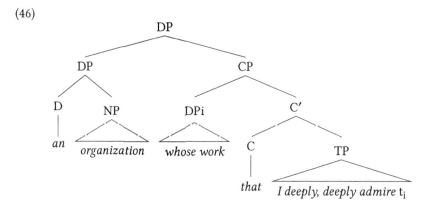

Given the distinct roles and positions of the determiner, dummy noun, interrogative pronoun and complementizer in the above English structures, we can now ask where the functionally equivalent morphology of Austronesian languages fits in, if at all.

Adelaar (1992) argues convincingly that the *ya* element in *yang* is cognate with the third person singular pronoun *ia* and that the following velar nasal is cognate with the Philippine linker, which we can treat as a type of complementizer.[26] The pronoun *ia* can furthermore be broken down into a person marking determiner element *i* (Ross 2006), plus *a*, a nominal head, as argued for by Reid (2002). The parts of the Malay/Indonesian

---

[25] Ellen Page, "Time to Thrive" Conference, 14 February 2014, Human Rights Campaign video, 0:26, posted and accessed 15 February 2014. Cited from Beatrice Santorini's doubly filled comp example webpage: http://www.ling.upenn.edu/~beatrice/examples/doublyFilledCompExamples.html.

[26] Reid (2002) argues for a similar analysis of Philippine case markers, in which they consist of a nominal head plus a linker. Translating Reid's proposal to the current framework, a case marker like Tagalog *ang* would have an extremely similar structure to Indonesian *yang*. This opens up a possibility whose implications I cannot fully address here, namely, that every Philippine-type DP is akin to a relative clause headed by a dummy nominal. There is some evidence to recommend such a view. Philippine-type DPs can contain a larger range of syntactic material than might naively be expected from an Indo-European perspective. For example, a case marking determiner can have as part of its complement negation and an independent tense domain, as shown in (i).

relativizer thus fit cleanly into the earlier template motivated by English, as shown in (47).

(47)
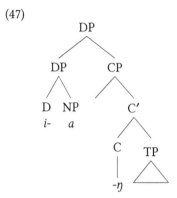

Similarly, Kähler (1974) shows that Ngaju Dayak and Old Javanese recruit demonstratives to play the role of relativizer, which can be located in the same DP occupied by *ia* above.

Other languages make use interrogative elements, which we locate on the left branch of CP. In two pioneering investigations of relative clauses in Indonesian languages, Gonda (1943) and Kähler (1974) note the frequency with which **anu* is used as a relativizer, as in (48).[27]

(48) Sundanese
Moal aja deui   hajam (a)nu bisa hibar lapas.
NEG EXT anymore chicken RELT can fly   fast
'In no case are there anymore chickens which can fly fast.' (Kähler 1974: 264)

In Sundanese, the relativizer is *anu*, a cognate of what Blust & Trussel (2010+) reconstruct as PMP **a-nu* "thing whose name is unknown, avoided, or cannot be remembered: what?"

(i) Tagalog
Ku~kun-in   ko   bukas   ang hindi mo   k<in>ain-Ø kahapon.
IMPRF~take-PV 1S.GEN tomorrow NOM NEG 2S.GEN <BEG>eat-PV yesterday
'I will take tomorrow what you didn't eat yesterday.'

Evidence against treating all DPs as full clauses in Philippine-type languages includes the impossibility of dependent form imperatives in DPs (§3 above) as well as the marked nature of topicalization within DPs. The latter argument, however, is weakened by the fact that relative clauses can also plausibly exclude a position for fronted topics. If a relative clause analysis is justified for Philippine-type DPs, then the typological division between languages like Tagalog and Indonesian would have to be characterized not as Philippine-type languages lacking relative clauses but rather lacking bare noun phrase arguments. Historically speaking, bare noun phrase arguments and dedicated relative clause markers clearly appear to be innovations in languages south of the Philippine area.

[27]Kähler (1974) further notes that it appears impossible to reconstruct a dedicated relativizer with any real time depth. I attribute this here to the fact that such elements are not necessary in Philippine-type languages whose event-denoting predicates are already noun-like and can thus serve as direct complements of determiners.

Sangirese *apa(n)*, on the other hand, is cognate with Blust & Trussel's reconstruction of PMP *apa 'what?' and shows evidence for a following nasal linker. The Sangirese relativizer thus fits into our schema as shown in (50).

(49) Sundanese
*I sire **apan** məm-pangasi' su səngkamisa naḷiu e, niuntung bue.*
PM 3P what:LNK AV-plant.rice in one.week past DET lucky EMPH
'They who planted rice last week, are lucky.' (Kähler 1974: 269 citing Adriani 1893-1894)

(50)
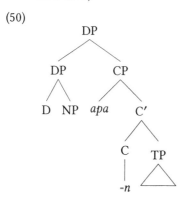

Yet other languages make use of a bleached noun alone. This strategy is extremely common in Sulawesi where we find various derivations of PMP *tau 'person', most often in the reduced form *to*, as in Kulawi (51). The presupposed portion of the clause can be analyzed simply as (52), where all the functional positions are left empty except for the bleached noun.

(51) Kulawi (Adriani & Esser 1939: 30)
*Ba bangkele **to** na-mate?*
QM woman RELT PRF-die
'Was it a woman who died?'

(52)
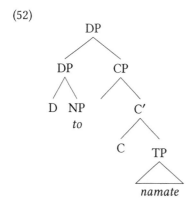

7 Austronesian predication and biclausal clefts in Indonesian languages

Balantak, a language of the Saluan-Banggai subgroup spoken in the eastern side of Central Sulawesi and recently described by van den Berg & Busenitz (2012), displays a fascinating combination of features that put it squarely between Philippine and Indonesian typologies. Like Philippine-type languages, it has a largely intact voice system and the remnants of a case marking system for NPs. The case marker *a* indicates the subject (i.e. the patient of patient voice, agent of agent voice, etc.) when it is post-verbal, as shown in (53). Just as in Tagalog and other Philippine languages, this marker also functions as a definite determiner.

(53) Balantak (van den Berg & Busenitz 2012: 47–48)
   a. *Ma-polos   tuu' a   sengke'-ku.*
      INTR.I-hurt very ART back-1S
      'My back really hurts.'
   b. *Boit-i-on   a   piso'-muu kabai sobii?*
      sharpen-APP-PV.I ART knife-2P or   let.it.be
      'Should your knife be sharpened or shall we just leave it?'

As in Philippine-type languages, the case marker still allows for complements of all lexical categories, as seen in (54). van den Berg & Busenitz (2012) term such constructions "semi-clefts".

(54) *...raaya'a a   mam-bayar.*
     3P   ART AV.I-pay
     '...they were the ones who paid.' (van den Berg & Busenitz 2012: 50)

Remarkably, Balantak has also developed a relative marker *men* from the bleached noun *mian* 'person' (adding further support to the etymology *to* RELT < *tau 'person' in other languages of Sulawesi). This is seen in (55), where both the case marking determiner *a* and the relativizer *men* co-occur in the presupposition of question.

(55) *Ai   ime a   men mae'?*
     EMPH.ART who ART RELT go
     'Who is going?' (van den Berg & Busenitz 2012: 50)

The functional structure of clefts in Balantak, shown in (56), would thus look not very different from Malay/Indonesian.

(56)
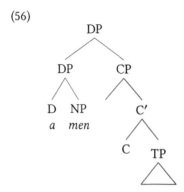

What is unique in Balantak is that the determiner in this structure maintains a robust NP case-marking function and can attach directly to verbs in many contexts. Balantak thus offers us a live view of what must have happened throughout Indonesia. The loss of case marking proceeds hand-in-hand with the rise of relativizers. In Balantak questions, it is still the case marker which is obligatory, not the relativizer, as van den Berg & Busenitz (2012) show explicitly in (57).

(57) Balantak

a. Pi-pii   takalan a   (men) ala-on-muu?
   RED-how.many liter   ART RELT take-PV.1-2P
   'How many liters will you take?'

b. *Pi-pii   takalan (men) ala-on-muu?
   RED-how.many liter   RELT take-PV.1-2P
   'How many liters will you take?'

But the functional scope of the case marker has also clearly shrunk in comparison to typical Philippine-type languages. Specifically, the nominative determiner *a* only occurs post-verbally in Balantak whereas in Philippine languages we find no such restriction. The loss of this domain would have given rise to the need for a relativizer *men* in positions where *a* was no longer licensed.[28]

5 Referentiality and predication

An idea was put forth earlier that the less referential half of a predication is assigned to the predicate position of a clause while the more referential half is packaged as the

---

[28]Like Balantak, Malagasy also instantiates an intermediate position between canonical Philippine-type languages and Indonesian. It is more complex than the languages considered here in possessing a distinct (i) focus complementizer *no*, (ii) relativizer *izay* and (iii) NP marker *ny*. Keenan's (2008) analysis of Malagasy is close to the one advocated here for Philippine-type languages although Paul (2001); Law (2007); Kalin (2009); Pearson (2009); Potsdam (2006b) show that the syntax of Malagasy cleft constructions is clearly non-equational. Potsdam's (2006b: 220–225) examination of the Malagasy CP in clefts is especially relevant here but space considerations preclude a full comparison.

subject, in line with work on copular clauses in English and other well studied languages. We have also seen in the above how the predicate position in Austronesian languages functions as a kind of de facto focus position by virtue of Austronesian languages tending to package presuppositions as subjects. The mechanics of this turn out to contain some surprises.

First, note that a bare predicate phrase in Tagalog, whether it is headed by an entity-denoting, property-denoting or event-denoting word, must precede the subject, as exemplified in (58) and (59).[29] The basic word order in Tagalog and the vast majority of Philippine-type languages is thus regularly described as predicate-initial on this basis.

(58) a. *Guro   ako.*
        teacher 1S.NOM
        'I am a teacher.'

   b. **Ako   guro.*   Cf. *A teacher is me.
        1S.NOM teacher

(59) a. *Matangkad ako.*
        tall   1S.NOM
        'I am tall.'

   b. **Ako   matangkad.* Cf. *Tall is me.
        1S.NOM tall

A paradox surfaces, however, when both parts of the predication are referential or definite. In such cases, it appears that the *more* referential portion of the predication must be located in the clause-initial predicate position. In a neutral context, *that* fills the subject position in the English translation of (60). In Tagalog, the demonstrative must be positioned in the clause-initial predicate position. In an English copular clause with a pronominal argument and a definite NP, the pronominal argument will be selected as the subject. In Tagalog, the pronominal argument must always be in predicate position when the other argument is definite, as seen in (61).[30]

(60) a. *Iyan   ang problema.*
        that.NOM NOM problem
        'That's the problem.' (Lit. 'The problem is that.')

---

[29]Topicalization is possible to achieve the subject initial orders here but it is marked either by the topic marker *ay* or a very clear intonational break after the subject. In short sentences like (62), the intonational break may be more difficult to hear. Speakers seem to agree however that for the order in (b) to be licit, there must be distinct phonological phrases while this is not true for the (a) sentences. It is in fact possible to make the judgments completely unambiguous through the use of clitics. Specifically, we can compare sentences like the following where the second position pronoun has two forms, a long form, *ikaw*, used in predicate position, and a clitic form *=ka*, used for arguments. When the second person is in a predication with a demonstrative, the clitic form is ungrammatical: *Ikaw iyan* 2S.NOM that.NOM 'That's you' versus **Iyan=ka* 'that.NOM=2SG.NOM'. When the demonstrative is topicalized, the second person pronoun retains its predicate form, *Iyan, ikaw* that.NOM 2SG.NOM 'That, is you'.

[30]As noted in fn.13, Kroeger (1993: 148–149) analyzes such constructions as inversions where the first constituent is the subject and the latter constituent is the predicate. All evidence, however, points to the initial constituents in such sentences behaving as predicates, leading Kroeger (2009) to revise his original analysis.

    b. *Ang problema iyan.
       NOM problem that.NOM

(61) a. *Ako ang guro.*
       1S NOM teacher
      'I am the teacher.'
    b. **Ang guro ako.* Cf. *The teacher is me.
       NOM teacher 1S

In (62), English and Tagalog again agree in placing the demonstrative in the subject position and the first singular pronoun in predicate position.

(62) a. *Ako iyan.*
       1S.NOM that.NOM
      'That's me.'
    b. ?*Iyan ako.*
       that.NOM 1S.NOM

Based on the above data, we can no longer say that Tagalog merely displays the mirror image of the English subject-predicate order. While both Austronesian languages and English enforce a familiarity condition on subjects (see Mikkelsen 2005: chap.8, for a summary of the English facts), there appears to be an additional role for an extended definiteness or animacy hierarchy in Tagalog and other Philippine languages. The involvement of an animacy hierarchy is clear from the following facts. Just like demonstratives, a third person pronoun must be in predicate position if the other half of the predication is definitely determined, as seen in (63). But when a third person pronoun is in competition with a first person pronoun for predicate position, it is the first person which wins, as shown in (64).

(63) a. *Siya ang problema.*
       3S.NOM NOM problem
      'S/he's the problem.' (Lit. 'The problem is s/he.')
    b. **Ang problema siya.*
       NOM problem 3S.NOM

(64) a. *Ako siya.*
       1S.NOM 3S.NOM
      'S/he's me.'
    b. **Siya ako.*
       3S.NOM 1S.NOM

Although space does not permit a full demonstration of all the possible interactions between NP types, the rules follow a slightly modified version of Aissen's (2003: 437) definiteness hierarchy, shown in (65). When both halves of a predication are referential, the portion higher on the scale in (65) will be selected as predicate.

7 Austronesian predication and biclausal clefts in Indonesian languages

(65) DEFINITENESS/ANIMATENESS HIERARCHY (Silverstein 1976; Aissen 1999; 2003)
local [1/2] person > third person pronouns > demonstratives/proper name > Definite NP > Indefinite Specific NP > Non-Specific

The only real optionality, as indicated by the lack of ranking above, is found with demonstratives and proper names. When these two types are in a predication relation, either order is acceptable, as seen in (66). This can potentially be linked to the ability of proper names in Tagalog to behave like pronominal clitics (Billings 2005).

(66) a. *Iyan   si   Boboy.*
    that.NOM NOM Boboy
    'That's Boboy.'

b. *Si   Boboy iyan.*
    NOM Boboy that.NOM
    'That's Boboy.'

In predications where the order is fixed by virtue of the definiteness hierarchy, information structure is flexible. For example, the sentence *ako ang guro* 'I am the teacher' can answer both the question in (5) as well as that in (5). This is unusual in Philippine languages, as the clause-initial predicate position is otherwise reserved for the focus of the sentence rather than the presupposition.[31]

(67) A: *Sino   ang guro?*
    who.NOM NOM teacher
    'Who is the teacher?'

B: *Ako   ang guro.*
    1S.NOM NOM teacher
    'I am the teacher.'

---

[31] Aldridge (2013) claims that in predications with two definite DPs (two *ang* phrases), the first is always the focus, exemplified with (i). I am not convinced that a focus reading is necessary or even unmarked on the first *ang* phrase in (i.b). Previous authors have disagreed on the pragmatic status of double *ang* phrase predications in Tagalog. Aldridge argues that predicate fronting in Tagalog (to derive the basic word order) is movement to a focus position. My feeling is rather that the focus interpretation of the predicate is a result of packaging presuppositions as definitely determined subjects. Once the presupposition is subtracted, the left-overs in clause-initial position canonically align with the focus. Examples such as (i) are critical to adjudicating between these two analyses but this must be left to further work.

(i) a. [*Ang lalaki*] *ang na-kita   ng babae.*
    NOM man   NOM NVOL.PV-see GEN woman
    'The man is who the woman saw.'

b. [*Ang na-kita   ng babae*] *ang lalaki.*
    NOM NVOL.PV-see GEN woman NOM man
    'The man is who the woman saw.'

(68) A: *Sino=ka?*
   who.NOM=2S.NOM
   'Who are you?'
   B: *Ako   ang guro.*
   1S.NOM NOM teacher
   'I am <u>the teacher</u>.'

I would like to offer a potential solution to the paradox of why it is the more definite or referential element that becomes the predicate when both elements are referential, in stark contrast to the canonical packaging of new information as predicate. The pattern can be accounted for by viewing it as the product of two potentially conflicting constraints. On one hand, presuppositions are packaged as *ang* phrases and what is left in the clause-initial position is the de facto focus. The only principle that predicate selection in the strict sense takes into account is whether an element is definite or not. If one element is definite and the other is not the story ends there; the definite element is packaged as subject while the remainder is placed in predicate position. If both elements are definite, another principle comes into play which only relates secondarily to the subject-predicate relation. This principle demands that elements higher on the definiteness/animacy hierarchy *linearly precede* those which are lower on the hierarchy. The clause-initial predicate position is then pressed into service to make the more animate element precede the less animate one.

Several pieces of evidence from other Austronesian languages support this analysis. First of all, as discussed in Kaufman (2014), many Indonesian languages have independently arrived at a split proclitic/enclitic system for agent marking.[32] In all attested examples, third person markers procliticize only if the local persons [1/2] have procliticized. First person furthermore tends to procliticize before second person. This can be seen clearly in the languages of Sumatra, as shown in Table 3 and equally compelling evidence is found in the languages of Sulawesi. On one end of the spectrum, all pronominal agents were enclitic in Old Malay. On the other side of the spectrum, Minangkabau, all such agents are expressed as proclitics. In between, Karo Batak, Gayo and Classical Malay which show a development that respects the animacy hierarchy such that the agents higher on the hierarchy must precede those which are lower.

In an independent development in several languages of Mindanao in the Philippines, the animacy hierarchy also determines the order of clitics within a clitic cluster (Billings & Kaufman 2004; Kaufman 2010a). For instance, in Maranao, a first person clitic always precedes a second person clitic and both first and second person clitics precede third person clitics, as seen in (69).

---

[32] Split proclitic/enclitic patterns in the languages of Sulawesi are argued by van den Berg (1996) to have developed from a full proclitic pattern and by Himmelmann (1996) from a full enclitic paradigm. The history and typology of pronominal proclisis is further discussed by Wolff (1996); Mead (2002); Kikusawa (2003); Billings & Kaufman (2004). I believe the comparative evidence points very clearly to split-paradigms resulting from partial accretion rather than loss, besides the obvious preference of Occam's razor for such an account, but the details do not concern us here.

Table 3: Person marking in the patient voice (Kaufman 2014)

	Old Malay	Karo Batak	Gayo	Clas. Malay	Minangkabau
1SG.	ni-V-(ŋ)ku	ku-V	ku-V	ku-V	den-V
2SG.	(ni-V-māmu)	i-V-əŋkō	i-V-kō	kau-V	aŋ-V
3SG.	ni-V-ña	i-V-na	i-V-é	di-V-ña	iño-V
1PL.EXCL	?	i-V-kami	kami-V	kami-V	kami-V
1PL.INCL	ni-V-(n)ta	si-V	kitö-V	kita-V	kito-V
2PL.	ni-V-māmu	i-V-kam	i-V-kam	kamu-V	kau-V
3PL.	ni-V-(n)da	i-V-na	i-V-é	di-V-mereka	iño-V

(69) Maranao (Kaufman 2010a)

a. *M<iy>a-ilay=ako=ngka.*
   <PRF>PV.NVOL-see=1S.NOM=2S.GEN
   'You saw me.'

b. *M<iy>a-ilay=ngka=siran.*
   <PRF>PV.NVOL-see=2S.GEN=3P.NOM
   'You saw them.'

Both of these phenomena offer support for the idea that there is an earliness principle at play which makes use of the definiteness/animacy hierarchy. A prediction of this analysis, which is driven by linear precedence, is that no subject-predicate paradox of the type found in Tagalog should exist in Austronesian languages with basic SVO word order. This is because the argument which is higher on the definiteness/animacy hierarchy will both make for a more natural subject and naturally precede the predicate in such languages. This prediction is at least borne out in Indonesian. As seen in (70), even a subject low on the animacy/definiteness hierarchy precedes the predicate in the unmarked word order. In a copular sentence such as that in (71), where a first person pronoun is in a predication relation with a definite NP, the pronouns still takes the canonical subject position. Unlike Tagalog, it cannot felicitously be positioned in predicate position without special topic-focus intonation.

(70) Indonesian
Serigala bisa membunuh orang.
wolf   can   AV:kill   person
'Wolves can kill people'

(71) Indonesian

a. *Aku guru-nya.*
   1S   teacher-DEF
   'I'm the teacher.'

b. #*Guru-nya   aku.*
   teacher-DEF 1S

Unfortunately, this topic has been left almost completely unexplored for other languages of Indonesia and so it is not yet possible to compare SVO languages of Indonesia with predicate-initial ones more broadly. The predictions of the current analysis are clear though that the unexpected inversions found in Tagalog should only occur in predicate-initial languages.

6 Conclusion

I have explored here several related aspects of predication and information structure in Austronesian languages. I began by arguing for a monoclausal analysis of apparent clefts in Philippine-type languages and tying this to the nominal nature of Philippine-type verbs. I then showed how true biclausal clefts emerge in Indonesian languages where the noun-verb contrast is more robust. In such languages, presupposed verbal material must be relativized before it can occupy subject position. While Indonesian relativizers come from varied sources (bleached nouns, interrogatives, pronouns in combination with the linker), it was shown that all patterns under examination fit neatly into a common syntactic template. Finally, I made an attempt at solving a paradox in the subject-predicate relation of Philippine-type languages. I argued that in addition to a canonical familiarity condition on subjects, there exists a linearity condition which requires that the part of a predication which is higher on the definiteness hierarchy precede the part which is lower. The prediction, which requires further exploration, is that SVO languages should not display these unexpected inversions.

It perhaps deserves emphasizing here that syntacticians have been too hasty in positing English-like constituency structures and lexical categories in the analysis of Austronesian languages. Consequently, important differences between Philippine-type and non-Philippine-type Austronesian languages have been masked. By stepping back from these assumptions, we can begin to explore fundamental problems in the relation between predication and information structure. Although the present work has only scratched the surface, it has hopefully opened a path for further research in how this relation varies across Austronesian languages. The resolution of this problem in Austronesian may very well contribute to answering the philosophical questions around predication first put forth by Plato and Aristotle over two millennia ago and debated today.

Abbreviations

APPL	applicative	BEG	begun aspect
ART	article	COMP	complementizer
AV	actor voice	COP	copula

DET	determiner	NVOL	non-voluntary mood
EMPH	emphatic	OBL	oblique case
EXT	existential	PM	personal marker
GEN	genitive case	PRF	perfective aspect
IMPRF	imperfective aspect	PST	past tense
INTR	intransitive	PV	patient voice
LNK	linker	QM	question marker
NEG	negation	RED	reduplication
NOM	nominative case	RELT	relative marker

References

Abbott, Barbara. 2000. Presuppositions as nonassertions. *Journal of Pragmatics* 32. 1419–1437.

Adelaar, K. Alexander. 1992. *Proto Malayic: The reconstruction of its phonology and parts of its lexicon and morphology*. Canberra: Dept. of Linguistics, Research School of Pacific Studies, the Australian National University.

Adriani, Nicolaus. 1893-1894. Sangireesche teksten. *Bijdragen tot de Taal-, Land- en Volkenkunde van Nederlandsch-Indië* 41/43. 1–168, 383–451, 461–524.

Adriani, Nicolaus & Samuel Jonathan Esser. 1939. *Koelawische taalstudien: Overzicht der spraakkunst, gesprekken en verhalen met vertaling*. Vol. 1. Bandoeng: Nix.

Aissen, Judith. 1999. Markedness and subject choice in optimality theory. *Natural Language and Linguistic Theory* 17. 673–711.

Aissen, Judith. 2003. Differential object marking: Iconicity vs. Economy. *Natural Language and Linguistic Theory* 21. 435–483.

Aldridge, Edith. 2002. Wh-movement in Seediq and Tagalog. In Andrea Rackowski & Norvin Richards (eds.), *Proceedings of AFLA 8: The 8th Meeting of the Austronesian Formal Linguistics Association*, vol. 44, 1–28. Cambridge, MA: MIT Press. MIT Working Papers in Linguistics.

Aldridge, Edith. 2004. *Ergativity and word order in Austronesian languages*. Cornell University (Doctoral dissertation).

Aldridge, Edith. 2013. Wh-clefts and verb-initial word order in Austronesian languages. *Linguistik Aktuell* 208. 71–96.

Ball, Catherine N. 1977. Th-clefts. *Pennsylvania Review of Linguistics* 2. 57–64.

Bauer, Winifred. 1991. Maori *ko* again. *Te Reo* 24. 31–36.

Bauer, Winifred. 1993. *Maori*. London: Routledge.

Besnier, Niko. 2000. *Tuvaluan*. London: Routledge.

Biggs, Bruce. 1974. Some problems of Polynesian grammar. *Journal of the Polynesian Society* 83. 401–426.

Billings, Loren A. 2005. Ordering clitics and postverbal R-expressions in Tagalog: A unified analysis? In Andrew Carnie, Heidi Harley & Sheila Ann Dooley (eds.), *Verb first: On the syntax of verb-initial languages*, vol. 73 (Linguistik Aktuell), 303–339. Amsterdam: John Benjamins Publishing Company.

Billings, Loren A. & Daniel Kaufman. 2004. Towards a typology of Austronesian pronominal clisis. In Paul Law (ed.), *Proceedings of AFLA 11* (ZAS Papers in Linguistics 34), 15–29. Berlin: Zentrum für Allgemeine Sprachwissenschaft.

Bloomfield, Leonard. 1917. *Tagalog texts*. Urbana: University of Illinois Press.

Blust, Robert. 2002. Notes on the history of focus in Austronesian languages. *The History and Typology of Western Austronesian Voice Systems* 518. 63–80.

Blust, Robert. 2015. Case markers of Proto-Austronesian. *Oceanic Linguistics* 54. 436–491.

Blust, Robert & Stephen Trussel. 2010+. *The Austronesian comparative dictionary*. http://www.trussel2.com/ACD.

Byma, Gary F. 1986. *Government and binding in Tagalog: An ergative analysis*. Calgary, Alberta: University of Calgary. (MA thesis).

Capell, Arthur. 1964. Verbal systems in Philippine languages. *Philippine Journal of Science* 93. 231–249.

Chang, Melody Y. 2000. On Tsou wh-questions: Movement or in situ? *Language and Linguistics* 1. 1–18.

Chung, Sandra. 2010. Six arguments for wh-movement in Chamorro. In Donna B. Gerdts, John C. Moore & Maria Polinsky (eds.), *Hypothesis A/Hypothesis B: Linguistic explorations in honor of David M. Perlmutter*, 49th edn. (Current Studies in Linguistics), 91–110. Cambridge, MA: MIT Press.

Cole, Peter & Gabriella Hermon. 2000. Partial wh-movernent: Evidence from Malay. In Uli Lutz, Gereon Müller & Arnim von Stechow (eds.), *Wh-scope marking* (Linguistik Aktuell), 101–130. Amsterdam & Philadelphia: John Benjamins Publishing Company.

Cole, Peter, Gabriella Hermon & Norhaida Aman. to appear. Clefted questions in Malay. *Malay/Indonesian Linguistics*.

Cole, Peter, Gabriella Hermon & Yassir Tjung. 2005. How irregular is wh in situ in Indonesian? *Studies in Language* 29. 553–581.

Constantino, Ernesto. 1965. The sentence patterns of twenty-six Philippine languages. *Lingua* 15. 71–124.

Curme, G. O. 1912. A history of English relative constructions. *The Journal of English and Germanic Philology* 11. 355–380.

Custis, Tonya. 2004. *Word order variation in Tongan: A syntactic analysis*. University of Minnesota. (Doctoral dissertation).

Davidson, Donald. 2005. *Truth and predication*. Cambridge, Massachusetts & London, England: The Belknap Press of Harvard University Press.

den Dikken, Marcel. 2006. *Relators and linkers*. Cambridge, MA: MIT Press.

DeWolf, Charles M. 1988. Voice in Austronesian languages of the Philippine type: Passive, ergative, or neither? In Masayoshi Shibatani (ed.), *Passive and voice*, vol. 16 (Typological Studies in Language), 143–193. Amsterdam & Philadelphia: John Benjamins Publishing Company.

Dukes, Michael. 1998. Evidence for grammatical functions in Tongan. In Miriam Butt & Tracy Holloway King (eds.), *Proceedings of the LFG98 Conference*. Stanford, CA: CSLI Publications.

Egerod, Soren. 1988. Thoughts on transitivity. *Bulletin Academia Sinica* 59. 369–384.

Foley, William A. 2008. The place of Philippine languages in a typology of voice systems. In Peter K. Austin & Simon Musgrave (eds.), *Voice and grammatical relation in Austronesian languages* (Studies in Constraint Based Lexicalism), 22–44. Stanford: CSLI Publications.

Foley, William A. & Robert D. Van Valin. 1984. *Functional syntax and universal grammar.* Vol. 38 (Cambridge Studies in Linguistics). Cambridge: Cambridge University Press.

Frege, Gottlob. 1892/1997. On concept and object. *The Frege Reader.* 181–193.

Georgopoulos, Carol. 1991. *Syntactic variables.* Dordrecht: Kluwer Academic Publishers.

Gil, David. 1993. Syntactic categories in Tagalog. In Sudapom Luksaneeyanawin (ed.), *Pan-Asiatic Linguistics: Proceedings of the Third International Symposium on Language and Linguistics, Bangkok, January 8–10, 1991*, 1136–1150. Bangkok: Chulalongkorn University Press.

Gonda, J. 1943. Indonesischerelativa. *Bijdragen tot de Taal-, Land- en Volkenkunde van Nederlandsche-Indig* 102. 501–537.

Heycock, Caroline. 2013. The syntax of predication. In Marcel Den Dikken (ed.), *The Cambridge handbook of generative syntax*, 322–352. Cambridge: Cambridge University Press.

Himmelmann, Nikolaus P. 1986. *Morphosyntactic predication: A functional-operational approach.* Vol. 62 (AKUP - Arbeiten des Kölner Univeralien Projekts). Cologne: Institut für Sprachwissenschaft der Universität zu Köln.

Himmelmann, Nikolaus P. 1987. *Morphosyntax und Morphologie. Die Ausrichtungsaffixe im Tagalog.* Vol. 8 (Studien zur theoretischen Linguistik). München: Wilhelm Fink.

Himmelmann, Nikolaus P. 1991. *The Philippine challenge to universal grammar.* Vol. 15. Cologne: Institut für Sprachwissenschaft der Universität zu Köln.

Himmelmann, Nikolaus P. 1996. Person marking and grammatical relations in Sulawesi. *Papers in Austronesian Linguistics* 84. 115–136. No. 3, Series A.

Himmelmann, Nikolaus P. 1997. *Deiktikon, Artikel, Nominalphrase: Zur Emergenz syntaktischer Struktur.* Vol. 362 (Linguistische Arbeiten). Tübingen: Niemeyer.

Himmelmann, Nikolaus P. 2005. Typological characteristics. In K. Alexander Adelaar & Nikolaus P. Himmelmann (eds.), *The Austronesian languages of Asia and Madagascar*, 110–181. London: Routledge.

Jespersen, Otto. 1965. *The philosophy of grammar.* New York: W. W. Norton & Company.

Jespersen, Otto. 1937/1984. *Analytic syntax.* Chicago: University of Chicago Press.

Kadmon, Nirit. 2000. *Formal pragmatics.* Oxford: Blackwell Publishers.

Kähler, Hans. 1974. Relative clause formation in some Austronesian languages. *Oceanic Linguistics* 13. 257–277.

Kalin, Laura. 2009. News about the *no*-phrase: Specificational pseudoclefts in Malagasy. In Sandy Chung, Daniel Finer, Ileana Paul & Eric Potsdam (eds.), *Proceedings of the sixteenth meeting of the Austronesian Formal Linguistics Association (AFLA)*, 61–75.

Kaufman, Daniel. Forthcoming. Response to commentators. *Theoretical Linguistics.*

Kaufman, Daniel. 2005. Aspects of pragmatic focus in Tagalog. In I Wayan Arka & Malcolm Ross (eds.), *The many faces of Austronesian voice systems: Some new empirical studies* (number 571 in Pacific Linguistics), 175–196. Canberra: Research School of Pacific & Asian Studies, ANU.

Kaufman, Daniel. 2009a. Austronesian nominalism and its consequences: A Tagalog case study. *Theoretical Linguistics* 35. 1–49.

Kaufman, Daniel. 2009b. Austronesian typology and the nominalist hypothesis. In K. Alexander Adelaar & Andrew Pawley (eds.), *Austronesian historical linguistics and culture history: A festschrift for Robert Blust* (Pacific Linguistics), 197–226. Canberra: ANU Press.

Kaufman, Daniel. 2010a. The grammar of clitics in Maranao. In Loren A. Billings & Nelke Goudswaard (eds.), *Piakandatu ami dr. Howard p. Mckaughan*, 132–157. Manila: Linguistic Society of the Philippines & SIL.

Kaufman, Daniel. 2010b. *The morphosyntax of Tagalog clitics: A typological approach.* Ithaca, NY: Cornell University (Doctoral dissertation).

Kaufman, Daniel. 2014. The syntax of Indonesian imposters. In Chris Collins (ed.), *Cross-linguistic studies of imposters and pronominal agreement* (Oxford Studies in Comparative Syntax), 89–120. New York: Oxford University Press.

Kaufman, Daniel. 2017. Lexical category and alignment in Austronesian. In Lisa Travis, Jessica Coon & Diane Massam (eds.), *Oxford handbook of ergativity*, 589–630. Oxford: Oxford University Press.

Keenan, Edward L. 1976. Towards a universal definition of "subject". In Charles Li & Sandra A. Thompson (eds.), *Subject and topic*, 303–333. New York: Academic.

Keenan, Edward L. 2008. Voice and relativization without movement in Malagasy. *Natural Language and Linguistic Theory* 26. 467–497.

Kikusawa, Ritsuko. 2003. The development of some Indonesian pronominal systems. In *Historical Linguistics 2001: Selected Papers from the 15th International Conference on Historical Linguistics, Melbourne, 13–17 August 2001*, 237–268. John Benjamins Publishing Company.

Kroeger, Paul. 1993. *Phrase structure and grammatical relations in Tagalog.* Stanford: Center for the Study of Language & Information, Stanford University.

Kroeger, Paul. 2007. McKaughan's analysis of Philippine voice. In Loren A. Billings & Nelleke Goudswaard (eds.), *Piakandatu ami Dr. Howard P. McKaughan*, 41–46. Manila: Linguistic Society of the Philippines & SIL Philippines.

Kroeger, Paul. 2009. Malagasy clefts from a Western Malayo-Polynesian perspective: Commentary on the paper by Hans-Martin Gärtner. *Natural Language and Linguistic Theory* 27. 817–838.

Lambrecht, Knud. 1994. *Information structure and sentence form: Topic, focus and the mental representations of discourse referents.* Cambridge, UK: Cambridge University Press.

Lambrecht, Knud. 2001. A framework for the analysis of cleft constructions. *Linguistics* 39. 463–516.

Law, Paul. 2007. The syntactic structure of the cleft construction in Malagasy. *Natural Language and Linguistic Theory* 25. 765–823.

Lemaréchal, Alain. 1991. Dérivation et orientation dans les langues des Philippines. *Bulletin de la Société de Linguistique de Paris* 86. 317–358.

Lopez, Cecilio. 1937/1977. Preliminary study of the affixes in Tagalog. *Selected writings of Cecilio Lopez in Philippine linguistics* 1. 28–104.

Mead, David. 2002. Proto-Celebic focus revisited. In Malcolm Wouk & Fay Ross (eds.), *The history and typology of Western Austronesian voice systems* (Pacific Linguistics), 143–177. Canberra: Research School of Pacific Asian Studies, ANU.

Mikkelsen, Line. 2005. *Copular Clauses: Specification, predication and equation*. Vol. 85 (Linguistik Aktuell). Amsterdam & Philadelphia: John Benjamins Publishing Company.

Mikkelsen, Line. 2011. Copular clauses. In Claudia Maienborn, Klaus von Heusinger & Paul Portner (eds.), *Semantics: An international handbook of natural language meaning*, vol. 2, 1805–1829. Berlin: Mouton de Gruyter.

Modrak, D. K. 1985. Forms and compounds. In James Bogen & James E. McGuire (eds.), *How things are: Studies in predication and the history of philosophy and science*, 85–99. Dordrecht, Boston & London: D. Reidel Publishing Company.

Nagaya, Naonori. 2007. Information structure and constituent order in Tagalog. *Language and Linguistics* 8. 343–372.

Naylor, Paz B. 1975. Topic, focus, and emphasis in the Tagalog verbal clause. *Oceanic Linguistics* 14. 12–79.

Naylor, Paz B. 1980. Linking, relation-marking, and Tagalog syntax. In Paz B. Naylor (ed.), *Austronesian Studies, papers from the 2nd Eastern Conference on Austronesian Languages*, 33–49. Ann Arbor: The University of Michigan.

Naylor, Paz B. 1995. Subject, topic, and Tagalog syntax. In D. Benett, T. Bynon & G. B. Hewitt (eds.), *Subject, voice and ergativity*, 161–201. London: SOAS.

Otsuka, Yuko. 2000. *Ergativity in Tongan*. University of Oxford (Doctoral dissertation).

Paul, Ileana. 2000. *Malagasy clause structure*. McGill University (Doctoral dissertation).

Paul, Ileana. 2001. Concealed pseudo-clefts. *Lingua* 111. 707–727.

Paul, Ileana. 2008. On the topic of pseudoclefts. *Syntax* 11. 91–124.

Pearson, Matthew. 2009. Another look at *no*: Pseudo-clefts and temporal clauses in Malagasy. In Sandy Chung, Daniel Finer, Ileana Paul & Eric Potsdam (eds.), *Proceedings of the sixteenth meeting of the Austronesian Formal Linguistics Association (AFLA)*, 165–179.

Potsdam, Eric. 2006a. More concealed pseudoclefts in Malagasy and the clausal typing hypothesis. *Lingua* 116. 2154–2182.

Potsdam, Eric. 2006b. The cleft structure of Malagasy wh-questions. In Hans-Martin Gärtner, Paul Law & Joachim Sabel (eds.), *In clause structure and adjuncts in Austronesian languages*, 195–232. Berlin: Mouton de Gruyter.

Potsdam, Eric. 2009. Austronesian verb-initial languages and *wh*-question strategies. *Natural Language and Linguistic Theory* 27. 737–771.

Rackowski, Andrea. 2002. *The structure of Tagalog: Specificity, voice and the distribution of arguments*. Cambridge, MA: MIT (Doctoral dissertation).

Reeve, Matthew. 2010. *Clefts*. University College London (Doctoral dissertation).

Reid, Lawrence Andrew. 2002. Determiners, nouns, or what? Problems in the analysis of some commonly occurring forms in Philippine languages. *Oceanic Linguistics* 41. 295–309.

Richards, Norvin. 1998. Syntax versus semantics in Tagalog wh-extraction. *UCLA occasional papers in linguistics* 21. 259–275.

Richards, Norvin. 2000. Another look at Tagalog subjects. In Ileana Paul, Vivianne Phillips & Lisa Travis (eds.), *Formal issues in Austronesian linguistics*, 105–116. Dordrecht, The Netherlands: Kluwer Academic Publishers.

Richards, Norvin. 2009a. Nouns, verbs, and hidden structure in Tagalog. *Theoretical Linguistics* 35. 139–152.

Richards, Norvin. 2009b. The Tagalog copula. In Sandy Chung, Daniel Finer, Ileana Paul & Eric Potsdam (eds.), *Proceedings of the sixteenth meeting of the Austronesian Formal Linguistics Association (AFLA)*, 181–195. London: AFLA Proceedings Project, University of Western Ontario.

Ross, Malcolm. 2002. The history and transitivity of western Austronesian voice and voice marking. In Fay Wouk & Malcolm Ross (eds.), *The history and typology of Western Austronesian voice systems* (Pacific Linguistics), 17–63. Canberra: Research School of Pacific & Asian Studies, ANU.

Ross, Malcolm. 2006. Reconstructing the case-marking and personal pronoun systems of Proto-Austronesian. In Yongli Zhang (ed.), *Streams converging into an ocean: Festschrift in honor of Professor Paul Jen-kuei Li on his 70th birthday*, vol. 5 (Language and Linguistics Monographs), 521–563. Taipei: Institute of Linguistics, Academica Sinica.

Ross, Malcolm. 2009. Proto-Austronesian verbal morphology: A reappraisal. In K. Alexander Adelaar & Andrew Pawley (eds.), *Austronesian historical linguistics and culture history: A festschrift for Robert Blust* (Pacific Linguistics), 295–326. Canberra: Research School of Pacific & Asian Studies, ANU.

Ross, Malcolm. 2015. Reconstructing Proto-Austronesian verb classes. *Language and Linguistics* 13. 279–315.

Schachter, Paul. 1976. The subject in Philippine languages: Topic, actor, actor- topic, or none of the above. In Charles Li (ed.), *Subject and topic*, 491–518. New York: Academic Press.

Schachter, Paul & Fe T. Otanes. 1982. *Tagalog reference grammar*. Berkeley, CA: University of California Press.

Scheerer, Otto. 1924. On the essential difference between the verbs of the European and the Philippine languages. *Philippine Journal of Education* 7. 1–10.

Seiter, William J. 1975. *Information questions in Philippine languages*. San Diego: University of California.

Seiter, William J. 1980. *Studies in Niuean syntax*. New York: Garland Publishingo.

Shibatani, Masayoshi. 2009. Elements of complex structures, where recursion isn't: The case of relativization. In Talmy Givon & Masayoshi Shibatani (eds.), *Syntactic complexity: Diachrony, acquisition, neuro-cognition, evolution*, vol. 85 (Typological Studies in Language), 163–198. Amsterdam: John Benjamins Publishing Company.

Silverstein, Michael. 1976. Hierarchy of features and ergativity. In R. M. W. Dixon (ed.), *Grammatical categories in Australian languages*, 112–171. Canberra: Australian Institute of Aboriginal Studies.

Starosta, Stanley, Andrew K. Pawley & Lawrence Reid. 1982. The evolution of focus in Austronesian. In Stephen A. Wurm & Lois Carrington (eds.), *Papers from the Third International Conference on Austronesian Linguistics, Vol.2. Tracking the travellers*, 145–170. Canberra: Pacific Linguistics.

Tchekhoff, Claude. 1981. *Simple sentences in Tongan*. Vol. 81. Canberra: ANU Press.

van den Berg, René. 1996. The demise of focus and the spread of conjugated verbs in sulawesi. *Papers in Western Austronesian Linguistics* 3. 89–114.

van den Berg, René & Robert I. Busenitz. 2012. *A grammar of Balantak: A language of Eastern Sulawesi*. Hein Steinhauer (ed.). Vol. 40 (SIL eBook). SIL International.

Williams, Edwin. 1997. The asymmetry of predication. *Texas Linguistic Forum* 38. 323–333.

Wolff, John U. 1973. Verbal inflection in Proto-Austronesian. *Philippine Journal of Linguistics Special Monograph*. Parangal kay Cecilio Lopez 4. 71–91.

Wolff, John U. 1996. The development of the passive verb with pronominal prefix in Western Austronesian langauges. In Bernd Nothofer (ed.), *Reconstruction, Classification, description: Festschrift in honor of Isidore Dyen*, 15–40. Hamburg: Abera.

Yap, Foong Ha. 2011. Referential and non-referential uses of nominalization construction in Malay. In Foong Ha Yap & Janick Wrona (eds.), *Nominalization in Asian languages: Diachronic and typological perspectives* (Typological Studies in Language), 627–658. Amsterdam/Philadelphia: John Benjamins Publishing Company.

Chapter 8

The role of information structure for morphosyntactic choices in Tagalog

Anja Latrouite
Heinrich-Heine-Universität Düsseldorf

Arndt Riester
Universität Stuttgart

> In this paper we investigate the influence of two information structure (IS) related aspects on the choice of voice form and sentence structure by Tagalog speakers. The first is the information status of argument referents. Tagalog is a multiple voice language, so almost every semantic argument in a sentence can be turned into the privileged syntactic argument (or subject) and be rendered salient. Information status of the undergoer has been argued to play an important role in voice and subject selection. The second IS-related aspect is the inherent structure of a discourse as determined by the implicit questions under discussion (QUDs) that are answered with each subsequent sentence in a text. The default sentence in Tagalog starts with a verb. Inversion constructions, i.e. sentences that start with an argument phrase instead of a verb, are described as motivated by information structure considerations such as focus-background or contrastive-topic-focus packaging. Based on a novel QUD approach, we will work out the discourse structure and at-issue contents of five short texts and show the important role of implicit QUDs and parallelisms on the choice of voice and constituent order.

1 Tagalog: Voice, information structure and inversion

1.1 Multiple voice system

Tagalog is a verb-initial language known for its multiple voice system. For an incremental theme verb like /sulat/ (actor voice: *sumulat*; undergoer voice: *sulatin*) 'to write' we find a set of voice affixes on the verb that may pick out the semantic core arguments or one of the peripheral arguments as the privileged syntactic argument (PSA) – the subject – of the respective sentence. The PSA is marked by *ang* if it is a common noun and *si* if it is a personal name. The *ang*- or *si*-marked reference phrases (RPs, cf. Van Valin 2008)

Anja Latrouite & Arndt Riester. 2018. The role of information structure for morphosyntactic choices in Tagalog. In Sonja Riesberg, Asako Shiohara & Atsuko Utsumi (eds.), *Perspectives on information structure in Austronesian languages*, 247–284. Berlin: Language Science Press. DOI:10.5281/zenodo.1402549

tend to receive a definite or at least specific interpretation, and usually appear after the other core arguments, as shown in (1). Actor and undergoer voice sentences differ in that undergoers[1] expressed by common nouns preferably get an indefinite (and maybe even non-specific) reading in actor voice sentences, e.g. *ng liham* in (1a), while they preferably receive a definite or specific reading in undergoer voice sentences, e.g. *ang liham* in (1b).[2] Note that the actor tends to receive a definite reading regardless of case marking.

(1) /sulat/ 'write'

    a. **um-: actor voice**
       *Hindi s<**um**>ulat*   [*ng liham*]$_{UG}$ *kay Lisa* [*ang babae*]$_{ACT}$.
       NEG <AV.RLS>write   GEN letter   DAT Lisa NOM woman
       'The woman did not write a(ny) letter/letters to Lisa.'

    b. **–in: (incremental) theme voice**
       *Hindi s<**in**>ulat*   [*ng babae*]$_{ACT}$ *kay Lisa* [*ang liham*]$_{UG}$.
       NEG <UV.RLS>write   GEN woman   DAT Lisa NOM letter
       'The woman did not write **the letter/a (certain) letter** to Lisa.'

As mentioned above, it is not only the agent or the theme argument that may be singled out as salient with a verb like *write*, as the examples in (2) show. Note that if an argument other than the agent or the theme is chosen as PSA, the information status of the theme argument is unspecified. Sentence (2b) exemplifies that thematic role labels (here: *theme*) are sometimes not fine-grained enough to capture the semantic properties that the voice affixes pick out. We will not be concerned with the intricacies of so-called peripheral voice forms in this paper. The examples are only meant to show that the voice system serves first and foremost to make different semantic arguments in a sentence salient and that only one argument at a time may be marked as salient in a sentence.

(2)   a. **–an: goal voice**
       *S<**in**>ulat-**an***   *ng babae ng liham si Lisa*.
       <UV.RLS>write-GV GEN woman GEN letter NOM Lisa
       'The woman wrote **Lisa** a/the letter/letters.'

    b. **i-: (transferred) theme voice**
       *I-s<**in**>ulat*   *ng babae **ang pangalan ni Lisa** sa papel*.
       TV-<UV.RLS>write GEN woman NOM name   GEN Lisa DAT paper
       'The woman wrote **Lisa's name** on (the) paper.'

---

[1] As it is common, we use the macro-role label *undergoer* to refer to various non-actor roles.
[2] The (specific) indefinite reading of the undergoer can be enforced by inserting the numeral *isa-ng* 'one'.

    (i) **–in: (incremental) theme voice**
       Hindi s<in>ulat   *ng babae kay Lisa **ang isa-ng liham**.*
       NEG <UV.RLS>write GEN woman DAT Lisa NOM one-LK letter
       'The woman did not write **a certain letter** to Lisa.'

c. i-pan(g)-: instrument voice
   I-p<in>an-sulat   ng babae kay Lisa ng liham **ang lapis**
   IV-APPL_INSTR<UV.RLS>-write GEN woman DAT Lisa GEN letter NOM pencil
   mo.
   your
   'The woman wrote the/a letter/letters to Lisa **with your pencil**.'

So far there are no elaborate corpus studies exploring whether the definiteness/specificity associated with *ang*-marking is about uniqueness, identifiability, familiarity, givenness, a certain kind of accessibility or other information-structurally relevant features. In this paper we are going to approach the problem from the other side. We will analyze the information structure and discourse structure of textual data and subsequently study the influence of information-structural constellations on voice selection. By *constellation* we mean, in particular, the focus-background structure of the entire clause within its discourse context rather than isolated properties such as the givenness of a single argument. The goal is to make further contributions to the investigation of which discourse properties exactly motivate voice and construction selection in a given text. To this end we will look at the results of a Tagalog translation and evaluation study aimed at getting speakers to produce and rate the same sentence in five contexts that differ with respect to the givenness of the arguments and the overall discourse structure. Before we turn to this study, however, a few more words need to be said about what has been found so far with respect to voice, constituent order and information structure coding in Tagalog.

1.2 Preliminary assumptions on information status, event type, information structure and the prominence of the undergoer

Philippine languages have been characterized as patient-prominent languages by Cena (1977), De Guzman (1992) and others, in the sense that undergoer voice has been said to be more frequent than actor voice in text counts, at least in transitive sentences (cf. Payne 1994; Sells 2001). Maclachlan (2002) among others argues that this observation does not hold unequivocally for Tagalog. Investigating several Philippine languages, Nolasco (2005), who proposes an ergative analysis of Tagalog, characterizes Philippine ergativity as speakers giving "the highest degree of prominence to the most affected entity" (ibid, p. 236), i.e. the entity viewed as most saliently affected by the event is said to receive the absolutive[3] case (*ang*-marking). For the most part, the most affected argument in transitive scenarios is the undergoer, but may be the actor if the undergoer is less identifiable. So, basically, he also recurs to the degree of referentiality (i.e. the information status) of the undergoer as one of the essential factors for voice selection. The idea of *ang*-marking as prominence marking is taken up by Latrouite (2011), who suggests three levels of evaluation with respect to the relative prominence of an argument: (i) the referential level, (ii) the event-structural level, and (iii) the information-structural level.

---

[3]Since we do not subscribe to the ergative analysis, we will gloss *ang* as *nominative* instead.

With respect to the referential level there are two possible scenarios: (i) one argument is higher on the scale of referentiality than the other (given > familiar > unfamiliar > non-unique > non-specific)[4] and, therefore, considered to be more prominent, or (ii) both are equally referential, but the referentiality of one of the arguments is less expected and, therefore, this information is treated as more salient. Expectancy is based on the frequency of a pattern. As Primus (2012) and others have pointed out, actors tend to be referentially independent and definite, while undergoers tend to be referentially dependent on the actor and are less often definite. Therefore, we find cross-linguistically a tendency to develop marked morphosyntactic coding for definite undergoers.

With respect to the level of event-structural prominence, we can distinguish undergoer- from actor-prominent and neutral verbs. Clearly undergoer-oriented verbs are change-of-state verbs like *to scare* or *to kill* that only provide information on the result state of the undergoer, but no information regarding the specific activity of the actor. Actor-oriented verbs are manner of action verbs (e.g. *to devour*) and certain stative verbs (e.g. *to fear*), and neutral verbs comprise punctual contact verbs like *to hit*. Schachter & Otanes (1972) provide examples showing that an undergoer-oriented verb like *to kill* or *to scare* cannot be used with actor voice in an unmarked, verb-initial sentence, as exemplified in (3a), but only with undergoer voice, as in (3b).

(3) a. * *T<um>akot   sa   mga babae   si   Lena.*
        <AV.RLS>scare DAT PL woman NOM Lena
        Intended: 'Lena scared the women.'

    b. *T<in>akot   ni   Lena ang   isa-ng   babae.*
        <UV.RLS>scare GEN Lena NOM ONE-LK woman
        'Lena scared a woman.'

This suggests that the voice alternation we are interested in is not available for these verbs. Note, however, that there are examples of actor voice forms of these verbs, even with definite undergoers, as example (4b) shows. The sequence in (4) is taken from a blog discussing a movie. The movie is about sisters that suffer from different kinds of traumas.

(4) a. *Kay Angel, ang multo ay ang pagiging alipin sa alak at sigarilyo.*
        DAT Angel, NOM ghost INV NOM developing slave DAT alcohol and cigarette
        'For Angel, the ghost is the developing addiction to alcohol and cigarettes.'

    b. [*Kay Sylvia,*]$_{UG}$ *t<**um**>a-takot*   [*sa   kaniya*]$_{UG}$ [*ang   pagpapalaglag sa*
        DAT Sylvia   <AV.RLS>IPFV.scare DAT her   NOM abortion   DAT
        kanya-ng magiging   anak]$_{ACT}$.
        her-LK   developing child
        'As for Sylvia, the abortion of her developing child scares (is haunting) her.'
                                    http://panitikanngpilipinas17.blogspot.de

---

[4]Compare also the givenness hierarchy by Gundel et al. (1993) and the comprehensive overview on information status by Baumann & Riester (2012).

8 The role of information structure for morphosyntactic choices in Tagalog

Latrouite (2011) observes that some kind of event-related markedness seems to be necessary to license actor voice of an inherently undergoer-oriented verb in a verb-initial clause. In her examples, the verb is always marked for imperfective aspect, inducing a habitual reading, and the actor argument is an inanimate causer rather than a volitional, controlling agent. She suggests that it is these divergent properties that license the use of the marked actor voice form. Note that in the example given in (4b), the sentence is also information-structurally marked, as the undergoer is a contrastive topic and appears in the left periphery. The new, focal information in (4b) is, thus, provided by the actor phrase *the abortion of her developing child*. The example is couched in a series of contrasting sentences, one of which is given in (4a), listing the afflictions and problems the – previously introduced – protagonists are haunted by. Latrouite (2011) suggests that considerations with respect to the level of information-structural prominence outrank considerations regarding the other two levels (event type and information status of arguments). Based on examples like (4b) as well as examples discussed further down below, it is argued that information structure plays an important role with respect to voice selection. However, there is no systematic corpus study to back-up the proposal as of yet and no detailed information-structural analysis of the data. This paper is meant to further investigate the claim that not only givenness and topicality, but also focality plays an important role for voice selection and, therefore, for PSA-marking.

Note that for the two not very frequent peripheral voice forms, instrument voice and causative voice, Nuhn (2016) finds textual givenness of the PSA to be a prerequisite in his preliminary corpus study. It seems to make sense that undergoer arguments can only be realized as the PSA if they are prementioned. However, note that the licensing of actor voice in (4b) rather points to focality of the actor as the decisive factor, since it is chosen over a given undergoer.

Latrouite (2016) finds that the textual givenness of undergoers is not sufficient to make speakers choose undergoer voice. For instance, in the target sentence (5c) the prementioned undergoer (experiencer) *mga negosyante* 'the negotiators' (see context in 5a) is not marked by *ang*; rather it is the inanimate actor argument *the rallies* which receives *ang*. As we have just pointed out, /takot/ (*tumakot, takutin*) 'to scare' is clearly undergoer-oriented. So not only based on the givenness of the undergoer but also based on event-structural prominence considerations, the undergoer argument would be expected to turn into the PSA. However, once again, we find actor voice and, once again, the sentence is information-structurally marked. It negates the truth of the previous sentence, and the follow-up sentence shows that the reason for the negotiators' fear is not the rallies but Erap.[5] It is therefore possible that it is the contrast between the actor arguments that licenses the chosen actor voice form.

---

[5] *Erap* is the nickname of Joseph Estrada, at the time President of the Philippines. Note, furthermore, that the form *yung* is very often used instead of *ang* in spoken Tagalog and seems to find its way into written Tagalog as well.

(5) Actor voice despite prementioned undergoer:

    a. **Context (undergoer voice) providing *rallies* and *negosyante*:**
Sabat naman ni Executive Sec. Ronaldo Zamora, t<in>a-takot lang
answer likewise GEN Executive Sec. Ronaldo Zamora <UV>IPFV-scare just
ng rallies ang mga negosyante.
GEN rallies NOM PL negotiators

'According to Executive Sec. Ronaldo Zamora, the rallies just frighten the negotiators/businessmen.'

    b. **Additional context:**
'And according to the postscript by Education Sec. Andrew Gonzales, it is forbidden for teachers to accompany the students to the rally, and a discussion regarding impeachment (from class) comes on top [...] What is this, martial law?'

    c. **Target sentence:**
Hindi totoo-ng t<um>a-takot   [*ng mga negosyante*]$_{UG}$ [*ang rallies*]$_{ACT}$.
Not true-LK <AV.RLS>IPFV-scare GEN PL negotiator NOM rallies

'It is not true that the rallies frighten the negotiators/businessmen.'

    d. **Continuation:**
Ang t<um>a-takot   [*sa kanila*]$_{UG}$, [*yung pananatili ni Erap sa*
NOM <AV.RLS>IPFV-scare DAT them   NOM staying GEN Erap DAT
puwesto]$_{ACT}$.
spot

'What scares them is Erap's staying on his spot.'
        (Pilipino Star Ngayon, December 12, 2000, *Mag – rally or tumahimik*)

The sentence in (6) shows an example pointing in a similar direction. The example is taken from the Tagalog translation of the *Hunger Games* by Suzanne Collins (2009). In the preceding paragraph the reader learns that the narrator is on her way to the woods to go hunting, which is illegal and may result in her getting killed. The narrator muses about the dangers she is putting herself into and how she cannot be open and truthful with anyone, not even her closest family members. In this context the following sentence is uttered.[6]

(6) *Nag-hi-hintay* [*sa akin*]$_{UG}$ *sa gubat* [*ang nagiisa-ng tao-ng puwede*
AV.RLS-IPFV-wait DAT 1SG DAT forest NOM alone-LK man-LK can
ko-ng pa-kita-an ng tunay na ako – si Gale]$_{ACT}$.
1SG.GEN-LK CAUS-visible-LV GEN true LK 1SG.NOM NOM Gale

'Waiting for me in the woods is the only person I can show my true self to – Gale' (*Yung Hunger Games*, p. 4)

---

[6]English original: "In the woods waits the only person with whom I can be myself: Gale."

8 The role of information structure for morphosyntactic choices in Tagalog

The actor phrase *the only person [I can show my true self to]: Gale* is newly introduced and, based on the relative clause, also starkly contrasted to the previously mentioned family members that the narrator cannot confide in. The undergoer argument is the narrator herself, so she is clearly given. Despite this fact, actor voice is chosen and the new, contrasted actor argument Gale is chosen as subject.[7] Examples like these lead Latrouite (2011) to the conclusion that the focality of the actor argument may result in actor voice selection, a pattern that cannot be predicted from the information status of the undergoer alone. It has been noted before that there is a default mapping between givenness/topicality and the macro-role *actor* on the one hand, and newness/focality and the macro-role *undergoer* on the other hand (e.g. Lambrecht 1994 among others), and that divergence from this default mapping often results in a specific morphosyntactic marking in the languages of the world, cf. Güldemann et al. (2015) on African languages.[8] Therefore, it is worthwhile exploring whether the sentences above are exceptions or whether they point to a more systematic pattern.

1.3 Hypotheses on information structure and voice marking

Given the asymmetry with respect to the default mapping of macro-roles and information-structural values, the characterization of information-structural prominence needs to be stated as follows:

(7) Information-structural prominence (characterization):
A core argument is IS-prominent if it has a non-default IS value (whereby the default value for actors is *+topical* and the default value for undergoers is *+focal* in a transitive sentence).

Based on the actor focus examples above and cross-linguistic findings that information-structural prominence as characterized in (7) is often-times reflected morphosyntactically in the languages of the world, we can formulate the hypothesis that information-structural prominence may indeed be a decisive factor for voice selection in Tagalog. If voice selection is influenced by prominence considerations and IS-prominence is an important factor, we expect the following correlation:

(8) IS-influenced tendencies w.r.t. voice selection with two-place predicates:

---

[7]Note that without further context the undergoer voice form would be preferred by speakers if the undergoer is highly referential (active, salient, given).

(i) H<in>intay ako   ng isa-ng lalaki / ni Gale.
    <UV.RLS>wait 1SG.NOM GEN one-LK man GEN Gale
    'A man/Gale waited for me.'

[8]The reason for this default mapping, at least in narratives, may very well be that stories tend to center around a small number of protagonists that engage in various activities with objects and people they encounter in the course of a story, so that the information packaging of a default sentence is Actor (topical) Verb (focal) Undergoer (focal).

a. If the undergoer is topical (given), undergoer voice is preferred.
   b. If the actor is focal (new), actor voice is preferred

It is important to note that research on information structure of the past decades has made it reasonably clear that the conceptual pairs *focal* vs. *new* (as well as *topical* vs. *given*) are closely related yet not identical to each other, see e.g. Beaver & Velleman (2011) or Riester & Baumann (2013). This is why, in §2.1, we are going to switch to a question-based definition of focus. In the current section, however, and with regard to the examples introduced so far, a novelty-based definition of focus is sufficient and, perhaps, easier to comprehend.

The tendencies stated in (8) render clear predictions if the actor and the undergoer do not differ in status with respect to information structure, i.e. if both are topical or both are focal. If both are topical, only the undergoer is considered information-structurally prominent based on (7). If both are focal, only the actor is considered prominent. As a first hypothesis to be checked we suggest the following:

Hypothesis (i)

If the actor is focal (contrary to the default mapping) and the undergoer is focal (in accordance with the default mapping), then actor voice is chosen:

Actor$_F$ Undergoer$_F$ → Actor Voice   (preliminary)

The situation described in Hypothesis (i) that will come to mind at first is probably so-called *broad focus* although the hypothesis can, for instance, also be applied to situations in which the undergoer is a (focus-like) contrastive topic and the actor is a focus, as witnessed in example (4b). We will say more on contrastive topics in §1.4. A second hypothesis to be checked is:

Hypothesis (ii)

If the actor is topical (according to the default mapping) and the undergoer is topical (contrary to the default mapping), then undergoer voice is chosen:

Actor$_T$ Undergoer$_T$ → Undergoer Voice

Undergoer voice could then be expected to be the preferred choice in sentences in which the verb or some non-core argument is focal, but both actor and undergoer are old information.

There are two more possible scenarios. The first scenario is the default mapping: actor (topical) – undergoer (focal). Neither argument is information-structurally prominent according to (7) in this scenario. Therefore, the choice of the respective voice form will have to be based on prominence considerations at a different level. The default for discourse-new undergoers is that they are indefinite, i.e. not referentially prominent. Based on the referential prominence considerations mentioned above, we expect actor voice to be frequent in this scenario, as shown, for instance, in (1a); cf. Primus (2012) on definiteness as a generally marked option for undergoers/objects. However, undergoer voice is also found in this constellation; compare (3b). Therefore, the only claim made in Hypothesis (iii) is that voice selection in this scenario involves information from a different level.

Hypothesis (iii)

If the actor is topical (according to the default mapping) and the undergoer is focal (according to the default mapping), then both voice forms may be used. The final choice will depend on prominence considerations at a different level (i.e. referential prominence or event-structural prominence).

Actor$_T$ Undergoer$_F$ → Actor Voice ∨ Undergoer Voice

The last possible scenario is a very marked one: both actor and undergoer are information-structurally prominent given the characterization in (7). In view of the fact that a given undergoer is not only IS-prominent but also prominent at the referential level, we might expect undergoer voice to be preferred over actor voice in this case. However, as we have already seen in examples (5d) and (6) above, a given undergoer does not necessarily enforce undergoer voice, so focality of the actor seems to outrank the topicality of the undergoer in quite a few instances.

Hypothesis (iv)

Actor$_F$ Undergoer$_T$ → Actor voice > Undergoer Voice   (preliminary)

Morphological marking on the verb is not the only possibility to overtly express IS-prominence. Many languages use fronting and inversion constructions as well as prosody to mark IS-prominence, and so does Tagalog. Therefore, we can expect that speakers may be able to express the IS-prominence of both arguments, albeit with different means: for instance, voice marking for one of the arguments and inversion for the other one. This is indeed found, as discussed in §1.4.

In order to factor out event-structural prominence and to highlight the role of information structure, Latrouite (2016) construed contexts for one and the same target sentence, containing the same verb and reference phrases. The contexts were meant to clearly determine the information status of the reference phrases and narrow down the set of possible implicit questions the target sentence could be an answer to. In this chapter, these contexts will be examined from a discourse-structural perspective. Before we turn to the study, however, we need to take a look at constituent order and information structure in Tagalog and lay out our question-under-discussion approach which we utilize to determine the information structure of an utterance.

1.4 Constituent order, prosody and inversion constructions

In this section, we turn our attention to other means of information-structure marking than voice. Kaufman (2005) puts forward what he calls the "double focus" construction in (9b), in which only the (non-focal) actor argument[9] is signalled on the verb via voice morphology, while the two focal undergoer arguments in-situ are marked by prosodic stress. Given what has been just laid out in §1.3, we would not expect focal undergoers

---

[9](9b) shows that a pronominal (in contrast to a nominal) PSA does not occur sentence-finally and is not *ang*-marked.

to trigger undergoer voice, so the data do not yet pose a challenge. There have been no claims so far with respect to how contrast should be marked. Prosody (indicated by capital letters) seems to be a possible option.

(9) "Double focus" (Kaufman 2005: 187ff.)

    a. *Dapat ba-ng mag-bigay ng pera sa mga guro?*
       should Q-LK AV-give GEN money DAT PL teacher
       'Should one give money to the teachers?'

    b. *Hinde, mag-bigay ka na lang* [*ng KENDI*]$_F$ [*sa mga BATA*]$_F$.
       NEG AV-give 2SG.NOM only GEN candy DAT PL child
       'No, (you) just give CANDY to the KIDS.'

Very often the phenomenon that some people call "double focus" is actually a combination of a contrastive topic (Büring 2003) plus a (contrastive) focus.[10] Contrastive topics have pragmatically a lot in common with foci (both of them give rise to alternatives, cf. Rooth 1992). We therefore expect that our hypotheses made with respect to focality (in particular, Hypothesis i) also cover contrastive topics. For instance, in (4b) we already saw actor-voice marking in combination with a contrastive topic and a focus.

A rather special means of focus/contrast marking is shown in example (10b), by Kaufman (2005: 194): the contrastive, genitive-marked actor appears in an extraordinary position at the end of the sentence and receives prosodic stress, while the undergoer is given. Thus, according to Hypothesis (iv), we would expect actor voice. However, in (10b) undergoer voice is found, indicating that special word order choices seem to have an influence on voice selection as well.

(10) a. *K<in>a-usap ng bawat propeso ang mga estudyante, di ba?*
       <UV>COM-speak GEN each professor NOM PL student, NEG Q
       'Each professor spoke with the students, right?'

    b. *Hindi. Hindi k<in>a-usap ang mga estudyante ni* [*PROPESOR MARTINEZ*]$_F$.
       NEG NEG <UV>COM-speak NOM PL student GEN Prof. Martinez
       'No. PROFESSOR MARTINEZ did NOT speak with the students.'

Note that the actual information structure of (10b) is in fact a bit unclear. It is quite likely that, other than what is assumed in Kaufman (2005), the extraposed phrase *ni Propesor Martinez* is actually the contrastive topic, while the focus is on the negation. Since we have no other piece of evidence for this particular construction, we shall have nothing more to say about it at this point.

---

[10] True instances of "double focus", which may also be characterized as two parts of a single, discontinuous *complex focus* (Krifka 1992), are rare in comparison with the rather frequent CT-F pairs. See also the discussion in Riester & Baumann (2013: 216).

8 The role of information structure for morphosyntactic choices in Tagalog

It is also possible for a contrasted core argument to appear with nominative marking in sentence-initial position followed by *ay*, while the other focal element appears in-situ with prosodic stress, as shown in (11). This construction is one of three inversion constructions mentioned in Schachter & Otanes (1972) and Van Valin & Latrouite (2015) and has also been linked to information packaging considerations. Inversion constructions are structures that diverge from the verb-initial default word order by starting off with a reference phrase in sentence-initial position. The three kinds of inversion constructions are the so-called *ay*-inversion construction, the *ang*-inversion construction and the adjunct fronting construction. In our study below, the *ay*-inversion construction was the most frequent one. According to Schachter & Otanes (1972), *ay*-inverted elements are for the most part topical arguments, but may be used for contrast. In the example in (11), the *ay*-inverted element can easily be construed as a contrastive topic and the argument realized in-situ as the (contrastive) focus.

(11) Contrastive topic – contrastive focus
 [Si Peter]_{CT} ay nag-ba-basa [ng LIBRO mo]_F.
 NOM Peter INV AV.RLS-IPFV-read GEN book 2SG.GEN
 'PETER is reading your BOOK.'

Note that, despite its nominative marking, the sentence-initial element followed by *ay* does not have to be the PSA of the verb; at least in undergoer voice sentences it can be the actor as well, see (12a). The particle *ay* may also be replaced by a pause here, signalling the clause-external position of the sentence-initial element. There are no corpus studies yet, but one can speculate that the construction in (12a) may be one of the ways to code both the topicality of the undergoer (undergoer voice) and the focality of the actor (*ay*-inversion) at the same time. We therefore tentatively assume the information structure indicated on the example. Note that it is not possible to *ay*-invert an undergoer in combination with actor voice, see (12b).[11]

(12) a. *Ay*-inversion sentence with two NOM-marked phrases
 [Si Peter]_F ay b<in>asa [ang libro mo]_T.
 NOM Peter INV <UV.RLS>read NOM book your
 'PETER read your book.'
 b. *Ang libro mo ay nag-basa si Peter.
 NOM book your INV <AV.RLS>read NOM Peter
 Intended: 'Peter read the BOOK.'

Based on these descriptions we can add a fifth hypothesis that we wish to check.

---
[11]Even with a resumptive pronoun, the sentence is considered ungrammatical by the consultants.

(i) *Ang libro mo ay nag-ba-basa nito si Peter.
 NOM book your INV <AV.RLS>read this.GEN NOM Peter
 Intended: 'The book, Peter is reading it.'

Hypothesis (v)

    Actor$_F$ +ay Undergoer$_T$ → Undergoer Voice   (preliminary)

Meanwhile, based on the problems with extraposition in (10b) and with *ay*-inversion in (12a), we change Hypothesis (iv) to exclude *ay*-inversion and non-default constituent order.

Hypothesis (iv)

    Undergoer$_T$ Actor$_F$ *(only default constituent order)* → Actor Voice   (final)

Finally, Hypothesis (i) will be stated more precisely to explicitly also cover *ay*-inversion and contrastive topics, i.e. examples like (11).

Hypothesis (i)

    Actor$_{F/CT}$ ±ay Undergoer$_F$ → Actor Voice   (final)

In the following, we mention a few more information-structurally relevant syntactic properties of Tagalog, which, however, we will not investigate any further. It should be noted that the *ay*-inversion may also be used in connection with framesetters, such as a temporal or local adverbial phrase, as shown in (13).

(13)   Kahapon ay nag-basa   ng libro mo si   Peter.
     yesterday INV AV.RLS-read GEN book your NOM Peter
     'Yesterday Peter read your book.'

If Tagalog speakers wish to put narrow focus on an obliquely marked argument or adjunct, they are also said to recur to adjunct inversion (Kroeger 1993), in which the adjunct is moved to the sentence-initial position and attracts clitics (if present) that appear between them and the verb. In (14) the pronoun *siya* is a clitic.

(14)   Adjunct/oblique inversion ("emphatic" inversion, Schachter & Otanes 1972, pp. 496–98)

    a. T<um>awa   siya   sa   kaniya kahapon.
        <AV.RLS>laugh 3SG.NOM DAT 3SG.OBL yesterday
       'She laughed at him yesterday.'

    b. Kahapon siya   t<um>awa   sa   kaniya.
        yesterday 3SG.NOM <AV.RLS>laugh DAT 3SG.OBL
       'It was yesterday that she laughed at him.'

    c. Sa   kaniya siya   t<um>awa   kahapon.
        DAT 3SG.OBL 3SG.NOM <AV.RLS>laugh yesterday
       'It was at him that she laughed yesterday.'

Another inversion construction is the nominative or *ang*-inversion, in which the PSA is put in sentence-initial position followed by a nominalized (*ang*-marked) predicate phrase, yielding an equative structure like in (15b). This construction is often translated by means of an English cleft construction, but can be shown to have a slightly different distribution (Latrouite & Van Valin 2016) and a different syntactic structure (e.g. Nagaya 2007).

(15) Nominative *(ang)* inversion

    a. *T<um>a-tawa*   *siya.*
       <AV.RLS>IPFV-laugh 3SG.NOM
       'He was laughing.'

    b. *Siya*   *ang t<um>a-tawa.*
       3SG.NOM NOM <AV.RLS>IPFV-laugh
       'He was the one laughing.'

Except for two instances of *ang*-inversion (see (39) in §3.5 and (40) in §3.6), speakers did not reproduce the last two inversion constructions in the study presented in this paper, although Latrouite & Van Valin (2016) could show that for the Hunger Games corpus the *ang*-inversion is more frequently used than the English *it*-cleft.

2 The pragmatics of information structure and discourse structure

2.1 Information structure theory: Basic assumptions and terminology

In this and the following section, we will define the information-structural concepts and terminology used in the case studies of §3 from a discourse perspective. At least two ways of describing information packaging have been proposed in the literature; the topic-comment structure and the focus–background structure. Lambrecht (1994) and others assume that the topic is the expression with respect to which the speaker aims to increase the hearer's knowledge, the comment being the part which provides this knowledge. The focus-background packaging, on the other hand, is about the distinction of "non-presupposed" vs. "presupposed" material.[12] This definition is close in spirit, though not in terminology, to Riester (to appear) or Riester, Brunetti, et al. (n.d.), building on the tradition of Alternative Semantics (Rooth 1992) and theories of *questions under discussion (QUD)* (Büring 2003; Büring 2016; Beaver & Clark 2008; Roberts 2012). It is assumed that

---

[12] This usage of the term *presupposed*, which can apply to denotations of non-clausal expressions and which is closely related to the notions *given* or *backgrounded*, stems from Chomsky (1971) and Jackendoff (1972). It is, however, in conflict with the use of the term in formal-pragmatic approaches, e.g. Karttunen (1974); Stalnaker (1974), which essentially define presuppositions as (abstract) propositional entities assumed to be part of the common ground, i.e. not necessarily as given. Compare also discussions in Lambrecht (1994: 150f.), Wagner (2012) or Riester & Piontek (2015: 237f.). For a contemporary picture of presupposition and other types of projective content see e.g. Tonhauser et al. (2013).

focus is the answer to the (current) QUD, while the background is the content used when formulating the QUD. Elements of the background that are not topical (here, interpreted as not referential, cf. Jacobs 2001) are sometimes called *tail* (cf. Vallduví & Engdahl 1996).

(16)   Question: What is Peter doing in the dark?
        Answer: Peter   is   dancing   in the dark.
                    [Aboutness Topic]   [Comment]   [Tail   ]
                    [Background   ]   [Focus]   [Background]
                    [Focus Domain ~   ]

As for the information-structural markup, we choose the conventions demonstrated in (17), following Riester, Brunetti, et al. (n.d.):

(17) Q_1: What is Peter doing in the dark?
      > A_1: [[Peter]$_T$ is [dancing]$_F$ in the dark]~.

(Q)uestions under discussion and their (A)nswers share the same index. The indentation (>) signals the fact that answers are subordinate to their QUD in discourse structure, i.e. they stand in a parent-child relation, as symbolized in Figure 1.

Figure 1: Simple question-answer discourse

The focus (F) is the part of the answer that corresponds to the question element of the QUD. QUDs which are implicit are enclosed in curly brackets, while overt questions are represented without brackets. The ~ symbol (Rooth 1992) indicates a focus domain, whose purpose it is to delimit the area comprising both the background and the focus. Focus domains "match" (Büring 2008) the QUD regarding their background, and they also allow for the easy identification of mutually contrastive assertions. All material inside the focus domain that is not focal is part of the background. There is no separate label for the background itself but we identify referential expressions in the background, e.g. *Peter* in example (16), as aboutness topics (T).[13]

A further category, which is not yet satisfactorily captured by the above grouping, is the contrastive topic (CT). Following Büring (2003), a contrastive topic is a hybrid category, which shares properties with both focus and background (or aboutness topic). We assume that contrastive topics can only occur in combination with a focus. They reflect a complex discourse strategy of the kind depicted in (18) or, more abstractly, in Figure 2.

---

[13] As for functional elements (e.g. the copula *is*, determiners, or prepositions), we leave it open when they should become part of the focus and when they should not.

(18) Q_1: {Who is doing what in the dark?}
   > $Q_{1.1}$: {What is Peter doing in the dark?}
   >> $A_{1.1}$: [[Peter]$_{CT}$ is [dancing]$_F$ in the dark]~.
   > $Q_{1.2}$: {What is Anna doing in the dark?}
   >> $A_{1.2}$: [[Anna]$_{CT}$ is [eating]$_F$ in the dark]~.

Figure 2: Question-subquestion discourse

The complex strategy consists in the fact that a question with two question elements (here: *who, what*) are answered by a sequence of answers to subquestions (indicated $Q_{1.1}$, $Q_{1.2}$). Now, the expressions *Peter/Anna* – which are backgrounded with respect to the subquestions but focal with respect to the main question Q_1 – are contrastive topics. Note that contrastive topics, as in (11), can function as aboutness topics (i.e. indicate a discourse referent) but they need not. Throughout the languages of world, it is the contrastive function of expressions that leads to stronger deviations from the default sentence realization than the aboutness function. In other words, it seems to be more important to signal that a change is expected or currently happening than to signal that there is a mere topical continuity. For that reason we expect contrastive topics to trigger more dramatic changes with regard to constituent order and prosody than (non-contrastive) aboutness topics.

2.2 Discourse structure trees, QUDs and well-formedness conditions

Recently, Riester, Brunetti, et al. (n.d.) (see also Reyle & Riester 2016, Riester to appear) have proposed a procedure for the identification of implicit questions under discussion (QUDs) in textual data. We will apply their methodology in the data analyses of Tagalog presented in §3. The method implements an insight, going back to at least Stutterheim & Klein (1989); van Kuppevelt (1995); Ginzburg (1996) and Roberts (2012), that the assertions made in a text can actually be thought of as answers to implicit questions, much like question-answer sequences in spoken dialogues. While in much of the previous work, QUDs have remained an object of theoretical investigation, Riester, Brunetti, et al. (n.d.) develop practical linguistic annotation guidelines, which are demonstrated on the basis of French, German and English corpus data.[14] Since the information structure of an

---

[14]See also Riester & Shiohara (2018 [this volume]) for an application of the QUD-tree method to Sumbawa (Austronesian, Malayo-Polynesian).

assertion is definable relative to its QUD, the benefit of enhancing a text with pragmatically defined implicit QUDs is that we gain access to the information structure of each clausal unit. This provides us with potential access to a large amount of data, which can be used to study the morphosyntactic marking of information structure in any language of interest. The method is more flexible, faster and cheaper than collecting data by means of experimental techniques, and comes with the additional advantage that the data under investigation are potentially more natural than, for instance, artificially produced question-answer responses. Without going into details, the reconstruction of the implicit QUDs of a text is enabled because it is constrained by a number of pragmatic principles derived and adapted from the literature on information structure; in particular Rooth (1992); Schwarzschild (1999); Büring (2003) and Büring (2008):

- For any assertion A identified in a text, its immediately dominating question Q must be directed at one of its constituents (Q-A-CONGRUENCE); i.e. QUDs which do not target any expression in the assertion are forbidden.

- The principle of Q-GIVENNESS says that Q can only consist of material that is salient at the point when A occurs, where *salient* means that the content is already active in the mind of the reader before A is processed. Typically, activation results from previous mention. In other words, material that is given in the discourse counts as salient and can be used to formulate Q.

- The Q-GIVENNESS constraint is complemented by the principle MAXIMIZE-Q-ANAPHORICITY, which says that all the content that is given in assertion A should be reflected in the QUD; i.e. A should have a maximal background and a minimal focus.

For instance, in (19) the appropriate QUD for A_1 must be the one indicated by Q_1, because it is this question which contains only given material *(rats)* and maximizes the background of A_1. By contrast, the reader is encouraged to check that other questions (e.g. *Is stress unhealthy? What about cats? What happened?*) violate one or several of the constraints mentioned above.

(19) A_0: The life of rats is stressful and dangerous.
      Q_1: {What about rats?}
      > A_1: [[They]$_T$ [get chased by cats]$_F$]~.

The final constraint, PARALLELISM, is designed to handle contrastive information in a text. When two assertions A' and A'' share semantic content while their remaining parts are interpreted as alternatives, then there is a common QUD, in which the shared material is reflected. In specific cases, PARALLELISM will override Q-GIVENNESS, which means that the QUD of two (or more) parallel assertions may contain some discourse-new material if it is (semantically) contained in both assertions. As an example, consider the sequence in (20). The information-structurally relevant QUD is $Q_{1.1}$ (a subquestion of Q_1) which includes the discourse-new (but semantically shared) material *chase*.[15]

(20) A_0: The life of rats is stressful and dangerous.
      Q_1: {What about rats?}
      > $Q_{1.1}$: {Who chases rats?}
      >> $A_{1.1'}$: [[Cats]$_F$ chase [rats]$_T$]~
      >> $A_{1.1''}$: and [[dogs]$_F$ go after [them]$_T$]~ as well.

Finally, example (21) introduces so-called non-at-issue (NAI) material (Potts 2005), which we define as linguistically optional expressions or, more precisely, as discourse-new material which is syntactically and semantically independent and which does not contribute in a direct manner to answering the current QUD. Typical NAI expressions are, for instance, appositions, non-restrictive relative clauses, speaker-oriented adverbs, evidentials or adjunct clauses like in (21).

(21) Q_0: {What do cats do?}
      > A_0: [When they are in the mood,]$_{NAI}$ [[cats]$_T$ [chase big rats]$_F$]~.

We will simply ignore non-at-issue material when it occurs at the beginning or in the middle of a clause. Non-at-issue material at the end of a clause will be treated as a new, independent assertion. Finally, note that discourse markers (e.g. *and, or, but, although*) or discourse particles (*also, as well, only, even*) are not marked as NAI but simply left unannotated; compare $A_{1.1''}$ in (20).

3 Case study 'The unhappy rats'

3.1 QUD approach to 'The unhappy rats'

Our case study is based on data elicited in Manila. Four speakers of Tagalog (three of which only speak Tagalog and no other Philippine language, and one who speaks Palawan and Tagalog) were asked to freely translate five short texts that differ in the givenness of the actor argument, the undergoer argument, the verb, and in the questions under discussion answered by the target sentence. The target sentences themselves vary slightly in their formulation in order to make the discourses sound more natural. In the following overview of the material we focus on the givenness of the arguments in the target sentences. The discourse structure of the texts will be worked out in detail in the next section.

In Text 1, the actor *cats* is the discourse topic. The verb and the undergoer provide the new information.

---

[15]This example demonstrates that it makes sense to distinguish between *topical* reference phrases, e.g. *[rats]$_T$*, and larger, non-referential *backgrounds* that may contain more material than just the aboutness topic, e.g. the phrase *[chase [rats]$_T$]*.

1. *Cats are silly creatures with nothing but nonsense on their minds. They climb up on curtains, bring home mice.* Cats also chase and catch big rats, *when they get a chance. Who wants to have a big rat in their house?*

In Text 2, the undergoer *rats* is the discourse topic, and there is a narrow contrastive focus on the actor *cats*.

2. *It is not only wolves and foxes that threaten rats and catch them.* Cats also catch rats *and eat them afterwards.*

In Text 3, the undergoer *rats* is the discourse topic. The actor *cats* and their activity with respect to the undergoer is the new information.

3. *Rats live stressful and dangerous lives. The noise of the traffic makes them nervous and sick. Dogs chase them. And also* (our domestic) cats catch and kill rats, *when they get the chance.*

In Text 4, the discourse topic is the cruel laws of nature. All sentences are about predators catching certain animals. Thus, the verb combination *chase and catch* is given, while the actor *cats* and undergoer *rats* are new/contrastive.

4. *Life in the wilderness is pretty cruel. Lions catch antelopes, sharks catch tunafish and happen to get caught and killed by humans themselves. Even here in the city these cruel laws of nature can be observed.* (Our domestic) cats also chase and catch rats, *and some also bring them home to continue playing with the bleeding creature.*

In Text 5, the discourse topic is the unhappiness and violence that the narrator witnesses. All follow-up sentences are all-new sentences that elaborate on what kind of violence the narrator observes.

5. *When I look out of the window, I see only unhappiness and violence. Dogs chase hens and make them lose their feathers. Old bitter women scream at children and make them cry. And also* (our domestic) cats catch and kill innocent rats, *when no one is looking.*

A PhD student and one of the authors presented the Tagalog translations to nine native speakers of Tagalog in Manila in a private setting. The consultants had different educational backgrounds and were aged 20–63. They were not aware of the original English texts and were asked to read, evaluate, correct and improve the Tagalog versions of the five texts. They were also asked which translations they liked better. Interestingly, the participants never corrected sentence structure or voice selection, but only vocabulary choices. When asked explicitly about variants that could be found in different texts with respect to syntax and voice, they stated their preferences, but none of the translations was rejected as awkward. We therefore consider the translations we got as acceptable and natural Tagalog.

The nature of the texts led to translations with a lot of parallelisms and the occurrence of the particle *rin* 'also' in the target sentence *Cats also catch rats*, regardless of whether or not this particle had been given in the English original. As pointed out by Krifka (1998), particles like *also* tend to have an associated constituent, which is often the contrastive topic.

The overall goal of the study was to find out how far the difference in textual givenness of the arguments would influence voice selection and construction choice in the target sentence. Recall that under the QUD approach (Riester, Brunetti, et al. n.d.) the crucial information-structural classes distinguished are focus, background (including aboutness topic), contrastive topic, and non-at-issue material, while a differentiation between new and contrastive focus is not made.

In the following sections we will provide an analysis of the discourse structures and the implicit questions under discussion giving rise to comprehensive information-structural analyses. Remember that the discourses shown in §3.2–§3.6 differ from the ones introduced above in this section, since we present the free Tagalog translations of the original texts as well as their re-translations into English. Based on the analyses we can check whether our expectations regarding the coding of the target sentence and the actual coding choices by native speakers match.

3.2 Text 1 – Intended: Actor (topical) Verb (focal) Undergoer (focal)

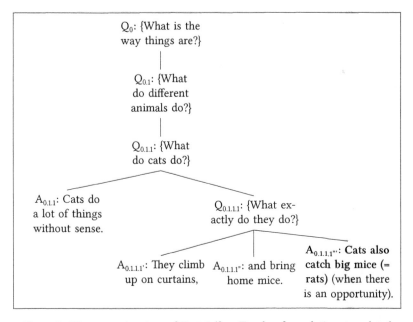

Figure 3: Discourse structure of Text 1 (free Tagalog formulation, translated back into English)

The first short text deals with the life of cats and the silly things they do. The QUD-tree analysis is shown in Figure 3 (target sentence in boldface). The actor *cat* was thus given, and intended was focus on the verb and the undergoer *rats*, i.e. *[[cats]$_T$ also [catch rats]$_F$]~*. The text was conceived in a way that no information-structural prominence in the sense of (7) for either argument needed to be marked morphosyntactically. Based on Hypothesis (iii) developed in §1.2, we predicted no special syntactic structure for the target sentence in this case, i.e. only the normal predicate-initial structure. But we expected actor voice to be the preferred choice for this scenario because the undergoers are non-specific and the verbs are not undergoer-oriented. This is indeed what we found, as $A_{0.1.1.1}$"', discussed below in (24), shows. While we only give the translation of one consultant here, all other consultants chose the same form, i.e. a predicate-initial sentence with actor voice.

According to Roberts (2012), any discourse addresses the so-called "Big Question" Q_0: *{What is the way things are?}* Many actual discourses, however, start *in medias res* (Firbas 1992), i.e. they use grammatical means (like presupposition triggers or non-default constituent order) to express that certain information should be accommodated (i.e. treated as if it were given), which boils down to answering a more specific subquestion (indicated in our example text by $Q_{0.1}$ and $Q_{0.1.1}$[16]). Since such grammatical means differ from language to language, we cannot be sure, at the outset, that our QUD-analysis for the initial sentence is correct. It is generally advisable not to draw any crucial conclusions from discourse-initial sentences (which we don't). In this example, we merely propose, without proving it, that the speaker has chosen to start a contrastive discourse strategy, analogous to the one in (18), §2.1, with the goal to provide information about different animals. We suggest therefore to analyse the expression *cats* in $A_{0.1.1}$ of (22) as a contrastive topic. Combinations of CT and F can be coded via *ay*-inversion in Tagalog, as shown in example (11) and suggested in Hypothesis (i), cf. Latrouite (2017).

(22) Q_0: {What is the way things are?}
      > $Q_{0.1}$: {What do different animals do?}
      >> $Q_{0.1.1}$: {What do cats do?}
      >>> $A_{0.1.1}$: [[*Ang mga pusa*]$_{CT}$ *ay* [*g<um>a-gawa   ng   mga wala-ng*
                  NOM PL   cat   INV   <AV.RLS>IPFV-do GEN PL   NEG-LK
             kabuluha-ng bagay]$_F$]~.
             sense-LK   thing
             'Cats do a lot of things without sense.'

Assertion $A_{0.1.1}$ is then elaborated by use of three partial answers to the question in $Q_{0.1.1.1}$ in (23). The three parallel answers, hence, all carry focus on the predicate and undergoer. Given that the actor is topical and the undergoer is focal, i.e. given that the arguments have their IS-default values, Hypothesis (iii) delegates the voice selection to the level of referentiality. As the referent of the undergoer argument is non-specific, like in example

---

[16] Note that the sub-numbering convention indicates that there is an entailment relation between the questions. For instance, every answer to $Q_{0.1.1}$ is, at the same time, an answer to $Q_{0.1}$ and, in turn, to Q_0.

(1a) in the introduction, actor voice is expected to be preferred, and this is also what we find in the translations of all four consultants. Note that the sentences in (23) and (24) have default constituent order. The reason why the PSA is not in final position here is its occurrence as a (clitic) pronoun.

(23) >>> $Q_{0.1.1.1}$: {What exactly do they do?}

>>>> $A_{0.1.1.1'}$: [[*Um-a-akyat*]$_F$ [*sila*]$_T$ [*sa mga kurtina*]$_F$]~
AV-IPFV-climb 3PL.NOM DAT PL curtain

'They climb up on curtains,'

>>>> $A_{0.1.1.1''}$: *at* [[*nag-da-dala* *ng mga daga sa bahay*]$_F$]~.
and AV.RLS-IPFV-carry GEN PL mouse DAT house

'and bring home mice.'

(24) **Target sentence:**

>>>> $A_{0.1.1.1'''}$: [*Kung may pagkakataon,*]$_{NAI}$ [[*nang-hu-huli*]$_F$ *rin* [*sila*]$_T$
if EXIST opportunity, AV.RLS-IPFV-catch also 3PL.NOM
[*ng malaki-ng daga*]$_F$]~.
GEN big-LK mouse

'Cats also catch big mice (= rats), when there is an opportunity.'

Note that, in the final assertion $A_{0.1.1.1'''}$ in (24) the preceding *if*-sentence, labelled as not at issue, does not answer the question under discussion $Q_{0.1.1.1}$, but rather expresses the relevance condition for the truth of the sentence containing the actual at-issue content. The target sentence *cats also catch rats* has a parallel structure to the two preceding sentences that answer the same question under discussion. All sentences have the same basic structure, i.e. they are predicate-initial and show actor voice. Note that the focus-sensitive particle *rin* appears directly in the postverbal position in $A_{0.1.1.1'''}$.

3.3 Text 2 – Intended: Narrow Actor Focus, i.e. Actor (focal) Verb (backgrounded) Undergoer (topical); Partly realized: Actor (contrastive topic) Verb (focus) Undergoer (topical)

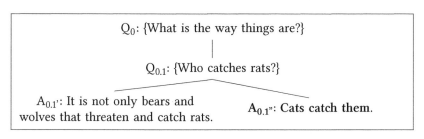

Figure 4: Discourse structure of free formulation based on Text 2

The second short text[17] (discourse structure given in Figure 4) was intended to yield a narrow focus on the actor argument in the target sentence *[[Cats]$_F$ also catch [rats]$_T$]*~ and, thus, represent one of the marked constructions mentioned in Hypotheses (iv) and (v), i.e. either Verb$_{AV}$ Undergoer$_T$ Actor$_F$ or Actor$_F$ +ay Verb$_{UV}$ Undergoer$_T$, because both arguments are information-structurally prominent according to (7). In order to force a context that would yield a narrow actor focus question as the natural implicit question under discussion for the target sentence, we provided a preceding sentence containing the focus sensitive particle *l(am)ang* 'only' with scope over those actor arguments that the actor *cat* in the target sentence was supposed to be contrasted with. The negation of the exhaustive particle in the first sentence was meant to be an indicator of the ensuing parallelism. In order to express the (negated) exhaustive narrow focus on the actor argument expressed in the context sentence, the *ang*-inversion construction (compare (15b) in §1.4) was chosen by all Tagalog translators, as shown in (25).

(25) Q$_0$: {What is the way things are?}
> Q$_{0.1}$: {Who catches rats?}
>> A$_{0.1'}$: [*Hindi lang* [*ang mga oso at lobo*]$_F$ *ang na-nakot at*
        NEG only NOM PL bear and wolf NOM AV.RLS.scare and
        nag-hu-huli [*ng mga daga*]$_T$]~.
        AV.RLS-IPFV-catch GEN PL rat
    'It is not only bears and wolves that threaten and catch rats.'

Subsequently, speakers did not continue with another *ang*-inversion but chose *ay*-inversion for the target sentence. As for *ay*-inverted narrow actor focus, Hypothesis (v) made us expect undergoer voice to mark the topicality of the undergoer. Indeed, two consultants offered this construction, which is given in (26).[18] The two other consultants suggested the construction in (27), i.e. *ay*-inversion of the actor combined with actor voice.

(26) Target sentence:
>> A$_{0.1"}$: [[*Ang mga pusa*]$_F$ *din ay h<in>u-huli* [*sila*]$_T$]~.
        NOM PL cat also INV <UV.RLS>-IPFV-catch 3PL.NOM
    'Cats also catch them.'

(27) Alternative realization of target sentence:
>> Q$_1$: {Who does what to rats?}
>>> Q$_{1.1}$ {What do cats do to rats?}

---

[17] For unknown reasons, the consultant changed the names of the animals from the original text.
[18] A predicate-initial construction as in (10b), with undergoer voice and the genitive-marked actor in sentence-final, i.e. a prosodically prominent position, was rejected as "not good" by all consultants, i.e. it was neither offered in the translations nor accepted as a possible option, when we asked the speakers in Manila about this. This adds to our suspicion that the construction in question does not express narrow contrastive focus.

>>>> A₁.₁: [[*Ang mga pusa*]_CT (*rin*) *ay* [*nang-hu-huli*   *at*
            NOM PL   cat   (also) INV AV.RLS-IPFV-catch and

       nag-ka-kain]_F [*ng mga daga*]_T]~.
       AV.RLS-IPFV-eat GEN PL rat

       'Cats (also) catch and eat rats.'

Note that the target sentence A₁.₁ in (27), which has a different label than the one in (26) due to a very different discourse structure, contains a given verb *catch* and a new verb *eat*. It is quite likely that the way Text 2 was formulated had the (unintended) effect that the consultants construed the verb coordination as being contrasted against the previous combination *threaten and catch*. Hence, we assume, as indicated in (27), that a CT+F structure was chosen with focus on the verb complex. This also leads us to diversify our inventory of hypotheses once more and to add a slight change to Hypothesis (v), restricting it to backgrounded verbs.

Hypothesis (v)

    Actor_F +ay Verb_BG Undergoer_T → Undergoer Voice   (*final*)

Hypothesis (vi)

    Actor_CT +ay Verb_F Undergoer_T → Actor Voice

While it may seem ad hoc to formulate a new hypothesis merely on the basis of a somewhat unclear example like (27), we will come across a very similar example in the next section, which seems to confirm that Hypothesis (vi) is on the right track.

Most of the Tagalog target sentences for Text 2 did not contain a word for *also*, which was contained in the original English text; somehow consultants seemed to feel that the *ay*-construction already conveyed an additive focus reading. Only one consultant paid heed to the focus sensitive particle in her translation and placed *rin* 'also' right after the actor in one instantiation of (27). As we have seen above and see again here, the positioning of *rin* indicates its scope. If the verb is part of the scope, *rin* appears after verb. If only the actor is in its scope, it appears right after the actor.

3.4 Text 3 – Intended: Actor (focal) Verb (focal) Undergoer (topical); Result: Actor (contrastive topic) Verb (focal) Undergoer (topical)

Next, we wanted to find out whether a truly new verb would make a difference for the construction chosen, so we construed a text in which both the actor and the verb were discourse-new. This text (discourse structure shown in Figure 5) is about the life of rats, i.e. it is about the undergoer of the target sentence. In the sentences preceding the target sentence there is a clear focus on the events that affect rats. The translation provided by one of our consultants contains simple predicate-initial structures. This is in line with our expectation regarding predicate focus sentences.

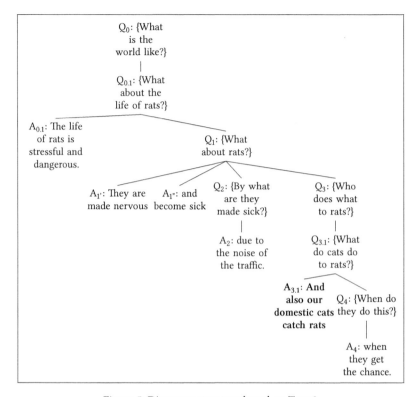

Figure 5: Discourse structure based on Text 3

(28) Q_0: {What is the world like?}

> $Q_{0.1}$: {What about the life of rats?}

>> $A_{0.1}$: [[*Delikado at ma-stress*]$_F$ [*ang buhay ng mga daga*]$_T$]~.
Dangerous and stressful NOM life GEN PL rats

'The life of rats is stressful and dangerous.'

(29) >> Q_1: {What about rats?}

>>> $A_{1'}$: [[*Ni-ni-nerbyos*]$_F$ [*sila*]$_T$]~
UV.RLS-IPFV-nervous 3PL.NOM

'They are made nervous'

>>> $A_{1''}$: *at* [[*nag-kakasakit*]$_F$]~
and AV.RLS-become.sick

'and become sick,'

(30) >>> Q_2: {By what are they made sick?}

8 The role of information structure for morphosyntactic choices in Tagalog

>>>> A$_2$: [[gawa ng ingay ng trapik]$_F$]~.
      done GEN noise GEN traffic
   'due to the noise of the traffic.'
   Orig: 'The noise of the traffic makes them nervous and sick.'

Interestingly, the consultant combines an undergoer voice verb and an actor voice verb in (29), realizing the affector-actor within an optional adjunct phrase, which we treat as a separate information unit at the end of the sentence. We therefore have narrow (contrastive) predicate focus on the verbs in (29) and a secondary focus on the actor phrase, which is not at issue with respect to Q$_1$ but at issue with respect to the separate subquestion Q$_2$ in (30). Note that the way the text was construed, we had expected to obtain a parallel structure between two actors (or affectors), the traffic and the cats. However, since the speaker chose to demote the traffic to a peripheral adjunct and used the intransitive verb *to fall sick*, a non-parallel discourse structure resulted.

Similarly to the narrow-actor-focus context, i.e. example (27) in §3.3, the actor phrase *our domestic cats* in the target sentence in (31) was not realized at the end of the sentence (hence, Hypothesis (iv) is not applicable), but in sentence-initial position before the inversion marker *ay* and, once again, actor voice instead of undergoer voice was chosen, despite the given undergoer.

(31) **Target sentence:**
   >>> Q$_3$: {Who does what to rats?}
   >>>> Q$_{3.1}$: {What do cats do to rats?}
   >>>>> A$_{3.1}$: At [[ang ating mga alagang pusa]$_{CT}$ ay [h<um>u-huli]$_F$
         and NOM our PL pet cat INV <AV.RLS>IPFV-catch
         rin [ng daga]$_T$]~
         also GEN rat
      'And also our domestic cats catch rats,'

(32) >>>>> Q$_4$: {When do they do this?}
   > > > > > A$_4$: [[kapag may pagkakataon]$_F$]~.
         if exist chance
      'when they get the chance.'

We cannot claim that the speakers simply gave the exact same structure to this utterance as to the narrow actor focus construction in (27), because the particle *rin* appears after the verb, not after the actor. Otherwise, however, the syntactic structure and voice are identical and, hence, in accordance with Hypothesis (vi). As witnessed above, the *ay*-inversion seems to express the first half of a contrastive discourse strategy, which is mirrored in the assumption of Q$_3$ and Q$_{3.1}$ in (31). (It is only now that the speaker realizes the contrastive potential between the negative effects of, respectively, the traffic and the cats on the well-being of the rats.) We, therefore, analyze the answer in (31) as a

CT-F structure.[19] This assumption is perhaps corroborated by a statement from one of the consultants who suggested the construction in $A_{3.1}$ and who explained her choice as follows: "Both parts of the sentence [i.e. $A_{3.1}$ and A_4] are about the cats, so we are talking about cats now", i.e. we have shifted the topic to the cats.

It is interesting to note that two people offered the construction given in (31), but two other consultants chose a predicate-initial construction with undergoer voice and the focal genitive-marked actor in the sentence-final position, as shown in (33).

(33) Alternative target sentence:

    >>> $Q_{1.1}$: {What do cats do to rats?}

    >>>> $A_{1.1}$: [[h<in>u-huli]$_F$ rin [ang mga daga]$_T$ [ng mga pusa]$_{CT}$]~.
            <UV.RLS>IPFV-catch also NOM PL rat   GEN PL cat

    'Also cats catch rats.'

This construction, in which the focal genitive-marked actor is in the marked, sentence-final position and the topical undergoer triggers undergoer voice, is an example comparable to (10b) in §1.4, in which the CT is clause-final. The speakers chose for the target sentence a structure identical to the sentence preceding it, i.e. they construed for the preceding sentence *(the noise of the traffic made them nervous)* an UV-sentence with *traffic* as genitive-marked actor argument, so that the two affectors *traffic* and *cats* were contrasted.

The focus sensitive particle *rin* appears in both realizations, (31) and (33), right after the verb indicating that the verb is included in its scope.

3.5 Text 4 – Intended: Actor (contrastive topic) Verb (background) Undergoer (focus)

The fourth text (Figure 6) deals with life in the wilderness and different kinds of predators that chase and catch animals and are chased themselves. Therefore, the text consists once again of a number of parallel sentences involving two variables (CT+F) that motivate the general question *Who catches whom?* and the specific questions *Whom do lions catch?* and *Whom do sharks catch?* Note that these parallel contrastive topic-focus sentences all show the same construction: *ay*-inversion and actor voice, as shown in (35), in accordance with Hypothesis (i).

(34) Q_0: {What is the way things are?}

    > $Q_{0.1}$: {What is life in the wilderness like?}

    >> $A_{0.1}$: [[Sa kalikasan]$_{CT}$ ay [may mga hindi patas na batas]$_F$]~.
            DAT wilderness INV exist PL neg fair LK law

    'In the wilderness there are unfair laws.'

---

[19] But we should keep in mind that the assumption of a single focus spanning both the actor and the verb, hence a direct answer to question Q_1, is also still an option.

8 The role of information structure for morphosyntactic choices in Tagalog

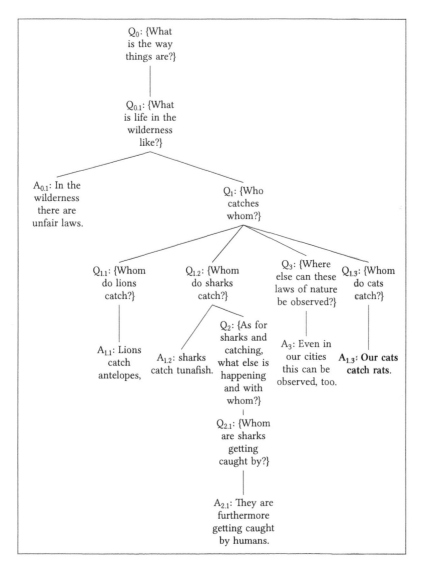

Figure 6: Discourse structure based on Text 4

(35) >> Q_1: {Who catches whom?}

>>> $Q_{1.1}$: {Whom do lions catch?}

>>>> $A_{1.1}$: [[*Ang mga leon*]$_{CT}$ *ay nag-hu-huli* [*ng mga bayawak*]$_F$]~.
NOM PL   lion   INV AV.RLS-IPFV-catch   GEN PL   antelope

'Lions catch antelopes.'

>>> $Q_{1.2}$: {Whom do sharks catch?}

>>>> $A_{1.2}$: [[*Ang mga pating*]$_{CT}$ *ay nang-hu-huli* [*ng mga tulingan*]$_F$]~.
NOM PL   shark   INV AV.RLS-IPFV-catch   GEN PL   tunafish

'sharks catch tunafish.'

The next sentence, $A_{2.1}$ in (36), signals, both in its original formulation and in the Tagalog version, a change in discourse strategy: both the (nominative-marked) sharks and the activity of catching are kept up from $A_{1.2}$ in (35) to $A_{2.1}$ in (36). However, the sharks change their role from actor to undergoer, which is expressed by a contrastive change to undergoer voice. Furthermore, a new actor *(humans)* is introduced. We tentatively propose the – unusual – information structure shown in (36), in which the voice infix is assigned the function of a contrastive topic, while the actor *humans* is the focus. This also explains the slightly cumbersome formulation of Q_2 and $Q_{2.1}$. Under this analysis, the *ay*-inverted pronoun is merely an aboutness topic; a constellation for which we have not formulated any hypothesis.

(36) >>>> Q_2: {As for sharks and catching, what else is happening and with whom?}

>>>>> $Q_{2.1}$: {Whom are sharks getting caught by?}

>>>>>> $A_{2.1}$: [[*Sila*]$_T$ *ay h*[*<in>*]$_{CT}$*u-huli din* [*ng mga tao*]$_F$]~.
3PL.NOM INV <UV>-IPFV-catch also GEN PL   man

'They are furthermore getting caught by humans'
Original: 'and they happen to also get caught by humans themselves.'

The speaker then jumps back up in the tree with a comment about cities, (37). What we see in A_3 is another *ay*-inversion expressing a narrow contrastive focus on a locative adjunct.[20]

(37) >>> Q_3: {Where else can these laws of nature be observed?}

>>>> A_3: *Kahit* [[*sa ating mga lungsod*]$_F$ *ay na-o-obersbahan din*
Even   DAT our-LK PL city   INV UV-IPFV-observe also

[*ito*]$_T$.]~.
DEM.NOM

'Even in our cities this can be observed, too.'
Original: 'Even here in the city these cruel laws of nature can be observed.'

---

[20]The verb *observe* is treated as salient here, although it has not been mentioned explicitly in the previous discourse.

8 The role of information structure for morphosyntactic choices in Tagalog

The target sentence *cats also catch rats* is then realized by three speakers as an *ay*-inversion with actor voice, i.e. the speaker is returning to the previously chosen discourse strategy, expressed by Q_1: *{Who catches whom?}* and the follow-up subquestion $Q_{1.3}$ in (38).

(38) **Target sentence:**
 >>> $Q_{1.3}$: {Whom do cats catch?}
 >>>> $A_{1.3}$: [[*Ang nating mga pusa*]$_{CT}$ *ay nang-hu-huli*   [*ng mga*
               NOM our   PL cat   INV AV.RLS-IPFV-catch GEN PL
  daga]$_F$]~.
  rat
  'Our cats catch rats.'

The fourth speaker suggested the *ang*-inversion in (39) – recall example (15) in §1.4 – thus either expressing the thought that the only ones who catch rats are cats – as indicated below – or, alternatively, that the only act of catching that takes place in the city is between cats and rats. The first option would mean that, in violation of the Q-GIVENNESS principle (§2.2), the rats would have to be accommodated as given. The second solution would inevitably mean that the *ang*-inversion construction is not restricted to exhaustive narrow argument focus, but may also be used for (exhaustive) complex focus spanning both the actor and the undergoer. The data here are too limited to finally settle this question. However, given that we are not aware of languages in which cleft sentences are restricted to narrow argument marking, the second solution seems quite plausible.

(39) **Alternative target sentence:**
 >>> Q_4: {Who catches rats (in the city)?}
 >>>> A_4: [[*Ang nating mga pusa*]$_F$ *ang nang-hu-huli*   [*ng mga*
               NOM our   PL cat   NOM <AV.RLS>IPFV-catch GEN PL
  daga]$_T$]~.
  rat
  '(Here) it is our cats that catch rats.'
  Original sentence: '(Our domestic) cats also chase and catch rats.'

3.6 Text 5 – Intended: Sentence focus, i.e. Actor (focal) Verb (focal) Undergoer (focal); Partly realized: Actor (contrastive topic) Verb (focal) Undergoer (focal)

Finally, we tried to construe a context for an all-new sentence, in order to elicit a clause-focus construction. In the text shown in Figure 7, a number of different scenes witnessed from a window were listed. Every sentence contained a new actor, a new verb and a new undergoer.

In the first assertion $A_{0.1}$ in (40), the *ang*-inverted narrow (exhaustive) focus on *panay-away at kaguluhan* 'constant fighting and turmoil' is motivated by the focus-sensitive

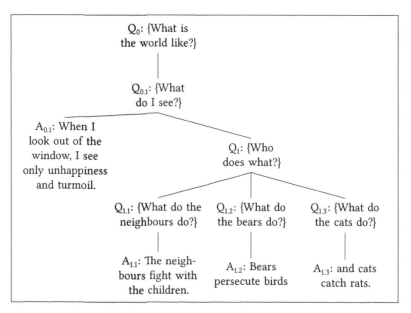

Figure 7: Discourse structure based on Text 5

particle *only*, i.e. the question $Q_{0.1}$: *{What do I see?}* is accommodated. Moreover, the *when*-clause is interpreted as a relevance condition which is not at issue.

(40) Q_0: {What is the world like?}

     > $Q_{0.1}$: {What do I see?}

     >> $A_{0.1}$: [Pag t<um>i-tingin ako sa bintana,]$_{NAI}$ [[panay-away
                 when   <AV.RLS>IPFV-look 1SG.NOM DAT window   constant fight
                  at kaguluhan]$_F$ lang ang na-ki-kita ko]~.
                  and turmoil   only NOM UV-IPFV-see 1SG.GEN

        'When I look out of the window, I see only constant fighting and turmoil.'

This sentence is followed by yet another sequence of *ay*-inversions (i.e. CT-F structures), describing who (CT) is performing which act of violence: the focused elements are, therefore, the AV-marked predicate and the undergoer. The construction fits the pattern described in Hypothesis (i).[21]

---

[21]What this example shows is that the construction of a text that consists of only new and unrelated sentences is in fact a very unnatural task. Instead, human interpreters will seize every opportunity to bring structure (here: CT-F pairs) – and therefore coherence – into what was originally intended to be an unstructured sequence of sentences.

(41) >> Q_1: {Who does what?}

>>> $Q_{1.1}$: {What do the neighbours do?}

>>>> $A_{1.1}$: [[*Ang mga kapitbahay*]$_{CT}$ *ay* [*nag-a-away*   *ng   mga bata*]$_F$]~.
          NOM PL   neighbour   INV AV.RLS-IPFV-fight GEN PL child

'The neighbours fight with the children.'

>>> $Q_{1.2}$: {What do the bears do?}

>>>> $A_{1.2}$: [[*ang mga oso*]$_{CT}$ *ay* [*t\<um\>u-tusig*   *ng   mga birds*]$_F$]~
          NOM PL   bear   INV \<AV.RLS\>IPFV-persecute GEN PL bird

'Bears persecute birds'

(42) Target sentence:

>>> $Q_{1.3}$: {What do the cats do?}

>>>> $A_{1.3}$: *at* [[*ang mga pusa*]$_{CT}$ *ay* [*nang-hu-huli*   *ng   mga daga*]$_F$].
          and NOM PL   cat   INV AV.RLS-IPFV-catch GEN PL rat

'and cats catch rats.'

Three speakers continued with a third *ay*-inverted CT-F assertion for the target sentence, as shown $A_{1.3}$ of (42). Only one speaker chose an all-focus existential construction for the target sentence.

(43) Alternative target sentence:

>> Q_2: {What other violent things are happening?}

>>> A_2: [[*May mga pusang h\<um\>a-habol   at p\<um\>a-patay ng mga*
       exist PL   cat-LK \<AV\>-IPFV-catch and \<AV\>-IPFV-kill GEN PL
       inosente-ng mga daga]$_F$]~.
       innocent-LK PL   rat

'There are cats chasing and killing innocent rats.'

4 Summary of findings, conclusions

Table 1 sums up our findings with respect to the target-sentence translations discussed in the paper. Note that the other (non-target) sentences discussed in the previous sections are not mentioned in the table, although their analyses, too, are in accordance with the described hypotheses.

In four of the texts (except for Text 1) the actor was focal (which includes contrastive topics) and thus IS-prominent, in two of them (Text 2 and 3) the undergoer was topical/backgrounded and thus IS-prominent. In our examples, actor voice was the preferred choice. As Table 1 shows, with the exception of Text 1, the actor argument was always conceived of as a contrastive topic or a focus. Contrastive topics (and, otherwise, narrow foci) were typically *ay*-inverted (Texts 2–5). Notable exceptions were the extraposed CT

Table 1: Information structure and morphosyntactic choices (voice, constituent order and inversion): target realizations in five sample texts

Structure	Voice	Example	Hypothesis	Text
[V UG]$_F$ ACT$_T$	AV	(24)	(iii)	1
ACT$_F$ ay V$_{BG}$ UG$_T$	UV	(26)	(v)	2
ACT$_{CT}$ ay V$_F$ UG$_T$	AV	(27)	(vi)	
ACT$_{CT}$ ay V$_F$ UG$_T$	AV	(31)	(vi)	3
V$_F$ UG$_T$ ACT$_{CT}$	UV	(33)	–	
ACT$_{CT}$ ay V$_{BG}$ UG$_F$	AV	(38)	(i)	4
ACT$_F$ ang V$_{BG}$ UG$_{T/F(?)}$	AV	(39)	–	
ACT$_{CT}$ ay [V UG]$_F$	AV	(42)	(i)	5
[may ACT V UG]$_F$	AV	(43)	(i)	

in (33), the existential construction in (43) as well as the *ang*-inversion in (39), whose information-structural analysis remains uncertain. Undergoer topicality did not generally lead to the selection of undergoer voice in the presence of a focal actor (Texts 2 and 3). The current data lead us, thus, to the conclusion that focality of the actor is definitely more salient, and has a greater morphosyntactic effect, than topicality of the undergoer.

In general, it has become clear that in order to describe the information-structural impact on voice selection, a more comprehensive approach is necessary rather than simply considering givenness and newness of arguments. This paper[22] is the first to apply the new *QUD-tree* method described in Riester, Brunetti, et al. (n.d.) to Austronesian language data. It, therefore, demonstrates a completely new way of studying the information structure of a lesser-described language on the basis of textual corpus data.

With respect to our hypotheses, we can specifically state the following based on our case study: Hypothesis (i) was confirmed in the data.

Hypothesis (i)

Actor$_{F/CT}$ ±ay Undergoer$_F$ → Actor Voice

However, we must add that, in our data, basic sentences structure was not chosen at all to encode two focused (or CT) core arguments. Rather we found the *ay*-inversion construction to be the predominant pattern (Texts 4 and 5).

Hypothesis (ii)

Actor$_T$ Undergoer$_T$ → Undergoer Voice

---

[22]See also the paper by Riester & Shiohara (2018 [this volume]).

8 The role of information structure for morphosyntactic choices in Tagalog

Hypothesis (ii) was not truly investigated here, as basically all undergoer voice sentences found and discussed in the literature are of this type. Therefore, it was not the most interesting case to look at. Our target sentence did not appear in a narrow verb-focus or adjunct focus context, and apart from one sentence with a focal locative adjunct, (37) in Text 4, which indeed showed undergoer voice, we have nothing to add to this particular issue.

Hypothesis (iii)

$Actor_T$ $Undergoer_F$ → decided at different level

Since Hypothesis (iii) left it open whether a default information structure would lead to actor or undergoer voice, it was not actually challenged by our data. In the undergoer-verb-focus scenario (Text 1), the participants provided actor-voice sentences; more specifically, they chose the expected unmarked verb-initial word order.

Hypothesis (iv)

$Undergoer_T$ $Actor_F$ (default order) → Actor Voice

Hypothesis (iv) was discussed in §1.4 and eventually restricted to cases with default constituent order, thus excluding patterns with *ay*-inversion and extraposed actors. Remember that narrow actor focus in our data was expressed by means of *ay*-inversion. Hence, Hypothesis (iv) did not apply to any of the cases found in the data.

Based on the great variety of cases involving *ay*-inversion in our data, we formulated two more hypotheses regarding *ay*-inverted actors and clause-final topical undergoers.

Hypothesis (v)

$Actor_F$ +ay $Verb_{BG}$ $Undergoer_T$ → Undergoer Voice

Hypothesis (v) specifies one way of realizing narrow actor focus, hence, the situation intended in Text 2, which was found in sentence (26).

Hypothesis (vi)

$Actor_{CT}$ +ay $Verb_F$ $Undergoer_T$ → Actor Voice

Finally, Hypothesis (vi) could be confirmed for all instances exhibiting the respective syntactic-pragmatic pattern, which, however, were produced by the consultants more or less by accident, since the CT-F structures they came up with deviated from the originally intended information-structural constellations. Notably, if we examine all examples that exhibit an *ay*-inverted contrastive topic and a focus on either the verb, the undergoer or both, we always witness actor voice.

The lesson we learn from our approach is that, on the one hand, it is quite difficult to steer participants to produce a very specific information-structural pattern and obtain a natural discourse at the same time. On the other hand, the QUD-tree method allows us to fruitfully analyze and interpret the actually produced data despite the deviations we gained.

In the current study we have presented many new facts about information structure marking in Tagalog and, in particular, about its relation to voice and inversion. We were able to specify a number of detailed hypotheses, and data that match them. We must leave it to future work, though, to test these hypotheses on a bigger scale and to identify a more general explanation why certain voice forms were chosen under specific information-structural constellations.

Acknowledgements

The authors would like to thank the editors of this volume and two anonymous reviewers. We also owe many thanks to the LingDy project in Tokyo for invitations to several workshops on the information structure of Austronesian languages, held at the Research Institute for Languages and Cultures of Asia and Africa (ILCAA) at Tokyo University of Foreign Studies. Furthermore, financial support of Deutsche Forschungsgemeinschaft (DFG) is kindly acknowledged. The authors are funded via the Stuttgart Sonderforschungsbereich 732, Project A6 and the Düsseldorf Sonderforschungsbereich 991, Project D4. Special thanks go to R.D. Van Valin, Jr., Katalin Balogh and Patrick Nuhn for comments on earlier versions of the paper.

Abbreviations

~	focus domain	IPFV	imperfective
ACT	actor	IV	instrumental voice
APPL$_{INSTR}$	instrumental applicative	LK	linker
AV	actor voice	NEG	negation
BG	background	NOM	nominative
BV	beneficiary voice	OBL	oblique
COM	comitative	PL	plural
CT	contrastive topic	Q	question marker
DAT	dative	RLS	realis
EXIST	existential	SG	singular
F	focus	T	aboutness topic
GEN	genitive	TV	theme voice
GV	goal voice	UG	undergoer
INV	inversion particle	UV	undergoer voice

References

Baumann, Stefan & Arndt Riester. 2012. Referential and lexical givenness: Semantic, prosodic and cognitive aspects. In Gorka Elordieta & Pilar Prieto (eds.), *Prosody and meaning* (Interface Explorations 25), 119–162. Berlin: Mouton de Gruyter.

Beaver, David & Brady Clark. 2008. *Sense and sensitivity. How focus determines meaning.* Oxford: Wiley-Blackwell.

Beaver, David & Dan Velleman. 2011. The communicative significance of primary and secondary accents. *Lingua* 121. 1671–1692.

Büring, Daniel. 2003. On D-trees, beans, and B-accents. *Linguistics & Philosophy* 26(5). 511–545.

Büring, Daniel. 2016. *Intonation and meaning.* Oxford: Oxford University Press.

Büring, Daniel. 2008. What's new (and what's given) in the theory of focus? In *Proceedings of the 34th Annual Meeting of the Berkeley Linguistics Society*, 403–424.

Cena, Resty M. 1977. Patient primacy in Tagalog. In *LSA annual meeting*. Chicago.

Chomsky, Noam. 1971. Deep structure, surface structure, and semantic interpretation. In Danny Steinberg & Leon Jakobovits (eds.), *Semantics. An interdisciplinary reader in philosophy, linguistics and psychology*, 183–216. Cambridge: Cambridge University Press.

Collins, Suzanne. 2009. *The hunger games.* New York: Scholastic.

De Guzman, Videa P. 1992. Morphological evidence for primacy of patient as subject in Tagalog. In Malcolm Ross (ed.), *Papers in Austronesian linguistics No. 2*, 87–96. Canberra: Australian National University.

Firbas, Jan. 1992. *Functional sentence perspective in written and spoken communication.* Cambridge: Cambridge University Press.

Ginzburg, Jonathan. 1996. Dynamics and the semantics of dialogue. In Jerry Seligman & Dag Westerståhl (eds.), *Logic, language and computation*, 221–237. Stanford: CSLI.

Güldemann, Tom, Sabine Zerbian & Malte Zimmermann. 2015. Variation in information structure with special reference to Africa. *Annual Review of Linguistics* 1. 155–178.

Gundel, Jeanette K., Nancy Hedberg & Ron Zacharski. 1993. Cognitive status and the form of referring expressions in discourse. *Language* 69(2). 274–307.

Jackendoff, Ray. 1972. *Semantic interpretation in Generative Grammar.* Cambridge: MIT Press.

Jacobs, Joachim. 2001. The dimension of topic-comment. *Linguistics* 39. 641–681.

Karttunen, Lauri. 1974. Presuppositions and linguistic context. *Theoretical Linguistics* 1. 181–194.

Kaufman, Daniel. 2005. Aspects of pragmatic focus in Tagalog. In Wayan Arka & Malcolm Ross (eds.), *The many faces of Austronesian voice systems: Some new empirical studies*, 175–196. Canberra: Pacific Linguistics.

Krifka, Manfred. 1992. A compositional semantics for multiple focus constructions. In Joachim Jacobs (ed.), *Informationsstruktur und Grammatik*, 17–53. Opladen: Westdeutscher Verlag.

Krifka, Manfred. 1998. Additive particles under stress. In Devon Strolovich & Aaron Lawson (eds.), *Proceedings of Semantics and Linguistic Theory (SALT VIII)*, 111–128. Ithaca: CLC Publications.

Kroeger, Paul. 1993. *Phrase structure and grammatical relations in Tagalog*. Stanford: CSLI.

Lambrecht, Knud. 1994. *Information structure and sentence form: Topic, focus and the mental representations of discourse referents*. Cambridge, UK: Cambridge University Press.

Latrouite, Anja. 2011. *Voice and case in Tagalog: The coding of prominence and orientation*. Heinrich-Heine-Universität Düsseldorf (Doctoral dissertation).

Latrouite, Anja. 2016. Shifting perspectives: Case marking restrictions and the syntax-semantics-pragmatics interface. In Jens Fleischhauer, Anja Latrouite & Rainer Osswald (eds.), *Explorations of the syntax-semantics interface*, 289–318. Düsseldorf: DUP.

Latrouite, Anja. 2017. Voice selection, inversions, discourse structure and at-issue-ness considerations in Tagalog. Talk given at Workshop LingDy Forum Questions under Discussion in Austronesian Corpus Data. Research Institute for Languages and Cultures of Asia and Africa, Tokyo University of Foreign Studies.

Latrouite, Anja & Robert D. Van Valin. 2016. Understanding construction choice in Tagalog. Talk at the 26th Meeting of the Southeast Asian Linguistics Society (SEALS), Manila.

Maclachlan, Anna. 2002. Optimality and three Austronesian case systems. In Mengistu Amberber & Peter Collins (eds.), *Language universals and variation* (Perspectives on Cognitive Science), 155–184. Westport: Praeger.

Nagaya, Naonori. 2007. Information structure and constituent order in Tagalog. *Language and Linguistics* 8(1). 343–372.

Nolasco, Ricardo. 2005. What ergativity in Philippine languages really means. In *Proceedings of the Taiwan-Japan Joint Workshop on Austronesian Languages*, 215–238. Taipei.

Nuhn, Patrick. 2016. *Towards a better understanding of peripheral voice in Tagalog: A case study*. Bachelor Thesis. Heinrich-Heine-Universität Düsseldorf.

Payne, Thomas. 1994. The pragmatics of voice in a Philippine language: Actor-focus and goal-focus in Cebuano narrative. In Talmy Givón (ed.), *Voice and inversion*, 317–364. Amsterdam: John Benjamins Publishing Company.

Potts, Christopher. 2005. *The logic of conventional implicatures*. Oxford: Oxford University Press.

Primus, Beatrice. 2012. Animacy, generalized semantic roles, and differential object marking. In Monique Lamers & Peter de Swart (eds.), *Case, word order, and prominence. Interacting cues in language production and comprehension*, 65–90. Dordrecht: Springer.

Reyle, Uwe & Arndt Riester. 2016. Joint information structure and discourse structure analysis in an underspecified DRT framework. In Julie Hunter, Mandy Simons & Matthew Stone (eds.), *Proceedings of the 20th Workshop on the Semantics and Pragmatics of Dialogue (JerSem)*, 15–24. New Brunswick, NJ, USA.

Riester, Arndt. to appear. Constructing QUD trees. In Malte Zimmermann, Klaus von Heusinger & Edgar Onea (eds.), *Questions in discourse. Vol. 2: Pragmatics* (CRiSPI). Leiden: Brill.

Riester, Arndt & Stefan Baumann. 2013. Focus triggers and focus types from a corpus perspective. *Dialogue and Discourse* 4(2). 215–248.

Riester, Arndt, Lisa Brunetti & Kordula De Kuthy. N.d. Annotation guidelines for questions under discussion and information structure. In Evangelia Adamou, Katharina Haude & Martine Vanhove (eds.), *Information structure in lesser-described languages: Studies in prosody and syntax*. Amsterdam: John Benjamins Publishing Company.

Riester, Arndt & Jörn Piontek. 2015. Anarchy in the NP. When new nouns get deaccented and given nouns don't. *Lingua* 165(B). 230–253.

Riester, Arndt & Asako Shiohara. 2018. Information structure in Sumbawa: A QUD analysis. In Sonja Riesberg, Asako Shiohara & Atsuko Utsumi (eds.), *Information structure in Austronesian languages*. Berlin: Language Science Press.

Roberts, Craige. 2012. Information structure: Towards an integrated formal theory of pragmatics. *Semantics and Pragmatics* 5(6). 1–69. Earlier version (1996) in OSU Working Papers in Linguistics, Vol. 49.

Rooth, Mats. 1992. A theory of focus interpretation. *Natural Language Semantics* 1(1). 75–116.

Schachter, Paul & Fe T. Otanes. 1972. *Tagalog reference grammar*. Berkeley: University of California Press.

Schwarzschild, Roger. 1999. GIVENness, AvoidF, and other constraints on the placement of accent. *Natural Language Semantics* 7(2). 141–177.

Sells, Peter. 2001. Form and function in the typology of grammatical voice systems. In Géraldine Legendre, Jane Grimshaw & Sten Vikner (eds.), *Optimality-theoretic syntax*, 355–392. Cambridge, MA: MIT Press.

Stalnaker, Robert. 1974. Pragmatic presuppositions. In Milton Munitz & Peter Unger (eds.), *Semantics and philosophy: Essays*, 197–214. New York: New York University Press.

Stutterheim, Christiane von & Wolfgang Klein. 1989. Referential movement in descriptive and narrative discourse. In Rainer Dietrich & Carl Graumann (eds.), *Language processing in social context*, 39–76. Amsterdam: North Holland.

Tonhauser, Judith, David Beaver, Craige Roberts & Mandy Simons. 2013. Toward a taxonomy of projective content. *Language* 89(1). 66–109.

Vallduví, Enric & Elisabet Engdahl. 1996. The linguistic realization of information packaging. *Linguistics* 34. 459–516.

van Kuppevelt, Jan. 1995. Discourse structure, topicality and questioning. *Journal of Linguistics* 31. 109–149.

Van Valin, Robert D. 2008. RPs and the nature of lexical and syntactic categories in Role and Reference Grammar. In Robert D. Van Valin (ed.), *Investigations of the syntax-semantics-pragmatics interface*, 161–178. Amsterdam: John Benjamins Publishing Company.

Van Valin, Robert D. & Anja Latrouite. 2015. A Role and Reference Grammar account of the information structure-syntax interface in Tagalog. Talk at the International Conference on Role and Reference Grammar (RRG), Düsseldorf.

Wagner, Michael. 2012. Focus and givenness: A unified approach. In Ivona Kučerová & Ad Neeleman (eds.), *Contrasts and positions in information structure*, 102–148. Cambridge: Cambridge University Press.

Chapter 9

Information structure in Sumbawa: A QUD analysis

Arndt Riester
Institute for Natural Language Processing (IMS), University of Stuttgart

Asako Shiohara
Research Institute for Languages and Cultures of Asia and Africa (ILCAA),
Tokyo University of Foreign Studies

> This paper describes the constituent ordering and other basic morphosyntactic properties of Sumbawa and their relation to information structure. Our study is based on conversational corpus data and makes use of a novel method of information-structural discourse analysis, which is based on the reconstruction of implicit questions under discussion (QUDs).

1 Introduction

Sumbawa (indigenous designation: Samawa; ISO-639-3 code: SMW) is a language spoken in the western part of Sumbawa Island, Indonesia. Sumbawa belongs to the Bali-Sasak-Sumbawa subgroup of the Malayo-Polynesian branch of the Austronesian language family (Adelaar 2005; Mbete 1990: 19). In this paper, we investigate the variation of constituent order in Sumbawa verbal clauses, using transcripts of a spoken conversation. In particular, we are interested in the question of how morphosyntactic variation (in particular, pre- and postverbal argument realization as well as the occurrence of clitics) is correlated with information structure, an aspect of Sumbawa about which so far relatively little is known.

In order to understand how information-structural variation is expressed, we use a novel method of textual analysis, developed in Reyle & Riester (2016); Riester et al. (in press), whose goal it is to identify for each elementary assertion the implicit *question under discussion (QUD)* (van Kuppevelt 1995; Büring 2003; Roberts 2012) to which the assertion provides an answer. Based on these QUDs the information structure of each assertion can be straightforwardly determined. The structure of this article is as follows: §2 provides an outline of the verbal clause structure in Sumbawa, with a special focus on

Arndt Riester & Asako Shiohara. 2018. Information structure in Sumbawa: A QUD analysis. In Sonja Riesberg, Asako Shiohara & Atsuko Utsumi (eds.), *Perspectives on information structure in Austronesian languages*, 285–311. Berlin: Language Science Press. DOI:10.5281/zenodo.1402551

syntactically possible constituent-order variation and its correlation with the presence or absence of a clitic pronoun on the predicate, whose dependence on information structure we will explore in the subsequent sections. In §3, we will introduce the annotation method we will apply to the conversational data in order to determine the information structure of each utterance. §4 and §5 provide the result of the application: §4 gives a rough picture how the three categories *focus, background*, and *contrastive topic* shape the general constituent order of Sumbawa, while §5 focuses on the order of argument and predicate in relation to the presence or absence of the clitic pronoun. In §6, we will give a summary of the sections and evaluate the effect of the method.

2 Constituent order and clitics in Sumbawa

In this section, we discuss the morphosyntax of Sumbawa verbal clauses, with a special focus on syntactically possible constituent order variation and its correlation with the presence or absence of a clitic pronoun on the predicate, largely based on Shiohara (2013b,a), drawing on elicited data.

In Sumbawa, as reported in Shiohara (2013a: 174), sentences can be formed using only a predicate which may carry clitics indicating, for instance, tense and subject/agent. One or several participants of the situation expressed by the predicate can be omitted when their identity is clear from the previous utterance or the utterance situation; see examples (1)-(6).

(1) ka=**ku**=teri'
PST=1SG=fall
'I fell.'

(2) ka=**mu**=teri'
PST=2SG=fall
'You fell.'

(3) ka=teri'
PST=fall
'He/She/They fell.'

(4) ka=**ku**=inum
PST=1SG=drink
'I drank it.[1]'

(5) ka=**mu**=inum
PST=2SG=drink
'You drank it.'

(6) ka=**ya**=inum
PST=3=drink
'He/She/They drank it.'

The occurrence of the subject/agent clitic is determined by three factors: (i) (in-)transitivity of the main verb, (ii) the person of the single core intransitive participant (S) or transitive agent (A), and (iii) the overt realization or absence of the argument and its position. The information structure of a clause has an influence on (iii) and, therefore, on the occurrence of the clitic.

Table 1 shows a list of the clitic and independent pronouns. There is no distinction between singular and plural in the third person. As can be seen in examples (1)-(6), the first and second person clitic pronoun may (but need not) occur both on intransitive and on transitive verbs. The third person clitic *ya* exhibits an exceptional behavior in that it can

---

[1] Something the referent of which is clear from the context.

9 Information structure in Sumbawa: A QUD analysis

Table 1: Sumbawa independent and clitic pronouns

Person & Number	Free pronoun	Clitic pronoun
1SG	aku	ku=
1PL.INCL	kita	tu=
1PL.EXCL	kami	
2SG	kau	mu=
2PL	nènè	nènè=
3	nya	ya=

only occur on transitive, e.g. (6), but not on intransitive verbs, e.g. (3). Sentence (7), in which *ya* co-occurs with an intransitive verb, is not accepted by the speakers.[2]

(7) * ka=ya=teri'
 PST=3=fell
 Intended meaning: 'He/She/They fell.'

The person of the transitive patient (P) is never coded on the predicate, but can be expressed by use of an independent pronoun (or, of course, a lexical NP). Pronouns and lexical NPs behave syntactically in the same way; see (8).

(8) ya=tari aku / kau / nya / tau nan
 3=wait 1SG 2SG 3 person that
 'She is waiting for me/you/him/that person.'

The constituents for S, A, or P may principally occur before or after the predicate. However, first and second person pronominal S arguments cannot occur after the predicate. Sentences (9) and (10) are not permitted by the speakers.

(9) * ka=ku=teri' aku (10) * ka=mu=teri' kau
 PST=1SG=fall 1SG   PST=2SG=fall 2SG
 Intended meaning: 'I fell.'   Intended meaning: 'You fell.'

By contrast, the S constituent for the third person can occur after the predicate, for instance, as the NP *tódé nan* 'that child' in sentence (11) or *nya* 'he/she/they' in (12).

---

[2] Unlike some other Austronesian languages, such as Acehnese (Durie 1985) and Tukang Besi (Donohue 1996), which exhibit so-called split-intransitivity, Sumbawa does not make a syntactic distinction between agentive intransitive verbs, which typically denote a volitional action, and non-agentive intransitive verbs, which typically denote a non-volitional situation. Thus, intransitive verbs such as *barari* 'run' or *barnang* 'swim' that denote a volitional action behave in the same way as the non-volitional verb *teri* 'fall', which we use as a representative of intransitive verbs throughout this section.

(11) ka=teri' tódé nan
    PST=fall child that
    'That child fell'.

(12) ka=teri' nya
    PST=fall 3
    'He/She/They fell'.

Sumbawa does not exhibit inflectional case marking. Yet, as for the post-predicate constituents, the case frame exhibits an ergative pattern, in that A occurs in a PP form with the preposition *ling*, as shown in examples (13)-(15), while an S constituent, as shown in examples (11) and (12) above, and P, as given in the NP *kawa nan* 'that coffee' in sentences (13)-(15), occurs in the form of an NP.[3]

(13) ka=ku=inum kawa nan ling aku
    PST=1SG=drink coffee that by 1SG
    'I drank that coffee.'

(14) ka=mu=inum kawa nan ling kau
    PST=2SG=drink coffee that by 2SG
    'You drank that coffee.'

(15) ka=ya=inum kawa nan ling nya Amin
    PST=3=drink coffee that by Mr. Amin
    'Amin drank that coffee.'

S, A and P may all occur before the predicate, as (16)–(21) show. All arguments are expressed by an NP (i.e. without preposition) in this position. (We omit the second person, since it is analogous to the first.)

(16) aku ka=teri'
    1SG PST=fall
    'I fell.'

(17) tódé nan ka=teri'
    child that PST=fall
    'That child fell.'

(18) aku ka=inum kawa nan
    1SG PST=drink coffee that
    'I drank that coffee.'

---

[3] Strictly speaking, it is only for the third person referent that the ergative pattern is fully observed since, as we already showed in examples (9) and (10), a first or second person S may not occur in post-predicate position. Another split in alignment, which we already mentioned in connection with (3) and (6), is observed with regard to clitic pronouns. The distribution of the first and second person clitic exhibits the accusative pattern in that it may code the person of S and A, but not that of P, while that of the the third person clitic exhibits the ergative pattern in that it may only code the person of A, not that of S and P. A split in alignment determined by person is commonly observed cross-linguistically, cf. Siewierska (2013).

(19) *nya Amin ka=inum kawa nan*
Mr. Amin PST=drink coffee that
'Amin drank that coffee.'

(20) *nya ka=inum kawa nan*
3   PST=drink coffee that
'He/She/They drank that coffee.'

(21) *kawa nan ka=ya=inum ling nya Amin*
coffee that PST=3=drink by Mr. Amin
'Amin drank that coffee.'

Whenever the S or A argument occur in pre-predicate position, there is no clitic pronoun on the predicate. In other words, the clitic and the pre-predicate argument are in complementary distribution. Examples (22)-(24) are all ungrammatical. Note that the post-predicate PP indicating A obligatorily occurs with the clitic pronoun, as shown in examples (13)-(15) and (21) above.

(22) * *aku ka=ku=teri'*
1SG PST=1SG=fall
Intended meaning: 'I fell.'

(23) * *aku ka=ku=inum kawa*
1SG PST=1SG=drink coffee

(24) * *nya Amin ka=ya=inum kawa*
Mr. Amin PST=3=drink coffee

Only one NP may be fronted at a time; examples (25) and (26), with two fronted NPs, are not permitted by speakers. This is the only purely syntactic constraint on the relative order of verb and arguments.

(25) * *nya Amin kawa nan inum*   (A P V)
Mr. Amin coffee that drink
Intended meaning: 'Amin is drinking that coffee.'

(26) * *kawa nan nya Amin inum*   (P A V)
coffee that Mr. Amin drink
Intended meaning: 'Amin is drinking that coffee.'

The following tables summarize the complex correlation between the type and location of the S/A argument on the one hand and the occurrence of a clitic pronoun on the verb on the other hand, for intransitive (Table 2) and transitive (Table 3) predicates. The symbols have the following meaning: - "no clitic pronoun", + "a clitic pronoun occurs", * "ungrammatical construction". The examples from above are indicated in brackets.

Table 2: Intransitive predicates: occurrence of clitics, subject type and subject position (examples indicated in brackets)

	1st person	2nd person	3rd person
No overt subject	+ (1)	+ (2)	- (3)
Post-predicate subject NP	* (9)	* (10)	- (11, 12)
Post-predicate "subject PP"	*	*	*
Pre-predicate subject NP	- (16)	-	- (17)

Table 3: Transitive predicates: occurrence of clitics, agent type and agent position

	1st person	2nd person	3rd person
No overt agent	+ (4)	+ (5)	+ (6)
Post-predicate agent NP	*	*	*
Post-predicate agent PP *(ling)*	+ (13)	+ (14)	+ (15, 21)
Pre-predicate agent NP	- (18)	-	- (19, 20)

3 Information structure theory and questions under discussion

In this section, we change from the grammatical description of Sumbawa to information structure theory, which, as we will show, will later help us account for the patterns described in the previous section. The central problem when studying the morphosyntactic realization of information structure in any language is the avoidance of circularity. Although variation in the constituent order of sentences often goes hand in hand with a variation of the discourse context in which these sentences occur, there is, at the surface, no syntactic focus-marking strategy that would universally apply in all situations to all languages. First of all, many languages have an *in-situ* focus as a default option, but some also have the possibility to explicitly realize focus clause-finally, by sorting constituents according to their information status or by applying extraposition. The opposite strategy, available in many languages, is the fronting or clefting of the focal constituent. Yet other languages exhibit no or very few morphosyntactic reflexes of information structure but instead mainly rely on intonation or prosodic phrasing to mark a focus that syntactically remains *in-situ*. For overviews and comparisons see e.g. Zubizarreta (1998); Büring (2009); Skopeteas & Fanselow (2010); Güldemann et al. (2015); Féry & Ishihara (2016). In general, it is methodologically questionable to use morphosyntactic (or prosodic) indicators for the identification of information structure if, at the outset, little is known about information-structure marking in a particular language.

9 Information structure in Sumbawa: A QUD analysis

Information structure is a pragmatic phenomenon, i.e. it is usually described in terms of meaning categories which relate to context. This is what accounts for both its universality and its somewhat enigmatic status. Throughout the literature, *focus* has – very inconsistently – been described as the answer to a question (Paul 1970 [1880]; Halliday 1967; Roberts 2012), as alternative-evoking (Rooth 1992), asserted (Lambrecht 1994), new (Halliday 1967; Schwarzschild 1999), identificational (Kiss 1998), exhaustive (van Rooij 2008) or contrastive (Katz & Selkirk 2011). A *topic* is usually defined – in a rather noncommittal way – as that which a sentence is "about" (Hockett 1958; Strawson 1964; Reinhart 1981; McNally 1998; Jacobs 2001; Krifka 2008), and the notion of *contrastive topic* has received a sophisticated characterization in terms of a speaker strategy (Büring 2003) to answer a complex question by working through a list of subquestions. Neither of these concepts easily connects to naturally occurring text or speech data. In order to study the information structure of language data gathered in fieldwork, people have, therefore, typically reverted to question-answer scenarios or other semi-spontaneous methods like the use of pictures or stories (cf. Skopeteas et al. 2006) to elicit controlled, information-structurally relevant material.

In the current study, we will apply a new annotation method based on implicit *questions under discussion* (QUDs), cf. Stutterheim & Klein (1989); van Kuppevelt (1995); Roberts (2012); Beaver et al. (2017), which enables a pragmatic information-structure analysis of textual fieldwork data. The method, so far, has mainly been applied to French and German (e.g. Riester in press).[4] Among the aforementioned definitions of focus, we adopt the one that takes focus to be the answer to the current question under discussion.

When investigating dialogues, as we do in this study on Sumbawa, explicit questions, of course, allow us to study the morphosyntactic realization of the background-focus divide. Examples of overt (Q)uestion-(A)nswer pairs are provided in the following Sumbawa examples (27).[5]

(27) Q$_7$: ada ke cabe nana
    exist Q chili over.there
    'Was there chili over there (in Japan)?'

   A$_7$: [ada [si]$_F$ [cabe,]$_T$]~
    exist PTC chili
    'There was chili.'

(27) is an example of a polarity question, which triggers a *yes*- or *no*-answer. In this case the addressee answers by means of a full clause, containing a verum focus, which is realized on the particle *si* within the predicate.

As for the information-structural categories and markup we assume the following definitions: the focus (F) of a sentence is that part which answers the question, whereas

---

[4]See also Latrouite & Riester (2018 [this volume]) on the use of QUDs for the description of voice selection in Tagalog.
[5]In this example, the question is signalled by a rising final intonation.

the remainder (the information already contained within the question itself) is the background. Following Reinhart (1981); Jacobs (2001) or Krifka (2008) we, furthermore, assume that aboutness topics (T) are referential entities (terms) that are properly contained in (and, therefore, potentially smaller than) the background.[6] Following standard assumptions in Alternative Semantics (Rooth 1992; Büring 2008; 2016), answers (consisting of an obligatory focus and an optional background) are so-called *focus domains*, which are marked by the ~ symbol.[7] Choice questions (also known as alternative questions) presented as disjunctions may trigger a constituent focus, which is why the answer in (3)[8] is not a polarity focus clause.

(28) Q_{27}: no   roa   tu=satoan tris   ke, atau ada   waya tu=satoan
          NEG possible 1PL=ask   always Q   or   exist time 1PL=ask

   'Can we never ask, or is there a (proper) time to ask?'

   A_{27}: [[*Ada   waya*]$_F$ *tu=katoan*]~
          exist time   1PL=ask

   'There is a time for asking.'

Since both alternatives contain the same verbal element *tu=satoan* '1PL=ask', this element is assumed to figure as the background of the answer. (We will say more on this below, e.g. example (35), when discussing parallel statements.)

Not all assertions, even in dialogues, are made in response to explicit questions, and not all explicit questions in dialogues receive a direct answer. In both cases we need to develop an idea of how to reconstruct the *intended* question, lest a large part of the assertions of the discourse will remain unanalyzed. Following Roberts (2012) and earlier work, e.g. by Stutterheim & Klein (1989) or van Kuppevelt (1995), we assume that every assertion in a text is actually the answer to a (typically implicit) *question under discussion (QUD)*. Thus, if we manage to determine the QUD of an assertion, its information-structural analysis (focus, background, aboutness topics) will follow, as in the case of overt questions.

The non-trivial part, of course, consists in the identification of the QUDs of predominantly monological passages of text. A solution to the problem is described at length in Riester et al. (in press), and we will only shortly sketch it here. First, we segment the text into separate speech acts (which are predominantly assertions). Besides orthographic sentence boundaries we also split coordinated phrases into separate semantic assertions (under the assumption that a coordination is an effective way of communicating a series of statements at one stroke). However, argument clauses will not be separated from their matrix clauses, since this would result in ungrammatical sentence fragments. For

---

[6]Usually, the "comment" is taken to be the complement of a topic. Since we see no use for such a category in our current work, we will ignore it.

[7]In Rooth (1992: 85ff.) ~ operators are used, among other purposes, to establish question-answer coherence: both questions and focused answers represent sets of alternatives, and the ~ operator identifies the question set as a proper subset of the focus alternatives.

[8]The alternation *satoan-katoan* seems due to dialectal variation.

instance, (29)-(32) is the result of the segmentation of a short paragraph, where a letter A is assigned to each separate assertion.

(29) A: seandai parak ne ketakit nya
   if   close ITJ scared 3
   'If someone approaches, they get scared.'

(30) A: min ada tau   asing   ne ketakit nya sate yang de sate
   if exist person foreign ITJ scared 3 want like REL want
   'If there is a foreigner, they are scared that he is after them like a kidnapper (lit. *a wanter*)'

(31) A: barari
   run
   'They run away.'

(32) A: nan luk model   nan
   that way character that
   'That's their character.'

As we can see, the conditional clauses in (29) and (30) are not split into parts because this would lead to ungrammaticality: neither of the clauses with the conjunctions *seandai* 'if' in (29) and *min* 'if' in (30) is grammatical in isolation.

The next step consists in the identification of the QUDs. The determination of QUDs in non-parallel text passages follows three basic principles (for a justification see Riester et al. in press and references therein):

  (i) Q-A-CONGRUENCE requires that the QUD for an assertion targets an actual constituent of the assertion. (It is not permitted to choose a question which does not ask for at least one constituent of the answer.)

  (ii) Q-GIVENNESS says that implicit QUDs can only contain linguistic material that has been mentioned or is salient in the current discourse context.

  (iii) Finally, MAXIMIZE-Q-ANAPHORICITY determines that all given material that occurs in the assertion is in fact mentioned in the question, thereby producing a maximally cohesive discourse (and, at the same time, a focus that is as narrow as possible).

For instance, in a small toy discourse A_0-A_1, the implicit QUD Q_1 is the one shown in example (33)[9] and its tree representation in Figure 1.

(33) A_0: Last Sunday, we had a picnic in the park.
   Q_1: {What about the picnic?}
   > A_1: [[The picnic]$_T$ [consisted of sandwiches]$_F$.]~

Arndt Riester & Asako Shiohara

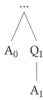

Figure 1: Tree representation of example (33)

In contrast to Q_1, the questions in (34) are all invalid because each of them violates at least one of the QUD constraints.

(34) a. Q: {Which park was it?} #Q-A-CONGRUENCE
      b. Q: {What about the sandwiches?} #Q-GIVENNESS
      c. Q: {What happened in the park?} #MAXIMIZE-Q-ANAPHORICITY

The question in (34a) violates Q-A-CONGRUENCE because it cannot have A_1 as its answer. (34b) contains the discourse-new expression *sandwiches*, thereby violating Q-GIVENNESS and, finally, (34c) and in fact all questions in (34) violate MAXIMIZE-Q-ANAPHORICITY, because neither of them contains the expression *picnic*, which is given in A_1, since it already occured in A_0.

However, a violation of the principle of Q-GIVENNESS is acceptable in two cases. The first one is the beginning of a text. Here, the implicit QUD sometimes needs to contain linguistic material that is discourse-new (for details on this process of *accommodation*, see citetriear17b).

The other acceptable violation is found in connection with parallelisms. When a QUD is answered by a series of structurally analogous assertions, the assertions are defined to be parallel. In that case, the corresponding QUD is allowed to contain the shared content, even though it may not be given in the preceding discourse. For example in (35) the verb *ate* is not given in the context, and Q-GIVENNESS would predict question Q_2. However, the double occurrence of the verb within two parallel statements (marked as $A_{2.1'}$ and $A_{2.1''}$) licenses the formulation of the more specific QUD $Q_{2.1}$. Note that it is generally the case that a sub-QUD like this is always entailed by the more general one, i.e. every answer to $Q_{2.1}$ is at the same time an answer to Q_2, even though $Q_{2.1}$ determines a narrower (here: object) focus.

(35) A_1: We had a lot of fun at our picnic.
      Q_2: {What did we do at the picnic?} (QUD licensed by Q-GIVENNESS)
      > $Q_{2.1}$: {What did we eat at the picnic?} (sub-QUD, def. by parallelism)
      ≫ $A_{2.1'}$: [[We]$_T$ ate [delicious sandwiches]$_F$]~.
      ≫ $A_{2.1''}$: and [[we]$_T$ even ate [sashimi]$_F$]~.

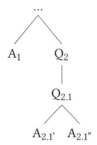

Figure 2: Tree representation of example (35)

Riester et al. (in press), following Büring (2003), also postulate a more complex case of parallelism that includes contrastive topics (indexed as CT in the annotation). This type involves two (or more) assertions, which are contrasted against each other at two different positions. An example is given in (36).

(36) Q_3: {Who ate what at the picnic?}
> $Q_{3.1}$: {What did my girlfriend eat?}
≫ $A_{3.1}$: [[My girlfriend]$_{CT}$ ate [delicious sandwiches]$_F$]~
> $Q_{3.2}$: {What did I eat?}
≫ $A_{3.2}$: and [[I]$_{CT}$ even ate [sashimi]$_F$]~.

Figure 3: Tree representation of example (36)

Analogous to example (35) above, the two statements $Q_{3.1}$ and $Q_{3.2}$ in (36) are parallel, because they both describe events of eating, and they answer the same QUD Q_3. However, the difference to (35) is that the assertions in (36) vary in two positions (here: subject and object), and that Q_3 contains two interrogative pronouns instead of one. This is typically a sign that Q_3 is not answered directly but broken down into subquestions about a list of salient individuals (here: my girlfriend and I). We shall assume that the elements of the answers which answer Q_3 but which are backgrounded with regard to one of the subquestions are so-called *contrastive topics*, whereas those elements which answer both the superquestion Q_3 and one of the subquestions are *foci*.

---

[9]The indentation symbol (>) before A_1 indicates that A_1 is subordinate to Q_1 in the corresponding discourse tree, whereas A_0 and Q_1 are at the same level. On different tree representation formats see Riester (in press).

Example (37), cited from the Sumbawa conversation, involves CTs. The conversation topic is about the difficulties Muslims face in connection with Japanese food. In this example, conditional clauses represent the topical options (Haiman 1978; Ebert et al. 2014) that the speakers are contrasting against each other.[10]

(37) Speaker S:

Q_3: {What if we ate pork unwittingly or knowingly?}

> $Q_{3.1}$: {What if we did it unwittingly?}

≫ $A_{3.1}$: [o ba terang,]$_{NAI}$ [[lamin nongka tu=sangaja]$_{CT}$ [terang]$_{NAI}$ [no
        ITJ clear   if   NEG.PST 1PL=act.deliberately clear   NEG
sikuda]$_F$]~
problem

'But it is clear, if we didn't act deliberately, it is clear that it is not a problem.'

Speaker I:

≫ $A_{3.1+}$: ya [[lamin nongka tu=sangaja]$_{CT}$ [no sikuda]$_F$]~
         yes if   NEG.PST 1PL=act.deliberately NEG problem

'Yes, if we didn't act deliberately, it's no problem.'

> $Q_{3.2}$: {What if we did it knowingly?}

≫ $A_{3.2}$: tapi [[lamin ka=tu=to]$_{CT}$ [kan]$_{NAI}$ [no roa]$_F$ [dean
        but if   PST=1PL=know you.know NEG comfortable that
nan]$_T$]~
that

'but if we knew, we are not comfortable with that.'

Finally, an assertion may contain phrases which neither form part of the QUD nor contribute to answering it, i.e. they are neither backgrounded nor focused. We classify such phrases as *non-at-issue (NAI) material*, cf. Tonhauser et al. (2013); AnderBois et al. (2015). More specifically, we are talking about triggers of conventional implicatures (Potts 2005), which include appositions, non-restrictive relative clauses, parentheticals, speaker-oriented adverbs, evidentials as well as adjunct phrases/clauses, cf. Riester et al. (in press) for more details and precise definitions. A few of these, namely the speaker- or addressee-oriented phrases *it is clear that* or *you know* are contained in (37). Another example is shown in (38).

(38) $Q_{19.1}$: {As for work, what attitude do people in Japan have?}

> $A_{19.1}$: **[maklum]**$_{NAI}$ [tau   [ana]$_{CT}$ [mega disiplin]$_F$]~ [sia]$_{NAI}$
            you.know   people over.there very disciplined 2PL.HON

'**You know, my friend**, people over there are very disciplined.'

---

[10] Note that speaker I. is repeating the statement made by speaker S., which is indicated by a '+' on the index. More on this in example (43) below.

4 Corpus analysis

4.1 The nature of conversational data

The data we are examining is the transcript of a Sumbawa conversation titled *Memory of Japan*, which consists of approximately 1500 words. The conversation took place between two Sumbawa speakers and Shiohara, one of the authors. The main speaker, I., had been working in Japan as a trainee, and is talking about his experiences to Speaker S., one of his friends, and to Shiohara, in reply to their questions.[11]

In the conversation, Speaker I. talks about Japanese people, culture and society. The nature of the conversation has a crucial influence on the syntactic and pragmatic properties of the discourse; many clauses have a first person A or S. Since the speaker talks about a number of situations as if they were general facts rather than his personal experiences, he often uses the generic first person plural form for the A and S arguments, especially the clitic *tu*; many verbal clauses carry the clitic pronoun *tu* or the independent pronoun *kita*. (Compare Table 1 in §2.) There are only few examples of a first person singular A or S, in which the speaker talks about a specific episode he was part of.

4.2 Focus identification

The conversation contains about 100 assertions (or discourse units), which were analyzed according to the guidelines in Riester et al. (in press). The general tendency observed in the conversation is that a referent or a situation that has been mentioned in the directly preceding discourse tends not to be expressed in the current clause. Thus, entities in the background are often left unexpressed, and a substantial amount of assertions are only formed by the focal expression itself. Nevertheless, because of the implicit referents, these are strictly speaking not all-focus assertions but rather elliptical clauses with narrow verb focus. A_{38} in example (39) is an example of an assertion that only consists of a focused expression. The silent A argument for this clause is co-referential with the S argument *tau* in A_{35} and *nya* in A_{36}.

(39) A_{35}:   *Toyama ta   mega tertutup tau*
              Toyama this very unsocial person

        'In Toyama people are very unsocial.'

   Q_{36}: {What about the people in Toyama?}

  > A_{36}':   [*seandai*   *parak*]$_{NAI}$ *ne* [[*ketakit*]$_F$ [*nya*]$_T$]~
             for.example close   ITJ   scared 3

        'For instance, if someone approaches, they get scared.'

        [...]

---

[11] A transcription and translation will be made available in Shiohara (in preparation). The video recording of the conversation, available on YouTube, was created in collaboration with the Sumbawa Literature Association (Yayasan Bungaku Sumbawa), of which the two speakers and Shiohara are members, cf. https://www.youtube.com/watch?v=D8gOyhJi1VI

> Q_{38}: {What do they do in such a case?}

≫ A_{38}: [[*barari*]$_F$]~
　　　　run

'They run away.'

A better example of a sentence focus, which shows that the default constituent order of intransitives is V S, is shown in A_{14} of (40).

(40) Q_{14}: {What is the situation in winter?}

> A_{14}: [[*kukir　　sarea apa　godong*]$_F$]~
　　　　withered all　what leaf

'All leaves are withered.'

The assertions can be classified according to the syntactic range of their focus constituents. In what follows, we will show examples of different types of focus, and we will examine the relative order of focus, background and contrastive topic in clauses with a narrow (or mid-size) focus. Our main interest in this research is the relative order of a predicate and its argument(s), and the effect this has on the presence of a clitic.

4.3 Information structure and constituent order

In an argument focus clause, the argument always precedes the background.[12] Two examples of preverbal (patient) argument focus can be observed in $A_{1.1''}$ in (41) and $A_{4.1'}$ in (42).

(41) $Q_{1.1}$: {What (else) can we not eat?}

> $A_{A.1''}$: *atau* [[*apa de terkait ke　　bawi nan*]$_F$ *no　tu=bau kakan*]~
　　　　or　　what REL related with pig　that　NEG 1PL=can eat

'also we cannot eat whatever is related to the pig.'

(42) $Q_{4.1}$: {How much salary do we get?}

> $A_{4.1'}$: [[*balu-pulu-ribu　　yen perbulan*]$_F$ *tu=terima*]~
　　　　eighty thousand yen per.month 1PL=receive

'we are getting eighty thousand yen per month'

---

[12] A fronted NP may be followed by the discourse particle *si*, as observed in elicited sentences like (i). The typical usage of *si* is the indication of a contrast or a situation that is counter to an expectation. This usage was not detected in the current conversation.

(i) *tódé nan si　ka=teri'*
　　child that PTC PST=fell

'That child fell.'

The precise conditions under which *si* occurs other than as a polarity particle need to be addressed in future research.

9 Information structure in Sumbawa: A QUD analysis

This generalization holds throughout our data. The only apparent exception occurs in the form of a repetition. The three assertions in (43) below convey the same assertion and are, therefore, labelled as $A_{25.1}$, $A_{25.1+}$ and $A_{25.1++}$.

(43) $Q_{25.1}$: {Which privacy-related issues – said the friend – can you not ask a Japanese person about?}

> $A_{25.1}$: [umpama]$_{NAI}$ [[umir,]$_F$]~
         for.example   age

'For example, about the age,'

> $A_{25.1+}$: [[umir nan]$_F$ na   coba-coba katoan]~ [ling]$_{NAI}$
         age   that NEG.IMP try   ask   HEARSAY

'don't try to ask about the age, he said.'

[...]

> $A_{25.1++}$: No roa   **tu=katoan umir** tau   jepang ta,
          NEG possible 1PL=ask   age person Japan this

'It is not possible that we ask about the age of a Japanese person'

Repetitions, in some sense, defy the rules of proper information transfer because, from a logical point of view, a speaker should not assert something which is already implied by the common ground – which would amount to making an all-given (or focus-less) assertion. Intuitively however, speakers repeat themselves precisely because they are not confident that their interlocutor has already accepted their previous statement. It is, therefore, reasonable to assume that, under normal circumstances, a structurally identical repetition has the same information structure as its previous mention. However, in example (43), the focus argument *umir* 'age' first occurs in an elliptical environment ($A_{25.1}$), it then precedes the background in the second statement $A_{25.1+}$ (an imperative), while in the third, assertive, statement $A_{25.1++}$ it suddenly follows the verb. We believe, since this is the only case of a potential focus argument following a backgrounded verbal predicate, that, by means of the repetition, the speaker frees himself from the pragmatic requirements of the discourse context; thereby performing a kind of "context reset" with regard to the contents of his statement. It is, therefore, possible that the actual information structure of $A_{25.1++}$ is that of an all-new assertion, in which the patient argument follows the verb, as shown below.

(44) Q: {What is the way things are?}

> A: [[No roa   tu=katoan umir tau   jepang ta,]$_F$]~
      NEG possible 1PL=ask   age person Japan this

'It is not possible that we ask the age of a Japanese person'

When an argument is backgrounded it follows the predicate in most cases, as shown in in $A_{2.1''''+}$ (a backgrounded subject argument following the focused stative verb *mogang* 'to be light'). Another example of the same kind is $A_{36'}$ / (39), discussed above.

(45) $Q_{2.1}$: {How was the work like?}
   [...]
   > $A_{2.1'''+}$: [[*mogang mogang*]$_F$ [*boat*]$_T$]~
           light   light   work
   'The work is easy, so easy.'

4.4 Contrastive topics

Apart from the conditional clauses previously discussed in (37), §3, we do not find in our data any paramount examples of overtly realized pairs of contrastive topics, i.e. those marked on referring argument expressions. What we do find is that, in a few cases, an argument that was given somewhere in the earlier discourse but didn't play a role in the preceding sentence, occurs in pre-predicate position. The question is now whether these entities should be assigned to the background (therefore representing aboutness topics) or not. For instance, in $A_{19.1}$ of (38), repeated in (46), the phrase *people over there* refers to a group given in a distant part of the discourse context. Obviously, the speaker is not using this phrase as a simple aboutness topic. Instead, what he does is implicitly contrast the referent with a different group of people (presumably, those at home). Since we need to account for the topic change anyway, we make use of the structure introduced in §3 in connection with contrastive topics, i.e. a question-subquestion tree of which, however, only the first half is overtly realized, compare Riester et al. (in press: Sect. 5.2). Since there is no essential discourse-structural difference between such a "new" topic and the contrastive topics introduced above, we also tentatively assign (the contrastive element of) the referring expression the label CT, in the style of Büring (2003: 526).

(46) Q_{19}: {As for work, what attitude do different people have?}
   > $Q_{19.1}$: {As for work, what attitude do people in Japan have?}
   ≫ $A_{19.1}$: [...] [*tau*] [*ana*]$_{CT}$ [*mega disiplin*]$_F$~ [...]
           people over.there very   disciplined
   'People over there are very disciplined.'

In the very similar case of $A_{17.1}$ / (47), the demonstrative *denan* 'that' is introduced by the form *lamin*, tentatively glossed 'as for' here, and refers to 'the time to get up', which is the P argument of the predicate *determine*. What the speaker wants to express is that this particular issue was not regulated, although other things were, like e.g. the working hours. Again, we represent this in the form of a contrastive / non-continuous topic, which is merely implicitly contrastive.

(47) Speaker S.:
   Q_{17}: {Which things were regulated?}

> Q₁₇.₁: [...] waya mleng tunung apa   waya, ada ke ya=tentukan kalis-kalis
           time get.up sleep what time exist Q 3=determine from
      ana   e
      over.there ITJ

'Is there a regulation when to get up from sleep over there?'

Speaker I.:

≫ A₁₇.₁: [Lamin [denan]_CT [no=soka]_F ya=tentukan,]~
      as.for that   NEG.PST   3=determine

'As for that, they didn't prescribe it.'

Note that examples like these represent a challenge to the rules currently formulated in the guidelines of Riester et al. (in press), since the lack of an overt alternative makes the identification of such "implicitly contrastive topics" very difficult. Obviously, the QUD-tree framework needs to be enhanced with clearer rules concerning the identification of such non-continuous, implicitly contrastive topics. Kroeger (2004: 136) provides a brief and clear discussion on a distinction of topic types similar to those observed here. He discusses that "(T)he topic of a sentence, when it is the same as the topic of the preceding sentence, needs no special marking. It can often be referred to with an unstressed pronoun, an agreement marker (as in the 'pro-drop' languages), or even by being omitted entirely ('zero anaphora'). But in certain contexts the topic may require more elaborate marking. This may happen when there is a change in topic, a contrast between one topic and another, or a choice among several available topics". See also Lambrecht (1994: 117ff.) for a detailed discussion on the distinctions among various types of topics, and *Centering Theory* (Walker et al. 1998) for a closely related discourse approach to topics (or "backward-looking centers").

4.5 Other focus types found in the data

In this section, we mention a few other focus types found in our data, before returning to our main issues defined in §2, constituent order and clitics. As observed in example (27), §4.3, repeated here as (48), a verum focus is realized on the particle *si*.

(48) Q₇: ada ke cabe nana
         exist Q chili over.there

'Was there chili over there (in Japan)?'

> A₇: [ada [si]_F [cabe,]_T]~
     exist PTC   chili

'There was chili.'

The negative counterpart, a falsum focus, can be seen in A₁₇.₁ of example (47) in the previous section or, using a slightly different negative element, in A₁₂ of (49). In both cases focus is realized on the negative element, which is followed by the predicate.

(49) Q$_{12}$: nka   kadu gita cabe pang Jepang ana?
         NEG.PST ever see chili in Japan over.there
       'Have you never seen chili over there in Japan?'

> A$_{12}$: [[nka]$_F$ kadu gita [puin cabe]$_T$]~
         NEG.PST ever see tree chili
      'I have never seen a chili tree.'

In the case of focus on an NP modifier, the modifier retains its canonical (post-nominal) position.[13]

(50) Q$_8$ {What kind of chili was there?}

> Q$_{8.1}$: {What about a lot of the chili?}

≫ A$_{8.1}$: cuma [de ka [peno]$_{CT}$ cabe ne, **cabe** [*instan*]$_F$]~
       only REL PST many   chili ITJ chili instant
      'It is just that a lot of chili was instant chili.'

Compare this to assertion A$_{33}$ in example (51), in which a modified phrase with the same word order occurs in an adjunct clause (classified as non-at-issue) that is all-new and, hence, not narrowly focused.

(51) Q$_{33}$: {What do we have to do?}

> A$_{33'}$: [*min sate parak* *ke* **tau** ***sowai gera***]$_{NAI}$ [...] [*harus*
      if want approach with person woman beautiful   have.to
     [*tu=tahan* *rasa-ate*]$_F$]~
     1PL=control emotion

     'If we want to approach a beautiful woman, we need to control our emotions.'

---

[13] The situation is different with numerals. In A$_{12}$ of example (50), the focal numeral *lima* 'five' precedes the head noun.

  (i) (Speaker talking to himself:)

     Q$_{12}$: *jadi ada pida*   *kamar*
          then exist how.many room
       'Then, how many rooms were there?'

    > A$_{12}$: [[*lima*]$_F$ *kamar*]~ [*amen no salah*]$_{NAI}$
          five   room   if   NEG wrong
       'There were five rooms, if I am not wrong.'

As Shiohara (2014) suggests, the position of a numeral relative to its head noun varies according to its focal status. If a numeral is not in focus, it follows the head noun, like a modifier does, though the data we examined in this article do not include any such example.

5 Grammatical relations, person, agreement and constituent order

5.1 Intransitives

In §2, we introduced the basic morphosyntactic rules of Sumbawa – based on elicited data – in which A, S and P are realized. In this section, we will look at how information structure, observed in our annotated data, can explain some of the variation found.

According to the rules postulated in Table 2 in §2, a first (or second) person S is expected to be realized either as a pronominal clitic or as a pre-predicate argument. The first case is exemplified by (52). The tendency that an entity that was mentioned in the directly preceding utterance or that is generally salient is not overtly expressed applies to all types of arguments. Thus, when the referent of S or A is topical, it is expected to be realized (only) as a clitic pronoun within the predicate in first and second person. This is the case with the first person plural subject in (52).

(52) Q_{33}: {What do we have to do?}

> $A_{33"}$: [*harus* [*tu=bersabar benar*]$_F$]~ [*ampa*]$_{NAI}$
  have.to 1PL=patient really ITJ
  'We need to be really patient.'

An unexpected CT-case, which runs counter to the predictions, is $A_{23.1}$ in example (53), in which S is doubly marked.

(53) Q_{23}: {Who does what in the morning?}

> $Q_{23.1}$: {What do we (Muslims) do in the morning?}

≫ $A_{23.1}$: [*kan*]$_{NAI}$ [[*kita*]$_{CT}$ [*tu=sembayang-subu*]$_F$ [*dunung,*]$_T$]~
  you.know 1PL.INCL 1PL=do.early-morning-prayer before
  'As you know, we first do the early morning prayer.'

As mentioned in §2, this construction was not accepted by participants in an elicitation task when asked for their grammatical judgment, and was therefore classified as non-canonical, if not ungrammatical. In many languages, the complementary distribution of clitic and argument has made way for a more canonical agreement system, in which the two forms co-occur. We may see the phenomenon in Sumbawa in an ongoing process of a grammatical change.[14] At the present stage of our research, though, we do not have enough data to say more about this.

The third person S is expected to be realized as either a pre-predicate argument, post-predicate argument, or left unexpressed, and all three types are observed in the conversation. Examples of post-predicate realization already discussed are the broad-focus

---

[14]In some Austronesian languages spoken in eastern Indonesia, such as Kambera (Klamer 1998: 69–70) and Bima (Satyawati 2009: 92), this type of co-occurrence of clitic pronoun and argument is permitted.

example (40) as well as the narrow-verb-focus clauses $A_{36'}$ / (39) and (45). A further example is (54). Zero marking was shown in A_{38} / (39) and can also be witnessed in (55). Finally, pre-predicate subject realization was demonstrated in connection with contrastive-topichood in (46). As expected, there is never a clitic on any of these predicates.

(54) $Q_{41.1}$: {How did the person who came look like?}

> $A_{41.1}$: [[*barangkali, lenge benar*]$_F$ [*ade datang ta*]$_T$]~
>   maybe   ugly really   REL come this

'Maybe the person who came was really ugly.'

(55) Q_{21}: {How was it to start working at 7:15 a.m.?}

> A_{21+}: [[*disiplin   benar*]$_F$]~
>   disciplined really

'It was really disciplined.'

5.2 Transitives

According to Table 3, §2, the A argument can be realized as either a pre-predicate argument, a post-predicate PP, or simply as a pronominal clitic. The post-predicate PP may co-occur with a clitic, while a pre-predicate argument may not. However, post-predicate PPs were not found in our data.[15]

The two remaining options, pre-predicate argument and clitic, are expected to occur in complementary distribution. In our data, clitics are particularly frequent in combination with a first person A, as shown, for instance, in (51) above. Another example, which shows a clitic on the predicate of the main clause and a preverbal pronoun (no clitic) in the embedded clause, is given in (56).

(56) Q_3: {What should we do towards the Japanese people concerning the consumption of pork?}

---

[15]It can be observed that the post-predicate PP argument typically occurs in narrative sentences, indicating a series of events in which several people take turns at being the agent. In such cases, an agent, despite being salient in the preceding utterance, needs to be expressed for the sake of disambiguation. (i) is a typical example cited from a folktale in Jonker (1934: 214).

(i) *ya=beang mo ling Salam lako guru;   meng ka=ya=kakan mo ling guru:*   "*e,*
   3=give   PTC by Salam to teacher; when PST=3=eat   PTC by teacher   ITJ
   nyaman tai asu ode"
   delicious shit dog small

'Salam gave (it) to the teacher. When the teacher ate (it), (he said): "Ah, the shit of the small dog is delicious."'

In our present conversation data the speaker is mainly talking about his own experiences. There are no comparable cases that would require agent disambiguation. Therefore, a broader analysis of narrative data, like folktales, is required to verify this particular function of the post-predicate PP.

> A_{3+}: [*harus* [*tu=bada*]$_F$ [*nya*]$_T$ *luk* **kita**   *no   bau kakan nan*]~
have.to 1PL=tell   3   that 1PL.INCL NEG can eat   that
'We must tell them that we can't eat that.'

Apparently, the speaker felt the need to realize the – given – agent of the embedded clause by use of the overt pronoun *kita*. Note that in this construction the entire clause is backgrounded. It is very likely that the occurrence of the preverbal pronoun is meant to convey a so-called secondary contrast,[16] i.e. "We must *tell* them that *we* can't eat that (although *you* can)." So, once more, the entity is not just topical but implicitly contrastive.

Furthermore, according to the rules spelled out in §2, clitics (in all persons) are expected to appear instead of "zero-marked" transitive clauses, but this is clearly not always the case in our conversation. There are several instances of transitive clauses in which neither a clitic nor an overt agent occurs, like (57).

(57) Q_9: {What kind of chili did the speaker see how often?}
> $Q_{9.1}$: {What kind of chili did the speaker see rarely?}
≫ $A_{9.1}$: [[*jarang*]$_{CT}$ **gita** *cabe* [*mira*]$_F$]~
rarely   see chili red
'I rarely saw red chili.'

There are also a few preverbal third person A arguments, like (58), which all seem to mark a contrastive (or at least a non-continuous) topic.

(58) Q_1: {What did the people in various places make?}
> $Q_{1.1}$: {What did the people at the factory make?}
≫ $A_{1.1}$: [*Jadi tau*   [*ana*]$_{CT}$ *pina,* [*mara leng   tau   nana,*]$_{NAI}$ *pina*
then person over.there make like   word person over.there make
[*peralatan untuk elepator*]$_F$]~
tool   parts elevator
'At the time, people there, as they said, were making parts for an elevator.'

Finally, the P argument may occur as either pre-predicate argument or post-predicate argument. In all cases found, pre-predicate P arguments either correspond to the focused constituent (argument focus), as in examples (41) and (42), or to the contrastive topic, $A_{17.1}$ / (47), while a post-predicate P argument either belongs to the background, (49) or (56), is included in a (wide or mid-size) focus spanning the entire VP constituent, (51), or represents the focus in a CT-F combination, as shown in (57) and (58). A zero marked P argument is, as one would expect, one that is always clear from the context, see A_{11} in example (59).

---

[16]The current QUD framework does not consider the phenomenon of *second-occurrence focus* (Beaver & Velleman 2011; Büring 2015; Baumann 2016) and will, therefore, not mark any secondary foci within the background, since there is no nesting of focus domains.

(59) Q_{11}: {How did we get there?}

> A_{11}: [[*olo*]$_F$ [*pang nan*]$_T$]~
>   put.in place that
> '(They) put (us) in that place.'

6 Summary and conclusions

We have investigated conversational corpus data from Sumbawa and demonstrated how information structure, determined on the basis of contextual-pragmatic constraints and the concept of questions under discussion, is related to constituent-ordering patterns known from earlier morphosyntactic descriptions of the language. In order to present the findings in a more systematic way, we revisit Table 2 (now Table 4) and Table 3 (now Table 5) from §2 and include our new findings about information structure.

Summarizing, we can say that, by default (i.e. in the case of broad focus), the arguments follow the verbal predicate. Arguments occur pre-predicatively whenever any of them is narrowly focused and there is no contrastive topic present. In addition to that, a contrastive topic may also occur pre-predicatively. We found several candidates for potential contrastive topics. Since in all the cases the contrast can only be construed implicitly, we acknowledge that some readers may prefer to use the terminology 'non-continuous topic' instead, although we see no essential difference between a contrastive topic (with or without an overt alternative) and the shift to a new topic, since from a pragmatic point of view, both require the formulation of a new QUD *about* this topical entity. In either case there is no topical continuity. As we said, both focus and contrastive/non-continuous topic may occur in the pre-predicate argument slot. This correspondence is very common cross-linguistically, since "the beginning of a sentence is a

Table 4: Intransitive predicates: constituent order, subject realization and information structure

	$1^{st}/2^{nd}$ person	3rd person
no overt subject	cf. (52)	[[V]$_F$]~ (39, 55)
post-predicate S-NP	*	[[V S]$_F$]~ (40,)
	*	[[V]$_F$ [S]$_T$]~ (39, 45, 54)
pre-predicate S-NP		[[S]$_F$ V]~ (not attested)
	(53)	[[S]$_{CT}$ [V]$_F$]~ (46)

Table 5: Transitive predicates: constituent order, agent realization and information structure

	1ˢᵗ/2ⁿᵈ person	3ʳᵈ person
no overt agent		[[V]_F]~ *(not attested)*
	[[V P]_F]~ (51)	
		[[P]_F V]~
	(41, 42)	
		[[P]_CT [V]_F]~ cf. (47)
	[[V]_F [P]_T]~ (56)	
post-predicate A-PP *(ling)*	*(not enough data)*	
pre-predicate A-NP	[[A]_CT V [P]_F]~ (58) *(no other patterns attested)*	

highly prominent position" (Kroeger 2004: 139) and both CT and F share the property of evoking alternatives (Büring 2003). However, the two pragmatic roles are usually distinguished phonologically in Sumbawa: a pre-predicate NP in focus occurs with a falling intonation, while the contrastive topic expression occurs with a rising intonation.

We have demonstrated how the use of the QUD-tree framework can be successfully applied to conversational data from a lesser-studied language like Sumbawa. This is the first comprehensive application of this method to a non-European language.[17] Not only were we able to provide an in-depth analysis of the information-structure system of the language but we could also show that the method is generally a valuable instrument to explain some of the constituent-order variation and the occurrence of clitics. With this method, we gain access to the information structure phenomena and corresponding syntactic properties contained in various kinds of text and dialogue data. This means that we are now able to investigate more potential variation on more natural data than when studying information structure only in elicitation experiments. Some of the variety may be explained by semantic-pragmatic factors, while others may reflect an ongoing grammatical change in Sumbawa.

We are confident that the phenomena and variety discovered in this study are the beginning of a series of new discoveries in the field of pragmatic data analysis on larger and more varied natural corpora.

---

[17]Compare also Latrouite & Riester (2018 [this volume]).

Acknowledgements

The authors would like to thank two anonymous reviewers for their comments. We are very grateful to Sonja Riesberg for her encouragement and support. We also would like to express our gratitude for the members of the Sumbawa Literature Association (Yayasan Bungaku Sumbawa); Syamsul Bahri (SMU3), Syamsul Bahri (SMK1), Ade Erma Lestari (SMU3), Iwan Irwansyah (SMA3), Sambahadi Kurniawan (SMU3), Nyoman Purayasa (SMU3), who worked with Asako Shiohara in recording and annotating the conversation we used as our data in our research. The financial support by the German Science Foundation (DFG), Collaborative Research Center (SFB) 732 Stuttgart, Project A6, the Linguistic Dynamics Science Project 3 (LingDy3) at ILCAA, Tokyo University of Foreign Studies (2016–2022AY), and JSPS Grants-in-Aid for Scientific Research: JP15K02472 are kindly acknowledged.

Abbreviations

~	focus domain	NEG	negation
CT	contrastive topic	PL	plural
EXCL	exclusive	PST	past tense
F	focus	Q	question particle
HON	honorific	QUD	question under discussion
IMP	imperative	REL	relativizer
INCL	inclusive	SG	singular
ITJ	interjection	T	aboutness topic
NAI	non-at-issue		

References

Adelaar, K. Alexander. 2005. Malayo-Sumbawan. *Oceanic Linguistics* 44(2). 357–388.

AnderBois, Scott, Adrian Brasoveanu & Robert Henderson. 2015. At-issue proposals and appositive impositions in discourse. *Journal of Semantics* 32(1). 93–138.

Baumann, Stefan. 2016. Second occurrence focus. In Caroline Féry & Shinichiro Ishihara (eds.), *The Oxford handbook of information structure*, 483–502. Oxford: Oxford University Press.

Beaver, David, Craige Roberts, Mandy Simons & Judith Tonhauser. 2017. Questions under discussion: Where information structure meets projective content. *Annual Review of Linguistics* 3(1). 265–284.

Beaver, David & Dan Velleman. 2011. The communicative significance of primary and secondary accents. *Lingua* 121. 1671–1692.

Büring, Daniel. 2003. On D-trees, beans, and B-accents. *Linguistics & Philosophy* 26(5). 511–545.

Büring, Daniel. 2009. Towards a typology of focus realization. In Malte Zimmermann & Caroline Féry (eds.), *Information structure*, 177–205. Oxford: Oxford University Press.
Büring, Daniel. 2015. A theory of second occurrence focus. *Language, Cognition and Neuroscience* 30(1-2). 73–87.
Büring, Daniel. 2016. *Intonation and meaning*. Oxford: Oxford University Press.
Büring, Daniel. 2008. What's new (and what's given) in the theory of focus? In *Proceedings of the 34th Annual Meeting of the Berkeley Linguistics Society*, 403–424.
Donohue, Mark. 1996. Split intransitivity in Tukang Besi. *Oceanic Linguistics* 35(2). 295–304.
Durie, Mark. 1985. *A grammar of Acehnese on the basis of a dialect of North Aceh*. Dordrecht: Foris Publications.
Kiss, Katalin É. 1998. Identificational focus versus information focus. *Language* 74(2). 245–273.
Ebert, Christian, Cornelia Ebert & Stefan Hinterwimmer. 2014. A unified analysis of conditionals as topics. *Linguistics and Philosophy* 37. 353–408.
Féry, Caroline & Shinichiro Ishihara. 2016. *The Oxford handbook of information structure*. Oxford: Oxford University Press.
Güldemann, Tom, Sabine Zerbian & Malte Zimmermann. 2015. Variation in information structure with special reference to Africa. *Annual Review of Linguistics* 1. 155–178.
Haiman, John. 1978. Conditionals are topics. *Language* 54(3). 564–589.
Halliday, M. A. K. 1967. Notes on transitivity and theme in English. Part 2. *Journal of Linguistics* 3. 199–244.
Hockett, Charles. 1958. *A course in modern linguistics*. New York: Macmillan.
Jacobs, Joachim. 2001. The dimension of topic-comment. *Linguistics* 39. 641–681.
Jonker, J. C. G. 1934. Soembawareesche teksten met vertaling. *Bijdragen tot de Taal-, Land- en Volkenkunde van Nederlandsch-Indië* 92(1). 211–335.
Katz, Jonah & Elisabeth O. Selkirk. 2011. Contrastive focus vs. discourse-new: Evidence from phonetic prominence in English. *Language* 87(4). 771–816.
Klamer, Marian. 1998. *A grammar of Kambera*. Berlin: Mouton de Gruyter.
Krifka, Manfred. 2008. Basic notions of information structure. *Acta Linguistica Hungarica* 55(3–4). 243–276.
Kroeger, Paul. 2004. *Analyzing syntax: A lexical-functional approach*. Cambridge: Cambridge University Press.
Lambrecht, Knud. 1994. *Information structure and sentence form: Topic, focus and the mental representations of discourse referents*. Cambridge, UK: Cambridge University Press.
Latrouite, Anja & Arndt Riester. 2018. The role of information structure for morphosyntactic choices in Tagalog. In Sonja Riesberg, Asako Shiohara & Atsuko Utsumi (eds.), *Information structure in Austronesian languages*. Berlin: Language Science Press.
Mbete, Aaron Meko. 1990. *Rekonstruksi protobahasa Bali-Sasak-Sumbawa [Reconstruction of the proto-language Bali-Sasak-Sumbawa]*. Universitas Indonesia, Jakarta dissertation.

McNally, Louise. 1998. On recent formal analyses of topic. In J. Ginzburg, Z. Khasidashvili, C. Vogel, J. Levi & E. Vallduví (eds.), *The Tbilisi Symposium on Language, Logic, and Computation*, 147–160. Stanford, CA, USA: CSLI Publications.

Paul, Herrmann. 1970 [1880]. *Prinzipien der Sprachgeschichte*. 8th edn. Tübingen: Niemeyer.

Potts, Christopher. 2005. *The logic of conventional implicatures*. Oxford: Oxford University Press.

Reinhart, Tanya. 1981. Pragmatics and linguistics: An analysis of sentence topics in pragmatics and philosophy I. *Philosophica* 27(1). 53–94.

Reyle, Uwe & Arndt Riester. 2016. Joint information structure and discourse structure analysis in an underspecified DRT framework. In Julie Hunter, Mandy Simons & Matthew Stone (eds.), *Proceedings of the 20th Workshop on the Semantics and Pragmatics of Dialogue (JerSem)*, 15–24. New Brunswick, NJ, USA.

Riester, Arndt. in press. Constructing QUD trees. In Malte Zimmermann, Klaus von Heusinger & Edgar Onea (eds.), *Questions in discourse. Vol. 2: Pragmatics* (CRiSPI). Leiden: Brill.

Riester, Arndt, Lisa Brunetti & Kordula De Kuthy. in press. Annotation guidelines for Questions under Discussion and information structure. In Evangelia Adamou, Katharina Haude & Martine Vanhove (eds.), *Information structure in lesser-described languages: Studies in prosody and syntax*. Amsterdam: John Benjamins Publishing Company.

Roberts, Craige. 2012. Information structure: Towards an integrated formal theory of pragmatics. *Semantics and Pragmatics* 5(6). 1–69. Earlier version (1996) in OSU Working Papers in Linguistics, Vol. 49.

Rooth, Mats. 1992. A theory of focus interpretation. *Natural Language Semantics* 1(1). 75–116.

Satyawati, Made Sri. 2009. *Valensi dan relasi sintaksis bahasa Bima [Valency and syntactic relation in Bahasa Bima]*. Udayana University dissertation.

Schwarzschild, Roger. 1999. GIVENness, AvoidF, and other constraints on the placement of accent. *Natural Language Semantics* 7(2). 141–177.

Shiohara, Asako. in preparation. Memory of Japan: A Sumbawa conversation annotated with QUDs and information structure.

Shiohara, Asako. 2013a. Tense, aspect, mood and polarity in the Sumbawa Besar dialect of Sumbawa. *NUSA: Linguistic Studies of Languages in and around Indonesia* 55. 173–192.

Shiohara, Asako. 2013b. Voice in the Sumbawa Besar dialect of Sumbawa. *NUSA: Linguistic Studies of Languages in and around Indonesia* 54. 145–158.

Shiohara, Asako. 2014. Numerals in Sumbawa. In Marian Klammer & František Kratochvíl (eds.), *Number and quantity in East Nusantara*, 15–26. Canberra: Asia-Pacific Linguistics.

Siewierska, Anna. 2013. Verbal person marking. In Matthew Dryer & Martin Haspelmath (eds.), *The world atlas of language structures online*. Leipzig: Max Planck Institute for Evolutionary Anthropology. http://wals.info/chapter/102. [Accessed 2018-01-24].

Skopeteas, Stavros & Gisbert Fanselow. 2010. Focus types and argument asymmetries: A cross-linguistic study in language production. In Carsten Breul & Edward Göbbel (eds.), *Comparative and contrastive studies of information structure*, 169–197. Amsterdam & Philadelphia: John Benjamins Publishing Company.

Skopeteas, Stavros, Ines Fiedler, Sam Hellmuth, Anne Schwarz, Ruben Stoel, Gisbert Fanselow, Caroline Féry & Manfred Krifka. 2006. *Questionnaire on information structure (QUIS)*. Vol. 4 (Interdisciplinary Studies on Information Structure). Potsdam: Universitätsverlag Potsdam.

Strawson, Peter. 1964. Identifying reference and truth-values. *Theoria* 30. 96–118.

Stutterheim, Christiane von & Wolfgang Klein. 1989. Referential movement in descriptive and narrative discourse. In Rainer Dietrich & Carl Graumann (eds.), *Language processing in social context*, 39–76. Amsterdam: North Holland.

Tonhauser, Judith, David Beaver, Craige Roberts & Mandy Simons. 2013. Toward a taxonomy of projective content. *Language* 89(1). 66–109.

van Kuppevelt, Jan. 1995. Discourse structure, topicality and questioning. *Journal of Linguistics* 31. 109–149.

van Rooij, Robert. 2008. Topic, focus, and exhaustive interpretation. In *Proceedings of the 18th International Congress of Linguists (CIL)*. Seoul.

Walker, Marilyn, Aravind Joshi & Ellen Prince. 1998. *Centering theory in discourse*. Oxford: Oxford University Press.

Zubizarreta, Maria Luisa. 1998. *Prosody, focus, and word order*. Cambridge: MIT Press.

Chapter 10

Preposed NPs in Seediq

Naomi Tsukida

Aichi Prefectural University

> Seediq is an Austronesian language spoken in northeastern Taiwan. Its word order is VXS in general (where X stands for adjuncts or arguments other than the subject), but an NP that has some semantic relation to the matrix clause can precede the matrix clause. This NP is followed by the particle *'u* and a non-final pause. I will call such NPs preposed NPs. This paper will investigate the nature of these preposed NPs. What is their semantics and function? What type of NPs can be preposed? What are their anaphoricity and topic-persistence properties? Preposed NPs are often coreferential with the matrix subject, which may or may not be overt. When a preposed NP is coreferential with the main clause subject, and the matrix subject is not overt, then the seeming word order is SVX. When the preposed NP is coreferential with the matrix subject, and that subject is overt, then the seeming word order is SVXS. How do SVX and SVXS differ? What is the function of this double reference in SVXS? In addition, how do these word orders differ from simple VXS order?

1 Introduction

Seediq is an Austronesian language, spoken in northeastern Taiwan and belonging to the Atayalic subgroup. There are three Seediq dialects: Teruku, Tekedaya, and Tuuda. The research reported here is based on the Teruku dialect, which is mainly spoken in Hualien County. The population of the Teruku subgroup is about 30,000, but the younger generations do not speak the language.

In what follows §1.1 explains Seediq word order. Subject and voice are covered in §1.2, non-subject arguments in §1.3, and the *'u* particle in §1.4.

1.1 Word order

The basic constituent order in Seediq is VXS (X stands for adjuncts or arguments other than the subject). In example (1), *kerut*[1] '<AV>cut' is the V, *bunga* 'sweet potato' is a non-subject argument, and *payi* 'old woman' is the subject. *Ka* is multi-functional. Its function here is to mark the subject.

---

[1] The phoneme inventory of Teruku Seediq is as follows: p, t, k, q, ', b, d, s, x, h, g (voiced velar fricative), c, l (voiced lateral fricative), r, m, n, ng (velar nasal), w, y, a, i, u, and e (schwa).

Naomi Tsukida. 2018. Preposed NPs in Seediq. In Sonja Riesberg, Asako Shiohara & Atsuko Utsumi (eds.), *Perspectives on information structure in Austronesian languages*, 313–344. Berlin: Language Science Press. DOI:10.5281/zenodo.1402553

(1) AV
    K\<em\>erut bunga   ka payi.
    \<AV\>cut sweet.potato SBJ old.woman
    'The old woman cuts sweet potato.'

In NPs, modifiers other than numbers typically follow the head. See §3.1 for details.

Seediq has two sets of clitic pronouns, NOMINATIVE and GENITIVE, and two sets of independent pronouns, NEUTRAL and OBLIQUE. While all the pronouns have a GENITIVE clitic, the NOMINATIVE clitic is limited to the first and second persons. Clitic pronouns are second-position clitics, following the first element of the predicate. Some of the examples are =ku in example (2) and =na in examples (6), (7), and (8).

(2) Clitic pronoun
    K\<em\>erut=ku   bunga   (ka yaku).
    \<AV\>cut=1SG.NOM sweet.potato SBJ 1SG
    'I cut sweet potato.'

One can omit adjuncts and arguments including the subject if they are recoverable from the context. Clitic pronouns are enough to indicate arguments, so when there is a nominative clitic in the sentence, it does not need to be referred to by an independent pronoun.

In addition to the basic VXS order, Seediq can have an NP preceding the matrix clause, followed by the particle 'u and a non-final pause. In example (3), *payi* 'old woman' is preposed and followed by the 'u particle and a non-final pause. The matrix subject *ka payi* may be omitted, because, even if it is omitted, it is identifiable as coreferential with the preposed NP.

(3) Preposed NP
    Payi   'u, k\<em\>erut bunga   (ka hiya).
    old.woman PRT \<AV\>cut sweet.potato SBJ 3SG
    'The old woman, she cuts sweet potato.'

As a result, SVX order (more precisely, S 'u, V X (ka S)) is realized, though I do not regard the preposed NP as a subject. This paper will investigate the nature of such preposed NPs.

1.2 Subject and voice

The subject appears in the Neutral case, preceded by the particle *ka*, in clause-final position. *Ka* is multi-functional; some of its functions are subject-marker, linker, and complementizer. Its usage as a linker is yet to be investigated.

In Seediq, thematic roles fall into three groups, according to the verb form they trigger when they are chosen as the subject. The first group, the A group, includes AGENT, THEME, and EXPERIENCER; these trigger AV forms, as in (1) in §1.1. The second group, the G group, includes PATIENT, GOAL, LOCATION, and RECIPIENT; these trigger GV forms, as in (4). The third group, the C group, includes CONVEYED THEME, INSTRUMENT, and

BENEFICIARY; these trigger CV forms, as in (5). In (4) and (5), the patient *bunga* 'sweet potato' and the instrument *yayu* 'knife' is the subject, respectively, and the Agent *payi* 'old woman' is not the subject anymore.

(4) GV
 Kerut-un payi ka bunga.
 cut-GV1 old.woman SBJ sweet.potato
 'The/An old woman will cut the sweet potato.'

(5) CV
 Se-kerut bunga payi ka yayu.
 CV-cut sweet.potato old.woman SBJ knife
 'The/An old woman cut the/a sweet potato with the knife.'

Patient and location are grouped together; forms suffixed with *-un* are GV1, and those with *-an* are GV2 forms. Corresponding forms in other languages are often regarded as a patient voice and a location voice, respectively (Huang & Hsinsheng 2016: 78, for example), but in Teruku-Seediq, their usage is not so straightforward. Even when the thematic role of the subject is location, if one wants to express a future event, the *-un* form is used, for example. Moreover, even when the thematic role of the subject is patient, the *-an* form may be used if one wants to express a progressive or habitual event. See Tsukida (2012) for more details.

When the subject is a pronoun, it triggers a nominative clitic pronoun after the first element of the predicate (see example (2)).

There are cases where the thematic role of a *ka*-marked NP and the verb form do not correspond. For example, the verb is in AV form but the thematic role of the *ka*-marked NP is patient. In such cases the *ka*-marked NP cannot be regarded as the subject. Such cases exist, though they are rare.

In addition to triggering the nominative clitic pronoun, subjects show several distinctive morpho-syntactic properties (see Tsukida 2009 for details).

1.3 Non-subject arguments

An NP belonging to the A group (the group of NPs with thematic roles that trigger AV) is realized by the genitive clitic if it is a pronoun, when it is not the subject. The A arguments in (4) and (5) are not subjects. If one replaces them with pronouns, they would be as (6) and (7), respectively.

(6) GV, with pronominal A
 Kerut-un=na ka bunga.
 cut-GV1=3SG.GEN SBJ sweet.potato
 'He/She will cut the sweet potato.'

(7) CV, with pronominal A
 Se-kerut=na   bunga   ka yayu.
 CV-cut=3SG.GEN sweet.potato SBJ knife
 'The/An old woman cut the/a sweet potato with the knife.'

As for nouns, they do not have a distinct genitive form; the genitive form is the same as the neutral form. We can regard *payi* 'old woman' in (4) and (5) as a genitive form, though it is formally the same as a neutral form.

When it is not the subject, an NP belonging to the G or C group (the group of NPs with thematic roles that trigger GV or CV) is realized as OBLIQUE. The oblique form, however, is not distinct from the neutral form, except for pronouns and nouns with high animacy. For pronouns and NPs with high animacy, the oblique form usually involves the suffix *-an*. The occurrences of *bunga* 'sweet potato' in (1), (2), (3), (5) and (7) are regarded as oblique forms, though they are homophonous with neutral forms. *Sediq-an* 'person-OBL' in (8) is an example of a distinct oblique form.

(8) CV
 Se-kerut=na   sediq-an   ka yayu niyi.
 CV-cut=3SG.GEN person-OBL SBJ knife PROX
 'He/She cuts the/a person with this knife.'

1.4 The *'u* particle

As mentioned in §1.1, an NP may appear preceding a matrix clause, followed by the particle *'u* and a non-final pause. The particle may be *ga*, *de'u*, or *dega*, in addition to *'u*. *Ga* is interchangeable with *'u*. I will use only *'u* in the remainder of the paper. *De'u* and *dega* are interchangeable, as they are derived from *'u* and *ga* by affixation of *de-*. *De'u* and *dega* are used differently from *'u* and *ga*. I will not treat the use of *de'u* and *dega* in this paper.

What can precede *'u* is not only an NP but also a clause. In example (9), two clauses are connected by *'u*.

(9) Clause-A 'u, clause-B.
 M-iyah=su   hini 'u, me-qaras=ku.
 AV-come=2SG.NOM   here PRT AV-be.glad=1SG.NOM
 'If you come, I will be glad.'

'u is multifunctional, and the two clauses connected by it may have several kinds of relationships. In this sentence, the preposed clause is a conditional for the event denoted by the matrix clause. One can add an appropriate adverb to express the relationship overtly. In example (10), for example, *nasi* 'if' is added to express the conditional meaning overtly.

(10) With *nasi* 'if'
Nasi=su   m-iyah   hini 'u, me-qaras=ku.
if=2SG.NOM AV-come here PRT AV-be.glad=1SG.NOM
'If you come here, I will be glad.'

1.5 Texts

In the next section, I will investigate the nature of the preposed NPs mentioned in §1.1 from the point of view of semantics/function, NP types, anaphoricity, and topic persistence, analyzing Seediq texts.

For my analysis, I used parts of *Sufferings of the Teruku church* written by Yudaw Pisaw (Tien Shin-de). In these texts, matrix clause subjects occur five times more frequently than preposed NPs. I started checking from the beginning and when I reached 3728 words, 262 matrix clause subjects and 55 preposed NPs had been found. I therefore stopped counting matrix clause subjects but continued counting preposed NPs, up to 7315 words, and found 38 more instances of preposed NPs. In total, I have 93 instances of preposed NPs.

Table 1: Matrix subjects and preposed NPs in texts

Words	Matrix subject	Preposed NP
1–3728	262	55
3729–7315	– (stopped counting)	38
Total	262	93

2 Semantics/function of preposed NPs

It is not the case that one can freely choose an NP to precede the matrix clause. Preposing is usually restricted to the following NPs:

- An NP that is coreferential with the matrix subject (preposed subject)

- An NP that is coreferential with the A-argument in the matrix clause (preposed A)

- An NP that expresses the place of existence in an existential construction, or the possessor in a possessive construction, or a possessor that is left-dislocated from the matrix subject (preposed possessor, see §2.3 for details)

- An NP that expresses time (preposed time)

• Choices in alternative questions are preposed even when they are not subjects, A-arguments, times, places, or possessors (preposed alternatives)

Some preposed NPs apparently do not fit the above criteria. They are not coreferential with a subject, an A argument, or a possessor in the matrix clause; nor are they frames or alternatives. These will be discussed in §2.6.

Among 93 instances of preposed NPs, 66 instances have a preposed NP that is coreferential with the subject of the clause (preposed subject); in four instances it is coreferential with an A-argument (preposed A), in one instance it is a possessor (preposed possessor), and in 16 instances it is time (preposed time). There were six instances where it was difficult to judge the exact function of the preposed NP. These 93 instances are summarized in Table 2.

Table 2: Semantics/function of preposed NP

	Token	%
Preposed Subject	66	70%
Preposed A	4	6%
Preposed Possessor	1	1%
Preposed Time	16	17%
Preposed alternative	0	0%
None of the above	6	6%
Total	93	100%

I will explain each of the above cases in turn.

2.1 Preposed subjects

One can prepose an NP that is coreferential with the matrix subject, as in (3) and (11). I will call such cases PREPOSED SUBJECTS, though preposed NPs are not subjects, actually.

(11) Preposed subject
 Niyi$_i$ 'u, 'adi 'utux=ta (ka kiya$_i$).
 PROX PRT NEG God=1PLIN.GEN SBJ it
 'As for this, it is not our God.'

One can omit the matrix subject, as shown in (11).

When an NP that is coreferential with the subject appears in pre-clausal position, the subject in the regular clause-final position is often omitted. In the text, 13 of 66 preposed subjects had overt subjects, and 53 instances had covert subjects. I will investigate in §3.3, §4.3, and §5.3 whether there is any difference between these two cases.

With a verbal predicate, "subject" means the NP that triggers the verb form, appearing in clause-final position preceded by the subject particle ka. Payi 'old woman' in (1), bunga 'sweet potato' in (4), and *yayu* 'knife' in (5) are examples of subjects. For sentence (1), one can put *payi* 'old woman' in front of the matrix clause, as in (12), but one cannot do the same for *bunga* 'sweet potato,' as in (13).

(12) One can prepose a subject argument
 Payi   'u, kerut bunga   (ka hiya).
 old.woman PRT <AV>cut sweet.potato SBJ 3SG
 'The old woman, she cuts sweet potato.'

(13) One cannot prepose a non-subject argument
 *Bunga   'u, kerut ka payi.
 sweet.potato PRT <AV>cut SBJ old.woman
 'The old woman cuts sweet potato.'

For sentence (4), one can prepose *bunga* 'sweet potato', as in (14).

(14) GV
 Bunga   'u kerut-un payi   (ka bunga).
 sweet.potato PRT cut-GV1 old.woman SBJ sweet.potato
 'The/An old woman will cut the sweet potato.'

A preposed subject is not an actual subject, as I have indicated, but only coreferential with the matrix subject. It seems to share some of the subject properties mentioned in §1.2, however. A nominative clitic that corresponds to the preposed NP appears in the main clause, for example.

(15) One can prepose a subject argument
 Yaku 'u, kerut=ku bunga   (ka yaku).
 1SG PRT <AV>cut=1SG.NOM sweet.potato SBJ 1SG
 'As for me, I cut sweet potato.'

We cannot tell, however, whether it is the preposed NP *yaku* or the subject of the matrix clause that triggers the clitic.

When the preposed NP is coreferential with the matrix subject, the matrix subject may either appear again or be omitted. For 13 of 66 preposed subject, matrix clause subject is overt and for 53 it was not overt. When it is overt, it is realized either by *hiya*, the 3rd person singular pronoun, by *dehiya*, the 3rd person plural pronoun, or by *kiya* 'it, so'. In example (16), *Karaw Wacih* (proper name) appears in preposed position and at the end of the matrix clause, it is referred to again by a pronoun *ka hiya*.

(16) Preposed subject with overt matrix subject
 Si'ida ka Karaw Watih niyi 'u adi ka balay=bi senehiyi Yisu Kiristu
 then LNK Karaw Wacih PROX PRT NEG LNK really=really AV.believe Jesus Christ
 ka hiya niyana.
 SBJ 3SG yet
 'At that time Karaw Wacih, he did not really believed in Gospel yet.'

I will call this pattern *S 'u, VX ka hiya*. In this denotation, *hiya* represents *hiya*, *dehiya* and *kiya*. The pattern where the matrix subject is not overt, on the other hand, will be labeled *S 'u, VX*.

2.2 Preposed A

Here by "A" I mean the group of NPs which are not the subject but whose thematic roles trigger AV when they become the subject. A pronoun is in the genitive case when it appears as non-subject, as in (6) and (7).

An A argument can be preposed to the matrix clause. In a sentence like (5), for example, one can prepose *payi* 'old woman', as in (17), because its thematic role is agent. The genitive clitic pronoun =*na*, which is coreferential with *payi* appears in the matrix clause.

(17) CV
Payi   'u, se-kerut=na   bunga   ka yayu.
old.woman PRT CV-cut=3SG.GEN sweet.potato SBJ knife
'As for the old woman, she will cut the/a sweet potato with the knife.'

There are four such instances among the 95 preposed NPs.

Preposing A is not allowed if there is no X (non-subject argument). In (18) there is only the A argument *Kumu* (a person's name) as a non-subject argument. From this sentence, one cannot prepose A, as shown in (19).

(18) A as non-subject argument
B<en>arig   Kumu ka patas niyi.
<CV.PRF>buy Kumu SBJ book PROX
'Kumu bought this book.'

(19) One cannot prepose A
*Kumu 'u, b<en>arig=na   ka patas niyi.
kumu PRT <CV.PRF>buy=3SG.GEN SBJ book PROX
'As for Kumu, she bought this book./As for Kumu, this book was bought by her.'

A time expression is not enough to enable preposing of A. Even if *sehiga* 'yesterday' is X, one cannot prepose A, as shown in (20).

(20) One cannot prepose A
*Kumu 'u, b<en>arig=na   sehiga   ka patas niyi.
Kumu PRT <CV.PRF>buy=3SG.GEN yesterday SBJ book this
'As for Kumu, she bought this book yesterday.'

2.3 Preposed possessor

One of the morphosyntactic properties of subjects is that they license possessor left-dislocation. From a subject NP consisting of a noun and a possessor, one can move out the possessor and put it in front of the clause. Examples (21) and (22) exemplify this. In (21) *Masaw* (the name of a male person) is part of the NP *tederuy Masaw* 'Masaw's car', which is the subject of the sentence. In (22), on the other hand, *Masaw* is preposed, and in the subject a genitive clitic pronoun is present which is coreferential with the preposed *Masaw*.

(21) Me-gerung   ka tederuy Masaw.
      AV-be.broken SBJ car   Masaw
      'Masaw's car is broken.'

(22) Masaw 'u, me-gerung   ka tederuy=na.
      Masaw PRT AV-be.broken SBJ car=3SG.GEN
      'As for Masaw, his car is broken.'

There is one such instance among the 93 preposed NPs.

2.4 Preposed time

Preposed time sets the temporal frame in which the following expression should be interpreted. An example is (23).

(23) Preposed time
      Ya'asa diyan   'u, m-iyah rigaw   sbu ka 'asu sekiya
      because day:time PRT AV-come <AV>hang:about <AV>hit SBJ ship sky
      'Amirika heki.
      America REASON
      'Because in the daytime, American airplanes come to make an air raid.'

There are 16 such instances among the 93 preposed NPs.

2.5 Preposed alternatives

For alternative questions, alternatives are preposed, as in (24).

(24) Preposed Alternatives
      Deha niyi 'u, 'ima ka sewayi=su?
      two PROX PRT who SBJ younger:sibling=2SG.GEN
      'Between these two, who is your younger sibling?'

There was no such example in the text I used in this investigation.

2.6 None of the above

Some preposed NPs apparently do not belong to any of the classifications listed above. Such NPs rarely become subjects, but examples do exist. In (25), *saw niyi* 'such things' is a patient, not A, of the verb *me-kela* 'to know', notionally. It is not a subject, either, because the predicate verb is AV, not GV, which would have a patient as its subject. Nor is it a possessor, time or expression of alternatives.

(25) None of the above
Saw niyi 'u, dima me-kela ka nihung.
like PROX PRT already AV-know SBJ Japan
'As for such things, Japan already knew.'

There were six such instances in the text I analyzed.

2.7 Discussion

Let us examine here whether these preposed NPs are "topics" of some sort.

Preposed subjects, preposed As, and preposed possessors, shown in §2.1, §2.2 and §2.3, seem to serve as aboutness topics (Krifka 2007: 40–41). They indicate what the information denoted by the matrix clause (=comment) is about. Examples (12) and (17), for example, are about *payi* 'old woman'. The matrix clause tells the information about the preposed NP.

Preposed time and preposed alternative, on the other hand, seem to serve as frame setters. The frame setter indicates that the information actually provided is restricted to the particular dimension specified (Krifka 2007: 47). In example (23), the information provided by the matrix clause 'American airplanes come to make an air raid' is restricted to the particular dimension specified by the preposed NP *diyan* 'daytime', for example.

For those elements that are neither preposed subjects, preposed As, preposed possessors, preposed time or preposed alternatives, still more research is necessary, but as for example (25), the preposed NP, *saw niyi* 'such things' seems to serve to set frame for the information provided by the matrix clause, 'Japan already knew'.

3 NP types

In this section, I will investigate the composition of preposed NPs.

3.1 Preliminaries

In Seediq NPs, a noun (a common noun or a proper noun) or a pronoun usually functions as the head, but demonstratives and VPs can also function as referential expressions, without any affix or particle. Seediq is quite flexible, in the sense of van Lier & Rijkhoff (2013).

(26) A noun as a referential expression
Qita=ku   kuyuh ka yaku.
<AV>see=1SG.NOM woman SBJ 1SG
'I saw a/the woman.'

(27) A demonstrative as a referential expression
Me-gerung   ka gaga.
AV-be:broken SBJ DIST
'That is broken.'

VPs also are used as referential expressions without any additional affixation or particle. AV forms mean 'one who does the action denoted by the verb'/'one who bears the state denoted by the verb'; GV forms mean 'the object to which the action denoted by the verb is done'/'the place where the action denoted by the verb takes place'/'the recipient who recieves something'/'the goal toward which the action denoted by the verb aims'/ etc.; CV forms mean 'the instrument by which the action is done'/'the beneficiary for whom the action is done'/'the object that is transferred'/etc." A CV-perfect form may mean 'what has been done as the action denoted by the verb' (see (48)). *Mpe-tegesa kari* 'the one who teaches language' in (28) is an example of an AV form used as a referential expression.

(28) A VP as a referential expression
Qita=ku   mpe-tegesa   kari   ka yaku.
<AV>see=1SG.NOM AV.FUT-teach language SBJ 1SG
'I saw the language teacher.'

When the head is a noun, it can be modified by demonstratives, numbers, genitive pronouns, another noun, or relative clauses. Modifiers, except for numbers, typically follow the head.

(29) A demonstrative modifying a noun
Qita=ku   kuyuh gaga ka yaku.
<AV>see=1SG.NOM woman DIST SBJ 1SG
'I saw that woman.'

(30) A number modifying a noun
Me-gerung   ka teru tederuy.
AV-be:broken SBJ three car
'The three cars are broken.'

(31) A genitive pronoun modifying a noun
Qita=ku   kuyuh=na   ka yaku.
<AV>see=1SG.NOM wife=3SG.GEN SBJ 1SG
'I saw his wife.'

(32) Another noun modifying a noun
Me-gerung   ka sapah qehuni.
AV-be:broken SBJ house wood
'The wooden house is broken.'

(33) A relative clause modifying a noun
Qita=ku   kuyuh mpe-tegesa kari   ka yaku.
<AV>see=1SG.NOM woman AV.FUT-teach language SBJ 1SG
'I saw the woman who will teach language.'

I classified NPs into the following types, and investigated how they appear in preposed position. I also investigated their distribution as subjects and made comparisons.

- Personal pronoun (PP)
- Demonstrative (D)
- Proper noun + *niyi* (this) (PD)
- Common noun + *niyi* (this) (CD)
- Bare proper noun (BPN)
- Common noun + Genitive (CG)
- Common noun + Relative clause/Attributive (CR)
- Common noun (CN)
- *Saw* nominal (*Saw*) 'Things like ...'
- VP

This classification and ordering are based in part on Gundel et al.'s (1993) classification which claims that the form of a given NP reflects the givenness of the NP and show the Givenness Hierarchy (Gundel et al. 1993: 275).

$$\text{in focus} > \text{activated} > \text{familiar} > \text{uniquely identifiable} > \text{referential} > \text{type identifiable}$$

$$\{it\} \quad \left\{ \begin{array}{c} that \\ this \\ this\ N \end{array} \right\} \quad \{that\ N\} \quad \{the\ N\} \quad \{\text{indefinite } this\ N\} \quad \{a\ N\}$$

Figure 1: Givenness hierarchy (Gundel et al. 1993: 275)

In Seediq, too, a personal pronoun (PP) may reflect *in focus* status, which is at the leftmost position in the hierarchy, demonstrative (D) may reflect *activated* status, common noun + demonstrative (CD) may reflect *activated* or *referential* status, and so on. As

Seediq does not have a definite article or an indefinite article, it is not easy to identify each NP as uniquely identifiable or type identifiable

At this stage, it is an open question whether and how the different composition in Seediq NPs reflects givenness. This is still under investigation, and the classification above is only a preliminary step. Though still to be examined more thoroughly, I tried ordering them so that it would correspond, at least partially, to the givenness hierarchy by Gundel et al. (1993).

I will explain my classification and ordering below.

First is an NP consisting of a personal pronoun. In Gundel et al. (1993), this is an indication of *in focus* status. An example of a personal pronoun preposed to a matrix clause:

(34) Personal pronoun (PP)
 Hiya 'u, ya'a=bi   teru 'idas ka ne-niq-un=na   hiya ni
 3SG PRT UNCERTN=really three month SBJ FUT-live-GV1=3SG.GEN there and
 'Then she, it was about three months that she would live there, and ....'

Next is an NP consisting of a demonstrative. In Gundel et al. (1993), this is an indication of *activated* status. An example of a demonstrative preposed to a matrix clause:

(35) Demonstrative (D)
 Niyi 'u, 'adi 'utux=ta ka niyi.
 PROX PRT NEG God=1PI.GEN SBJ PROX
 'This, this is not our God.'

I also treated the time expression *si'ida* 'then, at that time' as demonstrative.

(36) Demonstrative (D)
 Si'ida 'u, me-seseli ngangut sapah 'Umih Yadu.
 then PRT\ AV-gather outside house PN   PN
 'At that time, they gathered outside of the house of Umih Yadu.'

Next is an NP consisting of a proper name and a demonstrative (PD). Gundel et al. (1993) do not include such a form. An example of a proper noun modified by a demonstrative appearing in front of the matrix clause:

(37) Proper noun + *niyi* (PD)
 Ya'asa Tiwang niyi 'u, m-en-niq degiyaq qawgan.
 because Ciwang PROX PRT AV-PRF-live mountain Qawgan
 'Because this Ciwang, she was a Teruku, and she had lived at Mt. Qawgan.'

Proper nouns modified by demonstratives seem to be *activated* or *familiar*.

Next is an NP consisting of a common noun and a demonstrative. Gundel et al. (1993) point out the functional difference between *this* and *that* from the point of view of information structure. According to them, *this N* is an indication of *activated* status, but *that*

N indicates *familiarity*. I examined the corpus to determine whether the corresponding expressions in Seediq, *N niyi* (*this N*) and *N gaga* (*that N*), show a similar difference, but I found only instances of *N niyi*. There are no instances of *N gaga* in the text, but *N gaga* is often found in elicitation. An example of a preposed CD (common noun modified by a demonstrative):

(38) Common noun + *niyi* (CD)
Budi   pe-patas=mu   niyi 'u, biq-i=ku   haya
bamboo FUT-CV.write=1SG.GEN PROX PRT give-GV.NFIN=1SG.NOM BEN
kuyuh=mu   rubiq wilang ha.
wife=1SG.GEN PN   PN   GENTLE
'As for this fountain pen, please give it to my wife Rubiq Wilang.'

Common nouns modified by demonstratives (CDs) are supposed to be *activated, familiar* or *uniquely identifiable*.

Next is an NP consisting of a proper name. An example:

(39) Bare proper noun (BPN)
Kiya de'u, nihung 'u, hengkawas 19,14 m-adas hebaraw=bi merata ni kensat
so   PRT Japan PRT year   1914 AV-bring many=really soldier and police
m-iyah   keremux dexegal Teruku.
AV-come <AV>invade land   Teruku
'Then, Japan, in 1914, brought soldiers and police and came to invade the Truku territory.'

Things or persons denoted by proper names are at least *uniquely identifiable*.

Next is an NP consisting of a common noun and a genitive pronoun. The genitive expresses a possessor, as illustrated in (40).

(40) Common noun + Genitive pronoun (CG)
Bubu=na   'u, wada   m-arig bawa da.
mother=3SG.GEN PRT be:gone AV-buy bun   NS
'His/Her mother went to buy a bun.'

Common nouns modified by genitive pronouns (CGs) are supposed to be *uniquely identifiable* or *referential*.

Next is an NP consisting of a common noun and a relative clause or attributive expression. In Seediq, a noun may be modified by another noun, and the relationship between them is possessor-possessed, material-thing (e.g., paper napkin), purpose-thing (e.g., traveling shoes), whole-part (e.g., face tattoo), product-producer (e.g., his book, meaning 'the book he wrote'), etc. I collectively call those meanings that are expressed by the modifiers illustrated "attributive". "Relative clause" is actually a VP modifying a noun (see (42)). This type, therefore, is a class of NPs consisting of a noun and another noun or a VP modifying it. Examples are:

(41) Common noun + Other noun (CR)
Kana ka mensewayi de-senehiyi 'uri 'u, tetegeli'ing m-usa me-seseli
all LNK brother PL-believer also PRT AV.hide AV-go AV-gather
tehemuku.
AV.worship

'The brothers and sisters of believers went together hiding to worship as well.'

(42) Common noun + VP (CR)
Kensat nihung m-eniq Sekadang 'u, Matsudo-sang ni Motoyoshi-singsi 2
police Japan AV-live Sekadang PRT Matsudo-Mr. and Motoyoshi-teacher two
hiyi.
body

'The Japanese police who were at Skadang, they were Mr. Matsudo and Teacher Motoyoshi, two people.'

Common nouns modified by another noun or VP (CRs) are also supposed to be *uniquely identifiable*, *referential* or type *identifiable*.

Next is an NP consisting of a common noun alone, as illustrated in (43):

(43) Common noun (CN)
Ke'man 'u, pengkeku'ung sengkekingal m-usa 'ayug daya 'alang=deha
night PRT in:the:darkness one:by:one AV-go stream upwards village=3PL.GEN
ka se'diq senehiyi Kiristu.
SBJ person AV-believe Christ

'At night, people who believed in Christ went to the upper stream of their village, in the darkness, one by one.'

Bare common nouns may be *uniquely identifiable*, *referential*, or *type identifiable*. Seediq does not have any definite article or indefinite article, so it is often hard to tell.

Next is *saw* + noun. An NP is preceded by *saw*, a preposition meaning 'like ...'; *saw NP* means 'things like an NP' or 'things concerning NP.' Sometimes *ka* appears between *saw* and *NP*. An example:

(44) *Saw* nominals
Saw ka qaya samat 'u, des-un=deha be'nux, seberig-an
like LNK thing wild:animal PRT bring-GV1=3PL.GEN plain:land sell-GV2
kelemukan.
Taiwanese

'As for things concerning wild animals (animal skins, bones, horns, and the like), they brought them to the plains and sold them to Taiwanese.'

Saw + *noun* would correspond to *type identifiable* in givenness hierarchy by Gundel et al. (1993).

The last is VP. A VP can function as a referential expression, as in example (28). This type of expression may appear as the subject or as a non-subject argument, but rarely as a preposed element. (45) is another example of a VP functioning as a subject phrase. In this example, a VP *n-arig=mu sehiga* '<CV.PRF>buy=1SG.GEN yesterday' means 'what I bought yesterday.'

(45) VP as matrix subject
 Me-gerung ka n-arig=mu sehiga.
 AV-be:broken SBJ CV.PRF-buy=1SG.GEN yesterday
 'What I bought yesterday is broken.'

Such VPs used as referential expression may be *uniquely identifiable, referential* or *type identifiable*, depending on the adjuncts contained in them.

3.2 Results

I investigated what type of NP appears for each type of preposed NP classified in §2. The results are shown in Table 3.

Table 3: Types of preposed NPs, in terms of coreference

	Preposed				Others	Sum
	Subject	Time	A	Po		
PP	2	0	0	0	0	2
D	6	10	0	0	2	18
PD	12	0	0	0	0	12
CD	4	0	0	0	0	4
BPN	20	0	2	0	0	22
CG	6	0	1	1	0	8
CR	4	0	0	0	1	5
CN	4	6	1	0	0	11
Saw+ noun	7	0	0	0	3	12
VP	1	0	0	0	0	1
Interrogative	0	0	0	0	0	0
Total	66	16	4	1	6	

There are several things I can point out from the results above.

Personal pronouns rarely appear preposed. There are only two instances of them.

For preposed subjects, person names, accompanied by a demonstrative (PD) or not (BPN), appear more often than the other types of NPs.

For preposed time, there are 10 instances of *si'ida* 'then, at that time.' These are classified as demonstrative. The other six instances are bare common nouns (CN).

Among those six instances that were not S, A, Po, or Time, three are of the type *saw* + noun 'things concerning *noun*.' It seems easier for speakers to ignore the semantic relationship between the preposed NP and the voice of the predicate verb of the matrix clause when the preposed NP is *saw* + noun. Let us examine here the three cases more precisely. One is example (25). The other two are (46) and (47).

(46) Saw + noun
Saw niyi 'u, berah 'ini 'iyah   dexegal Taywan hini ka Nihung
like PROX PRT before NEG AV.NFIN.come land   Taiwan here SBJ Japan
han.
temporarily
'As for such things, it was before Japan came here to the land of Taiwan.'

(47) Saw + noun
Saw niyi 'u, 'adi=nami tegesa ka yami kensat Nihung 'uri pini,
like PROX PRT NEG=1PLEX <AV>teach SBJ 1PLEX police Japan also ANGER
mesa.
HEARSAY
'As for such things, we Japanese police do not teach, they say.'

In these examples, *saw niyi* 'such things' seems to indicate rather abstract situations, not concrete entities. Such lack of concreteness seems to lead to inconsistency of the voice form of the matrix verb.

Below, I will investigate whether the situation differs for preposed subjects if the matrix subject is overt or not. I will also compare the preposed subject situation with the situation of the matrix subject.

3.3 Comparison

Among sentences with preposed subjects, some have an overt matrix subject, and some do not. When the matrix subject is overt, the same referent is referred to twice, both in the topic position and in the regular subject position (S 'u, VX ka S). What is the function of this double reference?

The preposed subject is coreferential with the matrix subject. How does the appearance of an NP in preposed position differ from an NP that is the matrix subject, in internal constituency? I will compare the NPs in these cases.

3.3.1 When the matrix subject is overt and when it is not

Among 66 instances of preposed subjects, 13 instances are *S 'u, XV ka hiya* pattern (with overt matrix clause subject), and 53 instances are *S 'u, VX* pattern (without overt matrix subject). The types of preposed NPs are shown in Table 4.

There are considerable differences in internal constituency between *S 'u, VX ka hiya* pattern and *S 'u, VX* pattern.

Table 4: NP types of preposed subjects with overt matrix subjects and those without.

	Preposed subjects			
	S 'u, VX ka hiya.		S 'u, VX.	
PP	0	0%	2	4%
D	1	8%	5	9%
PD	4	31%	8	15%
CD	1	8%	3	6%
BPN	6	46%	14	26%
CG	0	0%	6	11%
CR	0	0%	4	8%
CN	0	0%	4	8%
Saw+ noun	1	8%	6	12%
VP	0	0%	1	2%
Total	13	100%	53	100%

We can first point out that what can appear as S of the *S 'u, VX ka hiya* pattern is very limited. Most of them (10 of 13) are PD or BPN. There is one example each of D, CD and *saw* + *noun*. There are no examples of PP, CR, CG, CN or VP.

As for the PP (personal pronoun) type, for all preposed subjects there are very few instances, as we saw in §3.2. The two that occur lack an overt subject. Clauses with a personal pronoun as preposed subject and a matrix clause with an overt subject seem to be avoided.

Among the 13 instances of preposed subjects with an overt regular-position subject (*S 'u, VX ka hiya* type), 10 (76%) are instances of PD or BPN; that is, a proper name, with or without a modifying demonstrative, is introduced as the preposed NP and then referred to again in the matrix subject position by a pronoun, as in (48).

(48) Tiwang niyi 'u, Teruku ka hiya.
 Ciwang PROX PRT Teruku SBJ 3SG
 'This Ciwang, she was a Teruku person.'

In the *S 'u, VX* pattern, on the other hand, PD and BPN represent only 41 percent of the cases. This is lower than the number of cases with the *S 'u, VX ka hiya* pattern (76%).

As for the CR, CG, and CN types (common nouns modified by a VP or another noun, those modified by a genitive pronoun, and bare common nouns), there is no instance of the *S 'u, VX ka hiya* pattern. There is only one instance of the CD type (common noun modified by a demonstrative). We can thus say that common nouns rarely appear as preposed subjects of the *S 'u, VX ka hiya* pattern.

For the S 'u, VX type, the proportion of common nouns as preposed NPs is higher (17 among 53) than for the S 'u, VX ka hiya type.

As for the saw + noun type, 6 of 7 instances of them occurred in the S 'u, VX type.

We see in Table 4 that most instances of saw NP 'u (6 out of 7) occurred in the S 'u, VX pattern.

There is one example of VP in preposed position (see the next section for this example).

3.3.2 Preposed subjects and matrix subjects

Now let us compare preposed subjects and matrix subjects. There are 262 overt matrix subject occurrences in the text. A comparison of NP types in preposed subjects and matrix subjects is given in Table 5 and visualized in Figure 2.

Table 5: NP types of preposed subjects with and without overt regular-position subjects and matrix subjects.

	Preposed-Subject				Matrix clause subjects	
	S 'u, VX ka hiya.		S 'u, VX.		XV ka S	
PP	0	0%	2	4%	52	20%
D	1	8%	5	9%	4	2%
PD	4	31%	8	15%	10	4%
CD	1	8%	3	6%	2	1%
BPN	6	46%	14	26%	64	24%
CG	0	0%	6	11%	49	19%
CR	0	0%	4	8%	10	4%
CN	0	0%	4	8%	48	18%
Saw+noun	1	8%	6	12%	2	1%
VP	0	0%	1	2%	21	8%
Total	13	100%	53	100%	262	100%

The PP type (personal pronouns) scarcely appears as a preposed subject, but for matrix subjects, the PP type is observed very often (20%).

Demonstratives (D), proper names modified by demonstratives (PD), and common nouns modified by demonstratives (CD) appear as preposed subjects (22 out of 66, 33%), but not as often in regular subject position (16 out of 262, 6%).

CD, CR, CG (common nouns modified by demonstratives, another noun, a VP, or a genitive pronoun) and CN (bare common nouns) are very common matrix subjects (109 out of 262, 41%). For preposed subjects, they are much fewer (1 out of 14, 7%, for S of the S 'u, VX ka hiya pattern and 17 out of 52, 32%, for the S of S 'u, VX pattern).

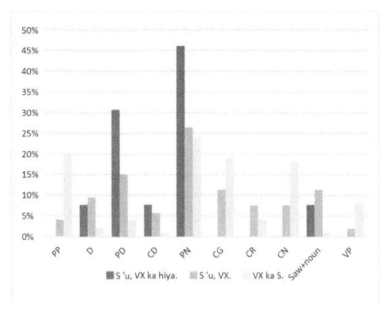

Figure 2: NP types of preposed subjects with and without overt regular-position subjects and matrix subjects.

Personal names, bare (BPN) or with modification by demonstratives (PD), are less common for matrix subjects (74 out of 262, 28%) than for preposed subjects (10 out of 13, 77%, for S of the *S 'u, VX ka hiya* pattern and 22 out of 53, 42%, for S of the *S 'u, VX* pattern).

VPs can function as referential expressions, as we saw at the beginning of §3. Such expressions appear in regular subject position, but rarely in preposed position. There were 21 instances in which a VP appeared as a matrix subject, but only one of a prepositional phrase in pre-clausal position. Example (49) shows a VP functioning as subject.

(49)   VP as the subject
       Laqi=na   'Ipay Yudaw ka q<en>ita.
       child=3SG.GEN Ipay Yudaw SBJ <AV><PRF>see
       'The one who saw it was her child Ipay Yudaw.'

We can say that NP *ka* VP is similar to a cleft or pseudocleft construction. Similar constructions are reported for Philippine languages (Himmelmann 2005: 140, Nagaya 2011: 604), and for many other Formosan languages as well.

A preposed VP is usually interpreted as an adverbial-clause predicate with the subject omitted, and not as a referential phrase. This is because *'u* is multifunctional and can mark adverbial clauses as well as preposed subjects, as we saw in §1.4. In the texts, there was one example of a preposed VP that could be interpreted as a referential expression (see example (50)).

(50) VP preceding the matrix clause
P<en>le'alay=bi senehiyi kari Kiristu ka 'alang Besuring 'u, Talug
<AV.PRF>first=really AV.believe word Christ LNK village Besuring PRT Talug
Payan.
Payab
'As for the first one to believe the gospel of Christ in the village of Besuring, it was Talug Payan.'

The VP preceding *'u* in (50), *p<en>le'alay=bi senehiyi kari Kiristu ka alang Besuring* cannot be interpreted as an adverbial, meaning 'as/because/if one was the first to believe the gospel of Christ in the Besuring village', but only as a referential phrase, meaning 'the first one to believe the gospel of Christ in the Besuring village'.

Instances of *saw* + noun 'such things as *noun*, such things related to *noun*' are very few for matrix subjects (1 out of 262). We can see more examples in preposed position (1 out of 13 for S of the *S 'u, VX ka hiya* pattern, 6 out 53 for S of the *S 'u, VX* pattern). This distribution seems to be the opposite of that with VPs.

4 Anaphoricity

In this section, I will investigate anaphoricity in preposed subjects.

4.1 Preliminaries

Anaphoricity is an index of the degree to which a referent can be said to have a discourse antecedent. Following Gregory & Michaelis (2001: 1687), I apply the label "anaphoricity" to an attribute with three possible values:

- 0: Tokens containing pre-clausal NPs whose referents have not been mentioned in the preceding discourse.

- 1: Tokens containing pre-clausal NPs whose referents are members of a set that was previously evoked.

- 2: Tokens containing pre-clausal NPs that denote entities that have been mentioned previously in the discourse.

Examples (51)–(53) illustrate the three possible anaphoricity scores, with referring expressions and their antecedents co-indexed in (52) and (53).

(51) is an example of an anaphoricity score of 0. The preposed NP in this example is *saw ka qaya samat* 'those things concerning wild animals.' In the previous text, it is not mentioned at all, so its anaphoricity score is 0.

(51) Anaphoricity score of 0 (not mentioned before)
Saw ka qaya samat 'u, des-un=deha be'nux, seberig-an
like LNK thing wild:animal PRT bring-GV1=3PL.GEN plain:land sell-GV2
kelemukan.
Taiwanese

'As for those things concerning wild animals (animal skins, bones, horns, and the like), they brought them to the plain and sold them to Taiwanese.'

(52) has an anaphoricity score of 1. The preposed NP in example (52b) is *duma* 'some, others.' It is a member of *dehiyaan* '3PL.OBL,' which was mentioned in (52a).

(52) Anaphoricity score of 1 (members of a set that was previously evoked)
  a. Bitaq saw m-ahu quyu peqeraqil dehiya'an$_i$.
     until like AV-wash snake AV.torture 3PL.OBL
     'They tortured them up to hitting snake (=expression of harshness).'
  b. **Duma**$_i$ 'u, pesa-'un=deha kulu m-banah.
     some PRT put-GV1=3PL.GEN box AV-red
     'Some were put into prison (=red box).'

(53) has an anaphoricity score of 2. The preposed NP in example (53b) is *dexegal Taiwan* 'land of Taiwan.' It is mentioned in the previous clause (53a).

(53) Anaphoricity score of 2 (Mentioned before)
  a. Saw niyi 'u, berah 'ini 'iyah **dexegal Taywan**$_i$ hini ka Nihung
     like this PRT before NEG AV.NFIN.come land Taiwan here SBJ Japan
     han.
     temporarily
     'Things like these, it was before Japan came here to Taiwan.'
  b. Kiya ni pa'ah hengkawas 1895 siida, **dexegal Taywan**$_i$ 'u diy-un
     so and from year 1895 then land Taiwan PRT have-GV1
     kelawa Nihung.
     <AV>govern Japan
     'Then, from 1895, the land of Taiwan was owned and governed by Japan.'

4.2 Results

For preposed subjects, 35 out of 66 had anaphoricity scores of 2, 1 out of 7 had a score of 1, and 24 of 66 had scores of 0. The results are summarized in Table 6.
In nearly half of the instances the score was 2.

Table 6: Anaphoricity of preposed subjects

	Preposed Subjects	%
0 (=no prior mention)	24	36%
1 (=member of an activated set)	7	11%
2 (=prior mention)	35	53%
Total	66	100%

4.3 Comparison

In this section I will compare the anaphoricity scores of preposed NPs with and without overt matrix subjects and also with matrix subjects.

4.3.1 When the matrix subject is overt and when it is not

A comparison of the anaphoricity of preposed subjects with and without overt matrix subjects is shown in Table 7.

Table 7: Anaphoricity of preposed subjects with and without overt matrix subjects

	Preposed subject			
	S 'u, VX ka hiya.		S 'u, VX.	
0 (=no prior mention)	7	54%	17	32%
1 (=member of an activated set)	0	0%	7	13%
2 (=prior mention)	6	46%	29	55%
Total	13	100%	53	100%

For S of the *S 'u, XV ka hiya* pattern, the anaphoricity score is either 0 or 2; there is no instance of an anaphoricity score of 1. Seven out of 13 are examples where the score is 0, the other 6 are examples where the score is 2. For S of the *S 'u, XV ka hiya* pattern, about a half of the instances (29 of 53) had scores of 2. We can say that the proportion of scores of 2 is similar when the matrix subject is present or absent. For scores of 0 and 1, two cases show a difference: for S of the *S 'u, XV* pattern, the anaphoricity score is 0 (17 out of 53) or 1 (7 out of 53), whereas there are no instances of anaphoricity scores of 1 for S of the *S 'u, XV ka hiya* pattern.

4.3.2 Preposed subjects and matrix subjects

A comparison of the anaphoricity of preposed subjects and matrix subjects is given in Table 8, and illustrated in Figure 3.

Table 8: Anaphoricity of preposed subjects with and without overt matrix subjects, and matrix subjects.

	Preposed subjects				Matrix subjects	
	S 'u, VX ka hiya.		S 'u, VX.		VX ka S.	
0 (=no prior mention)	7	54%	17	32%	98	37%
1 (=member of an activated set)	0	0%	7	13%	15	6%
2 (=prior mention)	6	46%	29	55%	149	57%
Total	13	100%	53	100%	262	100%

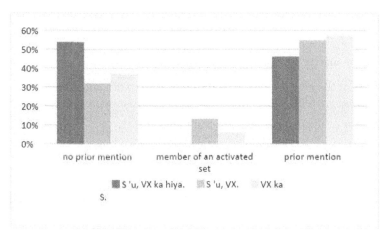

Figure 3: Anaphoricity of preposed subjects with and without overt matrix subjects, and matrix subjects.

For matrix subjects, the proportion of scores of 0, 1, or 2 is somewhat similar to the S of the *S 'u, XV* pattern. For both, more than half of the referents (57% for matrix subjects and 55% for S of the *S 'u, XV* pattern) had anaphoricity scores of 2 (mentioned in the previous discourse), and about one third (37% for matrix subjects and 33% for preposed subjects without overt matrix subjects) had scores of 0 (not mentioned at all). The percentage of NPs with scores of 1 is somewhat lower for matrix subjects (6%) than for S of the *S 'u, XV* pattern (13%).

For S of the *S 'u, XV ka hiya* pattern, the rate of each score differs from the other two types. There is no instance of score 1, and the percentage for score 0 is somewhat higher than for the other two. It may be a coincidence which originates from scarcity of the data.

4.4 Correlation between NP types and anaphoricity

Let us see the correlation between NP types and anaphoricity. It is summarized in Table 9.

Table 9: Type of NP and anaphoricity

	Anaphoricity score		
	0	1	2
PP	0	0	2
D	0	0	6
PD	1	0	11
CD	1	0	3
BPN	12	0	8
CG	4	0	2
CR	2	2	0
CN	1	3	0
Saw+ noun	2	2	3
VP	1	0	0
Total	24	7	35

It is interesting to see the anaphoricity difference between PD and BPN. For most of the PD (11 of 12), the anaphoricity score is 2, while more than half of BPN (12 of 20) had a score of 0. When something already referred to is mentioned again, it appears accompanied by demonstratives. This seems to support the idea that PDs are *activated* or *familiar* while BPN are at least *uniquely identifiable*. For all PP and D also, the anaphoricity score is 2. This seems to support the idea that PP and D correspond to *in focus* and *activated*, respectively.

For those that would correspond to lower givenness (CR, CN, *saw* + noun or VP), we can see that score of 2 is not observed very much.

5 Topic persistence

Lastly, I will examine the topic persistence of preposed subjects.

5.1 Preliminaries

I applied the label of persistence to an attribute with four possible values in the following way:

- 0: The pre-clausal NP denotatum is not referred to at all within five subsequent clauses.

- 1: The pre-clausal NP denotatum is referred to in subsequent clauses by means of a lexically headed NP rather than a pronoun.

- 2: The pre-clausal NP denotatum is expressed pronominally within the five following clauses.

- 3: The pre-clausal NP denotatum is referred to in subsequent clauses by means of a zero pronoun.

I added a fourth value to the classification in Gregory & Michaelis (2001: 1689), because in Seediq one can omit NPs that are recoverable from the context. I wanted to distinguish covert and overt pronouns, so I limited the score of 2 to those cases with overt pronouns and applied a score of 3 to those cases with covert pronouns. The examples in (54-57) illustrate the four possible persistence scores, with referring expressions and their antecedents co-indexed.

The preposed NP of (54a), *Tiwang niyi* 'this Ciwang,' is not referred to at all in at least the following five clauses (though the example below only shows the following two clauses), so the score is 0. From sentence (54b), the topic of the text is changed to *Bakan Hagay* and *Karaw Wacih*.

(54) Lack of persistence; score of 0
    a. *Tiwang niyi 'u, dima sedu'uy kari Kiristu ka hiya da.*
       Ciwang PROX PRT already AV.have words Christ SBJ 3SG NS
       'This Ciwang, she was already a Christian.'
    b. *Pa'ah d<en>ehuq-an=na   Ekedusan ka Bakan Hagay 'u*
       from <PRF>arive-GV=3SG.GEN Ekedusan SBJ Bakan Hagay PRT
       'Since Bakan Hagay arrived at Ekedusan,'
    c. *'ida sekuxul=bi m-uyas 'uyas 'Utux Baraw deha Karaw Watih*
       surely <AV>like=really AV-sing song God   Heaven with Karaw Wacih
       senaw=na.
       husband=3SG.GEN
       'she liked singing songs about God in heaven with her husband Karaw Wacih.'

The preposed NP of (55a), *Lebak Yudaw* 'Lebak Yudaw,' is referred to by a lexically headed NP *Lebak niyi* 'this Lebak' in sentence (55b), the following clause. The score is therefore 1.

(55) Repeated NP; score of 1
    a. *Si'ida ka* **Lebak Yudaw**$_i$ *'u, me-'ayung sapah kensat ka hiya ni*
       then LNK Lebak Yudaw PRT AV-assistant house police SBJ 3SG and
       'At that time, Lebak Yudaw was an assistant at the police station and,'

b. *m-bahang kari quri t<en>egesa   Kiristu ka **Lebak niyi**ᵢ 'uri,*
   AV-listen story about <CV>PRF.teach Christ SBJ Lebak PROX also
   'this Lebak also heard the story about what Christ taught.'

The preposed NP in (56a), *niyi* 'this,' is referred to by the pronoun *kiya* 'it, so' in sentence (56b), the following sentence. The score is therefore 2.

(56) Pronominal use; score of 2

   a. ***Niyi**ᵢ 'u, 'adi 'utux=ta   ka **kiya**ⱼ,*
      PROX PRT NEG God=1PI.GEN SBJ it
      'This, it is not our God,'

   b. *'utux 'amirika ka **kiya**ⱼ.*
      God America SBJ it
      'it is the American God.'

The preposed NP of (57a), *kari niyi* 'this story' is the patient of the predicate verb of clause (57b), *m-iyah tegesa* 'come to teach,' but it is not overt. The score is therefore 3.

(57) Zero pronoun use; score of 3

   a. ***Kari niyi**ᵢ 'u, n-eyah-an=na   m-angal pa'ah 'alang Besuring.*
      story PROX PRT PRF-come-GV=3SG.GEN AV-take from village Besuring
      'As for this story [=the gospel], it was taken from Besuring village.'

   b. *Pekelug m-iyah tgesa __ᵢ hiya ka Tiwang 'Iwal.*
      just AV-come <AV>teach   there SBJ Ciwang Iwal
      'Ciwang Iwal came to teach it just then.'

5.2 Results

For preposed subjects, the topic persistence score is 0 for 35%, 1 for 23%, 2 for 33%, and 3 for 9%. The incidence of score 3 is rather low. It is summarized in Table 10.

Table 10: Persistence of preposed subjects

	Preposed subject	%
0 (=no persistence)	23	35%
1 (=repeated NP)	15	23%
2 (=pronominal use)	22	33%
3 (=zero pronoun)	6	9%
Total	66	100%

5.3 Comparison

In this section I will compare the topic persistence scores of preposed NPs with and without overt matrix subjects, and also with matrix subjects.

5.3.1 When the matrix clause subject is and is not overt

A comparison of topic persistence of preposed subjects depending on the presence or absence of overt matrix subjects is given in Table 11.

Table 11: Persistence of preposed subjects with and without overt matrix subjects

	Preposed subjects			
	S 'u, VX ka hiya.		S 'u, VX.	
0 (=no persistence)	2	15%	21	40%
1 (=repeated NP)	3	23%	12	23%
2 (=pronominal use)	8	62%	14	26%
3 (=zero pronoun)	0	0%	6	11%
Total	13	100%	53	100%

Topic persistence differs considerably depending on the presence or absence of an overt matrix subject.

62% (8 out of 13) of the instances of the S of the *S 'u, VX ka hiya* pattern showed a score of 2, but only 26% (14 out of 53) of the S of the *S 'u, VX* pattern. In contrast, 15% of the instances (2 out of 13) of the S of the *S 'u, VX ka hiya* pattern showed a score of 0, while 40% of the S of the *S 'u, VX* (21 out of 53) showed a score of 0. There was no instance of an overt matrix subject (*S 'u, VX ka hiya*) that showed a score of 3; the six instances of score 3 (11%) are all S of *S 'u, VX*. For S of *S 'u, VX ka hiya*, the proportion of score 2 (62%) is the highest. For S of *S 'u, VX*, the proportion of score 0 (40%) is the highest.

5.3.2 Preposed subject and matrix subject

Now let us compare preposed subjects with matrix subjects. This is shown in Table 12 and Figure 4.

We can see that the matrix subject shows a tendency quite similar to S of *S 'u, VX*. In many instances of both types (45% and 40%, respectively), the referent is referred to only once in a single clause (for a score of 0). In contrast, many instances of S of *S 'u, VX ka hiya* (double reference) show a score of 2 (referred to again by a pronoun within the following five clauses). The doubly referenced entity somehow tends to persist longer.

Table 12: Persistence of preposed subjects with and without overt matrix subjects

	Preposed subjects				Matrix subjects	
	S 'u, VX ka hiya.		S 'u, VX.		VX ka S.	
0 (=no persistence)	2	15%	21	40%	117	45%
1 (=repeated NP)	3	23%	12	23%	51	19%
2 (=pronominal use)	8	62%	14	26%	65	25%
3 (=zero pronoun)	0	0%	6	11%	29	11%
Total	13	100%	53	100%	262	100%

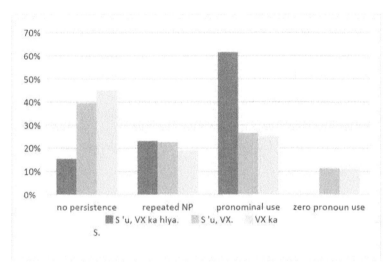

Figure 4: Persistence of preposed subjects with and without overt regular-position subjects

5.4 Correlation between NP types and topic persistence

Let us see the correlation between NP types and topic persistence, summarized in Table 13.

Table 13: NP types and Topic pessistence

	Topic persistence			
	0	1	2	3
PP	0	0	2	0
D	2	1	2	1
PD	2	2	6	2
CD	1	1	1	1
BPN	5	8	6	0
CG	4	0	1	1
CR	2	1	2	0
CN	2	2	0	0
Saw+ noun	4	0	2	1
VP	1	0	0	0
Total	23	15	22	6

As for topic persistence, the tendency is not as clear as in the case of anaphoricity. We can say that CR, CG, CN and *saw* + noun, which are supposed to be at the lower position in the givenness hierarchy of Gundel et al. (1993), the topic persistence score tends to be low (score of 0).

6 Summary

I examined the semantics/function of NP type, anaphoricity, and topic persistence in preposed NPs.

Semantically, more than two thirds of the preposed NPs are coreferential with the matrix subject. One sixth of them are preposed Time.

Preposed subjects, As, and possessors can be regarded to indicate aboutness topics, and the matrix clause denotes the comment about them. Preposed time, alternative, and those preposed NPs that are not classified as any of the above seem to set a frame to the information provided by the matrix clause.

As for NP types, this paper pointed out several characteristics of preposed NPs. We can say that preposed subjects tend to be proper names. About half of the preposed subjects are bare proper names (BPN) or proper names modified by a demonstrative (PD). Only 28% of the matrix subjects are BPN or PD, so BPN or PD is a characteristic of preposed subjects.

Another characteristic of the NP types of preposed subjects is that personal pronouns rarely appear preposed. Only 3% of preposed subjects are personal pronouns, but 20% of matrix subjects are personal pronouns.

We can point out one characteristic of S of the *S 'u, VX ka hiya* pattern: common nouns rarely appear. When the matrix subject is overt, there are few instances (7%) of common nouns (bare CN), modified by a demonstrative (CD), by another noun or a VP (CR), or by a genitive pronoun (CG). For S of the *S 'u, VX* pattern, one third of preposed subjects are CN, CD, CR, or CG. For matrix subjects, the rate of CN, CD, CR, and CG is higher; it is about 40%.

As for anaphoricity, there is no drastic difference between S of the *S 'u, VX ka hiya* pattern, S of the *S 'u, VX* pattern, or matrix subjects. Matrix subjects showed slightly more (57%) high scores (2) than preposed subjects (53%). Half of the instances of S of the *S 'u, VX ka hiya* pattern (50%) showed a score of 0, which is the highest proportion among the three.

This paper also examined coreference between types of NPs and anaphoricity. Difference in anaphoricity between PD and BPN seems worth noting. Most of the PD are already mentioned in the previous discourse, while BPN are not necessarily so. Also, PP and D are all mentioned in the previous discourse.

As for topic persistence, preposed S of the *S 'u, VX* pattern and matrix subjects showed similar tendencies (Table 12 in §5.3.2). Totally, 40% or 45% showed a score of 0, 23% or 19% showed a score of 1, 25% showed a score of 2, and 12% or 11% showed a score of 3. S of the *S 'u, VX ka hiya* pattern, on the other hand, showed a different tendency: only 14% showed a score of 0, 21% showed a score of 1, and 64% showed a score of 2. There are no instances of preposed subjects with overt matrix subjects that showed a score of 3.

To summarize, we can say that S of the *S 'u, VX* pattern and matrix subjects showed similar tendencies except for NP types. What type of NP it is determines whether it appears in preposed position or in regular subject position. S of the *S 'u, VX ka hiya* pattern, on the other hand, is used to give further information about a proper name. It tends to persist longer in the following clauses. As for anaphoricity, there is no drastic difference among the three.

Acknowledgments

I thank two anonymous reviewers for useful comments. Also I would like to thank Editage (www.editage.jp) for English language editing. For any mistakes in the present paper, however, solely the author is responsible.

Abbreviations

ANGER	anger	CNJ	conjunction
AV	actor voice	CV	conveyance voice
BPN	bare person name	CR	common noun modified by another noun or VP
CG	common noun modified with Genitive pronoun	D	demonstrative
CN	common noun	DIST	distant

EX	exclusive		by demonstrative
FUT	future	PL	plural
GEN	genitive	PO	Possessor
GENTLE	gentle	PP	personal pronoun
GV	goal voice	PRF	perfective
GV1	goal voice 1	PROX	proximant
GV2	goal voice 2	PRT	particle
HEARSAY	hearsay	REASON	reason
IN	inclusive	SBJ	subject
LNK	linker	SG	singular
NEG	negative	UNCERTN	uncertain
NFIN	non-finite	1	first
NOM	nominative	2	second
RDPL	reduplication	3	third
PD	person name modified		

References

Gregory, Michelle L. & Laura A. Michaelis. 2001. Topicalization and left-dislocation: A functional opposition revisited. *Journal of Pragmatics* 33. 1665–1706.

Gundel, Jeanette K., Nancy Hedberg & Ron Zacharski. 1993. Cognitive status and the form of referring expressions in discourse. *Language* 69(2). 274–307.

Himmelmann, Nikolaus P. 2005. The Austronesian languages of Asia and Madagascar: Typological characteristics. In Nikolaus P. Himmelmann & K. Alexander Adelaar (eds.), *The Austronesian languages of Asia and Madagascar*, 110–181. London: Routledge.

Huang, Lillian & Wu Hsinsheng. 2016. *An introduction to atayal grammar*. Shin-pei city, Taiwan: Council of Indigenous peoples.

Krifka, Manfred. 2007. Basic notions of information structure. In C. Fery & M. Krifka (eds.), *Interdisciplinary studies on information structure*, 13–56. Potsdam: Universitätsverlag.

Nagaya, Naonori. 2011. Rise and fall of referentiality: Articles in Philippine languages. In Foong Ha Yap, Karen Grunow-Hårsta & Janick Wrona (eds.), *Nominalization in Asian languages*, 589–626. Philadelphia, PA: John Benjamins Publishing Company.

Tsukida, Naomi. 2009. *Grammar of Seediq, Taiwan*. Tokyo: University of Tokyo (Doctoral dissertation).

Tsukida, Naomi. 2012. Goal Voice and Conveyance Voice of Seediq. In Nakamura & Kikusawa (eds.), *Objectivization and subjectivization: A typology of voice systems* (Senri Ethnological Studies 77), 77–95. Osaka: National Museum of Ethnology.

van Lier, Eva & Jan Rijkhoff. 2013. Flexible word classes in linguistic typology and grammatical theory. In Jan Rijkhoff & Eva van Lier (eds.), *Flexible word classes. Typological studies of underspecified parts of speech*, 1–30. Oxford & New York: Oxford University Press.

Part III

Information structure and prosody

Chapter 11

Some preliminary observations on prosody and information structure in Austronesian languages of Indonesia and East Timor

Nikolaus P. Himmelmann
Universität zu Köln

> This chapter provides a brief overview of what is known about prosody and information structure in the Austronesian languages of Indonesia and East Timor. It emphasizes the fact that the prosodic systems found in these languages appear to differ substantially from the better known systems found in languages such as English and German and finds that to date there is little evidence that prosody plays a major role in conveying information-structural distinctions. Of major import in this regard appears to be the fact that many Austronesian languages in the area appear to lack lexical stress as well as lexical tone. Consequently, intonational phrases lack (postlexical) pitch accents, the tonal inventory being restricted to a smallish number of edge tone combinations on the intonational phrase level plus a single boundary tone on the level of intermediate phrases. The chapter concludes with a brief discussion of a major exception to these generalisations, i.e. the group of (Austronesian) West New Guinea languages that show a bewildering variety of tonal and stress-related distinctions.

1 Introduction

Apart from some varieties of Malay, the prosodic systems found in Indonesian and East Timorese languages have not been investigated in detail to date. Still, from what is known from Malayic varieties[1] and the few studies on other languages that have been published (in particular, Stoel 2006 on Javanese and Himmelmann 2010 on Waima'a) it seems likely that prosodic PROMINENCE does not have a major role to play in marking information-structural categories. If at all, prosodic PHRASING may be of relevance in this regard inasmuch as it is not determined by syntactic or processing constraints.

---

[1]See Riesberg et al. (2018 [this volume]) for a brief summary of the relevant literature on Malayic varieties.

Nikolaus P. Himmelmann. 2018. Some preliminary observations on prosody and information structure in Austronesian languages of Indonesia and East Timor. In Sonja Riesberg, Asako Shiohara & Atsuko Utsumi (eds.), *Perspectives on information structure in Austronesian languages*, 347–374. Berlin: Language Science Press. DOI:10.5281/zenodo.1402555

Nikolaus P. Himmelmann

Current ideas on the prosodic marking of information-structural categories, in particular focus and activation status (i.e. the distinction between given, accessible and new discourse referents), are based on, and heavily biased towards, what is found in some western European languages, in particular the West Germanic languages English, German and Dutch. From a cross-linguistic point of view, the prosodic marking of information-structural categories in these languages is quite unusual and does not provide a good starting point for investigating the relationship between prosody and information structure in Austronesian languages of Indonesia. Rather, as it is argued here, it will be more productive to start with much simpler assumptions and only take on board more complex prosodic features, if the data require them.

Paradoxically, it will be useful to look at the basic ingredients of West Germanic systems in order to make clear what is meant by "simpler assumptions". Consequently, §2 briefly lists the essential features of a West Germanic system. §3 presents a general proposal for a stepwise build-up of prosodic systems, not necessarily confined to the languages under investigation. It starts from the most minimal assumptions about prosodic phrasing and stops at the level of complexity that appears to be widespread in the languages of Indonesia. §4 and §5 introduce complications to the relatively simple prosodic system sketched in §3. §4 is concerned with the further subdivision of intonational phrases (IPs) into smaller (lower-level) prosodic phrases, while §5 briefly looks at languages in eastern Indonesia where highly unusual word-prosodic systems are attested. §6 concludes.

The exposition is couched in the terminology and formalisms used in the autosegmental-metrical framework for prosodic analysis (Ladd 2008), and more specifically the Tone and Break Indices (ToBI) framework (Beckman et al. 2005). This framework is chosen because it is the currently most widely used and understood approach to prosodic analysis, and there are a number of cross-linguistic studies which make use of it (see for example the two volumes edited by Jun 2005; 2014). But the current argument does not depend on the autosegmental framework and can, in principle, also be expressed in other frameworks for prosodic analysis.

The limitation to Austronesian languages of Indonesia and East Timor is arbitrary in the sense that there are Austronesian languages outside this area that may show similar characteristics, in particular the ones in Brunei and Malaysia. However, the author is not sufficiently familiar with these other languages to be able to make useful observations with regard to western Austronesian languages more generally, not to mention Oceanic languages. This, in fact, also holds for the Indonesian part of Borneo, known as Kalimantan, where the generalizations put forward here possibly do not apply. The prosodic systems found in the languages of the Philippines very likely differ in important regards.[2]

---

[2]Thus, for example, Blust (2013: 175) notes: "The most distinctive typological feature in the sound systems of Philippine languages is the widespread occurrence of phonemic stress." The Sangiric languages in northern Sulawesi may show related contrasts. See Himmelmann & Kaufman (2018) for a more detailed assessment of this claim.

2 The West Germanic "prototype"

Abstracting away from many details, the phonological structure of an intonation phrase (IP) in West Germanic can be represented as in Figure 1. Using the conventions of the ToBI framework, the T here represents tonal targets which can be either H(igh) or L(ow). These targets can be anchored either to the edge of an IP (hence edge tones) or to a metrically strong syllable (represented by a bolded σ in Figure 1).[3] The latter are widely referred to as (postlexical) pitch accents. The difference between the two edge tone types, i.e. boundary tones and phrase accents, is further explained in §3.

$$\%T \quad T^* \quad T^*+T \quad T\text{-}T\%$$
$$\downarrow \quad \downarrow \quad \downarrow \quad \downarrow$$
$$[\sigma\sigma\sigma\boldsymbol{\sigma}\sigma\sigma\sigma\boldsymbol{\sigma}\sigma\sigma\sigma\sigma\sigma]$$

Metrically-anchored tones
T* = pitch accent (monotonal)
T*+T = pitch accent (bitonal)
Edge tones
T- = phrase accent
T% = IP boundary tone (final)
%T = IP boundary tone (initial)

Figure 1: Phonological structure of a West Germanic Intonation Phrase

The occurrence of (postlexical) pitch accents presupposes lexical stress, i.e. the phonologically organized highlighting of a syllable relative to adjacent ones by way of modulating phonetic parameters such as pitch, intensity and duration. It is doubtful that all languages have lexical stress in this sense,[4] and as further detailed in §3.2, this appears to be the case for most of the Austronesian languages of Indonesia and East Timor. Note also that even if all languages had lexical stress, it could be the case that the intonational system is organized independently of it. Thus, for example, Lindström & Remijsen (2005) claim for the Papuan language Kuot, spoken on New Ireland, that it is "a language where intonation ignores stress" (Lindström & Remijsen 2005: 839). In fact, it may be the case that the occurrence of postlexical pitch accents of the West Germanic type is rather rare cross-linguistically.

Most research on intonation, especially in the last three decades, has focussed on (postlexical) pitch accents and their function in marking information-structural cate-

---

[3] Actually, the division is not as straightforward as it is made out to be here. The placement of edge tones, in particular phrase accents, may also make reference to metrically strong syllables, as discussed in the Grice et al. (2000).

[4] The term *stress* is used throughout this chapter in exactly this sense. Note that *stress* as widely used in the literature often includes other notions such as regular rhythmic alternations between strong and weak syllables (foot structure). Claiming that Austronesian languages in the area under discussion usually do not make use of lexical stress hence does not necessarily imply that they do not make use of foot structure or other word-level prosodic distinctions.

gories, in particular focus and activation status (cf. Ladd 2008; Wagner & Watson 2010; Baumann & Kügler 2015; Zimmermann 2016 for recent reviews). While this makes sense with regard to West Germanic and possibly other European languages, it may be counterproductive simply to transfer this model to other languages, as further argued in the following section.

The major emphasis on postlexical pitch accents goes hand in hand with prioritizing information-structural categories among the three main functions that intonational marking may serve. The other two main functions are marking sentence mood (declarative vs. interrogative, etc.) and delimiting phrases on various levels (phrasing or chunking function). While the sentence mood marking function also has received considerable attention in the investigation of European languages, the phrasing function has not played a very prominent role. [5]

3 Start simple!

When looking at prosody in Austronesian languages of Indonesia (and perhaps also in many other parts of the world), it is useful to start with the simplest possible assumptions regarding a prosodic system rather than with the complex model provided by the West Germanic languages.

3.1 Lexical level

With regard to the lexical level, the simplest assumption would be that there is neither lexical stress nor lexical tone (including so-called lexical pitch accents). In the literature on Austronesian languages, as conveniently summarized in van Zanten et al. (2010), it has been widely assumed that these languages, including the ones spoken in Indonesia and East Timor, have lexical stress systems of various kinds, with a strong preference for stress to occur on the penultimate syllable. However, as van Zanten et al. remark in §4 of their survey (van Zanten et al. 2010: 99–102; see also van Heuven & van Zanten 2007a: 194), there are good reasons to doubt that the prominence phenomena discussed in the literature actually belong to the lexical level rather than to the phrasal level. As we will see further below, what has often been described as regular penultimate stress is in fact the regular occurrence of a rising-falling edge tone combination at the end of intonational phrases. The classic example is Standard Indonesian as spoken in Java, to which a wide variety of stress systems have been attributed, but where there is solid evidence that it actually lacks lexical stress (see Goedemans & van Zanten 2007 for a summary of the relevant research). The work by van Heuven and colleagues shows that this holds true for production (acoustics) as well as perception. With regard to the latter, van Zanten

---

[5]Féry (2013) argues that prosodic phrasing is actually more relevant for focus marking than prosodic prominence, hence questioning the emphasis on prosodic prominences in intonation research. However, the marking of information structure (in particular focus) is still considered the primary function of prosody in this line of argument. In line with much of the literature, it is assumed here that the phrasing function of prosody is not necessarily related to information-structural distinction. This does not preclude the possibility that phrasing sometimes may be indicative of focus domains. This issue is taken up again at the end of §3.2.

& van Heuven (1998) report a gating experiment which shows that Indonesian listeners were unable to make use of prosodic information in predicting word endings, unlike Dutch listeners who performed much better on the same (Indonesian!) stimuli.

Goedemans & van Zanten (2014) go a step further. Reflecting on the experiences accrued in over two decades of compiling and maintaining a database on stress systems attested in the world's languages (StressTyp) and in particular the fact that in more recent years a number of languages initially classified as having lexical stress had to be reclassified as having no stress, they propose the following list of criteria (or indicators) for descriptions of prominence phenomena where the proposed analysis as lexical stress is doubtful (Goedemans & van Zanten 2014: 88):

1. Stress is reported to vary in different utterances of the same word
2. Stress is reported to be a phenomenon related to phrases
3. Stress is reported to be very weak and unstable
4. Fundamental differences in stress use of various speakers reported
5. The reported stress rule makes no sense in any current metrical theory

The following three indicators are considered not to raise suspicion on their own but to strengthen doubts in case at least one of the above indicators holds true (Goedemans & van Zanten 2014: 88):

6. Position in the intonation contour influences stress location in an unexpected way
7. Numerous exceptions to the rule are reported
8. Only schwa in penultimate position rejects stress

A quick glance at the usually terse sections on stress in many a description of an Austronesian language makes it clear that more often than not several of these indicators apply and that therefore it is not advisable to assume the existence of lexical stress in a particular Austronesian language without further validation.

As for the Austronesian languages of Indonesia, the existence of lexical stress has been properly demonstrated only for very few of them. All of these languages are spoken in the easternmost part of the archipelago, in the Indonesian part of New Guinea and surrounding islands (henceforth simply called Papua in this chapter), as further discussed in §5 below.

Note also that it may be the case that there is sufficient evidence for stress-like distinctions in some languages of Sulawesi, in particular Central Sulawesi languages, as briefly discussed in Himmelmann & Kaufman (2018). Utsumi (2011) claims that in Bantik, a Sangiric language of northern Sulawesi, lexical pitch accents regularly occur on either the penultimate or the ultimate syllable (hence having a distinctive function).

3.2 Postlexical level

With regard to the postlexical level, the simplest assumption – apart from no use of prosody[6] – would be something like the structure depicted in Figure 2. It shows a string of syllables which is separated from adjacent strings of the same type by melodic and rhythmic cues. Typical rhythmic cues are lengthening the final syllable of the string and pausing. The basic melodic cue pertains to the fact that syllable strings in natural languages are produced with a coherent melody, one string being delimited from the preceding and following ones by the on- and offsets of a coherent pitch contour. Typically, there is a noticeable jump in pitch (up or down) between the offset and the next onset. Additional optional cues include non-modal voice quality such as devoicing at the end of the string or the occurrence of (non-phonemic) glottal stops at the beginning. See Himmelmann et al. (2018) for further discussion and experimentation.

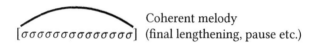

[σσσσσσσσσσσσσσ]   Coherent melody
                  (final lengthening, pause etc.)

Figure 2: A minimal prosodic structure

The minimal structure in Figure 2 can serve a basic phrasing function inasmuch as the units thus delimited are useful processing units (in terms of planning and/or comprehension). As such, their size would not be primarily determined by the exigencies of airflow management (breathing), but rather by other factors such as semantic and pragmatic considerations of information packaging. Thus, for example, Chafe (1994: 108–119) proposes that intonational phrases (intonation units in his terminology) are designed to introduce one new idea (one piece of new information) at a time into the ongoing discourse.[7] Such a function can easily be served by the units in Figure 2. To serve this function, there is no need to highlight the new information in some way, or to distinguish different types of boundaries. The only requirement is that such a unit never contain more than one piece of new information.[8] An alternative, though partially overlapping, hypothesis for the functional basis of the kind of unit depicted in Figure 2 is the idea that it corresponds to speech acts, i.e. each speech act is packaged as one prosodic unit.[9]

---

[6] "No prosody" would mean only purely physiologically conditioned variation in pitch and chunking of speech production. Speech chunks would then be completely determined by breathing requirements, with no regard for content or structure, each chunk probably starting on a relatively high pitch and gradually declining till the end of the unit. Lieberman's (1967) model of intonation is considerably more refined, but is based on a model of speech physiology which would roughly produce this kind of output, if the speaker were not allowed to control and thereby modulate the basic physiological necessities.

[7] A very similar proposal is Pawley & Syder's (2000) one-clause-at-a-time hypothesis.

[8] Obviously, the validity of Chafe's one-new-idea constraint depends on being able to provide an independent and operationalizable definition of how to identify one piece of new information. As this hypothesis only serves as an illustration of what kind of function the minimal structure in Figure 2 has, there is no need here to get into this quite complicated issue.

[9] This idea is suggested by the widely recognized sentence mood marking functions of intonation mentioned above. See Cresti (1996) for further elaboration.

A first maximally simple enrichment of the minimal structure in Figure 2 would be the addition of one type of tonal target, i.e. boundary tones, as shown in Figure 3.

%T   T%
↓   ↓
[σσσσσσσσσσσσσσ]

%T, T% = boundary tone(s) (initial, final)

Figure 3: Minimal tonal prosodic structure (boundary tones only)

In terms of function, units with the structure in Figure 3 would be capable of marking sentence mood-like distinctions in addition to the very basic information packaging function served by units of the type in Figure 2.

Further enrichment of the basic structure in Figure 3 would include the addition of a so-called phrase accent, i.e. a pitch target anchored to the edge of the phrase, but not necessarily to the very final segment.

T-T%
↓↓
[σσσσσσσσσσσσσσ]

Edge tones
T% = boundary tone
T- = phrase accent

Figure 4: Enriched minimal tonal prosodic structure (edge tones only)

The term *phrase accent* has been used for at least three, *prima facie* different kinds of phenomena:

1. for a postnuclear prominence occurring at the right edge of an intonational phrase which is part of a complex phrase-final edge tone and typically anchored to a metrically strong syllable (ToBI labels T-T%; cp. Grice et al. 2000; Ladd 2008: 142–147);

2. for the boundary tone of a so-called intermediate phrase, i.e. a phrase that is smaller than an IP but larger than a prosodic word (cf. Beckman & Pierrehumbert 1986 and much subsequent work);

3. for a major pitch excursion occurring at the right or – much more rarely – the left edge of an intonational phrase in some languages which otherwise do not appear to make phonological use of pitch changes, i.e. lacking lexical tone distinctions as well as postlexical pitch accents (e.g. French, Indonesian, Waima'a). This pitch excursion may, or may not, be accompanied by extra duration.

It is a matter for further research to determine whether these three phenomena have enough in common to warrant subsumption under a common notion. Alternatively, we are dealing with three phenomena which share the positional feature of edge placement but otherwise have different properties. Part of resolving this issue will be the question of which functions phrase accents serve. Type 2 phrase accents appear to have a boundary-marking function but is this also true for the other two types, both of which are followed by boundary tones proper? And, inasmuch as phrase accents have a boundary-marking function, what is the function of the units thus delimited?

Many Austronesian languages of Indonesia seem to have prosodic units of the basic type shown in Figure 4. The available descriptions report differences with regard to the exact placement of the phrase accents. Common options include:

- 'free' variation within a 2-syllable window (e.g. Javanese);
- mostly penultimate syllable, but sometimes also on ultima (e.g. Manado and Papuan Malay, Waima'a).

It is unclear whether these reported differences are actually factual differences. Alternatively, they arise from different analytical procedures and theoretical frameworks. With regard to Ambon Malay, Maskikit-Essed & Gussenhoven (2016) provide production evidence for an analysis which considers the configuration depicted in Figure 4 as free floating boundary tones not anchored to segmental landmarks in the same way as phrase accents in European languages (including, in particular, French). Although the pre-boundary pitch movement distinguishing this configuration from simple boundary tones as in Figure 3 is often perceived by Western researchers as being anchored to either the penultimate or the ultimate syllable, various measurements indicate that – at least in the case of Ambon Malay – the position of the peak of this pitch movement is highly variable and correlates much less strongly with potential segmental landmarks than typical European postlexical accents.

It is not clear whether this analysis for Ambon Malay also applies to other languages, which to date have not been investigated to the same degree of detail as Ambon Malay. Only such more detailed analyses will show whether the different descriptions reported above correspond to factual differences. In the remainder of this chapter, we will continue to use the term *phrase accent* to refer to the configuration in Figure 4, with the understanding that the details of the analysis, and in particular the specifics of tune-text association, are yet to be worked out.

In the current context, the question of what functions phrase accents may have in marking information structure is a major concern. In languages with relatively fixed word order, it is unlikely that the phrase accent directly marks information-structural categories such as focus, as its position is constrained to a relatively small window (usually two syllables) at the IP edge. The text occurring in this window is often just a single word (or part thereof) or the final syllable of a content word plus a phrase-final particle. Hence the phrase accent occurs on the word/word + particle that happens to be in edge position, regardless of its information-structural status. Insofar as speakers do not

11 Prosody and information structure in Indonesian and East Timor

have a choice with regard to determining which word occurs in edge position, they do not have a choice to determine which word (or syllable) is "highlighted" by the phrase accent. Compare the two examples from Papuan Malay in (1).

(1) Papuan Malay (elicited)

    a. *baju*
        shirt
        'shirt'

    b. *baju mera*
        shirt red
        'red shirt'

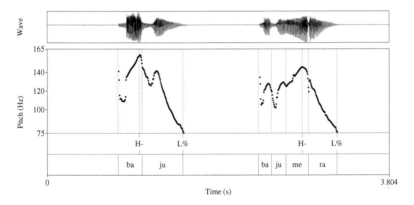

Figure 5: F0 and waveform for ex. (1a) [10]

As Figure 5 shows, the phrase accent remains at the right edge when another word is added to the phrase. That is, in a phrase such as *baju mera* the phrase accent cannot occur on *baju*, but necessarily occurs on *mera*, because the order of these two constituents cannot be changed. Consequently, in languages which make use of a phrase accent and have fixed word order in at least some phrase types, it is prosodically impossible to mark a difference in (contrastive) focus of the kind seen in English BLUE *car* vs. *blue* CAR. This is nicely illustrated by the following example provided in Stoel (2007), which comes from a corpus of Manado Malay spontaneous narrative speech.

---

[10] All acoustic analyses presented in this chapter were carried out and plotted with PRAAT (Boersma & Weenink 2015).

(2) Manado Malay (Stoel 2007: 121)
dorang mo cari   tiga: - tiga   oto (=) cuma: (0.4) kita cuma dapa satu oto
3P   ASP look.for three   three car   only   1S   only get one car
'(We planned to go to the wedding party by car.) They were looking for three ... three cars. But ... I only got one car.'

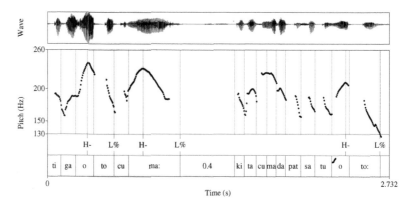

Figure 6: F0 and waveform for example (2) [11]

Despite the fact that in example (2) *tiga* 'three' is contrasted with *satu* 'one', the phrase accent occurs on *oto* in both instances, because this word takes up the final two syllables in both IPs.

The preceding examples should also make it clear why so many descriptions of Austronesian languages of Indonesia contain the assertion that lexical stress mostly/always occurs on the penultimate syllable. In elicitation, lexical items tend to be produced with the most unmarked declarative intonation pattern, which in many languages includes a phrase accent heard by the researcher to be located in the penultimate syllable, as illustrated by (1a). But when occurring in non-final position in larger structures as in (1b), more often than not no trace of this presumed lexical stress can be detected.

This also brings us back to the prosodic structure shown in Figure 1, which differs from the one in Figure 4 in that it includes metrically-anchored tonal targets in addition to edge tones. As already noted in §2, metrical anchoring presupposes lexically-based prominence differences (i.e. lexical stress) which specify the syllables that may serve as anchors for (postlexical) pitch accents. (Postlexical) pitch accents are a major way to prosodically mark the information status of individual words and phrases. Hence, the fact that prosody only plays a limited role in the expression of information structure in

---

[11] Only IP edge tones are tonally annotated here. The analysis of the rise across *kita cuma* is discussed in the following section.

many Austronesian languages of Indonesia is related to the lack of lexical stress (lexically encoded prominence differences) in many of these languages.

However, as shown by many languages around the globe including many African languages and Korean,[12] (postlexical) pitch accents may not be the only prosodic means to mark information-structural categories. Prosodic (re- or de-) phrasing may also serve this purpose. A classic and much discussed example comes from the Bantu language Chichewa as analysed by Kanerva (1990). While broad focus utterances tend to be presented in single prosodic phrases, narrow focus on one of the constituents requires the insertion of a prosodic boundary after the focussed word, as can be seen when comparing (3a) with (3b):

(3) Prosodic rephrasing in Chichewa(Kanerva 1990: 98)

    a. *(a-na-ményá   nyu^{m}bá ^{n}dí mwáála)*[13]
       1.SBJ-RECENT.PAST-hit 9.house with 3.rock

       'He hit the house with a rock.' (answering: What did he do?)

    b. *(anaméenya) (nyuú^{m}ba) (^{n}dí mwáála)*

       'He *hit* the house with a rock.' (answering: What did he do to the house with the rock?)

In fact, Féry (2013: 683) proposes "that the most common prosodic realization of focus can be subsumed typologically under the notion of alignment: a focussed constituent is preferably aligned prosodically with the right or left edge of a prosodic domain the size of either a prosodic phrase or an intonation phrase."

This view would appear to contradict our assessment above that phrase accents, which occur at the right edge of IPs, do not mark information-structural categories for the simple reason that most Austronesian languages of Indonesia do not freely allow to move focussed words into this position. While speakers thus cannot simply move words around so that they occur in IP-final position, speakers have great freedom in determining the size of an IP. So, in principle, there is the possibility to bring a focussed word into IP-final position by inserting a prosodic boundary behind it (similar to the Chichewa example (3)). However, this possibility does not appear to be systematically used in Austronesian languages of Indonesia. As we will see in the following section, there is some variability with regard to the placement of the phrase accent (at least in Manado Malay), but it is not the case that the word occurring in IP-final position always belongs to the focus domain. Furthermore, most instances of narrow focus are not signalled by inserting an IP boundary. Thus, looking again at example (2), there is no example known to this author where an IP boundary is inserted after a numeral in narrow contrastive focus (here *satu*), separating it from the following non-focussed nominal head of the phrase (here *oto*).

However, IP boundaries are not the only kind of prosodic boundary. In the literature, a fairly heterogeneous group of phrase types is distinguished in between the phonological

---

[12] See Jun (1998) for a detailed study of Korean dephrasing.
[13] Morpheme breaks and glossing from Downing & Pompino-Marschall (2013: 651). Numbers refer to noun classes.

word and the intonational phrase, these two levels being uncontroversially recognized in all frameworks and widely believed to be found in all languages (but see Schiering et al. 2010). Thus, for example, Kanerva (1990) speaks of *focus phrases* in reference to the smaller kind of phrases seen in example (3b) and argues that these are one level below the intonational phrase in Chichewa. Consequently, to provide a reasonably comprehensive survey of the relation between prosodic phrasing and information structure in Austronesian languages of Indonesia, we have to see whether there is evidence for phrasing units smaller than IPs but larger than phonological words. This will be the topic of the next section.

4 Where things get more complicated 1: Intonation (postlexical prosody)

The structure given in Figure 4 above is not the whole story for the Austronesian languages of Indonesia disposing of this basic type of prosodic structure. In addition to the pitch modulation occurring in a two syllable window at the right edge of an IP, which here is interpreted as a phrase accent, there tend to be further pitch rises earlier on in an IP which are not accounted for by Figure 4. Example (4) from Totoli illustrates this.

(4) Totoli (elicited)
 [[*i Ali*] *anu nangaan=ko*]
   PN REL AV.RLS:eat=AND
 'Ali was the one who ate it.' (Answering the question 'who ate the banana'.)

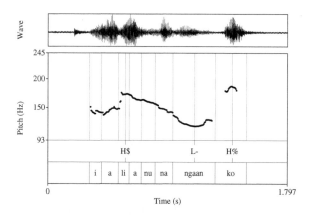

Figure 7: F0 and waveform for example (4)

That is, IPs can be prosodically chunked into smaller units which do not interrupt the melodic and rhythmic coherence of the larger IP. These smaller chunks here are called

11 Prosody and information structure in Indonesian and East Timor

intermediate phrases (ip) and the boundary tone that delimits their right edge is represented by H$ in the tonal tier. They exhibit the following features throughout the area of investigation:

- The major boundary marker for ips is a H(igh) tone on the unit-final syllable, the peak usually being located at the very end of it. This syllable is not markedly lengthened or otherwise prosodically highlighted in addition to bearing the boundary tone. In theory, the boundary marker for ips could also be a L(ow) tone, but in all the Austronesian languages of Indonesia and East Timor the author is familiar with, it is always H.

- In case there are two or more consecutive ips in an IP, the unit-final Hs tend to be downstepped. However, downstepping does not regularly include IP-final phrase accents and boundary tones, i.e. an IP-final high phrase accent or boundary tone is often (but not necessarily) higher than any of the preceding H$ targets. Example (4) illustrates this for a final H-boundary tone (H%).

- No pauses or other rhythmic boundary markers may occur at an ip boundary.

- Similarly, there is no interruption of the overall pitch contour (i.e. no offset-onset phenomena). However, there is always a tonal reset in that the beginning of the following unit always involves a (consecutive) fall to a lower pitch level. This ip-initial low(er) target is often reached within the first syllable of the following ip, but it may also occur somewhat later (2nd or even 3rd syllable). Cf. the discussion of example (5) below.

- While the rise towards the final H may begin earlier on in the unit, the penultimate syllable is not prosodically highlighted in any special way.

To date, the details of the more fine-grained prosodic structure of the ip in Austronesian languages of Indonesia are not yet well understood. There appears to be considerable variability both within and between languages. Stoel (2005; 2007) observes that in Manado Malay pitch tends to continuously rise across the ip, therefore postulating an initial L$-boundary tone. Figure 8 provides an abstract representation for the resulting structure.

The analysis shown in Figure 8 is of course only one of a number of different possible analyses for the observed state of affairs. A more standard ToBI analysis, for example, would not make use of a special symbol ($) for ip boundaries, but analyse these as phrase accents (T-) as well, i.e. conflating the 2nd and 3rd meanings of "pitch accent" distinguished in reference to Figure 8 above. A major reason for this alternative analysis is Selkirk's (1984) *Strict Layer Hypothesis* which predicts that each layer on the prosodic hierarchy is exhaustively parsed into constituents of the same type on the next lower level. Thus IPs should exclusively consist of ips. But in in Figure 8, the IP is parsed into two ips plus a third unit of an apparently different status rather than into three ips. The

$$[[\sigma\sigma\sigma\sigma\sigma]_{ip}[\sigma\sigma\sigma\sigma\sigma\sigma]_{ip}\sigma\sigma\sigma\sigma]_{IP}$$

with tones: L\$ H\$ L\$ H\$ T-T% (arrows pointing down to the respective edges)

T\$ = ip-boundary tone
T% = IP boundary tone
T- = IP phrase accent

Figure 8: The intermediate phrase (ip)

major reason for not following the more mainstream analysis here is that it is not clear that the boundary tones of ips and the phrase accent, which is a part of the edge tone combination marking IPs, really are similar enough to be considered tonal targets of the same type. We come back to this issue at the end of this section after providing more detail on the form and function of ips.

Intermediate phrases with the structure in Figure 8 are also found in East Timorese Waima'a. However, in Waima'a, ips are often essentially flat, the peak of the H\$ rise being followed by a short fall back to the base line, as seen in (5).[14]

(5) Waima'a ([pesawat_41][15])
    ne kara data naha barse ne whaka ige la   rihu ne'i wake nin(i)
    3s want alight if   seem 3s fly   PTL LOC fog PRX below POSS
    'if it were about to land, then it should fly below the clouds'

There are various possibilities for analysing the pitch trajectory in the two ips seen in Figure 9, including also an initial L(ow) boundary tone (the difference between the structure in Figure 8 and the one seen in Figure 9 would then have to be captured by different specifications for phonetic implementation). Alternatively, one could analyse this configuration as involving a final HL\$ boundary tone, with the low target usually being reached on the first or second syllable of the following unit. This is not the place to argue one or the other solution. The important point to keep in mind is that despite considerable variability regarding the details of the pitch contour, what all ips have in common is that there is an H target in the final syllable. While IPs may also end on a final H target, this final target is immediately preceded by another pitch target – the phrase accent – which is not found in ips.

As seen in example (5), an ip may be quite long and span a number of words and even complete (subordinate) clauses. It is thus clearly larger than the units analysed as *phonological words* and *accentual phrases* in the literature. Instead of *intermediary*

---

[14] This pattern is also found in Manado Malay, e.g. example 30 in Stoel (2007: 130).
[15] Examples from the corpora listed in the Sources section at the end are indexed for the recording and line they are taken from. Elision of syllables is common in natural Waima'a discourse. In (5), for example, the initial conditional clause *ne kara data naha* is shortened to *ne katatona*. The regularities of syllable elision and concomitant sound changes are, however, not yet understood.

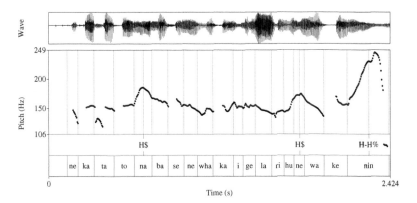

Figure 9: F0 and waveform for example (5)

phrase, the units under discussion could also be called *prosodic phrases* or *phonological phrases*.[16] All of these three terms are used in very different ways in the literature and it is not clear that the units thus labelled are actually instances of a common general type. Hence, *intermediate phrase* here specifically applies to the kinds of units defined at the beginning of this section. It is a matter for further research to determine whether these units have essential features in common with units referred to by the same label in other languages (English and Japanese, for example, as analysed in Beckman & Pierrehumbert 1986).

As a general rule, the size of ips is determined by syntax. That is, their boundaries usually match syntactic constituents such as NPs, VPs or clauses, with the possibility that heavy constituents such as NPs which include a relative clause are chunked into two ips. A fully worked out analysis of ip chunking is not yet available for any Austronesian language of Indonesia. The following patterns have been observed in the author's data for Totoli and Waima'a.

It is quite common that the initial word in an IP is chunked as an ip if it is a question word, a conjunction, or an imperative marker. In (6), the initial word is the question word *isei* 'who', in (7) it is the conjunction *tamba* 'because', and in (8) it is the negative imperative marker *deme'e* 'don't'. For such relatively short ips it appears to be the rule that pitch rises continuously throughout the ip, as seen in the corresponding figures.

---

[16] The latter term is used by Stoel (2007) who uses a slightly different analytical framework but his *phonological phrase* clearly matches what is labelled *intermediate phrase* here. To wit: "There are two prosodic constituents that are particularly relevant for the description of Manado Malay intonation: the Phonological Phrase (PhP) and the Intonation Phrase (IP). The PhP is defined here as a prosodic constituent that begins and/or ends with an edge tone. The IP is defined as a prosodic constituent that contains one or more PhPs, but no more than one pitch accent [i.e. phrase accent in the terminology used here, NPH]. IPs do not have any associated edge tones. A PhP corresponds roughly to an XP at the syntactic level, and an IP to a clause. An IP may be followed by a short pause, while a PhP may not. It is characteristic for Manado Malay that the accent-bearing unit is a relatively high-level unit, whereas in many European languages, not only the IP, but also the PhP, may have more than one accent" (Stoel 2007: 121).

(6) Totoli (elicited)
isei nangaanko saginna
who? AV.RLS:eat:AND banana:3S.POSS
'Who ate his/her banana?'

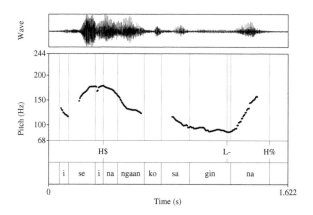

Figure 10: F0 and waveform for example (6)

(7) Waima'a (elicited)
tamba ai-sa'i aku bira
because yesterday 1S sick
'because I was sick yesterday'

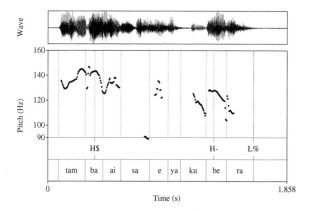

Figure 11: F0 and waveform for example (7)

(8) Waima'a (elicited)
deme'e sike mala ne'i
NEG.IMP touch box PRX
'Don't touch this box.'

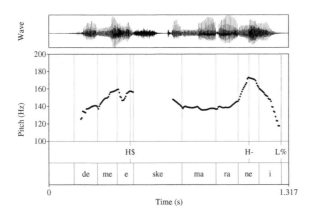

Figure 12: F0 and waveform for example (8)

Similarly, initial adverbial phrases such as *pas la n'iki* 'right here' in (9) form their own ip. In this example, the pronominal subject and the verb (*ne soke* 'he crashes') also form an ip of their own.

(9) Waima'a ([pearcarlito_101])
pas la n'iki ne soke la watu see
right LOC here 3S crash LOC stone one
'and right then he crashes into a stone.'

Initial subject or topic NPs also tend to be phrased as ips. In (10), *kii ba'an ke* 'the old man' exemplifies this preference. As opposed to the preceding example, here the following VP is not phrased independently but forms one longish final phrase together with the local adjunct *la kai-oo kai-oo ta* 'in the tree tops'. To date, the phrasing regularities for VPs and constituents following VPs are not yet well understood.

(10) Waima'a ([pearcarlito_79])
kii ba'an ke uhu naga kai-wuo la kai-oo kai-oo ta
person HON-N DEM pick CONT fruit LOC tree-top tree-top DIST
'the old man just keeps on picking fruits in the tree tops'

Finally, there is a strong tendency to phrase clauses separately in case a single IP contains more than one clause. This holds for subordinate clauses, as already exemplified with

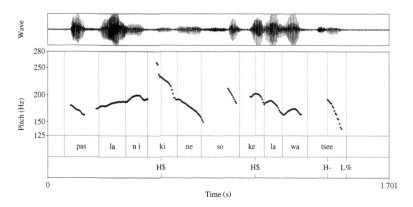

Figure 13: F0 and waveform for example (9)

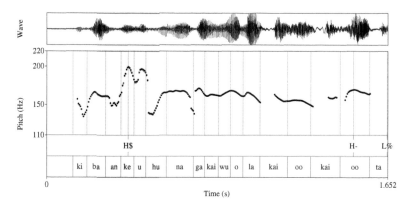

Figure 14: F0 and waveform for example (10)

example (5). Example (11) shows that the length of subordinate and main clauses does not appear to play a major role in this regard, i.e. ip boundaries are inserted even when the overall IP is relatively short.

(11) Waima'a ([pearcarlito_103])
 soke watu see ne lo'i
 crash stone one 3s fall

 'crashing into a stone, he falls'

Two clauses may also be combined in a single IP if they are parallel in structure. In example (12), the parallelism is emphasized by the preverbal particle *oo* 'too, as well' in both clauses.

11 Prosody and information structure in Indonesian and East Timor

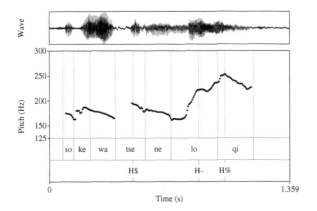

Figure 15: F0 and waveform for example (11)

(12) Waima'a ([pearcarlito_143])
wuo-telu ana oo laka ne oo laka
CLF-three DIM too go 3S too go

'the three of them walk off, (and) he also walks off'

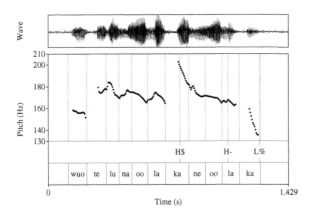

Figure 16: F0 and waveform for example (12)

The preceding examples illustrate strong tendencies where it seems reasonable to account for ip chunking in terms of syntactic structure. For these examples, it is not immediately obvious that information structure has a role to play. Nevertheless, it is also clear that a purely syntactic account will not suffice in all instances as none of these tendencies is actually obligatory (i.e. subordinate clauses do not have to be phrased as separate

365

ips, for example). It may thus very well turn out that some aspects of ip chunking are sensitive to information-structural factors.

A case in point are VPs and constituents following them. For this syntactic configuration, no clear syntactic tendencies have been detected so far (cf. examples (9) and (10) above). A particularly conspicuous example in this regard is example (5) where the final H$-boundary splits a complex PP/NP into two parts: *la rihu ne'i* 'LOC this fog('s)' and *wake nini* 'below POSS'. The first part of this PP, which contains the preposed possessor NP 'this fog', is chunked with the remainder of the clause (*barse ne whaka ige* 'it should fly' (= modal particle + subject pronoun + verb + particle). The second part consists of what is formally the head of the complex NP, the possessum 'below' (more literally: 'its underside'). Here, it may be speculated that ip chunking puts special emphasis on 'below', as flying below the fog may have prevented the plane crash reported in the narrative from which this segment is taken.

Another example for the possible influence of information structure on ip chunking comes from Manado Malay. Stoel (2007) observes the following possibility for prosodically highlighting a word which does not occur in IP-final position. In Manado Malay, it is possible to add one, and exactly one, ip after the word carrying the phrase accent. This post-accentual ip is characterized by a compressed pitch range, usually being almost flat on a low tonal level, with the possibility of ending with a smallish final fall. Example (13) can be produced in the two different prosodic shapes presented in Figure 17 and Figure 18, respectively (both elicited).[17]

(13) Manado Malay verb focus (Stoel 2007: 126)
    dia da   bamara pa Weni
    3S ASP angry   at Weni
    'She is angry at Weni.'

Note that in both instances, according to the analysis proposed by Stoel, the sentence is chunked into three ips, i.e. [dia] [da bamara] [pa Weni]. In Figure 17, the first two units are characterized by the rise from a low initial target to a H tone on the final syllable of the ip, as is typical for ips. In the third unit, *pa Weni*, there is a phrase accent on the penultimate syllable *We*, followed by a fall in the final syllable, i.e. the typical pattern marking the end of an IP. Information-structurally this is a relatively neutral rendering, compatible with broad focus and object focus contexts.

In Figure 18, on the other hand, the phrase accent occurs on the penultimate syllable of the second unit [*da baMAra*], followed by a fall which continues throughout the third unit [*pa Weni*]. The post-accentual ip is analysed by Stoel as involving only a single L boundary tone at the right edge, as opposed to the continuous L to H-rise typical for ips preceding the pitch accent. He calls it "encliticized" (Stoel 2007: 121), as it appears to contain (usually already) well-known information that is added to a unit which in itself is already complete. The rendering in Figure 18 is appropriate for contexts involving a

---

[17] The following three figures are directly quoted from Stoel (2007), hence the difference in layout and annotation detail. No sound files were available to the present author.

11 Prosody and information structure in Indonesian and East Timor

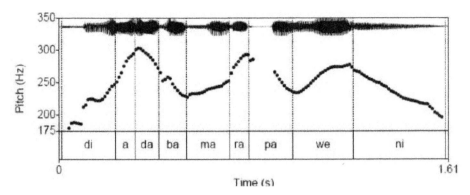

Figure 17: Example (13) with unmarked prosodic phrasing (= Figure 5 in Stoel 2007: 126)

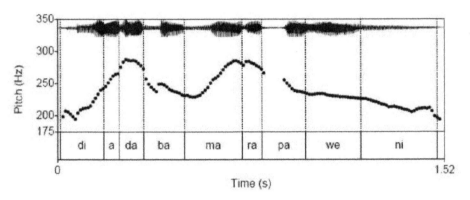

Figure 18: Example (13) with verb focus (= Figure 6 in Stoel 2007: 127)

narrow focus on the predicate. Example (14) illustrates narrow focus on the predicate from spontaneous speech.

(14) Manado Malay verb focus Stoel 2007: 126
 da orang cari pa ngana
 ASP person look.for at 2S
 'Somebody was looking for you.'

Finally, there are examples where the *lack* of expected ip chunking appears to be influenced by information-structural considerations. This is attested in utterances where the utterance-final word carries contrastive focus as in *she does not like* RED, *she likes* GREEN. The Waima'a example in (15) illustrates.

367

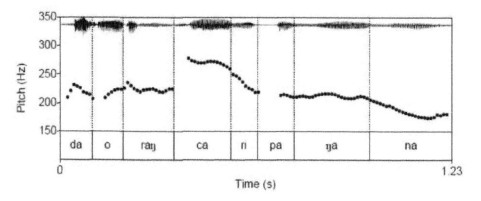

Figure 19: Example (14) with verb focus (= Figure 8 in Stoel 2007: 128)

(15) Waima'a (elicited)
      ne de   kara haru lumu
      3S NEG like shirt green
      'S/he doesn't like the green shirt.'

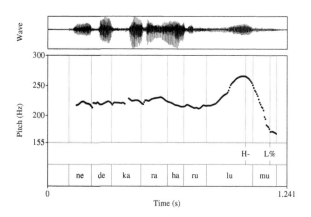

Figure 20: F0 and waveform for example (15)

However, that the lack of ip chunking may be a way to convey contrastive focus on the word it appears on is only a conjecture that needs more testing and research. Note that even if this conjecture turns out to be true, it would not allow for a consistent marking of contrastively focussed items because the phrase accent is confined to the phrase-final word. Hence, in the current example it would not be possible to contrast the SHIRT *green* with the SKIRT *green* because the word order requires the adjective to follow the noun (cf. example (2) above).

11 Prosody and information structure in Indonesian and East Timor

To sum up this section, the intonational structure in Austronesian languages of Indonesia and East Timor appears to be more complicated than suggested by Figure 4, because there is an additional level of intonational structure below the IP, i.e. the intermediate phrase. The regularities obtaining for ips are not yet well understood. This concerns both their tonal structure and the factors determining ip boundaries. The major tonal target in an ip is a H tone which consistently appears on the final syllable. What is not clear yet, is whether there is also an initial tonal target (in at least some of the languages in the region) and how to analyse the different trajectories for reaching the final H$ (continuous rise throughout the ip vs. rise over the last few syllables of the ip vs. steep rise on the final syllable only).

A further unresolved issue – briefly mentioned in connection with Figure 8 – is the question of how to analyse the (usually) final segment of an IP which follows the last H$ and contains the phrase accent and final boundary tone. Should this segment also be analysed as an ip (as the strict layer hypothesis Selkirk 1984 would demand)? But then, how can one explain the fact that tonal targets in this segment can be much more varied than in pre-final ips and obey different alignment regularities than the final boundary tone of ips? One option is to assume that ip-level tones are deleted at IP boundaries and overwritten by the higher-level IP edge tones, as proposed by Khan & Khan (2014: 83) for Bengali (similar proposals have also been made for other languages, as pointed out by Khan & Khan 2014). However, it is not clear what kind of empirical evidence would support such an analysis. Furthermore, inasmuch as IP-level boundary tones are of a different type and do not include ip-level tones as a constituent (as in the model of Beckman & Pierrehumbert 1986, for example), this can still be seen as a violation of the strict layer hypothesis.

As for boundary-determining factors, it is clear that ip boundaries generally obey major syntactic phrase boundaries such as NP, VP and PP. But exceptions occur, as seen in example (5). Furthermore, there appears to be a general tendency to phrase separately preverbal constituents of various types, including nominal and prepositional phrases and single word-constituents such as question words and conjunctions. The latter clearly show that constituent length is not a primary factor in ip chunking. There is also a clear tendency to phrase clauses separately if they occur in a single IP. No regularities for the VP and following constituents have been discovered so far. Similarly, it is not clear why expected ip boundaries are occasionally missing. It may well be the case that these types of examples involve information-structural influences on ip-phrasing.

5 Where things get more complicated 2: Tone and stress (lexical prosody)

In §3.1, it was noted that there is little or no evidence for word-prosodic distinctions in many Austronesian languages of Indonesia. In particular, there is little evidence for lexical stress, which is of primary concern here. The present section serves to briefly point out that, though comparatively rare, the Austronesian languages of Indonesia may show considerable prosodic complexity on the word level, in particular in the eastern parts of Indonesia.[18] Furthermore, and more importantly, it seems that wherever there are word-prosodic distinctions they tend to be highly constrained in terms of (a) the position within the word or phrase, (b) the types of contrast allowed for, and (c) the interaction with other prosodic subsystems.

Tonal contrasts have been reported primarily for a number of Austronesian West New Guinea languages (spoken in Indonesia's two easternmost provinces Papua and Papua Barat). Remijsen (2001) and Kamholz (2014: Chapter 5) provide succinct surveys as to what is known about tone in Austronesian Papua.[19] The languages analysed so far show a broad variety of tonal systems. Magey Matbat, spoken on Misol, one of the Raja Ampat islands, is analysed by Remijsen (2007) as a syllable tone language with six different tones. A large part of the Magey Matbat vocabulary appears to be monosyllabic, but bi- and trisyllabic words also occur. All monosyllabic words bear tone. From the few examples provided in Remijsen (2007) it appears that at least one syllable in polysyllabic words is toneless, but the position of tone-bearing syllables is not predictable. This contrasts with Moor, a language spoken in southern Cenderawasih Bay, which is analysed by Kamholz (2014: 101–106) as disposing of four tonal patterns. Tonal marking in Moor is largely confined to the final two syllables. More importantly, and rather unusually for a tone language, "tones are realized only on phrase-final words" (Kamholz 2014: 102). It seems likely that tonal marking here interacts with the phrase-accent+boundary tone typical for IPs in Austronesian languages of Indonesia, a topic not addressed by Kamholz.

A particularly complex – and cross-linguistically unusual – word-prosodic system is found in Ma'ya, the largest of the Raja Ampat languages. (Remijsen 2001; Remijsen 2002) makes a convincing case for an analysis in terms of both lexical stress and lexical tone. There are three tonal contrasts which, however, are confined to the final syllable. In addition, lexical bases differ in whether they are stressed on the penultimate or ultimate syllable. That is, there are minimal pairs which differ only with regard to tone, e.g. sa^{12} 'to sweep' vs. sa^3 'to climb' vs. toneless sa 'one' (Remijsen 2002: 596). And there are minimal pairs differing only in stress, e.g. $'mana^3$ 'light (of weight)' vs. $ma'na^3$ 'grease' (Remijsen 2002: 600). Note that Remijsen (2002: 602–610) provides detailed acoustic evidence for the proposed stress difference, which includes not only duration measures, but also differences in vowel quality and spectral balance.

Unfortunately, neither Remijsen nor Kamholz discuss postlexical prosody in the languages they investigate. Hence it is unclear whether the word-level prosodies interact with postlexical tonal marking. Consequently, it is also unclear whether word-level prosodies have any role to play in conveying information-structural distinctions.

---

[18]This is not intended to be a comprehensive survey of word prosodies in Austronesian languages of Indonesia, for which see van Zanten et al. (2010) (to be read with the caveats found in van Heuven & van Zanten 2007b and Goedemans & van Zanten 2014).

[19]It is quite likely that there are more tone languages in this area than listed in Kamholz (2014). Among the Raja Empat languages, Ambel also has tone (Arnold 2017). In Yapen, current work by the author points to tone in Wooi.

6 Conclusion

In this chapter, it has been argued that prosodic systems in the Austronesian languages of Indonesia work somewhat differently from what is known from West Germanic languages (on which most current prosodic theory is based), and should be approached accordingly. Most importantly perhaps, there is little evidence for lexical stress in many of these languages. And even if there are stress-like distinctions, it should not be presumed that these interact with the intonational system in a way similar to what has been found for Germanic languages (i.e. 'stressed' syllables do not necessarily serve as anchors for intonational tonal targets, recall Lindström & Remijsen's 2005 "a language where intonation ignores stress"). Intonational targets appear to be placed with reference to the boundaries of prosodic units. Two types of units need to be distinguished, the higher-level Intonational Phrase (IP) and the lower level intermediate phrase (ip). Regularities for phrasing on both levels are not yet very well understood. Information-structural factors such as focus and activation status may play a role here, but it is unlikely that they suffice for a full account of prosodic phrasing on either level.

Sources

Data on Totoli, Waima'a and Papuan Malay are from language documentation projects the author has participated in. They are all available in the *DoBeS Archive* (http://dobes.mpi.nl/) in the following subcollections:
Belo, Maurício C.A, John Bowden, John Hajek, Nikolaus P. Himmelman & Alexandre V. Tilman. 2002–2006. *DoBeS Waima'a Documentation*. DoBeS Archive MPI Nijmegen.
Leto, Claudia, Winarno S. Alamudi, Nikolaus P. Himmelmann, Jani Kuhnt - Saptodewo, Sonja Riesberg & Hasan Basri. 2005–2010. *DoBeS Totoli Documentation*, DoBeS Archive MPI for Psycholinguistics Nijmegen.

Acknowledgements

I gratefully acknowledge very pertinent and helpful comments by two anonymous reviewers who thoroughly read and commented on the draft of this chapter. Very special thanks to Gabriele Schwiertz and Patrick Coenen for help with the figures and the layout. I am also very grateful for a number of grants by the Volkswagen foundation I have had the privilege to receive since 2002 and without which the research on which this chapter is based would not have been possible. Many thanks to my colleagues and friends at the Center for Endangered Language Documentation (CELD) in Manokwari for much help and support in trying to understand the languages of West Papua. I am grateful to the Center of Excellence for the Dynamics of Language (CoEDL) at the Australian National University for providing a congenial environment to carry out the major revisions of this chapter. Work on this chapter was also supported by the SFB 1252 "Prominence in Language", project A03 "Prosodic prominence in cross-linguistic perspective".

Abbreviations

Conventions in the examples: each line is one IP; (=) indicates latching; pause length is given in ( ); - marks truncated IPs; < > surround false starts.

Glosses for grammatical categories:

AND	andative	N	phrase-final nasal in Waima'a with attributive function
ASP	aspectual particle		
AV	actor voice		
CLF	classifier	NEG	negation
CONT	continuative (aspect)	P	plural pronoun
DEM	demonstrative	POSS	possessive
DET	determiner	PN	personal name marker
DIM	diminutive	PRX	proximal (demonstrative)
DIST	distal (demonstrative)	PTL	particle
HON	honorific	REL	relative marker
IMP	imperative	RLS	realis
LOC	locative (preposition)	S	singular pronoun
		SBJ	subject

References

Arnold, Laura. 2017. *A Grammar of Ambel.* University of Edinburgh (Doctoral dissertation).

Baumann, Stefan & Frank Kügler. 2015. Prosody and information status in typological perspective. *Lingua* 165. 179–316.

Beckman, Mary E., Julia Hirschberg & Stefanie Shattuck-Hufnagel. 2005. The original ToBI system and the evolution of the ToBI framework. In Sun-Ah Jun (ed.), *Prosodic typology: The phonology of intonation and phrasing*, 9–54. Oxford: Oxford University Press.

Beckman, Mary E. & Janet B. Pierrehumbert. 1986. Intonational structure in Japanese and English. *Phonology Yearbook* 3. 255–309.

Blust, Robert. 2013. *The Austronesian languages.* Canberra. http://hdl.handle.net/1885/10191. Revised edition.

Boersma, Paul & David Weenink. 2015. *Praat: Doing phonetics by computer.* Vol. Version 5.4.09. http://www.praat.org/. Accessed 2015-09.

Chafe, Wallace L. 1994. *Discourse, consciousness, and time: The flow and displacement of conscious experience in speaking and writing.* Chicago: University of Chicago Press.

Cresti, Emanuela. 1996. Speech acts units and informational units. In Elisabetta Fava (ed.), *Speech acts and linguistic research*, 89–107. Padova: Edizioni Nemo.

Downing, Laura J. & Bernd Pompino-Marschall. 2013. The focus prosody of Chichewa and the stress-focus constraint: A response to Samek-Lodovici 2005. *Natural Language and Linguistic Theory* 31. 647–681.

Féry, Caroline. 2013. Focus as prosodic alignment. *Natural Language and Linguistic Theory* 31. 683–734.

Goedemans, Robert W. N. & Ellen van Zanten. 2007. Stress and accent in Indonesian. In Vincent J. van Heuven & Ellen van Zanten (eds.), *Prosody in Indonesian languages*, 35–63. Utrecht: LOT.

Goedemans, Robert W. N. & Ellen van Zanten. 2014. Above and beyond the segments: Experimental linguistics and phonetics. In Johanneke Caspers, Yija Chen, Willemijn F. L. Heeren, Jos J. A. Pacilly, Niels O. Schiller & Ellen van Zanten (eds.), *No stress typology*, 83–95. Amsterdam: John Benjamins Publishing Company.

Grice, Martine, Robert D. Ladd & Amalia Arvaniti. 2000. On the place of phrase accents in intonational phonology. *Phonology* 17. 143–185.

Himmelmann, Nikolaus P. 2010. Notes on Waima'a intonation. In Michael Ewing & Marian Klamer (eds.), *East Nusantara: Typological and areal analyses*, 47–69. Canberra: Pacific Linguistics.

Himmelmann, Nikolaus P. & Daniel Kaufman. 2018. Prosodic systems: Austronesia. In Carlos Gussenhoven & Aoju Chen (eds.), *The Oxford handbook of language prosody*. Oxford: Oxford University Press.

Himmelmann, Nikolaus P., Meytal Sandler, Jan Strunk & Volker Unterladstetter. 2018. On the universality of intonational phrases – a cross-linguistic interrater study. *Phonology* 35(2). 207–245.

Jun, Sun-Ah. 1998. The accentual phrase in the Korean prosodic hierarchy. *Phonology* 15. 189–226.

Jun, Sun-Ah (ed.). 2005. *Prosodic typology: The phonology of intonation and phrasing*. Oxford: Oxford University Press.

Jun, Sun-Ah (ed.). 2014. *Prosodic typology II: The phonology of intonation and phrasing*. Oxford: Oxford University Press.

Kamholz, David C. 2014. *Austronesians in Papua: Diversification and change in South Halmahera-West New Guinea*. Berkley: University of California dissertation.

Kanerva, Jonni M. 1990. *Focus and phrasing in Chichewa phonology*. New York: Garland.

Khan, Sameer & Volker Khan. 2014. The intonational phonology of Bangladeshi Standard Bengali. In Sun-Ah Jun (ed.), *Prosodic typology II: The phonology of intonation and phrasing*, 82–117. Oxford: Oxford University Press.

Ladd, Robert D. 2008. *Intonational phonology*. 2nd edn. Cambridge: Cambridge University Press.

Lieberman, Philip. 1967. *Intonation, perception, and language*. Cambridge: MIT Press.

Lindström, Eva & Bert Remijsen. 2005. Aspects of the prosody of Kuot, a language where intonation ignores stress. *Linguistics* 43. 839–870.

Maskikit-Essed, Raechel & Carlos Gussenhoven. 2016. No stress, no pitch accent, no prosodic focus: The case of Ambonese Malay. *Phonology* 33. 353–389.

Pawley, Andrew & Frances Syder. 2000. The one-clause-at-a-time hypothesis. In Heidi Riggenbach (ed.), *Perspectives on fluency*, 163–198. Ann Arbor: U. Michigan Press.

Remijsen, Bert. 2001. *Word-prosodic systems of Raja Ampat languages*. Leiden University dissertation.

Remijsen, Bert. 2002. Lexically contrastive stress accent and lexical tone in Ma'ya. In Carlos Gussenhoven & Natasha Warner (eds.), *Laboratory phonology VII*, 585–614. Berlin: de Gruyter.

Remijsen, Bert. 2007. Lexical tone in Magey Matbat. In Vincent J. van Heuven & Ellen van Zanten (eds.), *Prosody in Austronesian languages of Indonesia*, 9–34. Utrecht: LOT.

Riesberg, Sonja, Janina Kalbertodt, Stefan Baumann & Nikolaus P. Himmelmann. 2018. On the perception of prosodic prominences and boundaries in Papuan Malay. In Sonja Riesberg, Asako Shiohara & Atsuko Utsumi (eds.), *A cross-linguistic perspective on information structure in Austronesian languages*. Berlin: Language Science Press.

Schiering, René, Balthasar Bickel & Kristine A. Hildebrandt. 2010. The prosodic word is not universal, but emergent. *Journal of Linguistics* 46. 657–709.

Selkirk, Elisabeth O. 1984. *Phonology and syntax: The relation between sound and structure*. Cambridge: The MIT Press.

Stoel, Ruben B. 2005. *Focus in Manado Malay: Grammar, particles, and intonation*. Leiden: CNWS Publications.

Stoel, Ruben B. 2006. The intonation of Banyumas Javanese. In Hansjörg Mixdorff & Rüdiger Hoffmann (eds.), *Proceedings of the Speech Prosody 2006 conference*, 827–830. Dresden: TUDpress.

Stoel, Ruben B. 2007. The intonation of Manado Malay. In Vincent J. van Heuven & Ellen van Zanten (eds.), *Prosody in Indonesian languages*, 117–150. Utrecht: LOT.

Utsumi, Atsuko. 2011. Reduplication in the Bantik language. *Asian and African Languages and Linguistics* 6. 5–26.

van Heuven, Vincent J. & Ellen van Zanten. 2007a. Concluding remarks. In Vincent J. van Heuven & Ellen van Zanten (eds.), *Prosody in Indonesian languages*, 191–202. Utrecht: LOT.

van Heuven, Vincent J. & Ellen van Zanten (eds.). 2007b. *Prosody in Austronesian languages of Indonesia*. Utrecht: LOT.

van Zanten, Ellen, Ruben Stoel & Ruben Remijsen. 2010. Stress types in Austronesian languages. In Harry van der Hulst, Robert W. N. Goedemans & Ellen van Zanten (eds.), *A survey of word accentual patterns in the languages of the world*, 87–112. Berlin: de Gruyter.

van Zanten, Ellen & Vincent J. van Heuven. 1998. Word stress in Indonesian: Its communicative relevance. *Bijdragen tot de Taal-, Land- and Volkenkunde* 154. 129–147.

Wagner, Michael & Duane G. Watson. 2010. Experimental and theoretical advances in prosody: A review. *Language and cognitive processes* 25. 905–945.

Zimmermann, Malte. 2016. Information structure. *Oxford Bibliographies in Linguistics*. DOI:10.1093/obo/9780199772810-0130

Chapter 12

Focus and prosody in Tagalog

Naonori Nagaya
Tokyo University of Foreign Studies

Hyun Kyung Hwang
RIKEN Brain Science Institute

In this paper, we look into the interaction between focus and prosody in Tagalog. In this language, for most focus conditions regular correspondences between syntax and information structure are observed: canonical constructions are used for sentence focus and predicate focus conditions, while pseudocleft constructions are used for argument focus conditions. However, some wh-questions, in particular targeting non-agent arguments, can be answered by means of canonical constructions as well as pseudocleft constructions. In this experimental study, we examine production data in order to test how Tagalog speakers prosodically distinguish canonical sentences associated with different focus structures. The results reveal that F0 cues and intensity consistently differentiate focused conditions from all-old utterances throughout the entire sentence. However, the distinct focus conditions are not prosodically differentiated. As for the argument focus condition, there may be durational effects applying to the phrase in narrow focus, but this needs further confirmation.

1 Mismatch between syntactic and focus structure

Tagalog, an Austronesian language of the Philippines, has VSO word order, displaying VO word order correlates in a relatively consistent manner. Thus, in typical transitive clauses as in (1) a predicative verb appears in the clause-initial position, followed by arguments and adjuncts. Arguments and adjuncts are marked by either determiner-like case-markers or prepositions. In this paper, we refer to this type of verb-predicate clause as the canonical construction.

(1) Kumain si Mama ng mami sa kusina.
    K<um>ain si=Mama   nang=mami[1] sa= kusina.
    eat<AV> P.NOM=Mama GEN=noodles LOC= kitchen
    'Mama ate noodles in the kitchen.'

Naonori Nagaya & Hyun Kyung Hwang. 2018. Focus and prosody in Tagalog. In Sonja Riesberg, Asako Shiohara & Atsuko Utsumi (eds.), *Perspectives on information structure in Austronesian languages*, 375–388. Berlin: Language Science Press. DOI:10.5281/zenodo.1402557

Tagalog also has another construction type, where one of the arguments appears in the clause-initial position. We call this construction type a pseudocleft construction in the sense that it involves an equational clause structure with a *wh*-relative clause-like structure.[2] To illustrate, consider (2) and (3).

(2) *Si Mama ang kumain ng mami.*
    Si=   Mama ang=[k<um>ain nang= mami].
    P.NOM= Mama NOM=eat<AV> GEN= noodles
    'The one who ate noodles is Mama.'
    'Mama is the one who ate noodles.'

(3) *Ang mami ang kinain ni Mama.*
    (Ang=)mami   ang=[k<in>ain   ni=   Mama].
    NOM=noodles NOM=eat<PV.PFV> P.GEN= Mama
    'What Mama ate is noodles.'

As seen in these examples, canonical and pseudocleft constructions share the same propositional content. A contrast between the two construction types lies in the focus assignment patterns with which they are associated (Kaufman 2005, Nagaya 2007; see Lambrecht 1994 for the notion of focus structure used here). On the one hand, canonical constructions are employed for either sentence focus or predicate focus structures, see (4) and (5), respectively.

(4) Q: *Anong nangyari?*
       Ano ='ng nang-yari?
       what =NOM AV:PFV-happen
       'What happened?'
    A: *Kumain si Mama ng mami.*
       K<um>ain si=Mama   nang= mami.
       eat<AV> P.NOM=Mama GEN= noodles
       'Mama ate noodles.'

(5) Q: *Anong ginawa ni Mama?*
       Ano ='ng g<in>awa ni=   Mama?
       what =NOM do<PV:PFV> P.GEN= Mama
       'What did Mama do?'
    A: *Kumain siya ng mami.*
       K<um>ain=siya   nang=mami.
       eat<AV>=3SG.NOM GEN=noodles
       'She ate noodles.'

---

[1] In the commonly-used Tagalog orthography, the diagraph *ng* represents a velar nasal /ŋ/. An exception is the genitive case-marker for common nouns, which is pronounced as [naŋ] but spelled as *ng*. In this paper, however, it is presented as *nang* instead of *ng* for the sake of convenience.

[2] See Kaufman (2009; 2018 [this volume]) for another view of this construction type.

On the other hand, pseudocleft constructions are employed for narrow focus or argument focus, where the initial constituent of a clause is exclusively focused. In particular, this construction type is the only option in contrastive focus contexts. Example (6) illustrates an explicit contrast.

(6) A: *K<um>ain=daw si=Maria nang= mami.*
    eat<AV>=hearsay P.NOM=Maria GEN= noodles
    '(They say) Maria ate noodles.'

   B: *Hindi. Si=Mama ang=[k<um>ain nang= mami].*
   NEG P.NOM=Mama NOM=eat<AV> GEN= noodles
   'No. It is Mama (not Maria) who ate noodles.'

Not surprisingly, *wh*-questions must take the form of pseudocleft constructions, as in (7) and (8). Attention should be paid to the structural parallelism between (2)/(3) and (7)/(8).

(7) *Sino ang=[k<um>ain nang= mami]?* [*cf.* (2)]
    who.NOM NOM=eat<AV> GEN= noodles
    'Who is the one who ate noodles?'
    'Who ate noodles?'

(8) *Ano ang=[k<in>ain ni= Mama]?* [*cf.* (3)]
    what NOM=eat<PV:PFV> P.GEN= Mama
    'What is it that Mama ate?'
    'What did Mama eat?'

To summarize, in Tagalog, canonical constructions are used for predicate focus (henceforth PF) and sentence focus (henceforth SF), while pseudocleft constructions are employed for argument focus (henceforth AF). See Table 1 for a summary of these observations.

Table 1: Construction types and focus structures in Tagalog

Construction type	Focus structure	Contexts
Canonical construction	Predicate Focus (PF)	'What happened to X?' 'What did X do?'
Pseudocleft construction	Sentence Focus (SF) Argument Focus (AF)	'What happened?' 'only' focus of negation/correction *wh*-question

However, the summary in Table 1 slightly overstates the regularity of the correspondence between syntactic and focus structure because questions targeting an argument do not require a pseudocleft construction as the answer. Rather, a question such as 'What did Mama eat?' allows for three types of answers, as seen in (9).

(9) Q: *Ano ang kinain ni Mama?* [=(8)]
        <u>Ano</u> ang=[k<in>ain   ni=   Mama]?
        what NOM=eat<PV:PFV> P.GEN= Mama
      '<u>What</u> is it that Mama ate?'
      '<u>What</u> did Mama eat?'

    A0: <u>Mami</u>.
        noodles
      '<u>Noodles</u>.'

    A1: *Kumain siya ng <u>mami</u>.* [Canonical]
        K<um>ain=siya   nang= <u>mami</u>.
        eat<AV>=3SG.NOM GEN= noodles
      'She ate <u>noodles</u>.'

    A2: *<u>Mami</u> ang kinain niya.* [Pseudocleft]
        <u>Mami</u>   ang=k<in>ain=niya.
        noodles NOM=eat<PV:PFV>=3SG.GEN
      'What she ate is <u>noodles</u>.'

That is, the question *Ano ang kinain ni Mama?* 'What did Mama eat?' can be answered with a pseudocleft construction in (9A2) as well as with a canonical construction in (9A1), despite the fact that here only one argument is in focus. In (9A1), then, we see a mismatch between syntactic and focus structure deviating from the regularities stated in Table 1.

Note that such a mismatch is not possible when the agent NP is the target of a wh-question. Consider (10).

(10) Q: *Sino ang bumili ng mami?*
         Sino ang= b<um>ili nang= mami?
         who NOM= buy<AV> GEN= noodles
       'Who bought noodles?'

    A1: *Si Mama.*

    A2: *??Bumili si Mama ng mami.* [canonical]
        B<um>ili si=   Mama nang= mami.
        buy<AV> P.NOM= Mama GEN= noodles
      'Mama bought noodles.'

    A3: *Si Mama ang bumili.* [pseudocleft]
        Si=   Mama ang= b<um>ili.
        P.NOM Mama NOM= buy<AV>
      'It is Mama who bought noodles.'

To answer a question targeting the agent, one can employ an agent NP by itself as in (10A1) or a pseudocleft construction as in (10A3). However, the use of a canonical construction in (10A2) is not felicitous. So, canonical constructions are only legitimate answers to argument questions if the argument asked for does not bear the agent role.

With regard to the constructions where syntactic and focus structure do not properly match the generalizations captured in Table 1, the question arises whether in such constructions the narrowly focused constituents differ prosodically from non-focused constituents. That is, do Tagalog speakers prosodically distinguish argument focus (9A1) from predicate focus (5A) in the canonical construction?

In order to answer this question, we carried out a phonetic experiment. Our working hypothesis is that canonical constructions with different focus structures display the same syntax but with different prosodic cues, such as MaxF0 and duration. To the best of our knowledge, the interaction between focus and prosody in Tagalog has not been well explored in experimental studies (cp. Kaufman 2005). Our study will be the first experimental research on this matter.

The rest of this paper is organized as follows: in §2, we give a detailed description of the method employed for this experimental study. In §3, the results of the experiment and analyses of them are provided. §4 concludes this paper.

2 Method

In this experimental study, we look into the question of whether Tagalog speakers prosodically distinguish canonical sentences associated with different focus structures. To investigate this question, we make an acoustic comparison of the target sentence *Bumili siya nang mami* 'She bought noodles' in four different focus contexts: SF, PF, AF, and All-Old contexts (henceforth AO). See (11), (12), (13), and (14), respectively.

(11) Q: *Ano ='ng nang-yari?*
what =NOM AV:PFV-happen
'What happened?'

A: *B<um>ili =siya   nang= mami.*
buy<AV> =3SG.NOM GEN= noodles
'She bought noodles.'

(12) Q: *Ano ='ng g<in>awa   ni=   Mama?*
what =NOM do<PV:PFV> P.GEN= Mama
'What did Mama do?'

A: *B<um>ili =siya   nang= mami.*
buy<AV> =3SG.NOM GEN= noodles
'She <u>bought noodles</u>.'

(13) Q: Ano ='ng [b<in>ili   ni=   Mama]?
       what =NOM buy<PV:PFV> P.GEN= Mama
       'What did Mama buy?'
    A: B<um>ili=siya   nang= mami.
       buy<AV>=3SG.NOM GEN= noodles
       'She bought noodles.'

(14) Q: B<um>ili =ba si=   Mama nang= mami?
       buy<AV> =Q P.NOM= Mama GEN= noodles
       'Did Mama buy noodles?'
    A: Oo, b<um>ili =siya   nang= mami.
       yes buy<AV> =3SG.NOM GEN= noodles
       'Yes, she bought noodles.'

For this experiment, five male participants were recorded. See Table 2. All of them are college students in their twenties. They are native speakers of Tagalog but from different dialectal backgrounds: Quezon City (3), Rizal (1), Laguna (1). They also speak English as a second language. The recordings were made at the University of the Philippines, Diliman. All recording sessions were organized and supervised by the first author. A portable recorder (Zoom H5) with a head-mounted microphone (Shure Beta 54) was employed for the recordings.

Table 2: List of participants

Participant	Hometown	Gender	Age
Speaker 1	Laguna	male	21
Speaker 2	Quezon City	male	20
Speaker 3	Quezon City	male	21
Speaker 4	Rizal	male	23
Speaker 5	Quezon City	male	25

During the recording sessions, participants were asked to read the answers in a list of question-answer pairs. The four target pairs (SF, PF, AF and AO contexts) were randomly dispersed together with nine dummy pairs. See the Appendix for the complete list of question-answer pairs used for this experiment. Each participant repeated the whole list ten times.

At the recording, each participant was instructed to exchange a conversation with another participant. More precisely, one participant asked the questions, and another participant answered them.[3] Speaker 1 was paired with Speakers 2 and 3. Speakers 4 and 5 were paired. Only answers were recorded. Before the actual recording session, participants were asked to practice by reading the two sets of sentences.

3 Results and discussion

3.1 Impressionistic comparison of pitch contours

A total of 200 utterances (4 information status x 5 speakers x 10 repetitions) were analyzed. In analyzing the data, prosodic word boundaries were manually marked on each utterance. The target sentence *Bumili siya nang mami* 'She bought noodles' was divided into three prosodic words[4]:

- *bumili* 'bought' (P)
- *siya* 'she' (N)
- *nang mami* 'noodles' (A)

For impressionistic comparison of the pitch contours as a function of information status, time-normalized pitch tracks in semitone are plotted in Figure 1, averaging across all renditions by each speaker. Overall, the AO condition yielded lower F0s compared to all focused conditions across all speakers. In comparing different focus types, however, speakers exhibited slightly distinct patterns. As shown in the top-left panel of Figure 1, Speaker 1 produced the SF condition (dark solid line) with a slightly higher pitch than the other focus conditions, but no substantial difference was observed between PF (dotted line) and AF (dashed line) in terms of F0. On the other hand, Speaker 2 (top-right panel) exhibited somewhat higher F0 peaks of P and A in the PF condition (dotted line) than in the other focus conditions. The prosodic manifestation of information status of this particular speaker seems to be different from the other speakers in that the overall shapes of contours are quite distinct. Specifically, the contours of Speaker 2 in the PF and AO conditions show a different overall pattern from the ones found for AF or SF whereas those of the other speakers exhibit more or less similar overall contour shapes in all information conditions. Speaker 3 (mid-left panel) seems to be quite sensitive to the presence or absence of focus, but does not distinguish different types of focus; PF, SF and AF yielded nearly the same F0 contours. Speaker 4 (mid-right panel) and Speaker 5 (bottom panel) produced SF and PF with a somewhat higher F0 than AF but no remarkable difference was found between information conditions.

---

[3]We thank one of the reviewers who hinted at possible effects of convergence between two speakers (see Garrod & Pickering 2009; Kim et al. 2012; Gorisch et al. 2012) in this setting. However, it seems that such effects were not seriously large in our data because two speakers who exchanged conversations in the recording session exhibited quite different prosodic patterns.

[4]"P", "N", and "A" are labels for prosodic words. They are abbreviations of "predicate", "nominative", and "accusative". But this does not imply that Tagalog has a nominative-accusative case system.

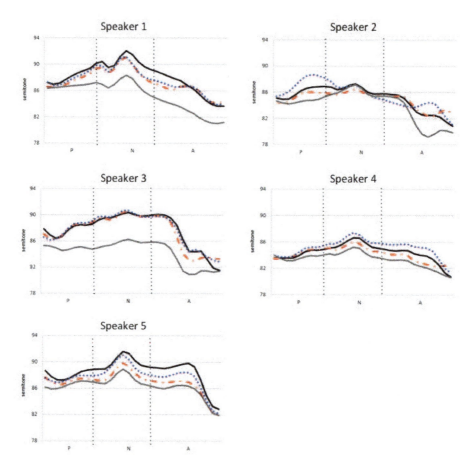

Figure 1: F0 contours of each speaker in semitone: SF, AF, PF and AO are represented by dark solid lines, dashed lines, dotted lines and light solid lines, respectively.

3.2 Statistical analyses

In order to compare prosodic characteristics of different information conditions, maximum F0 (MaxF0), minimum F0 (MinF0), mean F0, mean intensity, and duration values of each prosodic word were extracted using the Praat script ProsodyPro (Xu 2013).

For statistical analysis, linear mixed-effects analyses were conducted using JMP 9, with the speaker as random effects and information status as fixed effects. MaxF0, MinF0, meanF0, mean intensity, and duration were used as dependent measures. The analyses were performed separately for each phrase. All reported effects were significant at the $p < 0.05$ level. The results of our analyses are summarized in Table 3.

Table 3: Results of statistical analyses

	P (*bumili*)	N (*siya*)	A (*nang mami*)
MaxF0	PF=SF=AF>AO	SF=PF=AF>AO	SF=PF=AF>AO
MinF0	AF=PF=SF>AO	SF=PF=AF>AO	AF=PF=SF>AO
mean F0	PF=SF=AF>AO	SF=PF=AF>AO	SF=PF=AF>AO
intensity	PF=AF=SF>AO	PF=AF=SF>AO	PF=AF=SF>AO
duration	PF=AF=AO=SF	AF=PF=AO=SF	AF=PF=SF>AO

Prosodically, all the conditions show the same patterns for P (*bumili*) and N (*siya*); in these parts of the sentence, all the focus conditions were realized with significantly higher F0 and greater intensity than the AO condition while different types of focus were not prosodically differentiated. Interestingly, duration was not significantly different among the four information conditions.

Similar results are observed in the A phrase (*nang mami*). Focus conditions yielded highest F0, greater intensity, and longer duration compared to the AO condition. However, the four conditions did not differ significantly with respect to the acoustic measurements. Unlike the P phrase (*bumili*) and the N phrase (*siya*), this phrase was realized with longer duration when it received focus. It is conceivable this is an effect of narrow focus. Yet, further investigation involving more speakers and material would be necessary to confirm this effect.

3.3 Discussion

The results of our analyses reveal two important facts about the interaction between focus and prosody in Tagalog. First, it was observed that F0 and intensity consistently differentiated focused conditions from AO. This observation was also confirmed by the statistical analyses. Second, no significant prosodic differences were observed between the distinct focus constructions.

A general problem for these conclusions, however, pertains to the fact that the intonational contours of the target sentences vary from speaker to speaker to an extent that needs further explanation. The five speakers did utter the same sentence but with quite different contours, as demonstrated in Figure 1. The pitch contours of Speaker 4 may appear to be reasonably similar to that of Speaker 5 to be considered minor variants of the same overall pattern. But the similarities between the remaining contours are less easily amenable to a single underlying melody. It is not clear yet how to account for this variation among Tagalog speakers. Dialectal differences could be one factor to consider. However, the prosodic characteristics of different dialects in Tagalog are next to unknown, so this has to remain a speculation at this point. Further, Speakers 2, 3, and 5 produced noticeably different patterns though they are from the same region. Thus, it seems that this large between-speaker variation cannot be attributed solely to dialectal differences.

4 Conclusion

In this paper, we presented a preliminary experimental phonetic analysis of the interaction between focus and prosody in Tagalog. In particular, we highlighted mismatching patterns between syntax and information structure found in question-answer pairs. Some *wh*-questions, specifically ones targeting non-agent arguments, can be answered by means of canonical constructions as well as pseudocleft constructions, despite the fact that for most focus conditions Tagalog displays regular correspondences between syntax and information structure: canonical constructions are used for SF and PF conditions, while pseudocleft constructions are used for AF conditions.

Our working hypothesis was that there might be prosodic cues to distinguish canonical constructions associated with different focus structures. The results of our production study reveal that F0 cues and intensity consistently differentiate focused conditions from all-old utterances throughout the entire sentence. As for the argument focus condition, there may be durational effects applying to the phrase in narrow focus, but this needs further confirmation.

Acknowledgements

An earlier version of this paper was presented at the third International Workshop on Information Structure in Austronesian Languages held in ILCAA, Tokyo University of Foreign Studies, on February 18–20, 2016. We are thankful to the audience for the valuable comments and criticism that have helped in improving the manuscript. We are also grateful to three anonymous reviewers for valuable suggestions. Of course, any errors that remain are our responsibility. This work was supported by the Japan Society for the Promotion of Science (Grants-in-Aid #15K16734, #15H03206, #17H02331, and #17H02333).

Abbreviations

AV	actor voice		PFV	perfective
CV	circumstantial voice		PROS	prospective
DUP	reduplication		PV	patient voice
GEN	genitive		SG	singular
GER	gerund		PL	plural
IPFV	imperfective		1	first person
LK	linker		2	second person
LOC	locative		3	third person
LV	locative voice		"<>"	infix
NEG	negator		"="	cliticization
NOM	nominative		"~"	reduplication
P	personal name			

Appendix: Target sentences

Four target sentences and nine dummy sentences were employed in this experiment. Below is the list of the target and filler sentences: sentences (16), (21), (23), and (27) are targets (highlighted in bold so that they can be spotted more easily), while the others function as fillers. In the recording sessions, the entire list was repeated ten times. The participants were asked to read these sentences in this order. Only the parts in italics were presented to the participants (i.e., no morphological analyses, interlinear glossing, or translations).

(15) Q: *Saan ka pupunta?*
 Saan =ka pu~punta?
 where =2SG.NOM AV:PROS:go
 'Where are you going?'

 A: *Sa Ministop ako pupunta.*
 Sa= Ministop =ako pu~punta.
 LOC= Ministop =1SG.NOM AV:PROS:go
 'I am going to a Ministop.'

(16) Q: **Anong binili ni Mama?**
 Ano ='ng b<in>ili ni= Mama?
 what =NOM PV:PFV:buy P.GEN= Mama
 'What did Mama buy?'

 A: **Bumili siya ng mami.**
 B<um>ili =siya nang= mami.
 AV:buy =3SG.NOM GEN= noodles
 'She bought noodles.'

(17) Q: *Sino ang bumili ng mami?*
 Sino ang= b<um>ili nang= mami?
 who NOM= AV:buy GEN= noodles
 'Who bought noodles?'

 A: *Si Mama ang bumili.*
 Si= Mama ang= b<um>ili.
 P.NOM Mama NOM= AV:buy
 'It is Mama who bought noodles.'

(18) Q: *Ano pa binili ni Mama?*
 Ano =pa (=ang) b<in>ili ni= Mama?
 what =else =NOM PV:PFV:buy P.GEN= Mama
 'What else did Mama buy?'

A: *Mami lang ang binili niya.*
   Mami   =lang ang= b<in>ili   =niya.
   noodles =only NOM= PV:PFV:buy =3SG.GEN
   'She bought only noodles.'

(19) Q: *Saan ka pumunta?*
   Saan =ka   p<um>unta?
   where =2SG.NOM AV:go
   'Where did you go?'

   A: *Pumunta ako sa Ministop.*
   P<um>unta =ako   sa= Ministop
   AV:PFV:go =1SG.NOM LOC= Ministop
   'I went to Ministop.'

(20) Q: *Mani ba ang kinain niya?*
   Mani   =ba ang= k<in>ain =niya?
   peanuts =Q NOM= PV:PFV:eat =3SG.GEN
   'Did she eat peanuts?'

   A: *Hindi. Mami ang kinain niya.*
   Hindi. Mami   ang= k<in>ain   =niya
   NEG   noodles NOM= PV:PFV:eat =3SG.GEN
   'No. She ate noodles.'

(21) Q: **Anong ginawa ni Mama doon?**
   Ano ='ng g<in>awa ni=   Mama doon?
   what =NOM PV:PFV:do P.GEN Mama there
   'What did Mama do there?'

   A: **Bumili siya ng mami.**
   B<um>ili =siya   nang= mami.
   AV:buy   =3SG.NOM GEN= noodles
   'She bought noodles.'

(22) Q: *Anong paborito mong pagkain?*
   Ano =ng paborito mo=ng   pagkian?
   what =NOM favorite 2SG.GEN=LK food
   'What is your favorite food?'

   A: *Paborito ko ang mami.*
   Paborito =ko   ang= mami
   favorite =1SG.GEN NOM= noodles
   'Noodles are my favorite.'

(23) Q: *Anong nangyari?*
Ano ='ng nang-yari?
what =NOM AV:PFV:happen
'What happened?'

A: ***Bumili siya ng mami.***
B<um>ili =siya nang= mami.
AV:buy =3SG.NOM GEN= noodles
'She bought noodles.'

(24) Q: *Sino ang bumili ng mami?*
Sino ang= b<um>ili nang= mami?
who NOM= AV:buy GEN= noodles
'Who bought noodles?'

A: *Bumili si Mama ng mami.*
B<um>ili si= Mama nang= mami?
AV:buy P.NOM= Mama GEN= noodles
'Mama bought noodles.'

(25) Q: *Anong binili ni Mama?*
Ano ='ng b<in>ili ni= Mama?
what =NOM PV:PFV:buy P.GEN= Mama
'What did Mama buy?'

A: *Mami ang binili niya.*
Mami ang= b<in>ili =niya.
noodles NOM= PV:PFV:buy =3SG.GEN
'She bought noodles.'

(26) Q: *Masarap ba ang mami nila?*
Ma-sarap =ba ang= mami =nila?
ADJ-delicious =Q NOM= noodles =3PL.GEN
'Are their noodles delicious?'

A: *Oo. Masarap ang mami nila.*
Oo Ma-sarap ang= mami =nila.
yes ADJ-delicous NOM= noodles =3PL.GEN
'Yes, their noodles are delicious.'

(27) Q: ***Bumili ba si Mama ng mami?***
B<um>ili =ba si= Mama nang= mami?
AV:buy =Q P.NOM= Mama GEN= noodles
'Did Mama buy noodles?'

A: *Oo, bumili siya ng mami.*
   Oo, b<um>ili =siya   nang= mami.
   yes AV:buy =3SG.NOM GEN= noodles

   'Yes, she bought noodles.'

References

Garrod, S. & M. Pickering. 2009. Joint action, interactive alignment, and dialog. *Topics in Cognitive Science* 1. 292–304.

Gorisch, J., B. Wells & G. Brown. 2012. Pitch contour matching and interactional alignment across turns: An acoustic investigation. *Language and Speech* 55. 57–76.

Kaufman, Daniel. 2005. Aspects of pragmatic focus in Tagalog. In I Wayan Arka & Malcolm D. Ross (eds.), *The many faces of Austronesian voice systems: Some new empirical studies*, 175–196. Canberra: Pacific Linguistics.

Kaufman, Daniel. 2009. Austronesian nominalism and its consequences: A Tagalog case study. *Theoretical Linguistics* 35. 1–49.

Kaufman, Daniel. 2018. Austronesian predication and the emergence of biclausal clefts in Indonesian languages. In Sonja Riesberg, Asako Shiohara & Atsuko Utsumi (eds.), *A cross-linguistic perspective on information structure in Austronesian languages*. Berlin: Language Science Press.

Kim, M., W. Horton & A. R. Bradlow. 2012. Phonetic convergence in spontaneous conversations as a function of interlocutor language distance. *Laboratory Phonology* 2. 125–156.

Lambrecht, Knud. 1994. *Information structure and sentence form: Topic, focus and the mental representations of discourse referents*. Cambridge, UK: Cambridge University Press.

Nagaya, Naonori. 2007. Information structure and constituent order in Tagalog. *Language and Linguistics* 8. 343–372.

Xu, Yi. 2013. ProsodyPro: A tool for large-scale systematic prosody analysis. In *Proceedings of Tools and Resources for the Analysis of Speech Prosody (TRASP 2013)*, 7–10. Aix-en-Provence, France.

Chapter 13

On the perception of prosodic prominences and boundaries in Papuan Malay

Sonja Riesberg
Universität zu Köln & Centre of Excellence for the Dynamics of Language, The Australian National University

Janina Kalbertodt
Universität zu Köln

Stefan Baumann
Universität zu Köln

Nikolaus P. Himmelmann
Universität zu Köln

> This paper reports the results of two perception experiments on the prosody of Papuan Malay. We investigated how native Papuan Malay listeners perceive prosodic prominences on the one hand, and boundaries on the other, following the Rapid Prosody Transcription method as sketched in Cole & Shattuck-Hufnagel (2016). Inter-rater agreement between the participants was shown to be much lower for prosodic prominences than for boundaries. Importantly, however, the acoustic cues for prominences and boundaries largely overlap. Hence, one could claim that inasmuch as prominence is perceived at all in Papuan Malay, it is perceived at boundaries, making it doubtful whether prosodic prominence can be usefully distinguished from boundary marking in this language. Our results thus essentially confirm the results found for Standard Indonesian by Goedemans & van Zanten (2007) and various claims regarding the production of other local varieties of Malay; namely, that Malayic varieties appear to lack stress (i.e. lexical stress as well as post-lexical pitch accents).

Sonja Riesberg, Janina Kalbertodt, Stefan Baumann & Nikolaus P. Himmelmann. 2018. On the perception of prosodic prominences and boundaries in Papuan Malay. In Sonja Riesberg, Asako Shiohara & Atsuko Utsumi (eds.), *Perspectives on information structure in Austronesian languages*, 389–414. Berlin: Language Science Press. DOI:10.5281/zenodo.1402559

S. Riesberg, J. Kalbertodt, S. Baumann & N. Himmelmann

1 Introduction

Papuan Malay (henceforth PM) is a local variety of Indonesian/Malay, spoken in the two easternmost provinces of Indonesia – Papua Barat and Papua – by approximately 1,200,000 speakers (see Kluge 2014). It is spoken mostly in the coastal areas, and to a lesser extent in the mountainous inland. Indonesian Papua, with its more than 270 indigenous languages, is linguistically highly diverse, and most speakers are at least bilingual. Papuan Malay serves as the lingua franca in this area, and most native speakers speak PM in addition to one or more local languages.

This paper reports on two perception experiments that investigate the contribution of prosody with respect to how native speakers of PM perceive prosodic prominences and boundaries in natural speech. It thus stands alongside a growing number of recent papers that discuss the prosodic systems of different varieties of Indonesian, such as, for example, the study by Goedemans & van Zanten (2007) on Standard Indonesian and, most recently, the paper by Maskikit-Essed & Gussenhoven (2016) on Ambonese Malay.

For a long time, the standard assumption has been that (Standard) Indonesian displays lexical stress on the penultimate syllable, unless this syllable contains a schwa, in which case stress falls on the final syllable (cf. Alieva et al. 1991; Cohn 1989). Secondary stress has been claimed to fall on the first syllable and every odd syllable thereafter, but never on the one adjacent to the syllable that carries the main stress (Cohn & McCarthy 1994). Other authors have claimed that schwa in (some varieties of) Indonesian can be stressed just as well as any other vowel (Halim 1974; Laksman 1994).

However, in a growing number of studies, the claim that Indonesian displays lexical stress on the penultimate syllable has been challenged. While some authors found that there is a preference for stress to occur on the penultimate syllable but free variation – especially in longer words – is possible (cf. van Zanten 1994; van Zanten & van Heuven 2004), other authors came to the conclusion that there is no lexical stress at all (Zubkova 1966; Odé 1997). Especially in more recent publications, it has been pointed out that the aforementioned disagreement as to whether or not Indonesian displays lexical stress is probably due to the fact that "Indonesian" as a reasonably homogeneous language does not exist. Around 700 indigenous languages are spoken in the Republic of Indonesia (cf. Simons & Fennig 2018), with the great majority of people being at least bilingual, speaking a local language in addition to (some variety of) Indonesian. Often, Indonesian is learned as a second language, usually from the age of six or seven, when children enter primary school and are exposed to Indonesian as the language of education. Furthermore, in addition to standard Indonesian and the indigenous languages, local varieties of Malay are spoken in many regions of Indonesia (e.g. Ambonese Malay, Jambi Malay, Kupang Malay, Manado Malay, Papuan Malay, etc.). Often, these local varieties of Malay take the place of standard Indonesian and are the major means of everyday communication. It is thus very likely that studies on lexical stress in "Indonesian" are based on data from speakers with different substrate dialects and languages, which means that the contradictory results of such studies are probably due to the different prosodic properties of these substrates. More recent studies therefore make an effort to control for the linguistic background of the participants in their experiments. Yet even these more recent studies provide results that are not straightforward to interpret, an assessment which is also valid for our study, as further detailed in §5. This is in part due to the fact that more recent studies – even if they control for substrate influence – continue to have issues regarding the naturalness of the word tokens under investigation (often loan words four syllables in length or even longer) and adequate sampling. Many studies rely on non-natural lab speech, often produced by a single speaker, and evaluated by only a few more.

Goedemans & van Zanten (2007), for example, conducted a carefully designed perception experiment with two groups of participants with different linguistic profiles: one group consisted of speakers of Indonesian with Javanese as their substrate language, the other group consisted of speakers of Indonesian who were additionally native speakers of Toba Batak. These two languages were chosen because Toba Batak is said to exhibit clearly defined stress, while Javanese is said to have only weak stress, the location of which lacks consensus in the literature (Goedemans & van Zanten 2007: 40). As stimuli, the authors recorded material from one Toba Batak Indonesian speaker and one Javanese Indonesian speaker. This material was manipulated so that presumably prominence-lending phonetic cues, i.e. pitch excursions, duration and intensity, would occur on different syllables. It was then judged for acceptability by listeners of the two different groups. The Javanese listeners did not show any preference for stress on either the penultimate or the ultimate syllable for both the Javanese Indonesian and the Toba Batak Indonesian stimuli. The Toba Batak listeners, on the other hand, clearly preferred penultimate stress in the Toba Batak speech data, but showed no clear preferences for the Javanese data. Goedemans & van Zanten interpret these results as evidence against lexical stress in Javanese Indonesian. Though their experiment was explicitly *not* designed to investigate prominence above the word level, they do observe that phrasal prominence always occurs close to the boundary. They they come to the conclusion that "the distinction between accent lending and boundary marking intonation movements is very difficult to make in Indonesian" (Goedemans & van Zanten 2007: 57).

One of the few studies that address the issue of phrasal prominence in more detail is the work by Maskikit-Essed & Gussenhoven (2016) on Ambonese Malay (see also Stoel 2007 on Manado Malay, Himmelmann 2010 on Waima'a, and Clynes & Deterding 2011 on Brunei Malay). Maskikit-Essed & Gussenhoven conducted a production experiment with four native speakers of Ambonese Malay. They recorded 80 mini-dialogs consisting of read question-answer pairs, which contained eight target nouns in different positions (phrase- and IP-final as well as phrase- and IP-medial) and were controlled for different focus conditions. In these eight target words, no evidence for (post-)lexical stress in the putative stressed syllables (ultimate or penultimate, depending on the word) was found. Furthermore, the phrase-final pitch movement, which is a typical feature of declarative mood in many languages in the area (Himmelmann 2010: 67), is not tied to either the final or the prefinal syllable. Rather, it is sensitive to the available space and tends to be timed earlier when the word is longer. Finally, Maskikit-Essed & Gussenhoven tested two focus conditions, one in which the phrase-final target word was in focus, and one in which it occurred in post-focal position, i.e. a focal element preceded the phrase-final target word. In the latter condition, the authors could not find any signs of reduction of the post-focal target words, either in duration or in pitch height. Furthermore, the pitch contours were similar, not only on the target words, but also over the whole sentences (Maskikit-Essed & Gussenhoven 2016: 372). Taking these results together, Maskikit-Essed & Gussenhoven come to the conclusion that information focus in Ambonese Malay is not expressed by means of prosody.

For Papuan Malay, Kluge (2014) recorded 1,072 words in two different carrier sentences, one in which the target word occurs clause-finally, and one in which it appears in clause-medial position.[1] Kluge concludes that 964 (90%) of all words have penultimate stress (including both open and closed penultimate syllables), and only 108 (10%) show stress on the final syllable. Of those 108 words that displayed ultimate stress, 105 (97%) contained the front open-mid vowel /ɛ/ (the equivalent of Indonesian schwa) in the penultimate syllable. Yet, Kluge notes that /ɛ/ does not condition ultimate stress, since 65 of those words with penultimate stress, the stressed syllable also contained an /ɛ/. In addition, three words with ultimate stress contained /i/ and /u/ vowels in the penultimate syllable (Kluge 2014: 89).

Based on this analysis, Papuan Malay would appear to be very similar to Ambonese Malay as presented in the grammar by van Minde (1997), where it is claimed that Ambonese Malay has regular penultimate stress, with a small number of lexical items showing ultimate stress. Note that in both grammars, the analysis is based primarily on the auditory impression of the Western researcher who hears one or the other syllable as more prominent. It is unclear what Ambon and Papuan Malay native speakers actually hear. The present study is a first exploration of this question. Recall from above that Maskikit-Essed & Gussenhoven (2016) did not find clear acoustic evidence for (lexical) stress or (post-lexical) pitch accents in Ambonese Malay. Hence, it may very well be the case that Western ears tend to hear these languages according to the categories they know from their own prosodic systems, and not necessarily based on the 'objectively' available acoustic input. That is, if Maskikit-Essed & Gussenhoven's (2016) findings hold up to further scrutiny, the phrase-final pitch movement in Ambon Malay that is heard by Western researchers as being clearly located on either the penultimate or the ultimate syllable is actually most often (i.e. in terms of the measurable acoustic cues) located somewhere in between the final two syllables and thus, strictly speaking, is not properly anchored to either one, but rather to the phrase-final boundary.

In targeting perception rather than production, the current study takes up the line of research pioneered by Leiden phoneticians in the 1990s, though with a somewhat different methodology (see the book edited by van Heuven & van Zanten 2007 for a summary). With regard to these studies, Papuan Malay would appear to be most similar to Toba Batak, for which a system with predominantly penultimate and occasional ultimate stress has also been reported, though possibly with a higher functional load, as

---

[1] The two carrier sentences Kluge used are: *Sa blum taw ko pu kata itu, kata xxx.* 'I don't yet know that word of yours, the word xxx' and *Ko pu kata xxx itu, sa blum taw.* 'Your word xxx, I don't know yet.' (Kluge 2014: 57).

a fair number of minimal stress pairs are claimed to exist (Roosman 2007: 92ff provides a succinct summary of the literature). Unfortunately, Roosman (2007) does not investigate prominence perception by Toba Batak speakers of their native tongue. Moreover, the work by Goedemans & van Zanten (2007) discussed above only looks at the perception of different varieties of Indonesian by native Toba Batak speakers. Hence, the results here will not be directly comparable with the results reported by the Leiden group. It will nevertheless begin to sketch out one of the constellations not yet investigated in detail, i.e. the native perception of a prosodic system which – to Western ears – appears to have a fairly clear lexical stress system with predominantly penultimate stress.

In concluding these introductory remarks, it bears emphasizing that although much of the literature – and consequently also parts of this introduction – makes reference to phonological categories, including in particular "(lexical) stress", such categories only make sense as part of a comprehensive analysis of the prosodic system of a given language. Since such an analysis does not yet exist for Papuan Malay, the main purpose of the current chapter is to provide perceptual data for a more comprehensive investigation of the Papuan Malay system, which in addition will require a rigorous and detailed acoustic analysis, a task currently being undertaken by one of the authors (Himmelmann).

The present chapter is structured as follows: §2 describes the experimental setup and methods, before §3 and §4 report on the results of the two experiments (on prominences and boundaries, respectively). §5 summarizes the findings and draws some preliminary conclusions on the interrelation between the perception of prosodic cues and their interpretation by native listeners of Papuan Malay.

2 Methods

Given the growing amount of evidence in the literature to support the assumption that the prosodic systems of different varieties of Malay differ significantly from the better-known European systems, we wanted to address the question of how native speakers of one of these varieties – Papuan Malay – interpret prosodic cues if required to judge the presence or absence of prominences and boundaries. We therefore conducted two perception experiments using the *Rapid Prosody Transcription* (RPT) method, as introduced in different papers by Jennifer Cole and colleagues (cf. Mo et al. 2008; Cole, Mo & Hasegawa-Johnson 2010; Cole, Mo & Baek 2010; Cole & Shattuck-Hufnagel 2016: 7–13). In the RPT setup, ordinary listeners who are naïve with respect to prosodic analysis listen to excerpts of audio recordings. They are given minimal instructions (see below) and are allowed to play the audio recordings only twice. On a printed transcript of the recorded excerpts, in which punctuation and capitalization have been removed, the participants are either asked to underline those words which they perceive as prominent (prominence experiment), or to draw a vertical line after the word which they perceive to be the last word of a prosodic unit (boundary experiment).

The advantage of this method is its simplicity and directness, providing us with coarse-grained linguistic data: prosodic judgments by untrained listeners, which are based on the listeners' holistic perception of form and function. As noted by Cole and colleagues, the prominence and boundary judgments elicited in this task are clearly not based exclusively on prosodic factors, but also include morphosyntactic, semantic and pragmatic factors. Our main concerns here are prosodic factors, but some of our variables (for example, the distinction between content and function words) also target these other levels.

2.1 Subjects

The raters of our perception study were 44 native speakers of Papuan Malay (22 for the prominence experiment, 22 for the boundary experiment). Of the 22 participants in the prominence experiment, 15 were female. 15 were bilingual in Papuan Malay and standard Indonesian, and 7 participants were additionally proficient in another local language. Of the 22 participants in the boundary experiment, 12 were female. 17 subjects were speakers of Papuan Malay and standard Indonesian, and 5 spoke another local language. All 44 participants were students at the Universitas Papua (UNIPA) in Manokwari (West Papua), and between 18 and 28 years of age. All participants stated that Papuan Malay was (one of) their first language(s)[2] and that Papuan Malay was their first language of communication at home and at university, as well as when talking to friends. None of them had any experience in prosodic analysis or reported any hearing or reading problems.

2.2 Stimuli and procedure

The participants annotated 56 excerpts of audio recordings (the same for both the prominence and the boundary experiment). These excerpts were taken from a corpus of natural speech, consisting of speakers re-telling Chafe's *Pear Movie* (Chafe 1980) and playing the *Tangram Task*.[3] Excerpts thus consisted of both monologues (the pear movie recordings) and dialogues (the tangram recordings). They were of varying lengths, ranging from 1 to 15 seconds, and included 28 different native speakers of Papuan Malay (17 female, 11 male).

Instructions for the participants of the experiments were, as stated above, minimal. They included a short written description of what we mean by *prominence* and *boundaries*, respectively. For the prominences, it was explicitly stated that underlining more than one word per excerpt was allowed. No audio examples were given, but both instructions contained a written example that illustrated how to mark either prominences or boundaries, and how choices could be corrected, if necessary (see Appendix A for the original instructions in Indonesian, and Appendix B for English translations).

The data in (1) show an example of one of the excerpts, including glosses and translation (1a), and how it was presented to the participants of the experiment (1b). (1c) shows

---

[2] Four further participants that took part in the prominence experiment were excluded from the results because they had learned Papuan Malay only at a later age when they entered primary school. They were therefore not considered native speakers, even if they had lived in Manokwari for several years and their dominant language was Papuan Malay at the time of the experiment.

[3] The *Tangram Task* is an elicitation method that involves two speakers negotiating whether the picture described by speaker one is the same as the picture given to speaker two.

the prominence choices made by one of the participants (RW, female, 23 years), (1d) indicates the boundary positions perceived by another participant (JGL, female, 25 years).

(1) Papuan Malay

    a. *yang tiga orang ini pegang topi satu*
        REL three person DEM carry hat one

       'The three people are carrying a hat.'

    b. yang tiga orang ini pegang topi satu

    c. yang tiga orang ini pegang topi satu

    d. yang / tiga orang ini / pegang topi satu

2.3 Test variables

We tested the influence on the native listeners' judgments of a number of prosodic and morphosyntactic cues which have been found to have an effect on prominence or boundary perception in other (generally West Germanic) languages. For each test word in both experiments, we investigated the following prosodic factors: *word duration* (in ms), *mean duration of syllables* (in ms), *duration of the last syllable within a word* (in ms), *minimum*, *maximum* and *mean pitch* (in Hz), absolute *pitch range* (in semitones), *number of syllables* (both abstract phonological and actually realized) as well as *presence of a pause*. An increase in duration, pitch height and pitch range have been shown in many studies to correlate with higher perceived prominence in Germanic languages (e.g. Cole, Mo & Hasegawa-Johnson 2010; Rietveld & Gussenhoven 1985), while presence of a pause and domain-final lengthening has been shown to trigger the perception of a phrase break (e.g. Turk & Shattuck-Hufnagel 2007).

Furthermore, we analyzed the morphosyntactic cues *part-of-speech* (POS), *part-of-speech class* (i.e. content words vs. function words), whether the word is the *last verbal argument* in the excerpt, and *syntactic break* (three levels: no, weak or strong break). The label *weak break* was assigned to sentence-medial words that were followed by a subordinate clause (e.g. relative clause), while the label *strong break* was assigned to sentence-final words. Again, all these structural factors were chosen from a European point of view, since West Germanic languages are known to be sensitive to these parameters. In English and German, function words are usually less prominent than content words (Büring 2012: 31), while the last verbal argument in a sentence is of importance when it comes to focus projection, i.e. in the default intonation of a broad focus sentence, the last verbal argument receives the nuclear accent (Uhmann 1988: 66).

In addition to these linguistic factors, we correlated the experiment's outcome with an expert rating of prosodic boundaries, which represents the consensus judgments of the authors, all of them German natives. Boundaries in this version are based on the consensus of at least three of the four authors. In a pre-test, this expert rating was statistically analyzed with the same factors examined for the native raters, showing strong influences of pause, overall word duration, mean syllable duration and syntactic structure. The effect of syntactic structure is somewhat surprising, as two of the authors do not know the language and thus have no understanding of the syntax.

2.4 Data analysis

Both experiments consisted of binary classification tasks. In the prominence experiment (Experiment I), participants had a binary choice for each word in the transcript to rate it as either prominent or non-prominent. In the boundary experiment (Experiment II), there was a choice for each consecutive pair of words to either place a boundary between them or not. That is, for an excerpt containing n words, there were $(n - 1)$ consecutive word pairs and thus $(n - 1)$ potential boundaries the rater had to decide upon, since no judgment was needed after the last word of an excerpt. Given that our set of 56 excerpts consisted of 730 words altogether, each participant thus produced 730 data points in the prominence experiment and 674 data points in the boundary experiment.

For the statistical analysis of these data, a mixed effects logistic regression was performed using the *lme4-package* (Bates et al. 2015) in *R* (R Core Team 2015), which suits both continuous and categorical input variables. As this study is exploratory in nature, we only created single effect models (e.g. only *maximum pitch* or *part-of-speech*, but not both variables) with random effects for speaker, sentence and rater. Subsequently, odds ratios were calculated to enable a comparison of the factors by means of effect size in order to determine which cue had the strongest influence on the raters' judgments.

We further calculated both the Fleiss' kappa coefficient (plus its z-normalized score) and Cohen's kappa. Fleiss' kappa provides a single coefficient as a measure of agreement across all raters. Cohen's kappa calculates agreement between an individual pair of raters for each word/consecutive pair of words, comparing the labels (i.e. prominent – non-prominent, and boundary – no-boundary, respectively).

In addition, we calculated the prominence-score (p-score) and the boundary-score (b-score), which serve as relative measures representing the ratio of subjects that underlined a word, i.e. that perceived a word as prominent, or drew a vertical line, i.e. perceived a prosodic break, with respect to the total number of participants. An example showing p- and b-scores is given in Figure 1.

3 Results of the prominence experiment

3.1 Inter-rater and multi-rater agreement

As mentioned above, we measured the overall inter-rater agreement for both experiments by calculating Fleiss' and Cohen's kappa coefficients. These two measures allow us to compare the performance of the two rater groups between the two experiments. They also make it possible to compare our results with similar studies that used RPT to investigate native speakers' perception of prominences in American English and in German.

13 On the perception of prosodic prominences and boundaries in Papuan Malay

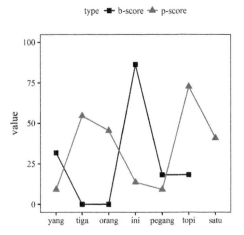

Figure 1: P- and b-scores for one PM excerpt (cf. (1) above). The higher the value, the more participants perceived a word as prominent (gray line with triangles) or perceived a boundary after the respective word (black line with squares). Recall that no b-score has been calculated for the last word of an excerpt.

The Fleiss' kappa score we calculated for the prominence experiment amounts to 0.103 ($z = 42.1$), a value that turns out to be surprisingly low in cross-linguistic comparison. In Table 1, we compare the PM inter-rater scores from the prominence experiment with those of two comparable studies on American English (Mo et al. 2008; Cole, Mo & Hasegawa-Johnson 2010) and German (Baumann & Winter to appear). The study by Cole and colleagues used spontaneous conversational speech from the *Buckeye Corpus*, which consists of interviews with adult speakers of American English from Columbus (Pitt et al. 2007). Baumann & Winter's study, on the other hand, used read sentences that displayed different focus structures and information status categories. Both made use of the RPT method as described above. The comparison clearly shows that the PM listeners perform significantly worse in the prominence task than English or German listeners.

Table 1: Fleiss' kappa for prominences in German, American English, and PM rating studies

	German	English	PM
Fleiss' Kappa	0.53	0.42	0.103
z	244	20.4	42.1

The slightly higher agreement of German raters compared to English raters is probably due to the different data types used in the respective experiments, i.e. read speech versus spontaneous conversational data. Considering that the naturalness of the stimuli might have an effect on the raters' level of agreement in their perception of prominences, the PM scores are probably best compared with the English scores. Still, the difference between English raters, with a Fleiss' kappa score of 0.42, and Papuan Malay, with a kappa score of only 0.103, is also striking.

To test whether the low score of the PM raters in the prominence experiment was just due to very low agreement between some individual participants, we calculated Cohen's kappa scores for every single rater pair. In Table 2, the pair-wise inter-rater agreement is summarized, using the agreement categories postulated by Landis & Koch (1977), who characterize kappa values between 0–0.20 as slight agreement, 0.21–0.40 as fair, 0.41–0.60 as moderate, 0.61–0.80 as substantial, and 0.81–1 as (almost) perfect agreement.

Table 2: Inter-rater agreement categories (based on Cohen's kappa scores) for PM subjects in the prominence experiment

inter-rater agreement	Prominences pairs	percentage
none	25	10.82%
slight	164	71.00%
fair	40	17.32%
moderate	2	0.87%
substantial	0	0.00%
(almost) perfect	0	0.00%
	231	100%

As we can see, more than 80% of the pairs showed either 'slight' or no agreement, and for only about 17% of pairs was the agreement 'fair'. The picture gained by the Fleiss' kappa study is thus confirmed. As we will see in §4.1, both the multi-rater agreement and the pair-wise inter-rater agreement in the prominence experiment is much lower than in the boundary experiment.

3.2 Factors determining perceived prominence

As already indicated by the low kappa values above, we observed a high degree of variability in the listeners' judgments, leading to predominantly low p-scores. In fact, the modal value in our data was a p-score of 13.6%, as shown in Figure 2. There was not a single item (out of 726[4]) that *all* raters considered prominent, the highest p-score being 81.8% (18 out of 22 participants agreeing on assigning prominence to a given word), which was achieved only three times. Furthermore, there were only twenty words which all participants judged as *not* prominent (out of 726 words altogether).

When examining which of the 14 test variables influenced the perception of prominence, only *part-of-speech* was *not* found to have a significant effect on prominence

---

[4]Four items had to be discarded because no pitch features could be calculated.

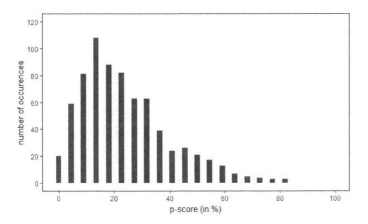

Figure 2: Distribution of p-scores in the PM data

judgments ($X^2(1)$ = 0.6444, p = 0.4221). Note, however, that the actual effect sizes of the various factors were found to be rather small, as indicated by the odds ratios. An odds ratio of 1 usually indicates that there is no change in the odds of receiving a certain outcome when manipulating the test variable. An odds ratio bigger than 1 indicates an increase in the odds of getting a certain outcome (cf. Field et al. 2012: 320, 923), in our case a prominence response. We have excluded variables with extremely small odds ratios from further consideration, in order to concentrate on those effects that are most likely to have noticeable effects on prominence judgments. Our threshold was set to an odds ratio of 1.5 to 1. This procedure led to the exclusion of all measures relating to pitch (*maximum, minimum, mean pitch* and *pitch range*) in addition to *part-of-speech, number of syllables (phonological)* and *duration of the last syllable*.

The strongest effect was found for *pause* ($X^2(1)$ = 156.26, p < 0.0001), increasing the odds of observing a prominence response in the presence of a pause as opposed to the absence of a pause by 2.7 to 1 (logit estimate: 1.01, SE = 0.08). Figure 3 shows the relation between prominence judgments on a word and a subsequent pause.

The second most influential factor for the perception of prominence by native speakers of Papuan Malay was *part-of-speech class* ($X^2(1)$ = 329.3, p < 0.0001), i.e. content vs. function word, as displayed in Figure 4. Being presented with a content word as opposed to a function word increases the odds of observing a positive response for prominence by 2.1 to 1 (logit estimate: 0.73, SE = 0.04).

As a third factor, overall *word duration* had an impact on the prominence ratings ($X^2(1)$ = 857.16, p < 0.0001). In this continuous parameter, a change by one standard deviation increases the odds of a prominence response by 1.9 to 1 (logit estimate: 0.62, SE = 0.02). Figure 5 shows this effect as a tendency of longer words to reach a higher p-score, i.e. the longer the word, the more participants marked it as prominent.

The remaining four test variables were found to be more marginally relevant and clearly overlap with one of the three preceding variables. Thus, *mean syllable duration* and *num-*

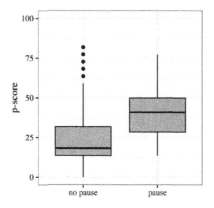

Figure 3: P-scores as a function of presence or absence of a subsequent pause

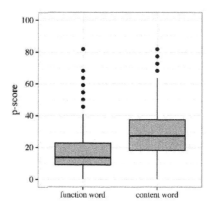

Figure 4: P-scores as a function of part-of-speech class

ber of syllables (actually realized) – both with odds ratios of 1.6 to 1 – are obviously related to word duration. Similarly, *syntactic break* (odds ratio 1.5 to 1) and *last verbal argument* (odds ratio 1.6 to 1) often overlap with pauses.

4 Results of the boundary experiment

4.1 Inter-rater and multi-rater agreement

The first result to note with regard to inter-rater agreement is that our participants performed much better in the boundary experiment (Experiment II) than they did in the prominence experiment (Experiment I). That is, inter-rater agreement was much higher

13 On the perception of prosodic prominences and boundaries in Papuan Malay

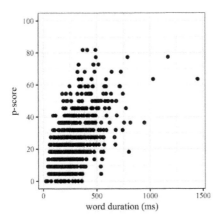

Figure 5: P-scores as a function of word duration

in the former than in the latter. Table 3 repeats the Fleiss' kappa scores for the prominence experiment (cf. §3.1) and contrasts them with the scores for the boundary experiment.

Table 3: Fleiss' kappa scores for prominences and boundaries in PM

Prominences	Boundaries
0.103	0.407
z = 42.1	z = 160

Comparing the boundary scores again with Mo et al.'s (2008) RPT results for American English, we see that – in contrast to the prominence scores – English listeners and Papuan Malay listeners are not too far apart in their perception of boundaries: 0.544 for American English vs. 0.407 for Papuan Malay.

As with the prominence experiment, we additionally looked at the pair-wise inter-rater agreement. Table 4 summarizes the Cohen's kappa values by using the agreement categories of Landis & Koch (1977). Compared with the results of the prominence experiment (repeated in the second and third columns of Table 4), we see a clear difference between the two experiments: while in the prominence experiment more than 80% of all rater pairs showed either no or only slight agreement, only about 18% of the rater pairs showed such low agreement in the boundary experiment. Instead, the majority of pairs who participated in the boundary experiment (more than 60%) showed moderate or even substantial agreement.

401

Table 4: Inter-rater agreement categories (based on Cohen's kappa scores) for PM subjects in both experiments

inter-rater agreement	Prominences		Boundaries	
	pairs	percentage	pairs	percentage
none	25	10.82%	4	1.73%
slight	164	71.00%	37	16.02%
fair	40	17.32%	51	22.08%
moderate	2	0.87%	106	45.89%
substantial	0	0.00%	33	14.29%
(almost) perfect	0	0.00%	0	0.00%
	231	100%	231	100%

4.2 Factors determining perceived boundaries

As we have seen in the previous section, the overall agreement of raters is better in the boundary experiment than in the prominence experiment. This is reflected in Figure 6, where we observe a modal value of 0, which is to be expected as there are usually many more word pairs with no boundaries between them than ones where the two words are separated by a boundary. We can also observe a longer tail to the right, indicating that higher scores are reached than in the prominence experiment. That is, the participants agreed more on the position of boundaries than on the position of prominences (top scores: 95.5% as opposed to 81.8%). However, even though the agreement among raters is higher for boundaries than for prominences, complete agreement (on the *presence* of a boundary) is never achieved.

When correlating the multiple possible factors introduced in §2 with the outcome, the only variable that does not reach significance is *part-of-speech class* ($X^2(1) = 0.7962$, $p = 0.3722$). In the same way as with the prominence results, however, we will concentrate only on the strongest effects, indicated by odds ratios bigger than 1.5 to 1. The variables not considered further are the morphosyntactic parameters *part-of-speech* and *last argument*, and the duration/syllable number measures *duration of last syllable*, *number of syllables (phonological)* and *number of syllables (actually realized)*. This also includes two of the pitch measures, i.e. *minimum* and *mean pitch*, but note that the other two pitch measures (*maximum pitch* and *pitch range*) are also only marginally effective (odds ratio 1.6 to 1 for *pitch range* and odds ratio 1.7 to 1 for *maximum pitch*).

The most significant factor affecting the perception of a boundary in this experiment was the presence of a *pause* ($X^2(1) = 1519$, $p < 0.0001$). As illustrated in Figure 7, the presence of a pause in contrast to a non-interrupted signal increased the odds of a positive response for boundary by 22.9 to 1 (logit estimate: 3.13, SE = 0.09).

Although much weaker, another major effect on the perception of boundaries was found in the *syntactic structure* of the utterances ($X^2(1) = 1514.2$, $p < 0.0001$). As Figure 8 indicates, the type of syntactic break influences the perception of a boundary. Thus, a change

13 On the perception of prosodic prominences and boundaries in Papuan Malay

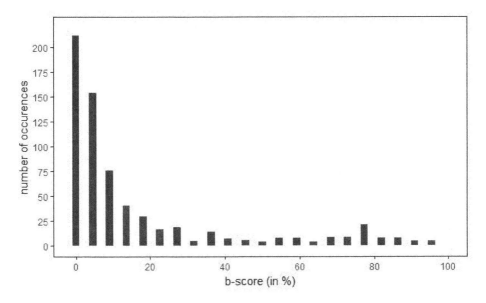

Figure 6: Distribution of b-scores in the PM data

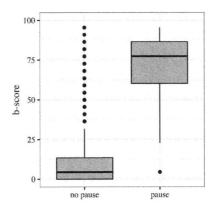

Figure 7: B-score as a function of pause

of one unit increases the odds of observing a boundary response by 3.4 to 1 (logit estimate: 1.23, SE = 0.03). The effect size can be explained by the amount of variability shown in the plot and the overly coarse values for this parameter. Thus, there are quite a few instances where participants agreed on the presence of a boundary even though there was no major (clausal) syntactic break. Such boundaries typically involve a clause-internal syntactic break such as the right edge of a topic or subject NP. Recall that the syntactic break parameter only distinguishes subordinate clause and sentence boundaries from no boundary (= all syntactic boundaries within a clause). Furthermore, participants did not always agree on perceiving a prosodic boundary at sentence boundaries (= strong syntactic breaks), which in part is due to the fact that sentence boundaries are often not easy to determine in spontaneous discourse. The high variability, especially in cases of a strong syntactic break, leads to a relatively small effect of *syntax*, although the mean values of the two categories *weak* and *strong break* are far apart from each other.

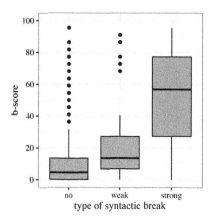

Figure 8: B-score as a function of syntactic structure

Next to *pause* and *syntax*, the *mean duration of syllables* was found to be the third most important factor for the perception of boundaries, but the effect here is relatively weak ($X^2(1) = 1415.1$, $p < 0.0001$; see Figure 9). Thus, a change of one standard deviation increases the odds of getting a boundary response by 2.6 to 1 (logit estimate: 0.95, SE = 0.029).

We found almost the same effect size for the parameter *word duration* ($X^2(1) = 1423.7$, $p < 0.0001$), where a change of one standard deviation increases the odds of observing a boundary response by 2.5 to 1 (logit estimate: 0.90, SE = 0.028).

5 Discussion

If we compare the results gained in the two RPT-experiments, we find a high degree of variability for prominence judgments, but less variability for boundary judgments.

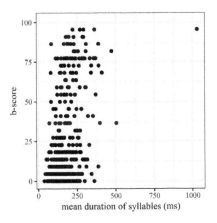

Figure 9: B-score as a function of mean syllable duration

The lack of agreement with regard to prominence judgments is reflected in overall low Kappa values and low p-scores (best p-score achieved: 81.8%; modal value: 13.6%). The considerably stronger agreement in the perception of prosodic boundaries is shown by much higher Kappa values and more consistent b-scores at both ends of the scale (best b-score achieved: 95.5%; modal value: 0%).

When correlating the native judgments of Experiment I and II with the various parameters that might affect the perception of prominences and boundaries, respectively, we observe an interesting pattern (see Table 5): the two *prosodic* factors most important in influencing prominence and boundary ratings are basically the same; namely, *pause* and *word duration/mean syllable duration*.[5] Apart from the considerable difference in effect size with regard to the parameter *pause*, the major difference between the two experiments pertains to the *non-prosodic* factor found to be most influential for the relevant judgment. *Part-of-speech class* was found to be a relevant cue for prominence but not for boundaries. This is not surprising, as content words are generally claimed to be more prominent than function words, due to their higher semantic weight or structural strength (see Büring 2012) and to their (commonly) lower word frequency (see Cole, Mo & Hasegawa-Johnson 2010). In contrast, *syntactic structure* becomes more important when it is the participants' task to judge the position of boundaries. This, again, is in line with findings for other languages (see, for example, Cole, Mo & Baek 2010).

Table 5 lists the three most important factors determining prominence and boundary judgments in descending order. Importantly, and somewhat surprisingly from a European perspective, the relevant prosodic factors are not only (almost) the same across

---

[5]For boundaries, *word duration* is the fourth most influential parameter with an odds ratio of 2.5, and *mean syllable duration* is the third-most effective cue, with an odds ratio of 2.6. As this difference is extremely small, we regard these two factors as equally effective with regard to prosodic boundaries. In the case of prominences, the difference between *word duration* (odds ratio of 1.9) and *mean syllable duration* (odds ratio 1.6) is somewhat more pronounced, but still not very large.

both experiments, but the ranking is also the same, i.e. *pause* in first and *word duration/ mean syllable duration* in third position.

Table 5: Major effects for both experiments in terms of their effect size (odds ratio =OR)

Experiment I: Prominences	OR	Experiment II: Boundaries	OR
pause	2.7	pause	22.9
part-of-speech class	2.1	syntactic structure	3.4
word duration	1.9	mean syllable duration /word duration	2.6/2.5

When comparing the odds ratios, it is obvious that the effect sizes for the prominence-lending parameters are smaller than their counterparts for boundary perception. The rather small effect sizes are linked to the very high degree of variability in the prominence ratings (low Kappa values). That is, the effects these parameters may have on prominence judgments clearly do not lead to substantial agreement with regard to these judgments. In fact, the high degree of variability raises the question of whether the notion of prominence makes any sense to PM speakers, a point we will return to below.

For boundaries, by contrast, the effects seem to be more robust. Furthermore, the variability observed here is within the range of variability observed for other languages (see §4.1 above). Major phonetic cues for prosodic boundaries are pauses and longer word and syllable durations, which are widely attested cross-linguistically (see, for example, Turk & Shattuck-Hufnagel 2007). In fact, with regard to boundary perception, native hearing and Western auditory analysis appear to be quite similar, as revealed by the comparison of the expert rating by the four authors (cf. §2) and native listeners' judgments in Figure 10. In most cases in which experts did not perceive a prosodic boundary, the native raters also tended towards the perception of no boundary, which is indicated in the plot by larger dots for lower b-scores. However, in some cases where non-native experts did not perceive a boundary, there was a considerable agreement among native raters that they perceived a boundary. The opposite pattern can be observed for instances in which the experts did perceive a boundary: there are fewer instances of low b-scores but (slightly) more instances of higher b-scores. Statistically, this pattern is mirrored by a strong correlation for the perception of boundaries between the two groups ($X^2(1) = 2949.9$, $p < 0.0001$). When the experts observed a boundary in contrast to no boundary, the odds of a boundary response by the native listeners increased by 26.8 to 1 (logit estimate: 3.3, SE = 0.07), which is higher than the strongest factor influencing native speakers' boundary judgments (i.e. *pause* with an odds ratio of 22.9).

Given the very weak inter-rater agreement results for prominence judgments and the fact that the same prosodic cues appear to play a role in judging prominences and boundaries, we tentatively conclude that the perception of prominence is to some extent conflated with the – more clearly conceptualized – perception of (prosodic) boundaries

13 On the perception of prosodic prominences and boundaries in Papuan Malay

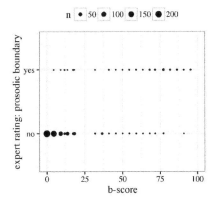

Figure 10: Correlation between non-native (German) experts' and native (PM) listeners' boundary perception (indicated by binary scores and b-scores, respectively). The size of the dots indicates the number of compatible observations (the more observations, the larger the dot).

in PM. This conclusion is in line with similar observations quoted from the literature in §1, which also raise doubts as to the feasibility of separating prosodic prominences from prosodic boundaries in other Malayic varieties.

It should be noted, however, that there is no perfect match between prominences and boundaries in that natively perceived boundaries are not reliable predictors for prominences. Testing the effect of b-scores on p-scores, we found an odds ratio of only 1.1 to 1, although the likelihood-ratio test revealed significance. The small effect size is mainly due to the fact that substantially more prominences were marked than boundaries. Recall from §3.2 that only 20 of the 726 words (i.e. 2.75%) occurring in the test items were unanimously judged to *lack* prominence. In contrast, of the 674 non-final words in the test utterances, 212 were unanimously judged *not* to precede a boundary (i.e. 31.45%).

Perhaps the most surprising result of our preliminary exploration is the fact that pitch-related parameters do not appear to play a role for PM speakers in judging prominences and boundaries. Recall from §3.2 and §4.2 that only *maximum* and *mean pitch* were found to be marginally effective in the case of boundary judgments, but well below the more effective parameters *pause, syntactic break*, and *mean syllable/word duration*. This finding is particularly relevant because the claims of Western researchers regarding lexical stress differences in Malayic varieties appear to be primarily based on differences in pitch alignment, with high pitch targets being heard as located on either the penultimate or the ultimate syllable of a word. The production study by Maskikit-Essed & Gussenhoven (2016) for Ambonese Malay already questioned whether there is in fact a clear alignment of pitch targets with respect to syllable boundaries. Our study suggests that, although modulations of pitch are clearly present (acoustically as well as perceptually to the Western ear), these do not appear to play a role either in the perception of boundaries or in the marking of prosodic prominences in PM – and possibly other Malayic varieties.

In fact, prosodic prominence may not be a relevant category in PM and other Malayic varieties in general, which would thus represent further instances of what has been termed *stress deafness* (see e.g. Peperkamp & Dupoux 2002, Dupoux et al. 2010 for French). However, our results are not directly comparable with this line of work as the methods used quite clearly differ. It is also far from clear whether stress deafness is a homogeneous phenomenon. Hence, it may turn out that the French and PM cases only partially overlap, if at all.

We need more data to answer the question of whether PM listeners are really insensitive to prominence-lending pitch modulations. This includes the further question of whether they do not respond to pitch modulations at all, i.e. also when rating languages that are known to primarily use pitch in the marking of prosodic prominence (a study presenting German stimuli to Papuan Malay listeners is currently under way). If we were to find higher prominence scores when PM listeners rate German data, the present results would only support the conclusion that pitch modulations are not systematically employed in prominence marking in PM, thus confirming similar findings in the literature reported in §1. If prominence scores by PM listeners prove to be similar across different languages, this would suggest a more general account in terms of stress deafness for PM listeners.

We would also like to add a cautionary note regarding the notion of "(post-) lexical stress" as it has been used in this chapter and in much of the previous descriptive and experimental literature. Inasmuch as 'stress' is understood to be a phenomenon that pertains to the phonologically organized highlighting of a syllable relative to adjacent ones by way of modulating phonetic parameters such as pitch and duration, the current study supports the conclusions of earlier studies that lexical stress is not part of the prosodic system of Malayic varieties. As pointed out in the introduction, the cases of Papuan and Ambon Malay are particularly interesting in this regard, because pitch modulations here appear to be – both acoustically and perceptually to the Western ear – very regular and clearly anchored to different syllables (penultimate or final), unlike in the Indonesian spoken by Javanese native speakers, where pitch modulations are much more variable.

In this context, it should be noted that it is very well possible that in PM pitch targets are clearly aligned with syllables, in contrast to Maskikit-Essed & Gussenhoven's (2016) claims for Ambonese Malay. If this were to be the case, we would need a stress-like notion to be able to account for differing alignments of pitch targets with penultimate and final syllables which, however, would differ from the standard understanding of "lexical stress", as this distinction does not appear to be perceived as a prominence distinction by native speakers.

While it thus seems very likely that prosodic prominence is organized differently in these languages, a number of phenomena may still need to be accounted for in stress-related metrical categories. To give just one more example, Kluge (2014) makes the occasional reference to stress distinctions in discussing segmental alternations in PM. An example is the observation that /s/ is only palatalized in unstressed syllables (Kluge 2014: 73). If one denies lexical stress distinctions in the standard sense given above, one needs to identify another factor that adequately constrains the palatalization rule. Furthermore, lexical stress in the sense of phonologically organized prominence distinctions is of course not the only possible prosodic organization at word level. Foot structure, for example, may be evident in terms of phenomena not directly reflected in phonetic differences. Thus, it should be clearly understood that denying the existence of lexical stress in these languages does not mean that there is no word-prosodic organization at all.

Acknowledgements

Work on this chapter by Riesberg and Himmelmann was generously supported by the Volkswagen Foundation within the scope of the project "Documentation Summits in the Central Mountains of Papua" (Az 85892). We are grateful to the Centre of Endangered Languages Documentation (CELD) in Manokwari, particularly to Yusuf Sawaki, Jean Lekeneny and Anna Rumaikeuw, for providing support and the facilities for conducting the experiments. Special thanks to Jan Strunk and Christoph A. Bracks for computing the kappa statistics, and to Katherine Walker for improving style and grammar.

Abbreviations

b-score	boundary-score	p-score	prominence-score
DEM	demonstrative	REL	relative pronoun
PM	Papuan Malay	RPT	Rapid Prosody Transcription

Appendix A

Instructions for Experiment I (Prominences)

Pertama-tama kami mengucapkan terima kasih karena Anda bersedia berpartisipasi dalam eksperimen tentang bagaimana Anda memahami bahasa. Jawaban yang Anda berikan tidak ada yang salah atau benar karena semuanya bergantung pada rasa bahasa.

Dalam berbicara seseorang akan mengucapkan beberapa atau banyak kata dalam sebuah kalimat dengan nada yang lebih menonjol dibandingkan dengan kata-kata lain yang terdapat dalam kalimat tersebut. Kata-kata dengan nada yang menonjol ini biasanya dapat dirasakan oleh pendengarnya. Tugas Anda adalah menandai (menggarisbawahi) kata-kata yang nadanya Anda dengar lebih menonjol dibandingkan dengan kata-kata lain dalam rekaman kalimat yang akan Anda putar.

Berikut ini Anda akan diputarkan 56 kalimat. Setiap kalimat juga akan disajikan dalam bentuk tertulis. Untuk mulai silakan klik **Contoh 1**, dst.

Tugas Anda adalah menggarisbawahi **semua** kata yang nadanya Anda anggap lebih menonjol (mis. lebih tinggi) dibandingkan dengan kata-kata lain pada setiap rekaman kalimat yang Anda dengarkan. Silakan garis bawahi kata tersebut dengan cara seperti ini:

Dia melihat sapi

Dalam hal ini, Anda dimungkinkan untuk memilih lebih dari satu kata pada setiap rekaman kalimat!

Dia melihat sapi dan kuda makan rumput

Anda dapat memutar setiap rekaman kalimat sebanyak dua kali. Akan tetapi, tidak memungkinkan untuk menghentikan rekaman pada saat contoh kalimat sedang diputar.

Jika Anda harus mengoreksi pilihan Anda, silakan coret kata yang telah Anda garis bawahi dengan cara seperti ini:

sapi

Selamat mengikuti eksperimen ini!

Instructions for Experiment II (Boundaries)

Ketika seseorang berbicara, dia akan membagi ucapan mereka menjadi potongan-potongan. Potongan-potongan tersebut membentuk kelompok kata-kata yang memudahkan pendengar untuk memahami ucapan pembicara. Potongan-potongan tersebut penting terutama saat pembicara memproduksi ucapan yang panjang.

Contoh potongan yang mungkin Anda ketahui adalah potongan nomor ketika Anda memberi tahu nomor telepon Anda kepada orang lain. Biasanya, Anda tidak setiap kali memberi satu nomor (0, 8, 1, 3 ...), tetapi Anda akan memotong nomor hp tersebut menjadi kelompok-kelompok yang terdiri atas dua, tiga, atau empat angka (081, 358, 772 ...).

Untuk rekaman yang akan Anda dengar, Anda diminta untuk menandai potongan dengan cara menyisipkan garis tegak lurus atau vertikal (pada cetakan) untuk bagian yang Anda dengar sebagai satu potongan. Batas antara dua potongan tidak harus sama dengan lokasi tempat Anda akan menulis tanda koma, titik, atau tanda baca lainnya. Jadi, Anda harus benar-benar hati-hati mendengar ujaran dan tandai batas yang Anda dengar sebagai akhir sebuah potongan.

Sebuah potongan mungkin saja berupa satu kata, atau mungkin terdiri atas beberapa kata, dan ukuran (jumlah kata) dalam setiap potongan dari para pembicara bisa saja berbeda-beda dalam satu ujaran. Beberapa ujaran mungkin Anda dengar konsisten, yaitu terdiri atas satu potongan saja. Jika demikian, Anda tidak perlu menandai batas potongan.

Contoh:

081|358|772...
0813|5877|2...
Bapak saya | sudah datang
Bapak | saya sudah datang

13 On the perception of prosodic prominences and boundaries in Papuan Malay

Appendix B

Instructions for Experiment I (Prominences)

First of all, we want to say thank you for participating in our experiment on how people perceive language. There is no right or wrong answer - we are just interested in your innate sense of language.[6]

When talking, people will stress or emphasize some words within a sentence more than others. These stressed words can usually be perceived by the hearer. Your task in this experiment is to point out (underline) all words that you perceive to be more emphasized compared to the rest of the utterance in the recordings that we will play to you.

You will hear 56 sentences. You will also receive each sentence as a written transcript. To start, please click **Example 1**, and so on.

Your task is to underline **all** words that you perceive to stick out (e.g. because they are higher/louder) compared to the other words in each recording that you will hear. Please underline your choice in the following way:

He sees a <u>cow</u>

It is possible to choose more than one word for each recording!

He sees a <u>cow</u> and a horse <u>eating</u> grass

You can play each recording twice. It will not be possible to stop the recording while it is playing.

If you want to make a correction to your choice, please cross out the underlined word.

<u>c̶o̶w̶</u>

Enjoy the experiment!

Instructions for Experiment II (Boundaries)

When people speak, they chunk their utterances into units. These chunks of words help the hearer to understand the utterance. They are especially important if the speaker produces longer, coherent speech.

An example you might be familiar with is the chunking of digits when giving somebody your telephone number. Instead of spelling one digit after another (0, 8, 1, 3 ...), it is common to divide the number into units consisting of two, three, or four digits each (081, 358, 772 ...).

For the recordings you will hear, you are asked to mark those chunks by inserting a vertical line (on the printout) to divide what you perceive to be a unit. The boundary between two chunks does not necessarily have to coincide with where one would write

---

[6]Note that the English transations are free rather than literal translations of the Indonesian original.

a comma, a full stop or any other punctuation, so please listen carefully and draw the line where you hear the end of one unit.

One unit might consist of one word only, or it can contain several words - the size of a unit might vary from utterance to utterance. Some recordings might consist of one unit only. If this is the case, you don't have to draw a boundary.

Examples:

081|358|772...
0813|5877|2...
let's eat grandpa
let's eat | grandpa

References

Alieva, Natalia F., Vladimir D. Arakin, Alexander K. Ogloblin & Yu H. Sirk. 1991. *Bahasa Indonesia: Descripsi dan teori*. Yogyakarta: Kanisius.

Bates, D., M. Maechler, B. Bolker & S. Walker. 2015. Lme4: Linear mixed-effects models using Eigen and S4. *R package version* 1.1-8. http://CRAN.R-project.org/package=lme4.

Baumann, Stefan & Bodo Winter. to appear. What makes a word prominent? Predicting untrained German listeners' perceptual judgments. *Journal of Phonetics*.

Büring, Daniel. 2012. Predicate integration - phrase structure or argument structure? In Ivona Kucerova & Ad Neeleman (eds.), *Contrasts and positions in information structure*, 27–47. Cambridge: Cambridge University Press.

Chafe, Wallace L. 1980. *The Pear Stories: Cognitive, cultural, and linguistic aspects of narrative production*. Norwood, New Jersey: Ablex.

Clynes, Adrian & David Deterding. 2011. Standard Malay (Brunei). *Journal of the International Phonetic Association* 41(2). 259–268.

Cohn, Abigail C. 1989. Stress in Indonesian and bracketing paradoxes. *Natural Language and Linguistic Theory* 7. 167–216.

Cohn, Abigail C. & John J. McCarthy. 1994. Alignment and parallelism in Indonesian phonology. *Working Papers of the Cornell Phonetics Laboratory* 12. 53–137.

Cole, Jennifer, Yoonsook Mo & Soondo Baek. 2010. The role of syntactic structure in guiding prosody perception with ordinary listeners and everyday speech. *Language and Cognitive Processes* 25. 1141–1177.

Cole, Jennifer, Yoonsook Mo & Mark Hasegawa-Johnson. 2010. Signal-based and expectation-based factors in the perception of prosodic prominence. *Laboratory Phonology* 1. 425–452.

Cole, Jennifer & Stefanie Shattuck-Hufnagel. 2016. New methods for prosodic transcription: Capturing variability as a source of information. *Journal of the Association for Laboratory Phonology* 7(1). 8. DOI:10.5334/labphon.29

Dupoux, Emmanuel, Sharon Peperkamp & Núria. Sebastián-Gallés. 2010. Limits on bilingualism revisited: Stress 'deafness' in simultaneous French-Spanish bilinguals. *Cognition* 114. 266–275.

Field, Andy, Jeremy Miles & Zoë Field. 2012. *Discovering statistics using R*. Los Angeles: Sage.

Goedemans, Robert W. N. & Ellen van Zanten. 2007. Stress and accent in Indonesian. In Vincent J. van Heuven & Ellen van Zanten (eds.), *Prosody in Indonesian languages*, 35–63. Utrecht: LOT.

Halim, Amran. 1974. *Intonation in relation to syntax in Bahasa Indonesia*. Jakarta: Djambatan.

Himmelmann, Nikolaus P. 2010. Notes on Waima'a intonation. In Michael Ewing & Marian Klamer (eds.), *East Nusantara: Typological and areal analyses*, 47–69. Canberra: Pacific Linguistics.

Kluge, Angela. 2014. *A grammar of Papuan Malay*. Utrecht: LOT.

Laksman, Myrna. 1994. Location of stress in Indonesian words and sentences. In Cecilia Odé & Vincent J. van Heuven (eds.), *Experimental studies of Indonesian prosody* (Semaian 9), 108–139. Leiden: Leiden University, Vakgroep Talen en Culturen van Zuidoost-Azië en Oceanië).

Landis, J. Richard & Gary G. Koch. 1977. The measurement of observer agreement for categorical data. *Biometrics* 33. 159–174.

Maskikit-Essed, Raechel & Carlos Gussenhoven. 2016. No stress, no pitch accent, no prosodic focus: The case of Ambonese Malay. *Phonology* 33. 353–389.

Mo, Yoonsook, Jennifer Cole & Eun-Kyung Lee. 2008. *Naïve listeners' prominence and boundary perception*. http://www.isca-speech.org/archive.

Odé, Cecilia. 1997. On the perception of prominence in Indonesian: An experiment. In Cecilia Odé & Wim Stokhof (eds.), *Proceedings of the Seventh International Conference on Austronesian Linguistics*, 151–166. Amsterdam: Rodopi.

Peperkamp, Sharon & Emmanuel Dupoux. 2002. A typological study of stress 'deafness'. *Laboratory Phonology* 7. 203–240.

Pitt, Mark A., Laure Dilley, Keith Johnson, Scott Kieslin, William Raymond & Elizabeth Hume. 2007. *Buckeye corpus of conversational speech*. Columbus, OH: Department of Psychology, Ohio State University.

R Core Team. 2015. *R: A language and environment for statistical computing*. Vienna, Austria: R Foundation for Statistical Computing. Version 3.2.2.

Rietveld, Toni C. M. & Carlos Gussenhoven. 1985. On the relation between pitch excursion size and pitch prominence. *Journal of Phonetics* 15. 273–285.

Roosman, Lilie. 2007. Melodic structure in Toba Batak and Betawi Malay word prosody. In Vincent J. van Heuven & Ellen van Zanten (eds.), *Prosody in Indonesian languages*, 89–116. Utrecht: LOT.

Simons, Gary F. & Charles D. Fennig (eds.). 2018. *Ethnologue: Languages of the world*. Dallas, Texas. https://www.ethnologue.com/. Online version.

Stoel, Ruben B. 2007. The intonation of Manado Malay. In Vincent J. van Heuven & Ellen van Zanten (eds.), *Prosody in Indonesian languages*, 117–150. Utrecht: LOT.

Turk, Alice E. & Stefanie Shattuck-Hufnagel. 2007. Multiple targets of phrase-final lengthening in American English words. *Journal of Phonetics* 35. 445–472.

Uhmann, Susanne. 1988. Akzenttöne, Grenztöne und Fokussilben. Zum Aufbau eines phonologischen Intonationssystems für das Deutsche. In Hans Altmann (ed.), *Intonationsforschungen*, 65–88. Tübingen: Niemeyer.

van Heuven, Vincent J. & Ellen van Zanten. 2007. Prosody in Austronesian languages of Indonesia: Concluding remarks. In Vincent J. van Heuven & Ellen van Zanten (eds.), *Prosody in Austronesian languages of Indonesia*, 191–207. Utrecht: LOT.

van Minde, Don. 1997. *Malayu Ambong: Phonology, morphology, syntax*. Leiden: University of Leiden. (Doctoral dissertation).

van Zanten, Ellen. 1994. The effect of sentence position and accent on the duration of Indonesian words: A pilot study. In Cecilia Odé & Vincent J. van Heuven (eds.), *Experimental studies of Indonesian prosody* (Semaian 9), 140–180. Leiden: Leiden University, Vakgroep Talen en Culturen van Zuidoost-Azië en Oceanië.

van Zanten, Ellen & Vincent J. van Heuven. 2004. Word stress in Indonesian: Fixed or free? *NUSA Linguistic Studies of Indonesian and other Languages in Indonesia* 53. 1–20.

Zubkova, Ludmila G. 1966. *Vokalizm Indonezijskogo jazyka*. St Petersburg: Leningrad University. (Doctoral dissertation).

Name index

Abadiano, Helen R., 5, 22
Abbott, Barbara, 214
Adelaar, K. Alexander, 43, 124, 228, 285
Adriani, Nicolaus, 230
Aissen, Judith, 234, 235
Aldridge, Edith, 213, 224, 227, 235
Alieva, Natalia F., 390
Alsagoff, Lubna, 43
AnderBois, Scott, 296
Ariel, Mira, 6, 88
Arka, I Wayan, 161, 162, 166, 181, 190
Arnold, Laura, 370
Astini, Ida Ayu Putu, 140
Aziz, Yellow Y., 5

Baek, Soondo, 393, 405
Bakhtin, Mikhail M., 6
Ball, Catherine N., 218
Barešová, Ivona, 47
Bates, D., 396
Bauer, Winifred, 227
Baumann, Stefan, 43, 47–49, 250, 254, 256, 305, 350, 397
Beaver, David, 254, 259, 291, 305
Beckman, Mary E., 348, 353, 361, 369
Benn, Keith Laurence, 5, 7
Besnier, Niko, 227
Biber, Douglas, 6, 22, 23
Bible Society in Taiwan, 12, 15, 31
Bickel, Balthasar, 141
Biggs, Bruce, 211
Billings, Loren A., 235, 236
Bloomfield, Leonard, 213
Blust, Robert, 141, 208, 212, 229, 230, 348
Boersma, Paul, 355
Bresnan, Joan, 162, 170

Brunetti, Lisa, 259–261, 265, 278
Bühler, Karl, 81, 82, 86, 98
Büring, Daniel, 259, 260, 262, 290, 292, 305, 395, 405
Busenitz, Robert I., 231, 232
Butt, Miriam, 170
Byma, Gary F., 213
Büring, Daniel, 256, 259, 260, 262, 285, 291, 295, 300, 307

Capell, Arthur, 213
Carlier, Anne, 120, 133
Carlson, Katy, 198
Carroll, Alice, 43, 45, 46
Cena, Resty M., 249
Chafe, Wallace L., 42, 44, 46, 184, 352, 394
Chang, Melody Y., 227
Choi, Hye-Won, 146
Chomsky, Noam, 259
Chung, Sandra, 48, 227
Chung, Siaw-Fong, 48
Clark, Brady, 259
Cleary-Kemp, Jessica, 48
Clynes, Adrian, 391
Cohn, Abigail C., 390
Cohn, Dorrit, 197
Cole, Jennifer, 389, 393, 395, 397, 405
Cole, Peter, 48, 178, 181, 226, 227
Collins, Suzanne, 252
Comrie, Bernard, 141, 145, 146, 162
Connor, Ulla, 5
Conrad, Susan, 6
Constantino, Ernesto, 219, 220
Cresti, Emanuela, 352
Croft, William, 141

Name index

Crossley, Scott A., 5
Cruse, D. A., 201
Cumming, Susanna, 69, 71, 177–179, 181, 182, 185, 186, 190, 191, 194, 199, 202, 203
Curme, G. O., 228
Custis, Tonya, 227
Cutfield, Sarah, 81

Dalrymple, Mary, 145–147, 159, 170
Davidson, Donald, 208
Daw, Khin Khin Aye, 43
Dawuda, Carmen, 81
De Busser, Rik, 9–14, 25
De Guzman, Videa P., 249
De Mulder, Walter, 120, 133
DeLancey, Scott, 76
Delpada, Benidiktus, 68
den Dikken, Marcel, 212
Deterding, David, 391
DeWolf, Charles M., 213
Diessel, Holger, 62, 81, 82, 87, 91, 100, 101, 109
Dixon, R. M.W, 141
Djenar, Dwi Noverini, 63, 71
Donohue, Mark, 287
Downing, Laura J., 357
Dowty, D., 141
Du Bois, John W., 42, 62, 67
Dukes, Michael, 211
Dupoux, Emmanuel, 408
Duranti, Alessandro, 41
Durie, Mark, 287

Ebert, Christian, 296
Ebert, Karen H., 133
Egerod, Soren, 213
Enç, M., 170
Enfield, N. J., 50, 82, 87, 91, 92, 109
Engdahl, Elisabet, 144–147, 260
Englebretson, Robert, 42, 124
Erteschick-Shir, Naomi, 145, 151, 154, 155, 160
Esser, Samuel Jonathan, 230

Evans, Nicholas, 68
Ewing, Michael, 133
Ezard, Bryan, 5

Fanselow, Gisbert, 290
Fennig, Charles D., 390
Féry, Caroline, 290, 350, 357
Field, Andy, 399
Firbas, Jan, 266
Flaming, Rachel, 5
Fludernik, Monika, 197
Foley, William A., 8, 145, 163, 167, 185, 212, 213
Forker, Diana, 69–71
Fox, Barbara A., 7
Fox, James J., 161
François, Alexandre, 83, 90
Fraund, Kari, 123
Frege, Gottlob, 209
French, Koleen Matsuda, 8
Fretheim, Thornstein, 42, 179, 182–184, 195, 200

Garrod, S., 381
Georgopoulos, Carol, 227
Gerland, Doris, 123
Gil, David, 213
Ginzburg, Jonathan, 261
Givón, Talmy, 7, 157, 158, 160, 183, 184
Goddard, Cliff, 69, 71–73
Goedemans, Robert W. N., 350, 351, 370, 389–391, 393
Gonda, J., 229
Gorisch, J., 381
Gregory, Michelle L., 333, 338
Grice, Martine, 349, 353
Grimes, Charles E, 161
Güldemann, Tom, 253, 290
Gundel, Jeanette K., 42, 67, 74, 155, 179, 182–184, 195, 200, 250, 324, 325, 327, 342
Gussenhoven, Carlos, 354, 390–392, 395, 407, 408

Name index

Haig, Geoffrey, 84
Haiman, John, 23, 296
Halim, Amran, 390
Halliday, M. A. K., 3–7, 12–16, 21, 22, 85, 291
Hasan, Ruqaiya, 3–7, 12–16, 21, 22, 85
Hasegawa-Johnson, Mark, 393, 395, 397, 405
Haspelmath, Martin, 141
Hassel, R. Chris, 5
Hasselgård, Hilde, 13
Haviland, John B., 67
Hawkins, John A., 120, 123, 129, 132, 133
Heine, Bernd, 120, 153
Hendriks, Henriëtte, 5
Heritage, John, 54, 72, 76
Hermon, Gabriella, 48, 226
Heycock, Caroline, 212
Hickmann, Maya, 5
Himmelmann, Nikolaus P., 20, 48, 62, 63, 81, 82, 85–88, 90, 91, 98, 99, 101, 107, 120, 210, 213, 219, 236, 332, 347, 348, 351, 352, 391
Hockett, Charles, 291
Hoey, Michael, 7
Holmes, Janet, 68
Hopper, Paul J., 48, 49, 52, 53, 181, 190, 196
Hsinsheng, Wu, 315
Huang, Hui-chuan J. (黃慧娟), 9–11
Huang, Lillian, 315
Huang, Yan, 14, 85

Ishihara, Shinichiro, 290

Jackendoff, Ray, 259
Jacobs, Joachim, 260, 291, 292
Jernudd, Björn H., 43
Jespersen, Otto, 212
Jonker, J. C. G., 304
Jun, Sun-Ah, 348, 357

Kadmon, Nirit, 214
Kähler, Hans, 229, 230

Kalin, Laura, 232
Kalyan, Siva, 83
Kamholz, David C., 370
Kanerva, Jonni M., 357, 358
Karina, Sitta, 191, 193, 194, 196, 197
Karttunen, Lauri, 259
Kaswanti Purwo, 180, 181, 185, 190, 199, 202
Katz, Jonah, 291
Kaufman, Daniel, 213, 215, 219, 221, 224, 225, 236, 237, 255, 256, 348, 351, 376, 379
Keenan, Edward L., 162, 211, 232
Kehler, Andrew, 5
Khan, Sameer, 369
Khan, Volker, 369
Kikusawa, Ritsuko, 236
Kim, M., 381
King, Tracy Holloway, 170
Kiss, Katalin É., 291
Klamer, Marian, 303
Klein, Wolfgang, 261, 291, 292
Kluge, Angela, 124, 390, 392, 408
Koch, Gary G., 398, 401
Kratochvíl, František, 68
Krifka, Manfred, 100, 108, 119, 146–148, 154, 160, 162, 256, 265, 291, 292, 322
Krisna, Asbari-Nurpatria, 181, 192, 193, 195
Kroeger, Paul, 181, 190, 212, 215, 218, 227, 233, 258, 301, 307
Kruger, Alet, 5
Kügler, Frank, 350
Kuipers, J. C., 161
Kumalasari, Ade, 181
Kuo, Eddie C. Y., 43
Kurniawan, Eka, 182, 185–188, 200, 201
Kuteva, Tania, 120, 153

Ladd, Robert D., 348, 350, 353
Laksman, Myrna, 390
Lambrecht, Knud, 6, 42, 100, 108, 144, 147, 155, 159, 167, 179, 182–185, 193,

Name index

194, 214, 216, 217, 253, 259, 291, 301, 376
Landis, J. Richard, 398, 401
LaPolla, Randy J., 142, 170, 183–185
Latrouite, Anja, 249, 251, 253, 255, 257, 259, 266, 291, 307
Law, Paul, 232
Lee, Nala Huiying, 43
Lehmann, Christian, 123
Lemaréchal, Alain, 213
Li, Paul Jen-Kuei, 7, 8
Lieberman, Philip, 352
Lindström, Eva, 349, 371
Litamahuputty, Betty, 124
Lopez, Cecilio, 213
Lyons, Christopher, 119–121, 133

Maclachlan, Anna, 249
Maier, Emar, 197
Majid, Asifa, 124
Malah Zubairu, Helen Tan, 7
Malau, Catriona, 83
Mann, William C., 5
Manning, Christopher, 181, 190
Margetts, Anna, 82, 90, 92
Martin, James R., 5, 6, 15, 21
Maskikit-Essed, Raechel, 354, 390–392, 407, 408
Matić, Dejan, 101, 108
Matthiessen, Christian M. I. M., 3, 5
Mayer, Mercer, 42, 45, 46
Mbete, Aaron Meko, 285
McCarthy, John J., 390
McNally, Louise, 291
McNamara, Danielle S., 5
Mead, David, 236
Merrell, Floyd, 16
Michaelis, Laura A., 333, 338
Mikkelsen, Line, 209, 234
Mo, Yoonsook, 393, 395, 397, 401, 405
Modrak, D. K., 209
Mosel, Ulrike, 82, 90, 97, 107
Musan, Renate, 119, 146–148, 154, 160, 162
Mycock, Louise, 170

Nagaya, Naonori, 223, 259, 332, 376
Naylor, Paz B., 213, 215
Nikolaeva, Irina, 145–147, 159
Nolasco, Ricardo, 249
Nomoto, Hiroki, 69, 72
Nuhn, Patrick, 251
Nuranindya, Dyan, 180

Odé, Cecilia, 390
Otanes, Fe T., 213, 250, 257
Otsuka, Yuko, 227
Ozerov, Pavel, 101, 108

Paauw, Scott H., 115, 116
Pastika, I Wayan, 140, 157, 160
Paul, Herrmann, 291
Paul, Ileana, 218, 227, 232
Pawley, Andrew, 352
Payne, Thomas, 249
Pearson, Matthew, 232
Peperkamp, Sharon, 408
Pickering, M., 381
Pierrehumbert, Janet B., 353, 361, 369
Piontek, Jörn, 259
Pitt, Mark A., 397
Pompino-Marschall, Bernd, 357
Potsdam, Eric, 218, 227, 232
Potts, Christopher, 263, 296
Prentice, David J., 43, 116–118, 124
Primus, Beatrice, 250, 254
Prince, Ellen F., 42

Quick, Phil, 140, 157
Quine, Willard V., 20

Rackowski, Andrea, 213
Rashid, Sabariah Md, 7
Reeve, Matthew, 217
Reid, Lawrence Andrew, 228
Reinhart, Tanya, 154, 291, 292
Remijsen, Bert, 349, 370, 371
Reyle, Uwe, 261, 285
Richards, Norvin, 213, 227
Riesberg, Sonja, 8, 347

Name index

Riester, Arndt, 43, 47–49, 250, 254, 256, 259–261, 265, 278, 285, 291–293, 295–297, 300, 301, 307
Rietveld, Toni C. M., 395
Rijkhoff, Jan, 322
Roberts, Craige, 259, 261, 266, 285, 291, 292
Rommetveit, Ragnar, 41
Roosman, Lilie, 393
Rooth, Mats, 256, 259, 260, 262, 291, 292
Rosch, Eleanor, 155
Ross, Malcolm, 212, 220, 221, 228
Rubin, Aaron D., 48, 123

Sacks, Harvey, 47, 72, 75, 76
Salehuddin, Khazriyati, 48
San Roque, Lila, 42, 44, 46
Sasi Rekha d/o Muthiah, 43
Satyawati, Made Sri, 303
Schachter, Paul, 210, 213, 250, 257
Scheerer, Otto, 213
Schegloff, Emanuel A., 47, 72, 75, 76
Schiering, René, 358
Schnell, Stefan, 84
Schwarzschild, Roger, 262, 291
Sedeng, I Nyoman, 140–142, 162
Seiter, William J., 227
Selkirk, Elisabeth O., 291, 359, 369
Sells, Peter, 249
Shattuck-Hufnagel, Stefanie, 389, 393, 395, 406
Shibatani, Masayoshi, 221
Shih, Chao-kai (施朝凱), 9–11
Shiohara, Asako, 185, 202, 261, 278, 286, 297, 302
Siewierska, Anna, 288
Silverstein, Michael, 235
Simons, Gary F., 390
Singapore Department of Statistics, 43
Skopeteas, Stavros, 290, 291
Sneddon, James N., 52, 65, 66, 69, 180
Stalnaker, Robert, 259
Starosta, Stanley, 213, 220
Stivers, Tanya, 42, 75

Stoel, Ruben B., 347, 355, 356, 359–361, 366–368, 391
Strawson, Peter, 291
Stubbe, Maria, 68
Stutterheim, Christiane von, 261, 291, 292
Sukamto, Katharina Endriati, 51, 67
Sumitri, Ni Wayan, 161
Syder, Frances, 352

Tannen, Deborah, 198
Tanskanen, Sanna-Kaisa, 5
Taylor, John R., 155
Tchekhoff, Claude, 211
Terrill, Angela, 81
Thompson, Sandra A., 5
Thurgood, Elzbieta A., 124
Toer, Pramoedya Ananta, 180
Tomasello, Michael, 62, 74
Tonhauser, Judith, 259, 296
Trussel, Stephen, 229, 230
Tsukida, Naomi, 315
Turk, Alice E., 395, 406
Tversky, Barbara, 20

Uhmann, Susanne, 395
Utsumi, Atsuko, 351

Vallduví, Enric, 108, 144–147, 260
van den Berg, René, 231, 232, 236
Van Heuven, Vincent J., 350, 370, 390, 392
van Kuppevelt, Jan, 261, 285, 291, 292
van Lier, Eva, 322
Van Minde, Don, 48, 392
van Rooij, Robert, 291
Van Valin, Robert D., 142, 170, 183–185, 212, 247, 257, 259
Van Zanten, Ellen, 350, 351, 370, 389–393
Velleman, Dan, 254, 305

Wagner, Michael, 259, 350
Wald, Benji, 99
Walker, Marilyn, 301
Watson, Duane G., 350

Name index

Wedgwood, Daniel, 101, 108
Weenink, David, 355
Williams, Edwin, 212
Williams, Nicholas, 48, 62, 63
Winskel, Heather, 48
Winter, Bodo, 397
Witzlack-Makarevich, Alena, 141
Wolff, John U., 221, 236
Wouk, Fay, 157, 190

Xu, Yi, 382

Yap, Foong Ha, 225

Zacks, Jeffrey M., 20
Zeitoun, Elizabeth, 9, 11
Zimmermann, Malte, 350
Zlatev, Jordan, 41
Zubizarreta, Maria Luisa, 290
Zubkova, Ludmila G., 390

Language index

Abui, 68[17]
Acehnese, 287[2]
African, 253, 357
Afrikaans, 5
Ambon, 124, 354, 392, 408
Ambonese, 390–392, 407, 408
American English, 396, 397, 401
Amharic, 123
Arabic, 5, 139[1]
Australian, 81, 110
Austronesian, 5, 7, 8, 43, 76, 83, 140, 141, 157, 165, 208, 208[1], 212[6], 214[10], 215, 216, 219, 220, 220[14], 221, 221[16], 226, 227, 227[24], 228, 233, 234, 236–238, 261[14], 278, 280, 285, 287[2], 303[14], 313, 348, 349, 349[4], 350, 351, 354, 356–359, 361, 369, 370, 370[18], 371, 375, 384

Baba Malay, 43, 124
Balantak, 208, 231, 232, 232[28]
Bali, 139, 140, 285
Balinese, 139, 139[1], 139[2], 140, 141, 141[3], 142, 144, 145, 145[4], 146–148, 150, 151, 153, 155, 156[9], 157, 158, 160–166, 170–172
Bantik, 351
Bantu, 357
Batak, 236, 391–393
Bazaar Malay, 43
Bengali, 369
Bima, 303[14]
Bislama, 83, 104
Brunei Malay, 391
Bunun, 6–9, 9[3], 10–12, 14, 15, 20–23, 25, 28, 31, 33

Chichewa, 357, 358
Chinese, 15, 43, 124
Cirebon Javanese, 133
Classical Malay, 177, 181, 182, 194, 196, 236

Dalabon, 81
Dutch, 348, 351

English, 4[1], 5, 7, 43, 43[3], 44, 64, 66, 71, 72, 76, 83, 86, 95, 99, 107, 119, 119[4], 120[5], 121, 121[6], 122, 132, 139[1], 151, 159–163, 167, 186[10], 192, 208, 211–217, 217[11], 218, 218[12], 219, 221, 222, 226–229, 233, 234, 238, 252[6], 259, 261, 264, 265, 269, 343, 348, 355, 361, 380, 394, 395, 397, 398, 401
European, 84, 223[17], 228[26], 348, 350, 354, 361[16], 393, 395, 405

Formosan, 221, 332
French, 5, 261, 291, 353, 354, 408

German, 5, 261, 291, 308, 348, 395–397, 408
Germanic, 348–350, 371, 395

Hokkien, 43

Indian Malay, 43
Indonesian, 42[1], 51[9], 63[13], 66, 67, 116, 119[4], 120, 123, 124, 127, 139[1], 139[2], 177, 177[1], 178, 178[3], 179, 181, 181[7], 182[9], 185, 189, 190, 194, 202, 208, 216, 217, 219, 225, 226, 227[24], 228, 228[26], 229, 229[26], 231, 232[28],

Language index

236–238, 347, 348, 350, 351, 353, 390–394, 408
Isbukun, 7–9, 9³, 10–12, 17, 18

Japanese, 199, 296, 297, 299, 304, 327, 329, 361
Javanese, 43, 139¹, 229, 347, 354, 391, 408

Kambera, 303¹⁴
Korean, 22, 357, 357¹²
Kulawi, 230
Kuot, 349

Lao, 82, 87, 92, 110
Lavukaleve, 81

Magey Matbat, 370
Maksím, 145
Malagasy, 218¹², 227²⁴, 232²⁸
Malay, 42, 42¹, 43, 43², 43³, 44, 47, 48, 48⁵, 49⁷, 50, 53, 56, 62–64, 66–69, 69¹⁸, 69¹⁹, 72–76, 115, 116, 118, 119, 124, 125, 177, 177¹, 181, 208, 216, 219, 225, 225¹⁹, 226, 227²⁴, 228, 231, 236, 347, 354, 355, 357, 359, 360¹⁴, 361¹⁶, 366, 371, 390–394, 394², 398, 399, 401, 407–409
Malayic, 43, 347, 347¹, 407, 408
Malayo-Polynesian, 261¹⁴, 285
Malaysian, 177, 177¹
Manado Malay, 356, 366, 367
Mandarin, 5, 43
Maranao, 236
Minahasan, 115
Moor, 370
Mwotlap, 83, 90

Ngaju Dayak, 229
Norwegian, 5, 195

Oceanic, 81–83, 90, 108, 348

Palawan, 263
Papuan Malay, 355

Pendau, 140, 157
Pidgin, 124
Polynesian, 211
Puyuma, 221

Qiang, 221¹⁶
Quechua, 221¹⁶

Russian, 145

Samoan, 82, 90, 97, 107
Sangiric, 115, 348², 351
Seediq, 227²⁴, 313, 313¹, 314, 315, 317, 322, 324–327, 338
Singapore Malay, 47–52, 55–58, 60, 61, 63–74
Singaporean, 43, 64, 76
Singlish, 43
Sumbawa, 261¹⁴, 285, 286, 287², 288, 290, 291, 296, 297, 297¹¹, 303, 306–308
Sundanese, 43, 229

Tagalog, 210, 211, 212⁶, 213, 213⁹, 215, 216, 218¹², 219, 219¹³, 222, 223¹⁷, 224, 227²⁴, 228, 229²⁶, 231, 233–235, 235³¹, 237, 238, 247, 249, 251⁵, 252, 253, 255, 258, 261, 263–266, 268, 269, 274, 280, 291⁴, 375, 376, 376¹, 377, 379, 380, 381⁴, 383, 384
Taiwanese, 327, 334
Takbanuaz, 7, 12
Takituduh, 7, 12
Takivatan, 7–9, 9³, 10–12, 15, 17–20, 25, 28
Talaud, 115, 125
Tamil, 43
Tawala, 5
Teruku, 313, 313¹, 315, 317, 325, 326, 330
Tongan, 211, 227²⁴
Totoli, 358, 361, 362, 371
Tukang Besi, 287²
Tuuda, 313

Language index

Waima'a, 347, 353, 354, 360, 360[15], 361–365, 367, 368, 371, 372, 391
Wandamen, 5
Wooi, 370[19]

Yucatec, 123

Subject index

aboutness topic, 260, 263^{15}, 265, 274, 280, 300, 308
actor argument, 251, 253, 255, 263, 268, 272, 277
actor focus, 253
actor voice, 8, 24, 173, 210, 220^{14}, 225, 238, 247–251, 253–257, 266–268, 271, 272, 275, 277, 279, 280, 343, 372, 384
anaphoric, 7, 9, 14, 16, 18, 20, 24, 56, 65, 66, 72, 81, 91, 120, 120^5, 121, 121^6, 123, 124, 129–133
anaphoricity, 317, 333–337, 342, 343
argument focus, 275, 298, 305, 377, 379, 384
assertion, 159, 183, 184, 192, 214, 262, 263, 267, 275, 277, 285, 292, 293, 296, 297, 299, 302, 356
AV, 141, 142, 144, 160, 161, 165, 166, 314, 315, 320, 322, 323

backgrounded, 261, 269, 277, 295, 296, 299, 305
biclausal focus, 208
boundary tone, 349, 353, 359, 360, 366, 369, 370
broad focus, 306, 357, 366, 395

categorisation, 42, 43, 47–51, 53, 55, 58, 60–66, 75
classifier phrase, 48–50, 52–54, 58
clause, 3, 4, 6, 20, 52, 56, 69, 72^{21}, 84, 89, 90, 93, 94, 97, 102, 105–108, 117, 127, 141–143, 150–152, 154, 155, 157–159, 161, 164, 171, 178, 178^2, 179–182, 186–202, 207, 210, 211, 213, 215–217, 221, 222, 224, 230, 232, 233, 249, 251, 263, 276, 285, 286, 292, 297, 298, 302, 304, 305, 314, 316–322, 324–326, 329–332, 334, 338–340, 342, 360^{15}, 361^{16}, 363, 366, 375–377, 395, 404
cleft construction, 217, 223^{17}, 259
climactic portion, 178, 185, 189–191, 193, 202
clitic, 8, 157, 159, 160, 181, 191, 223, 224, 224^{18}, 233^{29}, 236, 258, 267, 286, 288^3, 289, 297, 298, 303–305, 314, 315, 319
clitic pronoun, 286, 289, 297, 303, 303^{14}, 315, 320, 321
cohesion, 3, 5–7, 12–15, 17, 21, 22
cohesive density, 7, 15, 22, 22^5, 23, 24
completive focus, 145, 148, 171
constituent order, 8, 177, 182, 203, 249, 255, 258, 261, 266, 267, 279, 285, 286, 290, 298, 301, 313
continuing topic, 157, 159
contrastive, 69, 140, 146–148, 150, 152, 154, 158–163, 165, 167, 169, 172, 254, 256–258, 260–262, 264, 266, 271, 272, 274, 277, 286, 291, 295, 300, 301, 305, 306, 355
contrastive focus, 142, 145, 146, 148, 150–153, 160, 164–166, 167^{11}, 168, 169, 184, 265, 367, 368, 377
contrastive topic, 142, 143, 148, 160–162, 164–166, 169–171, 215, 251, 254, 256, 257, 260, 265, 266, 274, 277, 279, 280, 298, 305–308

default mapping, 253, 253^8, 254, 255

Subject index

default topic, 155, 155[7], 156–158, 172
deictic, 9, 14, 16, 18–20, 62, 65, 75, 81, 86, 91, 99, 100, 102, 107, 116
demonstrative, 10, 14, 16, 18, 23, 24, 54, 61, 63–66, 74, 77, 82, 83, 85–88, 91, 92, 99, 103, 111, 116, 117, 123[9], 126–128, 132, 133, 218, 225[20], 233, 233[29], 234, 300, 323–326, 328, 330, 342–344, 372, 409
discourse, 3–7, 13, 20, 21, 23, 42, 43, 47, 48, 49[7], 51, 53, 62, 63, 63[13], 64, 65, 66[14], 67, 69, 71, 75, 81–83, 86, 88, 89, 92, 94, 100, 101, 104, 106–109, 111, 120, 126, 132, 133, 141, 142, 144–147, 149, 150, 156, 157, 164, 167, 170, 172, 178, 181–183, 185, 186, 188, 197, 198, 200, 201, 203, 210, 211, 215, 249, 259–263, 265, 266, 271, 274, 274[20], 275, 279, 290, 292–294, 295[9], 297, 298[12], 299–301, 333, 336, 343, 348, 352, 360[15], 404
discourse structure, 47, 84, 108, 249, 260, 263, 268, 269, 271
discourse topic, 108, 263, 264

edge tone, 349, 350, 353, 360, 361[16]
emphatic focus, 146, 153, 154
epistemic stance, 42, 47, 48, 50, 51, 53, 57, 58, 60, 61, 63, 65–67, 69, 75
eventiveness, 71, 71[20], 72, 177, 178, 181, 182, 202
exophoric, 4, 16, 20[4], 81–83, 85–87, 91, 92, 98, 99, 102, 107–109

focus domain, 260, 280, 308, 357
focus marker, 144, 151, 153, 159, 161
focus position, 142, 144, 215, 233, 235[31]
focus structure, 5, 184, 376–379
frame setter, 162–165, 167, 169, 171, 322
free pronoun, 8, 181, 182, 196, 198, 201

givenness, 103, 119[4], 146, 162, 172, 249, 250[4], 251, 253, 263, 265, 278, 324, 325, 327, 337, 342

identity, 14, 17, 21, 118, 286
information packaging, 101, 107, 108, 253[8], 257, 259, 352, 353
information status, 132, 199, 248, 249, 250[4], 251, 253, 255, 290, 356, 381, 382, 397
interrogative, 133, 149, 217, 218, 218[12], 219, 224, 226, 226[23], 227–229, 295, 350
intonation, 102, 104, 108, 215, 237, 290, 291[5], 307, 349, 350[5], 351, 352, 352[6], 352[9], 356, 357, 361[16], 371, 391, 395
intonational phrase, 353, 358
intransitive clause, 57, 179, 186, 189, 193, 223[17]

joint attention, 62, 63, 68–72, 74, 74[22], 75, 76, 82, 83, 98, 100, 102, 107

left periphery, 144, 162, 164, 166, 167, 207, 215, 228, 251
lexical cohesion, 14, 17
lexical stress, 349, 349[4], 350, 351, 356, 357, 369–371, 390, 391, 393, 407–409
locative voice, 8, 24, 384

narrow actor focus, 268, 271, 279
narrow contrastive focus, 264, 268[18], 274, 357
narrow focus, 184, 258, 268, 357, 367, 377, 383, 384
new focus, 144, 145, 148–150, 152, 154, 155, 159, 167, 168, 170, 172, 178, 179, 186, 190, 192, 194, 198, 201, 202
new topic, 66[14], 157, 170, 172, 306
nominative, 173, 210, 210[5], 211, 219, 224, 232, 239, 257, 259, 280, 314, 315, 319, 344, 381[4], 384

oral narrative, 7, 11, 15, 19, 21, 23
OV, 181, 182, 197–202

Subject index

patient voice, 210, 221, 231, 239, 315, 384
penultimate stress, 350, 391–393
phrase accent, 349, 353–360, 361[16], 366, 368, 369
pivot, 47, 141, 142, 144, 145, 152, 155, 159–163, 165, 166, 171, 172, 179, 212[6]
pragmatic assertion, 183, 184, 192, 214
pragmatic presupposition, 149, 183, 184, 214
predicate focus, 269, 271, 376, 377, 379
presupposition, 105, 149, 183, 184, 194, 207, 209, 214–218, 227, 231, 235, 235[31], 259[12], 266
primary topic, 155, 159, 160, 170
prominence, 49[7], 150, 159, 170–172, 249–251, 253–255, 266, 350, 351, 353, 356, 357, 391, 393, 394, 394[2], 395–402, 404–409
prominence-score, 409
pronoun, 18, 21, 24, 53[11], 54, 59, 72, 85, 86, 100, 101, 108, 111, 118, 119[4], 121, 123[9], 126, 127, 139[2], 155, 156, 156[9], 157–159, 163, 164, 178, 179, 181, 181[7], 183, 186, 197, 198, 211, 217, 218, 228, 233[29], 234, 237, 257[11], 258, 267, 274, 287, 297, 301, 304, 305, 314, 315, 319, 320, 322–326, 330, 331, 338–341, 343, 344, 366, 372, 409
prosodic boundary, 357, 404, 406
prosodic phrasing, 290, 348, 350[5], 358, 371
prosodic prominence, 151, 350[5], 408
prosodic word, 224, 353, 381, 382
prosody, 13, 145, 145[4], 160, 185, 255, 261, 348, 350, 350[5], 352, 352[6], 356, 370, 379, 383, 384, 390, 392
pseudocleft, 376–378, 384
pseudocleft construction, 332, 376, 378, 379

QUD, 259, 260, 262, 263, 265, 285, 292–296, 305[16], 306

referent, 4, 14, 42, 47–50, 52–54, 58, 60, 62–66, 66[14], 67, 68, 71, 74–76, 81–83, 87, 91–95, 97, 98, 100–102, 104, 106–109, 116, 118, 119, 119[4], 120–123, 123[9], 124, 126–130, 132, 133, 155–160, 162, 164, 169, 170, 178[2], 182–188, 191, 192, 194–196, 198–201, 211, 214, 261, 266, 286[1], 288[3], 297, 300, 303, 329, 333, 340
referential cohesion, 7, 12–14, 17, 19, 21, 22
referential density, 23
referentiality, 84, 208, 209, 212, 213, 215, 249, 250, 266
RefLex, 43, 47, 48, 48[6], 49–53, 57, 64, 71, 73
relative clause, 52, 57, 69, 197, 203, 208, 216–218, 222, 223[17], 225–227, 228, 229[26], 253, 324, 326, 361, 395
rhythmic effect, 187, 188, 198, 202
right edge, 353, 355, 357–359, 366, 404

secondary topic, 155, 155[7], 159, 160, 170, 172
sentence focus, 193, 196, 298, 376, 377
stance, 42, 47–50, 53, 58, 62, 63, 67, 74, 75
stress deafness, 408
syntactic break, 402, 404

tonal marking, 370
topic status, 186, 195, 200
topicalisation, 100, 163, 164, 167, 169
topicality, 156, 160, 185, 251, 253, 255, 257, 268, 278

ultimate stress, 392
Undergoer, 188, 253[8], 254, 255, 258, 268, 269, 278, 279
undergoer, 8, 188, 190, 202, 248[2], 249–253, 253[7], 254–257, 263, 264, 266, 268, 269, 271, 272, 274–280

427

Subject index

undergoer voice, 25, 173, 247–252, 253[7], 254–257, 268, 268[18], 271, 272, 274, 278–280
UV, 142, 160, 168

verb focus, 297
voice, 61, 71[20], 77, 89, 140, 141, 155, 157, 160, 165, 170, 173, 181, 185, 208[1], 210[5], 212[6], 220, 221, 231, 247–252, 254–256, 264, 271, 274, 279, 280, 313, 315, 329, 343, 344, 352, 384
voice selection, 249, 251, 253, 254, 256, 264–266, 278, 291[4]
voice system, 8, 141, 145, 172, 231, 247, 248

word class, 14–17, 27, 30, 35–37
word duration, 395, 400, 405, 406
word order, 55, 76, 117, 142, 185, 233, 235[31], 237, 256, 257, 279, 302, 313, 354, 355, 368, 375